New Zealand's
South Island
(Te Waipounamu)

Nelson &
Marlborough
(p274)

The
West
Coast
(p236)

Christchurch
& Canterbury
(p58)

Queenstown
& Wanaka
(p192)

Dunedin
& Otago
(p114)

Fiordland &
Southland
(p148)

Peter Dragicevich, Brett Atkinson, Andrew Bain,
Samantha Forge, Anita Isalska

PLAN YOUR TRIP

ON THE ROAD

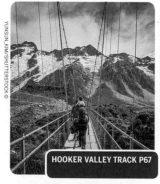

HOOKER VALLEY TRACK P67

YUNSUN_KIM/SHUTTERSTOCK ©

STIRLING POINT, BLUFF P168

DMITRY PICHUGIN/SHUTTERSTOCK ©

KAWARAU BRIDGE BUNGY JUMPING P205

BENNG/SHUTTERSTOCK ©

LUPINS AT LAKE TEKAPO P106

NADLY AIZAT/SHUTTERSTOCK ©

Contents

UNDERSTAND

SURVIVAL GUIDE

SPECIAL FEATURES

Welcome to the South Island

From turquoise lakes and lush peninsulas to snowcapped mountains and sparkling glaciers, the South Island's majestic landscapes offer awe and adventure in equal measure.

Wandering Wild

With just over a million people scattered across 151,215 sq km, you'll have no trouble finding your own slice of wilderness on New Zealand's 'mainland'. The only problem will be choosing between the sublime forests, mountains, lakes, beaches and fiords that make this island one of the best outdoor destinations on the planet. Lace up your boots and tackle one of the South Island's six Great Walks, or choose from countless other options ranging from short nature strolls to multiday, backcountry epics. The Department of Conservation's track and hut network makes it easy to find a way in.

Adventure Ahoy

Hiking (known as 'tramping' here) may be the South Island's quintessential activity, but there are racier ways to immerse yourself in its landscapes. Tumble down the Buller or Rangitata Rivers in a raft, or paddle the glassy coves of the Marlborough Sounds, Abel Tasman National Park or Fiordland. In winter, slice up the slopes around Wanaka, Queenstown or Mt Hutt, while in warmer weather the Alps 2 Ocean Cycle Trail and Central Otago Rail Trail beckon to those on two wheels. For the hardcore thrill-seekers, Queenstown's gravity-defying menu of bungy, paragliding or skydiving is sure to get your adrenalin pumping.

Meet the Locals

Prepare to meet the South Island's idiosyncratic wildlife. Whales, fur seals, dolphins and penguins all frequent the coastal waters around Kaikoura; endangered Hector's dolphins cavort alongside penguins in Akaroa Harbour and the Catlins; and the Otago Peninsula shelters penguins, sea lions and even a colony of royal albatrosses. Further south, remote Stewart Island is the perfect place to spot the iconic but shy kiwi, alongside a profusion of other feathered friends. The South Island is also home to two special parrots, the kaka and the kea – the latter is particularly partial to car aerials and unattended tramping boots.

Tantalise Your Tastebuds

Epicurious travellers will delight in the South Island's smorgasbord of produce, from luscious berries, stone fruit, asparagus and root vegetables, to local seafood, lamb, beef and a plethora of artisanal dairy delights. Roadside kiosks sell everything from farm eggs to grandma's tomato relish, while world-class restaurants skim the cream of local crops for innovative tasting menus. Add some of the world's best cool-climate wines, from Central Otago's pinot noir to Marlborough's renowned sauvignon blanc, as well as some of the most exciting breweries in the country, and you have a recipe for a foodies' paradise.

Why I Love the South Island

By Samantha Forge, Writer

It's hard to pinpoint exactly when I first fell in love with the South Island. It could have been while watching dolphins leap out of the water in Akaroa Harbour, or wandering the sunlit paths of Peel Forest, or perhaps when I rounded a bend and saw the glittering turquoise waters of Lake Tekapo. Maybe it was when the clouds parted right on sunset to give me my first glimpse of the peaks of Aoraki/Mt Cook. Whenever it was, these landscapes are seared into my soul now, and I know that they'll continue to draw me back time after time.

For more about our writers, see p384

Above: Aoraki/ Mt Cook (p108) and Hooker Lake (p67)

New Zealand – South Island

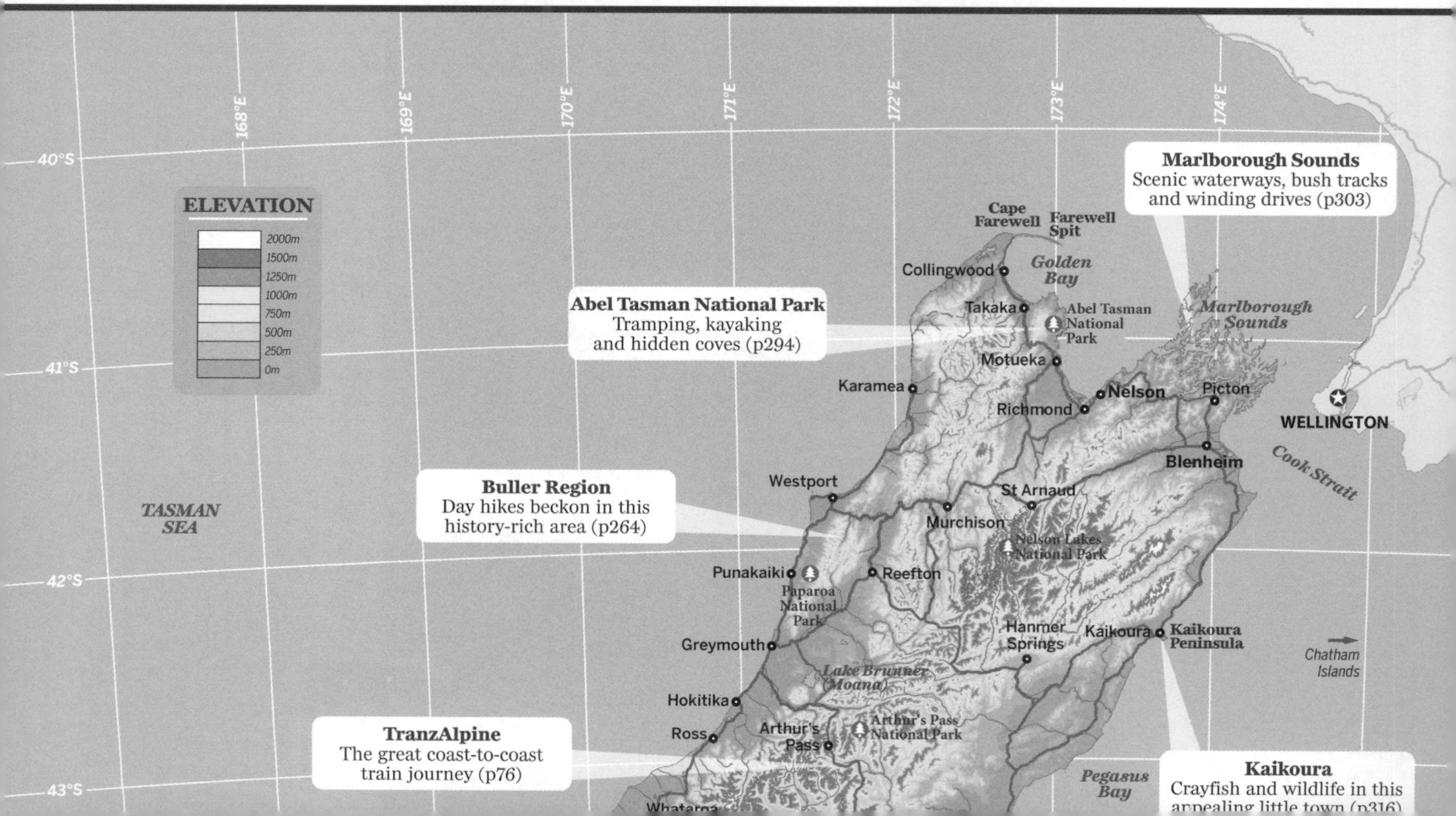

ELEVATION

2000m
1500m
1250m
1000m
750m
500m
250m
0m

Marlborough Sounds
Scenic waterways, bush tracks and winding drives (p303)

Abel Tasman National Park
Tramping, kayaking and hidden coves (p294)

Buller Region
Day hikes beckon in this history-rich area (p264)

TranzAlpine
The great coast-to-coast train journey (p76)

Kaikoura
Crayfish and wildlife in this appealing little town (p316)

WELLINGTON

Cook Strait

Chatham Islands

Marlborough Sounds

Picton

Blenheim

Nelson

Abel Tasman National Park

Golden Bay

Farewell Spit

Cape Farewell

Collingwood

Takaka

Motueka

Richmond

St Arnaud

Nelson Lakes National Park

Murchison

Hanmer Springs

Kaikoura Peninsula

Kaikoura

Pegasus Bay

Karamea

Reefton

Lake Brunner (Moana)

Arthur's Pass National Park

Westport

Punakaiki

Paparoa National Park

Greymouth

Arthur's Pass

Hokitika

Ross

Whataroa

TASMAN SEA

200 km
100 miles

174°E
173°E
172°E
171°E
170°E
169°E
168°E

40°S
41°S
42°S
43°S

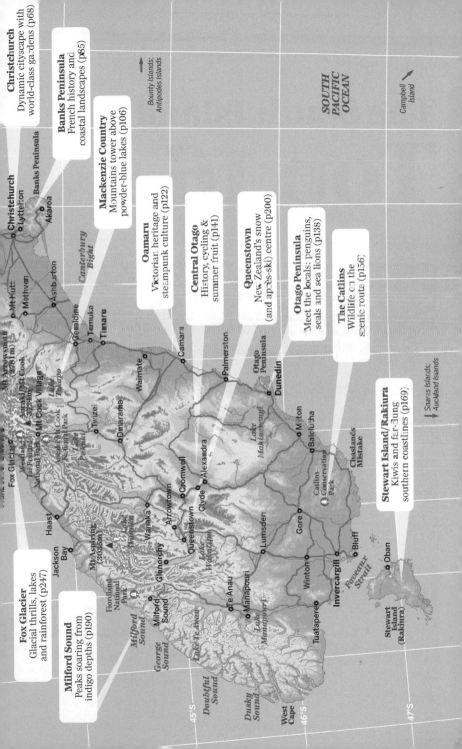

Christchurch
Dynamic cityscape with world-class gardens (p68)

Banks Peninsula
French history and coastal landscapes (p85)

Mackenzie Country
Mountains tower above powder-blue lakes (p106)

Oamaru
Victorian heritage and steampunk culture (p122)

Central Otago
History, cycling & summer fruit (p141)

Queenstown
New Zealand's snow (and après-ski) centre (p200)

Otago Peninsula
Meet the locals: penguins, seals and sea lions (p138)

The Catlins
Wildlife on the scenic route (p156)

Stewart Island/Rakiura
Kiwis and far-flung southern coastlines (p169)

Fox Glacier
Glacial thrills, lakes and rainforest (p247)

Milford Sound
Peaks soaring from indigo depths (p190)

SOUTH PACIFIC OCEAN

Bounty Islands;
Antipodes Islands

Campbell Island

Snares Islands;
Auckland Islands

Christchurch
Lyttelton
Banks Peninsula
Akaroa
Canterbury Bight

Mt Hutt
Methven
Ashburton
Geraldine
Temuka
Timaru
Waimate
Oamaru
Palmerston
Otago Peninsula
Dunedin
Milton
Balclutha
Chaslands Mistake
Catlins Conservation Park
Gore
Lumsden
Winton
Invercargill
Bluff
Foveaux Strait
Oban
Stewart Island (Rakiura)

Mt Arrowsmith (2781m)
Aoraki/Mt Cook (3724m)
Mt Cook Village
Westland/Tai Poutini National Park
Aoraki/Mt Cook National Park
Lake Tekapo
Twizel
Omarama
Pukaki
Lake Benmore
Cromwell
Alexandra
Clyde
Lake Manuherikia
Fox Glacier
Haast
Jackson Bay
Mt Aspiring (3033m)
Lake Wanaka
Wanaka
Arrowtown
Glenorchy
Queenstown
Lake Wakatipu
Fiordland National Park
Milford Sound
Milford Sound
George Sound
Te Anau
Lake Te Anau
Manapouri
Lake Manapouri
Tuatapere
Doubtful Sound
Dusky Sound
West Cape

45°S
46°S
47°S

The South Island's
Top 16

Abel Tasman National Park

1 This is New Zealand at its most glorious and seductive: lush green hills fringed with golden sandy coves, slipping gently into warm shallows before meeting a crystal-clear sea of cerulean blue. Abel Tasman National Park (p294) is the quintessential postcard paradise and you can put yourself in the picture in an endless number of poses: kayaking, swimming, sunbathing and of course tramping the Abel Tasman Coast Track. This sweet corner of the South Island raises the bar and effortlessly keeps it there.

Milford Sound

2 Fingers crossed you'll be lucky enough to see Milford Sound (p190) on a clear, sunny day, when the world-renowned collage of waterfalls, verdant cliffs and peaks, and dark cobalt waters is at its best. More likely, though, is the classic Fiordland scenario of rain, with the landscape an arguably more dramatic scene of gushing waterfalls and Mitre Peak revealed slowly through swirling mist. It's awesome either way, particularly when special inhabitants such as seals, dolphins and birds show up alongside a boat cruise or kayak trip.

Queenstown

3 Queenstown (p200) may be known as the birthplace of bungy jumping, but there's more to do in New Zealand's adventure capital than just leaping off a bridge tied to a giant rubber band. Amid the ridiculously beautiful scenery of Lake Wakatipu, the Shotover River and the Remarkables mountain range, travellers can spend their days tramping, mountain biking, paragliding, skydiving, rafting or heading cross-country on a 4WD tour. The lively hospitality hubs of Queenstown and nearby Arrowtown are stimulating places to relive the adventures over a drink or dinner.

Marlborough Sounds

4 Way more than just the place where the Interislander ferry docks, Picton is a vibrant hang-out and hub for adventure trips into the serpentine Marlborough Sounds (p303), four different waterways linked by bush tracks and winding drives. Boat trips allow the deepest penetration into the area's countless nooks and crannies. Tramp or bike the Queen Charlotte Track, or paddle a kayak between back-to-nature campsites. A host of boat trips offer everything from activity combos to lunch cruises and trips to Motuara Island to meet precious rare birds.

Akaroa & Banks Peninsula

5 Infused with a dash of Gallic ambience, Francophile Akaroa village sits within one of the prettiest harbours on the Banks Peninsula (p85). Dainty dolphins and plump penguins inhabit clear waters that are perfect for sailing and exploring. Elsewhere on the peninsula, the spidery Summit Rd traces the rim of an ancient volcano, with winding offshoots that descend to hidden bays and coves. Spend your days tramping and kayaking amid the improbably beautiful land- and seascapes, unwinding at night in cosy town bistros or atmospheric rural B&Bs.
Bottom right: Akaroa (p87)

8

Christchurch

6 Many travellers merely pass through Christchurch (p68) on their way to the South Island's outdoor playgrounds, but those who linger will discover a creative, cosmopolitan city full of culture and heart. Firmly back on its feet after the devastation of the 2011 earthquake, Christchurch's city centre has been transformed into an open, pedestrian-friendly space, with multiple green zones and an astonishing array of street art. A world-class art gallery, blissful botanical gardens and fascinating museums all combine to make Christchurch a must-see stop on any southerly sojourn.

Kaikoura

7 First settled by Māori, with their keen nose for seafood, Kaikoura (p316) meaning 'eat crayfish' – is NZ's best spot for both consuming and communing with marine life. While whales are definitely off the menu, you're almost guaranteed a good gander at Moby's mates on a whale-watching tour. There's also swimming with seals and dolphins, or spotting albatrosses, petrels and other seabirds. When it comes to seafood, crayfish is king, but on fishing tours you can hook into other edible wonders of the unique Kaikoura deep. Bottom left: Humpback whale at Kaikoura (p317)

Stewart Island

8 Stewart Island (p169), the country's rugged southern addendum, is a paradise for trampers, bird-watchers and travellers seeking an authentic NZ experience. Test yourself on the challenging North West Circuit Track or spend three days on the easier, but still spectacular, Rakiura Track. Compete against friendly locals in NZ's southernmost pub quiz at the South Sea Hotel in Oban, before making plans to explore the abundant birdlife on nearby Ulva Island. Leave time for a kiwi-spotting tour, to see NZ's shy feathered icon mooching around at twilight on isolated beaches.

Oamaru

9 A wonderfully restored Victorian townscape, a celebration of steampunk culture and the nightly arrival of hundreds of little blue penguins: surprising Oamaru (p122) has plenty of reasons for inclusion on your South Island itinerary. Explore the town's historic harbourside precinct on a penny-farthing bicycle before adjourning for high tea or a homemade pie in one of the charming cafes. At dusk, grab a grandstand seat to greet penguins returning home after a day's fishing, before toasting their ocean-going bravery with a beer at the nearby brewery. Left: Harbour St Bakery (p125)

Mackenzie Country

10 Canterbury's Mackenzie Country (p106) is the star of scenic Hwy 8 between Christchurch and Queenstown, serving up icons such as Lake Tekapo (pictured) and Aoraki/Mt Cook. Ringed by mountain ranges and infilled with golden tussock and surreal blue hydro lakes, this unique basin offers plenty of options for soaking up the scenery, from the gentle Alps 2 Ocean Cycle Trail to horse trekking, scenic flights and tramping. There are also stargazing tours that take advantage of the basin's status as the southern hemisphere's only International Dark Sky Reserve.

© MARTYN ANNETTS / ALAMY STOCK PHOTO

Otago Peninsula

11 Few cities have such remarkable wildlife on their doorstep as Dunedin. Only 15 minutes' drive of the city centre, the Otago Peninsula (p138) is a narrow strip of land lined with peaceful beaches, craggy coves and cliffs. It's a haven for seals and sea lions, but its seabirds – including rare yellow-eyed penguins (hoiho; pictured), and the world's most northerly royal albatross colony at Tairoa Head – are what make it so special. Visit in January or February to see the huge albatrosses soaring above the cliffs and making clumsy landings.

Fox Glacier

12 Unusually close to both the Tasman Sea and the loftiest peaks of the Southern Alps, the twin glaciers of Franz Josef and Fox (p244) are a must-see for their crazy valleys and spectacular ice flows. Tramping on the ice is a great way to view them, as are scenic flights soaring over the glaciers and up to Aoraki/Mt Cook. Fox Glacier's amazing extras are Lake Matheson, the famous 'mirror' lake fringed with rainforest, and wild Gillespies Beach, with its rusting mining relics and a walkway to a remote seal colony.

Central Otago

13 Central Otago (p142) presents a chance to balance virtue and vice alongside some of NZ's most beautiful landscapes. Cycle the easygoing Otago Central Rail Trail or the spectacularly scenic Roxburgh Gorge Trail. Slake your thirst with a beer in laid-back country pubs, or linger for lunch in the vineyard restaurants of Bannockburn and Gibbston Valley. Other foodie diversions include Cromwell's weekly farmers market, and the summer fruit harvest – starring nectarines, peaches, plums and cherries. Left: Clutha River (p145)

Buller Region

14 Most West Coast travellers turn south from Westport, missing the opportunity to explore the Buller Region (p264) to the north. An incredible array of sights and experiences are on offer: tramp and cycle around ghostly Denniston Plateau, discover regional history at Charming Creek – one of NZ's best day walks – and gaze at the limestone arches of Oparara Basin. Beyond the town of Karamea is the Kohaihai end of the Heaphy Track, where there's a half-day tramp to raw, empty Scotts Beach. Right: Oparara Basin (p269)

13

The Catlins

15 Even for many New Zealanders, the rugged Catlins (p156) coast is unknown territory. Avoid the functional inland route linking Dunedin and Invercargill, and traverse the Catlins' diverse procession of isolated bays and coves, dramatic landforms such as waterfalls and caves, and opportunities to chinwag with friendly locals and spot local wildlife. The Catlins' highlights include the quirky Lost Gypsy Gallery at Papatowai, swimming (or surfing) with dolphins at Curio Bay, and the walk to windswept Slope Point, the southernmost tip of the South Island. Top right: Nugget Point (p156)

TranzAlpine

16 New Zealand's most scenic train route is the *TranzAlpine* (p76), a five-hour journey from the Pacific Ocean to the Tasman Sea. After leaving Christchurch and the bucolic Canterbury Plains (pictured), it heads into the foothills of the Southern Alps, negotiating tunnels and viaducts to reach the Waimakariri Valley. A stop within Arthur's Pass National Park is followed by the Otira tunnel, burrowing through the bedrock of the South Island's alpine spine. Then it's down through the Taramakau River Valley, past Lake Brunner, and finally into sleepy Greymouth. Unforgettable.

Need to Know

For more information, see Survival Guide (p353)

Currency
New Zealand dollar ($)

Language
English, Māori

Visas
Citizens of 60 countries, including Australia, the UK, the US and most EU countries, don't need visas for NZ (length-of-stay allowances vary). See www.immigration.govt.nz.

Money
Credit cards are used for most purchases in NZ, and are accepted in most hotels and restaurants. ATMs are widely available in cities and larger towns.

Mobile Phones
European phones should work on NZ's network, but most American or Japanese phones will not. It's straightforward to buy a local SIM card and prepaid account at outlets in airports and large towns (provided your mobile is unlocked).

Time
New Zealand time (GMT/UTC plus 12 hours)

When to Go

Nelson
GO Jan–Mar

Franz Josef Glacier
GO Feb–Mar

Christchurch
GO Jan–Mar

Queenstown
GO Jun–Aug

Te Anau
GO Oct–Apr

Warm to hot summers, mild winters

High Season (Dec–Feb)

➡ Best weather and conditions for beach-time and outdoor adventures.

➡ Domestic holidaymakers fill up hot spots and keep roads busy.

➡ Major international tourist influx fills all available gaps.

Shoulder (Mar–Apr & Sep–Nov)

➡ Generally settled weather; a great time to travel.

➡ Locals in school and work so lighter traveller volumes.

➡ The south may be cool from September to November, especially at night.

Low Season (May–Aug)

➡ Unpredictable weather, ranging from glorious to ghastly.

➡ No crowds, easy bookings, but quiet towns go into hibernation.

➡ High season in the ski towns, especially around Queenstown.

Useful Websites

100% Pure New Zealand (www.newzealand.com) Comprehensive official tourism site.

Department of Conservation (www.doc.govt.nz) DOC parks, trail conditions and camping info.

Lonely Planet (www.lonely planet.com/new-zealand) Destination information, hotel bookings, traveller forum and more.

Destination New Zealand (www.destination-nz.com) Event listings and info from NZ history to fashion.

Important Numbers

Regular NZ phone numbers have a two-digit area code followed by a seven-digit number. When dialling within a region, the area code is still required. Drop the initial 0 if dialling from abroad. If you're calling the police but don't speak English well, ask for Language Line, which may be able to hook you up with a translator.

NZ country code	64
International access code from NZ	00
Emergency (Ambulance, Fire, Police)	111
Directory Assistance (charges apply)	018

Exchange Rates

Australia	A$1	NZ$1.10
Canada	C$1	NZ$1.14
China	Y10	NZ$2.21
Euro zone	€1	NZ$1.72
Japan	¥100	NZ$1.29
Singapore	S$1	NZ$1.08
UK	UK£1	NZ$1.97
US	US$1	NZ$1.46

For current exchange rates, see www.xe.com.

Daily Costs

Budget: Less than $150

➡ Dorm beds or campsites: $25–40 per night

➡ Main course in a budget eatery: less than $15

➡ InterCity or Naked Bus pass: 15 hours or five trips $125–159

Midrange: $150–250

➡ Double room in a midrange hotel/motel: $110–200

➡ Main course in a midrange restaurant: $15–32

➡ Car rental: from $40 per day

Top End: More than $250

➡ Double room in an upmarket hotel: from $200

➡ Three-course meal in a classy restaurant: $80

➡ Domestic flight: from $100

Opening Hours

Opening hours vary seasonally depending on where you are. Most places close on Christmas Day and Good Friday.

Banks 9am–4.30pm Monday to Friday, some also 9am–noon Saturday

Cafes 7am–4pm

Post Offices 8.30am–5pm Monday to Friday; larger branches also 9.30am–noon Saturday

Pubs & Bars noon–late ('late' varies by region, and by day)

Restaurants noon–2.30pm and 6.30pm–9pm

Shops & Businesses 9am–5.30pm Monday to Friday and 9am to noon or 5pm Saturday

Supermarkets 8am–7pm, often 9pm or later in cities

Arriving on the South Island

Christchurch Airport Christchurch Metro Purple Line runs into the city regularly from around 7am to 11pm. Door-to-door shuttles run 24 hours (from $23). A taxi into the city costs around $45 to $65 (20 minutes).

Queenstown Airport Taxis charge around $50 for trips between the airport and town. Ritchies Connectabus has an airport service that runs every 15 minutes ($12). Door-to-door shuttle services cost around $20.

Entry & Exit Formulas

Disembarkation in New Zealand is generally a straightforward affair, with only the usual customs declarations and luggage-carousel scramble to endure. Under the Orwellian title of 'Advance Passenger Screening', documents that used to be checked after you touched down in NZ (passport, visa etc) are now checked before you board your flight – make sure all your documentation is in order so that your check-in is stress-free. There are no restrictions when it comes to foreign citizens entering NZ. If you have a current passport and visa (or don't require one), you should be fine.

For information on **getting around**, see p32

PLAN YOUR TRIP NEED TO KNOW

What's New

Canterbury Earthquake National Memorial

Unveiled on the sixth anniversary of the 22 February 2011 earthquake that claimed 185 lives in Christchurch, this peaceful new memorial provides a place to reflect and remember. (p71)

Bill Richardson Transport World

Operate a digger for the day, or spend hours perusing gleaming motorbikes and classic cars at this shiny new museum. It's so much fun it may just put the under-loved town of Invercargill back on the map. (p164)

Franz Josef Clay Target Shooting

Exhilarating two-hour sessions at this new clay-target shooting outfit are the perfect way to spend your time while you're wait-ing for the skies to clear around Franz Josef Glacier. (p250)

Alpine Fault Tours

Experience the might of Mother Nature on this tour out of Whataroa, which brings you right to the place where the Australian and Pacific plates meet. (p253)

Wildwire Wanaka

This new via ferrata climbs high beside Twin Falls, on the slopes of Treble Cone in Wanaka. Its newest trip, the Lord of the Rungs, is the world's highest waterfall *via ferrata*, with climbers descending by helicopter at the end. (p228)

Emerson's Brewery

Opened in 2016, Emerson's flash new Dunedin home is a brewery, gastropub and cellar door all rolled into one stylish package. Drop in for a tour, fill a flagon with your favourite brew, or linger awhile on the sunny front deck. (p129)

Whitestone City

Celebrating Oamaru's Victorian heritage, this new interactive museum has been a labour of love for the Oamaru Whitestone Civic Trust. Opened in 2017, its quirky at-tractions include a penny-farthing carousel and a replica streetscape. (p123)

Little High Eatery

You're sure to find something to tickle your tastebuds at this snazzy new hipster food hall, home to eight delicious and disparate gourmet purveyors. Many of the businesses have relocated from the now-defunct Re:START mall, making the complex a perfect symbol of Christchurch's ongoing regeneration. (p79)

Suter Art Gallery

Following a two-year makeover, Nelson's historic Suter Art Gallery has reopened as a modern 21st-century institution featur-ing fascinating NZ art, with the added bonus of a wonderful river-side cafe. (p282)

Kaikoura Museum

Kaikoura Museum has reopened as one of NZ's best provincial museums. Of par-ticular interest is the poignant exhibition covering the 7.8 magnitude earthquake that struck the town in November 2016. (p316)

For more recommendations and reviews, see lonelyplanet.com/New-Zealand

If You Like...

Skiing & Snowboarding

Treble Cone Challenging downhill terrain within a stone's throw of Wanaka. (p228)

Canterbury Ski Mt Hutt, and stacks of smaller fields like Ohau, Roundhill, Porters and Broken River. (p96)

Coronet Peak Ski or snowboard Queenstown's oldest field then join the resort town's legendary après-ski scene. (p203)

Cardrona More great skiing in the Queenstown/Wanaka area, with slopes to suit all levels of experience. (p233)

Tramping

Milford Track Touted as the greatest of the Great Walks – 54km of fiords, sounds and peaks. (p152)

Routeburn Track The Great Walk competing with the Milford as the best of the bunch. (p196)

Mt Robert Circuit Nelson Lakes' premier day walk with stupendous views earned via the Pinchgut Track. (p288)

Old Ghost Road Built for bikers, this new multiday wilderness epic is also a tramper's delight. (p266)

Tuatapere Hump Ridge Track Traverse rugged tops and a remote coast in the deep south. (p180)

Abel Tasman Coast Track Stroll past sparkling seas, pristine beaches and coastal forests on this well-trodden track. (p279)

Māori Culture

Te Ana Māori Rock Art Centre Learn about traditional Māori rock art both in the museum and at nearby sites. (p104)

Okains Bay Māori & Colonial Museum View an outstanding array of heritage treasures including *waka taua* (war canoes). (p86)

Hokitika Watch the masters carve stone, bone, paua (shell) and *pounamu* (greenstone) in traditional Māori designs. (p254)

Ko Tane See a replica Māori village and an evening cultural show at Willowbank Wildlife Reserve. (p72)

Beaches

Wharariki No ice-cream van, no swimming. Just an enthralling, empty beach for wanderers and ponderers. (p302)

Anchorage Forget Photoshop, these surreal golden sands, blue waters and verdant green hills are for real. (p294)

Kaka Point A sweeping surf beach on a coast home to seals, sea lions and myriad seabirds. (p156)

Colac Bay A top spot for surfing, but this far south be sure to pack a wetsuit. (p175)

Okarito A wild, empty West Coast gem backed by a bird-filled lagoon. (p252)

Sumner The perfect spot for swimming, surfing and a sundowner, a short bus ride from Christchurch. (p73)

Wine Regions

Marlborough Superb sauvignon blanc and pretty winery restaurants are just the start of the story. (p314)

Nelson Marlborough's near neighbour is smaller in scale but equally scenic. (p282)

Waitaki Valley Truly boutique producers wrangle tricky terroir in New Zealand's edgiest wine region. (p121)

Central Otago Dozens of cellar doors nestle amid schist landscapes producing sublime pinot noir. (p142)

Waipara Valley North Canterbury's up-and-coming region produces spectacular pinot noir and riesling. (p94)

Extreme Activities

Queenstown Bungy with the world's originals at AJ Hackett's Kawarau Bridge, Ledge or Nevis sites. (p202)

Skydive Franz If you're going to do it, go for the highest –19,000ft above alps and glaciers. (p250)

Abel Tasman Canyons Paddle, swim, slide and leap through a hidden gorge in the national park. (p294)

Raft the Buller Bounce through the thrilling rapids on this mighty West Coast river. (p272)

Museums & Galleries

Christchurch Art Gallery Better than ever after post-quake restoration, with world-class permanent and temporary exhibitions. (p71)

vCanterbury Museum A wide-ranging collection of historical exhibits presented in a splendid earthquake survivor. (p69)

World of WearableArt Museum Home to the world-famous, wonderfully weird and wacky wearable-art show. (p282)

Eastern Southland Gallery Houses impressive works by iconic New Zealand artists Ralph Hotere and Rita Angus. (p161)

Shantytown Delve into the West Coast's flinty gold- and coal-mining past at this replica pioneer village. (p260)

Cities

Christchurch Cosmopolitan cafes, gorgeous gardens and surprising street art – post-quake Christchurch is brimming with activity. (p68)

Top: First Church of Otago (p129), Dunedin.

Bottom: Historic stone hut at Arrowtown's Chinese Settlement (p221).

Dunedin Gothic architecture, edgy arts, vibrant nightlife and wildlife on the doorstep. (p128)

Nelson Art, culture, cuisine and beaches – it's no wonder this is touted as the lifestyle capital of New Zealand. (p282)

Invercargill Not rock and roll, but gloriously retro, friendly and full of neat old buildings. (p164)

Queenstown Petite but rollicking tourism centre with a sophisticated arts and dining scene. (p200)

Pubs, Bars & Beer

Nelson Tour pubs and breweries on a craft-beer trail throughout New Zealand's original home of hops. (p286)

Christchurch Pubs such as Pomeroy's and the Brewery show commitment to the craft cause. (p81)

Dunedin Home to lively student bars and two big-name breweries – Speight's and Emerson's. (p129)

Queenstown Quench your thirst after a day's mountain biking, bungy jumping or skiing. (p215)

Invercargill Brewery A workhorse with its own range that also brews drops for some of NZ's best. (p164)

History

Arrowtown Gold rush–era town crammed with heritage buildings and the remains of one of NZ's earliest Chinese settlements. (p221)

Oamaru Victorian Precinct Beautifully restored whitestone buildings and warehouses, now housing eclectic galleries, restaurants and artisan workshops. (p123)

Waiuta South of Reefton on the South Island, explore the rusty relics of a ghost town, abandoned to nature in 1951. (p271)

Shantytown Embrace goldrush nostalgia at this authentic recreation of an 1860s mining town, south of Greymouth on the West Coast. (p260)

Toitū Otago Settlers Museum Human settlement on the South Island, told through interactive displays and a 100,000-object collection. (p128)

Off-the-Beaten-Track Experiences

Stewart Island The end of the line! Catch the ferry to Oban and get lost for a few days. (p169)

Karamea Lesser-trodden marvels like the Oparara Arch and secluded Scotts Beach reward tramps on the northern West Coast. (p268)

Molesworth NZ's largest cattle farm traverses some seriously remote terrain – take a Molesworth tour. (p95)

Haast Chat to fishermen and drive to lonely Jackson Bay on the South Island's land of no phone signal. (p242)

Foodie Experiences

Central Otago vineyard restaurants Eye-popping scenery combined with the best of NZ food and wine. (p147)

Christchurch city scene The southern CBD dining and bar scene is burgeoning (again). (p79)

Bluff oysters Guzzle silky, salty oysters between March and August; time your visit for May's oyster festival. (p169)

West Coast whitebait Whitebait fritters, bound in egg, are a South Island obsession. Try them on pizza, too. (p272)

NZ lamb Carnivores won't want to miss NZ's best-loved meat; Queenstown's local-minded Public Kitchen & Bar is a good place to start. (p213)

Road Trips

Milford Hwy Gasp at alpine peaks, sigh along thrilling forest-wrapped roads...the drive from Te Anau to Milford Sound is one of the world's finest. (p186)

Great Coast Road Overhanging cliffs and otherworldly rock formations feature on this route along the wild, windswept West Coast. (p263)

Arthur's Pass Between Canterbury and the West Coast, the Southern Alps' highest pass is a feat of engineering. (p97)

Southern Scenic Route Allow a week to do justice to this meandering route between Queenstown and Dunedin. (p159)

Month by Month

January

New Zealand peels its eyes open after New Year's Eve, gathers its wits and prepares for another year. Great weather, the cricket season is in full swing, and it's happy holidays for the locals.

☆ Nelson Jazz Festival

Get your jazz and blues groove on at rocking venues and ad hoc street corners. Acts range from Kiwi funkateers through to local hipsters, and Nelson's reputation for great wine and beer makes it very easy to enjoy the diverse beats. (p283)

☆ World Buskers Festival

Christchurch throngs with jugglers, musicians, tricksters, puppeteers, mime artists and dancers. Shoulder into the crowd, watch the performances and leave a few dollars. Avoid if you're scared of audience participation. (p77)

February

The sun is shining, the days are long and the drinks are chillin' in the fridge: this is prime party time across New Zealand (NZ). Book your festival tickets (and beds) in advance.

🍷 Marlborough Wine & Food Festival

Revel in mandatory over-indulgence at NZ's biggest and best wine festival, featuring tastings from more than 40 Marlborough wineries, plus fine food and entertainment. We hope you like sauvignon blanc. (p282)

☆ TUKI

Wanaka's super-relaxed alternative-music festival has a new name and location (at Glendhu Bay), but the same well-curated selection of NZ sounds with a dance, reggae, rock and electronica spin as always. (p229)

March

March brings a hint of autumn, along with harvest time in the vineyards of Marlborough and the orchards of Central Otago. Expect long dusky evenings and plenty of festivals filling out the calendar.

🍴 Hokitika Wildfoods Festival

Chow down on worms, hare's testicles or stallion's semen at Hokitika's comfort-zone-challenging food fest. Not for the mild-mannered or weak-stomached... But even if you are, it's still fun to watch! There are plenty of quality NZ brews to cleanse the palate. (p256)

🍷 Gibbston Wine & Food Festival

Head to the Queenstown Gardens in mid-March to sample products from the rugged and meandering river valley to the east of Queenstown. Look forward to fine wines, cheese, chocolate, food trucks and

cooking masterclasses from celebrated NZ chefs (www.gibbstonwincand-food.co.nz).

April

April is when canny travellers hit NZ: the ocean is swimmable and the weather still mild, with nary a tourist or queue in sight. The exception is Easter, when accommodation prices soar.

🍷 Clyde Wine & Food Festival

The main street of sleepy Clyde comes to life on Easter Sunday, as locals rub shoulders with foodie fanatics come to sample an abundance of local prod-ucts, including renowned cool-climate pinot noir (www.promotedunstan.org.nz).

👁 Warbirds Over Wanaka

Held every second Easter in even-numbered years, Warbirds over Wanaka is an internationally renowned air show set against the rugged Central Otago landscape. Heritage and iconic aircraft pull crazy manoeuvres for up to 50,000 spectators. (p229)

May

Party nights are long gone and a chilly NZ winter beckons. Thank goodness for the Comedy Festival. May is also your last chance to explore Fiordland and Southland in reasonable weather.

Top: Fireworks at the Queenstown Winter Festival (p210).

Bottom: Aerial display at Warbirds Over Wanaka (p229)

✗ Bluff Oyster & Food Festival

Bluff and oysters go together like, well, like a bivalve. Truck down to the deep south for some slippery, salty specimens at this local fest. It's chilly down here in May, but the live music and oyster eating/opening competitions warm everybody up. (p169)

☆ New Zealand International Comedy Festival

This three-week laughfest (www.comedyfestival.co.nz) kicks off on the North Island, but then hits the South Island with a travelling troupe of international and local talent. Venues include Christchurch, Oamaru and Invercargill.

June

Time to head south: it's ski season. Queenstown and Wanaka hit their strides, and international legions descend on Coronet Peak, the Remarkables, Treble Cone and Cardrona. On the coast some places take a winter hiatus.

☆ New Zealand Gold Guitar Awards

We like both kinds of music: country *and* western! These awards in Gore cap off a week of everlovin' country twang and bootscootin' good times, with plenty of concerts and buskers. (p161)

July

It's chilly all across the South Island, but the alps are still a hot ticket. Queenstown gets crazy with its annual winter festival. The less active can combine cinema, chocolate and craft beer in Dunedin.

☆ New Zealand International Film Festival

After seasons in Dunedin and Christchurch, this festival (www.nziff.co.nz) hits the road for screenings in regional towns from July to November. Film buffs in Greymouth and Invercargill get very excited at the prospect.

☆⛷ Queenstown Winter Festival

This four-day snow fest attracts around 45,000 snow bunnies to Queenstown for fireworks, jazz, street parades, comedy, a Mardi Gras, a masquerade ball and lots of snow-centric activities on the slopes. Book your bed in advance. (p210)

August

Land a good deal on accommodation pretty much anywhere except the ski towns. Winter is almost spent, but there's still not much happening outdoors: music, art and rugby games are your saviours.

☆ Christchurch Arts Festival

The South Island's biggest arts festival takes place in odd-numbered years. Celebrate with cultured Cantabrians at a wide array of venues right across the city. Music, theatre and dance all feature. (p77)

🏃 Snowsports

Forget Europe or South America. Here's your chance to experience the widest range of snowsports activities in the southern hemisphere. Focus on your downhill at Coronet Peak, achieve snowboarding nirvana at Cardrona, or go heliskiing at Mt Hutt.

September

Spring has sprung, blossoms burst across the South Island, and baby lambs are running amok. There are accommodation bargains to be had, but be ready for four seasons in one day. The snow often lingers.

October

Post-rugby and precricket sees sports fans twiddling their thumbs: a trip to Kaikoura, Akaroa or Nelson perhaps? October is 'shoulder season', with reasonable accommodation rates and smaller crowds. Weather can be changeable; pack your umbrella.

☆⛷ French Fest

Allez à toute vitesse to Akaroa's French Fest (www.akaroa.com/akaroa-french-fest), held in odd-numbered years in early October to celebrate the peninsula's Gallic heritage. Quirky events include a waiters' race and a French cricket tournament, as well as plenty of food and wine, of course.

 Kaikoura Seafest

Kaikoura is a town built on crayfish. Well, not literally, but there sure are plenty of crustaceans, many of which find themselves on plates at Seafest (www.seafest.co.nz), which is also a great excuse to drink a lot and dance around.

November

Another NZ summer approaches as days lengthen following the introduction of daylight saving. Now's a good time to tramp the Great Walks, but you'll need to book ahead.

☆ Highlands 501

Get your motor running for Highlands 501, a super-charged rev-fest in Cromwell featuring 40-odd cars racing over a 501km endurance circuit, as well as stacks of other events and entertainment. (p147)

✯✯ NZ Cup & Show Week

Christchurch's iconic annual NZ Cup & Show Week (www.nzcupandshow.co.nz) is a great opportunity for the good people of Christchurch to celebrate, with fashion shows, horse racing and the country-comes-to-town appeal of the A&P (agricultural and pastoral) Show.

✯✯ Oamaru Victorian Heritage Celebrations

Hark back to the good old days when Queen Vic sat on the throne, hems were low, collars high and civic decency was *de rigueur*. Oamaru pays tongue-in-cheek homage to the past with dress-ups, penny-farthing races, performances and a grand fete. (p125)

December

Summertime! The crack of leather on willow echoes across the nation's cricket pitches and office workers surge towards the finish line. Everyone gears up for Christmas: avoid shopping centres like the plague.

✯ Queen Charlotte Track

Beat the summer rush on the popular Queen Charlotte Track, either on two legs or two wheels, or even integrate a spot of sea kayaking into your journey. (p303)

PLAN YOUR TRIP MONTH BY MONTH

Itineraries

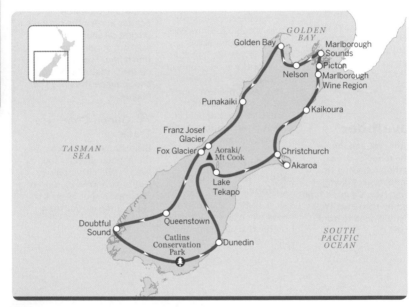

3 WEEKS Southern Circuit

This tour of South Island highlights takes in a remarkable range of landscapes, offering diverse experiences from wine tasting to whale-watching to ice tramping.

Begin in **Christchurch**, the South Island's culture capital. Get a caffeine buzz at Supreme Supreme, then stroll through the pedestrian-friendly CBD to Christchurch Art Gallery and Canterbury Museum. Wander along the Avon River in the Botanic Gardens, and tour the city on the historic tram before heading up the Gondola for excellent views.

City-saturated? Take a day trip to pretty **Akaroa** on the Banks Peninsula, then head north for whale-watching in **Kaikoura**. Continue through the **Marlborough wine region** and the harbour town of **Picton**, before whiling away a day or two in the **Marlborough Sounds**.

Detour west past artsy **Nelson** to ecofriendly **Golden Bay** before heading down the West Coast where **Punakaiki** and the glaciers – **Franz Josef** and **Fox** – are just the tip of the iceberg. Go crazy in adventurous **Queenstown**, be mesmerised by **Doubtful Sound** and chill out around the sleepy **Catlins**. Back up the East Coast, drop in to Scottish-flavoured **Dunedin**, then detour through the Waitaki Valley to the snowy heights of **Aoraki/Mt Cook** and **Lake Tekapo**, before rolling back into Christchurch.

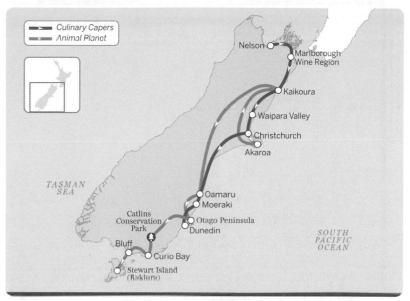

 Culinary Capers

 Animal Planet

Fruits, vegetables, seafood, dairy, game, grapes, hops – the fertile South Island is paradise for foodies. If you want to tantalise your tastebuds then this is your place.

Hop into gear around **Nelson**, widely regarded as the nation's craft-brewing capital and home to microbreweries such as Hop Federation and Townshend. Head over to **Marlborough,** NZ's best wine touring territory, then down the South Island's rugged East Coast to **Kaikoura** for delicious seafood at rustic eateries. Graduate to classier dining at the vineyard restaurants of the **Waipara Valley** – Pegasus Bay and Black Estate are great for leisurely lunches.

Head into **Christchurch** to sample the restaurants around Victoria and New Regent Sts, and Lyttelton, and don't miss the Christchurch Farmers Market on Saturday mornings. Craft heaven awaits beer buffs at Pomeroy's Old Brewery Inn and the Brewery.

From Christchurch continue south to North Otago and award-winning eateries such as Riverstone Kitchen in **Oamaru** and Fleur's Place in **Moeraki**. Emerson's and Speight's are the breweries to check out further south in **Dunedin** before loading up the car with locavore goodies from Dunedin's Otago Farmers Market.

Cast adrift from ancient Gondwanaland and uninhabited by humans until around 800 years ago, the South Island boasts a remarkable range of land and sea creatures. Experience this veritable menagerie on this tour.

From **Christchurch**, travel to **Akaroa** to swim with Hector's dolphins, New Zealand's smallest and rarest. Squeeze in a return trip up the coast to **Kaikoura** for whale-watching and swimming with NZ fur seals, before travelling south to **Oamaru**. A wonderful historic precinct and a fascination with steampunk draw visitors, but nature buffs should make a beeline for the little blue penguin colony, which comes alive at dusk.

From Oamaru continue south to the **Otago Peninsula** to spot more little blue penguins, as well as their extremely rare, shuffling cousin, the yellow-eyed penguin (hoiho). Join a tour to meet seals and sea lions before admiring the royal albatross colony on nearby Taiaroa Head. A seaborne journey with Elm Wildlife Tours is another essential Otago Peninsula experience.

Continue to the rugged, **Catlins**, where penguins, Hector's dolphins and sea lions are all visitors at **Curio Bay**. Leave the Island at **Bluff** for kiwi-spotting on wild and idiosyncratic **Stewart Island/Rakiura**.

Off the Beaten Track

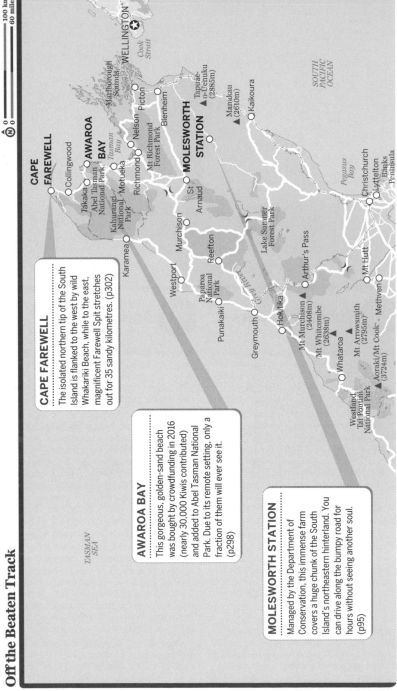

CAPE FAREWELL

The isolated northern tip of the South Island is flanked to the west by wild Whakariki Beach, while to the east, magnificent Farewell Spit stretches out for 35 sandy kilometres. (p302)

AWAROA BAY

This gorgeous, golden-sand beach was bought by crowdfunding in 2016 (nearly 30,000 Kiwis contributed) and added to Abel Tasman National Park. Due to its remote setting, only a fraction of them will ever see it. (p298)

MOLESWORTH STATION

Managed by the Department of Conservation, this immense farm covers a huge chunk of the South Island's northeastern hinterland. You can drive along the bumpy road for hours without seeing another soul. (p95)

ST BATHANS

There's not much left of this historic goldmining town but a haunted pub, a handful of heritage houses and a curious blue lake. (p144)

JACKSON BAY

This remote fishing village, nestled in the shadow of the Southern Alps, is literally the end of the road on the rugged West Coast. You're likely to have its walking tracks all to yourself. (p244)

MACETOWN

There's something hugely intriguing about goldmining ghost towns, especially ones reached by either an arduous trek or an arse-numbing 4WD ride. (p225)

PARADISE

Who doesn't want to say that they've been to Paradise! There's not much to do there but it's all about the journey, after all – along a river valley with mountain views in every direction. (p219)

MAVORA LAKES CONSERVATION PARK

Enclosed within a state forest, this remote area features two blissful lakes separated by an expanse of golden meadow: a perfect setting for Lord of the Rings fantasies. (p183)

Getting Around

For more information, see Transport (p366)

Travelling by Car

Nothing beats the freedom that travelling around the South Island by car provides. You'll be able to access beautifully remote areas that are impractical to reach otherwise. For the most part the roads are excellent and the going is easy. That said, a surprising number of tourists come unstuck while driving in New Zealand.

The major problems seem to be: drivers temporarily forgetting which side of the road they should be driving on (the left); fatigued drivers hiring cars after long flights and embarking on lengthy road journeys; and inexperience in driving on winding country roads, particularly in the South Island's famous mountainous terrain.

Note, if you're spotted driving erratically it's not unknown for locals to confiscate your keys and call the police; this happens several times a year, and generally the police will contact the hire company who will cancel your contract, potentially leaving you stranded. So, while driving in NZ isn't especially difficult, if you're an inexperienced driver or your experience is limited to cities only, consider other alternatives.

New Zealanders may come across as friendly and polite, but many seem to save their rage for the roads. Kiwi motorists are notoriously unaccommodating if you find you need to change lanes, although this is more pronounced in the bigger cities than country areas. If you're driving a slower vehicle such as a caravan, pull

RESOURCES

Automobile Association (www.aa.co.nz/travel) Emergency breakdown services, distance calculators, maps and accommodation guides. Has reciprocal arrangements with similar overseas organisations.

NZ Transport Agency (www.nzta.govt.nz) Real-time traffic reports, journey planner, and information on walking, cycling and public transport. It also handles online payment for the toll roads heading north of Auckland and around Tauranga.

Nga Haerenga: The New Zealand Cycle Trail (www.nzcycletrail.com) Cycling information including suggested itineraries, track details, outlines of 23 'Great Rides', and cycling events.

over when you can to allow faster vehicles to overtake.

If you're flying into Christchurch on a long flight, we highly recommend that you give yourself a day or two to recover and see the sights (by public transport, taxi or Uber) before hiring a car.

Car Hire

It's easy to rent a car from any of the main centres, with the major international agencies having offices both at the airports and in the city centres. In most cases it's cheaper to hire from a local agency, where the cars may be a little older or slightly battered.

Driving Conditions

All major routes are sealed and well-maintained, but in more remote, off-the-beaten-track areas you may strike some unsealed roads. Many of the mountain roads, including some of the major routes out of Queenstown, are windy and narrow. Snow chains are required for many of the mountain routes in winter; if you're travelling without them, you'll be turned back.

No Car?

Bus

Buses connect all of the major towns, however services can be expensive, slow and infrequent. Various tour companies offer guided coach trips to the main destinations. The larger cities have extensive local bus networks.

Air

Aside from Christchurch and Queenstown, the main air-travel hubs, there are airports in Kaikoura, Blenheim, Nelson, Hokitika, Westport, Timaru, Dunedin, Invercargill and Oban (Stewart Island). It's often possible to pick up a cheap domestic fare.

Train

The South Island's two train lines exist more as scenic journeys than as an effective transport mode. The *Coastal Pacific* connects Picton to Christchurch, while the *TranzAlpine* heads clear across the Southern Alps from Christchurch to Greymouth.

Bicycle

While plenty of people do it, New Zealand isn't the easiest country for cycle touring: the terrain is hilly and the traffic can be unforgiving and unaccommodating. The plains east of the Southern Alps are much easier going than the West Coast.

DRIVING FAST FACTS

➡ Drive on the left.

➡ All vehicle occupants must wear a seatbelt.

➡ Minimum age for a full licence is 18 years.

➡ Carry your licence at all times.

➡ Maximum speed 100km/h on motorways, 50km/h in built-up areas.

➡ Blood alcohol limit 50mg per 100ml (0.05).

ROAD DISTANCES (KM)

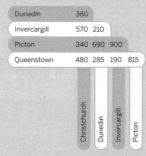

	Christchurch	Dunedin	Invercargill	Picton
Dunedin	360			
Invercargill	570	210		
Picton	340	690	900	
Queenstown	480	285	190	815

Tramper on the Routeburn Track (p19...

Hiking on the South Island

Hiking (aka bushwalking, trekking or tramping, as Kiwis call it) is the perfect activity for a close encounter with the South Island's natural beauty. There are thousands of kilometres of tracks here – some well marked (including the six South Island Great Walks), some barely a line on a map – plus an excellent network of huts and campgrounds.

Best Walks

Top Multiday Hikes

Routeburn Track, Fiordland and Mt Aspiring National Parks

Abel Tasman Coast Track, Abel Tasman National Park

Heaphy Track, Kahurangi National Park

Top Day Hikes

Mt Robert Circuit, Nelson Lakes National Park

Avalanche Peak, Canterbury

Key Summit, Fiordland National Park

Top Wildlife Encounters

Bird life, St Arnaud Range Track, Nelson Lakes

Seals, Cape Foulwind Walkway, West Coast

Kiwi, Rakiura Track, Stewart Island

Best Hikes for Beginners

Queen Charlotte Track, Marlborough Sounds

Abel Tasman Coast Track, Abel Tasman National Park

Rob Roy Track, Mt Aspiring National Park

Planning Your Tramp

When to Go

Mid-December–late January Tramping high season is during the school summer holidays, starting a couple of weeks before Christmas – avoid it if you can.

January–March The summer weather lingers into March: wait until February if you can, when tracks are (marginally) less crowded. Most non-alpine tracks can be walked enjoyably at any time from about October through to April.

June–August Winter is not the time to be out in the wild, especially at altitude – some paths close in winter because of avalanche danger and reduced facilities and services.

What to Bring

Primary considerations: your feet and your shoulders. Make sure your footwear is as tough as old boots and that your pack isn't too heavy. If you're camping or staying in huts without stoves, bring a camping stove. Also bring insect repellent to keep sandflies away, and don't forget your scroggin – a mixture of dried fruit and nuts (and sometimes chocolate) for munching en route.

Maps

The topographical maps produced by Land Information New Zealand (LINZ) are a safe bet. Bookshops don't often have a good selection of these, but LINZ has map sales offices in major cities and towns, and DOC offices often sell LINZ maps for local tracks. Outdoor stores also stock them. The LINZ map series includes park maps (national, state and forest), dedicated walking track maps, and detailed 'Topo50' maps (you may need two or three of these per track).

Hiking Books

The DOC publishes detailed books on the flora and fauna, geology and history of NZ's national parks, plus leaflets (50c to $2) detailing hundreds of NZ walking tracks.

Lonely Planet's *Hiking & Tramping in New Zealand* describes around 50 walks of various lengths and degrees of difficulty. Mark Pickering and Rodney Smith's *101 Great Tramps* has suggestions for two- to six-day tramps around the country. The companion guide, *202 Great Walks: the Best Day Walks in New Zealand,* by Mark Pickering, is handy for shorter, family-friendly excursions. New trampers should check out *Don't Forget Your Scroggin* by Sarah Bennett and Lee Slater – all about being safe and happy on the track. Bird's Eye Tramping Guides from Potton & Burton Publishing have fab topographical maps, and there are countless other books covering tramps and short urban walks around NZ – scan the bookshops.

Online Resources

www.freewalks.nz Descriptions, maps and photos of long and short tramps all over NZ.

Mackay Falls, Milford Track (p152)

Track Classification

Tracks in NZ are classified according to various features, including level of difficulty. We loosely refer to the level of difficulty as easy, medium, hard or difficult. The widely used track classification system is as follows:

Short Walk Well formed; possibly allows for wheelchair access or constructed to 'shoe' standard (ie walking boots not required). Suitable for people of all ages and fitness levels.

Walking Track Easy and well-formed longer walks; constructed to 'shoe' standard. Suitable for people of most ages and fitness levels.

Easy Tramping Track or Great Walk Well formed; major water crossings have bridges and track junctions have signs. Light walking boots and average fitness required.

Tramping Track Requires skill and experience; constructed to 'boot' standard. Suitable for people of moderate physical fitness. Water crossings may not have bridges.

Route Requires a high degree of skill, experience and navigation skills. Well-equipped, fit trampers only.

www.tramper.co.nz Articles, photos, forums and excellent track and hut information.

www.trampingnz.com Region-by-region track info with readable trip reports.

www.peakbagging.org.nz Find a summit and get up on top of it.

www.topomap.co.nz Online topographic maps of the whole country.

Responsible Tramping

If you went straight from the cradle into a pair of hiking boots, some of these tramping tips will seem ridiculously obvious; others you mightn't have considered. Online, the Leave No Trace website (www.lnt.org) is a great resource for low-impact hiking, and the DOC site (http://

TRACK SAFETY

Thousands of people tramp across NZ without incident, but every year too many folks meet their maker in the mountains. Some trails are only for the experienced, fit and well equipped – don't attempt these if you don't fit the bill. Ensure you are healthy and used to walking for sustained periods.

The South Island's volatile climate subjects high-altitude walks to snow and ice, even in summer, and rivers can rise rapidly: always check weather and track conditions before setting off, and be prepared to change your plans or sit out bad weather. Resources include:

www.doc.govt.nz DOC's track info, alerts and a lot more.

www.adventuresmart.org.nz Log your walk intentions online (and tell a friend or local!).

www.mountainsafety.org.nz Tramping safety tips.

www.metservice.co.nz Weather forecasts.

Lake Te Anau, as viewed from the Kepler Track (p153)

freedomcamping.org) has plenty more responsible camping tips. When in doubt, ask DOC or i-SITE staff.

The ridiculously obvious:

➡ Time your tramp to avoid peak season: fewer people equals less stress on the environment and fewer snorers in the huts.

➡ Carry out all your rubbish. Burying rubbish disturbs soil and vegetation, encourages erosion, and animals will probably dig it up anyway.

➡ Don't use detergents, shampoo or toothpaste in or near watercourses (even if they're biodegradable).

➡ Use lightweight kerosene, alcohol or Shellite (white gas) stoves for cooking; avoid disposable butane gas canisters.

➡ Where there's a toilet, use it. Where there isn't one, dig a hole and bury your by-product (at least 15cm deep, 100m from any watercourse).

➡ If a track passes through a muddy patch, just plough straight on through – skirting around the outside increases the size of the bog.

You mightn't have considered:

➡ Wash your dishes 50m from watercourses; use a scourer, sand or snow instead of detergent.

➡ If you really need to scrub your bod, use biodegradable soap and a bucket, at least 50m from any watercourse. Spread the waste water around widely to help the soil filter it.

➡ If open fires are allowed, use only dead, fallen wood in existing fireplaces. Leave any extra wood for the next happy camper.

➡ Keep food-storage bags out of reach of scavengers by tying them to rafters or trees.

➡ Feeding wildlife can lead to unbalanced populations, diseases and animals becoming dependent on humans. Keep your food to yourself.

Great Walks

NZ's nine official Great Walks are the country's most popular tracks: six of them are on the South Island. A 10th Great Walk (also on the South Island) joins the party in 2019. Natural beauty abounds, but prepare yourself for crowds, especially over summer.

All of the South Island's Great Walks are described in Lonely Planet's *Hiking & Tramping in New Zealand,* and are detailed in pamphlets provided by DOC visitor centres and online at www.greatwalks.co.nz.

THE SOUTH ISLAND'S GREAT WALKS

WALK	DISTANCE	DURATION	DIFFICULTY	DESCRIPTION
Abel Tasman Coast Track *	60km	3-5 days	Easy to intermediate	NZ's most popular walk (or sea kayak); beaches and bays in Abel Tasman National Park
Heaphy Track *	78km	4-6 days	Intermediate	Forests, beaches and karst landscapes in Kahurangi National Park
Kepler Track **	60km	3-4 days	Intermediate	Lakes, rivers, gorges, glacial valleys and beech forest in Fiordland National Park
Milford Track **	53.5km	4 days	Easy to intermediate	Rainforest, sheer valleys and peaks, and 580m-high Sutherland Falls in Fiordland National Park
Paparoa Track and Pike29 Memorial Track *	55km	2-4 days	Intermediate	Opens in 2019. Limestone cliffs, mining history and majestic sunsets amid the Paparoa Range
Rakiura Track *	39km	3 days	Intermediate	Bird life (kiwi!), beaches and lush bush on remote Stewart Island (Rakiura)
Routeburn Track **	32km	2-4 days	Intermediate	Eye-popping alpine scenery around Mt Aspiring and Fiordland National Parks

* Bookings required year-round

** Booking required peak season only (October to April)

Tickets & Bookings

To tramp these tracks you'll need to book online or at DOC visitor centres and some i-SITEs before setting out. These track-specific tickets cover you for hut accommodation (from $22 to $70 per adult per night, depending on the track) and/or camping ($6 to $20 per adult per night). You can camp only at designated camping grounds; note there's no camping on the Milford Track.

In the off-peak season (May to September) you can use Backcountry Hut Passes or pay-as-you-go Hut Tickets on all Great Walks except for the Heaphy Track, Abel Tasman Coast Track and Rakiura Track (advance bookings required year-round).

You can book at DOC visitor centres by phoning ☎0800 694 732 or ☎03-249 8514, using the online booking system on www.greatwalks.co.nz, or by emailing greatwalksbookings@doc.govt.nz. Book as far in advance as possible, especially if you're planning on walking during summer.

Backcountry Huts

The DOC maintains more than 950 backcountry huts in NZ's national and forest parks. Hut categories comprise:

Basic huts Just a shed!

Standard huts No cooking equipment and sometimes no heating, but mattresses, water supply and toilets.

Serviced huts Mattress-equipped bunks or sleeping platforms, water supply, heating, toilets and sometimes cooking facilities.

Details about the hut services can be found on the DOC website. Backcountry hut fees per adult, per night range from $5 to $15, with tickets bought in advance at DOC visitor centres (some huts can also be booked online: visit www.doc.govt.nz). Children under 10 can use huts for free; 11- to 17-year-olds are charged half price. If you do a lot of tramping, DOC sells a six-month Backcountry Hut Pass applicable to most huts except Great Walk huts in peak season (October to April, during which time you'll need Great Walk tickets). In the low season (May to September), Backcountry Hut Tickets and Passes can also be used to procure a bunk or campsite on some Great Walks.

Depending on the hut category, a night's stay may use one or two tickets. Date your tickets and put them in the boxes provided at huts. Accommodation is on a first-come, first-served basis.

Conservation Campsites

The DOC also manages 220-plus 'Conservation Campsites' (often vehicle accessible) with categories as follows:

Basic campsites Basic toilets and water; free and unbookable

Standard campsites Toilets and water supply, and perhaps barbecues and picnic tables; $6 to $13 and unbookable.

Serviced campsites Full facilities: flush toilets, tap water, showers and picnic tables. They may also have barbecues, a kitchen and laundry; $18; bookable via DOC visitor centres.

Children aged five to 17 pay half price for Conservation Campsites; kids four and under stay free.

TE ARAROA

Epic! Te Araroa (www.teararoa.org.nz) is a 3000km trail from Cape Reinga in NZ's north to Bluff in the south (or the other way around). The route links up existing tracks with new sections. Built over almost 20 years, mostly by volunteers, it's one of the longest hikes in the world: check the website for maps and track notes, plus blogs and videos from hardy types who have completed the end-to-end epic.

Trailhead Transport

Getting to and from trailheads can be problematic, except for popular trails serviced by public and dedicated trampers' transport. Having a vehicle only helps with getting to one end of the track (you still have to collect your car afterwards). If the track starts or ends down a dead-end road, hitching will be difficult.

Of course, tracks accessible by public transport are also the most crowded. An alternative is to arrange private transport, either with a friend or by chartering a vehicle to drop you at one end, then pick you up at the other. If you intend to leave a vehicle at a trailhead, don't leave anything valuable inside – theft from cars in isolated areas is a significant problem.

Plan Your Trip

Skiing & Snowboarding

New Zealand (NZ) is a premier southern-hemisphere destination for snow bunnies, where wintry pursuits span all levels: family-friendly ski areas, cross-country (Nordic) skiing, daredevil snowboarding terrain and pulse-quickening heliskiing. The NZ ski season varies between areas but it's generally mid-June through September, though it can run as late as mid-October.

BE HEYS / SHUTTERSTOCK ©

Best Skiing & Snowboarding

Best for Beginners or with Kids

Mt Hutt, Central Canterbury

Cardrona, Queenstown

The Remarkables, Queenstown

Mt Dobson, South Canterbury

Roundhill, South Canterbury

Coronet Peak, Queenstown

Best Snowboarding

Mt Hutt, Central Canterbury

Treble Cone, Wanaka

Cardrona, Wanaka

Ohau, South Canterbury

Best Après-Ski Watering Holes

Dubliner, Methven

Cardrona Hotel, Cardrona

Lalaland, Wanaka

Rhino's Ski Shack, Queenstown

Planning
Where to Go

The variety of locations and conditions makes it difficult to rate NZ's ski fields in any particular order. Some people like to be near Queenstown's party scene; others prefer the quality high-altitude runs on Mt Hutt, uncrowded Rainbow or less-stressed club skiing areas. Club areas are publicly accessible and usually less crowded and cheaper than commercial fields, even though nonmembers pay a higher fee.

Practicalities

New Zealand's commercial ski areas aren't generally set up as 'resorts' with chalets, lodges or hotels. Rather, accommodation and après-ski carousing are often in surrounding towns, connected with the slopes via daily shuttles. It's a bonus if you want to sample a few different ski areas, as you can base yourself in one town and day trip to a few different resorts. Many club areas have lodges where you can stay, subject to availability.

Visitor information centres in NZ, and Tourism New Zealand (www.newzealand. com) internationally, have info on the various ski areas and can make bookings and organise packages. Lift passes usually cost $65 to $120 per adult per day (half price for kids) but more for major resorts. Lesson-and-lift packages are available at most areas. Ski and snowboard equipment rental starts at around $50 a day (cheaper for multiday hire). Private/group lessons start at around $120/60 per hour.

Websites

www.snow.co.nz Reports, webcams and ski info across the country.

www.nzski.com Reports, employment, passes and webcams for Mt Hutt, Coronet Peak and the Remarkables.

www.skiandride.nz Good all-round online portal for South Island ski areas with road conditions, school holiday dates and other practical info.

www.chillout.co.nz Portal to info on 13 ski areas and sales of ski passes that access them all. The 'Chill Travel Pass' areas are Awakino, Broken River, Cheeseman, Craigieburn, Fox Peak, Hanmer Springs, Mt Dobson, Mt Lyford, Mt Olympus, Rainbow and Temple Basin (plus a couple of days on Treble Cone and Porters).

South Island Ski Regions
Queenstown & Wanaka

Coronet Peak (p203) At the Queenstown region's oldest commercial ski field, snow-making systems and treeless slopes provide excellent skiing and snowboarding for all levels, with plenty of family-friendly options. There's night skiing on Fridays and Saturdays (and on

Winter Sports Areas

Wednesdays in July). Shuttles run from Queenstown, 16km away.

The Remarkables (p203) Visually remarkable, this ski field is also near Queenstown (24km away) – shuttle buses run during ski season. It has a good smattering of intermediate, advanced and beginner runs. Kids' club offered for five- to 15-year-old snow bunnies, and childcare options for younger pups.

Treble Cone (p228) The highest and largest of the southern lakes ski areas is in a spectacular location 26km from Wanaka, with steep slopes suitable for intermediate to advanced skiers (a rather professional vibe). There are also halfpipes and a terrain park for boarders.

Cardrona (p233) Around 34km from Wanaka, with several high-capacity chairlifts, beginners tows and the southern hemisphere's biggest park and pipe playground for the freestylers. Buses run from Wanaka and Queenstown during ski season. A friendly scene with good services

for skiers with disabilities, plus an on-mountain crèche for under-fives.

Snow Farm New Zealand (p233) New Zealand's only commercial Nordic (cross-country) ski area is 33km from Wanaka on the Pisa Range, high above the Cardrona Valley. There are 55km of groomed trails, huts with facilities and thousands of hectares of open snow.

South Canterbury

Mt Dobson (p105) The 3km-wide basin here, 26km from Fairlie, has a terrain park and famously dry powder. There's a huge learners' area and plenty for intermediates (and up high, dry powder and challenging terrain to suit more experienced snowheads). On a clear day you can see Aoraki/Mt Cook and the Pacific Ocean from the summit.

Roundhill (p106) A small field with wide, gentle slopes, perfect for beginners and intermediates,

Skiing at Coronet Peak (p203), near Queenstown

with a trump card of NZ's largest vertical drop (783m). It's 32km from Lake Tekapo village.

Ohau (p113) This commercial ski area with a secluded feel is on Mt Sutton, 42km from Twizel There are intermediate and advanced runs, excellent snowboarding, two terrain parks and sociable Lake Ohau Lodge, overlooking glorious views.

Fox Peak (p105) An affordable, uncrowded club ski area 40km from Fairlie in the Two Thumb Range. Expect rope tows, good cross-country skiing and dorm-style accommodation.

Central Canterbury

Mt Hutt (p99) One of the highest ski areas in the southern hemisphere, as well as one of NZ's best. It's close to Methven; Christchurch is 118km to the east – ski shuttles service both towns. Road access is steep – be extremely cautious in lousy weather. The ski area is exposed to the mercy of the elements (leading locals to dub it 'Mt Shut') but the season is long. Plenty of beginner, intermediate and advanced slopes, with chairlifts, heliskiing and wide-open faces that are good for learning to snowboard. Kids aged under 10 ski free.

Porters (p96) The closest commercial ski area to Christchurch (96km away on the Arthur's Pass road). The 'Big Mama' run boasts a 680m drop, but there are wider, gentler slopes, too. There's also a terrain park, good cross-country runs along the ridge, and lodge accommodation.

Temple Basin (p96) A club field with a cult following, 4km from the Arthur's Pass township. It's a 50-minute walk uphill from the car park to the ski-area lodges. There's floodlit skiing at night and excellent backcountry runs for snowboarders. Diehard snowheads only.

Craigieburn Valley (p96) Centred on Hamilton Peak, Craigieburn Valley is no-frills backcountry heaven, 40km from Arthur's Pass. It's one of NZ's most challenging club areas, with upper intermediate and advanced runs (no beginners). Accommodation in please-do-a-chore lodges.

Broken River (p96) Not far from Craigieburn Valley, this club field is a 15- to 20-minute walk from the car park and has a real sense of isolation. Reliable snow, laid-back vibe and sheltered enough to minimise bad-weather closures. Catered or self-catered lodge accommodation available.

HELISKIING

New Zealand's remote heights are tailor-made for heliskiing, with operators covering a wide off-piste area along the pristine slopes of the Southern Alps, including extreme skiing for the hardcore. Costs range from around $900 to $1450 for three to eight runs. Heliskiing is available at Coronet Peak, Treble Cone, Cardrona, Mt Hutt, Ohau and Hanmer Springs; independent operators include the following:

➡ **Alpine Heliski** (p202)

➡ **Harris Mountains Heli-Ski** (p202)

➡ **Methven Heliski** (☎03-302 8108; www.methvenheli.co.nz; Main St; 5-run day trips $1075)

➡ **Over The Top** (p208)

➡ **Southern Lakes Heliski** (p202)

Cheeseman (p96) A club area in the Craigieburn Range, this smallish family-friendly operation is around 100km from Christchurch. Based on Mt Cockayne, it's a wide, sheltered basin with drive-to-the-snow road access. Lodge accommodation available.

Mt Olympus (p96) Difficult to find (but worth the search), 2096m Mt Olympus is 58km from Methven and 12km from Lake Ida. This club area has intermediate and advanced runs, and there are solid cross-country trails to other areas. Access is sometimes 4WD-only, depending on conditions. Lodge accommodation available.

Northern South Island

Hanmer Springs (p92) A friendly commercial field based on Mt St Patrick, 17km from Hanmer Springs township (linked by shuttles), with mostly intermediate and advanced runs.

Mt Lyford (p94) Around 60km from both Hanmer Springs and Kaikoura, and 4km from Mt Lyford village, this is more of a 'resort' than most NZ ski fields, with accommodation and eating options. There's a good mix of runs and a terrain park.

Rainbow (☎03-521 1861, snow phone ☎0832 226 05; www.skirainbow.co.nz; daily lift passes adult/child $80/39) Borders Nelson Lakes National Park (100km from Nelson, a similar distance from Blenheim), with varied terrain, minimal crowds and good cross-country skiing. Chains are often required. St Arnaud is the closest town (32km).

Coronet Peak (p203), near Queenstown

Otago

Awakino (p122) A small player in North Otago, but worth a visit for intermediate skiers. Oamaru is 45km away; Omarama is 66km inland. Weekend lodge-and-ski packages available.

Plan Your Trip
Surfing, Cycling & Extreme Sports

From midair adventures to deep dives, New Zealand (NZ) is pure adrenaline. Inspired by NZ's rugged landscape, even the meekest travellers muster the courage to dangle on a bungy rope, skydive above mountains or thunder down river rapids. New Zealand pioneered thrills like bungy jumping and jetboating, and locals' daredevil attitude is infectious. There's nowhere better than NZ to see what you're made of...

On the Land

Bungy Jumping

Bungy jumping was made famous by Kiwi AJ Hackett's 1987 plunge from the Eiffel Tower, after which he teamed up with champion NZ skier Henry van Asch to turn the endeavour into an accessible pursuit for anyone.

Today their original home base of Queenstown is a spiderweb of bungy cords, including AJ Hackett's triad: the 134m Nevis Bungy (the highest in NZ); the 43m Kawarau Bungy (the original); and the Ledge Bungy (at the highest altitude – diving off a 400m-high platform). There's another scenic jump at Thrillseekers Canyon near Hanmer Springs. Huge rope swings offer variation on the theme; head to Queenstown's Shotover Canyon or Nevis Swing for that swooshy buzz.

Caving

Caving (aka spelunking) opportunities abound in NZ's honeycombed karst (limestone) regions. You'll find local clubs and organised tours around Charleston and Karamea. Golden Bay also has some mammoth caves.

Top Adrenaline Rushes

Best Skydive Drop Zones
Queenstown

Fox & Franz Josef Glaciers

Top White-Water Rafting Trips
Shotover Canyon, Queenstown

Buller Gorge, Murchison

Top Mountain Biking Tracks
Old Ghost Road, Westport

Queen Charlotte Track, Marlborough

West Coast Wilderness Trail, Hokitika

Alps 2 Ocean, South Canterbury

Top Surfing Spots
Kaikoura Peninsula

Taylors Mistake & New Brighton, Christchurch

St Clair Beach, Dunedin

Punakaiki Beach

Tauranga Bay, Westport

Colac Bay, Riverton

For comprehensive information including details of specific areas and clubs, see the website of the New Zealand Speleological Society (www.caves.org.nz).

Paragliding & Hang Gliding

A surprisingly gentle but still thrilling way to take to the skies, paragliding involves setting sail from a hillside or clifftop under a parachute-like wing. Hang gliding is similar but with a smaller, rigid wing. Most flights are conducted in tandem with a master pilot, although it's also possible to get lessons to go it alone. To give it a whirl, try a tandem flight in Queenstown, Wanaka, Nelson, Motueka or Christchurch. The New Zealand Hang Gliding and Paragliding Association (www.nzhgpa.org.nz) rules the roost.

Horse Trekking

Treks in NZ offer a chance to explore some remarkable landscapes – from farms to forests and along rivers and beaches. Rides range from one-hour jaunts (from around $60) to week-long, fully supported treks.

South Island options include beachy trips in Golden Bay and adventures around mountain foothills near Aoraki/ Mt Cook, Lake Tekapo, Queenstown and Glenorchy – as a bonus, you can canter through several *Lord of the Rings* filming locations. Spectacular treks are offered from Punakaiki into Paparoa National Park. For info and operator listings, check out True NZ Horse Trekking (www.truenz. co.nz/horsetrekking).

Mountain Biking & Cycle Touring

Jaw-dropping mountains interlaced with farm tracks and old railway lines...it would be hard to design better mountain biking terrain than New Zealand. The New Zealand Cycle Trail (www.nzcycletrail.com), some 2500km of tracks, helped mountain biking grow from a weekend sport to a national craze. Its popularity among outdoors enthusiasts of a certain age (and the potential for gear oneupmanship) has led mountain biking to be dubbed 'the new golf'. But no age group is immune, and the variety of trails in NZ brings a choice of gentle pootles in meadows to multiday cycle tours, half-day downhill thrill rides to challenging week-long MTB adventures.

Mountain bike parks – most with various trail grades and skills areas (and handy bike hire, usually) – are great for trying mountain biking NZ style. The South Island's most famous is Queenstown's downhill park, fed by the Skyline Gondola.

Classic trails include the Rameka on Takaka Hill and the trails around Christchurch's Port Hills – but this is just the tip of the iceberg. An increasing number of DOC hiking trails are being converted to dual use – such as the tricky but epic Heaphy Track and challenging, history-rich Old Ghost Road – but mountain biking is often restricted to low season due to hiker numbers. Track damage is also an issue, so check with DOC before starting out.

Your clue that there's some great biking around is the presence of bike-hire outfits. Bowl on up and pick their brains. Most likely cycle-obsessed themselves, they'll soon point you in the direction of a ride appropriate to your level. The go-to book is *Classic New Zealand Mountain Bike Rides* (from bookshops, bike shops and www. kennett.co.nz).

If cycle touring is more your pace, check out the *Pedallers' Paradise* booklets by Nigel Rushton (www.paradise-press.co.nz). Changeable weather and road conditions mean cycle touring is less of a craze but there are remarkable road journeys, such as the Southern Scenic Route in the deep south.

Mountaineering

NZ has a proud mountaineering history – this was, after all, the home of Sir Edmund Hillary (1919–2008), who, along with Tenzing Norgay, were the first two mountaineers confirmed to summit Mt Everest. When he came back down, Sir Ed famously uttered to friend George Lowe, 'Well, George, we knocked the bastard off!'

The Southern Alps are studded with amazing climbs. The Aoraki/Mt Cook region is outstanding; but there are other zones extending throughout the spine of the South Island from the Kaikoura Ranges and the Nelson Lakes peaks all the way through to the hotbeds of Mt Aspiring National Park and Fiordland. Be warned, though: this is rugged and often remote stuff, and climber deaths are a regular occurrence. Even confident climbers are

NGA HAERENGA, THE NEW ZEALAND CYCLE TRAIL

The New Zealand Cycle Trail (www.nzcycletrail.com) – known in Māori as Nga Haerenga, 'the journeys' – is a 22-strong series of off-road trails known as Great Rides. Spread from north to south they are of diverse length, terrain and difficulty, with many following history-rich old railway lines and pioneer trails, while others are freshly cut, flowing and big fun. Almost all penetrate remarkable landscapes.

There are plenty of options for beginner to intermediate cyclists, with several hardcore exceptions including the Old Ghost Road, which is growing to international renown. The majority are also well supported by handy bike hire, shuttles, and dining and accommodation options, making them a mighty desirable way to explore NZ.

strongly advised to seek out a local guide, whatever the route.

The Christchurch-based New Zealand Alpine Club (www.alpineclub.org.nz) has background, news and useful links, and produces the annual *NZAC Alpine Journal* and the quarterly *The Climber* magazine. It also has details on upcoming climbing courses.

Rock Climbing

Time to chalk-up your fingers and don some natty little rubber shoes. Try the Port Hills area above Christchurch or Castle Hill on the road to Arthur's Pass. West of Nelson, the marble and limestone mountains of Golden Bay and Takaka Hill provide prime climbing. Other options are Long Beach (north of Dunedin), and Mihiwaka and Lovers Leap on the Otago Peninsula. Raining? You'll find an indoor climbing wall in Christchurch.

Climb New Zealand (www.climb.co.nz) has the low-down on the gnarliest overhangs around NZ, plus access and instruction info. Needless to say, instruction is a must for all but the most seasoned climbing pros.

Skydiving

With some of the most scenic jump zones in the world, NZ is a fantastic place to take a leap. First-time skydivers can knock off this bucket-list item with a tandem jump, strapped to a qualified instructor, experiencing up to 75 seconds of free fall before the chute opens. The thrill is worth every dollar, from $249 for a 9000ft jump to $559 for NZ's highest free-fall jump (a nerve-jangling 19,000ft, on offer in Franz Josef). Extra costs apply for a DVD or photographs capturing your mid-air terror/delight. Check out the New Zealand Parachute Federation (www.nzpf.org) for more info.

On the Water
Surfing

Big swells, golden sand, uncrowded beaches...are you scrambling for a surfboard yet? NZ's surf scene is world class, and the long coastline means there's heaps of variety for beginners and experienced surfers: point breaks, reefs, rocky shelves, hollow sandy beach breaks, and islands with swells from all points of the compass. If you're willing to travel off the beaten track, you can score waves all to yourself. A number of hostels and holiday parks double as surf schools and gear-rental outfits, making it easy to roll straight from bed to beach.

Regardless of the season, you'll need a wetsuit and some weather research. Water temperatures and climate vary greatly from north to south. In summer on the South Island you can get away with a 2mm–3mm steamer wetsuit. In winter you'll need a 3mm–5mm with extras like a hood and booties. Be rip tide aware: don't fight strong currents that sweep you away from the shore and swim parallel to the beach to get beyond the rip's reach before making your way back to land.

Surfing New Zealand (www.surfingnz.co.nz) has a list of approved surf schools where you can learn to catch waves, along with a calendar of competitions and events where you can go slack-jawed at the pros.

Jetboating

The jetboat was invented in NZ by an engineer from Fairlie – Bill Hamilton (1899–1978) – who wanted a boat that could navigate shallow, local rivers. He credited his eventual success to Archimedes, but as most jetboat drivers will inevitably tell you, Kiwi Bill is the hero of the jetboat story.

Top: Shotover Jet (p206), Arthurs Point/ Shotover Canyon

Bottom: Kayaking in Doubtful Sound (p181)

River jetboat tours can be found throughout NZ, and while much is made of the hair-raising 360-degree spins that see passengers drenched and grinning from ear to ear, they are really just a sideshow. Just as Bill would have it, jetboat journeys take you deep into wilderness you could otherwise never see, and as such they offer one of NZ's most rewarding tour experiences. In Haast and Whataroa, jetboat tours plunge visitors into pristine wilderness, aflutter with birds.

Big ticket trips such as Queenstown's Shotover, Kawarau and Dart live up to the hype. But the quieter achievers will blow your skirt up just as high. Check out the Buller and Wilkin in Mt Aspiring National Park.

Parasailing & Kiteboarding

Parasailing (dangling from a modified parachute over the water, while being pulled along by a speedboat) is perhaps the easiest way for humans to achieve assisted flight. There are operators in Wanaka and Queenstown.

Kiteboarding (aka kitesurfing), where a mini parachute drags you across the ocean on a mini surfboard, can be attempted at Nelson.

Though it's less adrenaline-soaked, stand-up paddleboarding (SUP) is increasingly popular across NZ.

Sea Kayaking

Sea kayaking offers a wonderful perspective of the coastline and gets you close to marine wildlife you may otherwise never see. Meanwhile tandem kayaks, aka 'divorce boats', present a different kind of challenge.

There are ample places to paddle. Hotspots include the Marlborough Sounds (from Picton) and Abel Tasman National Park. Kaikoura is exceptional for wildlife spotting, and Fiordland for jaw-dropping scenery.

The Kiwi Association of Sea Kayakers (www.kask.org.nz) gives a good primer on paddling techniques, plus resources for kayakers with a disability.

Scuba Diving & Snorkelling

New Zealand is just as enchanting under the waves, with warm waters in the north, interesting sea life all over and some impressive shipwrecks.

In the Marlborough Sounds, the MS *Mikhail Lermontov* is one of the world's largest diveable cruise-ship wrecks. In Fiordland, experienced divers can head for Dusky Sound, Milford Sound and Doubtful Sound, which have clear conditions and the occasional friendly fur seal or dolphin.

Expect to pay anywhere from $160 for a short, introductory, pool-based scuba course, and around $600 for a four-day, PADI-approved, ocean-dive course. One-off organised boat- and land-based dives start at around $170.

New Zealand Underwater Association (www.nzunderwater.org.nz) Clean seas and diving-safety advocates whose website has safety info, diving tips, gear maintenance advice and more.

Dive New Zealand (www.divenewzealand.com) NZ's only dedicated dive magazine, plus safety info and listings of dive clubs and shops.

White-Water Rafting, Kayaking & Canoeing

Epic mountain ranges and associated rainfall mean there's no shortage of great rivers to raft, nor any shortage of operators ready to get you into the rapids. Rivers are graded from I to VI (VI meaning they can't be safely rafted), with operators often running a couple of different trips to suit ability and age (rougher stretches are usually limited to rafters aged 13 or above).

Queenstown's Shotover and Kawarau Rivers are deservedly popular, but the Rangitata (Geraldine), Buller (Murchison) and the Arnold and Waiho rate just as highly. For a multiday epic, check out the Landsborough.

Kayaking and canoeing are rampant, particularly on friendly lake waters, although there are still plenty of places to paddle the rapids.

New Zealand Rafting Association (www.nz-rafting.co.nz) River conservation nonprofit; river gradings and listings of rafting operators.

New Zealand Kayak (www.kayaknz.co.nz) Community-based kayaking magazine.

Green-lipped mussel

Plan Your Trip
Eat & Drink
Like a Local

Travellers, start your appetites! Eating is a highlight of any visit to New Zealand. You can be utilitarian if money is tight, or embrace NZ's full bounty, from fresh seafood and gourmet burgers to farmers market fruit-and-veg and crisp-linen fine dining. Eateries range from fish and chip shops and pub bistros to retro cafes and ritzy dining rooms. Drinking, too, presents boundless opportunities to have a good time, with Kiwi coffee, craft beer and wine at the fore.

The Year in Food

Summer (December to February)

Gorge yourself on Central Otago stonefruit. Sup on sauvignon blanc at the Marlborough Wine & Food Festival.

Autumn (March to May)

Hokitika hosts its Wildfood Festival, while Central Otago's Clyde and Gibbston both have wine and food festivals. Bluff's famous oysters come into season in May, heralding a local food festival and a nationwide frenzy.

Winter (June to August)

The prime time for fireside comfort food.

Spring (September to November)

In October South Island foodies ping-pong between Kaikoura's Seafest and Akaroa's French Fest.

influx of migrants from Europe, Asia and the Middle East – as has an adventurous breed of local restaurant-goers and the elevation of Māori and Pacific Islander flavours and ingredients to the mainstream.

In order to wow the socks off increasingly demanding diners, restaurants must now succeed in fusing contrasting ingredients and traditions into ever more innovative fare. The phrase 'Modern NZ' has been coined to classify this unclassifiable technique: a melange of East and West, a swirl of Atlantic and Pacific Rim, and a dash of authentic French and Italian.

Traditional staples still hold sway (lamb, beef, venison, green-lipped mussels), but dishes are characterised by interesting flavours and fresh ingredients rather than fuss, clutter or snobbery. Spicing ranges from gentle to extreme, seafood is plentiful, and meats are tender and full flavoured. Enjoy!

Cafes & Coffee

Somewhere between the early 1990s and now, New Zealand cottoned on to coffee culture in a big way. Caffeine has become a nationwide addiction: there are Italian-style espresso machines in virtually every cafe, boutique roasters are de rigueur and, in urban areas, a qualified barista (coffee maker) is the norm. The cafe and bean-roasting scenes in Christchurch and student-filled Dunedin are world-class, very inclusive and family friendly.

Modern NZ

Once upon a time (yet not so long ago) NZ subsisted on a modest diet of 'meat and three veg'. Though small-town country pubs still serve their unchanging menu of roasted meats and battered fish, overall NZ's culinary sophistication has evolved dramatically. In larger towns, kitchens thrive on bending conventions and absorbing gastronomic influences from around the planet, all the while keeping local produce central to the menu.

Immigration has been key to this culinary rise – particularly the post-WWII

Pubs, Bars & Beer

Kiwi pubs were once male bastions with dim lighting, smoky air and beer-soaked carpets – these days they're more of a family affair. Sticky floors and pie-focused menus still abound in rural parts of NZ but pubs are generally where parents take their kids for lunch, friends mingle for sav blanc and tapas, and locals of all ages congregate to roar at live sports screenings. Food has become integral to the NZ pub experience, along with the inexorable rise of craft beer in the national drinking consciousness.

Myriad small, independent breweries have popped up around the country in the

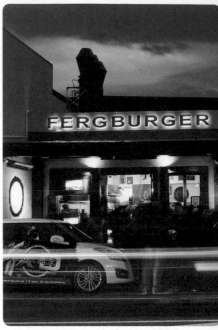

Fergburger (p213), Queenstown

LOCAL DELICACIES

Touring the menus of NZ, keep an eye out for these local delights: kina (sea urchin), paua (abalone; a type of sea snail), kumara (sweet potato, often served as chips), whitebait (tiny fish, often cooked into fritters or omelettes) and the humble kiwifruit.

last decade. The bigger centres all have dedicated craft-beer bars, with revolving beers on tap and passionate bar staff who know all there is to know about where the beers have come from, who made them and what's in them.

Wine Regions

Like the wine industry in neighbouring Australia, the New Zealand version has European migrants to thank for its status and success – visionary visitors who knew good soils and good climate when they saw it, and planted the first vines in the 1850s.

But it wasn't until the 1970s that things really got going, with traditional agricultural exports dwindling, Kiwis travelling more and the introduction of BYO ('Bring Your Own' wine) restaurant licensing conspiring to raise interest and demand for local wines.

Since then, New Zealand cool-climate wines have conquered the world, a clutch of key regions producing the lion's share of bottles. Organised day tours via minivan or bicycle are a great way to visit a few select wineries.

Marlborough NZ's biggest and most widely known wine region sits at the top of the South Island, where a microclimate of warm days and cool nights is perfect for growing sauvigon blanc. You could spend many days touring the many cellar doors here (and why not?).

Central Otago Reaching from Cromwell in the north to Alexandra in the south and Gibbston near Queenstown in the west, the South Island's Central Otago region produces sublime riesling and pinot noir.

Waipara Valley Not to be left out of proceedings, Christchurch has its own nearby wine region – the Waipara Valley just north of the city – where divine riesling and pinot noir come to fruition.

Vegetarians & Vegans

More than 10% of New Zealanders are vegetarian (more on the North than the South Island), and numbers are rising. Most large urban centres have at least one dedicated vegetarian cafe or restaurant: see the Vegetarians New Zealand website (www.vegetarians.co.nz) for listings. Beyond this, almost all restaurants and cafes offer some vegetarian menu choices (although sometimes only one or two). Many eateries also provide gluten-free and vegan options.

Plan Your Trip
Travel with Children

New Zealand's a dream for family travel: kid-centric activities, family-friendly accommodation, a moderate climate and very few critters that can bite or sting. Cuisine is chilli-free and food servers are clued up on dietary requirements. Base yourself in a sizeable town for amenities galore and excursions within a short drive.

South Island for Kids

Fabulous wildlife parks, beaches, parks, snowy slopes and interactive museums proliferate across NZ. There are countless attractions and amenities designed specifically for kids but families needn't stick to playgrounds and holiday parks. Kid-appropriate adventures, from glaciers to white-water rafting, are everywhere...if parents are brave enough, that is.

Admission Fees & Discounts

Kids' and family rates are often available for accommodation, tours, attraction entry fees, and air, bus and train transport, with discounts up to as much as 50% off the adult rate. Note that the definition of 'child' can vary from under 12 to under 18 years; toddlers (under four years old) usually get free admission and transport.

Eating Out with Children

If you sidestep the flashier restaurants, children are generally welcome in NZ eateries. Cafes are kid-friendly, and you'll see families getting in early for dinner in pub dining rooms. Most places can supply high chairs. Dedicated kids' menus are common, but selections are usually uninspiring (pizza, fish fingers, chicken nuggets etc). If a restaurant doesn't have a kids' menu,

Best Regions for Kids

Queenstown & Wanaka

New Zealand's winter sports scene suits pro snowheads (and après-ski fans) but it's just as easy to enjoy with kids...actually, it's more fun. Cardrona has kid-friendly skiing, and there's Wanaka's Puzzling World for ski-free days.

Christchurch & Canterbury

Nature parks, rowboats, the International Antarctic Centre and botanic gardens In the big city, and the amazing Banks Peninsula not far away (penguins, dolphins and pretty birds).

Marlborough & Nelson

Beautiful beaches, plus horseriding in the Abel Tasman National Park, and dolphin- and whale-spotting in Kaikoura.

Dunedin & Otago

Penguins waddle ashore in Oamaru and the Otago Peninsula, while seals sun themselves on beaches and albatrosses circle overhead.

TOP TIPS

➡ Book accommodation far in advance: many motels and hotels have adjoining rooms that can be opened up to form large family suites, but they are snapped up fast, especially in peak season.

➡ If you're planning to roam between locations, stock up on food in larger towns. There's much more choice, and prices in smaller food shops in remote locations can be sky high.

➡ Plan stops in advance if you're travelling by road. Distances can feel long but fortunately NZ is rich in gorgeous lookouts, roadside water-falls and many towns have promi-nent public toilets, hurrah!

find something on the regular menu and ask the kitchen to downsize it. It's usually fine to bring toddler food in with you. If the sun is shining, hit the farmers markets and find a picnic spot. New Zealand's res-taurants are decent at catering for gluten-free and dairy-free diners – one less thing to worry about if kids follow a special diet.

Breastfeeding & Nappy Changing

Most Kiwis are relaxed about public breast-feeding and nappy changing: wrestling with a nappy (diaper) in the open boot of a car is a common sight! Alternatively, most major towns have public rooms where par-ents can go to feed their baby or change a nappy. Infant formula and disposable nap-pies are widely available.

Babysitting

For babysitters who have been fully inter-viewed, have supplied child-care references and undergone a police check, try www.rockmybaby.co.nz (from $16 per hour). Alternatively look under 'baby sitting' in the *Yellow Pages* (www.yellow.co.nz).

Children's Highlights
Getting Active

Queenstown (p210) Everything from kids' rafting trips to paragliding, bungee jumping, ziplines, ice skating and (of course) skiing.

Abel Tasman Horse Trekking (p293) Paddock rides for little ones and beach horse treks for those aged 12 and up.

The Catlins (p156) Flat rambles a few minutes long, rewarded by waterfalls...no tired little legs here.

St Kilda & St Clair Beaches (p132) Kids don't mind chilly Dunedin, parents can warm up in the saltwater pool.

Wildlife Encounters

Kiwi Birdlife Park, Queenstown (p202) Spot a kiwi and myriad squawking birds.

Akaroa Dolphins (p89) Watch dolphins from a catamaran, in the company of a wildlife-spotting dog.

West Coast Wildlife Centre, Franz Josef (p249) Meet the world's rarest kiwi and tuatara (pint-sized dinosaurs).

Royal Albatross Centre (p139) Watch little penguins waddle ashore at dusk from Pilots Beach on the Otago Peninsula.

Cultural & Culinary Experiences

Canterbury Museum, Christchurch (p69) A mummy, dinosaur bones and a cool Discovery Centre.

Shantytown, Greymouth (p260) All aboard a steam train for gold-panning in a recreated gold-rush town.

Motueka Sunday Market (p292) Pick up a ripe bag of kiwifruit at harvest time.

Sweet Alice's Fudge Kitchen, Hokitika (p257) Candies, ice cream and fudge on the West Coast.

Regions at a Glance

Get ready for an oft-changing selection of some of the planet's most surprising scenery. From the labyrinthine marine idylls of the Marlborough Sounds to the craggy volcanic hills of the Banks Peninsula, the South Island packs a stunning scenic punch. Kayak through the mist of Doubtful Sound, or test yourself on the Milford or Routeburn Tracks – often in the company of New Zealand's quirky wildlife – before strapping on some skis and hitting the world-renowned slopes around Queenstown and Wanaka. Spend some time strolling the newly restored pavements of creative Christchurch, or head back in time along the streets of historic Oamaru and gothic Dunedin. Along the way, taste-test the best of the country's gourmet gastronomy at a profusion of regional restaurants, alongside world-class wineries and exciting breweries.

Christchurch & Canterbury

Architecture
Outdoor Activities
Scenery

....

Old and New Christchurch

Restoration may still be underway following the 2011 earthquake, but much of Christchurch's architectural heritage is back on display, alongside new buildings that pay homage to the city's history.

Tramping & Kayaking

Tramp the alpine valleys around Arthur's Pass, kayak with dolphins on Akaroa Harbour, or head inland for heart-pumping exertion amid the glacial lakes of Aoraki/Mt Cook National Park.

Banks Peninsula & the Southern Alps

Descend the Peninsula's Summit Rd to explore hidden bays and coves, or experience nature in the river valleys, soaring peaks and glaciers of the Southern Alps.

p58

Dunedin & Otago

Wildlife
Wine Regions
History

....

Birds, Seals & Sea Lions

Members of the Otago Peninsula's wild menagerie – seals, sea lions and penguins – patrol the rugged coastline, while rocky Taiaroa Head is the world's only mainland breeding location for the magnificent royal albatross.

Bannockburn & Waitaki Valley

Descend into the craggy valleys of Bannockburn for excellent vineyard restaurants and the world's best pinot noir, or delve into the up-and-coming Waitaki Valley wine scene for riesling and pinot gris.

Victoriana

Explore the arty and storied streets of Scottish-flavoured Dunedin, or escape by foot or pennyfarthing bicycle into the heritage ambience of Oamaru's restored Victorian Precinct.

p114

Fiordland & Southland

Scenery
Wilderness
Outdoor
Activities

Epic Landscapes

The star of the show is remarkable Milford Sound, but take time to explore the peculiar landforms around the rugged Catlins coast or experience the remote, end-of-the-world appeal of Stewart Island.

National Parks

Fiordland National Park comprises much of New Zealand's precious Te Wāhipounamu (Southwest New Zealand) World Heritage Area. Further south, Rakiura National Park showcases Stewart Island's beauty.

Tramping & Sea Kayaking

Test yourself by tramping a Great Walk such as the Milford or Kepler Tracks, or by negotiating a sea kayak around gloriously isolated Doubtful Sound.

p148

Queenstown & Wanaka

Outdoor
Activities
Scenery
Wine Regions

Queenstown Adrenaline

Nowhere else on earth offers so many adventurous activities: bungy jumping, river rafting and mountain biking only scratch the surface of Queenstown. Could this be the ultimate skydiving drop zone?

Mountains & Lakes

Queenstown's combination of Lake Wakatipu and the soaring Remarkables is a real jaw-dropper, or venture into the wilderness around Glenorchy and Mt Aspiring National Park.

Central Otago Wineries

Lunch at award-winning restaurants in Arrowtown, explore the unique terroir of the Gibbston Valley and finish with a riesling tasting at Rippon, overlooking gorgeous Lake Wanaka.

p192

The West Coast

Natural Wonders
Outdoor
Activities
History

Crazy Rock Formations

This region is replete with prehistoric wonders: don't miss Oparara's famous arches, Punakaiki's Pancake Rocks and the sublime Hokitika Gorge.

Tramping

The West Coast offers tracks from an easy hour's stroll through to hard-core epics. Old mining and milling routes like Charming Creek Walkway and Mahinapua Tramline entice beginners and history buffs.

Pioneer Tales

The West Coast's pioneering history comes vividly to life at places such as Denniston, Shantytown, Reefton and Jackson Bay.

p236

Nelson & Marlborough

Wilderness
Food & Wine
Wildlife

National Parks

Not satisfied with just one national park, the Nelson region has three – Nelson Lakes, Kahurangi and Abel Tasman. You could tramp in all three over a week.

Marlborough Wine Touring

Bobbing in Marlborough's sea of sauvignon blanc, riesling, pinot noir and bubbly are barrel-loads of quality cellar-door experiences and some fine food as well.

Kaikoura

The top of the South Island is home to myriad creatures, both in the water and on the wing. Kaikoura is a great one-stop shop for spotting whales or swimming with dolphins and seals.

p274

On the Road

Nelson & Marlborough (p274)

The West Coast (p236)

Christchurch & Canterbury (p58)

Queenstown & Wanaka (p192)

Dunedin & Otago (p114)

Fiordland & Southland (p148)

Christchurch & Canterbury

Best Places to Eat

→ Pegasus Bay (p95)

→ Supreme Supreme (p79)

→ Little High Eatery (p79)

→ Oxford (p104)

→ Twenty Seven Steps (p80)

Best Places to Stay

→ Halfmoon Cottage (p87)

→ Eco Villa (p78)

→ Peel Forest DOC Campsite (p101)

→ Woodbank Park Cottages (p93)

→ Lake Tekapo Lodge (p107)

Why Go?

Nowhere in New Zealand (NZ) is changing and developing as fast as post-quake Christchurch. The scaffolding is coming down, the hospitality scene is flourishing and the central city is once again drawing visitors to its pedestrian friendly streets.

A short drive from the city, Banks Peninsula conceals idyllic hidden bays and beaches that provide the perfect backdrop for wildlife cruises, with a sunset return to the attractions of pretty Akaroa. To the north are the vineyards of the Waipara Valley and the relaxed ambience of Hanmer Springs, while westwards, the Canterbury Plains morph quickly into the dramatic wilderness of the Southern Alps.

Canterbury's attractions include tramping along alpine valleys and over passes around Arthur's Pass, and mountain biking around the turquoise lakes of Mackenzie Country. During winter (June to September), attention switches to the ski fields. Throughout the seasons, Aoraki/Mt Cook, the country's tallest peak, stands sentinel over this diverse region.

When to Go

→ Canterbury is one of NZ's driest regions, as moisture-laden westerlies from the Tasman Sea dump their rainfall on the West Coast before hitting the eastern side of the South Island. Visit from January to March for hot and settled weather, with plenty of opportunities to get active amid the region's spectacular landscapes.

→ The shoulder seasons of October to November and March to May can be cool and dry, and blissfully uncrowded. Come prepared for all weather; snow is still possible on the mountains.

→ Hit the winter slopes from July to October at Mt Hutt or on one of Canterbury's smaller club ski fields.

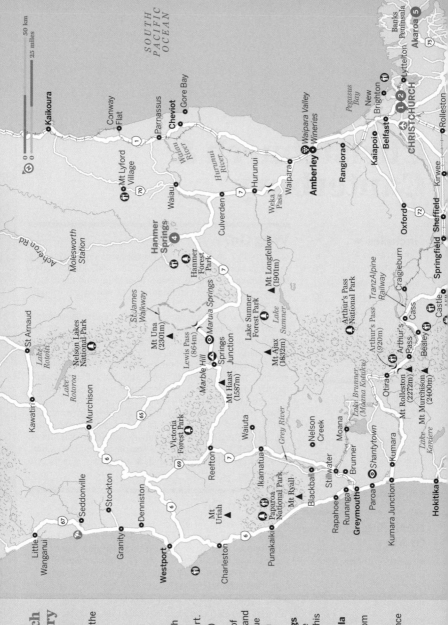

Christchurch & Canterbury Highlights

1 Christchurch
(p59) Experiencing the dynamic rebuilding and re-emergence of the city post-earthquake.

2 Botanic Gardens (p68)
Meandering through Christchurch's beautiful green heart.

3 Mt John (p106)
Marvelling at the otherworldly views of Mackenzie Country and the surreal azure blue of Lake Tekapo from the top.

4 Hanmer Springs
(p92) Soaking in the soothing waters at this famous hot spring.

5 Banks Peninsula
(p85) Admiring the surf-bitten edges from Summit Rd before descending to the quaint Gallic ambience of Akaroa.

TASMAN SEA

Lake Ellesmere

Dunsandel

Rakaia

Glentunnel

Windwhistle

Ashburton

Tinwald

Porters Pass (945m)

Glenavy

Pukeuri

Waitaki River

1

Waimate

82

83

Timaru

Pleasant Point

Temuka

Mt Hutt

Methven

Mayfield

Rakaia Gorge

Mt Somers

72

72

77

Rangitata

Rangitata River

Geraldine

Peel Forest

Fairlie

Albury

79

8

Hunter Hills

53

8

Lake Benmore

7 Twizel

8

30

Hokitika Gorge

Mt Bryce (2188m)

Mt Whitcombe (2538m)

Craigieburn Forest Park

Lake Coleridge

Lake Heron

Mesopotamia

Mt Arrowsmith (2795m)

Sommers Arps

The Thumbs (2545m)

Mt McLeod (1922m)

Fox Peak (2331m)

Two Thumb Range

Lake Tekapo

Lake Tekapo

Tekapo

Mt John 3

Foss

Hariharl

Mt Tyndall (2524m)

Mt D'Archiac (2865m)

Elie de Beaumont (3116m)

Westland Tai Poutini National Park

Mt Tasman (3498m)

MalteBrun (3154m)

6

Aoraki/Mt Cook (3775m)

Mt Cook Village

Glentanner

Lake Pukaki

Ben Ohau Range

Lake Ohau

Lake Iarithe

Whataroa

Okarito

Franz Josef

Fox Glacier

Aoraki/Mt Cook National Park

Mt Sefton (3151m)

Ruataniwha Conservation Park

4

6

Mahinapua

Bruce Bay

Pariga

Haast

6

DAY TRIPS FROM CHRISTCHURCH

LYTTELTON

Christchurch's historic port lies just over the prosaically named Port Hills from the city proper. Although it was badly hit during the earthquakes, it's well worth a trip through the 2km road tunnel during the day to explore its revitalised shopping strip, or at night to have a slap-up meal and catch a band.

☆ Best Things to See/Do/Eat

◉ **Christchurch Gondola** Stop before you reach the tunnel for a 862m ride on the cable car to the top of Mt Cavendish. The views over Christchurch, Lyttelton, Banks Peninsula and the Canterbury Plains are extraordinary. (p72)

✕ **London St Shopping** Lyttelton has long had a bohemian edge. The best time to visit its compact shopping street is on a Saturday morning, when the farmers' market is fizzing. (p84)

✕ **Roots** Lyttelton is home to one of Christchurch's most acclaimed restaurants. Roots sprung up post-quake, with an emphasis on local and seasonal produce, much of it foraged. (p85)

☆ How to Get There

Car From the city centre head southeast on Ferry Rd and veer onto Tunnel Rd (SH74). The journey takes around 20 minutes.
Bus Catch bus 28 or 535, which takes 30 minutes.

BANKS PENINSULA

You only need look at a map of this oddly shaped protuberance to realise what an absolutely unique place this is. Thumb shaped and with enough indents, whorls and contours to give it a fingerprint, this spectacular peninsula offsets rippling hills with sparkling waters. At its heart is a historic anomaly: the sweet little Frenchified village of Akaroa.

☆ Best Things to See/Do/Eat

◉ **Giant's House** Akaroa's most unusual attraction is this artsy garden, jam-packed with sculpture and mosaics made of broken china, mirrors and tiles. The pretty pink 1880 house at its centre is full of yet more of the owner's art. (p89)

🥾 **Walk around Akaroa** Pick up a pamphlet from the i-SITE and meander around Akaroa's heritage houses and churches. If you're after something more challenging, embark on the six-hour Skyline Circuit. (p89)

✕ **Hilltop Tavern** As you crest the hill and begin the descent to Akaroa Harbour, stop for a wood-fired pizza and craft beer at this historic pub. The views are spectacular. (p87)

☆ How to Get There

Car It takes less than an hour and a half to reach Akaroa from central Christchurch. The quickest route is to head southeast on Lincoln Rd and onto SH75. A more scenic route heads due south via Governors Bay. Alternatively, catch a shuttle.

WAIPARA VALLEY

The North Canterbury Wine Region is conveniently spread along either side of SH1, about an hour north of Christchurch. While it's one of New Zealand's smaller wine-producing areas, it's developing a reputation for cool-climate wines such as riesling, gewürztraminer and pinot noir.

☆ Best Things to See/Do/Eat

◉ **Willowbank Wildlife Reserve** As you're leaving the city, take a five-minute detour to the suburb of Northwood. This low-key zoo features a stellar roster of Kiwi critters and a recreated Māori village. (p72)

◉ **Wine Tasting** About a dozen of the region's wineries have public tasting rooms. Our favourite is pretty Pegasus Bay, set in verdant gardens and home to one of Canterbury's best restaurants. (p95)

✕ **Little Vintage Espresso** If you're in the mood for a more low-key lunch – or just a coffee to see you on your way – stop off at this whitewashed cottage as you pass through Amberley. (p95)

☆ How to Get There

Car Head north from the city centre on Sherborne St, Cranford St and Main Rd (SH74). If you're detouring to Willowbank, look for the signs to your left. SH74 joins SH1 at the northern edge of town. Buses aren't a viable option for visiting the wineries

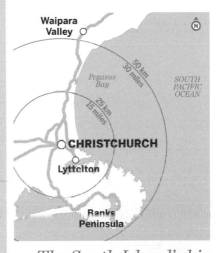

The South Island's big smoke is well positioned for day trips to beaches, mountains and wine regions. In winter you can even head out for a day's skiing on Mt Hutt.

TRAMPING IN CANTERBURY

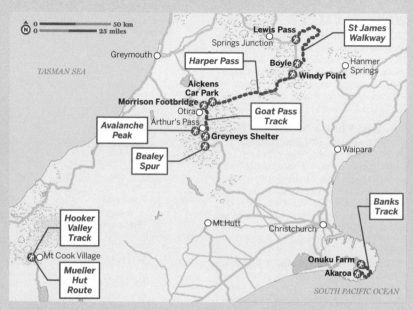

BANKS PENINSULA

☆ Banks Track
START ONUKU FARM
END AKAROA
DURATION 3 DAYS
DISTANCE 29KM
DIFFICULTY EASY TO MODERATE

The first private walk established in NZ, the Banks Track takes you across private farmland and forest and along the peninsula's remote outer bays. The route takes in a spectacular volcanic coastline, native bush, waterfalls and sandy beaches, with two crossings of the crater rim high above Akaroa Harbour.

Other than two steep climbs of nearly 700m each, this is a relatively leisurely tramp, which allows plenty of time to take in the marvellous scenery. For the more energetic, cutting the tramp to two days is an option.

Bookings are essential and should be made through **Banks Track** (☎03-304 7612; www.bankstrack.co.nz; ☉Oct-Apr). Tramper numbers

are limited to just 16 setting out each day, so book early for peak summer and NZ holiday periods. The three-day package ($260) includes transport from Akaroa to Onuku, three nights accommodation, landowners' fees, track registration and a copy of *Banks Peninsula Track: A Guide to the Route, Natural Features and Human History*. The two-day package ($195) covers the same route, but just the one night on the track, staying at Stony Bay (plus the night before the tramp at Onuku).

LEWIS PASS

☆ St James Walkway
START LEWIS PASS
END BOYLE
DURATION 5 DAYS
DISTANCE 65KM
DIFFICULTY EASY TO MODERATE

Built in 1981, the St James Walkway begins in the Lewis Pass National Reserve, traverses

For heavy-duty hikers, Canterbury is all about the mountains, be it the tightly packed peaks of Arthur's Pass National Park or the valleys and view points that unveil Aoraki/Mt Cook.

the western side of the St James Conservation Area, and ends in the Lake Sumner Forest Park. Despite taking in two mountain passes – Ada Pass (1008m) and Anne Saddle (1136m) – it's not particularly challenging, though there is one 17km day and some stream crossings. The climbs are not steep, and the rest of the walk is spent tramping through open valleys and beech forests.

The walkway follows historic pack tracks, is well benched and has an excellent series of serviced huts. The heart of the track, from Ada River along Anne River to upper Boyle River, runs through the St James Conservation Area. Vegetation within this area includes red, mountain and silver beech forests, manuka/kanuka and matagouri scrublands, numerous alpine plants, at least five species of tussock and a vast expanse of valley floor native grasslands. It is also home to around 430 indigenous species of flora and 30 native bird species.

ARTHUR'S PASS NATIONAL PARK

☆ Avalanche Peak
START/END ARTHUR'S PASS
DURATION 6–8 HOURS
DISTANCE 7KM
DIFFICULTY MODERATE

In this park of peaks, Avalanche Peak is without question the most popular one to climb and is the only mountain marked with a poled route to the summit. Its location is ideal, looming directly above Arthur's Pass village and just south of Mt Rolleston.

The alpine world experienced during this tramp is stunning on a clear day. Many experienced trampers will claim that this is in fact NZ's best day tramp, outshining the dramatic volcanic peaks and steamy vents of the Tongariro Alpine Crossing.

Unequivocal is the fact that Avalanche Peak is an alpine climb that should only be attempted by the fleet of foot in good conditions. The total climb and descent is 1100m, and although the route is clearly marked

and well trodden, it's still an arduous climb with a climax of 200m of narrow, crumbly ridge. People have died on Avalanche Peak when they failed to heed weather warnings.

Two routes, Avalanche Peak Track and Scotts Track, depart from SH73 and lead towards the peak, merging just before reaching it. Avalanche Peak Track is a much steeper climb, and at times you need to scramble up rock faces. Scotts Track is a more gradual and easier route. It's best to use Avalanche Peak Track to reach the summit and Scotts Track for the return, when your legs will be tired. Of course, the easiest return route to the peak is to simply use Scotts Track both ways, but that's not as much fun or as varied.

☆ Goat Pass Track
START GREYNEYS SHELTER
END MORRISON FOOTBRIDGE
DURATION 2 DAYS
DISTANCE 25KM
DIFFICULTY MODERATE

Goat Pass Track, also referred to as the Mingha-Deception Route (the two rivers the route follows), is an excellent introduction to tramping in Arthur's Pass. It is also one of the least complicated routes in the park, as long as the rivers run in your favour. Typical of the Southern Alps, the Bealey, Mingha and Deception Rivers can be very dangerous when in flood, and the Deception alone requires up to 30 compulsory crossings. This tramp should therefore not be attempted during periods of rain. Should the crossings start to look too difficult, backtrack or stay put – attempting a dicey crossing just isn't worth the risk.

This track forms the running leg of the Coast to Coast (p258), NZ's most famous multisport race, which crosses the South Island from the Tasman Sea to the Pacific Ocean by a gruelling combination of cycling, kayaking and running. On your travels, you may come across some competitors training for the event. With luck you'll also encounter whio, the nationally vulnerable and very cute blue duck.

The Goat Pass Track can be tramped in either direction, but the Mingha-Deception direction allows for a shorter day first up.

☆ Harper Pass

START AICKENS CAR PARK
END WINDY POINT
DURATION 5 DAYS
DISTANCE 77KM
DIFFICULTY MODERATE

Māori often travelled over Harper Pass as they crossed to the West Coast in search of *pounamu* (greenstone), and it was that knowledge and experience that would eventually see them lead the first Europeans through the area in 1857. Two guides, Wereta Tainui and Terapuhi, took Leonard Harper across the pass that now bears his name. By 1862, just three years after the first bridle paths were surveyed, the route was serving as the main gateway to the West Coast goldfields, with stores and liquor shops along the way. When the gold rush ended, however, the track fell into disrepair, until its reinvention as a tramping trail.

Today it is one of NZ's classic tramps, connecting Arthur's Pass to Lewis Pass, and is part of the country-length Te Araroa route (p39), making it a particularly busy tramp during the summer months. The track crosses the Main Divide over Harper Pass, a low saddle at just 963m above sea level. The segment in Arthur's Pass National Park is a valley route along the Taramakau River, but in Lake Sumner Forest Park the track is well cut and marked.

Trampers need to be cautious with the Taramakau. It is a large and unruly river in a high-rainfall area, making it prone to sudden flooding. The track can be walked in either direction, but a west-to-east crossing is recommended as you can be surer of good conditions as you cross the Otira, Otehake and Taramakau rivers, all of which are prone to flooding during rain. On the eastern side, the track is well defined along the Hurunui and Hope Rivers, and bridged at all major crossings.

☆ Bealey Spur

START/END CLOUDESLEY RD
DURATION 4–6 HOURS
DISTANCE 13.5KM
DIFFICULTY EASY TO MODERATE

To climb almost anything in Arthur's Pass National Park is to submit to steep ground. Bealey Spur is a rare exception, climbing

Southern rātā, Arthur's Pass National Park (p98)

steadily but not steeply to a historic hut at around 1230m above sea level. Add to this the fact that the tramp doesn't climb above the bushline, and that it sits east of the Main Divide, making it often drier than other park tracks even when northwesterly winds are bringing rain to Arthur's Pass, and it's a comfort hike of sorts.

It's also a tramp where the rewards far exceed the effort, with expansive views over the national park and the valleys that cut so deeply into it. Though it's not steep, the tramp does climb around 600m from SH73 to Bealey Spur Hut.

AORAKI/MT COOK NATIONAL PARK

☆ Mueller Hut Route

START/END AORAKI/MT COOK VILLAGE
DURATION 2 DAYS
DISTANCE 10KM
DIFFICULTY DEMANDING

This route passes through a dynamic landscape, simultaneously uplifted and eroded in the never-ending battle between powerful natural forces. Rock beds of schist, sandstone, siltstone and greywacke have

YUNSUN_KIM / SHUTTERSTOCK ©

Tramping the Hooker Valley Track

been carved out by glaciation, dramatically illustrated on the climb to Mueller Hut. Hanging glaciers, moraines and U-shaped valleys are all classic landmarks of icy geological transformation. Populating this inhospitable environment are alpine flowers and herb fields, of which there are many to see during the 1000m climb to the rocky ridge and hut atop it.

Mueller Glacier was named by Julius Haast in 1862, after the Danish explorer and writer Ferdinand von Mueller. A series of Mueller Huts have perched above it since the first one was built between 1914 and 1915.

☆ Hooker Valley Track

START/END WHITE HORSE HILL CAMPSITE
DURATION 3 HOURS
DISTANCE 10KM
DIFFICULTY EASY

Aoraki/Mt Cook National Park's signature tramp, the Hooker Valley Track, is a visual extravaganza to the base of NZ's highest mountain. A journey on foot into a glacial valley where moraines, glacial lakes and the glaciers themselves stand front and centre, it culminates just 10 straight-line kilometres from the summit of Aoraki/Mt Cook, on the shores of iceberg-laden Hooker Lake. And once you're standing beside the lake, the mountain actually looks even closer than that.

The tramp follows a wide and remarkably flat track (given its proximity to a 3724m-high mountain) through the stunning valley, making this a simple wander into mountain magnificence. All of which adds up to one small price to pay – popularity – with more than 80,000 people hiking through the Hooker Valley each year. Beat the crowds by setting out early in the blue light of dawn, or take the chance to spread out along the shore of Hooker Lake, claiming a private audience with the grandest NZ mountain of all.

CHRISTCHURCH

POP 375,000

Welcome to a vibrant city in transition, coping creatively with the aftermath of NZ's second-worst natural disaster. Traditionally the most English of NZ cities, Christchurch's heritage heart was all but hollowed out following the 2010 and 2011 earthquakes that left 186 people dead.

Today Christchurch is in the midst of an epic rebuild that has completely reconstructed the city centre, where over 80% of buildings needed to be demolished after the quake. Scaffolding and road cones will be part of Christchurch's landscape for a while yet, but don't be deterred; exciting new buildings are opening at an astonishing pace, and most sights are open for business.

Curious travellers will revel in this chaotic, crazy and colourful mix, full of surprises and inspiring in ways you can't even imagine. And despite all the hard work and heartache, the locals will be only too pleased to see you.

History

The first people to live in what is now Christchurch were moa (bird) hunters, who arrived around 1250. Immediately prior to colonisation, the Ngāi Tahu tribe had a small seasonal village on the banks of the Avon called Ōtautahi.

When British settlers arrived in 1850 it was an orderly Church of England project; the passengers on the 'First Four Ships' were dubbed 'the Canterbury Pilgrims' by the British press. Christchurch was meant to be a model of class-structured England in the South Pacific, not just another scruffy colonial outpost. Churches were built rather than pubs, the fertile farming land was deliberately placed in the hands of the gentry, and wool made the elite of Christchurch wealthy.

In 1856 Christchurch officially became NZ's first city, and a very English one at that. Town planning and architecture assumed a close affinity with the 'Mother Country' and English-style gardens were planted, earning it the nickname, the 'Garden City'. To this day, spring is a glorious time to visit.

◎ Sights

◉ City Centre

Starting from the ground up after the earthquakes, the Gap Filler folks fill the city's empty spaces with creativity and colour. Projects range from temporary art installations, performance spaces and gardens, to a minigolf course scattered through empty building sites, to the world's first giant outdoor arcade game. Gaps open up and get filled, so check out the Gap Map on the website (www.gapfiller.org.nz), or simply wander the streets and see what you can find.

Hagley Park PARK

(Map p74; Riccarton Ave) Wrapped around the Botanic Gardens, Hagley Park is Christchurch's biggest green space, stretching for 165 hectares. Riccarton Ave splits it in two, while the Avon River snakes through the northern half. It's a great place to stroll, whether on a foggy autumn morning, or a warm spring day when the cherry trees lining Harper Ave are in flower. Joggers make the most of the tree-lined avenues year-round.

★ Botanic Gardens GARDENS

(Map p74; www.ccc.govt.nz; Rolleston Ave; ⊙ 7am-9pm Nov-Feb, to 8.30pm Oct & Mar, to 6.30pm Apr-Sep) FREE Strolling through these 30 blissful riverside hectares of arboreal and floral splendour is a consummate Christchurch experience. Gorgeous at any time of the year, the gardens are particularly impressive in spring when the rhododendrons, azaleas

---

THE CANTERBURY EARTHQUAKES

Christchurch's seismic nightmare began at 4.35am on 4 September 2010. Centred 40km west of the city, a 40-second, 7.1-magnitude earthquake jolted Cantabrians from their sleep, and caused widespread damage to older buildings in the central city. Close to the quake's epicentre in rural Darfield, huge gashes erupted amid grassy pastures, and the South Island's main railway line was bent and buckled. Because the tremor struck in the early hours of the morning when most people were home in bed, there were no fatalities, and many Christchurch residents felt that the city had dodged a bullet.

Fast forward to 12.51pm on 22 February 2011, when central Christchurch was busy with shoppers and workers enjoying their lunch break. This time the 6.3-magnitude quake was much closer, centred just 10km southeast of the city and only 5km deep. The tremor was significantly greater, and many locals report being flung violently and almost vertically into the air. The peak ground acceleration exceeded 1.8, almost twice the acceleration of gravity.

When the dust settled after 24 traumatic seconds, NZ's second-largest city had changed forever. The towering spire of the iconic ChristChurch Cathedral lay in ruins; walls and verandas had cascaded down on shopping strips; and two multistorey buildings had pancaked. Of the 185 deaths (across 20 nationalities), 115 occurred in the six-storey Canterbury TV building, where many international students at a language school were killed. Elsewhere, the historic port town of Lyttelton was badly damaged; roads and bridges were crumpled; and residential suburbs in the east were inundated as a process of rapid liquefaction saw tons of oozy silt rise from the ground.

In the months that followed literally hundreds of aftershocks rattled the city's traumatised residents (and claimed one more life), but the resilience and bravery of Cantabrians quickly became evident. From the region's rural heartland, the 'Farmy Army' descended on the city, armed with shovels and food hampers. Social media mobilised 10,000 students, and the Student Volunteer Army became a vital force for residential clean-ups in the city's beleaguered eastern suburbs. Heartfelt aid and support arrived from across NZ, and seven other nations sent specialised urban-search-and-rescue teams.

The impact of the events of a warm summer's day in early 2011 will take longer than a generation to resolve. Entire streets and neighbourhoods in the eastern suburbs have had to be abandoned, and Christchurch's heritage architecture is irrevocably damaged. Families in some parts of the city have been forced to live in substandard accommodation, waiting for insurance claims to be settled. Around 80% of the buildings within the city centre's famed four avenues have been or are still due to be demolished. Amid the doomed, the saved, and the shiny new builds are countless construction sites and empty plots still strewn with rubble.

Plans for the next 20 years of the city's rebuild include a compact, low-rise city centre, large green spaces, and parks and cycleways along the Avon River. It's estimated that the total rebuild and repair bill could reach $40 or even $50 billion.

To find out more about the effects of the quakes, and to hear survivors tell their experiences of that time in their own voices, visit the highly recommended **Quake City** (p71).

---

and daffodil woodland are in riotous bloom. There are thematic gardens to explore, lawns to sprawl on, and a playground adjacent to the **Botanic Gardens Visitor Centre** (Map p74; ☑03-941 7590; ⊙9am-4pm), which also contains a lovely **cafe** and gift shop.

Guided walks ($10, 1½ hours) depart at 1.30pm (October to May) from the gate near Canterbury Museum (p69), or hop aboard the **Caterpillar** (Map p74; ☑0800 88 22 23; www.welcomeaboard.co.nz; adult/child $20/9; ⊙10am-3.30pm Oct-Mar, 11am-3pm Apr-Sep) electric shuttle.

Canterbury Museum MUSEUM
(Map p74; ☑03-366 5000; www.canterbury museum.com; Rolleston Ave; ⊙9am-5.30pm Oct-Mar, to 5pm Apr-Sep; ⊕) FREE Yes, there's a mummy and dinosaur bones, but the highlights of this museum are more local and more recent. The Māori galleries contain some beautiful *pounamu* (greenstone) pieces, while Christchurch Street is an atmospheric walk through the colonial past. The reproduction of Fred & Myrtle's gloriously kitsch Paua Shell House embraces Kiwiana at its best, and kids will enjoy the interactive displays in the

Christchurch

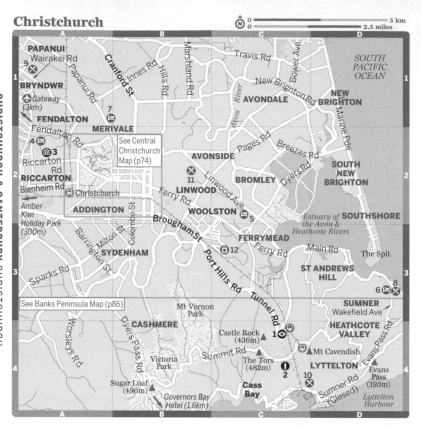

Discovery Centre (admission $2). Free guided tours (one hour) depart from the foyer at 3.30pm on Tuesdays and Thursdays.

Arts Centre   HISTORIC BUILDING
(Map p74; www.artscentre.org.nz; 2 Worcester Blvd; ⊙10am-5pm) FREE Dating from 1877, this enclave of Gothic Revival buildings was originally Canterbury College, the forerunner of Canterbury University. The buildings are slowly reopening to the public after extensive restoration work due to quake damage, with the entire site due to reopen by 2019. Inside you'll find an array of shops, cafes and museums and galleries, as well as the i-SITE (p83). Exhibition spaces play host to regular concerts, markets and events.

➡ Central Art Gallery
(Map p74; ☑03-366 3318; www.thecentral.co.nz; Arts Centre, 2 Worcester Blvd; ⊙10am-5pm Tue-Sun) FREE Housed in the Arts Centre's beautifully restored 1916 Library building, the Central Art Gallery exhibits contemporary works by established and emerging NZ artists.

➡ Teece Museum of Classical Antiquities
(Map p74; www.arts.canterbury.ac.nz; Old Chemistry Bldg, Arts Centre, 3 Hereford St; entry by donation; ⊙11am-3pm Wed-Sun) Part of the University of Canterbury, this petite, well-designed museum has an interesting collection of Greek, Roman and Egyptian antiquities.

➡ Rutherford's Den
(Map p74; ☑03-363 2836; www.rutherfordsden. org.nz; Arts Centre, 2 Worcester Boulevard; adult/ child $20/10; ⊙10am-5pm) Canterbury College's most famous alumnus was the father of nuclear physics, Lord Ernest Rutherford, the NZ physicist who first split the atom in 1917 (that's him on the $100 bill). The rooms where Rutherford worked have now been turned into a small interactive science museum, with displays on the scientist's many important discoveries, as well as a room dedicated to renewable energy.

Christchurch

★ **Christchurch Art Gallery** GALLERY
(Te Puna o Waiwhetu; Map p74; ☑03-941 7300; www.christchurchartgallery.org.nz; cnr Montreal St & Worcester Blvd; ⊙10am-5pm Thu-Tue, to 9pm Wed; 🅿️) Damaged in the earthquakes, Christchurch's fantastic art gallery has reopened brighter and bolder, presenting a stimulating mix of local and international exhibitions. Collection items range from the traditional to the startlingly contemporary – think light installations and interactive sculptures.

Free guided tours (one hour) take place at 11am and 2pm daily.

★ **Quake City** MUSEUM
(Map p74; ☑03-366 5000; www.quakecity.co.nz; 299 Durham St N; adult $20, child accompanied/unaccompanied free/$8; ⊙10am-5pm) A must-visit for anyone interested in understanding the impact of the Canterbury earthquakes, this compact museum tells stories through photography, video footage and various artefacts, including the remnants of ChristChurch Cathedral's celebrated rose window and other similarly moving debris. There are exhibits aimed at engaging both adults and children. Most affecting of all is the film featuring survivors recounting their own experiences.

Canterbury Earthquake National Memorial MEMORIAL
(Oi Manawa; Map p74; www.canterburyearth quakememorial.co.nz; Oxford Tce) Unveiled in 2017, this moving monument comprises a 100m-long memorial wall, curved along the south bank of the Avon and engraved with the names of the 185 people who died as a result of the 22 February 2011 earthquake. On the opposite bank, a shady park provides a space for reflection and remembrance. The memorial's Māori name, Oi Manawa, means 'tremor or quivering of the heart'.

Cathedral Square SQUARE
(Map p74) Christchurch's city square stands at the heart of the rebuilding efforts, with the remains of ChristChurch Cathedral emblematic of what has been lost. The February 2011 earthquake brought down the 63m-high spire, while subsequent earthquakes in June 2011 and December 2011 destroyed the prized stained-glass rose window. Other heritage buildings around the square were also badly damaged, but one modern landmark left unscathed is the 18m-high metal sculpture *Chalice*, designed by Neil Dawson. It was erected in 2001 to commemorate the new millennium.

The much-loved Gothic cathedral has been at the centre of a battle between those who seek to preserve what remains of Christchurch's heritage, the fiscal pragmatists, and those ideologically inclined to things new. In 2012 the Anglican Diocese announced that the cathedral was to be demolished, but work was stayed when heritage advocates launched court proceedings. Eventually, in September 2017, the church leadership voted to preserve the building after the government and Christchurch City Council banded together to offer significant financial support. It's thought that the rebuild could take up to 10 years, with an estimated cost of $104 million.

WORTH A TRIP

ORANA WILDLIFE PARK

This **wildlife park** (⌨03-359 7109; www.oranawildlifepark.co.nz; 793 McLeans Island Rd, McLeans Island; adult/child $34.50/9.50; ⊙10am-5pm) is an 'open range' zoo, and you'll know exactly what that means if you opt to jump in the cage for the lion encounter (per person $45). There's an excellent, walk-through native bird aviary, a nocturnal kiwi house, and a reptile exhibit featuring tuatara. Most of the 80-hectare grounds are devoted to Africana, including rhinos, giraffes, zebras, cheetahs and gorillas.

Transitional Cathedral   CHURCH
(Map p74; www.cardboardcathedral.org.nz; 234 Hereford St; entry by donation; ⊙9am-5pm Apr-Oct, to 7pm Nov-Mar) Universally known as the Cardboard Cathedral due to the 98 cardboard tubes used in its construction, this interesting structure serves as both the city's temporary Anglican cathedral and as a concert venue. Designed by Japanese 'disaster architect' Shigeru Ban, the entire building was constructed in 11 months.

◎ Surrounds

Willowbank Wildlife Reserve   ZOO
(⌨03-359 6226; www.willowbank.co.nz; 60 Hussey Rd, Northwood; adult/child $29.50/12; ⊙9.30am-7pm Oct-Apr, to 5pm May-Sep) 🐾 Willowbank focuses on native NZ critters (including kiwi), heritage farmyard animals and hands-on enclosures with wallabies, deer and lemurs. There's also a recreated Māori village, the setting for the evening **Ko Tane** (www.kotane.co.nz; adult/child $135/67.50; ⊙5.15pm). It's 10km north of town, near the airport.

International Antarctic Centre   MUSEUM
(⌨0508 736 4846, 03-357 0519; www.iceberg.co.nz; Christchurch Airport, 38 Orchard Rd; adult/child $39/19; ⊙9am-5.30pm; 🅿) As one of only five 'gateway cities' to Antarctica, Christchurch has played a special role in Antarctic exploration since expeditionary ships to the icy continent began departing from Lyttelton in the early 1900s. This huge complex, built for the administration of the NZ, US and Italian Antarctic programs, gives visitors the opportunity to learn about Antarctica in a fun, interactive environment.

Attractions include the Antarctic Storm chamber (where you can get a taste of -18°C wind chill), face-to-face encounters with resident little blue penguins, and a meet-and-greet with rescue huskies (Friday to Sunday only). The 'Xtreme Pass' (adult/child $59/29) includes the '4D theatre' (a 3D film with moving seats and a water spray) and a joy-ride on a Hägglund all-terrain amphibious Antarctic vehicle. An optional extra is the Penguin Backstage Tour (adult/child $25/15), which allows visitors behind the scenes of the Penguin Encounter.

A free shuttle to the centre departs from outside Canterbury Museum (p69) at 9am, 11am, 1pm and 3pm, returning at 10am, noon, 2pm and 4pm.

Riccarton House & Bush   HISTORIC BUILDING
(Map p70; www.riccartonhouse.co.nz; 16 Kahu Rd, Riccarton; ⊙9am-4pm Sun-Fri, to 1pm Sat) **FREE** Historic Riccarton House (1856) sits proudly amid 12 hectares of pretty parkland and forest beside the Avon River. The grounds host the popular Christchurch Farmers Market (p81) on Saturdays; the rest of the week you can visit the lovely restaurant on the ground floor.

The biggest draw, however, is the small patch of bush behind the house. Enclosed by a vermin-proof fence, this is the last stand of kahikatea floodplain forest in Canterbury.

Kahikatea is NZ's tallest native tree, growing to heights of 60m; the tallest trees here are a mere 30m and around 300 to 600 years old. A short loop track heads through the heart of the forest.

The majority of the house is only accessible on a guided tour, departing at 2pm Sunday to Friday (adult/child $18/5, one hour); shorter tours (adult/child $8/free) run every half hour between 10am and 12.30pm on Saturdays.

Christchurch Gondola   CABLE CAR
(Map p70; www.welcomeaboard.co.nz/gondola; 10 Bridle Path Rd; return adult/child $28/12; ⊙10am-5pm; 🅿) Take a ride to the top of Mt Cavendish (500m) on this 862m cable car for wonderful views over the city, Lyttelton, the Banks Peninsula and the Canterbury Plains. At the top there's a cafe and the child-focused *Time Tunnel* ride, which recounts the history of the area. You can also walk to Cavendish Bluff Lookout (30 minutes return) or the **Pioneer Women's Memorial** (Map p70), one hour return.

🏃 Activities

Boating

Antigua Boat Sheds
BOATING, KAYAKING

(Map p74; ☑ 03-366 5885; www.boatsheds.co.nz; 2 Cambridge Tce; ☺9am-5pm) Dating from 1882, the photogenic green-and-white Antigua Boat Sheds hires out rowing boats ($35), kayaks ($12), canoes ($35) and bikes (adult/child $10/5), all prices are per hour. There's also a good cafe.

Punting on the Avon
BOATING

(Map p74; www.punting.co.nz; 2 Cambridge Tce; adult/child $28/12; ☺9am-6pm Oct-Mar, 10am-4pm Apr-Sep) 🖋 If rowing your own boat down the Avon sounds a bit too much like hard work, why not relax in a flat-bottomed punt while a strapping lad in Edwardian clobber glides you peaceably through the Botanic Gardens. Tours depart year-round from the Antigua Boat Sheds; during the warmer months alternative trips run from sites at Mona Vale and Worcester Bridge.

Walking

The i-SITE (p83) provides information on walking tours as well as self-guided options, including the rewarding Avon River Walk, which takes in major city sights, and several excellent trails around the Port Hills.

For long-range city views, take the walkway from the Sign of the Takahe on Dyers Pass Rd. The various 'Sign of the...' places in this area were originally roadhouses built during the Depression as rest stops. This walk leads up to the Sign of the Kiwi, through Victoria Park and then along the view-filled Summit Rd to Scotts Reserve.

You can walk to Lyttelton on the Bridle Path (1½ hours), which starts at Heathcote Valley (take bus 28). The Godley Head Walkway (two hours return) begins at Taylors Mistake, crossing and recrossing Summit Rd, and offers beautiful views on a clear day.

Walks in Christchurch and throughout Canterbury are well detailed at www.christchurchnz.com.

Cycling

Being mostly flat and boasting more than 300km of cycle trails, Christchurch is a brilliant place to explore on two wheels. For evidence, look no further than the free Christchurch City Cycle Map, available around town or downloadable from www.ccc.govt.nz/cycling.

The i-SITE (p83) can advise on bicycle hire and guided tours.

There's some great off-road riding around the Port Hills, while towards Banks Peninsula you'll find the best section of the Little River Trail (p87), one of NZ's Great Rides.

Swimming & Surfing

Despite having separate names for different sections, it's one solid stretch of sandy beach that spreads north from the estuary of the Avon and Heathcote Rivers. Closest to the city centre is New Brighton, with a distinctive pier reaching 300m out to sea. On either side, South New Brighton and North Beach are quieter options. Waimairi, a little further north, is our personal pick.

The superstar is Sumner, 12km from the city centre on the south side of the estuary. Its beachy vibe, eateries and art-house cinema make it a satisfying spot for a day trip.

Further east around the headland, isolated Taylors Mistake has the cleanest water of any Christchurch beach and some good surf breaks. Beginners should stick to Sumner or New Brighton.

🎫 Tours

★Tram
TRAM

(Map p74; ☑ 03-366 7830; www.welcomeaboard.co.nz; adult/child $25/free; ☺9am-6pm Sep-Mar, 10am-5pm Apr-Aug) Excellent driver commentary makes this so much more than just a tram ride. The beautifully restored old dears trundle around a 17-stop loop, departing every 15 minutes, taking in a host of city highlights, including Cathedral Sq and New Regent St. The full circuit takes just under an hour, and you can hop on and hop off all day.

ℹ️ COMBO TICKETS

Christchurch Attractions (www.christchurchattractions.nz) is the company that runs the Avon River punting, tram, gondola (p72) and botanic gardens tour (p69), as well as attractions in Hanmer Springs (☑03-315 7046, 0800 661 538; www.welcomeaboard.co.nz; 839 Hanmer Springs Rd; ☺9am-5pm). A baffling array of combo tickets are available, which will save you some money if you're considering doing more than one activity. All four Christchurch attractions are included on the five-hour Grand Tour (adult/child $129/69), as well as a stop in Sumner.

Central Christchurch

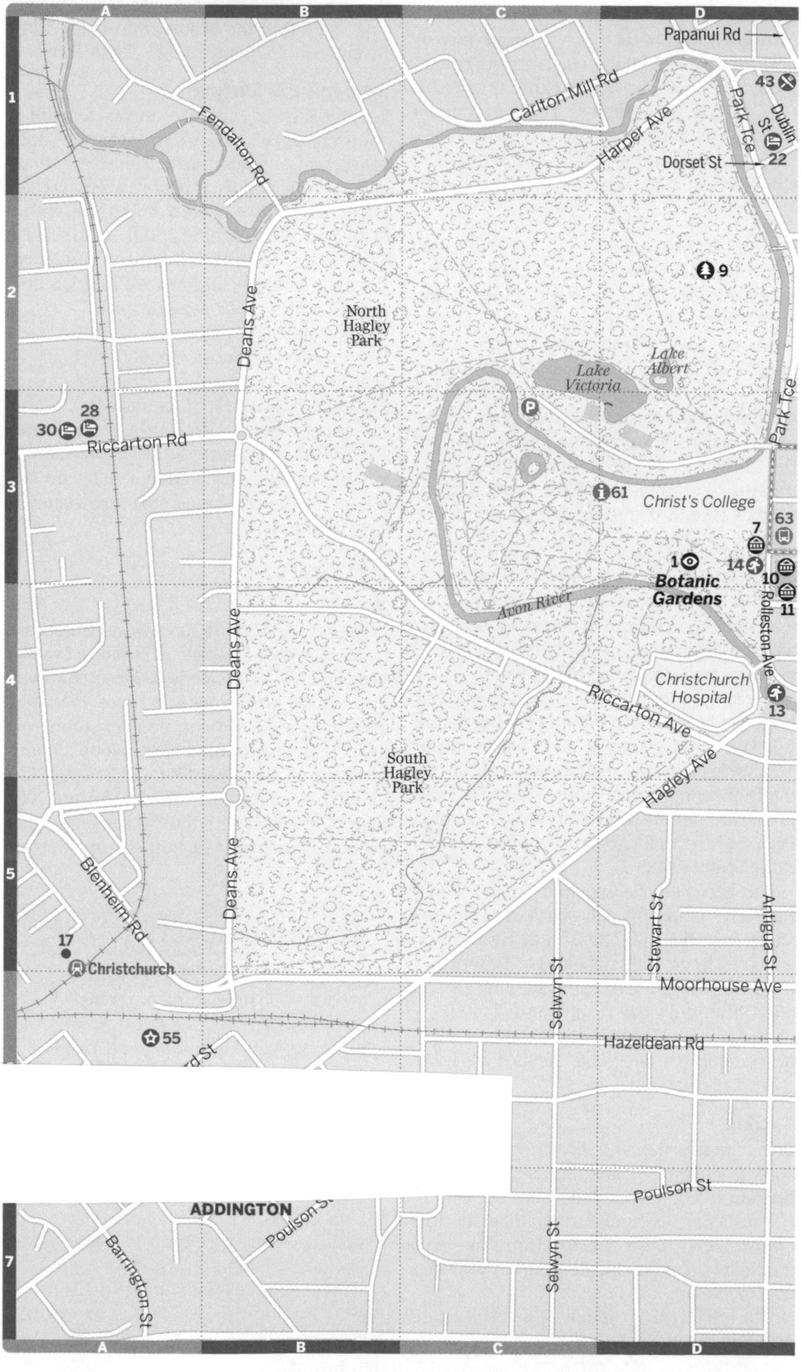

Papanui Rd

Carlton Mill Rd

Fendalton Rd

Harper Ave

Park Tce

Dublin St

43

Dorset St — 22

9

North Hagley Park

Deans Ave

Lake Albert

Lake Victoria

Park Tce

30 28

Riccarton Rd

61 Christ's College

7 63

1 Botanic Gardens

14

10

11

Avon River

Deans Ave

Rolleston Ave

Christchurch Hospital

Riccarton Ave

13

South Hagley Park

Hagley Ave

Deans Ave

Stewart St

Antigua St

Blenheim Rd

17

Christchurch

Moorhouse Ave

Selwyn St

55

d St

Hazeldean Rd

ADDINGTON

Poulson St

Poulson St

Selwyn St

Barrington St

Central Christchurch

TranzAlpine　　　　　　　　　　RAIL
(Map p74; ☑ 03-341 2588, 0800 872 467; www.ki-wirailscenic.co.nz; one way from $119) The *TranzAlpine* is one of the world's great train journeys, traversing the Southern Alps between Christchurch and Greymouth, from the Pacific Ocean to the Tasman Sea, passing through Arthur's Pass National Park. En route is a sequence of dramatic landscapes, from the flat, alluvial Canterbury Plains to narrow alpine gorges, an 8.5km tunnel, beech-forested river valleys, and a lake fringed with cabbage trees.

The 4½-hour journey is unforgettable, even in bad weather (if it's raining on one coast, it's probably fine on the other). The train departs Christchurch at 8.15am and Greymouth at 2.05pm.

CHRISTCHURCH FOR CHILDREN

There's no shortage of kid-friendly sights and activities in Christchurch. If family fun is a priority, consider planning your travels around NZ's biggest children's festival, **KidsFest** (www.kidsfest.org.nz; ⊙ Jul). It's held every July and is chock-full of shows, workshops and parties. The annual **World Buskers Festival** (p77) is also bound to be a hit with young 'uns.

The impressive **Margaret Mahy Family Playground** (Map p74; cnr Manchester & Armagh Sts) is a must for anyone with small people in tow. For picnics and open-air frolicking, visit the **Botanic Gardens** (p68); there's a playground beside the cafe, and little kids will love riding on the Caterpillar train. Extend your nature-based experience with a wildlife encounter at **Orana Wildlife Park** (p72) or the **Willowbank Wildlife Reserve** (p72), or get them burning off excess energy in a rowing boat or kayak from the **Antigua Boat Sheds** (p73). Fun can be stealthily combined with education at the **International Antarctic Centre** (p72), the Discovery Centre at **Canterbury Museum** (p69) and **Quake City** (p71). If the weather's good, hit the beaches at Sumner or New Brighton.

Guided City Walks   WALKING

(Map p74; ☑ 0800 423 783; www.walkchristchurch.nz; Rolleston Ave; adult/child $20/free; ⊙ 10.30am & 1pm) Departing from the red kiosk outside Canterbury Museum, these 2½-hour tours offer a leisurely stroll around the city's main sights in the company of knowledgable guides.

Hassle Free Tours   BUS

(Map p74; ☑ 03-385 5775; www.hasslefree.co.nz) Explore Christchurch in an open-top double-decker bus on a one-hour highlights tour ($35) or three-hour discovery tour ($69). Tours depart outside Canterbury Museum. Regional options include a 4WD alpine safari, Kaikoura whale-watching, and visiting the location of Edoras from the *Lord of the Rings* trilogy.

✪ Festivals & Events

Check www.ccc.govt.nz/events and www.christchurchnz.com/events for comprehensive festivals and events listings.

World Buskers Festival   PERFORMING ARTS

(www.worldbuskersfestival.com; ⊙ Jan) National and international talent entertain passers-by for 10 days in mid-January. Shows span stand-up comedy, burlesque, music and circus arts. Check the website for locations – and don't forget to throw money in the hat.

Christchurch Arts Festival   PERFORMING ARTS

(www.artsfestival.co.nz; ⊙ mid-Aug–mid-Sep) Month-long biennial arts extravaganza celebrating music, theatre and dance. The next festival will be held in 2019.

🛌 Sleeping

🛏 City Centre

Dorset House Backpackers   HOSTEL $

(Map p74; ☑ 03-366 8268; www.dorset.co.nz; 1 Dorset St; dm $31, d $81 80; 🅿 @ 🖥) 🏠 Built in 1871, this tranquil wooden villa has a sunny deck, a large regal lounge with a pool table, and great kitchen facilities. Dorms feature beds instead of bunks, and private rooms are small but spotless. It's a short stroll to Hagley Park and the Victoria St restaurant strip.

YHA Christchurch   HOSTEL $

(Map p74; ☑ 03-379 9536; www.yha.co.nz; 36 Hereford St; dm/s/d from $30/75/90; @ 🖥) Smart, well-run 100-plus-bed hostel conveniently located near Canterbury Museum and the Botanic Gardens. Dorms and doubles include many with en suite bathrooms. If it's full, Christchurch's other YHA is one street away (5 Worcester Blvd).

Around the World Backpackers   HOSTEL $

(Map p74; ☑ 03-365 4363; www.aroundtheworld.co.nz; 314 Barbadoes St; dm $25-41, d $74-85; 🅿 @ 🖥) Friendly, well-run hostel with good facilities, Kiwiana decor and sunny back garden (complete with hammock and barbecue). Rooms are small but clean; doubles have TVs and homey decorative touches.

All Stars Inn on Bealey   HOSTEL $

(Map p74; ☑ 03-366 6007; www.allstarsinn.com; 263 Bealey Ave; dm $34-39, d $85, with bathroom $110; 🅿 @ 🖥) Large, well-designed rooms are the hallmark of this purpose-built complex on the city fringe. Dorms have fridges, USB points and individual lights; some have en suites, too. Private rooms are similarly well equipped. It's a 25-minute walk to the centre of town.

★ Eco Villa
GUESTHOUSE $$

(Map p74; ☑ 03-595 1364; www.ecovilla.co.nz; 251 Hereford St; d $116-270, without bathroom $95-150; P 🛜) 🌱 There are only eight rooms in this beautifully renovated villa, each individually decorated with luxe fittings and muted colours. The lovely shared lounge, kitchen and dining room all emphasise the focus on sustainable, ecofriendly design, as does the lush edible garden (with twin outdoor bathtubs!). Be sure to try the delicious vegan breakfasts (per person $20).

BreakFree on Cashel
HOTEL $$

(Map p74; ☑ 03-360 1064; www.breakfreeon cashel.co.nz; 165 Cashel St; d $115-248; P 🛜) 🌱 This large, modern hotel in the heart of the CBD has options to suit all budgets. Rooms are compact and sharply designed, with high-tech features like smart TVs and sci-fi pod bathrooms.

Pomeroy's on Kilmore
B&B $$

(Map p74; ☑ 03-374 3532; www.pomeroysonkil more.co.nz; 282 Kilmore St; r $145-195; P 🛜) Even if this cute wooden house wasn't the sister and neighbour of the city's best craft-beer pub, it would still be one of our favourites. Three of the five elegant, en suite rooms open onto a sunny garden. Rates include breakfast at Little Pom's (p81) cafe next door.

Focus Motel
MOTEL $$

(Map p74; ☑ 03-943 0800; www.focusmotel.com; 344 Durham St N; r $160-250; P 🛜) Sleek and centrally located, this friendly motel offers studio, one- and two-bedroom units with big-screen TVs, iPod docks, kitchenettes and super-modern decor. There's a guest barbecue and laundry, and pillow-top chocolates sweeten the deal.

★ George
HOTEL $$$

(Map p74; ☑ 03-379 4560; www.thegeorge.com; 50 Park Tce; r $490-525, ste $795-1050; P @ 🛜) 🌱 The George has 53 luxe rooms in a defiantly 1970s-looking building on the fringe of Hagley Park. Discreet staff attend to every whim, and ritzy extras include huge TVs, luxury toiletries and two highly rated in-house restaurants – Pescatore and 50 Bistro.

Hotel Montreal
HOTEL $$$

(Map p74; ☑ 03-943 8547; www.hotelmontreal.co.nz; 363 Montreal St; d from $550; P 🛜) Handy to all the city sights and Victoria St's restaurants, this upmarket hotel occupies a revamped apartment building. Swanky suites are boldly styled in black, grey and gold, with plush lounge areas, kitchenettes and balconies in all rooms. There's also a light-filled in-house restaurant and a gym. Good deals are available in the low season.

Classic Villa
B&B $$$

(Map p74; ☑ 03-377 7905; www.theclassicvilla. co.nz; 17 Worcester Blvd; s $199, d $289-409, ste $569; P 🛜) 🌱 Pretty in pink, this 1897 house is one of Christchurch's most elegant accommodation options. Rooms are trimmed with antiques and Turkish rugs, and the Mediterranean-style breakfast is a shared social occasion.

🛏 Riccarton

Lorenzo Motor Inn
MOTEL $$

(Map p74; ☑ 03-348 8074; www.lorenzomotor lodge.co.nz; 36 Riccarton Rd; d $160-175, apt $250; P ❄ 🛜) There's a Mediterranean vibe to this trim two-storey motel – the best of many on the busy Riccarton Rd strip. There are a number of options available including studio and two-bedroom apartments; some have spa baths and little balconies, or sweet sitting areas.

Roma on Riccarton
MOTEL $$

(Map p74; ☑ 03-341 2100; www.romaonriccarton. co.nz; 38 Riccarton Rd; d $143-183, apt $260; P ❄ 🛜) One of the many motels along the Riccarton Rd strip, this modern two-storey block offers clean, well-proportioned units ranging from studios to two-bedroom apartments.

🛏 Other Areas

★ Jailhouse
HOSTEL $

(Map p74; ☑ 03-982 7777, 0800 524 546; www.jail. co.nz; 338 Lincoln Rd, Addington; dm $30-39, s/d $85/89; @ 🛜) From 1874 to 1999 this was Addington Prison; it's now one of Christchurch's most appealing and friendly hostels. Private rooms are a bit on the small side – they don't call them cells for nothing – but there are plenty of communal spaces to relax outside of your room. Perks include a TV room, unlimited free wi-fi and bikes for rent.

Haka Lodge
HOSTEL $

(Map p70; ☑ 03-980 4252; www.hakalodge.com; 518 Linwood Ave, Woolston; dm/d/apt $29/79/170; P 🛜) 🌱 Sprawled across three floors of a charming suburban house, Haka Lodge offers colourful bunk-free dorms and cheery doubles. Bonuses include a comfy lounge with wood-burning fireplace, large communal kitchen, and a bird-filled garden with barbecue. It's the kind of place you could happily stay awhile.

Merivale Manor
MOTEL $$

(Map p70; ☑03-355 7731; www.merivalemanor.co.nz; 122 Papanui Rd; d $169-249; ℗☎) A gracious 19th-century Victorian mansion is the hub of this elegant motel, with units both in the main house and in the more typical motel-style blocks lining the drive. Accommodation ranges from studios to two-bedroom apartments.

Le Petit Hotel
B&B $$

(Map p70; ☑03-326 6675; www.lepetithotel.co.nz; 16 Marriner St, Sumner; d $139-179; ℗@☎) Relaxed coffee-and-croissant breakfasts, friendly owners, elegant furnishings and close proximity to Sumner Beach make this charming B&B a definite *oui*. Request an upstairs room with a view.

Fendalton House
B&B $$

(Map p70; ☑03-343 1661; www.fendaltonhouse.co.nz; 28a Kotare St; r $195; ℗⊖☎) There's only one guest room at this friendly, homestay-style B&B nestled among the leafy streets of Fendalton. Rates include a generous cooked breakfast.

Eating

City Centre

★ Supreme Supreme
CAFE $

(Map p74; ☑03-365 0445; www.supremesupreme.co.nz; 10 Welles St; mains breakfast $7-20, lunch $12-22; ⊘7am-3pm Mon-Fri, 8am-3pm Sat & Sun; ☑) With so much to love, where to start? Perhaps with a cherry and pomegranate smoothie, a chocolate-fish milkshake or maybe just an exceptional espresso, alongside a fresh bagel, a goji bowl or even pulled corn-beef hash. One of NZ's original and best coffee roasters comes to the party with a right-now cafe of splendid style, form and function.

C1 Espresso
CAFE $

(Map p74; www.c1espresso.co.nz; 185 High St; mains $10-22; ⊘7am-10pm; ☎) 🥐 C1 sits pretty in a grand former post office that somehow escaped the cataclysm. Recycled materials fill the interior (Victorian oak panelling, bulbous

1970s light fixtures) and tables spill onto a little square. Eggy brekkies and bagels are available all day, while sliders and curly fries slip onto the menu at lunch.

Caffeine Laboratory
CAFE $

(Map p74; www.caffeinelab.co.nz; 1 New Regent St; mains $10-22; ⊘7am-3pm Mon-Fri, from 8am Sat & Sun; ☑) The small-scale, corner C-lab is hooked on coffee, but also cooks up delicious brunches like brioche French toast, house-smoked salmon or chipotle pulled pork. Around lunch, the menu switches to tasty hipster classics like fried chicken and mac 'n' cheese.

Vic's Cafe
CAFE $

(Map p74; www.vics.co.nz; 132 Victoria St; mains $9-22; ⊘7.30am-4.30pm; ☑) Pop in for a hearty breakfast at the big shared tables or linger over lunch on the front terrace. Otherwise grab baked goodies and still-warm artisanal bread for a DIY riverside picnic.

★ Little High Eatery
FOOD HALL $$

(Map p74; www.littlehigh.co.nz; 255 St Asaph St; dishes $5-20; ⊘7am-10pm Mon-Wed, 9am-midnight Thu-Sat, 8am-10pm Sun; ☎) Can't decide whether you want sushi, pizza or Thai for dinner? At Little High, you won't have to choose – this stylish new food hall is home to eight different gourmet businesses, offering everything from dumplings to burgers. Stop in for your morning coffee or swing by for a late-night mojito in the beautifully outfitted space.

Unknown Chapter
CAFE $$

(Map p74; www.unknownchaptercoffee.co.nz; 254 St Asaph St; mains $14-22; ⊘6.30am-4pm; ☑) Polished concrete, reclaimed timber tables, hanging plants and floor-to-ceiling windows give this newcomer an urban hipster vibe. Drop in for your morning caffeine hit, or visit at lunchtime for gourmet sandwiches, tasty salads and an irresistible cake cabinet.

Fiddlesticks
MODERN NZ $$

(Map p74; ☑03-365 0533; www.fiddlesticksbar.co.nz; 48 Worcester Blvd; mains breakfast $12-20, lunch $20-40, dinner $25-45; ⊘8am-late Mon-Fri, from 9am Sat & Sun; ☎) Sidle into Fiddlesticks for sophisticated, hearty meals from breakfast to supper. The cosy formal dining room is perfect for intimate dinners, but we like the glassed-in patio attached to the curvy cocktail bar – especially during weekend brunches, when you might be tempted to order a cheeky mimosa alongside your eggs.

Black Betty · CAFE $$
(Map p74; ✐ 03-365 8522; www.blackbetty.co.nz; 165 Madras St; mains $14-20; ⊙ 7.30am-4pm Mon-Fri, from 8am Sat & Sun; 🐾) Black Betty's industrial-chic warehouse is a popular destination for students from the nearby college. Friendly service, great food and a laid-back atmosphere are all pluses, but the biggest attraction is the coffee from specialty roaster Switch Espresso – try pour-over, syphon, aeropress or traditional espresso brews.

Rangoon Ruby BURMESE $$
(Map p74; ✐ 022 028 0920; www.facebook.com/RangoonRubyChch; 819 Colombo St; dishes $13-21; ⊙ 5.30-9.30pm Mon-Sat; 🍴) Rangoon Ruby is the latest iteration of longtime Christchurch fave Bodhi Tree, which has been wowing locals with the nuanced flavours of Burmese cuisine for more than a decade. Feel-good food comes in sharing-sized dishes and sings with zing. Standouts include *le pet thoke* (pickled tea-leaf salad) and *ameyda nut* (slow-cooked beef curry).

Lotus Heart VEGETARIAN $$
(Map p74; ✐ 03-377 2727; www.thelotusheart.co.nz; 363 St Asaph St; mains $14-25; ⊙ 7.30am-3pm Tue-Sun & 5-9pm Fri & Sat; 🍴) 🌱 Run by students of Indian spiritual leader Sri Chinmoy, this colourful vegetarian eatery serves a range of cuisines, from tasty curries and dosas, to pizzas, nachos and burgers. Organic, vegan and gluten-free options abound, and you can quench your thirst with freshly squeezed juices, smoothies and a wide tea selection.

⭐**Twenty Seven Steps** MODERN NZ $$$
(Map p74; ✐ 03-366 2727; www.twentysevensteps.co.nz; 16 New Regent St; mains $34-40; ⊙ 5pm-late) 🌱 Overlooking the pastel-coloured New Regent St strip, this elegant restaurant showcases locally sourced seasonal ingredients. Mainstays include modern renditions of lamb, beef, venison and seafood, as well as outstanding risotto. Delectable desserts and friendly waitstaff seal the deal; reservations are advised.

King of Snake ASIAN $$$
(Map p74; ✐ 03-365 7363; www.kingofsnake.co.nz; 145 Victoria St; mains $27-43; ⊙ 11am-late Mon-Fri, 4pm-late Sat & Sun) Dark wood, gold tiles and purple skull-patterned wallpaper fill this hip restaurant and cocktail bar with just the right amount of sinister opulence. The interesting fusion menu gainfully

plunders the cuisines of Asia – from India to Korea – to delicious, if pricey, effect.

Saggio di Vino EUROPEAN $$$
(Map p74; ✐ 03-379 4006; www.saggiodivino.co.nz; 179 Victoria St; mains $40-46; ⊙ 5pm-late) An elegant Italo-French restaurant that's up there with Christchurch's best. Expect delicious, modern takes on classics like duck *a l'orange* or fillet of beef, plus seasonal degustation menus (five courses from $105, with paired wines $155). The well-laden cheese trolley offers the perfect finale.

🍴 Sydenham

Hello Sunday CAFE $$
(Map p74; ✐ 03-260 1566; www.hellosundaycafe.co.nz; 6 Elgin St, Sydenham; mains $13-23; ⊙ 7.30am-4.30pm Mon-Fri, from 8.30am Sat & Sun; 🐾🍴) Spread across two rooms of a restored old post office building, this popular cafe is a great spot for all-day brunches, spectacular salads and excellent coffee. If you're feeling decadent, try the white chocolate and peanut butter waffles, topped with vanilla candy floss – wow!

Burgers & Beers Inc BURGERS $$
(Map p74; www.burgersandbeersinc.co.nz; 355 Colombo St, Sydenham; burgers $14-18; ⊙ 11am-late) Quirky gourmet burgers – try the Woolly Sahara Sand Hopper (Moroccan-spiced lamb with lemon yoghurt) or the Shagged Stag (venison with plum chutney) – and an ever-changing selection of Kiwi craft beers give you reason to head south.

🍴 Other Areas

Addington Coffee Co-op CAFE $
(Map p74; ✐ 03-943 1662; www.addingtoncoffee.org.nz; 297 Lincoln Rd, Addington; meals $7-22; ⊙ 7.30am-4pm Mon-Fri, from 9am Sat & Sun; 🐾🍴) You will find one of Christchurch's biggest and best cafes packed to the rafters most days. A compact shop selling fair-trade gifts jostles for attention with delicious cakes, gourmet pies, legendary breakfasts (until 2pm) and excellent coffee. An on-site launderette completes the deal for busy travellers.

Bohemian Bakery BAKERY $
(Map p70; ✐ 021 070 6271; www.bohemianbakery.co.nz; 43 Nayland St, Sumner; pastries $4-6; ⊙ 7.30am-4pm Wed-Sun) The kitchen at this petite bakery is entirely open, so you can see the bakers at work crafting delicious yeasty treats

all day long. Grab one of their famed cinnamon rolls and head to the beach.

Christchurch Farmers Market
MARKET $

(Map p70; www.christchurchfarmersmarket.co.nz; 16 Kahu Rd, Riccarton; ⊙9am-1pm Sat) 🌿 Held in the pretty grounds of Riccarton House (p72), this excellent farmers market offers a tasty array of organic fruit and veg, South Island cheeses and salmon, local craft beer and ethnic treats.

Kinji
JAPANESE $$

(Map p70; ☑03-359 4697; www.kinjirestaurant. com; 279b Greers Rd, Bishopdale; mains $16-24; ⊙5.30-10pm Mon-Sat) Despite being hidden away in suburbia, this acclaimed Japanese restaurant has a loyal following, so it's wise to book. Tuck into the likes of sashimi, grilled ginger squid and venison *tataki*, but save room for the green tea tiramisu, a surprising highlight.

Under the Red Verandah
CAFE $$

(Map p70; www.utrv.co.nz; 29 Tancred St, Linwood; mains $15-25; ⊙7.30am-3pm Mon-Fri, 8.30am-3pm Sat & Sun; 🌿) This lucky suburban backstreet boasts a lovely sunny cafe, beloved by locals and travellers alike. Take a seat under the namesake veranda and tuck into baked goodies, oaty pancakes, homemade pies and eggs multiple ways.

Gatherings
MODERN NZ $$$

(Map p74; ☑021 02 93 5641; www.gatherings. co.nz; 2 Papanui Rd, Merivale; lunch mains $10-14, dinner 5-course tasting menu $65, with matched wines $110; ⊙noon-2pm & 4-11pm Wed-Sat; 🌿) 🌿 Thoughtful, seasonal vegetarian dishes are the focus at this petite restaurant on the edge of the Papanui Rd dining strip. The set five-course tasting menu changes regularly, with a focus on sustainable, local produce and unique flavour combinations. At lunch, offerings include simple but well-executed staples like grilled cheese or soup.

🍷 **Drinking & Nightlife**

★ Smash Palace
BAR

(Map p74; ☑03-366 5369; www.thesmashpalace. co.nz; 172 High St; ⊙3pm-late Mon-Thu, from noon Fri-Sun) Epitomising the spirit of transience, tenacity and resourcefulness that Christchurch is now known for, this deliberately downcycled and ramshackle beer garden is an intoxicating mix of grease-monkey garage, trailer-trash park and proto-hipster hang-out, complete with a psychedelic school bus, edible garden and blooming roses.

There's craft beer, chips, Cheerios, and burgers made from scratch ($11 to $15).

★ Pomeroy's Old Brewery Inn
PUB

(Map p74; ☑03-365 1523; www.pomspub.co.nz; 292 Kilmore St; ⊙3pm-late Tue-Thu, from noon Fri-Sun) For fans of great beer, Pomeroy's is perfect for supping a drop or two alongside a plate of proper pork crackling. Among this British-style pub's many endearing features are regular live music, a snug, sunny courtyard and **Victoria's Kitchen**, serving comforting pub food (mains $25 to $40). The newest addition, pretty **Little Pom's** cafe, serves excellent brunch fare ($9 to $25) until mid-afternoon.

Fat Eddie's
BAR

(Map p74; ☑03-595 5332; www.fateddiesbar.co.nz; cnr Hereford St & Oxford Tce; ⊙2pm-late) Seven years after the quakes, jazz bar Fat Eddie's has reopened in a brand-new building on the riverfront. With comfy couches, retro styling, a big dance floor, live music most nights and a wraparound balcony perfect for sunset drinks, there's no doubt this new iteration will be more popular than ever.

Vesuvio
WINE BAR

(Map p74; ☑03-355 8530; www.vesuvio.co.nz; 4 Papanui Rd, Merivale; ⊙3pm-late) Half-hidden at the back of a busy cluster of eateries, this European-style wine bar is the perfect spot for a pre-dinner *aperitivo* – though the thoughtful selection of local and imported wines, excellent antipasti boards (from $19) and regular live jazz might mean you end up settling in for the night.

Allpress Espresso
COFFEE

(Map p74; 110 Montreal St, Sydenham; ⊙7.30am-3.30pm Mon-Fri) Hidden behind a nondescript facade down the industrial end of Montreal St, the Christchurch branch of this famous Kiwi coffee roastery does a mean espresso – just as you'd expect. If you're feeling peckish, there are also fresh light lunch options and smoothies on offer.

Dux Central
BAR

(Map p74; ☑03-943 7830; www.duxcentral.co.nz; 6 Poplar St; ⊙11am-late) Pumping a whole lot of heart back into the flattened High St precinct, the epic new Dux complex comprises a brew bar serving its own and other crafty drops, the Emerald Room wine bar, Upper Dux restaurant and the Poplar Social Club cocktail bar, all housed within the confines of a lovingly restored old building.

Boo Radley's   BAR
(Map p74; ☑03-366 9906; www.booradleys.co.nz; 98 Victoria St; ⊙4pm-late) An intimate, speak-easy vibe makes Boo's an alluring late-night hang-out. Southern-style decor meshes with bourbons galore and American comfort food like sliders, fried chicken and curly fries (snacks $7 to $24). There's regular live music, too.

The Brewery   CRAFT BEER
(Map p70; www.casselsbrewery.co.nz; 3 Garlands Rd, Woolston; ⊙8am-late) An essential destination for beer-loving travellers, the Cassels & Sons' brewery crafts beers using a wood-fired brew kettle, resulting in big, bold ales. Tasting trays are available for the curious and the indecisive, live bands perform regularly, and the food – including wood-fired pizzas ($20 to $26) – is top-notch, too.

☆ Entertainment

For live music and club listings, see www.undertheradar.co.nz and www.christchurch music.org.nz.

darkroom   LIVE MUSIC
(Map p74; www.darkroom.bar; 336 St Asaph St; ⊙7pm-late Thu-Sat) A hip combination of live-music venue and bar, darkroom has lots of Kiwi beers and great cocktails. Live gigs are frequent – and frequently free.

Isaac Theatre Royal   THEATRE
(Map p74; ☑03-366 6326; www.isaactheatre royal.co.nz; 145 Gloucester St; ⊙box office 10am-5pm Mon-Fri) This century-old dear survived the quakes and emerged restored to full glory in 2014. Its heritage features are enjoyed by patrons venturing inside for everything from opera and ballet to contemporary theatre and rock concerts.

Court Theatre   THEATRE
(Map p74; ☑03-963 0870; www.courttheatre. org.nz; Bernard St, Addington; ⊙box office 9am-8.15pm Mon-Thu, to 10.15pm Fri, 10am-10.15pm Sat) Christchurch's original Court Theatre was an integral part of the city's Arts Centre, but it was forced to relocate to this warehouse after the earthquakes. The new premises are much more spacious; it's a great venue to see popular international plays and works by NZ playwrights.

Alice Cinema   CINEMA
(Map p74; ☑03-365 0615; www.alice.co.nz; 209 Tuam St; adult/child $15/11) This delightful two-screen art-house cinema can be found within the long-standing and excellent Alice In Videoland video-store.

Shopping

★Tannery   SHOPPING CENTRE
(Map p70; www.thetannery.co.nz; 3 Garlands Rd, Woolston; ⊙10am-5pm) In a city mourning the loss of its heritage, this post-earthquake conversion of a 19th-century tannery couldn't be more welcome. The Victorian buildings have been beautifully restored, and are crammed with all manner of delightful boutiques selling everything from surfboards to vintage clothing to exquisite homewares.

When you're tired of shopping, stop by The Brewery (p82) for an afternoon pick-me-up. There are also several cafes and an art-house cinema on site.

New Regent St   MALL
(Map p74; www.newregentstreet.co.nz) This pretty little stretch of pastel Spanish Mission–style shops was described as NZ's most beautiful street when it was completed in 1932. Fully restored post-earthquake, it's once again a delightful place to stroll, and has become something of a hub for quality cafes, bars and restaurants.

Ballantynes   DEPARTMENT STORE
(Map p74; www.ballantynes.com; cnr Colombo & Cashel Sts; ⊙9am-5.30pm Mon-Fri, to 5pm Sat, 10am-5pm Sun) A venerable Christchurch department store selling men's and women's fashions, cosmetics, travel goods, stationery and speciality NZ gifts.

Scorpio Books   BOOKS
(Map p74; ☑03-379 2882; www.scorpiobooks.co.nz; BNZ Centre, 120 Hereford St; ⊙9am-6pm Mon-Fri, 10am-5pm Sat & Sun) Excellent independent bookstore Scorpio Books is now back in the inner city after six years in Riccarton.

ℹ Information

INTERNET ACCESS
Christchurch City Council offers free wi-fi in its libraries (no membership required), and Spark telecom company has set up numerous free wi-fi hot spots around the city. A limited number of internet cafes catering to gaming junkies are scattered about the city centre and suburbs, while many cafes and restaurants also offer free wi-fi; just ask for the password with your flat white.

MEDICAL SERVICES
24-Hour Surgery (☑03-365 7777; www.24hour surgery.co.nz; 401 Madras St) No appointment necessary.

Christchurch Hospital (☑ 03-364 0640, emergency dept 03-364 0270; www.cdhb.govt. nz; 2 Riccarton Ave) Has a 24-hour emergency department.

Urgent Pharmacy (☑ 03-366 4439; cnr Bealey Ave & Colombo St; ☺ 9am-11pm)

TOURIST INFORMATION

Airport i-SITE (☑ 03-741 3980; www. christchurchnz.com; International Arrivals Hall; ☺ 8am-6pm)

Christchurch i-SITE (Map p74; ☑ 03-379 9629; www.christchurchnz.com; Arts Centre, 28 Worcester Blvd; ☺ 8.30am-5pm)

ChristchurchNZ (www.christchurchnz.com) Official tourism website for the city and region.

DOC Visitor Centre (Map p74; ☑ 03-379 4082; www.doc.govt.nz; Arts Centre, 28 Worcester Blvd; ☺ 9am-4.45pm) Information on South Island national parks, including walk and hut bookings; located within the i-SITE.

ⓘ Getting There & Away

As the South Island's largest city, Christchurch is a major domestic and international air hub. It also has excellent road and rail links.

AIR

Christchurch Airport (p367) The South Island's main international gateway, with regular flights to Australia, China, Fiji and Singapore. Facilities include baggage storage, car rental counters, ATMs, foreign-exchange offices and an **i-SITE**.

Air New Zealand (p367) Direct flights to/from Auckland, Wellington, Dunedin and Queenstown. Code-share flights with smaller regional airlines head to/from Blenheim, Hamilton, Hokitika, Invercargill, Napier, Nelson, New Plymouth, Palmerston North, Paraparaumu, Rotorua and Tauranga.

Jetstar (p367) Flies to/from Auckland and Wellington.

BUS

Tourist-oriented services generally stop outside the Canterbury Museum on Rolleston Ave; local and some long-distance services depart from the inner-city **Bus Interchange** (Map p74; cnr Lichfield & Colombo Sts).

Akaroa French Connection (Map p74; ☑ 0800 800 575; www.akaroabus.co.nz; Rolleston Ave; return $50) Daily service to Akaroa.

Akaroa Shuttle (Map p74; ☑ 0800 500 929; www.akaroashuttle.co.nz; Rolleston Ave; one way/return $35/50) Daily service to Akaroa.

Atomic Shuttles (Map p74; ☑ 03-349 0697; www.atomictravel.co.nz; Lichfield St) Destinations include Picton ($40, 5¼ hours), Greymouth ($50, 3¾ hours), Timaru ($25, 2½ hours), Dunedin ($35, 5¾ hours) and Queenstown ($55, seven hours).

Budget Buses & Shuttles (Map p74; ☑ 03-615 5119; www.budgetshuttles.co.nz; Rolleston Ave; ☺ Mon-Sat) Offers a door-to-door shuttle to Geraldine ($57) and Timaru ($50), along with cheaper scheduled runs (from $27).

Hanmer Connection (Map p74; ☑ 0800 242 663; www.hanmerconnection.co.nz; Rolleston Ave; one way/return $30/50) Daily coach to/from Hanmer Springs via Amberley and Waipara.

InterCity (Map p74; ☑ 03-365 1113; www.intercity.co.nz; Lichfield St) New Zealand's widest and most reliable coach network. Coaches head to Timaru (from $14, 2½ hours), Dunedin (from $21, six hours), Queenstown (from $47, eight to 11 hours), Te Anau (from $63, 10¾ hours) and Picton (from $26, 5¼ hours), at least daily.

West Coast Shuttle (Map p74; ☑ 03-768 0028; www.westcoastshuttle.co.nz; Lichfield St) Daily bus to/from the West Coast stopping at Springfield ($32, 1¼ hours), Arthur's Pass ($42, 2¾ hours) and Greymouth ($55, four hours).

TRAIN

Christchurch Railway Station (www.greatjourneysofnz.co.nz; Troup Dr, Addington; ☺ ticket office 6.30am-3pm) Is the terminus for two highly scenic train journeys, the hero of which is the **TranzAlpine** (p70). The other, the *Coastal Pacific*, runs along the east coast from Christchurch to Picton, stopping at Waipara, Kaikoura and Blenheim. The service was not operating at the time of research due to damage sustained in the 2016 quake, but was expected to recommence in mid-2018. Contact **Great Journeys of New Zealand** (☑ 0800 872 467; www.greatjourneysofnz.co.nz) for updates.

ⓘ Getting Around

Christchurch's flat topography and gridlike structure make getting around on foot or by bike a breeze. The city's extensive bus network is a cheap and convenient way of reaching the city's suburban attractions.

TO/FROM THE AIRPORT

Christchurch Airport is 10km from the city centre. A taxi into town costs $45 to $65. Alternatively, the airport is well served by public buses (www.metroinfo.co.nz). The purple line bus heads through Riccarton (20 minutes) to the central Bus Interchange (30 minutes) and on to Sumner (1¼ hours). Bus 29 heads through Fendalton (10 minutes) to the Bus Interchange (30 minutes). Both services cost $8.50 (pay the driver) and run every 30 minutes from approximately 7am to 11pm. Shuttle services include **Steve's Shuttle** (☑ 0800 101 021; www.steveshuttle.co.nz; to city centre per 1/2/3 passengers $23/28/33) and **Super Shuttle** (☑ 0800 748 885; www.supershuttle.co.nz; to city centre per 1/2/3 passengers $25/31/37).

CAR & MOTORCYCLE

Hire

Most major car- and campervan-rental companies have offices in Christchurch, as do numerous smaller local companies. Operators with national networks often want cars from Christchurch to be returned to Auckland because most renters travel in the opposite direction, so you may find a cheaper price on a northbound route.

Local options include the following:

Ace Rental Cars (☎03-360 3270; www.ace rentalcars.co.nz; 20 Abros Pl, Burnside)

Hitch Car Rental (☎03-357 3074; www.hitch carrentals.co.nz; 545 Wairakei Rd)

New Zealand Motorcycle Rentals & Tours (☎09-486 2472; www.nzbike.com)

New Zealand Rent a Car (☎03-961 5880; www.nzrentacar.co.nz; 26b Sheffield Cres, Burnside)

Omega Rental Cars (☎03-377 4558; www. omegarentalcars.com; 158 Orchard Rd, Harewood)

Pegasus Rental Cars (☎03-358 5890; www. rentalcars.co.nz; 154 Orchard Rd, Harewood)

Purchase

Scour hostel noticeboards and check out **BPC Cars** (☎03-342 3434; www.bpccars.co.nz; 196 Yaldhurst Road, Avonhead; ⊙9.30am-5pm Mon-Fri, from 9.30am Sat) and **Turners Auctions** (☎03-343 9850; www.turners.co.nz; 1 Detroit Pl; ⊙8am-6pm Mon-Fri, 9am-5pm Sat, 10am-5pm Sun), or the websites www.trademe. co.nz and www.autotrader.co.nz.

PUBLIC TRANSPORT

Christchurch's **Metro bus network** (☎03-366 8855; www.metroinfo.co.nz) is inexpensive, efficient and comprehensive. Most buses run from the inner-city **Bus Interchange** (p83).

Pick up timetables from the **i-SITE** (p83) or the Interchange. Tickets (adult/child $4/2) can be purchased on board and include one free transfer within two hours. Alternatively, Metrocards allow unlimited travel for two hours/one day/one week for $2.55/5.10/25.50. Cards are available from the Interchange; they cost $10 and must be loaded with a minimum of $10 additional credit.

TAXI

Blue Star (☎03-379 9799; www.bluestartaxis. org.nz)

First Direct (☎03-377 5555; www.firstdirect. net.nz)

Gold Band (☎03-379 5795; www.goldbandtaxis. co.nz)

AROUND CHRISTCHURCH

Lyttelton

POP 3100

Southeast of Christchurch, the prominent Port Hills slope down to the city's port on Lyttelton Harbour. Christchurch's first European settlers landed here in 1850 to embark on their historic trek over the hills. Nowadays a 2km road tunnel makes the journey considerably quicker.

Lyttelton was badly damaged during the 2010 and 2011 earthquakes, and many of the town's heritage buildings along London St were subsequently demolished. Today, however, Lyttelton has re-emerged as one of Christchurch's most interesting communities. The town's arty, independent and bohemian vibe is stronger than ever, and it is once again a hub for great bars, cafes and shops. It's well worth catching the bus from Christchurch and getting immersed in the local scene, especially on a sunny Saturday morning when the farmers market's buzzing.

✖ Eating

Lyttelton Farmers Market   MARKET **$**
(Map p70; www.lyttelton.net.nz; London St; ⊙10am-1pm Sat) Every Saturday morning food stalls take the place of cars on Lyttelton's main street. Stock up alongside locals on fresh bread, baked goods, flowers, cheeses, local produce and good coffee.

Lyttelton Coffee Company   CAFE **$$**
(Map p70; ☎03-328 8096; www.lytteltoncoffee. co.nz; 29 London St; mains $12-20; ⊙7am-4pm Mon-Fri, 8am-4pm Sat & Sun; 🚗🖐) Local institution Lyttelton Coffee Company has risen from the rubble and continues its role as a stalwart of the London St foodie scene, serving consistently great coffee and wholesome food in its cavernous, exposed-brick warehouse space.

Freemans   ITALIAN **$$**
(Map p70; ☎03-328 7517; www.freemansdining room.co.nz; 47 London St; mains breakfast $16-18, lunch $20-27, dinner $24-39; ⊙3pm-late Wed-Fri, from 9am Sat, from noon Sun; 🚗) Freemans consistently pleases with fresh pasta, top-notch pizzas, local wines and craft beers from Christchurch's Three Boys Brewery. Grab a spot on the deck for great harbour views and Sunday afternoon jazz from 3pm.

★ **Roots** MODERN NZ $$$

(Map p70; ☑ 03-328 7658; www.rootsrestaurant.
co.nz; 8 London St; 5-/8-/12-course degustation
$90/125/185, incl wine $140/205/305; ☺6-
11pm Tue-Sat, plus noon-2pm Fri & Sat) 🍴 Let
chef-owner Giulio Sturla take you on a mag-
ical tasting tour with his renowned degusta-
tion menus, which champion all things local
and seasonal. Dishes can also be accompa-
nied by carefully paired wines, should you
choose to splurge. Reserve ahead.

🍷 Drinking & Nightlife

Civil and Naval BAR

(Map p70; ☑ 03-328 7206; www.civilandnaval
co.nz; 16 London St; ☺10am-11pm Sun-Thu, to 1am
Fri & Sat) Steadfast staff at this compact, bi-
jou bar serve a quality selection of cocktails,
fine wines and craft beers, while the kitchen
keeps patrons civil with an eclectic range of
tapas ($6 to $18).

Spooky Boogie COFFEE

(Map p70; 54 London St; ☺8am-4pm Wed-Fri, from
9am Sat & Sun) More sweet than spooky, this
hip new coffee shop cum record store at the
top end of London St does a roaring trade in
silky coffee and smooth beats alike.

Wunderbar BAR

(Map p70; ☑ 03-328 8818; www.wunderbar.co.nz;
19 London St; ☺5pm-late Mon-Fri, 1pm-3am Sat &
Sun) Wunderbar is a top spot to get down,
with regular live music covering all spectra,
and clientele to match. The kooky decor and
decapitated dolls' heads alone are worth the
trip. Enter via the stairs in the rear car park.

🛍 Shopping

Henry Trading ARTS & CRAFTS

(Map p70; ☑ 03-328 8088; www.henrytrading.
co.nz; 33 London St; ☺10am-4pm Tue-Sun) This
tiny but perfectly curated store stocks a
range of lovely homewares and gifts, many
made by local producers, as well as a sweet
line in artisanal Lyttelton souvenirs.

London St Bookshop BOOKS

(Map p70; 48 London St; ☺10am-4pm Tue-Sun)
Dimly lit and crammed full of intriguing vol-
umes, this charming second-hand bookshop
is a bibliophile's dream.

ℹ Information

Lyttelton Visitor Information Centre (Map
p70; ☑ 03-328 9093; www.lytteltonharbour.
info; 20 Oxford St; ☺10am-4pm) Friendly staff

WORTH A TRIP

GOVERNORS BAY

A scenic 9km drive from Lyttelton is
Governors Bay Hotel (Map p86; ☑ 03-
329 9433; www.governorsbayhotel.co.nz;
52 Main Rd, Governors Bay; ☺11am-late;
🔊), one of NZ's oldest operational pubs
(1870). You couldn't ask for a more invit-
ing deck and garden in which to quaff an
afternoon tipple. The food is good, too,
covering all the classic pub-grub bases
(mains $25 to $39).

Upstairs are chicly renovated rooms
with shared bathrooms (double rooms
$119 to $169).

can provide information on accommodation,
local walks and ferry departures.

ℹ Getting There & Away

Lyttelton is 15km from Christchurch CBD via the
Lyttelton Tunnel. At the time of writing, Summit
Rd between Sumner and Lyttelton was still
closed.

Bus Buses 28 and 535 run from Christchurch to
Lyttelton (adult/child $4/2, 30 minutes).

Ferry From Lyttelton, **Black Cat** (Map p70;
☑ 03-328 9078; www.blackcat.co.nz; 5 Nor-
wich Quay) provides ferries to sheltered Quail
Island (adult/child return $30/15, 10 minutes,
once daily October to April only), as well as to
sleepy Diamond Harbour (adult/child one way
$6.50/3.20, 10 minutes, hourly).

Banks Peninsula

POP 4750

Gorgeous Banks Peninsula (Horomaka)
was formed by two giant volcanic eruptions
about eight million years ago. Harbours and
bays radiate out from the peninsula's cen-
tre, giving it an unusual cogwheel shape.
The historic town of **Akaroa**, 80km from
Christchurch, is a highlight, as is the absurd-
ly beautiful drive along Summit Rd around
the edge of one of the original craters. It's
also worth exploring the little bays that dot
the peninsula's perimeter.

The waters around Banks Peninsula are
home to the smallest and one of the rarest
dolphin species, the Hector's dolphin, found
only in NZ waters. A range of tours depart
from Akaroa to spot these and other sealife,
including white-flippered penguins, orcas
and seals.

Banks Peninsula

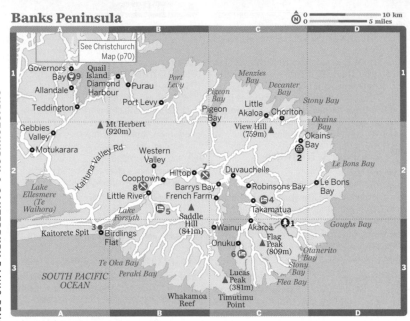

Banks Peninsula

History

James Cook sighted the peninsula in 1770, believing it to be an island. He named it after the naturalist Sir Joseph Banks.

In 1831, Onawe pā (fortified village) was attacked by the Ngāti Toa chief Te Rauparaha and in the massacres that followed, the local Ngāi Tahu population was dramatically reduced. Seven years later, whaling captain Jean Langlois negotiated the purchase of Banks Peninsula from the survivors and returned to France to form a trading company. With French-government backing, 63 settlers headed for the peninsula in 1840, but only days before they arrived, panicked British officials sent their own ship to raise the flag at Akaroa, claiming British sovereignty under the Treaty of Waitangi. Had the settlers arrived two years earlier, the entire South Island could have become a French colony, and NZ's future might have been quite different.

The French did settle at Akaroa, but in 1849 their land claim was sold to the New Zealand Company, and in 1850 a large group of British settlers arrived. The heavily forested land was cleared and soon farming became the peninsula's main industry.

◉ Sights & Activities

Okains Bay Māori & Colonial Museum   MUSEUM
(Map p86; www.okainsbaymuseum.co.nz; 1146 Okains Bay Rd, Okains Bay; adult/child $10/2; ☉10am-5pm) Northeast of Akaroa, this museum has a respectable array of European pioneer artefacts, but it is the nationally significant Māori collection, featuring a replica *wharenui* (meeting house), *waka* (canoes), stone tools and personal adornments, that

make this a worthwhile detour. Note the cute shop down the road.

Hinewai Reserve
FOREST

(Map p86; www.hinewai.org.nz; 632 Long Bay Rd) 🌿 Get a glimpse of what the peninsula once looked like with a stroll through this privately owned 1250-hectare nature reserve, which has been replanted with native forest. Pick up a map outlining the walking tracks at the visitor centre, a short walk from the main entrance.

Bone Dude
ART

(Map p86; ☑03-329 0947; www.thebonedude.co.nz; 111 Poranui Beach Rd, Birdlings Flat; from $60; ☺1-4pm Fri, 10am-1pm Sat) Creative types should consider booking a session with the Bone Dude, who'll show you how to carve your own bone pendant (allow three hours). Sessions are limited to seven participants, so book ahead.

🛏 Sleeping

★Onuku Farm Hostel
HOSTEL $

(Map p86; ☑03-304 7066; www.onuku.co.nz; Hamiltons Rd, Onuku; sites per person from $12.50, dm/d from $20/70; ☺Oct-Apr; 🅿@🛜) Set on a working farm 6km south of Akaroa, this blissfully isolated backpackers has a grassy camping area, simple, tidy rooms in a farmhouse and 'stargazer' cabins with translucent roofing ($40 for two, BYO bedding). Tonga Hut affords more privacy and breathtaking sea views ($80). Ask about the swimming-with-dolphins tours (from $110), kayaking trips (from $40) and the Skytrack walk.

★Halfmoon Cottage
HOSTEL $

(☑03-304 5050; www.halfmoon.co.nz; SH75, Barrys Bay; dm/s/d $33/64/80; ☺closed Jun-Aug; 🅿@🛜) This pretty 1896 cottage, 12km from Akaroa and right on the water, is a blissful place to spend a few days lazing on the big verandas or in the hammocks dotting the gardens. It offers proper home comforts and style, with the bonus of bicycles and kayaks to take exploring.

Coombe Farm
B&B $$

(Map p86; ☑03-304 7239; www.coombefarm.co.nz; 18 Old Le Bons Track, Takamatua Valley; d $180-220; 🅿🛜) Choose between the private and romantic Shepherd's Hut – complete with outdoor bath – or the historic farmhouse lovingly restored in shades of Laura Ashley. After a luxe breakfast you can take a walk to

---

LITTLE RIVER TRAIL

One of the Great Rides of the NZ Cycle Trail, this easy-graded, 49-km cycle trail (www.littleriverrailtrail.co.nz) runs from Hornby, on the outskirts of Christchurch, to Little River at the base of the Banks Peninsula. It rolls across rural plains, past weathered peaks and along the shores of Lake Ellesmere – home to NZ's most diverse bird population – and its smaller twin, Lake Forsyth. The best section of track can be enjoyed as a return ride from Little River, where there is a cafe and bike hire.

the nearby waterfall, or drive the five minutes into Akaroa.

🍴 Eating

Little River Cafe & Gallery
CAFE $

(Map p86; ☑03-325 1944; www.littlerivergallery.com; SH75, Little River; mains $12-22; ☺7.30am-4pm Mon-Fri, to 4.30pm Sat & Sun) On SH75 between Christchurch and Akaroa, the flourishing settlement of Little River is home to this fantastic combo of contemporary art gallery, shop and cafe. It's top-notch in all departments, with some particularly delectable home baking on offer as well as yummy deli goods to go.

★Hilltop Tavern
PUB FOOD $$

(Map p86; ☑03-325 1005; www.thehilltop.co.nz; 5207 Christchurch-Akaroa Rd; pizzas $24-26, mains $22-30; ☺10am-late, reduced hours May-Sep) Craft beer, wood-fired pizzas, a pool table and occasional live bands seal the deal for locals and visitors alike at this historic pub. Enjoy stunning views of Akaroa harbour and the peninsula – especially at sunset.

Akaroa

POP 624

Akaroa (Long Harbour) was the site of the country's first French settlement and descendants of the original French pioneers still reside here. It's a charming town that strives to recreate the feel of a French provincial village, down to the names of its streets and houses. Generally it's a sleepy place, but the peace is periodically shattered

Akaroa

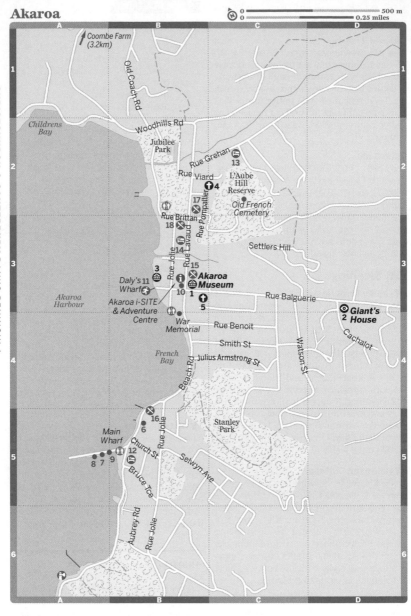

by hordes descending from gargantuan cruise ships. The ships used to dock in Lyttelton but since the earthquakes Akaroa has been a popular substitute. Even when Lyttelton's back on its feet, the ships will be reluctant to leave.

◉ Sights

★ Akaroa Museum
MUSEUM

(Map p88; www.akaroamuseum.org.nz; cnr Rues Lavaud & Balguerie; ⊙10.30am-4.30pm) **FREE** An arduous post-quake revamp has rewarded Akaroa with a smart, contemporary regional

Akaroa

⊙ **Top Sights**
1 Akaroa Museum...................................... B3
2 Giant's House... D3

⊙ **Sights**
3 Customs House B3
4 St Patrick's Catholic Church................. C2
5 St Peter's Anglican Church.................. B3

➌ **Activities, Courses & Tours**
6 Akaroa Dolphins.................................... B5
7 Akaroa Sailing Cruises A5
8 Black Cat Cruises A5
9 Coast Up Close B5

10 Eastern Bays Scenic Mail Run.............. B3
11 Fox II Sailing.. B3

🛏 **Sleeping**
12 Akaroa Village Inn................................. B5
13 Beaufort House C2
14 Chez la Mer B3

🍴 **Eating**
15 Akaroa Boucherie & Deli....................... B3
16 Bully Hayes B5
17 Little Bistro B2
18 Peninsula General Store....................... B3

museum. Learn about the phases of the peninsula's settlement, from the Māori to the French, and view interesting temporary exhibitions. The 20-minute historical film screening in the adjacent restored courthouse is worth a look, too. Note the donation box.

⭐ Giant's House   GARDENS
(Map p88; www.thegiantshouse.co.nz; 68 Rue Balguerie, adult/child $20/10; ⊙12-5pm Jan-Apr, 2-4pm May-Dec) An ongoing labour of love by local artist Josie Martin, this whimsical garden is really one giant artwork, a combination of sculpture and mosaics that cascades down a hillside above Akaroa. Echoes of Gaudí and Miró can be found in the intricate collages of mirrors, tiles and broken china, and there are many surprising nooks and crannies to discover. Martin also exhibits her paintings and sculptures in the lovely 1880 house, the former residence of Akaroa's first bank manager.

St Peter's Anglican Church   CHURCH
(Map p88; 46 Rue Balguerie) Graciously restored in 2015, this 1864 Anglican gem features extensive exposed timbers, stained glass and an historic organ. Well worth a peek whether you're godly or not.

Customs House   HISTORIC BUILDING
(Map p88; Rue Balguerie) Erected in 1858 near Daly's Wharf, this diminutive historic building helped to control the smuggling of alcohol into the town.

St Patrick's Catholic Church   CHURCH
(Map p88; www.akaroacatholicparish.co.nz; 29 Rue Lavaud; ⊙8am-7pm) Akaroa's Catholic church (1863) is a cute, frilly edged old dear, featuring richly coloured stained glass imported from Stuttgart.

🏃 Activities & Tours

Akaroa i-SITE (p90) stocks pamphlets on walks around Akaroa township, taking in the old cottages, churches and gardens that lend Akaroa its character. The six-hour Skyline Circuit also starts from town, and there are many more rewarding walks throughout the peninsula.

Fox II Sailing   BOATING
(Map p88; ☑0800 369 7245; www.akaroafoxsail. co.nz; Daly's Wharf; adult/child $80/40; ⊙departs 10.30am & 1.30pm Jan-May) Enjoy the scenery, observe the marine wildlife, learn some history and try your hand at sailing on Fox II, a gaff-rigged ketch built in 1922.

Akaroa Sailing Cruises   BOATING
(Map p88; ☑0800 724 528; www.aclasssailing. co.nz; Main Wharf; adult/child $75/37.50; ⊙departs 10.15am & 1.15pm Oct–mid-May) Set sail for a 2½-hour hands-on cruise around the harbour on a gorgeous 1946 A-Class yacht.

Akaroa Dolphins   BOATING
(Map p88; ☑03-304 7866; www.akaroadolphins.co.nz; 65 Beach Rd; adult/child $80/40; ⊙12.45pm year-round, plus 10.15am & 3.15pm Oct-Apr) Two-hour wildlife cruises on a comfortable 50ft catamaran, complete with a complimentary drink, home baking and, most importantly, the company of an extraordinary wildlife-spotting dog.

Black Cat Cruises   BOATING
(Map p88; ☑03-304 7641; www.blackcat.co.nz; Main Wharf; nature cruises adult/child $75/30, dolphin swims adult/child $160/130) As well as a two-hour 'nature' cruise, Black Cat offers a three-hour 'swimming with dolphins' experience. Wetsuits and snorkelling gear are provided, plus hot showers back on dry land.

Observers can tag along (adult/child $85/45) but only 12 people can swim per trip, so book ahead.

Coast Up Close BOATING
(Map p88; ☑ 0800 126 278; www.coastupclose. co.nz; Main Wharf; adult/child from $80/30; ⊙ departs 10.30am & 2pm Oct-Apr) Scenic boat trips with an emphasis on wildlife watching. Fishing trips can be arranged.

Akaroa Guided
Sea Kayaking Safari KAYAKING
(☑ 021 156 4591; www.akaroakayaks.com; per person from $115) Paddle serenely around the harbour on these guided kayaking tours, which cater for beginners and experienced paddlers alike. Slip into the water at 7.30am for a three-hour sunrise safari, or if early starts aren't your thing, try the 11.30am highlights tour.

Pohatu Plunge WILDLIFE
(☑ 03-304 8542; www.pohatu.co.nz; tours adult/ child $75/55, self-drive $25/12) 🏊 Runs three-hour evening tours from Akaroa to the Pohatu white-flippered penguin colony (a self-drive option is also available). The best time to see the penguins is during the breeding season from August to January, but it is possible throughout the year. Sea kayaking and 4WD nature tours are also available, as is the option of staying overnight in a secluded cottage.

Eastern Bays Scenic Mail Run DRIVING
(Map p88; ☑ 03-304 8526; tours $80; ⊙ departs 9am Mon-Fri) Travel along with the ex-conservation-ranger postie to visit isolated communities and bays on this 120km, five-hour mail delivery service. Departs from the i-SITE; bookings are essential as there are only eight seats available.

🛏 Sleeping

Chez la Mer HOSTEL $
(Map p88; ☑ 03-304 7024; www.chezlamer.co.nz; 50 Rue Lavaud; dm $34, d $76, with bathroom $86; 🛜) Pretty in pink, this historic building houses a friendly backpackers with well-kept rooms and a shaded garden, complete with fish pond, hammocks and barbecue. There's also a cosy lounge and kitchen, and free bikes for loan.

Akaroa Village Inn APARTMENTS $$
(Map p88; ☑ 03-304 1111; www.akaroavillageinn. co.nz; 81 Beach Rd; units $135-245; P 🛜) Right on the harbour front, this sprawling complex offers one- and two-bedroom units of varying

levels of luxury. The water-view apartments are obviously the pick of the bunch, but ask to see a few, as they are individually owned, and furnishings vary widely.

★**Beaufort House** B&B $$$
(Map p88; ☑ 03-304 7517; www.beauforthouse. co.nz; 42 Rue Grehan; r $395; ⊙ closed Jun-Aug; P 🛜) Tucked away on a quiet street behind gorgeous gardens, this lovely 1878 house is adorned with covetable artwork and antiques. Of the five individually decorated rooms only one is without an en suite, compensated by a large private bathroom with a claw-foot tub just across the hall. A lovely breakfast is included.

Eating

Peninsula General Store CAFE, DELI $
(Map p88; ☑ 03-304 8800; www.peninsulageneral store.co.nz; 40 Rue Lavaud; ⊙ 9am-4pm Thu-Mon) 🏊 Not only does this darling little corner store sell fresh bread, organic local produce and groceries, it also does the best espresso in the village.

Akaroa Boucherie & Deli DELI $
(Map p88; 67 Rue Lavaud; ⊙ 10am-5.30pm Mon-Fri, 9am-4pm Sat) A dream scenario for picnickers and self-caterers, this sharp butcher's shop and deli peddles all manner of local produce from bread, salmon, cheese and pickles, to delicious pies, smallgoods and, of course, meat.

Bully Hayes CAFE $$
(Map p88; www.bullyhayes.co.nz; 57 Beach Rd; mains $22-43; ⊙ 8am-9pm; 🛜) Named after a well-travelled American buccaneer, Bully Hayes is a bustling restaurant serving hearty if basic meals all day long, from breakfast to dinner. The seafood is fresh and the beers are cold, and the sunny spot overlooking the harbour is a winner in good weather.

Little Bistro FRENCH $$$
(Map p88; ☑ 03-304 7314; www.thelittlebistro. co.nz; 33 Rue Lavaud; mains $22-40; ⊙ 5.30-11pm Tue-Sat) A decent bet for refined food, this place serves a classic bistro-style menu featuring local seafood, South Island wines and Canterbury craft beers. The menu changes seasonally, but usually includes favourites such as crusted lamb or local salmon.

ℹ️ Information

Akaroa i-Site (Map p88; ☑ 03-304 7784; www. akaroa.com; 74a Rue Lavaud; ⊙ 9am-5pm) A helpful hub offering free maps, info and bookings for activities, transport etc. Doubles as the post office.

❶ Getting There & Away

From October to April the **Akaroa Shuttle** (☏ 0800 500 929; www.akaroashuttle. co.nz; adult/child one way $35/30, return $50/40; ☺ Oct-Apr) runs daily services from Christchurch to Akaroa (departs 8.30am), returning to Christchurch at 3.45pm. Check the website for Christchurch pick-up options. Scenic tours from Christchurch exploring Banks Peninsula are also available.

French Connection (☏ 0800 800 575; www. akaroabus.co.nz; return adult/child $50/35) has a year-round daily departure from Christchurch at 9am, returning from Akaroa at 4pm.

NORTH CANTERBURY

South of Kaikoura, SH1 crosses the Hundalee Hills and heads into Hurunui District, an area known for its wine and for the thermal resort of Hanmer Springs. It's also the start of the Canterbury Plains, a vast, flat, richly agricultural area partitioned by distinctive braided rivers. The region is bounded to the west by the Southern Alps. If you're crossing into Canterbury from either Westport or Nelson, the most direct route cuts through the Alps on the beautiful Lewis Pass Hwy (SH7).

Lewis Pass

The northernmost of the three main mountain passes connecting the West Coast to the east, 864m-high Lewis Pass is not as steep as the others (Arthur's and Haast), but the drive is arguably just as scenic. Vegetation comprises mainly beech (red and silver) and kowhai trees growing along river terraces.

From Lewis Pass the highway wiggles east for 62km before reaching the turn-off to Hanmer Springs.

❂ Sights & Activities

The area has some interesting **tramps**, passing through beech forest backed by snow-capped mountains, lakes and alpine tarns. Popular tracks include the **St James Walkway** (p64) and those through **Lake Sumner Forest Park**; see the DOC pamphlet *Lake Sumner & Lewis Pass* ($2). Subalpine conditions apply; make sure you sign the intentions books at the huts.

Marble Hill FOREST
(www.doc.govt.nz; SH7) Located within Lewis Pass Scenic Reserve, Marble Hill is home to one of NZ's most beautiful DOC camping grounds – a row of sites tucked into beech forest, overlooking a grassy meadow and encircled by snow-capped mountains.

MĀORI CANTERBURY

Only 14% of NZ's Māori live on the South Island, and of those, half live in Canterbury. The first major tribe to become established here were Waitaha, who were subsequently conquered and assimilated into the Ngāti Māmoe tribe in the 16th century. In the following century, they in turn were conquered and subsumed by Ngāi Tahu (www.ngaitahu.iwi. nz), a tribe that has its origins in the East Coast of the North Island.

In 1848 most of Canterbury was sold to the crown under an agreement which stipulated that an area of 10 acres per person would be reserved for the tribe; less than half of that actually was. With so little land left to them, Ngāi Tahu were no longer able to be self-sufficient and suffered great financial hardship. It wasn't until 1997 that this injustice was addressed, with the tribe receiving an apology from the crown and a settlement valued at $170 million. Part of the deal was the official inclusion of the Māori name for the most spiritually significant part of the tribe's ancestral land: Aoraki/Mt Cook.

Today, Ngāi Tahu is considered to be one of Māoridom's great success stories, with a reputation for good financial management, sound cultural advice and a portfolio including property, forestry, fisheries and many high-profile tourism operations.

There are many ways to engage in Māori culture in Canterbury. Artefacts can be seen at **Canterbury Museum** (p69), **Akaroa Museum** (p88), **Okains Bay Māori & Colonial Museum** (p86) and **South Canterbury Museum** (p103). **Willowbank Wildlife Reserve** (p72) in Christchurch has a replica Māori village and an evening cultural show. Further south in Timaru, the **Te Ana Māori Rock Art Centre** (p104) has interactive displays and arranges tours to see centuries-old work in situ.

This special place represents a landmark victory for NZ's conservation movement. Back in the 1970s, this significant forest was saved from the chop by a 341,159-signature petition known as the 'Maruia Declaration', which played a part in the Department of Conservation's establishment in 1987.

A more concrete feature of the reserve is **Evison's Wall**. A highly unsuccessful geological experiment begun in 1964, the 24m-long wall was built along the Alpine Fault to establish how the fault was moving. Such measuring methods have clearly been superseded, so now it's just a straight-as-a-die wall in an out-of-the-way place.

For a spot of exercise, head out on the **Lake Daniell Track**. You don't have to go all the way – it's four to six hours return – but even a short foray will reveal all sorts of native flora, such as matagouri, mistletoe and sweet-smelling beech trees.

Maruia Springs   HOT SPRINGS

(☑ 03-523 8840; www.maruiasprings.co.nz; SH7; adult/child $40/18; ☉ 8am-9pm) Maruia Springs is a small hot spring resort on the banks of the Maruia River. The water temperature varies between 36°C and 42°C across a variety of pools, including outdoor rock pools, indoor baths, a sauna and a cold plunge pool. It's a magical setting during winter (June to September) but mind the sandflies in summer (December to March).

ⓘ Getting There & Away

East West Coaches (☑ 03-789 6251; www. eastwestcoaches.co.nz) runs between Christchurch and Westport via the Lewis Pass daily except Saturday (adult/child $60/45, five hours), stopping at Maruia Springs and the St James Walkway.

Hanmer Springs

POP 840

Ringed by mountains, pretty Hanmer Springs has a slightly European feel, enhanced by the fact that many of the streets are named after English spa towns (Bath, Harrogate, Leamington). The town is the main thermal resort on the South Island, and it's a pleasantly low-key spot to indulge yourself, whether by soaking in hot pools, dining out, or being pampered in the spa complex. If that all sounds too soporific, fear not; there are plenty of family-friendly outdoor activities on offer, including a few to get the adrenaline pumping.

🏃 Activities

★**Hanmer Springs**
Thermal Pools   HOT SPRINGS

(Map p93; ☑ 03-315 0000; www.hanmersprings. co.nz; 42 Amuri Ave; adult/child $24/12, locker per 2hr $2; ☉ 10am-9pm; 🚗) Māori legend has it that these hot springs are the result of embers from Mt Ngauruhoe on the North Island falling from the sky. Whatever their origin, visitors flock to Hanmer Springs year-round to soak in the warming waters. The main complex consists of a series of large pools of various temperatures.

There are also smaller, adult-only landscaped rock pools, a freshwater 25m lap pool, private thermal pools ($32 per 30 minutes), a cafe and an adjacent spa. Kids of all ages will love the water slides and the whirl-down-the-plughole-thrill of the Superbowl ($10).

Hanmer Springs Spa   SPA

(Map p93; ☑ 03-315 0029, 0800 873 529; www. hanmersprings.co.nz; 42 Amuri Ave; ☉ 10am-7pm) If you're looking to be pampered, you've come to the right place. Hanmer Springs Spa offers every kind of treatment you would expect from an international-standard spa, from facials (from $90) to hot-stone massages ($180) to full-body treatments ($320).

Hanmer Forest Park   TRAMPING, MOUNTAIN BIKING

(www.visithurunui.co.nz) Trampers and mountain bikers will find plenty of room to move within the 130 sq km expanse of forest abutting Hanmer Springs. The easy Woodland Walk starts 1km up Jollies Pass Rd and goes through Douglas fir, poplar and redwood stands before joining Majuba Walk, which leads to Conical Hill Lookout and then back towards town (1½ hours).

The Waterfall Track is an excellent half-day tramp starting at the end of McIntyre Rd. The i-SITE (p94) stocks a *Forest Park Walks* booklet and a mountain-biking map (both $3).

Hanmer Springs Ski Area   SKIING

(☑ 027 434 1806; www.skihanmer.co.nz; daily lift passes adult/child/family $60/30/130) Only 17km from town via an unsealed road, this small complex has runs to suit all levels of ability. The **Adventure Centre** (Map p93; ☑ 0800 368 7386, 03-315 7233; www.hanmeradventure.co.nz; 20 Conical Hill Rd; ☉ 9am-5pm) provides shuttles during the ski season (adult/child return $40/32) and also has gear for hire.

🛏 Sleeping

Hanmer Springs has a wide range of accommodation options, from basic camping through to luxury B&Bs and swanky apartments. If you're planning on staying awhile, check out websites like www.alpineholidayhomes.co.nz and www.hanmerholidayhomes.co.nz for local rentals.

Kakapo Lodge
HOSTEL $

(Map p93; 📞 03-315 7472; www.kakapolodge.co.nz; 14 Amuri Ave; dm $33, d $76, with bathroom $95; P 🛜) The YHA-affiliated Kakapo has a cheery owner, a roomy kitchen and lounge, chill-busting underfloor heating and a 1st-floor sundeck. Bunk-free dorms (some with bathrooms) and spotless double rooms are available.

Jack in the Green
HOSTEL $

(📞 03-315 5111; www.jackinthegreen.co.nz; 3 Devon St; sites per person $20, dm $32, d $76, with bathroom $92; P 🛜) This charming converted old home is a 10-minute walk from the town centre. Large rooms (no bunks), relaxing gardens and a cosy lounge area are the main drawcards. For extra privacy, book an en suite garden 'chalet'.

Hanmer Springs Top 10
HOLIDAY PARK $

(Map p93; 📞 03-315 7113, 0800 904 545; www.hanmerspringstop10.co.nz; 5 Hanmer Springs Rd; sites $40-48, units from $89, with bathroom from $145; P @ 🛜) This family-friendly park is just a few minutes' walk from the town's eponymous pools. Kids will love the playground and jumping pillow. Take your pick from basic cabins (BYO everything) to attractive motel units with everything supplied.

★ Woodbank Park Cottages
COTTAGE $$

(📞 03-315 5075; www.woodbankcottages.co.nz; 381 Woodbank Rd; d $190-225; P ❄) Nestled among the trees, these two plush cottages are a six-minute drive from Hanmer but feel a million miles away. Decor is crisp and modern, with wraparound wooden decks that come equipped with gas barbecues and rural views. Log-burning fireplaces and well-stocked kitchens seal the deal.

Chalets Motel
MOTEL $$

(Map p93; 📞 03-315 7097; www.chaletsmotel.co.nz; 56 Jacks Pass Rd; d $160-195; P 🛜) Soak up the mountain views from these tidy, reasonably priced, freestanding wooden chalets, set on the slopes behind the town centre. All chalets have full kitchens; the larger spa unit is the pick of the bunch.

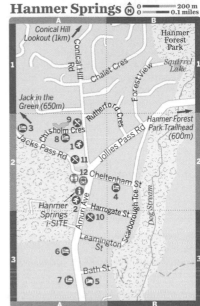

Hanmer Springs

⊙ Activities, Courses & Tours
1 Hanmer Springs Adventure
   Centre A2
   Hanmer Springs Spa .... (see 2)
2 Hanmer Springs Thermal Pools A2

⊜ Sleeping
3 Chalets Motel A2
4 Cheltenham House B2
5 Hanmer Springs Top 10 ....A3
6 Kakapo Lodge A3
7 Scenic Views A3
8 St James A2

⊗ Eating
9 Coriander's A2
10 No. 31 ....A3
11 Powerhouse Cafe A2

ℹ Transport
   Hanmer Connection ....(see 12)
   Hanmer Tours & Shuttle ....(see 12)
12 Main Bus Stop A2

Scenic Views
MOTEL $$

(Map p93; 📞 03-315 7419, 0800 843 974; www.hanmerscenicviews.co.nz; 2 Amuri Ave; d $160-235, apt from $245; P ❄ 🛜) An attractive timber-and-stone complex offering modern studios and apartments, most with sunny balconies

MT LYFORD

Around 60km from both Hanmer Springs and Kaikoura, **Mt Lyford Alpine Resort** (☑0274 710 717, 03-366 1220; www.mt-lyford.co.nz; day passes adult/child $75/35; ⊙lifts 9am-4pm) is more of a 'resort' than most NZ ski fields, with accommodation and eating options. There's a good mix of runs and a terrain park.

A shuttle service runs from Mt Lyford village (a 45-minute drive from Hanmer Springs) during the season – enquire at **Hanmer Springs Adventure** (p92).

or patios. Try for one of the two spa rooms, which have heavenly mountain views.

Cheltenham House　　　　B&B **$$$**
(Map p93; ☑03-315 7545; www.cheltenham.co.nz; 13 Cheltenham St; r $235-280; P🛜) This large 1930s house has room for both a billiard table and a grand piano. There are four art-filled suites in the main house and two in cosy garden cottages. Cooked gourmet breakfasts are delivered to the rooms and wine is served in the evening.

St James　　　　APARTMENT **$$$**
(Map p93; ☑0508 785 2637, 03-315 5225; www.thestjames.co.nz; 20 Chisholm Cres; d $225-270, apt from $320; P❄🛜) Luxuriate with all the mod cons, including an iPod dock and fully equipped kitchen. Sizes range from studios to two-bedroom apartments; most have mountain views.

Eating

Coriander's　　　　INDIAN **$$**
(Map p93; ☑03-315 7616; www.corianders.co.nz; Chisholm Cres; mains $16-22; ⊙noon-2pm & 5-10pm Tue-Sun, 5-10pm Mon; 🍴) Spice up your life at this brightly painted North Indian restaurant complete with *bhangra*-beats soundtrack. There are plenty of tasty lamb, chicken and seafood dishes to choose from, plus a fine vegetarian selection. The lunch special ($14) is good value.

Powerhouse Cafe　　　　CAFE **$$**
(Map p93; ☑03-315 5252; www.powerhousecafe.co.nz; 8 Jacks Pass Rd; brunch mains $15-24; ⊙7.30am-3pm) Delicious cakes and good-quality coffee are on the menu at this local favourite, tucked away off the main street. Power up with a huge High Country

breakfast or try the Highland Fling – caramelised, whisky-sodden porridge topped with banana. Lunch offerings are equally palatable.

No. 31　　　　MODERN NZ **$$$**
(Map p93; ☑03-315 7031; www.restaurant-no31.nz; 31 Amuri Ave; mains $37-40; ⊙5-11pm) Substantial servings of good-quality, albeit conservative, cuisine are on offer in this pretty wooden cottage. The upmarket ambience befits the prices, though you're also paying for the location, directly opposite the hot springs. Book ahead on weekends.

❶ Information

Hanmer Springs i-SITE (Map p93; ☑03-315 0020, 0800 442 663; www.visithanmersprings.co.nz; 40 Amuri Ave; ⊙10am-5pm) Books transport, accommodation and activities.

❶ Getting There & Away

The **main bus stop** (Map p93) is near the corner of Amuri Ave and Jacks Pass Rd.

Hanmer Connection (Map p93; ☑03-382 2952, 0800 242 663; www.hanmerconnection.co.nz; adult/child one way $30/20, return $50/30) Runs a daily bus to/from Christchurch via Waipara and Amberley, departing Christchurch at 9am and Hanmer Springs at 4.30pm.

Hanmer Tours & Shuttle (Map p93; ☑03-315 7418; www.hanmertours.co.nz) Runs daily buses to/from Culverden ($15, 30 minutes), Waikari ($15, 45 minutes), Waipara ($20, one hour), Amberley ($20, one hour), Christchurch city centre ($35, two hours) and Christchurch Airport ($45, two hours).

Waipara Valley

Conveniently stretched along SH1 60km north of Christchurch, this resolutely rural area makes for a tasty pit stop. The valley's warm dry summers followed by cool autumn nights have proved a winning formula for growing grapes, olives, hazelnuts and lavender. While Waipara accounts for less than 3% of NZ's vines, it nonetheless produces some of the country's finest cool-climate wines, including riesling, pinot noir and gewürztraminer.

Of the region's 30 or so wineries, around a dozen have cellar doors to visit, four with restaurants. To explore the valley's bounty fully, pick up a copy of the *North Canterbury Wine Region* map (or download it from www.waiparavalleynz.com). Otherwise, you'll spot

MOLESWORTH STATION

Filling up 1807 mountainous sq km between Hanmer Springs and Blenheim, Molesworth Station is NZ's largest farm, with the country's largest cattle herd (up to 10,000). It's also an area of national ecological significance and the entire farm is now administered by **DOC** (☑ 03-572 9100; www.doc.govt.nz; Gee St, Renwick).

Visits are usually only possible when the Acheron Rd through the station is open from November to early April, weather permitting; check with DOC or at the Hanmer Springs i-SITE (p94). Note that the gates are only open from 7am to 7pm. Pick up DOC's *Molesworth Station* brochure from the i-SITE or download it from the website.

Getting There & Away

You will need to have your own wheels or go on a tour. The 207km drive from Hanmer Springs north to Blenheim on the narrow, unsealed Acheron Rd takes around six hours.

Molesworth Heritage Tours (☑ 027 201 4536, 03-315 7401; www.molesworth.co.nz; tours $198-770; ☉ Oct-May) leads 4WD coach trips to the station from Hanmer Springs. Day tours include a picnic lunch, but there's also a five-hour 'no frills' option. From the Blenheim side, **Molesworth Tours** (☑ 03-572 8025; www.molesworthtours.co.nz) offers one- to four-day all-inclusive heritage and 4WD trips ($220 to $1487), as well as four-day fully supported (and catered) mountain-bike adventures ($1460).

---

several of the big players from the highway. The area's main town are tiny Waipara and slightly larger Amberley, but you're likely to spend most of your time in the countryside between the two.

◉ Sights

★ Pegasus Bay
WINERY

(☑ 03-314 6869; www.pegasusbay.com; Stockgrove Rd; ☉ restaurant noon-4pm Thu-Mon, tastings 10am-5pm daily) It's fitting that Waipara Valley's premier winery should have the loveliest setting and one of Canterbury's best restaurants (mains $34 to $43). Verdant manicured gardens set the scene, but it's the contemporary NZ menu and luscious paired wines that steal the show.

Black Estate
WINERY

(☑ 03-314 6085; www.blackestate.co.nz; 614 Omihi Rd, SH1; ☉ 10am-5pm, shorter hours Jun-Oct) ◢ Perched on a hillside overlooking the valley, this striking black barn is home to some excellent drops – try the pinot noirs from the winery's three nearby vineyards, each of which have a distinctive terroir of their own. The attached light-filled restaurant offers stunning views and food that champions local producers (mains $38 to $44).

Brew Moon
BREWERY

(☑ 03-314 8036; www.brewmoon.co.nz; 12 Markham St, Amberley; ☉ 3pm-late Wed-Fri, from noon Sat & Sun) The variety of craft beers available to taste at this wee brewery never

wanes. Stop in to fill a rigger (flagon) to take away, or sup an ale alongside a tasty wood-fired pizza in the cosy bar area (pizzas $10 to $20).

🍴 Sleeping & Eating

Old Glenmark Vicarage
B&B $$$

(☑ 03-314 6775; www.glenmarkvicarage.co.nz; 161 Church Rd, Waipara; d $230, barn d $210; P �ᷛ 🏊) There are two divine options in this beautifully restored vicarage: cosy up with bed and breakfast in the main house, or lounge around in the character filled, converted barn that sleeps up to six (perfect for families or groups). The lovely gardens and swimming pool are a blessed bonus.

★ Little Vintage Espresso
CAFE $

(20 Markham St, Amberley; breakfast $10-19; ☉ 7am-4pm Mon-Sat; �ᷛ) This petite whitewashed cottage just off SH1 has the best coffee in town, with food to match. All-day breakfasts, gourmet sandwiches and delectable homemade cakes are all on offer.

Pukeko Junction
CAFE, DELI $$

(☑ 03-314 8834; www.pukekojunction.co.nz; 458 Ashworths Rd, SH1, Leithfield; mains $7.50-20; ☉ 9am-4.30pm Tue-Sun; ◢) A deservedly popular roadside stop, this bright, friendly cafe in Leithfield (south of Amberley) serves delicious bakery fare, like gourmet sausage rolls and tarts filled with goat's cheese, leek and walnut. The attached shop stocks an excellent selection of local wines.

WORTH A TRIP

CRAIGIEBURN FOREST PARK

Just off the highway, this **mountainous area** (www.doc.govt.nz) becomes a mecca for ski bunnies from June to October, with several fields in its midst, including Broken River and Craigieburn Valley. Craigieburn Picnic Area and Campsite (sites per adult/child $6/3) is set in the park's beech-forested lower slopes.

From around October to April, a track network offers various tramps from 20-minute nature trails to the classic four-hour-return hike to Helicopter Hill. Mountain biking is also possible; see www.craigieburntrails.org.nz for details.

Waipara Springs   CAFE $$
(www.waiparasprings.co.nz; 409 Omihi Rd, SH1, Waipara; mains $25-29; ⊙10am-4pm) Slightly north of Waipara township, one of the valley's oldest vineyards has a fine line in righteous rieslings. The casual cafe serves platters and bistro fare in the lovely family-friendly garden on sunny days, or inside by the cosy wood-burning fire in winter.

ⓘ Getting There & Away

Hanmer Connection (☑ 0800 242 663; www.hanmerconnection.co.nz) One daily bus stops in Waipara on request on the road between Hanmer Springs ($20, 50 minutes) and Christchurch ($20, 1¼ hours).

Hanmer Tours & Shuttle (☑ 03-315 7418; www.hanmertours.co.nz) Runs a daily shuttle to/from Hanmer Springs ($20), Christchurch city centre ($15) and Christchurch Airport ($25).

InterCity (☑ 03-365 1113; www.intercity.co.nz) Coaches head to/from Picton (from $34, five hours), Kaikoura (from $28, 1¾ hours) and Christchurch (from $11, one hour) at least daily.

CENTRAL CANTERBURY

While the dead-flat agricultural heartland of the Canterbury Plains blankets the majority of the region, there's plenty of interest for travellers in the west, where the Southern Alps soar to snowy peaks. Here you'll find numerous ski fields and some brilliant wilderness walks.

Unusually for NZ, the most scenic routes avoid the coast, with most places of interest accessed from one of two spectacular roads:
the Great Alpine Highway (SH73), which wends from the Canterbury Plains deep into the mountains and over to the West Coast, and the Inland Scenic Route (SH72), which skirts the mountain foothills on its way south towards Tekapo.

Selwyn District

Named after NZ's first Anglican bishop, this largely rural district has swallowed an English map book and regurgitated place names such as Lincoln, Darfield and Sheffield. Yet any illusions of Britain are quickly dispelled by the looming presence of the snow-capped Southern Alps, providing a rugged retort to 'England's mountains green'.

The highly scenic Great Alpine Hwy pierces the heart of the district on its journey between Christchurch and the West Coast. On the Canterbury Plains, it passes through the small settlement of Springfield, notable for a monument to local Rewi Alley (1897–1987), who became a great hero of the Chinese Communist Party.

Selwyn's numerous ski fields may not be the country's most glamorous, but they provide plenty of thrills for ski bunnies. **Porters** (☑ 03-318 4731; www.skiporters.co.nz; daily lift passes adult/child weekend $99/69, midweek $79/49; ⊙lifts 9am-4pm) is the main commercial field; club fields include **Mt Olympus** (☑ 03-318 5840; www.mtolympus.co.nz; daily lift passes adult/child $75/35), **Cheeseman** (☑ 03-344 3247, snow phone 03-318 8794; www.mtcheeseman.co.nz; daily lift passes adult/child $79/39; ⊙lifts 9am-4.30pm, shorter hours midweek), **Broken River** (☑ 03-318 8713; www.brokenriver.co.nz; daily lift passes adult/child $75/35; ⊙lifts 9am-4pm), **Craigieburn Valley** (☑ 03-318 8711; www.craigieburn.co.nz; daily lift passes adult/child $75/35) and **Temple Basin** (☑ 03-377 7788; www.templebasin.co.nz; daily lift passes adult/child $69/35).

🏃 Activities

Rubicon Valley Horse Treks   HORSE RIDING
(☑ 03-318 8886; www.rubiconvalley.co.nz; 534 Rubicon Rd, Springfield) Operating from a sheep farm 6km from Springfield, Rubicon offers a variety of horse treks to suit both beginner and advanced riders, including hour-long farm rides ($55), two-hour river or valley rides ($98), two-hour sunset rides ($120) and six-hour mountain trail rides ($285).

🛏 Sleeping & Eating

Smylies Accommodation HOSTEL $
(☏ 03-318 4740; www.smylies.co.nz; 5653 West
Coast Rd, Springfield; dm/s/d $38/60/90; P 🕸)
🏄 This well-seasoned, welcoming, YHA-
associated hostel has a piano, manga comics
galore, a DVD library and a wood-burning
fire in the large communal kitchen. As
well as traditional dorms, there are also
self-contained motel units ($105) and a
three-bedroom cottage ($280). Winter
packages (June to September), including
ski-equipment rental and ski-field transport,
are available.

Famous Sheffield Pie Shop BAKERY $
(☏ 03-318 3876; www.sheffieldpieshop.co.nz; 51
Main West Rd, Sheffield; pies $5-6; ⊙ 6.30am-4pm
Mon-Fri, from 7.30am Sat & Sun) Blink and you'll
miss this stellar roadside bakery, a purveyor of
more than 20 varieties of pies, from traditional beef to more experimental flavour combi-
nations – think whisky and venison, or chick-
en, camembert and apricot. While you're here,
snaffle a bag of the exemplary afghan biscuits
– such cornflakey, chocolatey goodness!

ℹ Getting There & Away

Public transport is limited in Selwyn District, so
it's best have your own transport.

Arthur's Pass

POP 30

Having left the Canterbury Plains at Springfield, the Great Alpine Hwy heads over Por-
ter's Pass through the mountainous folds of
the Torlesse and Craigieburn Ranges and
into Arthur's Pass.

Māori used this pass to cross the Southern Alps long before its 'discovery' by Arthur
Dobson in 1864. The Westland gold rush created the need for a dependable crossing over
the Alps from Christchurch, and the coach
road was completed within a year. Later, the
coal and timber trade demanded a railway,
duly completed in 1923.

Today it's an amazing journey. Successive
valleys display their own character, not least
the spectacular braided Waimakariri River
Valley, encountered as you enter the national
park proper.

Arthur's Pass village is 4km from the actual pass. At 900m, it's NZ's highest-altitude
settlement and a handy base for tramps,
climbs and skiing. The weather, however, is
a bit of a shocker. Come prepared for rain.

◉ Sights

Castle Hill/Kura Tawhiti LANDMARK
Scattered across lush paddocks around 33km
from Springfield, these limestone formations
reach up to 30m high, and look so otherworldly they were named 'treasure from a
distant land' by early Māori. A car park (with
toilets) provides easy access to a short walk
into the strange rock garden (10 minutes), favoured by rock climbers and photographers.

Cave Stream Scenic Reserve CAVE
(www.doc.govt.nz) Near Broken River Bridge,
2km northeast of Castle Hill, you'll find
this 594m-long cave. As indicated by the information panels in the car park, the walk
through the cave is an achievable adventure,
but only with a foolproof torch and warm
clothing, and definitely only if the water level is less than waist deep where indicated.
Heed all notices, take necessary precautions
and revel in the spookiness.

Failing that, just wander around the
15-minute loop track for a gander at the surrounds, including limestone formations that
featured in the *Chronicles of Narnia* movie.

🛏 Sleeping & Eating

Camping is possible near the basic **Avalanche
Creek Shelter** (www.doc.govt.nz; SH73; adult/
child $8/4; P), opposite the DOC, where there's
running water, tables, a sink and toilets. You
can also camp for free at **Klondyke Corner**
(www.doc.govt.nz; SH73) or **Hawdon Shelter**
(www.doc.govt.nz; Mount White Rd, off SH37), 8km
and 24km south of Arthur's Pass respectively, where facilities are limited to toilets and
stream water for boiling. If you're not camping, there are plenty of accommodation options in Arthur's Pass village and surrounds.

Mountain House YHA HOSTEL $
(☏ 03-318 9258; www.trampers.co.nz; 83 Main Rd;
dm/d $33/92, motel units $165; P 🕸) Spread
around the village, this excellent suite of
accommodation includes a well-kept hostel, two upmarket motel units and two
three-bedroom cottages with log fires ($340,
for up to eight people). The enthusiastic
manager runs a tight ship and can provide
extensive local tramping information.

Arthur's Pass Village B&B B&B $$
(☏ 021 394 776; www.arthurspass.org.nz; 72 School
Tce; d $140-160; P 🕸) This lovingly restored
former railway cottage is now a cosy B&B,
with two well-appointed guest rooms. Break-
fast on free-range bacon and eggs, pancakes

DON'T MISS

ARTHUR'S PASS NATIONAL PARK

Straddling the Southern Alps, known to Māori as Kā Tiritiri o Te Moana (steep peak of glistening white), this vast alpine wilderness became the South Island's first national park in 1929. Of its 1144 sq km, two-thirds lies on the Canterbury side of the main divide; the rest is in Westland. It is a rugged, mountainous area, cut by deep valleys, and ranging in altitude from 245m at the Taramakau River to 2408m at Mt Murchison.

There are plenty of well-marked day tramps throughout the park, especially around Arthur's Pass village. Pick up a copy of DOC's *Discover Arthur's Pass* booklet to read about popular tramps, including: the **Arthur's Pass Walkway**, a reasonably easy track from the village to the Dobson Memorial at the summit of the pass (2½ hours return); the one-hour return walk to **Devils Punchbowl** falls; and the steep walk to beautiful views at **Temple Basin** (three hours return).

More challenging options include the **Bealey Spur** (p66) track, the classic summit hike to **Avalanche Peak** (p65) and the multiday **Goat Pass** (p65) and **Harper Pass** (p60) tracks; see Hiking in Canterbury (p65). These require previous tramping experience as flooding can make the rivers dangerous and the weather is extremely changeable. Always seek advice from DOC before setting out.

and freshly baked bread, while enjoying the company of the friendly owners. Delicious home-cooked dinners are also available ($35).

Wilderness Lodge LODGE **$$$**
(☑ 03-318 9246; www.wildernesslodge.co.nz; Cora Lynn Rd, Bealey; half board s $569-770, d $938-1240; P ⊚) ✦ For tranquillity and natural grandeur, this midsize alpine lodge tucked into beech forest just off the highway takes some beating. It's a class act, with a focus on immersive, nature-based experiences. Two daily guided activities (such as tramping and kayaking) are included in the tariff, along with gourmet breakfast and dinner.

Arthur's Pass Store & Cafe CAFE **$**
(85 Main Rd; breakfast & lunch $7-24; ⊙ 8am-5pm; ⊚) If you want to stock up on supplies, this is your best chance, with odds-on for egg sandwiches, hot chips, decent coffee, basic groceries and petrol.

ⓘ Information

DOC Arthur's Pass Visitor Centre (☑ 03-318 9211; www.doc.govt.nz; 80 Main Rd; ⊙ 8.30am-4.30pm) Helpful staff can provide advice on suitable tramps and the all-important weather forecast. Detailed route guides and topographical maps are also available, as are locator beacons for hire. Before you leave, log your trip details on AdventureSmart (www.adventuresmart.org.nz) via the on-site computer.

ⓘ Getting There & Away

Fill your fuel tank before you leave Springfield (or Hokitika or Greymouth, if you're coming from the west). There's a pump at **Arthur's Pass Store** but it's expensive and only operates from 8am until 5pm.

Buses depart from various stops all a stone's throw from the store – check with the bus company for the latest information.

Atomic Shuttles (☑ 03-349 0697; www.atomic travel.co.nz) From Arthur's Pass buses head to/from Christchurch ($40, 2¼ hours), Springfield ($40, one hour), Lake Brunner ($40, 50 minutes) and Greymouth ($40, 1¼ hours).

West Coast Shuttle (☑ 03-768 0028; www. westcoastshuttle.co.nz) Buses stopping at Arthur's Pass head to/from Christchurch ($42, 2¾ hours) and Greymouth ($32, 1¾ hours).

TranzAlpine (☑ 04-495 0775, 0800 872 467; www.greatjourneysofnz.co.nz/tranzalpine; fares from $119) One train daily in each direction stops in Arthur's Pass, heading to/from Springfield (1½ hours) and Christchurch (2½ hours), or Lake Brunner (one hour) and Greymouth (two hours).

Methven

POP 1700

Methven is busiest in winter (June to September), when it fills up with snow bunnies heading to nearby Mt Hutt. At other times tumbleweeds don't quite blow down the main street – much to the disappointment of the wannabe gunslingers arriving for the raucous October rodeo. Over summer (December to March) it's a low-key and affordable base for trampers and mountain bikers heading into the spectacular mountain foothills.

⚡ Activities

Most people come to Methven for the nearby ski slopes, but there are plenty of other activities nearby. Ask at the i-SITE about local walks (including the town heritage trail and Methven Walk/Cycleway) and longer tramps, horse riding, mountain biking, fishing, clay-shooting, archery, golfing, scenic helicopter flights, and jetboating through the nearby Rakaia Gorge.

🛏 Sleeping

Alpenhorn Chalet   HOSTEL $
(☑ 03-302 8779; www.alpenhorn.co.nz; 44 Allen St; dm $30, d $65-85; Ⓟ @ 🛜) This small, inviting home has a leafy conservatory housing an indoor spa pool, a log fire and complimentary espresso coffee. Bedrooms are spacious and brightly coloured, with lots of warm, natural wood; one double room has an en-suite bathroom.

Rakaia Gorge Camping Ground   CAMPGROUND $
(☑ 03-302 9353; 6686 Arundel-Rakaia Gorge Rd; sites per adult/child under 12yr $8.50/free) There are no powered sites here, only toilets, showers and a small kitchen shelter, but don't let that put you off. This is the best camping ground for miles, perched picturesquely above the ultra-blue Rakaia River, and a good base for exploring the area. Amenities closed May to September.

Redwood Lodge   HOSTEL, LODGE $$
(☑ 03-302 8964; www.redwoodlodge.co.nz; 3 Wayne Pl; s $55-65, d $86-149; Ⓟ @ 🛜) Expect a warm welcome and no dorms at this charming and peaceful family-friendly lodge. Most rooms are en suite, and bigger rooms can be reconfigured to accommodate families. The large shared lounge is ideal for resting ski-weary limbs.

Whitestone Cottages   RENTAL HOUSE $$$
(☑ 03-928 8050; www.whitestonecottages.co.nz; 3016 Methven Hwy; cottages $175-255; Ⓟ 🛜) When you just want to spread out, cook a meal, do your laundry and have your own space, these four large freestanding cottages in leafy grounds are just the ticket. Each sleeps six in two en suite bedrooms. Rates are for two people; each extra person is $35

✕ Eating

Cafe 131   CAFE $
(131 Main St; mains $10-19; ☺ 7.30am-5pm; 🛜) Polished timber and leadlight windows lend

WORTH A TRIP

MT HUTT & RAKAIA GORGE

Mt Hutt (☑ 03-302 8811; www.nzski.com/mt-hutt; daily lift passes adult/child $99/50; ☺ 9am-4pm) One of the highest ski areas in the southern hemisphere, Mt Hutt has the largest skiable area of any of NZ's commercial fields (365 hectares). The ski field is only 26km from Methven but in wintry conditions the drive takes about 40 minutes; allow two hours from Christchurch. Road access is steep: be extremely cautious in lousy weather.

Rakaia Gorge Walkway (www.doc.govt.nz; Rakaia Gorge Bridge, SH72) Following river terraces into the upper gorge, this well-graded tramp passes through forest and past the historic ferryman's cottage and coal mines, with plenty of pretty picnic spots. The highlight is the lookout at the end with epic alpine views. The walk is four hours return, but a shorter tramp to the lower lookout (one hour return) is also worthwhile.

atmosphere to this conservative but reliable local favourite. Highlights include good coffee, hearty all-day breakfasts and tasty home baking, with a tipple on offer should you fancy it. Free wi-fi is a nice bonus.

★ Dubliner   BISTRO $$
(☑ 03-302 8259; www.dubliner.co.nz; 116 Main St; meals $19-34; ☺ 4.30pm-late) This atmospheric Irish bar and restaurant is housed in Methven's lovingly restored old post office. Great food includes pizza, Irish stew and other hearty fare suitable for washing down with a pint of craft beer.

ⓘ Information

Medical Centre (☑ 03-302 8105; The Square, Main St; ☺ 8.30am-5.30pm)

Methven i-SITE (☑ 03-302 8955; www.methvenmthutt.co.nz; 160 Main St; ☺ 9.30am-5pm daily Jul-Sep, 9am-5pm Mon-Fri, 10am-3pm Sat & Sun Oct-Jun; 🛜) Provides info about local walks and other activities, and can book accommodation.

ⓘ Getting There & Away

Methven Travel (☑ 0800 684 888, 03-302 8106; www.methventravel.co.nz; 160 Main St) Runs shuttles between Methven and

Christchurch Airport (adult/child $45/27.50) four times a week from October to June, increasing to three times daily during the ski season. Also runs shuttles up to Mt Hutt ski field from June to September (adult return $20, kids free with paying adult).

Mt Somers

The small settlement of Mt Somers sits on the edge of the Southern Alps, beneath the mountain of the same name. The biggest drawcard to the area is the **Mt Somers track** (26km), a two-day tramp circling the mountain, linking the popular picnic spots of Sharplin Falls and Woolshed Creek. Trail highlights include volcanic formations, Māori rock drawings, deep river canyons and botanical diversity. The route is subject to sudden weather changes, so precautions should be taken.

There are two DOC huts on the track: Pinnacles Hut and Woolshed Creek Hut (adult/child $15/7.50). Hut tickets and information are available at **Mt Somers General Store** (☑ 03-303 9831; 61 Pattons Rd; ☺ 7am-5.30pm Mon-Fri, 8am-5.30pm Sat, 9am-5pm Sun) and Staveley Store.

🛏 Sleeping & Eating

Staveley Store & Cafe   CAFE **$$**
(☑ 03-303 0859; 2 Burgess Rd, Staveley; mains $6-11; ☺ 9am-4pm Apr-Nov) Call into this cute little country store for the best coffee for miles around, as well as tasty lunch rolls, delectable cakes, gourmet ice cream and locally sourced groceries. Also sells hut tickets for the Mt Somers track.

Stronechrubie   BISTRO **$$**
(☑ 03-303 9814; www.stronechrubie.co.nz; cnr Hoods Rd & SH72; mains bistro $18-28, restaurant $39-41; ☺ bistro 5.30pm-late Thu-Sat, restaurant 6.30pm-late Wed-Sat, Sun lunch by appointment; P ☎) This motel complex offers comfortable chalets overlooking bird-filled gardens (doubles $120 to $160), but it's the up-and-coming culinary hub that's the main draw here. Enjoy a more formal meal in the lauded, long-standing restaurant, or head to the flash new bar and bistro for modern, tapas-style fare alongside lovely wines and craft beer. Reservations recommended.

❶ Getting There & Away

There are no public buses to/from Mt Somers village, so you will need your own transport.

SOUTH CANTERBURY

After crossing the Rangitata River into South Canterbury, SH1 and the Inland Scenic Route (SH72) narrow to within 8km of each other at the quaint town of Geraldine. Here you can choose to take the busy coastal highway through the port city of Timaru, or continue inland on SH79 into Mackenzie Country, where NZ's tallest peaks rise above powder-blue lakes.

The Mackenzie Basin is a wild, tussock-strewn bowl at the foot of the Southern Alps, carved out by ancient glaciers. It takes its name from the legendary James 'Jock' McKenzie, who ran his stolen flocks in this then-uninhabited region in the 1840s.

Director Sir Peter Jackson made the most of this rugged and untamed landscape while filming the *Lord of the Rings,* choosing Mt Cook Village as the setting for Minas Tirith and a sheep station near Twizel as Gondor's Pelennor Fields.

Peel Forest

POP 180

Tucked away between the foothills of the Southern Alps and the Rangitata River, Peel Forest is a small but important remnant of indigenous podocarp (conifer) forest. Many of the totara, kahikatea and matai trees here are hundreds of years old and are home to an abundance of bird life, including riflemen, kereru (wood pigeons), bellbirds, fantails and grey warblers. There's a small settlement, mostly to serve the visitors who come to tramp, ride and raft the beautiful surrounds.

A road from nearby Mt Peel sheep station leads to Mesopotamia, the run of English writer Samuel Butler in the 1860s. His experiences here partly inspired his famous satire *Erewhon* ('nowhere' backwards, almost).

❍ Sights & Activities

Big Tree Walk (30 minutes return) is a gentle stroll through the forest to a particularly fine example of a totara, which is 31m tall, has a circumference of 9m and is over 1000 years old. There are also trails to **Emily Falls** (1½ hours return), **Rata Falls** (two hours return) and **Acland Falls** (one hour return). Pick up the *Peel Forest Area* brochure from **Peel Forest Store** (☑ 03-696 3567; www.peelforest.co.nz; 1202 Peel Forest Rd; mains lunch $6-19, dinner $20-29; ☺ cafe 9.30am-4.30pm daily, bar 6pm-late Wed-

Sat; 🐾) or download it from the DOC website (www.doc.govt.nz).

St Stephen's Church   CHURCH
(1200 Peel Forest Rd) Sitting in a pretty glade right next to the general store, this gorgeous little Anglican church (1885) has a warm wooden interior and some interesting stained glass. Look for St Francis of Assisi surrounded by NZ flora and fauna (get the kids to play spot the tuatara).

★ Rangitata Rafts   RAFTING
(📞 0800 251 251; www.rafts.co.nz; Rangitata Gorge Rd; ⊙ Oct-May) Begin your adventure in the stupendously beautiful braided Rangitata River valley before heading on an exhilarating two-hour ride through the gorge's Grade V rapids ($215, minimum age 15). A gentler alternative route encounters only Grade II rapids ($175, minimum age six).

Hidden Valleys   RAFTING
(📞 03 696 3660; www.hiddenvalleys.co.nz; ⊙ Sep-May) They may be based in Peel Forest but this crew doesn't limit itself to rafting the Rangitata. Multiday expeditions head to the Waimakariri, Waiau, Landsborough, and Grey and Waiatoto Rivers, peaking with a five-day trip ($1650) down the Clarence near Kaikoura. Shorter, child-friendly trips on the Rangitata River are also available (adult $105 to $200, child $75 to $180).

Peel Forest Horse Trekking   HORSE RIDING
(📞 03-696 3703; www.peelforesthorsetrekking. co.nz; 1hr/2hr/half day/full day $65/120/220/320, multiday $800-1450) Ride through lush forest on short rides or multiday treks with experienced guides. Accommodation packages are available in conjunction with Peel Forest Lodge.

🛏 Sleeping

★ Peel Forest DOC Campsite   CAMPGROUND $
(📞 03-696 3567; www.peelforest.co.nz; sites per adult/child powered $21/10.50, unpowered $18/9, cabins $50-80) Near the Rangitata River, around 3km beyond Peel Forest Store, this lovely camping ground is equipped with basic two- to four-berth cabins (bring your own sleeping bag), hot showers and a kitchen. Check in at the store.

Peel Forest Lodge   LODGE $$$
(📞 03-696 3703; www.peelforestlodge.co.nz; 96 Brake Rd; d $380, additional adult/child $40/20; 🅿🐾) This delightful log cabin hidden in the forest has four rooms and sleeps eight

people. It only takes one booking at a time, so you and your posse will have the place to yourself. The cabin is fully self-contained, but meals can be arranged, as can horse treks, rafting trips and other explorations of the beautiful surrounds.

❶ Getting There & Away
Atomic Shuttles (p102) and **InterCity** (p102) buses will get you as close as Geraldine, but you'll need your own transport or a lift to get to Peel Forest itself.

Geraldine
POP 2300

Consummately Canterbury in its dedication to English-style gardening, pretty Geraldine has a village vibe and an active arts scene. In spring (September to November), duck behind the war memorial on Talbot St to the River Garden Walk, where green-fingered locals have gone completely bonkers planting azaleas and rhododendrons. If you've still got energy to burn, try the well-marked trails in Talbot Forest on the town fringe.

◉ Sights

Geraldine Historical Museum   MUSEUM
(📞 03-693 7028; 5 Cox St; ⊙ 10am-3pm Mon-Sat, from 12.30pm Sun) **FREE** Occupying the photogenic Town Board Office building (1885), this cute little museum tells the town's story with an eclectic mix of exhibits, including an extensive collection of photographs.

Geraldine Vintage Car & Machinery Museum   MUSEUM
(📞 03-693 8756; 178 Talbot St; adult/child $15/ free; ⊙ 9.30am-4pm Oct-May, 10am-4pm Sat & Sun Jun-Sep) Rev-heads will enjoy this lovingly maintained vintage car collection, featuring a 1907 De Dion-Bouton and a gleaming 1926 Bentley. There's also a purpose-built Daimler used for the 1954 royal tour, plus some very nice Jags, 1970s muscle cars and all sorts of farm machinery.

Talbot Forest Scenic Reserve   FOREST
(www.doc.govt.nz; Tripp St) On the town's northwestern fringe, Talbot Forest Scenic Reserve is a good place for a peaceful wander. Leafy delights include lofty kahikatea (white pines) and a massive tōtara estimated to be around 800 years old. This remnant lowland podocarp (conifer) and hardwood forest contains the last stands of trees that once covered the entire Geraldine area.

🛏 Sleeping

Geraldine Kiwi Holiday Park HOLIDAY PARK **$**
(☑ 03-693 8147; www.geraldineholidaypark.co.nz;
39 Hislop St; sites $36-40, d $52-135; P @ ⑧)
🗲 This top-notch holiday park is set amid
well-established parkland right in the centre
of town. Tidy accommodation ranges from
budget cabins to plusher motel units, plus
there's a TV room and playground.

🍴 Eating

Long overdue to be lauded 'Cheese & Pick-
le Capital of NZ, Geraldine is paradise for
self-caterers. Numerous artisan producers
line the Four Peaks Plaza; seek out a bag of
Heartland potato chips, made just down the
road. There's an excellent **farmers market**
(St Mary's Church car park; ⊙ 9am-12.30pm Sat Oct-
Apr) 🗲, and, if you're not in the mood to DIY,
there are also a few good cafes in town.

Verde CAFE **$**
(☑ 03-693 9616; 45 Talbot St; mains $9-18; ⊙ 9am-
4pm; 🖋) Down the lane beside the old post
office and set in beautiful gardens, this excellent cafe is one of Geraldine's best eateries.
Drop in for coffee and cake, or linger over a
lazy lunch of salads, soup, sandwiches and
the like.

Running Duck BURGERS **$$**
(☑ 03-693 8320; www.therunningduck.co.nz; 1 Peel
St; burgers $8-19; ⊙ 8am-4pm Mon, Wed & Thu,
8am-8pm Fri, 9am-4pm Sat & Sun) A welcome
addition to the Geraldine culinary scene,
this hipster burger joint is the perfect set-
ting to feast on tasty gourmet burgers and
crispy fries, topped with chef Al's special
spicy sauce.

ℹ Information

Geraldine Visitor Information Centre (☑ 03-
693 1101; www.southcanterbury.org.nz; 38 Waihi
Tce; ⊙ 8am-5.30pm) Inside the Kiwi Country
visitor complex. See also www.gogeraldine.co.nz.

ℹ Getting There & Away

Atomic Shuttles (☑ 03-349 0697; www.atomic
travel.co.nz) runs daily services to the following:

DESTINATION	FARE	DURATION (HR)
Christchurch	$30	2
Cromwell	$35	4½
Lake Tekapo	$25	1¼
Queenstown	$35	5
Twizel	$30	2

Budget Buses & Shuttles (☑ 03-615 5119;
www.budgetshuttles.co.nz; ⊙ Mon-Sat) offers a
door-to-door shuttle to Christchurch ($57), along
with a cheaper scheduled run ($47).

InterCity (☑ 03-365 1113; www.intercity.co.nz)
runs daily services to the following:

DESTINATION	FARES FROM	DURATION (HR)
Christchurch	$32	2¼
Cromwell	$40	4¾
Lake Tekapo	$21	1¼
Mt Cook Village	$38	3
Queenstown	$42	5¾

Timaru

POP 26,000

Trucking on along the SH1 through Timaru,
travellers could be forgiven for thinking that
this small port city is merely a handy place for
food and fuel halfway between Christchurch
and Dunedin. Drop the anchors, people!
Straying into the CBD reveals a remarkably
intact Edwardian precinct boasting some
good dining and interesting shopping, not to
mention a clutch of cultural attractions and
lovely parks, all of which sustain at least a
day's stopover.

The town's name comes from the Māori
name Te Maru, meaning 'place of shelter'.
No permanent settlement existed here un-
til 1839, when the Weller brothers set up
a whaling station. The *Caroline,* a sailing
ship that transported whale oil, gave the
picturesque bay its name.

◉ Sights

★Aigantighe Art Gallery GALLERY
(Map p103; www.timaru.govt.nz/community/
facilities/art-gallery; 49 Wai-iti Rd; ⊙ 10am-4pm Tue-
Fri, from noon Sat & Sun) **FREE** One of the South
Island's largest public galleries, this 1908 man-
sion houses a notable collection of NZ and
European art across various eras, alongside
temporary exhibitions staged by the gallery's
ardent supporters. The Gaelic name means 'at
home' and is pronounced 'egg-and-tie'.

The gallery housing the permanent collec-
tion was closed for structural strengthening
when we visited, but there are still the excel-
lent changing exhibitions to explore, plus the
lovely sculpture garden.

Caroline Bay Park PARK, BEACH
(Map p103; Marine Pde) Fronting the town, this
expansive park ranges over an Edwardian-

Timaru

style garden under the Bay Hill cliff, then across broad lawns to low sand dunes and the beach itself. It has something for everyone between the playground, skate park, soundshell, ice-cream kiosk, minigolf, splash park and myriad other attractions.

Don't miss the **Trevor Griffiths Rose Garden** (Map p103), a triumphant collection of heritage varieties, and consider an evening picnic making the most of the late sun. If you're lucky enough to spot a seal or penguin on the beach, do keep your distance.

South Canterbury Museum   MUSEUM
(Map p103; http://museum.timaru.govt.nz; Perth St; admission by donation; ⏰10am-4.30pm Tue-Fri, 1-4.30pm Sat & Sun) Historic and natural artefacts of the region are displayed here. Highlights include the Māori section, a full-scale model of a ship's cabin from 1859, and a replica of the aeroplane designed and flown by local pioneer aviator and inventor Richard Pearse. It's speculated that

his mildly successful attempts at flight came before the Wright brothers' famous achievement in 1903.

Te Ana Māori Rock Art Centre   MUSEUM

(Map p103; ☑03-684 9141; www.teana.co.nz; 2 George St; adult/child $22/11, tours $130/52; ☺10am-3pm) Passionate Ngāi Tahu guides bring this innovative multimedia exhibition about Māori rock paintings to life. You can also take a three-hour excursion (departing at 2pm, November to April) to see isolated rock art in situ; prior booking is essential.

Sacred Heart Basilica   CHURCH

(7 Craigie Ave, Parkside) Roman Catholic with a definite emphasis on the Roman, this beautiful neoclassical church (1911) impresses with multiple domes, Ionian columns and richly coloured stained glass. Its architect, Francis Petre, also designed the large basilicas in Christchurch (now in ruins) and Oamaru. Inside, there's an art-nouveau feel to the plasterwork, which includes intertwined floral and sacred-heart motifs. There are no set opening hours; try the side door.

Timaru Botanic Gardens   GARDENS

(cnr King & Queen Sts; ☺8am-dusk) Established in 1864, these gardens are a restful place to while away an hour or two, with a pond, lush lawns, shady trees, a playground and vibrant floral displays. With luck you'll arrive during rhododendron or rose bloom time. Enter from Queen St, south of the city centre.

🛏 Sleeping

Timaru Top 10 Holiday Park   HOLIDAY PARK $

(☑03-684 7690; www.timaruholidaypark.co.nz; 154a Selwyn St, Marwiel; sites $40-44, units from $65, with bathroom from $99; ℗🕾) ✔ Tucked away in the suburbs, this excellent holiday park has clean, colourful amenities and a host of accommodation options throughout mature, leafy grounds. Helpful staff go out of their way to assist with local advice and bookings.

Grosvenor   HOTEL $

(Map p103; ☑03-687 9190; www.thegrosvenor.co.nz; 26 Cains Tce; s/d from $90/115; ℗🕾) In a heritage building right in the centre of town, this good-value budget hotel offers clean, no-frills rooms with comfy beds, fridge and TV. The quirky Mondrian-styled corridors give the place a hip vibe.

Sefton Homestay   B&B $$

(Map p103; ☑03-688 0017; www.seftonhomestay.co.nz; 32 Sefton St, Seaview; r $130-140; 🕾) Set back behind a pretty garden, this imposing heritage house has two guest rooms: one with an en suite, and a larger bedroom with an adjoining sun lounge and a bathroom across the hall. Swap travel stories over a glass of port in the guest sitting room.

Pleasant View   B&B $$

(☑03-686 6651; www.pleasantview.co.nz; 2 Moore St, Waimataitai; r $135-160; 🕾) Spot Hector's dolphins over breakfast from this modern clifftop house overlooking Caroline Bay. The two guest rooms are very comfortable, but only one gets the views. No matter, the large guest lounge has them in abundance, as well as a espresso machine and a mammoth TV.

Glendeer Lodge   B&B $$$

(☑03-686 9274; www.glendeer.co.nz; 51 Scarborough Rd, Scarborough; d $210-260; ℗🕾) ✔ Set on 5 acres 4km south of Timaru, this purpose-built lodge is a peaceful option away from busy SH1. Walk to the lighthouse, relax in the garden watching fallow deer nibbling the paddock, then retire to the plush, self-contained lodge offering three en suite rooms. The owners' fly-fishing guiding business lends a wilderness vibe.

🍴 Eating

Arthur Street Kitchen   CAFE $

(Map p103; www.arthurstkitchen.co.nz; 8 Arthur St; mains $9-19; ☺7am-5pm Mon-Fri, 9am-3pm Sat; 🖉) Timaru's hippest coffee house follows the recipe for success: namely great coffee, contemporary cafe fare, good tunes and a mix of arty inside and sunny outside seating. Made with flair and care, the food offering includes grainy salads, refined sandwiches and pastry treats, plus an à la carte breakfast and lunch menu.

⭐ Oxford   MODERN NZ $$

(Map p103; ☑03-688 3297; www.theoxford.co.nz; 152 Stafford St; mains $26-32; ☺10am-late Mon & Wed-Fri, 9.30am-late Sat & Sun) This sophisticated corner restaurant honours its 1925 building with stylish monochrome decor and a feature wall commemorating the day Timaru went bust. The menu offers high-class comfort food, starring local produce like venison, beef and salmon, while an alluring drinks list encourages you to pop in for pinot and cheese, or a glass of sticky wine alongside golden syrup pudding.

Koji   JAPANESE $$

(Map p103; ☑03-686 9166; 7 George St; mains $21-31; ☺11.30am-2pm & 5-9pm) Despite its unassuming exterior, this split-level restaurant does a jolly good job of creating a Japanese vibe. Sit in the downstairs dining room or at the cute bar, or better still head up to the upper level and watch flames rise from the teppanyaki grill. Delicious dishes include sashimi, tempura, *gyoza* and *takoyaki* complete with dancing bonito flakes.

ⓘ Information

Timaru Information Centre (Map p103; ☑ 03-687 9997; www.southcanterbury.org.nz; 2 George St; ☺10am-4pm Mon-Fri, to 3pm Sat & Sun; ☏) Across from the train station (trains in this area only carry freight, not passengers), the visitor centre shares its building with the **Te Ana Māori Rock Art Centre** (p104). There's free wi-fi throughout Timaru's CBD and Caroline Bay Park.

ⓘ Getting There & Away

AIR
Air New Zealand (☑ 0800 737 000; www.air newzealand.co.nz) Flies from Timaru's Richard Pearse Airport to/from Wellington and Auckland at least once daily.

BUS
Atomic Shuttles (Map p103; ☑ 03-349 0697; www.atomictravel.co.nz) Stops by the Timaru Information Centre twice daily, en route to Christchurch ($25, 2½ hours), Oamaru ($20,1¼ hours) and Dunedin ($25, 2¾ hours).

Budget Buses & Shuttles (Map p103; ☑ 03-615 5119; www.budgetshuttles.co.nz; ☺Mon-Sat) Offers shuttles to Christchurch, either door-to-door ($47) or scheduled runs from Timaru Information Centre to Christchurch's Canterbury Museum ($27).

InterCity (Map p103; ☑ 03-365 1113; www. intercity.co.nz) Stops outside the train station. Services run to the following destinations:

DESTINATIONS	FARES FROM	DURATION (HR)
Christchurch	$29	2½
Dunedin	$34	3
Gore	$49	6
Oamaru	$23	1
Te Anau	$52	8

Fairlie
POP 720

Leafy Fairlie describes itself as 'the gateway to the Mackenzie', but in reality this wee, rural town feels a world away from tussocky Mackenzie Country over Burkes Pass, to the west.

The bakery and picnic area make it a good lunchtime stop.

◎ Sights & Activities

The information centre can provide details on nearby tramping and mountain-biking tracks. The main ski resort, **Mt Dobson** (☑ 03-281 5509; www.mtdobson.co.nz; daily lift passes adult/child $82/28), lies in a 3km-wide treeless basin 26km northwest of Fairlie. There's also a club ski field 29km northwest at **Fox Peak** (☑ 03-685 8539, snow phone 03-688 0044; www.foxpeak. co.nz; daily lift passes adult/child $60/10) in the Two Thumb Range.

Fairlie Heritage Museum MUSEUM
(www.fairlieheritagemuseum.co.nz; 49 Mt Cook Rd; adult/child $6/free; ☺9.30am-5pm) A somewhat dusty window on to rural NZ of old, this museum endears with its farm machinery, model aeroplanes, dodgy dioramas and eclectic ephemera. Highlights include the homespun gyrocopter, historic cottage and new automotive wing featuring mint-condition tractors. The attached cafe bakes a good biscuit.

⛉ Sleeping & Eating

Musterer's MOTEL $$
(☑ 03-685 8284; www.musterers.co.nz; 9 Gordon St; units $110-260; ⓟ☏) On the western edge of Fairlie, these stylish self-contained cottages afford all mod cons with the bonus of a shared barbecue area and woolshed 'lounge' – complete with donkeys, goats and a pony to pet. Units are plush and spacious; the larger ones come complete with their own wood-fired hot tub ($45 extra) for a stargazing soak.

★**Fairlie Bakehouse** BAKERY $
(☑ 03-685 6063; www.liebers.co.nz; 74 Main St; pies $5-7; ☺7.30am-4.30pm Mon-Sat, to 4pm Sun; ☑) Famous for miles around and probably the top-ranking reason to stop in Fairlie, this terrific little bakery turns out exceptional pies, including the legendary salmon and bacon. On the sweet side, American doughnuts and raspberry cheesecake elbow their way in among Kiwi classics, such as custard squares and cream buns. Yum.

ⓘ Information

Fairlie Heartland Resource & Information Centre (☑ 03-685 8496; www.fairlienz.com; 67 Main St; ☺10am-4pm Mon-Fri) Has maps and brochures, and can advise on nearby activities.

❶ Getting There & Away

Atomic Shuttles (✉ 03-349 0697; www.atomic-travel.co.nz) runs daily services to the following:

DESTINATION	FARE	DURATION
Christchurch	$30	2½hr
Cromwell	$35	3½hr
Geraldine	$20	40min
Lake Tekapo	$20	40min
Queenstown	$50	4½hr

InterCity (✉ 03-365 1113; www.intercity.co.nz) runs daily services to the following:

DESTINATION	FARES FROM	DURATION
Christchurch	$33	3¼hr
Cromwell	$39	4hr
Lake Tekapo	$13	40min
Mt Cook	$87	2½hr
Queenstown	$40	5hr

Lake Tekapo

POP 369

Born of a hydropower scheme completed in 1953, today Tekapo is booming off the back of a tourism explosion, although it has long been a popular tour-bus stop on the route between Christchurch and Queenstown. Its popularity is well deserved: the town faces out across the turquoise lake to a backdrop of snow-capped mountains.

DARK SKY GAZING

The stars really do seem brighter in Mackenzie Country. A unique combination of clear skies and next to no light pollution makes this region one of the best stargazing sites in the world – a fact that led to 4367 sq km of Aoraki/Mt Cook National Park and the Mackenzie Basin being declared the southern hemisphere's only International Dark Sky Reserve in 2012.

If you're up for some amateur stargazing, all you'll need are a cloud-free night and some warm clothes. For best results, time your visit to coincide with a new moon, when the skies will be at their darkest. For those who'd like a bit more guidance, your best bet is to join one of the nightly tours of the Mt John Observatory run by **Earth & Sky** (p107).

Such splendid Mackenzie Country and Southern Alps views are reason enough to linger, but there's infinitely more to see if you wait till dark. In 2012 the Aoraki Mackenzie area was declared an International Dark Sky Reserve, one of only 12 in the world, and Tekapo's Mt John – under light-pollution-free skies – is the ultimate place to experience the region's glorious night sky.

◉ Sights

Church of the Good Shepherd   CHURCH
(Pioneer Dr; ⊙9am-5pm) The picture window behind the altar of this pretty stone church (built in 1935) gives worshippers a distractingly divine view of the lake and mountains; needless to say, it's a firm favourite for weddings. Come early in the morning or late afternoon to avoid the peace-shattering crowds – this is the prime disembarkation point for tour buses.

Nearby is a statue of a collie, a tribute to the sheepdogs that helped develop Mackenzie Country.

☀ Activities

Tramping

When the Mackenzie Basin was scoured out by glaciers, **Mt John** (1029m) remained as an island of tough bedrock in the centre of a vast river of ice. Nowadays, a road leads to the summit, or you can tramp via a circuit track (2½ hours return) for rewarding views. To extend it to an all-day tramp, continue on to **Alexandrina** and **McGregor Lakes**.

The free town map details this and other walks in the area, along with cycling tracks, including **Cowan's Hill** and those in **Lake Tekapo Regional Park**.

Skiing

Lake Tekapo is a great base for outdoor activities enthusiasts. In winter (June to September), snow bunnies can go downhill skiing at Mt Dobson (p105) and **Roundhill** (✉ 021 680 694, snow phone 03-680 6977; www.roundhill.co.nz; daily lift passes adult/child $84/36), and cross-country skiing on the **Two Thumb Range**.

Other Activities

Mackenzie Alpine Horse Trekking   HORSE RIDING
(✉ 0800 628 269; www.maht.co.nz; Godley Peaks Rd; 30min/1hr/2hr/day $45/70/110/310; ⊙Oct-May) Located on the road to Mt John, these

folks run various treks taking in the area's amazing scenery, catering for everyone from novice to experienced riders.

Tekapo Springs
SPA

(☏03-680 6550; www.tekaposprings.co.nz; 6 Lakeside Dr; pools adult/child $25/14, ice skating $18/13; ⊙10am-9pm) There's nothing nicer on a chilly day than soaking in the thermal waters of these landscaped outdoor pools, with views over the lake to the snow-capped mountains beyond. Pools range in temperature from 28°C to 40°C, and include an artificial beach and aqua play area. There's also a steam room and sauna ($6 extra), along with a day spa.

During the colder months (May to September) the attached ice-skating rink and snow-tubing slide are available, while in summer (December to March) there's the world's largest inflatable slide and slippery-slope tubing.

⚐ Tours

Earth & Sky
TOURS

(☏03-680 6960; www.earthandsky.co.nz; SH10) ✎ A recognised 'International Dark Sky Reserve', the Mackenzie region is one of the best places in the world for stargazing. Nightly tours head up to the University of Canterbury's observatory on Mt John (adult/child $150/85), where you'll get a guided tour of the sky from qualified astronomers.

For those on a tighter budget or with small children in tow (the minimum age for Mt John tours is eight years), there are 75-minute night tours to the smaller Cowan Observatory (adult/child $95/55) during summer (December through February).

Air Safaris
SCENIC FLIGHTS

(☏03-680 6880; www.airsafaris.co.nz; SH8) Awe-inspiring views of Aoraki/Mt Cook National Park's peaks and glaciers are offered on the 'Grand Traverse' fixed-wing flight (adult/child $370/250); there are also various other flights available, including similar trips in a helicopter.

Tekapo Helicopters
SCENIC FLIGHTS

(☏03-680 6229; www.tekapohelicopters.co.nz; SH8) For a bird's-eye view of the surrounds, check out the five different options here, from a 20-minute flight ($215) to an hour-long trip taking in Aoraki/Mt Cook, and Fox and Franz Josef Glaciers ($525). All flights include an alpine landing.

LAKE PUKAKI LOOKOUT

The largest of the Mackenzie's three alpine lakes, Pukaki is a vast jewel of surreal colour. On its shore, just off SH8 between Twizel and Lake Tekapo, is a well-signed and perennially popular lookout affording picture-perfect views across the water all the way up to snow-capped Aoraki/Mt Cook and its surrounding peaks.

Beside the lookout, the **Lake Pukaki Visitor Centre** (www.mtcookalpinesalmon.com; SH8; ⊙8.30am-5.30pm Oct-Jun, 9am-5pm Jul-Sep) is an outpost of Mt Cook Alpine Salmon, the highest salmon farm on the planet, which operates in a hydroelectric canal system some distance away. The visitor centre offers the opportunity to pick up some sashimi ($10) or a smoked morsel for supper.

🛏 Sleeping

Lake Tekapo

Motels & Holiday Park
HOLIDAY PARK, MOTEL $

(☏03-680 6825; www.laketekapo-accommodation.co.nz; 2 Lakeside Dr; sites $44-56, dm $36-40, d $100-170; [P]🐾) With a prime position right on the lakefront, this sprawling complex has something for everyone. Backpackers get the cosy, log-cabin lodge, while others can enjoy cute Kiwi 'bachs', basic cabins, and smart en suite units with particularly good views. Campervaners and campers are spoilt for choice, and share the sparkling amenities block.

Tailor Made Tekapo Backpackers
HOSTEL $

(☏03-680 6700; www.tekapohostelnz.com; 11 Aorangi Cres; dm $28-40, d $87-100, d without bathroom $77-99; 🐾) Spread over three well-tended houses on a peaceful street five minutes' walk from town, this sociable hostel offers bright dorms (with no bunks) and cosy doubles. There's also a large garden complete with barbecue, hammock, chickens and bunnies, plus tennis and basketball courts next door for the energetic.

★**Lake Tekapo Lodge**
B&B $$$

(☏03-680 6566; www.laketekapolodge.co.nz; 24 Aorangi Cres; r $300-495; 🐾) This fabulously designed, luxurious B&B is filled to the brim with covetable contemporary Kiwi art, and boasts painterly views of the lake and mountains from the sumptuous rooms and lounge. Fine-dining evening meals are available by prior arrangement.

Chalet Boutique Motel APARTMENT $$$
([☎]03-680 6774; www.thechalet.co.nz; 14 Pioneer Dr; units $205-330; [P][☎]) The 'boutique motel' tag doesn't do justice to this collection of attractive accommodation options in three adjacent properties beside the lake. The wonderfully private 'Henkel hut' is a stylish option for lovebirds. Charming hosts will happily provide all the local information you need.

✖ Eating

★ Astro Café CAFE $
(Mt John University Observatory; mains $6-14; ⊙9am-6pm Oct-Apr, 10am-5pm May-Sep, weather dependent) This glass-walled pavilion atop Mt John has spectacular 360-degree views across the entire Mackenzie Basin – it's quite possibly one of the planet's best locations for a cafe. Tuck into bagels with local salmon or fresh ham-off-the-bone sandwiches; the coffee and cake are good, too.

Kohan JAPANESE $$
([☎]03-680 6688; www.kohannz.com; SH8; dishes $6-20, bento $28-39; ⊙11am-2pm daily, plus 6-9pm Mon-Sat; [☎]) Despite its basic decor, this is one of Tekapo's best dining options, both for its distracting lake views and its authentic Japanese food, including fresh-off-the-boat sashimi. Leave room for the handmade green-tea ice cream.

ℹ Information

Kiwi Treasures & Information Centre ([☎]03-680 6686; SH8; ⊙8am-5.30pm Mon-Fri, to 6pm Sat & Sun) This little gift shop doubles as the post office and info centre with local maps and advice, plus bookings for nearby activities and national bus services.

Tekapo Springs Sales & Information Centre ([☎]03-680 6579; SH8; ⊙10am-6pm) The folks from Tekapo Springs dispense brochures and advice, as well as taking bookings for their own complex down the road.

See also www.tekapotourism.co.nz.

ℹ Getting There & Away

Atomic Shuttles ([☎]03-349 0697; www.atomic travel.co.nz) runs daily services to the following:

Destination	Fare	Duration
Christchurch	$35	3¼hr
Cromwell	$30	3hr
Geraldine	$25	1¼hr
Queenstown	$45	4hr
Twizel	$20	40min

Cook Connection ([☎]0800 266 526; www.cookconnect.co.nz) has a shuttle service to Mt Cook Village ($40, 2¼ hours).

InterCity ([☎]03-365 1113; www.intercity.co.nz) runs daily services to the following:

DESTINATION	FARES FROM	DURATION
Christchurch	$35	3¾hr
Cromwell	$35	2¾hr
Geraldine	$20	1hr
Mt Cook Village	$84	1½hr
Queenstown	$35	4hr

Aoraki/Mt Cook National Park

POP 200

The spectacular 700-sq-km Aoraki/Mt Cook National Park is part of the Southwest New Zealand (Te Wāhipounamu) World Heritage Area, which extends from Westland's Cook River down to Fiordland. More than one-third of the park has a blanket of permanent snow and glacial ice; of the 23 NZ mountains over 3000m, 19 are in this park. The highest is mighty Aoraki/Mt Cook – at 3724m, the tallest peak in Australasia. Among the region's other great peaks are Sefton, Tasman, Silberhorn, Malte Brun, La Perouse, Hicks, De la Beche, Douglas and the Minarets.

Aoraki/Mt Cook is a wonderful sight, assuming there's no cloud in the way. Most visitors arrive on tour buses, stop at the Hermitage hotel for photos, and then zoom off back down SH80. Hang around to soak up this awesome peak and the surrounding landscape, and to try the excellent short walks in the area, including to the Tasman Glacier.

History

Known to Māori as Aoraki (Cloud Piercer), after an ancestral deity in Māori mythology, the mountain was given its English name in 1851, in honour of explorer Captain James Cook.

This region has always been the focus of climbing in NZ. On 2 March 1882 William Spotswood Green and two Swiss alpinists failed to reach the summit after an epic 62-hour ascent. Two years later a trio of local climbers – Tom Fyfe, George Graham and Jack Clarke – were spurred into action by the news that two well-known European alpinists were coming to attempt the peak, and set off to climb it before the visitors. On Christmas

Day 1894 they ascended the Hooker Glacier and north ridge to stand on the summit.

In 1913 Australian climber Freda du Faur became the first woman to reach the summit. New Zealander Edmund Hillary first climbed the south ridge in 1948; Hillary went on to become one of the first two people to reach the summit of Mt Everest. Since then, most of the daunting face routes have been climbed.

◉ Sights

★ Aoraki/Mt Cook

National Park Visitor Centre   MUSEUM
(Map p110; ☑ 03-435 1186; www.doc.govt.nz; 1 Larch Grove; ⊙ 8.30am-5pm Oct-Apr, to 4.30pm May-Sep) **FREE** Arguably the best DOC visitor centre in NZ. It not only dispatches all necessary information and advice on tramping routes and weather conditions, it also houses excellent displays on the park's natural and human history. It's a fabulous place to commune with the wilderness, even on a rainy day. Most activities can be booked here.

Sir Edmund Hillary Alpine Centre   MUSEUM
(Map p110; www.hermitage.co.nz; Hermitage, Terrace Rd; adult/child $20/10; ⊙ 7am-8.30pm Oct-Mar, 8am-7pm Apr-Sep) This multimedia museum opened just three weeks before the 2008 death of the man regarded by many as the greatest New Zealander of all time. The main attraction is a cinema and domed digital planetarium that screens films all day, including the *Mt Cook Magic* 3D movie and a fascinating 75-minute documentary about Sir Ed's conquest of Everest. The foyer houses memorabilia both from St Ed's various expeditions and from the **Hermitage** (☑ 03-435 1809; www. hermitage.co.nz; Terrace Rd; r $235-525; P @ 🛜) hotel itself, which was originally built in 1884.

Tasman Glacier   GLACIER
(Map p110; www.doc.govt.nz) At 27km long and up to 4km wide, the Tasman is the largest of NZ's glaciers, but it's melting fast, losing hundreds of metres of length each year. It is also melting from the surface, shrinking around 150m in depth since it was first surveyed in 1891. Despite this considerable shrinkage, at its thickest point the ice is still estimated to be over 600m deep.

In its lower section the melts have exposed rocks, stones and boulders, which form a solid unsightly mass on top of the ice.

Tasman Lake, at the foot of the glacier, started to form only in the early 1970s and now stretches to 7km. The ongoing effects of climate change are expected to extend it

much further in the next decade. The lake is covered by a maze of huge icebergs, which are continuously being sheared off the glacier's terminal face. On 22 February 2011 the Christchurch earthquake caused a 1.3km-long, 300m-high, 30-million-tonne chunk to break off, causing 3.5m waves to roll into the tourist boats on the lake at the time (no one was injured). You can kayak on Tasman Lake with **Glacier Kayaking** (Map p110; ☑ 03-435 1890; www.mtcook.com; Old Mountaineers' Cafe, Bowen Dr; per person $250; ⊙ Oct-Apr).

In the glacier's last major advance (17,000 years ago), the glacier crept south far enough to carve out Lake Pukaki. A later advance did not reach out to the valley sides, so there's a gap between the outer valley walls and the lateral moraines of this later advance. The unsealed Tasman Valley Rd, which branches off Mt Cook Rd 800m south of Mt Cook Village, travels through this gap. From the Blue Lakes shelter, 8km along the road, the **Tasman Glacier View Track** (30 minutes return) climbs interminable steps to an aptly rewarding viewpoint on the moraine wall, with a side trip to Blue Lakes on the way.

🏃 Activities

Various easy tramps from the village are outlined in the (multilingual) *Walking & Cycling Tracks* pamphlet available from the Aoraki/Mt Cook National Park Visitor Centre (p109) and online. On the trails, look for the thar, a Himalayan goat; the chamois, smaller and of lighter build than the thar, and originally hailing from Europe; and red deer, also European. Summertime (December through March) brings into bloom the Mt Cook lily, a large mountain buttercup, and mountain daisies, gentians and edelweiss.

Longer tramps are only recommended for those with mountaineering experience, as tracks and conditions at higher altitudes can become dangerous. Highly changeable weather is typical: Aoraki/Mt Cook is only 44km from the coast and weather conditions rolling in from the Tasman Sea can mean sudden storms.

As for climbing, there's unlimited scope for the experienced, but those without experience must go with a guide. Regardless of your skills, take every precaution – more than 200 people have died in climbing accidents in the park. The bleak *In Memoriam* book in the Visitor Centre begins with the first death on Aoraki/Mt Cook in 1907; since then more than 80 climbers have died on the peak.

Aoraki/Mt Cook National Park

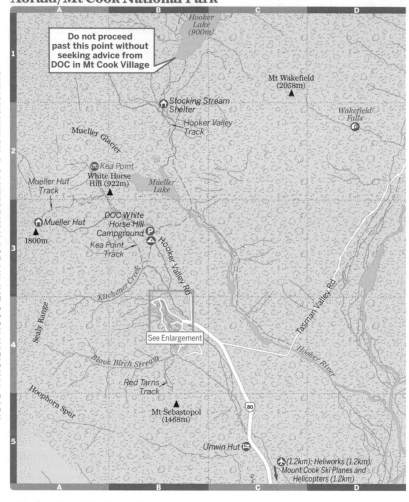

Do not proceed past this point without seeking advice from DOC in Mt Cook Village

Aoraki/Mt Cook National Park

◎ Top Sights
1 Aoraki/Mt Cook National Park Visitor Centre E4

◎ Sights
2 Sir Edmund Hillary Alpine Centre E4
3 Tasman Glacier E1

◎ Activities, Courses & Tours
Glacier Kayaking .... (see 6)
Kea Point Track .... (see 1)
Southern Alps Guiding .... (see 6)

◎ Sleeping
4 Aoraki/Mt Cook Alpine Lodge E5
5 Mt Cook YHA F5

◎ Eating
6 Old Mountaineers' Cafe E4

◎ Transport
7 Cook Connection E4
InterCity .... (see 7)

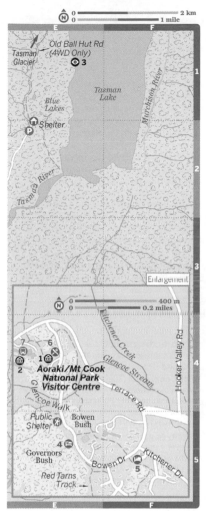

Check with the park rangers before attempting any climb and always heed their advice. If you're climbing, or even going on a longer tramp, fill out an intentions card before starting out so rangers can check on you if you're overdue coming back. Sign out again when you return. The Visitor Centre also hires locator beacons (per three/seven days $30/40).

If you intend to stay at any of the park's huts, it's essential to register your intentions at the Visitor Centre and pay the hut fees. Walkers can use the public shelter in Mt Cook Village, which has running water, toilets and

coin-operated showers. Note that this shelter cannot be used for overnight stays.

For details on the exceptional Hooker Valley and Mueller Hut tracks, see Hiking in Canterbury (p67).

Kea Point Track TRAMPING
(Map p110) The trail to Kea Point (two hours return from the visitor centre) is lined with native plants and ends with excellent views of Aoraki/Mt Cook, the Hooker Valley, and the ice faces of Mt Sefton and the Footstool. Despite the name, you're no more likely to see a kea (bird) here than anywhere else. If you do, don't feed it.

Southern Alps Guiding ROCK CLIMBING, SNOW SPORTS
(Map p110; ☏ 03-435 1890; www.mtcook. com; Old Mountaineers' Cafe, Bowen Dr) Offers mountaineering instruction and guiding, plus three- to four-hour helihiking trips on Tasman Glacier year-round ($550). From June to October heliskiers can head up the Tasman, Murchison and Mannering Glaciers for a series of 5km to 15km runs (four runs, from $1150; extra runs per person from $125).

Mount Cook Ski Planes and Helicopters SCENIC FLIGHTS
(☏03-430 8026; www.mtcookskiplanes.com; Mt Cook Airport) Get an aerial view of Mt Cook and surrounding glaciers via ski plane or helicopter with this outfit, based at Mt Cook Airport. Most flights include a snow or glacier landing; options include the 45-minute Grand Circle (adult/child $560/425) and the 35-minute Tasman Experience (adult/child $310/245). Flight-seeing without a landing is a cheaper option – for a taster, try the 10-minute Lower Tasman Loop ($99).

Sleeping & Eating

Mt Cook YHA HOSTEL $
(Map p110; ☏ 03-435 1820; www.yha.co.nz; 1 Bowen Dr; dm/d $40/140; ⓟ�飞) ⊘ Handsomely decked out in pine, this excellent hostel has a free sauna, a drying room, log fires, a large kitchen and friendly, helpful staff. Rooms are clean and warm, although some are a tight squeeze (particularly the twin bunk rooms).

★Aoraki/Mt Cook Alpine Lodge LODGE $$
(Map p110; ☏ 03-435 1860; www.aorakialpine lodge.co.nz; Bowen Dr; d $169-240; ⓟ⟩) This lovely family-run lodge has en suite rooms,

DON'T MISS

ALPS 2 OCEAN CYCLE TRAIL

One of the best Great Rides within the New Zealand Cycle Trail (www.nzcycletrail.com), the 'A2O' serves up epic vistas on its way from the foot of the Southern Alps all the way to the Pacific Ocean at Oamaru.

New Zealand's highest mountain – Aoraki/Mt Cook – is just one of many stunning sights. Others include braided rivers, glacier-carved valleys, turquoise hydro-lakes, tussock-covered highlands and lush farmland. Off-the-bike activities include wine tasting, penguin spotting, glider flights and soaking in al fresco hot tubs. Country hospitality, including food and accommodation, along with shuttles and other services, make the whole trip easy to organise and enjoy.

The trail is divided into nine easy-to-intermediate sections across terrain varying from canal paths, quiet country roads, old railway lines and expertly cut cross-country track, to some rougher, hilly stuff for the eager. The whole journey takes around four to six days, but it can easily be sliced into short sections.

Twizel is an excellent base for day rides. Options include taking a shuttle to Lake Tekapo (p106) for a five- to six-hour, big-sky ride back to Twizel, or riding from Twizel out to **Lake Ohau Lodge** (p113) for lunch or dinner. Both rides serve up the sublime lake and mountain scenery for which the Mackenzie is famous.

The trail is well supported by tour companies offering bike hire, shuttles, luggage transfers and accommodation. These include Twizel-based **Cycle Journeys** (☑03-435 0578, 0800 224 475; www.cyclejourneys.co.nz; 3 Benmore Pl; all-inclusive packages from $1250) and **Jollie Biker** (☑027 223 1761, 03-435 0517; www.thejolliebiker.co.nz; 193 Glen Lyon Rd; bike hire per day from $50). The Alps 2 Ocean website (www.alps2ocean.com) has comprehensive details.

including some suitable for families and two with kitchenettes; most have views. The huge lounge and kitchen area also has a superb mountain outlook, as does the barbecue area – a rather inspiring spot to sizzle your dinner.

Old Mountaineers' Cafe CAFE $$
(Map p110; www.mtcook.com; Bowen Dr; mains breakfast $9-15, lunch $14-26, dinner $24-35; ⏰10am-9pm; 🛜) 🍴 Encouraging lingering with books, memorabilia and mountain views through picture windows, the village's best eatery also supports local and organic suppliers via an all-day menu offering salmon and bacon pies, cooked breakfasts, burgers and pizza.

❶ Information

The **Aoraki/Mt Cook National Park Visitor Centre** (p109) is the best source of local information. The nearest ATM and supermarket are in Twizel.

❶ Getting There & Away

Mt Cook Village's small airport only serves aerial sightseeing companies. Some of these may be willing to combine transport to the West Coast (ie Franz Josef) with a scenic flight, but flights are heavily dependent on weather.

If you're driving, fill up at Lake Tekapo or Twizel. There is a self-service pump at Mt Cook, but it's expensive.

Cook Connection (Map p110; ☑0800 266 526; www.cookconnect.co.nz) runs shuttle services to Lake Tekapo ($40, 1½ hours) and Twizel ($28, 45 minutes).

InterCity (Map p110; ☑03-365 1113; www.intercity.co.nz) coaches stop at the Hermitage; however, they are operated as part of a 'tour' and can be pricey – you might be better off catching a shuttle back to Twizel and picking up an InterCity connection from there.

DESTINATION	FARES FROM	DURATION (HR)
Christchurch	$213	5¼
Lake Tekapo	$87	1¼
Queenstown	$184	4¾

Twizel

POP 1200

Pronounced 'twy-zel' but teased with 'Twizzel' and even 'Twizzelsticks' by outsiders, Twizel gets the last laugh. The town was built in 1968 to service construction of the nearby hydroelectric power station, and was due for obliteration in 1984 when the project was completed. But there was no way the locals were upping their twizzlesticks and relinquishing their relaxed, mountain country lifestyle.

Today the town is thriving with a modest boom in holiday-home subdivisions and recognition from travellers that – as plain Jane as it may be – Twizel is actually in the middle of everything and has almost everything one might need (within reason).

🏃 Activities

Twizel sits amid some spectacular country offering all sorts of adventure opportunities. **Lake Ruataniwha** is popular for rowing, boating and windsurfing. Nearby tramping and cycling trails are illustrated on the excellent town map, available from the information centre, including a nice river ramble. Twizel is also the best hub for rides on the Alps 2 Ocean Cycle Trail (p112).

Ruataniwha
Conservation Park   TRAMPING, MOUNTAIN BIKING
(www.doc.govt.nz) Stretched between Lake Pukaki and Lake Ohau, this 368 sq km protected area includes the rugged Ben Ohau Range along with the Dobson, Hopkins, Huxley, Temple and Maitland Valleys. It offers plenty of tramping and mountain-biking opportunities, as detailed in DOC's *Ruataniwha Conservation Park* pamphlet (available online), with several day trails close to Twizel.

Ohau Snow Fields   SNOW SPORTS
(☑ 03-438 9885; www.ohau.co.nz; daily lift passes adult/child $90/36) This commercial ski area lines the flanks of Mt Sutton, 42km from Twizel. Expect a high percentage of intermediate and advanced runs, excellent terrain for snowboarding, two terrain parks, and Lake Ohau Lodge (p113) for après-ski relaxation.

🛌 Sleeping

⭐ Lake Ohau Lodge   LODGE $$
(☑ 03-438 9885; www.ohau.co.nz; Lake Ohau Rd; s $110-216, d $118-237; ⓟ🐕) Idyllically sited on the western shore of Lake Ohau, 42km west of Twizel, accommodation ranges from budget rooms with shared facilities to upmarket rooms with decks and mountain views.

Omahau Downs   LODGE, COTTAGE $$
(☑ 03-435 0199; www.omahau.co.nz; SH8; d $150-165, cottages from $155; ⊗ closed Jun-Aug; ⓟ🐕) This farmstead, 2km north of Twizel, has three cosy, self-contained cottages (one sleeping up to 15), and a lodge with sparkling, modern rooms and a deck looking out at the Ben Ohau Range.

Heartland Lodge   B&B, APARTMENT $$$
(☑ 03-435 0008; www.heartland-lodge.co.nz; 19 North West Arch; d $300-360, apt $190; ⓟ🐕) On the leafy outskirts of town, this elegant modern house offers spacious, en suite rooms and a comfortable, convivial communal space. Friendly hosts prepare a cooked breakfast using organic, local produce where possible. The adjacent 'retreat' apartment sleeps up to six and has its own kitchenette (breakfast is not provided).

⭐ Shawty's   CAFE $$
(☑ 03-435 3155; www.shawtys.co.nz; 4 Market Pl; mains brunch $12-20, dinner $28-36; ⊗ 8.30am-late; 🐕) The town centre's social hub and hottest meal ticket serves up big breakfasts, gourmet pizzas and fancy lamb racks as the sun goes down. A considerate kids' menu, cocktails, al fresco dining and occasional live music make it all the more appealing.

ⓘ Information

Twizel Information Centre (☑ 03-435 3124; www.twizel.info; Market Pl; ⊗ 8.30am-5pm Mon-Fri, 10am-3pm Sat) Can advise on tramping and cycling paths in the area, as well as book accommodation. Also offers bike hire (one hour/three hours/full day $25/35/45).

ⓘ Getting There & Away

Atomic Shuttles (☑ 03-349 0697; www.atomic travel.co.nz) runs daily services to the following:

DESTINATION	FARE	DURATION
Christchurch	$35	4hr
Cromwell	$30	2hr
Geraldine	$25	2hr
Lake Tekapo	$20	45min
Queenstown	$30	3hr

Cook Connection (☑ 0800 266 526; www.cook connect.co.nz) runs daily shuttle services to Mt Cook Village (one way/return $28/51, one hour).

InterCity (☑ 03-365 1113; www.intercity.co.nz) runs daily services to the following:

DESTINATION	FARES FROM	DURATION
Christchurch	$38	5¼hr
Cromwell	$28	2hr
Lake Tekapo	$13	50min
Mt Cook Village	$78	1hr
Queenstown	$40	3hr

Naked Bus (www.nakedbus.com) services Christchurch and Queenstown/Wanaka.

Dunedin & Otago

Best Places to Eat

➡ Riverstone Kitchen (p127)

➡ Fleur's Place (p128)

➡ No 7 Balmac (p136)

➡ Bracken (p135)

➡ Courthouse Cafe & Larder (p144)

Best Places to Stay

➡ Pen-y-bryn Lodge (p125)

➡ Oliver's (p146)

➡ Pitches Store (p144)

➡ Old Bones Backpackers (p125)

➡ Hogwartz (p133)

Why Go?

Otago has attractions both urban and rural, from quirky towns to world-class wineries and some of the country's most accessible wildlife. Its historic heart is Dunedin, home to a vibrant student culture and arts scene. From the town's stately Edwardian train station it's possible to catch the famous Taieri Gorge Railway inland, and continue on two wheels along the craggily scenic Otago Central Rail Trail.

Those seeking colonial New Zealand can soak up the frontier atmosphere of gold-rush towns such as Clyde, St Bathans, Naseby and cute-as-a-button Ophir. For wildlife, head to the Otago Peninsula, where penguins, albatross, sea lions and seals are easily sighted. Seaside Oamaru has a wonderful historic precinct, resident penguin colonies and a quirky devotion to steampunk culture.

Unhurried and overflowing with picturesque scenery, Otago is generous to explorers who are after a more leisurely style of holiday.

When to Go

➡ February and March have sunny, settled weather (usually...), and the juicy appeal of fresh apricots, peaches and cherries.

➡ At Easter, hook yourself a 'Southern Man' at the biennial Middlemarch Singles Ball, or drown your sorrows at the Clyde Wine & Food Festival.

➡ Take to two wheels on the Otago Central Rail Trail during the quieter month of September.

➡ In November, watch the pros battle it out at the Highlands Motorsport Park, then ride graciously into the past on a penny farthing bicycle at Oamaru's Victorian Heritage Celebrations.

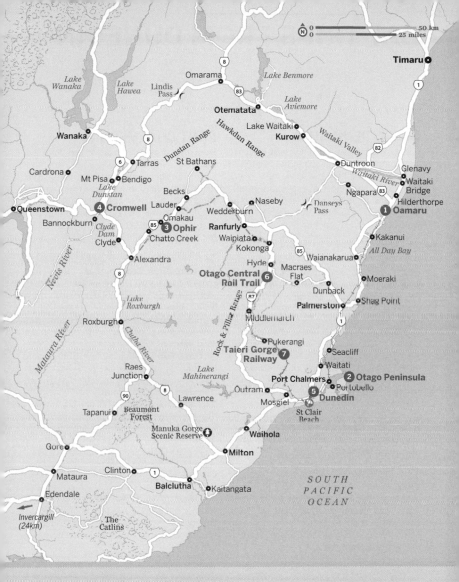

Dunedin & Otago Highlights

1 Oamaru (p122) Delving into its heritage past and a possible steampunk future.

2 Otago Peninsula (p138) Peering at penguins, admiring albatross and staring at seals.

3 Ophir (p143) Exploring New Zealand's gold-mining heritage in a quaint backcountry village.

4 Cromwell (p146) Tasting some of the planet's best pinot noir at the wineries in the fruit bowl of the south.

5 Dunedin (p128) Sampling local beers and bopping to local bands in the city's bars and cafes.

6 Otago Central Rail Trail (p118) Cycling through breathtaking vistas of brown and gold on the route of a defunct train line.

7 Taieri Gorge Railway (p132) Winding through gorges, alongside canyons and across tall viaducts on this snaking heritage railway.

DAY TRIPS FROM DUNEDIN

OTAGO PENINSULA

It's remarkable that one of the best places to spot some of New Zealand's most unique and endangered wildlife is so close to a major city. While the peninsula's most high-profile attractions are quite pricey, there's plenty of enjoyment to be had for free on coastal walkways and secluded beaches.

☆ Best Things to See/Do/Eat

◉ **Larnach Castle** This wonderfully out-of-place Gothic Revival manor house sits grandly atop a hill at the centre of the peninsula, surrounded by gorgeous gardens. It's a jarring juxtaposition to the wildness that surrounds it. (p139)

🌿 **Nature's Wonders Naturally** Penguins (both the little and the incredibly rare yellow-eyed) and NZ fur seals have the beaches all to themselves on this end-of-the-earth sheep farm. You can invade their privacy (from a discreet distance) on a bumpy Argo ride. (p138)

✖ **1908 Cafe** The best refuelling stop is this charming cafe and bistro, midway along the peninsula, in the main settlement of Portobello. (p141)

☆ How to Get There

Car It takes 25 minutes to drive to Portobello from central Dunedin, and a further 15 to reach Harrington Point at the peninsula's tip.
Bus Buses head to Portobello every half-hour during weekdays, with some continuing on to Harrington Point.

PORT CHALMERS

Dunedin's historic port town was long ago infiltrated by alternative types. It's well worth the short drive to take a walk along its modest main street where the heritage shopfronts are now home to cafes, galleries, design stores and thrift shops. However, there's an altogether wilder attraction hiding in the mountainous hinterland.

☆ Best Things to See/Do/Eat

◉ **Orokonui Ecosanctuary** Rare bird species finding sanctuary in this vast predator-free expanse of cloud forest include kiwi, takahe and kaka, while reptiles include tuatara and Otago skinks. Orokonui is a well-signposted 6km drive from the main road into Port Chalmers. (p137)

🌿 **Hare Hill** Explore the beautiful, remote beaches of Aramoana on horseback from this riding stable, just along the coastal road from Port Chalmers. (p138)

✖ **Carey's Bay Hotel** It's hard to top this historic waterfront pub for hearty meals topped with outstanding harbour views. (p138)

☆ How to Get There

Car You can drive from central Dunedin to Port Chalmers in less than 20 minutes; head northeast on Anzac Ave which becomes Ravensbourne Rd as it heads along the coast.
Bus Buses ply this route every half-hour but you'll need your own car to get to Orokonui.

MOERAKI

A pleasant drive north from Dunedin will bring you to this sleepy little place where even the name perfectly reflects its lethargy (it means 'a place to sleep by day'). We recommend booking ahead for a late lunch, getting the active stuff out of the way first and snoozing it off on the beach afterwards.

☆ Best Things to See/Do/Eat

◉ **Moeraki Boulders** Yet another of the truly weird geological features of New Zealand, this set of nearly perfectly round boulders lie lodged in the sand, just waiting to star in your social media feed (#wtf). (p128)

🌿 **Kaiks Wildlife Trail** Follow this track south from the village and you'll eventually reach a historic wooden lighthouse. Keep your eyes peeled for penguins and seals along the way. (p127)

✕ **Fleur's Place** Perhaps even more than the boulders, this ramshackle seafood restaurant, beloved by superchef Rick Stein, is one of Moeraki's main attractions. (p128)

☆ How to Get There

Car Allow an hour for the drive from Dunedin's city centre along SH1; head north on Great King St and keep going until you see the signs pointing right to Moeraki.

Train Catch the scenic *Seasider* train but note that it's a 3km walk to Fleur's from the station, which doesn't leave long for lunch.

Base yourself in Dunedin for a few days to explore the rugged coast surrounding it. You might even spot some of the world's rarest penguins.

CYCLING IN OTAGO

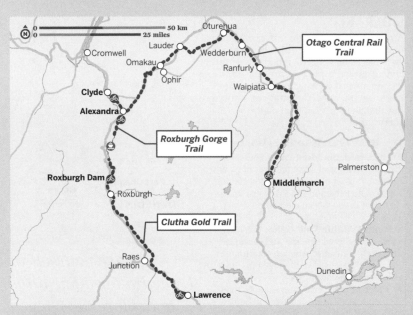

OTAGO CENTRAL RAIL TRAIL

START CLYDE OR MIDDLEMARCH
END MIDDLEMARCH OR CLYDE
DURATION 3 TO 5 DAYS
DISTANCE 152KM
DIFFICULTY EASY

Stretching from Dunedin to Clyde, the Central Otago rail line linked small inland goldfield towns with the big city from the early 20th century through to the 1990s. After the 150km stretch from Middlemarch to Clyde was permanently closed, the rails were ripped up and the trail resurfaced. The result is a year-round, mainly gravel trail that takes cyclists, walkers and horse riders along a historic route containing old rail bridges, viaducts and tunnels.

With excellent trailside facilities (toilets, shelters and information), few hills, gob-smacking scenery and profound remoteness, the trail attracts well over 25,000 visitors annually. March is the busiest time, when there are so many city slickers on the track that you might have to wait 30 minutes at cafes en route for a panini. Consider September for a quieter ride.

The trail can be followed in either direction. The entire trail takes approximately four to five days to complete by bike (or a week on foot), but you can obviously choose to do as short or as long a stretch as suits your plans. There are also easy detours to towns such as Naseby and St Bathans.

Mountain bikes can be hired in Dunedin, Middlemarch, Alexandra and Clyde. Any of the area's i-SITEs can provide detailed information. See www.otagocentralrailtrail.co.nz and www.otagorailtrail.co.nz for track information, recommended timings, accommodation options and tour companies.

Due to the popularity of the trail, a whole raft of sleeping and eating options have sprung up in remote locales en route, although some stops are less well served than others.

Otago is the most popular destination for cycle touring in the whole of New Zealand. These three trails can easily be linked together to make one mega ride.

ROXBURGH GORGE TRAIL

START ALEXANDRA
END ROXBURGH DAM
DURATION 4 TO 5 HOURS
DISTANCE 21KM CYCLE, 13KM BOAT RIDE
DIFFICULTY MODERATE

Opened to considerable fanfare in 2013, this well-constructed mountain-biking and walking **track** (p144) was intended to connect Alexandra to Roxburgh Dam. As access through some of the farmland in the middle section wasn't successfully negotiated, however, riding the 'full trail' requires prearranging a scenic 13km jet-boat ride (adult/child $95/55) through the local information centres or directly with **Clutha River Cruises** (p144).

An alternative is to make a return trip from each end: Alexandra–Doctors Point (20km return) or Roxburgh Dam–Shingle Creek (22km return).

It's requested that you purchase a $10 day tag to assist with the maintenance of the track, although this is not compulsory. They can be bought at i SITEs, cycle shops and tour operators, or online at www.central otagonz.com.

CLUTHA GOLD TRAIL

START ROXBURGH DAM
END LAWRENCE
DURATION 2 TO 4 DAYS
DISTANCE 73KM
DIFFICULTY EASY

From Roxburgh Dam you can continue on this far easier trail that follows the turquoise Clutha (Mata-au) River through Roxburgh to Beaumont and then on to Lawrence. The same voluntary maintenance fee tag system covers both tracks, although you're best to buy a $25 season tag (valid for a year).

Look out for evidence of the area's gold-mining past during the 10km ride from the dam to the Roxburgh township. The following 20km stretch to Millers Flat is flanked by unusual rock formations and native kanuka (tea tree); stop for a cooling dip at Pinders Pond. From Millers Flat it's 25km to Beaumont, passing through farmland and beneath

the Horseshoe Bend suspension bridge. The trail climbs from Beaumont to the highest point of the track on then heads through 434m Big Hill Tunnel on its way to Lawrence.

InterCity has direct buses from Lawrence to Dunedin. Bikes are allowed as checked luggage as long as they are collapsed down (both wheels removed, the handlebars turned sideways and the chain covered).

BIKE HIRE & LOGISTICS

☆ Dunedin

Cycle World   CYCLING

(Map p130; ☑ 03-477 7473; www.cycleworld.co.nz; 67 Stuart St; per day from $50; ☉ 8.30am-6pm Mon-Fri, 9.30am-3.30pm Sat, 10am-3pm Sun) Bike hire, repair and information.

☆ Middlemarch & Clyde

Trail Journeys   CYCLING

(☑ 03-464 3213; www.trailjourneys.co.nz; 20 Swansea St; per day from $45; ☉ depot Oct-Apr) Provides bike hire and logistical support to riders on the Otago Central Rail Trail, including shuttles, bag transfers and accommodation booking. Also has a depot in **Clyde** (☑ 03-449 2150; 16 Springvale Rd; rental per day from $45; ☉ 9am-5pm Mon-Fri May-Oct, 8am-5pm daily Nov-Apr) ✈, at the other end of the trail.

Cycle Surgery   CYCLING

(☑ 03-464 3630; www.cyclesurgery.co.nz; Swansea St; per day from $35; ☉ depot Oct-Apr) Hires bikes and serves coffee to Rail Trailers, as well as offering shuttles and guided cycling tours. Also has a drop-off depot at the Clyde trailhead.

☆ Alexandra

Altitude Bikes   CYCLING

(☑ 03-448 8917; www.altitudeadventures.co.nz; 88 Centennial Ave; per day from $30; ☉ 8.30am-5.30pm Mon-Fri, 9am-1pm Sat) Hires bikes in conjunction with Henderson Cycles and organises logistics for riders on the Otago Central, Clutha Gold and Roxburgh Gorge Trails.

WAITAKI DISTRICT

The broad, braided Waitaki River provides a clear dividing line between Otago and Canterbury to the region's north. The Waitaki Valley is a direct but less-travelled route from the Southern Alps to the sea, featuring freaky limestone formations, Māori rock paintings and ancient fossils. The area is also one of NZ's newest winemaking regions, and a major component of the new Alps 2 Ocean Cycle Trail (p112), which links Aoraki/Mt Cook National Park to the coast. The district's main town, Oamaru, is a place of penguins, steampunk and glorious heritage architecture.

Omarama

POP 270

At the head of the Waitaki Valley, sleepy Omarama is surrounded by mountain ranges and fabulous landscapes. Busy times include the rodeo (28 December) and the sheepdog trials (March).

◉ Sights & Activities

Wrinkly Rams FARM

(☑ 03-438 9751; www.thewrinklyrams.co.nz; 24-30 Omarama Ave, SH8; adult/child $25/12.50) A regular stop for tour buses, Wrinkly Rams stages 30-minute shearing and sheepdog

---

ESSENTIAL OTAGO

Eat nectarines, apricots, peaches, plums and cherries from Central Otago.

Drink pinot noir from Central Otago and the Waitaki Valley.

Read *To the Is-land* (1982), the first volume of Otago author Janet Frame's lyrical autobiography.

Listen to *Tally Ho! Flying Nun's Greatest Bits*, a 2011 compilation marking the 30th anniversary of Dunedin's iconic record label.

Watch *In My Father's Den* (2004), set in Central Otago.

Celebrate at Oamaru's Victorian Heritage Celebrations (p125) in late November.

Go green and tiptoe down to Otago Peninsula beaches in search of rare yellow-eyed penguins.

Go online www.dunedinnz.com, www.centralotagonz.com

---

shows, including lamb-feeding in season. Phone ahead to check show times, as they change daily based on group bookings. Attached is one of Omarama's better **cafes** (mains $12-30; ◷ 7am-4.30pm; 🛜).

Clay Cliffs Paritea LANDMARK

(Henburn Rd; vehicles $5) This bizarre moonscape is the result of two million years of erosion on layers of silt and gravel that were exposed along the active Ostler fault line. The cliffs are on private land; pay your entrance fee via the honour box at the gate. To get to the cliffs, head north from town for 3km on SH8, turn left onto Quailburn Rd, and then turn left after 3km onto unsealed Henburn Rd (the route is well signposted).

Omarama Hot Tubs SPA

(☑ 03-438 9703; www.hottubsomarama.co.nz; 29 Omarama Ave, SH8; per 1-/2-/3-/4-person tub $52/90/114/136, pod $75/140/180/200; ◷ 11am-late) If your legs are weary after mountain biking or tramping, or you just want to cosy up with your significant other, these private, wood-fired hot tubs could be just the ticket. Choose between a 90-minute soak in a tub (each has its own dressing room) or a two-hour session in a 'wellness pod', which includes a sauna.

🛏 Sleeping

Buscot Station FARMSTAY $

(☑ 027 222 1754; www.bbh.co.nz; 912 SH8; campsite/dm/s/d $10/26/44/63; 🅿) For a completely different and uniquely Kiwi experience, grab a room in the home-style farmhouse attached to a huge sheep and cattle station, or a bed in the large dormitory out the back. The sunset views are terrific and there's plenty of acreage for quiet explorations. Look for it on SH8, 10km north of Omarama.

ⓘ Information

Omarama Hot Tubs (p120) doubles as the tourist office, and can assist with accommodation and transport info. See www.discoveromarama.co.nz for more details.

ⓘ Getting There & Away

The road from Omarama to Cromwell heads over the striking Lindis Pass.

Atomic Shuttles (☑ 03-349 0697; www.atomictravel.co.nz) Services stop in Omarama for a break before continuing on to Christchurch ($40, five hours), Lake Tekapo ($20, 1¾ hours), Twizel ($20, 20 minutes), Cromwell ($25, 1½ hours) and Queenstown ($35, 2½ hours).

InterCity (☑ 03-471 7143; www.intercity.co.nz) Two coaches a day head to/from Christchurch (from $30, 4¾ hours), Twizel (from $10, 25 minutes), Cromwell (from $23, 1½ hours) and Queenstown (from $32, 2½ hours), and one heads to/from Mt Cook Village ($78, 1¼ hours).

Naked Bus (https://nakedbus.com) Daily services to/from Christchurch (4¾ hours), Lake Tekapo (1¼ hours), Cromwell (2½ hours) and Queenstown (3¼ hours). Prices vary.

Waitaki Valley

Wine, waterskiing and salmon-fishing are just some of the treats on offer along this little-travelled route. Coming from Omarama, the winding SH83 passes a series of glassy blue lakes. For a scenic detour along the north bank, leave the highway at Otematata and cross over Benmore Dam, then cross back over Aviemore Dam to rejoin the route.

A succession of sleepy little towns line the highway, peppered with rustic old bank buildings and pubs. One of the most appealing is tiny **Kurow**, the home town of world Cup–winning retired All Blacks captain Richie McCaw. From almost-as-cute **Duntroon**, adventurous (and appropriately insured) drivers can take the unsealed road over Danseys Pass to Naseby.

Although they've got a way to go to attain the global reputation enjoyed by their colleagues in Central Otago, winemaking pioneers in Waitaki Valley are producing wine of which international experts are taking notice.

☉ Sights & Activities

Kurow Heritage &
Information Centre   MUSEUM
(☑ 03-436 0950; www.kurow.org.nz; 57 Bledisloe St, Kurow; ☉ 9.30am-4pm Mon-Fri year-round, plus 11am-3pm Sat & Sun Nov-Mar) FREE Local hero Richie McCaw rates a mention at this very sweet community-run museum, which mostly features artefacts and curios from Kurow's more distant past. Staff are knowledgable and friendly, and can give excellent advice on local activities and routes.

Vintner's Drop   WINERY
(☑ 03-436 0545; www.ostlerwine.co.nz; 45 Bledisloe St, Kurow; tastings 3/5 wines $10/15, redeemable against purchase; ☉ 11am-5pm Nov-Mar, noon-3pm Mon-Fri Apr-Oct) Housed in Kurow's old post office, Vintner's Drop acts as a tasting room for Ostler Vineyards, along with other small local producers.

MĀORI OTAGO

The early Māori history of Otago echoes that of Canterbury (p91), with Ngāi Tahu the dominant tribe at the time the British arrived. One of the first parcels of land that Ngāi Tahu sold was called the Otago block, a 1618-sq-km parcel of land that changed hands in 1844 for £2400. The name Otago reflects the Ngāi Tahu pronunciation of Ōtākou, a small village on the far reaches of the Otago Peninsula, where there's still a *marae* (meeting place).

Dunedin's **Otago Museum** (p131) has the finest Māori exhibition on the South Island, including an ornately carved *waka taua* (war canoe) and finely crafted *pounamu* (greenstone). Māori rock art can still be seen in situ in the **Waitaki Valley** (p122).

Pasquale Kurow Winery   WINERY
(☑ 03-436 0443; www.pasquale.co.nz; 5303 Kurow-Duntroon Rd, SH83; ☉ 10am-5pm Nov-Mar) The valley's most impressive winery, Pasquale produces killer pinot noir, pinot gris and riesling, as well as less common varietals such as Gewürztraminer and *arnets*. Drop in for a tasting session ($10, refundable upon purchase) and an antipasto and cheese platter.

Takiroa Māori
Rock Painting Site   ARCHAEOLOGICAL SITE
(SH83) FREE Hidden within the honeycomb cliffs lining the highway, this well-signposted site, 3km west of Duntroon, features centuries-old drawings of mystical creatures, animals and even a sailing ship.

Vanished World Centre   MUSEUM
(www.vanishedworld.co.nz; 7 Campbell St, Duntroon; adult/child $10/free; ☉ 10am-4pm) Perhaps there wouldn't be quite so many bad dolphin tattoos and dancing penguin films if more people stopped in Duntroon to check out this small but interesting volunteer-run centre. Once you see the 25-million-year-old fossils of shark-toothed dolphins and giant penguins, they suddenly don't seem so cute.

Pick up a copy of the *Vanished World Trail* map ($6.50) outlining 20 different interesting geological locations around the Waitaki Valley and North Otago coast.

**Maerewhenua Māori
Rock Painting Site** ARCHAEOLOGICAL SITE
(Livingstone-Duntroon Rd) FREE Sheltered by
an impressive limestone overhang, this site
contains charcoal-and-ochre paintings dating to before the arrival of Europeans in NZ.
Head east from Duntroon and take the first
right after crossing the Maerewhenua River;
the site is on the left after about 400m.

Elephant Rocks LANDMARK
Sculpted by wind, rain and rivers, the huge
limestone boulders of this bizarre landscape
were utilised as Aslan's Camp in the NZ-
filmed *Narnia* movies (2005–2010). They're
located on farmland about 5.5km south of
the highway; follow the signs after crossing
the Maerewhenua River.

Awakino Skifield SKIING
(☑ 021 890 584; www.skiawakino.com; Awakino
Skifield Rd; daily lift passes adult/child $55/27) Sit-
uated high above Kurow, Awakino is a small
player on the NZ ski scene, but worth a visit for intermediate skiers who fancy some
peace and quiet. Weekend lodge-and-ski
packages are available.

❶ Getting There & Away

There's no public transport along this route.
You'll need your own car or bike.

Oamaru
POP 13,000

Nothing moves very fast in Oamaru. Tourists saunter, locals linger and penguins
waddle. Even the town's recently resurrect-
ed heritage modes of transport – penny
farthings and steam trains – reflect an
unhurried pace. Most travellers come here
for the penguins, but hang around and
you'll sense the wellspring of eccentricity
bubbling under the surface. Put simply,
Oamaru is *cool*.

Down by the water, a neighbourhood of
once-neglected Victorian buildings now
swarms with oddballs, antiquarians and bo-
hemians of all stripes, who run offbeat galleries, quirky shops, hip music venues and
even an 'urban winery'. Most visible are the
steampunks, their aesthetic boldly celebrating the past and the future with an ethos of
'tomorrow as it used to be'.

Away from the docks, Oamaru's whitestone buildings harbour an increasing array of
cafes and bars, while up on the clifftops a few
excellent accommodation options have taken

hold. You may find yourself lingering longer
than expected in this laid-back coastal town.

History

Oamaru used to be rich and ambitious. In its
1880s heyday, Oamaru was about the same
size as Los Angeles was at the time. Refrig-
erated meat-shipping had its origins nearby and the town became wealthy enough
to erect the imposing buildings that grace
Thames St today. However, the town over-
reached itself and spent the end of the 19th
century teetering on the verge of bankruptcy.

Economic decline in the 20th century
meant that there wasn't the impetus to swing
the wrecking ball here with the same reckless
abandon that wiped out much of the built
heritage of NZ's main centres. It's only in recent decades that canny creative types have
cottoned on to the uniqueness of Oamaru's
surviving Victorian streetscapes and have
started to unlock this otherwise unremarka-
ble town's potential for extreme kookiness.

◉ Sights & Activities

★**Blue Penguin Colony** BIRD SANCTUARY
(Map p124; ☑ 03-433 1195; www.penguins.co.nz;
2 Waterfront Rd; adult/child $30/15; ◷ 10am-
2hr after sunset) ✿ Every evening the tykes
from the Oamaru little penguin colony surf
in and wade ashore, heading to their nests
in an old stone quarry near the waterfront.
Stands are set up on either side of the waddle route. General admission will give you
a good view of the action but the premium
stand (adult/child $45/22.50), accessed by
a boardwalk through the nesting area, will
get you closer.

You'll see the most penguins (up to 250)
in November and December. From March
to August there may be only 10 to 50 birds.
They arrive in groups called rafts just before dark (around 5.30pm in midwinter and
9.30pm midsummer), and it takes about an
hour for them all to come ashore; nightly viewing times are posted at the i-SITE
(p126). Use of cameras is prohibited and
you're advised to dress warmly.

To understand the centre's conservation
work and its success in increasing the penguin population, take the daytime behind-
the-scenes tour (adult/child self-guided
$10/5 or guided $16/8); packages that combine night viewing and the daytime tour are
also available.

Do not under any circumstances wander
around the rocks beside the sea here at night

looking for penguins. It's damaging to their environment and spoils studies into the human effects on the birds.

★ Victorian Precinct AREA

(Map p124) Consisting of only a couple of blocks centred on Harbour and Tyne Sts, this atmospheric enclave has some of NZ's best-preserved Victorian commercial buildings. Descend on a dark and foggy night and it's downright Dickensian. It's also ground zero for all that is hip, cool and freaky in Oamaru, and one of the best places to window-shop in the entire South Island.

Wander around during the day and you'll discover antiquarian bookshops, antique stores, galleries, vintage-clothing shops, kooky gift stores, artist studios, old-fashioned lolly shops and artisan bookbinders. At night there are some cute little bars, and you might even see a penguin swaggering along the street – we did!

The precinct is at its liveliest on Sundays when the excellent Oamaru farmers market is in full swing. Note that some shops and attractions are closed on Mondays.

Friendly Bay Playground PARK

(Map p124; Wansbeck St; 🚼) Steampunk for kiddies: this unusual playground includes swings suspended from a giant penny farthing, a slippery pole accessed from an armoured elephant, and a giant hamster wheel.

Whitestone City MUSEUM

(Map p124; ☑0508 978 663; www.whitestone city.com; 12 Harbour St, Seaward Side; adult/child $20/10; ◷10am-6pm) Opened in 2017, this brand-new attraction brings Oamaru's heyday to life. Stroll through the replica Victorian streetscape, visit the schoolroom complete with slates and schoolmistress, play old-fashioned games in the dimly lit saloon, and take a ride on the pièce de résistance – a penny-farthing carousel.

Steampunk HQ GALLERY

(Map p124; ☑027 778 6547; www.steampunkoama ru.co.nz; 1 Itchen St; adult/child $10/2; ◷10am-5pm) Discover an alternative past – or maybe a quirky version of the future – at this fascinating art project celebrating steampunk culture. Ancient machines wheeze and splutter, and the industrial detritus of the last century or so is repurposed and reimagined to creepy effect. Bring a $2 coin to fire up the sparking, space-age locomotive out the front.

Thames Street AREA

(Map p124) Oamaru's main drag owes its expansive girth to the need to accommodate the minimum turning circle of a bullock cart. The town's grand pretensions reached their peak in the late 19th century in a series of gorgeous buildings constructed from the milky local limestone (known as Oamaru stone or whitestone), with their forms reflecting the fashion of the times; there's a particular emphasis on the neoclassical.

Impressive examples include the Forrester Gallery (at No 9, built 1883), the ANZ Bank (No 11, 1871), the Waitaki District Council building (No 20, 1883), the North Otago Museum (No 60, 1882), the Courthouse (No 88, 1883) and the Opera House (No 92, 1907).

Forrester Gallery GALLERY

(Map p124; ☑03-433 0853; www.culturewaitaki. org.nz; 9 Thames St; ◷10.30am-4.30pm Mon-Fri, from 1pm Sat & Sun; 🚼) **FREE** Housed in a temple-like former bank building, the Forrester Gallery stages excellent temporary exhibitions of local and NZ art. The 'wonderlab', upstairs, hosts interactive exhibitions especially designed for children.

Oamaru Public Gardens GARDENS

(Map p124; Severn St; ◷dawn-dusk) Opened in 1876, these beautiful gardens are a lovely place to stroll and relax, with expansive lawns, waterways, bridges and a children's playground.

St Patrick's Basilica CHURCH

(Map p124; ☑03-434 8543; www.cdd.org.nz/ st-patrick-oamaru; 68 Reed St) If you've ever

> ### WILDLIFE SPOTTING: LITTLE PENGUINS
>
> Nowhere near as rare as their yellow-eyed cousins, little penguins sometimes pop up in the oddest places (window-shopping in Oamaru's Victorian Precinct, for instance). Also known as blue penguins, little blue penguins, kororā (in Māori) and fairy penguins (in Australia), these little cuties can spend days out at sea before returning to their colony just before dusk.
>
> Although you might chance upon one at night in Oamaru or on the Otago Peninsula, the best places to see them arrive en masse are at Oamaru's **Blue Penguin Colony** (p122) or at the **Royal Albatross Centre** (p139) on the Otago Peninsula.

DUNEDIN & OTAGO OAMARU

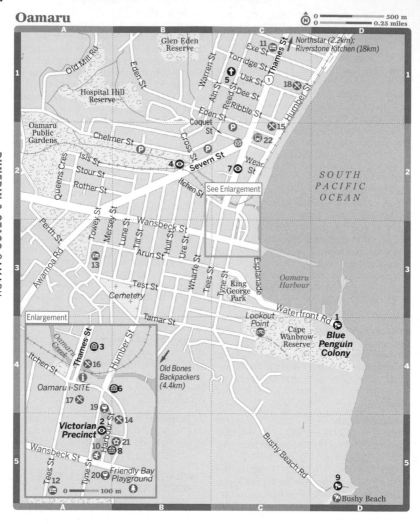

fantasised about being transported back to Ancient Rome, stroll through the Corinthian columns and into this gorgeous Catholic church (built in 1873). Renowned architect Francis Petre went for the full time warp with this one, right down to a coffered ceiling and cupola above the altar.

Yellow-Eyed Penguin Colony   BIRD SANCTUARY
(Map p124; Bushy Beach Rd) FREE Larger and much rarer than their little blue cousins, yellow-eyed penguins waddle ashore at Bushy Beach in the late afternoon to feed their young. In order to protect these endangered birds, the beach is closed to people from

3pm onwards, but there are hides set up on the cliffs (you'll need binoculars for a decent view). The best time to see them is two hours before sunset.

Vertical Ventures   CYCLING, ROCK CLIMBING
(Map p124; ☑ 03-434 5010; www.verticalventures. co.nz; 4 Wansbeck St) Hire a mountain bike (from $45 per day), or join guided mountain-biking trips, including the Alps 2 Ocean Cycle Trail (seven days including transport, food and accommodation from $2995). The 'vertical' part comes in the form of rock-climbing day trips (from $150 per person).

Oamaru

DUNEDIN & OTAGO OAMARU

🎉 Festivals & Events

Victorian Heritage Celebrations CULTURAL
(www.vhc.co.nz, ⓒmid-Nov) Five days of costumed capers and historical hijinks, culminating in a grand fete.

🛌 Sleeping

★Old Bones Backpackers HOSTEL $
(☑03-434 8115; www.oldbones.co.nz; Beach Rd; r $100, campervans per person $25; @🛜) Five kilometres south of Oamaru on the coast road, this top-notch dorm-free hostel has tidy rooms off a huge, sunny, central space. Listen to the surf crashing over the road while relaxing in front of the wood-burning fire, or book one of the hot tubs (from $90) and drift into ecstasy while gazing at the stars.

Oamaru Backpackers HOSTEL $
(Map p124; ☑021 190 0069; www.oamarubackpackers.co.nz; 47 Tees St; dm/s $30/50, d $75-90; P🛜) A stone's throw from the Victorian quarter, this recently renovated hostel has lovely, individually decorated rooms and a great dorm with privacy curtains and individual outlets. Best of all is the view of the harbour from the giant windows in the airy, light-filled lounge.

Highfield Mews MOTEL $$
(Map p124; ☑03-434 3437; www.highfieldmews.co.nz; 244 Thames St; units from $190; P@🛜) 🐾 The units at this flash new motel are basically smart apartments, with kitchens, desks, stereos, tiled bathrooms and outdoor furniture. The larger, one-bedroom units come with spa baths.

★Pen-y-bryn Lodge B&B $$$
(Map p124; ☑03-434 7939; www.penybryn.co.nz; 41 Towey St; r $600-725; P🛜) Well-travelled foodie owners have thoroughly revitalised this beautiful 1889 residence. There are two rooms in the main house but we prefer the three recently and luxuriously refurbished ones in the rear annexe. Predinner drinks and canapés are served in the antique-studded drawing room, and you can arrange a four-course dinner in the fabulous dining room (from $125 per person).

🍴 Eating

Steam CAFE $
(Map p124; www.facebook.com/steamoamaru; 7 Thames St; mains $10-13; ⓒ7.30am-4.30pm Mon-Fri, 8am-2.30pm Sat & Sun; 🛜) This popular little cafe near the Victorian quarter specialises in coffees and fruit juices, and it's a good spot to stock up on freshly ground beans for your own travels. Check the counter cabinet for the day's culinary choices, including freshly baked muffins, croissants and the like.

Harbour St Bakery BAKERY $
(Map p124; ☑03-434 0444; www.harbourstreetbakery.com; 4 Harbour St; pies $5.50; ⓒ10am-4pm Tue-Sun) Selling both European-style bread and pastries and NZ meat pies, this petite Dutch bakery covers its bases well. Grab a seat outside and watch Oamaru's heritage streetlife scroll past like an old-time movie.

Whitestone Cheese Factory   DELI, CAFE $

(Map p124; ☑ 03-434 8098; www.whitestonecheese. com; 3 Torridge St; platters $14.50; ⊗ 9am-5pm Mon-Fri, 10am-4pm Sat & Sun) The home of award-winning artisanal cheeses, Whitestone is a local culinary institution and the factory-door cafe is a fine place to challenge one's arteries. As well as fulfilling self-caterers' cheese dreams, the petite cafe offers a couple of cheesy options to eat-in, including cheese scones, cheesecake, and tasting platters of six different cheeses, as well as tea and coffee.

Tees St   CAFE $$

(Map p124; ☑ 03-434 7004; www.teesst.com; 3 Tees St; mains $13-18; ⊗ 7am-3pm Mon-Fri, from 8.30am Sat & Sun; ☜) An ornate Victorian draper's shop provides a suitably gracious ambience for this hip little cafe. A concise brunch menu offers the usual suspects, from eggs to pancakes to a delectable chia pudding. Great coffee and homemade pastries complete the picture.

Midori   JAPANESE $$

(Map p124; ☑ 03-434 9045; www.facebook.com/ MidoriJapaneseSushiBarAndRestaurant; 1 Ribble St; sushi $12-17, mains $18-29; ⊗ 10.30am-8.30pm Mon-Wed, 10.30am-9pm Thu-Fri, 11am-9pm Sat, noon-8.30pm Sun) Midori, housed in a heritage stone building, serves sashimi and sushi that make the most of fresh local seafood. Other carefully prepared dishes include teriyaki salmon and blue cod, udon soup and a variety of bento boxes. If you just want to grab and go, there's also a takeaway menu available.

♟ Drinking & Nightlife

Scott's Brewing Co.   BREWERY

(Map p124; ☑ 03-434 2244; www.scottsbrewing. co.nz; 1 Wansbeck St; ⊗ 11am-8.30pm Mon-Tue, to 9.30pm Wed & Sun, to 11pm Thu-Sat) Drop into this old waterfront warehouse to sample the output of Oamaru's premier craft brewers. Slouch against the counter for a tasting or head out onto the sunny deck for a pint and a pizza.

Criterion Hotel   PUB

(Map p124; ☑ 03-434 6247; www.criterionhotel. co.nz; 3 Tyne St; ⊗ 11am-late Mon-Fri, from 10am Sat & Sun) The most Victorian of the Victorian Precinct's watering holes, this corner beauty has a good beer selection and plenty of local wines. There's usually live music on Fridays.

☆ Entertainment

★ Penguin Club   LIVE MUSIC

(Map p124; www.thepenguinclub.co.nz; Emulsion Lane, off Harbour St; cover charge varies) Tucked down an atmospheric alley off a 19th-century street, the Penguin's unusual location matches its acts: everything from touring Kiwi bands to punky/grungy/rocky/country locals.

Oamaru Opera House   THEATRE

(Map p124; ☑ 03-433 0779; www.oamaruoperahouse.co.nz; 90 Thames St; ⊗ ticket office 10am-4pm Mon-Fri, to 1pm Sat) First opened in 1907 and now beautifully restored to its original glory, Oamaru's opera house hosts a variety of shows, including music, dance, theatre and comedy. The main auditorium seats 500-plus patrons under the stunning 1900s cupola and chandelier, while the smaller **Inkbox** theatre is home to more intimate performances.

ⓘ Information

Oamaru i-SITE (Map p124; ☑ 03-434 1656; www.visitoamaru.co.nz; 1 Thames St; ⊗ 9am-5pm; ☜) Friendly staff here can offer mountains of information including details on local walking trips and wildlife, plus daily penguin-viewing times. There's also bike hire ($28/40 per half/full day) and an interesting 10-minute film on the history of the town.

WILDLIFE SPOTTING: YELLOW-EYED PENGUINS

One of the world's rarest penguins, the endangered hoiho (yellow-eyed penguin) is found along the Otago coast. It's estimated that fewer than 4000 of these penguins remain in the wild, with around 150 breeding pairs resident on deserted beaches in the southeast of the South Island during the 2016–17 breeding season.

The encroachment of humans on their habitat is one of the main causes of the penguins' decline. Penguins have been badly distressed by tourists using flash photography or traipsing through the nesting grounds; under no circumstances should you approach one. Even loud voices can disturb them. For this reason, the best way to see a hoiho in the wild is through an organised tour onto private land, such as through **Nature's Wonders Naturally** (p138) or **Penguin Place** (p139) on the Otago Peninsula, or from the cliffs at **Bushy Beach** (p124) near Oamaru or **Roaring Bay** in the Catlins.

RIVERSTONE

It's well worth taking the 14km trip from Oamaru to this idiosyncratic complex, hidden along the unassuming short stretch of SH1 between the braided mouth of the Waitaki River and THE SH83 turn-off.

First and foremost it's the home of **Riverstone Kitchen** (☑03-431 3505; www.riverstonekitchen.co.nz; 1431 Glenavy-Hilderthorpe Rd, SH1, Waitaki Bridge; breakfast $16-22, lunch $22-32, dinner $28-34; ☺9am-late Thu-Sat, to 5pm Sun-Mon), a sophisticated restaurant that outshines any in Oamaru itself. A riverstone fireplace and polished concrete floors set the scene for a menu that's modern without being overworked. Much of the produce comes from the extensive on-site kitchen gardens (go for a stroll, they're impressive), plus locally sourced venison, pork, salmon and beef. It's a smashing brunch option, with excellent coffee and legendary truffled scrambled eggs. Save room for dessert, too.

Next door, behind a set of fake heritage shopfronts, **Riverstone Country** (☑03-431 3872; 1431 Glenavy-Hilderthorpe Rd, SH1, Waitaki Bridge; ☺9am-5.30pm) is literally packed to the rafters with gifts, crafts, homewares, fake flowers, garden ornaments and Christmas decorations. Outside, there's an aviary stocked with canaries, lorikeets and guinea pigs.

If this all points to an eccentric mind at the helm, take a look at the moated **castle** at the rear of the complex. The castle is the brainchild of Dot Smith, one of the owners of Riverstone, and is destined to be a private home – construction was completed in mid-2017. At the time of research there was no public access to the castle itself, but that is due to change; check with the restaurant for an update during your visit.

If you're looking for a good place to stay nearby, **Waitaki Waters** (☑03-431 3880; www.campingoamaru.co.nz; 305 Kaik Rd, Waitaki Bridge; sites/cabins from $15/45; ℗☎) is a holiday park with sparkling facilities, manicured hedges and a peaceful location 3km off SH1. Cabins are simple but well maintained; bring your own bedding.

❶ Getting There & Away

Oamaru sits on the main SH1 coastal route between Christchurch (3¼ hours) and Dunedin (1½ hours).

Most buses and shuttles depart from the **Lagonda Tearooms** (Map p124; ☑03-434 8716; www.facebook.com/LagondaTeaRooms; 191 Thames St; ☺9am-4.30pm; ☎). Both the tearooms and the i-SITE take bookings.

Atomic Shuttles (Map p124; ☑03-349 0697; www.atomictravel.co.nz) Buses to/from Christchurch ($35, four hours), Timaru ($20,1¼ hours) and Dunedin ($20, 1½ hours), twice daily.

Coast Line Tours (☑03-434 7744; www.coastline-tours.co.nz) Shuttles to/from Dunedin (adult/child $30/12); pick up at your accommodation. Detours to Moeraki and Dunedin Airport can be arranged.

InterCity (Map p124; ☑03-471 7143; www.intercity.co.nz) Two daily coaches to/from Christchurch (from $22, four hours), Timaru (from $15, one hour), the Moeraki turn-off (from $11, 28 minutes) and Dunedin (from $15, 1½ hours), and one to Te Anau (from $30, 6½ hours).

Naked Bus (https://nakedbus.com) Daily buses head to/from Christchurch (four hours), Timaru (1¼ hours), Moeraki (35 minutes) and Dunedin (1¾ hours). Fares fluctuate widely; check the website for deals.

The *Seasider* tourist train, operated by **Dunedin Railways** (p132), is a scenic way to travel to Dunedin.

Moeraki

The name Moeraki means 'a place to sleep by day', which should give you some clue as to the pace of life in this little fishing village. You might be surprised to learn that this was one of the first European settlements in NZ, with a whaling station established here in 1836. Since then, Moeraki has nurtured the creation of several national treasures, from Frances Hodgkins' paintings to author Keri Hulme's *The Bone People,* and Fleur Sullivan's cooking.

Apart from Fleur's eponymous restaurant, the main reason travellers stop in town is the Moeraki Boulders, (p128) beloved of photographers and children alike. It's a pleasant 45-minute walk along the beach from the village to the boulders. Head in the other direction on the **Kaiks Wildlife Trail** and you'll reach a cute old wooden **lighthouse**. You might even spot yellow-eyed penguins and fur seals (be sure to keep your distance).

⊙ Sights

Moeraki Boulders NATURAL FEATURE
(Te Kaihinaki) The main drawcard in Moeraki is this collection of large spherical boulders, scattered along a beautiful stretch of beach like a giant's discarded marbles. The famed rocks lie just off SH1, 1km north of the Moeraki turn-off. Try to time your visit with low tide.

🛏 Sleeping & Eating

**Riverside Haven
Lodge & Holiday Park** CAMPGROUND $
(☑ 03-439 5830; www.riversidehaven.nz; 2328 Herbert Hampden Rd/SH1, Waianakarua; sites from $8, dm $28-33, d with/without bathroom from $98/88; 🛜) ⌀ Nestled in a loop of the Waianakarua River, 12km north of the Moeraki turn-off, this pretty riverside property offers both bucolic camping sites and colourful lodge rooms, some with en suites. Kids will love the playground and farm animals; parents will love the spa and peaceful vibe.

★**Fleur's Place** SEAFOOD $$$
(☑ 03-439 4480; www.fleursplace.com; Old Jetty, 169 Haven St; mains $18-44; ⊙ 10.30am-late Wed-Sun) There's a rumble-tumble look about it, but this quirky tin-and-timber fishing hut houses one of the South Island's best – and most popular – seafood restaurants. Head for the upstairs deck and tuck into fresh shellfish, tender blue cod and other recently landed ocean bounty. Bookings are strongly recommended.

❶ Getting There & Away

Moeraki is on SH1, a 30-minute drive from Oamaru and one hour from Dunedin. All of the buses travelling between the two stop on SH1 by the Moeraki turn-off. From here it's about a 2km walk to both the centre of the village and to the boulders.

DUNEDIN

POP 127,000
Two words immediately spring to mind when Kiwis think of their seventh-largest city: 'Scotland' and 'students'. The 'Edinburgh of the South' is immensely proud of its Scottish heritage, never missing an opportunity to break out the haggis and bagpipes on civic occasions. In fact the very name Dunedin is derived from the Scottish Gaelic name for Edinburgh – Dùn Èideann – and the city even has its own tartan.

Just like the Scots, Dunedin locals love a drink, and none more so than the students that dominate Dunedin in term time. The country's oldest university provides plenty of student energy to sustain the local bars.

Dunedin is an easy place in which to while away a few days. Weatherboard houses ranging from stately to ramshackle pepper its hilly suburbs, and bluestone Victorian buildings punctuate the compact city centre. It's a great base for exploring the wildlife-rich Otago Peninsula, which officially lies within the city limits.

History

The first permanent European settlers, two shiploads of pious, hard-working Scots, arrived at Port Chalmers in 1848, including the nephew of Scotland's favourite son, Robbie Burns. A statue of the poet dominates The Octagon, the city's civic heart.

In the 1980s Dunedin spawned its own internationally influential indie music scene, with Flying Nun Records and the 'Dunedin sound'. Music is not Dunedin's only creative outlet. In 2014, the city became the first in New Zealand to be designated a UNESCO City of Literature, reflecting the city's literary heritage and culture.

⊙ Sights

⊙ City Centre

Dunedin Railway Station HISTORIC BUILDING
(Map p130; 22 Anzac Ave) Featuring mosaic-tile floors and glorious stained-glass windows, Dunedin's striking bluestone railway station (built between 1903 and 1906) claims to be NZ's most photographed building. Head upstairs for the **New Zealand Sports Hall of Fame** (Map p130; ☑ 03-477 7775; www. nzhalloffame.co.nz; adult/child $6/2; ⊙ 10am-4pm), a small museum devoted to the nation's obsession, and the **Art Station** (Map p130; ☑ 03-477 9465; www.otagoartsociety.co.nz; ⊙ 10am-4pm) FREE, the local Art Society's gallery and shop. The station is the departure point for several popular scenic rail journeys (p132).

★**Toitū Otago Settlers Museum** MUSEUM
(Map p130; ☑ 03-477 5052; www.toituosm.com; 31 Queens Gardens; ⊙ 10am-5pm) FREE Storytelling is the focus of this excellent interactive museum, which traces the history of human settlement in the South Island. The engrossing Māori section is followed by a large gallery where floor-to-ceiling portraits of Victorian-era settlers stare out from behind their whiskers and lace. Other displays include a

recreated passenger-ship cabin, an impressive vintage car collection and a fascinating array of obsolete technology, like the first computer used to draw the lottery in Dunedin.

Dunedin Chinese Garden GARDENS
(Map p130; ☑ 03-477 3248; www.dunedinchinese garden.com; cnr Rattray & Cumberland Sts; adult/ child $9/free; ☺10am-5pm) Built to recognise the contribution of Dunedin's Chinese community, this walled garden was constructed in Shanghai before being dismantled and re-assembled in its current location. The tranquil confines contain all of the elements of a classical Chinese garden, including ponds, pavilions, rockeries, stone bridges and a tea house. There's also a small display on the history of the local Chinese community. An informative audioguide is included in the entry price.

First Church of Otago CHURCH
(Map p130; ☑ 03-477 7118; www.firstchurchotago. org; 415 Moray Pl; ☺church 10am-4pm Mon-Sat, museum 10.30am-2.30pm Mon-Sat) Dunedin's original Scottish settlers founded Otago's first Presbyterian congregation upon their arrival in 1848 and built this grand church 25 years later. Constructed in the Gothic style out of Oamaru's famous white stone, the church has a soaring wooden ceiling and some magnificent stained-glass windows. At the rear is an interesting little **museum** devoted to the history of the congregation, which is inextricably linked to that of the city.

Speight's Brewery BREWERY
(Map p130; ☑ 03-477 7697; www.speights.co.nz; 200 Rattray St; adult/child $29/13; ☺tours noon, 2pm, 4pm Apr-Sep, plus 5pm, 6pm & 7pm Oct-Mar) Speight's has been churning out beer on this site since the late 19th century. The 90-minute tour gives an insight into the history of the building, the company and the brewing process, and finishes up in the tasting room for a guided sampling session.

St Joseph's Cathedral CHURCH
(Map p130; www.cdd.org.nz/st-joseph-cathe dral-dunedin; cnr Rattray & Smith Sts) Completed in 1886, Dunedin's bluestone Gothic-revival Catholic cathedral sits halfway up the hill above the town centre.

Dunedin Public Art Gallery GALLERY
(Map p130; ☑ 03-474 3240; www.dunedin.art.mu seum; 30 The Octagon; ☺10am-5pm) **FREE** Gaze upon local and international art – including a small collection of Impressionists – at this expansive and airy gallery. Only a fraction of the collection is displayed at any given time, with most of the space given over to often-edgy temporary exhibitions.

St Paul's Cathedral CHURCH
(Map p130; www.stpauls.net.nz; Moray Pl; ☺10am-4pm Oct-Apr, to 3pm May-Sep) Even in Presbyterian Dunedin, the 'established church' (aka the Church of England) gets the prime spot on The Octagon. A Romanesque portal leads into the Gothic interior of this beautiful Anglican cathedral, where soaring white Oamaru-stone pillars spread into a vaulted ceiling. The main part of the church dates from 1919 although the sanctuary was left unfinished until 1971, hence the slightly jarring modern extension. The massive organ (3500 pipes) is said to be one of the finest in the southern hemisphere.

Emerson's Brewery BREWERY
(Map p140; ☑ 03 477 1812; www.emersons. co.nz; 70 Anzac Ave; tour per person $28; ☺tours 10.30am, 12.30pm, 3.30pm & 5.30pm, restaurant

DUNEDIN & OTAGO DUNEDIN

UNESCO CITY OF LITERATURE

Dunedin was designated a UNESCO City of Literature in 2014, in recognition of the profound creative energy of this small southern city. If you'd like to explore Dunedin's literary side during your stay, check out the City of Literature office's website (www.cityofliterature. co.nz) for information about readings, launches and other literary events.

Nowhere is Dunedin's bookishness more evident than in the city's bookstores, whose number seems at odds with Dunedin's relatively small population. As well as the usual chain stores and the excellent **University Book Shop** (Map p130; ☑ 03-477 6976; www.unibooks. co.nz; 378 Great King St, North Dunedin; ☺8.30am-5.30pm Mon-Fri, 10am-4pm Sat, 11am-3pm Sun), be sure to seek out some of the city's abundant secondhand bookshops, which are all packed to the ceiling with intriguing volumes. Our favourites include **Dead Souls** (Map p130; ☑ 021 0270 8540; www.deadsouls.co.nz; 393 Princes St; ☺10am-6pm), **Scribes** (Map p130; ☑ 03-477 6874; 546 Great King St; ☺10am-5pm Mon-Fri, to 4.30pm Sat & Sun) and **Hard to Find Books** (Map p130; ☑ 03-471 8518; www.hardtofind.co.nz; 20 Dowling St; ☺10am-6pm).

Central Dunedin

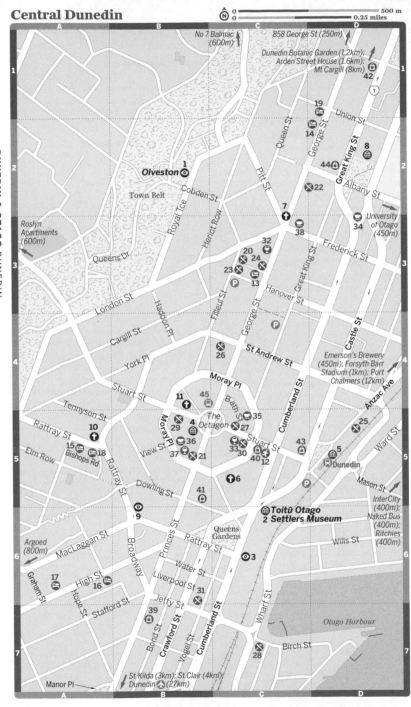

N

0 ——————————— 500 m
0 ——————————— 0.25 miles

No 7 Balmac
(600m)

858 George St (250m)

Dunedin Botanic Garden (1.2km);
Arden Street House (1.6km);
Mt Cargill (8km)

DUNEDIN & OTAGO DUNEDIN

Olveston

Town Belt

Roslyn
Apartments
(600m)

Queens Dr

Cobden St

Royal Tce

Heriot Row

Pitt St

Queen St

George St

Union St

Great King St

Albany St

University
of Otago
(450m)

Frederick St

London St

Cargill St

Haddon Pl

Filleul St

George St

Hanover St

Great King St

Castle St

Emerson's Brewery
(450m); Forsyth Barr
Stadium (1km); Port
Chalmers (12km)

York Pl

Stuart St

St Andrew St

Moray Pl

Cumberland St

Anzac Ave

Tennyson St

Rattray St

Elm Row

Bishops Rd

Moray Pl

View St

The
Octagon

Bath St

Stuart St

Ward St

Dowling St

MacLaggan St

Argoed
(800m)

Graham St

High St

Hope St

Broadway

Princes St

Stafford St

Rattray St

Water St

Liverpool St

Jetty St

Bond St

Crawford St

Vogel St

Queens
Gardens

**Toitū Otago
Settlers Museum**

Dunedin

Wills St

InterCity
(400m);
Naked Bus
(400m);
Ritchies
(400m)

Mason St

Cumberland St

Wharf St

Otago Harbour

Birch St

St Kilda (3km); St Clair (4km);
Dunedin ✈ (27km)

Manor Pl

Central Dunedin

10am-late, cellar door 10am-6pm Sun-Wed, to 8pm Thu-Sat) Opened in 2016, this impressive brick-and-glass structure is the flash new home of Emerson's, the microbrewery founded by local-boy-made-good Richard Emerson in 1992. Forty-five-minute tours take you behind the scenes of the brewing process, ending with the all-important tasting. There's also a cellar door where you can fill a rigger with your favourite drop – or, if you'd like to linger longer, drop into the cavernous restaurant for hearty meals (mains $28 to $32).

◉ North Dunedin

Knox Church   CHURCH
(Map p130; www.knoxchurch.net; 449 George St, North Dunedin; ☺8.30am-5pm) Dunedin's second grand Presbyterian church sprang up in 1876, only three years after the equally imposing First Church, and quickly became an emblem of the city. Built in the Gothic Revival style out of bluestone edged in white Oamaru stone, its most striking feature is its soaring 50m steeple. Inside there's a beautiful wooden ceiling and such good acoustics that the church is regularly used for concerts and other events.

Otago Museum   MUSEUM
(Map p130; ☎03-474 7474; www.otagomuseum.nz; 419 Great King St, North Dunedin; ☺10am-5pm) 🆓 FREE The centrepiece of this august institution is Southern Land, Southern People, showcasing Otago's cultural and physical past and present, from geology and dinosaurs to the modern day. The Tāngata Whenua Māori gallery houses an impressive *waka taua* (war canoe), wonderfully worn old carvings, and some lovely *pounamu* (greenstone) weapons, tools and jewellery. Other major galleries include Pacific Cultures, People of the World (including the requisite mummy), Nature, Maritime and the Animal Attic.

The newly renovated Tūhura Otago Community Trust Science Centre reopened in December 2017 to much fanfare, boasting 45 new hands-on interactive science displays, a refreshed Tropical Forest butterfly enclosure and a 7.5m-high double helix slide.

Guided tours depart from the information desk at 11am, 1pm, 2pm and 3pm daily (per person $15).

University of Otago

HISTORIC BUILDING

(Map p140; www.otago.ac.nz; 362 Leith St) Founded in 1869, the University of Otago is New Zealand's oldest. Today the university is home to some 18,000 students, and is well worth a wander, with many magnificent bluestone buildings to admire. The historic heart – bounded by Leith, St David and Castle Sts – is the most photogenic part of the campus. Check the university website for a self-guided tour map.

Dunedin Botanic Garden

GARDENS

(Map p140; ☑03-471 9275; www.dunedinbotanicgarden.co.nz; cnr Great King St & Opoho Rd, North Dunedin; ◷dawn-dusk) FREE Dating from 1863, these 30 hectares of peaceful, grassy and shady green space include rose gardens, rare natives, a rhododendron dell, an exotic bird aviary, a playground and a cafe. Kids love the Community Express 'train' (adult/child $3/1) and feeding the ducks (pick up free duck food at the park information centre).

⊙ Other Areas

★ Olveston

HOUSE

(Map p130; ☑03-477 3320; www.olveston.co.nz; 42 Royal Tce, Roslyn; adult/child $20/11; ◷tours 9.30am, 10.45am, noon, 1.30pm, 2.45pm & 4pm) Although it's a youngster by European standards, this spectacular 1906 mansion provides a wonderful window into Dunedin's past. Entry is via fascinating guided tours; it pays to book ahead. There's also a pretty little garden to explore (entry free).

Baldwin Street

LANDMARK

(Map p140; North East Valley) The world's steepest residential street (according to the *Guinness Book of World Records*), at its peak Baldwin St has a gradient of 1 in 2.86 (19°). The slope is the setting for several local events, the most amusing being the annual Jaffa Race, during which some 25,000 jaffas are rolled down the street each July for charity.

🏃 Activities

Swimming & Surfing

St Clair and St Kilda are both popular swimming beaches (though you need to watch for rips at St Clair). Both have consistently good left-hand breaks, and you'll also find good surfing further south at Blackhead, and at Aramoana on Otago Harbour's North Shore.

St Clair Hot Salt Water Pool

SWIMMING

(Map p140; www.dunedin.govt.nz; Esplanade, St Clair; adult/child $6.50/3; ◷6am-7pm Mon-Fri, from 7am Sat & Sun Oct-Mar) This heated outdoor pool sits on the western headland of St Clair Beach.

Esplanade Surf School

SURFING

(Map p140; ☑0800 484 141; www.espsurfschool.co.nz; 1 Esplanade, St Clair; 90min group lesson $60, private instruction $120) Operating from a van parked at St Clair Beach in summer whenever the surf is up (call at other times), this experienced crew provides board hire and lessons to suit all levels.

Walking

The **Otago Tramping & Mountaineering Club** (www.otmc.co.nz) organises regular day and overnight tramps in the surrounding area, including to the Silver Peaks Reserve north of Dunedin. Nonmembers are welcome, but must contact trip leaders beforehand.

Tunnel Beach Walkway

WALKING

(Tunnel Beach Rd, Blackhead) This short but extremely steep pathway (15 minutes down, 30 back up) brings you to a dramatic stretch of coast where the wild Pacific has carved sea stacks, arches and unusual formations out of the limestone. Strong currents make swimming here dangerous, but the views are spectacular.

Mt Cargill-Bethunes Gully Walkway

WALKING

(Map p140; www.doc.govt.nz; Norwood St, Normanby) Yes, it's possible to drive up 676m Mt Cargill, but that's not the point. The track (four hours, 8.5km return) starts from Norwood St, which is accessed from North Rd. From Mt Cargill, a trail continues to the 10-million-year-old, lava-formed Organ Pipes and, after another half-hour, to Mt Cargill Rd on the other side of the mountain.

Download the DOC's *Walks Around Dunedin* brochure for more information.

Heritage Train Rides

Dunedin Railways

RAIL

(Map p130; ☑03-477 4449; www.dunedinrailways.co.nz; Dunedin Railway Station, 22 Anzac Ave;

⊘office 8am-5pm Mon-Fri, 8.30am-3pm Sat & Sun) Two scenic heritage train journeys set off from Dunedin's railway station. The best is the **Taieri Gorge Railway**, with narrow tunnels, deep gorges, winding tracks, rugged canyons and viaduct crossings. The four-hour return trip aboard 1920s heritage coaches travels to Pukerangi (Mt Cargill–Bethunes Gully Walkway one way/return $61/91), 58km away. Some trains carry on to Middlemarch ($77/115, six hours return) – handy for the Otago Central Rail Trail.

The **Seasider** heads north, partly along the coast, as far as Oamaru (one way/return $72/109, seven hours return), although it's possible to get off the train at Moeraki ($66/99) for a two-hour stop before hopping on the return train. Shorter trips head as far as Palmerston ($59/89, four hours return). Aim for a seat on the right-hand side of the train for better sea views.

🛏 Sleeping

Dunedin has the whole gamut of places to lay your head, from backpacker hostels to luxury hotels. Most accommodation is within easy walking distance of the city centre, though some spots include an uphill stroll that will get your calves burning. Beds get scarce at the beginning of the new academic year (mid-to-late February), when helicopter parents book up beds to case their darlings (or, more likely, themselves) into their new lives.

🛏 City Centre

★Hogwartz   HOSTEL $
(Map p130; ☑03-474 1487; www.hogwartz.co.nz; 277 Rattray St; dm/s/d from $32/50/74, d with bathroom $86, studio $120; P@🅿🛜) The Catholic bishop's residence from 1872 to 1999, this beautiful building is now a fascinating warren of comfortable and sunny rooms, many with harbour views. Shared bathrooms include welcome touches like waterfall showers and underfloor heating. The old coach house and stables house swankier en suite rooms and apartments.

315 Euro   MOTEL $$
(Map p130; ☑03-477 9929; www.eurodunedin.co.nz; 315 George St; apt from $160; P@🛜) This sleek complex is accessed by an unlikely looking alley off Dunedin's main retail strip. Choose from modern studios or larger one-bedroom apartments with full kitchens and laundries. Double glazing keeps George St's incessant buzz at bay.

Dunedin Palms Motel   MOTEL $$
(Map p130; ☑03-477 8293; www.dunedinpalmsmotel.co.nz; 185-195 High St; units from $169; P🛜) Located a mercifully short stroll up from the city centre, the Palms has smartly renovated studios and one- and two-bedroom units arrayed around a central car park.

Fletcher Lodge   B&B $$$
(Map p130; ☑03-474 5551; www.fletcherlodge.co.nz; 276 High St; s/d/apt from $310/355/650; P🛜) 🌿 Originally home to one of NZ's wealthiest industrialists, this gorgeous red-brick mansion is just minutes from the city, but the secluded gardens feel wonderfully remote. Rooms are elegantly trimmed with antique furniture and ornate plaster ceilings.

Brothers Boutique Hotel   HOTEL $$$
(Map p130; ☑03-477 0043; www.brothershotel.co.nz; 295 Rattray St; r $190-395; P🛜) Rooms in this 1920s Christian Brothers residence have been refurbished beyond any monk's dreams, while still retaining many unique features. The chapel room even has its original arched stained-glass windows. There are great views from the rooftop units. Rates include a continental breakfast and an evening drink.

🛏 North Dunedin

Kiwi's Nest   HOSTEL $
(Map p130; ☑03-471 9540; www.kiwisnest.co.nz; 597 George St, North Dunedin; dm $28, s with/without bathroom $68/48, d $88/68, apt $105; P@🛜) This wonderfully homey two-storey house has a range of tidy centrally heated rooms, some with en suites, fridges and kettles. Plus it's a flat walk to The Octagon – something few Dunedin hostels can boast.

★858 George St   MOTEL $$
(Map p140; ☑03-474 0047; www.858georgestreetmotel.co.nz; 858 George St, North Dunedin; units from $150; P🛜) 🌿 Designed to blend in harmoniously with the neighbourhood two-storey Victorian houses, this top-quality motel complex has modern units ranging in size from studios to two bedrooms. Studios are fitted with microwaves, fridges, toasters and kettles, while the larger units also have stove tops or full ovens.

★Bluestone on George   APARTMENT $$$
(Map p130; ☑03-477 9201; www.bluestonedunedin.co.nz; 571 George St, North Dunedin; apt from $230; P@🛜) 🌿 If you're expecting an imposing old bluestone building, think again: this four-storey block couldn't be more

contemporary. The elegant studio units are decked out in muted tones, with kitchenettes, laundry facilities and decks or tiny balconies – some with harbour views. There's also a small gym and a guest lounge.

St Clair

Majestic Mansions APARTMENT $$
(Map p140; ☎03-456 5000; www.st-clair.co.nz; 15 Bedford St, St Clair; 1-/2-bedroom apt from $139/199; P 📶) One street back from St Clair Beach, this venerable 1920s apartment block has been thoroughly renovated, keeping the layout of the original little flats but sprucing them up with feature wallpaper and smart furnishings. Each has kitchen and laundry facilities.

Hotel St Clair HOTEL $$$
(Map p140; ☎03-456 0555; www.hotelstclair.com; 24 Esplanade, St Clair; r $214-409; P 📶) Soak up St Clair's surfy vibe from the balcony of your chic room in this contemporary medium-rise hotel. All but the cheapest rooms have ocean views, and the beach is only metres from the front door.

Other Areas

Leith Valley Touring Park HOLIDAY PARK $
(Map p140; ☎03-467 9936; www.leithvalleytouringpark.co.nz; 103 Malvern St, Woodhaugh; sites per person $19, units with/without bathroom from $99/49; P @ 📶) 🍃 This holiday park is surrounded by native bush studded with walks, glow-worm caves and a creek. Self-contained motel units are spacious, while flats are smaller but have a more rustic feel (BYO linen).

Argoed B&B $$
(Map p140; ☎03-474 1639; www.argoed.co.nz; 504 Queens Dr, Belleknowes; s/d from $150/210; P 📶) Roses and rhododendrons encircle this gracious two-storey wooden villa, built in the 1880s. Each of the three charmingly old-fashioned bedrooms has its own bathroom, though only one is en suite. Guests can relax in the conservatory or tinkle the ivories of the grand piano in the lounge.

Arden Street House B&B $$
(Map p140; ☎03-473 8860; www.ardenstreethouse.co.nz; 36 Arden St, North East Valley; s $75, d with/without bathroom $130/120, studio $140; P @ 📶) With crazy artworks, friendly kitties, charming hosts and a lived-in feeling, this 1930s hilltop house makes a wonderfully eccentric base. Some of the rooms have great views, while the more expensive studios have access to a shared lounge and kitchen. To get here from the city, drive up North Rd, turn right into Glendining Ave and then left into Arden St.

Roslyn Apartments APARTMENT $$$
(Map p140; ☎03-477 6777; www.roslynapartments.co.nz; 23 City Rd, Roslyn; apt from $225; P 📶) Unbeatable city and harbour views are the trump card at these modern apartments, just a short walk from Roslyn's eating strip. Each has full kitchen and laundry facilities.

Eating

Cafes and restaurants are clustered around The Octagon and all along George St. Uphill from the centre, Roslyn has some good eating choices, while the beachy ambience of St Clair is great for a lazy brunch or sunset drinks.

City Centre

★ **Otago Farmers Market** MARKET $
(Map p130; www.otagofarmersmarket.org.nz; Dunedin Railway Station; ⏲8am-12.30pm Sat) This thriving market is all local, all edible (or drinkable) and mostly organic. Grab a freshly baked pastry and a flat white to sustain you while you browse, and stock up on fresh meat, seafood, vegies and cheese for your journey. Sorted.

Perc CAFE $
(Map p130; ☎03-477 5462; www.perc.co.nz; 142 Stuart St; brunch $8-20; ⏲7am-4pm Mon-Fri, from 8am Sat & Sun; 📶) Hanging plants, flower-filled vases and large art-deco windows give this central cafe a creative, artsy vibe. The well-executed brunch options, fresh salads and counter full of tempting baked goods woo local students and office-workers alike, who set up camp here all day long for the flat whites and free wi-fi.

Modaks Espresso CAFE $
(Map p130; ☎03-477 6563; 337-339 George St; mains $9-21; ⏲7.30am-2.30pm Mon-Fri, from 8am Sat & Sun; 🖉) This funky little place with mismatched formica tables, plastic animal heads, and lounge chairs for slouching in is popular with students and those who appreciate sweet indie pop while they nurse a pot of tea. Plump, toasted bagels warm the insides in winter.

Miga KOREAN $$
(Map p130; ☎03-477 4770; www.facebook.com/migadunedin; 4 Hanover St; mains lunch $10-15, dinner $16-42; ⏲11.30am-2pm & 5pm-late Mon-Sat) Settle into a booth at this attractive

brick-lined eatery, and order claypot rice or noodle dishes from the extensive menu. Japanese dishes include tempura, *katsu* and incredible ramen soups, made with fresh noodles. Otherwise go for broke and cook a Korean barbecue right at your table.

Etrusco at the Savoy   ITALIAN **$$**
(Map p130; ☑03-477 3737; www.etrusco.co.nz; 8a Moray Pl; mains $15-27; ☺5.30pm-late) New Zealand has very few dining rooms to match the Edwardian elegance of the Savoy, with its moulded ceilings, stained-glass crests, brass chandeliers, Ionian columns and fabulously over-the-top lamps. Pizza and pasta might seem like an odd fit, but Etrusco's deliciously rustic Italian dishes absolutely hold their own.

Vogel St Kitchen   CAFE **$$**
(Map p130; ☑03-477 3623; www.vogelstkitchen. co.nz; 76 Vogel St; brunch $13-25, pizzas $24; ☺7.30am-3pm Mon-Thu, to 4pm Fri, 8.30am-4pm Sat & Sun; ☞) In the heart of Dunedin's warehouse precinct, Vogel St Kitchen offers smashing breakfasts and wood-fired pizzas in a cavernous two-storey redbrick building. It gets especially busy on weekends, when local residents make the most of large shared tables for long lazy brunches.

Paasha   TURKISH **$$**
(Map p130; ☑03-477 7181; www.paasha.co.nz; 31 St Andrew St; mains lunch $12-24, dinner $21-36; ☺11.30am-3pm & 5-9pm Mon-Wed, 11.30am-late Thu-Sun; ☞) Authentic kebabs, dips and salads are on the menu at this long-running favourite. It's a top place for takeaways, and most nights the spacious and warm interior is filled with groups drinking Efes beer and sharing heaving platters of tasty Turkish goodness.

Nova Cafe   CAFE **$$**
(Map p130; ☑03-479 0808; www.novadunedin. co.nz; 29 The Octagon; breakfast $12-24, lunch $18-27, dinner $18-34; ☺7am-late Mon-Fri, from 8.30am Sat & Sun) Not surprisingly, this extension of the art gallery has a stylish look about it. Start the day with the interesting breakfast selections, dabble in some Asian flavours for lunch, then finish the day with quality bistro-style mains and a glass of wine.

★**Bracken**   MODERN NZ **$$$**
(Map p130; ☑03-477 9779; www.bracken restaurant.co.nz; 95 Filleul St; 5/7/9-course menu $79/99/120, with matched wines $134/164/200; ☺6-9pm Tue-Sat) 🍽 Bracken's seasonal tasting menus offer a succession of pretty little plates bursting with flavour. While the dishes are intricate, nothing's overly gimmicky,

and the setting, in an old wooden house, is classy without being too formal.

Plato   MODERN NZ **$$$**
(Map p130; ☑03-477 4235; www.platocafe.co.nz; 2 Birch St; mains lunch $20-28, dinner $29-38; ☺noon-2pm Wed-Sat, from 11am Sun, plus 6pm-late daily) The kooky decor (including collections of toys and beer tankards) gives little indication of the seriously good food on offer at this relaxed eatery by the harbour. Fresh fish and shellfish feature prominently in a lengthy menu full of international flavours and subtle smoky elements. Servings are enormous.

Two Chefs Bistro   FRENCH **$$$**
(Map p130; ☑03-477 7293; www.twochefsbistro. com; 121 Stuart St; mains $34-42; ☺5.30pm-late Tue-Sat) French bistro dishes flirt with Asian and North African flavours on the plate, while high ceilings and dark wood conjure up a romantic ambience. Serves are small, but at least you'll be able to save room for one of the delectable desserts. The *plat du jour* option offers two courses and a glass of wine for $58.

Scotia   SCOTTISH **$$$**
(Map p130; ☑03-477 7704; www.scotiadunedin. co.nz; 199 Stuart St; mains $31-38; ☺5pm-late Tue-Sat) Occupying a cosy heritage townhouse, Scotia toasts all things Scottish with a wall full of single-malt whisky and hearty gourmet fare like sous vide duck breast and smoked beef fillet. The two Scottish Robbies – Burns and Coltrane – look down approvingly on a menu that also includes haggis and whisky-laced pâté.

✕ St Clair

Starfish   CAFE **$$**
(Map p140; ☑03-455 5940; www.starfishcafe.co.nz; 7/240 Forbury Rd, St Clair; mains $11-30; ☺7am-5pm Sun-Tue, to late Wed-Sat) Part of the growing restaurant scene at St Clair Beach, Starfish is a popular all-day eatery offering decadent brunch dishes, good coffee and a great buzz. Pop in for a quick lunch on the balcony overlooking the beach, or drop by in the evening for a hearty dinner accompanied by a glass of wine or wide selection of craft beer.

Esplanade   ITALIAN **$$**
(Map p140; ☑03-456 2544; www.esplanade.co; 2 Esplanade, St Clair; mains $21-26; ☺9am-late Mon-Fri, from 8.30am Sat & Sun) A prime position overlooking St Clair Beach is only the beginning at this relaxed Italian cafe-restaurant. Drop in during the morning for an espresso and a *panino*, or come by in the evening for

authentic thin-crust pizzas washed down with an aperol spritz. At sunset the windows offer the perfect frame as lavender twilight descends over the beach.

✕ Other Areas

Everyday Gourmet
CAFE, DELI $

(Map p130; www.everydaygourmet.net.nz; 466 George St, North Dunedin; mains $10-19; ⏱7.40am-4.30pm Mon-Fri, 8am-3.30pm Sat; 🛜) Apart from cooked breakfasts and pasta, most of the good stuff beckons from the counter of this excellent bakery-style cafe and deli. It's light, bright and extremely popular, with good coffee and friendly staff.

★ No 7 Balmac
CAFE $$

(Map p140; ☑03-464 0064; www.no7balmac.co.nz; 7 Balmacewen Rd, Maori Hill; mains brunch $14-26, dinner $29-45; ⏱7am-late Mon-Fri, 8.30am-late Sat, 8.30am-5pm Sun; 🛜) We wouldn't recommend walking to this sophisticated cafe at the top of Maori Hill, but luckily it's well worth the price of a cab. The fancy cafe fare stretches from smashing brunches to the likes of confit duck and slow-braised lamb. If you're on a diet, avoid eye contact with the cake cabinet.

🍺 Drinking & Nightlife

★ Aika + Co
BAR

(Map p130; www.facebook.com/aikaandcompany; 357 George St; ⏱10am-late Mon-Sat) With a new name but the same tiny space, 'Dunedin's littlest bar' might only be 1.8m wide, but it's still big enough to host regular live bands. There are just six bar stools, so patrons spill out into an adjacent laneway. By day, it's a handy coffee spot, as well as offering juices, milkshakes, baked goods and simple bar snacks.

Inch Bar
BAR

(Map p140; ☑03-473 6496; 8 Bank St, North East Valley; ⏱3pm-late) Make the short trek from town to this cavelike little bar for its selection of Kiwi craft beers and tapas, and the cute little indoor/outdoor beer garden. Despite its diminutive dimensions, it often hosts live music on Thursday, Friday and Saturday nights.

Albar
BAR

(Map p130; ☑03-479 2468; 135 Stuart St; ⏱11am-late) This former butcher is now a bohemian bar, with a dark, atmospheric interior and cosy booths, illuminated by a single chandelier. Punters are drawn in by the many single-malt whiskies and interesting tap beers, as well as the cheap tapas-style snacks (from $7).

Carousel
COCKTAIL BAR

(Map p130; ☑03-477 4141; www.carouselbar.co.nz; 141 Stuart St; ⏱5pm-late Wed-Sat) Monochrome tartan wallpaper, a roof deck and great cocktails leave the classy clientele looking pleased to be seen somewhere so deadly cool. DJs spin deep house until late from Thursday to Saturday, and there's often live jazz on Friday evenings from 8.30pm. It's upstairs.

Pequeno
COCKTAIL BAR

(Map p130; ☑03-477 7830; www.pequeno.co.nz; behind 12 Moray Pl; ⏱7pm-late Tue, Wed & Sat, from 6pm Thu, from 5pm Fri) Down the alley opposite the Rialto Cinema, Pequeno attracts a sophisticated crowd with leather couches, a cosy fireplace and an excellent wine and cocktail list. Music is generally laid-back, with regular live acts.

🛍 Shopping

Gallery De Novo
ART

(Map p130; ☑03-474 9200; www.gallerydenovo. co.nz; 101 Stuart St; ⏱9.30am-5.30pm Mon-Fri, 10am-3pm Sat & Sun) This interesting, contemporary, fine-art gallery is worth a peek whether you're likely to invest in a substantial piece of Kiwi art or not.

Stuart Street
Potters Co-operative
ARTS & CRAFTS

(Map p130; ☑03-471 8484; 14 Stuart St; ⏱10am-5pm Mon-Fri, 9am-3pm Sat) If you're after a unique souvenir, this sweet store stocks locally crafted pottery and ceramic art.

JUST GIVE ME THE COFFEE & NO ONE WILL GET HURT

Dunedin has some excellent coffee bars in which you can refuel and recharge:

The Fix (Map p130; www.thefixcoffee. co.nz; 15 Frederick St; ⏱7am-4pm Mon-Fri, 8am-noon Sat)

Mazagran Espresso Bar (Map p130; 36 Moray Pl; ⏱8am-6pm Mon-Fri, to 2pm Sat)

Insomnia by Strictly Coffee (Map p130; ☑03-479 0017; www.strictlycoffee. co.nz; 23 Bath St; ⏱7am-4pm Mon-Fri)

Allpress (Map p130; ☑03-477 7162; www. nz.allpressespresso.com; 12 Emily Siedeberg Pl; ⏱8am-4pm Mon-Fri)

ⓘ Information

MEDICAL SERVICES

Dunedin Hospital (☑ 03-474 0999; www. southerndhb.govt.nz; 201 Great King St)

Urgent Doctors (☑ 03-479 2900; www.dunedin urgentdoctors.co.nz; 95 Hanover St; ☺ 8am-10pm) There's also a late-night pharmacy next door.

TOURIST INFORMATION

The **Dunedin i-SITE** (Map p130; ☑ 03-474 3300; www.isitedunedin.co.nz; 50 The Octagon; ☺ 8.30am-5pm Apr-Oct, to 6pm Nov-Mar) incorporates the **DOC Visitor Centre** (Department of Conservation; Map p130; ☑ 03-474 3300; www. doc.govt.nz, ☺ 8.30am-5.30pm), providing a one-stop shop for all of your information needs, including Great Walks and hut bookings.

ⓘ Getting There & Away

AIR

Air New Zealand (☑ 0800 737 000; www. airnewzealand.co.nz) flies to/from Auckland, Wellington and Christchurch.

Jetstar (☑ 0800 800 995; www.jetstar.com) flies to/from Auckland and Wellington.

Virgin Australia (☑ 0800 670 000; www.virgin australia.com) flies to/from Brisbane, Australia.

BUS

Buses and shuttles leave from the Dunedin Railway Station, except where we've noted otherwise.

Atomic Shuttles (Map p130; ☑ 03-349 0697; www.atomictravel.co.nz) Buses to/from Christchurch ($35, six hours), Queenstown ($45, 4½ hours), Timaru ($25, three hours) and Oamaru ($20, two hours), twice daily.

Catch-a-Bus (☑ 03-449 2150; www.trailjour neys.co.nz) Bike-friendly shuttles to/from key Rail Trail towns, including Middlemarch ($45, one hour), Ranfurly ($49, two hours), Alexandra ($56, 3¼ hours), Clyde ($56, 3½ hours) and Cromwell ($60, 3¾ hours).

Coast Line Tours (Map p130; ☑ 03-434 7744; www.coastline-tours.co.nz) Shuttles to Oamaru depart from The Octagon (one way/return $30/55, two hours); detours to Dunedin Airport and Moeraki can be arranged.

InterCity (Map p140; ☑ 03-471 7143; www.inter city.co.nz) Coaches to/from Christchurch (from $42, six hours), Oamaru (from $23, 1½ hours), Cromwell (from $23, 3¼ hours), Queenstown (from $26, 4¼ hours) and Te Anau (from $38, 4½ hours) daily. Departs 7 Halsey St.

Naked Bus (Map p140; https://nakedbus. com; prices vary) Daily buses head to/from Christchurch (six hours), Timaru (three hours), Gore (2½ hours) and Invercargill (3¾ hours).

Ritchies (Map p140; ☑ 03-443 9120; www. alpineconnexions.co.nz) Shuttles head to/from Clyde ($50, three hours), Cromwell ($50, 3¼

hours), Wanaka ($50, four hours) and Queenstown ($50, 4½ hours), as well as key stops on the Otago Central Rail Trail.

TRAIN

The heritage tourist trains operated by **Dunedin Railways** (p132) can be used as a transport connection. The *Taieri Gorge Railway* heads to Middlemarch twice a week, while the *Seasider* is an option for Moeraki and Oamaru.

ⓘ Getting Around

TO/FROM THE AIRPORT

Dunedin Airport (p367) is 27km southwest of the city. There is no public transport to the airport. A standard taxi ride to/from the city costs around $90. For door-to-door shuttles, try **Kiwi Shuttles** (☑ 03-487 9790; www.kiwishuttles. co.nz; per 1/2/3/4 passengers $20/36/48/60) or **Super Shuttle** (☑ 0800 748 885; www. supershuttle.co.nz; per 1/2/3/4 passengers $25/40/50/60) – book in advance.

BUS

Dunedin's **GoBus** (☑ 03-474 0287; www.orc. govt.nz; adult $2.60-15.30) network extends across the city. It's particularly handy for getting to St Clair, St Kilda and Port Chalmers, and as far afield as Palmerston or the Otago Peninsula. Buses run regularly Monday to Friday, with reduced services on weekends.

Individual tickets are available from the bus driver; for longer stays, invest in a GoCard – purchase from bus drivers, from the council offices in The Octagon, or from **University Book Shop** (p129) – which offers reduced fares.

CAR

The big car-hire companies all have offices in Dunedin; local outfits include **Hanson Rental Vehicles** (☑ 03-453 6576; www.hanson.net.nz; 313 Kaikorai Valley Rd) and **Ezi Car Rental** (☑ 03-486 1245; www.ezicarrental.co.nz; Dunedin Airport).

TAXI

There are several taxi companies in Dunedin; options include **Dunedin Taxis** (☑ 0800 505 010; ☑ 03-477 7777; www.dunedintaxis.co.nz), **Southern Taxis** (☑ 03-476 6300; www.south erntaxis.co.nz) and **Green Cabs** (☑ 0800 46 47 336; www.greencabs.co.nz).

AROUND DUNEDIN

Port Chalmers

POP 1370

Little Port Chalmers is only 13km from central Dunedin but it feels a world away. Somewhere between working class and bohemian, Port Chalmers has a history as a port town

DON'T MISS

OROKONUI ECOSANCTUARY

From the impressive visitors centre there are great views over this 307-hectare predator-free nature **reserve** (Map p140; 03-482 1755; www.orokonui.org. nz; 600 Blueskin Rd; adult/child $19/9.50; 9.30am-4.30pm), which encloses cloud forest on the ridge above Port Chalmers and stretches to the estuary on the opposite side. Its mission is to provide a mainland refuge for species usually exiled to offshore islands for their own protection. Visiting options include self-guided explorations, hour-long 'highlights' tours (adult/child $35/17.50; 11am and 1.30pm daily) and two-hour 'forest explorer' tours (adult/child $50/35; 11am daily).

but has long attracted Dunedin's arty types. The main drag, George St, is home to a handful of cafes, design stores and galleries, perfect for a half-day's worth of wandering, browsing and sipping away from the city crush.

🏃 Activities

Traditional rock climbing (nonbolted) is popular at Long Beach and the cliffs at Mihiwaka, both accessed via Blueskin Rd north of Port Chalmers.

Hare Hill   HORSE RIDING
(Map p140; 03-472 8496; www.horseriding-dunedin.co.nz; 207 Aramoana Rd, Deborah Bay; treks $95-195) Horse treks include thrilling beach rides and harbour views.

🛏 Sleeping & Eating

Billy Brown's   HOSTEL $$
(Map p140; 03-472 8323; www.billybrowns.co.nz; 423 Aramoana Rd, Hamilton Bay; d $150, additional person $50; Sep-May) On a farm 5km along the road from Port Chalmers, this backpacker fave no longer offers dorm accommodation, but the whole rustic lodge is available to rent for groups from one to eight people. There's a lovely lounge with a cosy wood-burner and plenty of retro vinyl to spin.

Union Co.   CAFE $
(Map p140; 2 George St; mains $8-15; 8am-3pm) Great coffee, delicious baked goods and a sunny corner position make this the pick for your morning caffeine fix.

Carey's Bay Hotel   PUB FOOD $$
(Map p140; 03-472 8022; www.careysbayhotel. co.nz; 17 Macandrew Rd, Carey's Bay; mains $19-30;

10am-late) Just around the corner from Port Chalmers you'll find this historic pub, popular with locals for its hearty meals and unbeatable location – on sunny days grab a table out the front for first-class views over the water.

Portsider   PUB FOOD $$
(Map p140; 03-472 8060; www.portsider.co.nz; 31 George St; mains $18-30) Duck into this snug gastropub for good-value meals, a wide range of tap beers and friendly service.

🛈 Getting There & Away

On weekdays buses (adult/child $6/3.60, 30 minutes, half-hourly) travel between Dunedin and Port Chalmers between 6.30am and 9.30pm (11.30pm on Friday). On weekends buses run hourly between 8.30am and 11.30pm on Saturday, and 9.30am and 5.30pm on Sunday.

Otago Peninsula

POP 4210

It's hard to believe that the Otago Peninsula – a picturesque haven of rolling hills, secluded bays, sandy beaches and clifftop vistas – is only half an hour's drive from downtown Dunedin. As well as interesting historical sites and wild walking trails, this small sliver of land is home to the South Island's most accessible diversity of wildlife, including albatross, penguins, fur seals and sea lions. The peninsula's only town is the petite Portobello and, despite a host of tours exploring the region, it maintains its quiet rural air.

👁 Sights

⭐ **Nature's Wonders**
Naturally   WILDLIFE RESERVE
(Map p140; 03-478 1150; www.natureswonders. co.nz; Taiaroa Head; adult/child Argo $99/45, coach $45/22.50; tours from 10.15am) What makes the improbably beautiful beaches of this coastal sheep farm different from other important wildlife habitats is that (apart from pest eradication and the like) they're left completely alone. Many of the multiple private beaches haven't suffered a human footprint in years. The result is that yellow-eyed penguins can often be spotted (through binoculars) at any time of the day, and NZ fur seals laze around rocky swimming holes, blissfully unfazed by tour groups passing by.

Depending on the time of year, you might also see whales and little penguin chicks.

The tour is conducted in 'go-anywhere' Argo vehicles by enthusiastic guides, at least some of whom double as true-blue Kiwi farmers. A less bumpy coach option is also available, though you won't see as much.

Glenfalloch Woodland Garden   GARDENS
(Map p140; ☑ 03-476 1006; www.glenfalloch.co.nz; 430 Portobello Rd, Macandrew Bay; ⊘ 8am-dusk) **FREE** Make time to pause at these lush, well-tended gardens, filled with flowers and swaying mature trees, including a 1000-year-old matai. Walking tracks meander through dense forest, with peeks of the harbour visible from all angles. There's also a good restaurant on site. The Portobello bus stops out the front.

Larnach Castle   CASTLE
(Map p140; ☑ 03-476 1616; www.larnachcastle.co.nz; 145 Camp Rd; adult/child castle & grounds $31/10, grounds only $15.50/5; ⊘ 9am-7pm Oct-Mar, to 5pm Apr-Sep) 🖉 Standing proudly on top of a hill overlooking the peninsula, this gorgeous Gothic Revival mansion was built in 1871 by Dunedin banker, merchant and Member of Parliament William Larnach. The castle fell into disrepair after Larnach's death, until it was purchased by the Barker family in 1967, and a long period of restoration began. The four floors are now filled with intricate woodwork and exquisite antique furnishings, and the crenellated tower offers expansive views.

A self-guided tour brochure is provided, or you can buy an iPhone app ($6) that digitally peoples the rooms with costumed actors. After lording it about in the mansion, take a stroll through the pretty gardens or settle in for high tea in the ballroom cafe.

Penguin Place   BIRD SANCTUARY
(Map p140; ☑ 03-478 0286; www.penguinplace.co.nz; 45 Pakihau Rd, Harington Point; adult/child $54/16; ⊘ tours from 10.15am Oct-Mar, 3.45pm Apr-Sep) On private farmland, this reserve protects nesting sites of the rare yellow-eyed penguin (hoiho). The 90-minute tours focus on penguin conservation and close-up viewing from a system of hides. Bookings recommended.

Royal Albatross Centre & Fort Taiaroa   BIRD SANCTUARY
(Map p140; ☑ 03-478 0499; www.albatross.org.nz; Taiaroa Head; adult/child albatross $50/15, fort $25/10, combined $55/20; ⊘ 10.15am-dusk) Taiaroa Head, at the peninsula's northern tip, has the world's only mainland royal albatross colony, along with a late-19th-century military fort. The only public access to the area is by guided tour. There's an hour-long albatross tour and a 30-minute fort tour available, or the two can also be combined. Otherwise you can just call into the centre to look at the displays and have a bite in the cafe.

Albatross are present on Taiaroa Head throughout the year, but the best time to see them is from December to March, when one parent is constantly guarding the young while the other delivers food throughout the day. Sightings are most common in the afternoon when the winds pick up; calm days don't see as many birds in flight.

Little penguins swim ashore at Pilots Beach (just below the car park) around dusk to head to their nests in the dunes. For their protection, the beach is closed to the public every evening, but viewing is possible from a specially constructed wooden platform (adult/child $35/10). Depending on the time of year, 50 to 300 penguins might waddle past.

Fort Taiaroa was built in 1885 in response to a perceived threat of Russian invasion. Its **Armstrong Disappearing Gun** was designed to be loaded and aimed underground, then popped up like the world's slowest jack-in-the-box to be fired.

🏃 Activities & Tours

A popular walking destination is beautiful **Sandfly Bay**, reached from Seal Point Rd (one hour return). You can also follow a track from the end of Sandymount Rd to the **Sandymount summit** and on to the impressive **Chasm and Lovers Leap** (one hour return). Note that this track is closed from September to mid-October for lambing. Pick up or download the helpful DOC *Dunedin Walks* brochure to plan your tramp.

Wild Earth Adventures   KAYAKING
(☑ 03-489 1951; www.wildearth.co.nz; per person $115) Offers guided tours in double sea kayaks, with wildlife often sighted en route. Tours take between three hours and a full day, with pick-ups from The Octagon in Dunedin.

Back to Nature Tours   BUS
(☑ 0800 286 000; www.backtonaturetours.co.nz) 🖉 The full-day Royal Peninsula tour (adult/child $193/125) heads to points of interest

> **WILDLIFE SPOTTING: SEA LIONS**
>
> Sea lions are most easily seen on a tour, but are regularly present at Sandfly Bay, Allans Beach and Victory Beach on the Otago Peninsula. They are predominantly bachelor males vacationing from Campbell Island or the Auckland Islands. Give them plenty of space, as these beasts can really motor over the first 20m.

Dunedin & the Otago Peninsula

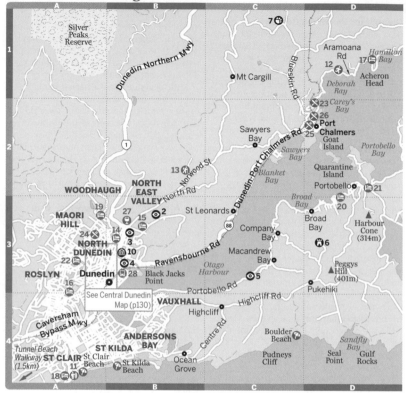

around Dunedin before hitting the Otago Peninsula. Stops include Larnach Castle's (p139) gardens (castle entry is extra), Penguin Place (p139) and the Royal Albatross Centre (p139). There's a half-day option that visits various beaches ($83/55) and another tackling the Lovers Leap walking track ($89/55). Will pick up from your accommodation.

Elm Wildlife Tours   WILDLIFE
(☑ 03-454 4121; www.elmwildlifetours.co.nz; tours from $103) 🖉 Well-regarded, small-group, wildlife-focused tours, with options to add the Royal Albatross Centre (p139) or a Monarch Cruise. Pick-up and drop-off from Dunedin is included.

🛏 Sleeping & Eating

McFarmers Backpackers   HOSTEL $
(Map p140; ☑ 03-478 0389; mcfarmers@xtra.co.nz; 774 Portobello Rd, Broad Bay; s/d $55/70) On a working sheep farm with harbour views, the

timber lodge and self-contained cottage here are steeped in character and feel instantly like home. The Portobello bus goes past the gate.

★**Portobello Motel**   MOTEL $$
(Map p140; ☑ 03-478 0155; www.portobellomotels. com; 10 Harington Point Rd, Portobello; units from $160; 🅿 🛜) These sunny, modern units are thoughtfully decorated and outfitted with all mod cons. The studio units are the pick of the bunch, each with small private decks overlooking the bay. Spacious one- and two-bedroom versions are also available, but lack the views.

Larnach Castle   B&B $$$
(Map p140; ☑ 03-476 1616; www.larnachcastle. co.nz; 145 Camp Rd; d stable/lodge/estate $160/320/510; 🅿 @ 🛜) 🖉 Larnach Castle's pricey back-garden lodge has 12 unique, whimsically decorated rooms with views. Less frivolous are the atmospheric rooms in the 140-year-old stables (bathrooms are

shared). A few hundred metres from the castle, Camp Estate has luxury suites worthy of a romantic splurge. Each option includes breakfast and castle entry; dinner in the castle is extra ($70).

1908 Cafe   CAFE, BISTRO $$
(Map p140; ☑ 03-478 0801; www.1908cafe.co.nz; 7 Harington Point Rd, Portobello; mains lunch $14-24, dinner $31-34; ⊙ noon-2pm & 6-10pm, closed Mon & Tue Apr-Oct) Salmon, venison and steak are joined by fresh fish and blackboard specials at this casual eatery. Cafe fare, such as soup and toasted sandwiches, is served at lunch. As the name suggests, the building originally opened as a tearoom in 1908, and many of the original features are still in place.

❶ Getting There & Away

Portobello is a scenic 20km drive from Dunedin along the harbour. On weekdays, buses make the journey from Dunedin's Cumberland St to Portobello Village from 7.30am to 10.30pm (adult/ child $6/3.60, one hour, half-hourly), with four services continuing to Harrington Point at the tip of the peninsula. On Saturdays the service reduces to hourly from 8.30am.

Once on the peninsula, it's tough to get around without your own transport. Most tours will pick you up from your Dunedin accommodation.

There's no petrol available on the peninsula.

CENTRAL OTAGO

Rolling hills that turn from green to gold in the relentless summer sun provide a backdrop to a succession of tiny, charming gold-rush towns where farmers mingle with Lycra-clad cyclists in lost-in-time pubs. As well as being one of the country's top wine regions, the area provides fantastic opportunities for those on two wheels, whether mountain biking along old gold-mining trails or traversing the district on the Otago Central Rail Trail.

Middlemarch

POP 153

With the Rock and Pillar Range as an impressive backdrop, the small town of Middlemarch is the terminus of both the Taieri Gorge Railway and the Otago Central Rail Trail. It's famous in NZ for the Middlemarch Singles Ball (held over Easter in odd-numbered years), where southern men gather to entice city gals to the country life.

Activities

Both Cycle Surgery (p119) and Trail Journeys (p119) have depots on Middlemarch's main street, providing bike hire and logistical support to riders on the Otago Central Rail Trail (p118). This includes shuttles, bag transfers and an accommodation booking service. They also have depots in Clyde, at the other end of the trail, to drop off your bikes.

Sleeping & Eating

Otago Central Hotel　　　　　B&B $$
(☑027 544 4800; www.otagocentralhotelhyde.com; SH87, Hyde; d with/without bathroom from $170/130; ☺Oct-Apr) Most of the tidy rooms in this cool old hotel, 27km along the trail from Middlemarch, have private bathrooms, but only some are en suite. It's no longer a working pub, and the $50 set dinner is the only meal option for many miles around.

Kissing Gate Cafe　　　　　　CAFE $
(☑03-464 3224; 2 Swansea St; mains $8-18; ☺8.30am-4pm; 🛜) Sit out under the fruit trees in the pretty garden of this cute little wooden cottage and tuck into a cooked breakfast, meat pie, zingy salad or some home baking. Nana-chic at its best.

Getting There & Away

Middlemarch is an hour's scenic drive from Dunedin.

Both of the main cycle companies offer shuttles to Dunedin, Pukerangi and the Rail Trail towns. In the warmer months, Trail Journey's **Catch-a-Bus** (☑03-449 2150; www.trailjourneys.co.nz; ☺Oct-Apr) has scheduled daily services to/from Dunedin ($45, one hour), Ranfurly ($27, one hour), Alexandra ($55, 2¼ hours), Clyde ($55, 2½ hours) and Cromwell ($59, three hours).

The scenic **Taieri Gorge Railway** (☑03-477 4449; www.dunedinrailways.co.nz; ☺Sun May-Sep, Fri & Sun Oct-Apr) has only limited runs between Dunedin and Middlemarch (one way/return $77/115, three hours); most services end at Pukerangi Station, 20km away.

Ranfurly

POP 663

After a series of fires in the 1930s, Ranfurly was rebuilt in the architectural style of the day, and a few attractive art-deco buildings still line its sleepy main drag. The teensy town is trying hard to cash in on its meagre legacy, calling itself the 'South Island's art-deco capital'. There's even an **Art Deco Museum** in the admittedly fabulous Centennial Milk Bar building on the main street.

Most travellers come through Ranfurly on the Otago Central Rail Trail (p118), which passes right through town.

Sleeping

Hawkdun Lodge　　　　　　MOTEL $$
(☑03-444 9750; www.hawkdunlodge.co.nz; 1 Bute St; s/d from $113/150; 🛜) 🌱 This smart boutique motel is the best option in the town centre by far. Even studio units are spacious, with kitchenettes, sitting areas and en suites. Travelling chefs can flex their skills in the smart guest kitchen and dining area.

Peter's Farm Lodge　　　　　LODGE $$
(☑03-444 9811; www.petersfarm.co.nz; 113 Tregonning Rd, Waipiata; per adult/child $60/45) On a sheep farm 13km south of Ranfurly, this rustic 1882 farmhouse offers comfy beds, hearty barbecue dinners ($25) and free pick-ups from the Rail Trail. Kayaks, fishing rods and gold pans are all available, so it's worth staying a couple of nights. Further beds are available in neighbouring Tregonning Cottage (1882).

Kokonga Lodge　　　　　　B&B $$$
(☑03-444 9774; www.kokongalodge.co.nz; 33 Kokonga-Waipiata Rd; s/d $240/295; @🛜) Just off SH87 between Ranfurly and Hyde, this upmarket rural property offers six contemporary en suite rooms, one of which was

occupied by Sir Peter Jackson when he was filming *The Hobbit* in the area. The Rail Trail passes nearby.

ℹ Information

Call into the **Ranfurly i-SITE** (☑ 03-444 1005; www.centralotagonz.com; 3 Charlemont St; ⊘ 9am-5pm; ☎) in the old train station to pick up a copy of the free *Rural Art Deco – Ranfurly Walk* brochure. While there, check out the short film about the Rail Trail and local history displays.

ℹ Getting There & Away

Ranfurly sits on route 85, 1¾ hours drive from Dunedin. In the warmer months, Trail Journey's **Catch-a-Bus** (☑ 03-449 2150; www.trailjourneys.co.nz; ⊘ Oct-Apr) passes through Ranfurly on its way between Cromwell ($52, two hours) and Dunedin ($49, two hours).

Naseby

POP 120

Cute as a button, surrounded by forest and dotted with 19th-century stone buildings, Naseby is the kind of small settlement where life moves slowly. That the town is pleasantly obsessed with the fairly insignificant world of NZ curling (a Winter Olympic sport resembling shuffleboard on ice) indicates there's not much else going on. It's that lazy small-town vibe, along with good mountain-biking and walking trails through the surrounding forest, that makes Naseby an interesting stopover for Rail Trailers.

🏃 Activities

Maniototo Curling International ICE SKATING (☑ 03-444 9878; www.curling.co.nz; 1057 Channel Rd; adult/child per 90min $35/15; ⊘ 10am-5pm May-Oct, 9am-7.30pm Nov-Apr) All year round you can shimmy after curling stones at this indoor ice rink; tuition is available. In winter there's also an outdoor ice rink to skate around.

Naseby Ice Luge SNOW SPORTS (☑ 03-444 9270; www.lugenz.com; 1057 Channel Rd; adult/child $35/25; ⊘ 10am-4pm Jun-Aug) Hurtle 360m down a hillside on a wooden sled during winter. Weather dependent; call ahead, bookings recommended.

🛏 Sleeping

Old Doctor's Residence B&B $$$ (☑ 03-444 9775; www.olddoctorsresidence.co.nz; 58 Derwent St; r/ste $295/350; ☎) 🖉 Old

doctors take note: this is how to reside! Sitting behind a pretty garden, this gorgeous 1870s house offers two luxurious guest rooms and a lounge where wine and nibbles are served in the evening. The suite has a sitting room and an en suite bathroom, while the smaller room's bathroom is accessed from the corridor.

ℹ Information

Ernslaw One Forestry Office (☑ 03-444 9995; www.ernslaw.co.nz/naseby-recreational-area-2; 34 Derwent St; ⊘ 9am-4pm Mon-Fri) Administers the 500-hectare recreation reserve within the privately owned Naseby Forest. Call in for maps of walking tracks and mountain-bike trails around town.

Naseby Information Centre (☑ 03-444 9961; www.nasebyinfo.org.nz; Old Post Office, Derwent St; ⊘ 11am-2pm Fri, Sun & Mon, to 4pm Sat, extended hours summer)

ℹ Getting There & Away

The Ranfurly–Naseby Rd leaves SH85, 4km north of Ranfurly. There's no public transport and cyclists should factor in a 12km detour from the Rail Trail (many accommodation providers will collect you if you ask). From Naseby, you can wind your way on unsealed roads northeast through spectacular scenery to Danseys Pass and through to Duntroon in the Waitaki Valley.

Lauder, Omakau & Ophir

Separated by 8km of SH85, tiny **Lauder** (population 12) and larger **Omakau** (population 260) are good stops if you're a hungry cyclist in need of a feed and a bed. However, the area's real gem is **Ophir** (population 50), 2km from Omakau across the Manuherikia River.

Gold was discovered here in 1863 and the town swiftly formed, named after the biblical place where King Solomon sourced his gold. By 1875 the population had hit over 1000 but when the gold disappeared, so did the people. Ophir's fate was sealed when the railway bypassed it in 1904, leaving its main street trapped in time.

The most photogenic of Ophir's heritage buildings is the 1886 **post office** (www.historic.org.nz; 53 Swindon St, Ophir; ⊘ 9am-noon Mon-Fri). At the far end of town, the road heads over the heritage-listed 1870s **Dan O'Connell Bridge**, a bumpy but scenic crossing that loops back to SH85.

OFF THE BEATEN TRACK

ST BATHANS

A 17km detour north from SH85 heads into the foothills of the Dunstan Mountains and on to diminutive St Bathans. This once-thriving gold-mining town of 2000 people is now home to only half a dozen residents living amid a cluster of cute 19th-century buildings, almost all of which have 'For Sale' signs. There's not much in town but the historic **pub** (☑ 03-447 3629; stbathans.vulcanhotel@xtra.co.nz; Main St; r per person $60).

The **Blue Lake** is an accidental attraction: a large hollow filled with blue water that has run off abandoned gold workings. Walk along the sculpted cliffs to the lookout for a better view of the alien landscape (one hour return).

Sleeping & Eating

★ Pitches Store B&B $$$
(☑ 03-447 3240; www.pitches-store.co.nz; 45 Swindon St, Ophir; r $295; ☺ restaurant 10am-late daily Dec-Apr, 10am-3pm Mon, Sun & Thu, 10am-late Fri & Sat May & Aug-Nov) Formerly a general store and butcher, this heritage building has been sensitively transformed into six elegant guest rooms and a humdinger of a **cafe-restaurant** (mains: lunch $15 to $18 and dinner $33 to $37). Exposed stone walls may speak of the past but the menu offers contemporary gourmet fare – it was named Silver Fern Farms Best Regional Restaurant in 2016 and 2017.

Stationside Cafe CAFE $
(☑ 03-447 3580; Lauder-Matakanui Rd, Lauder; mains $8-18; ☺ 8am-5pm Oct-Apr) Country hospitality is on show at this great little trailside place with wonderfully charming hosts. Options include tasty breakfasts, healthy salads and soups, as well as a mouth-watering selection of just-baked scones, cakes and muffins.

Getting There & Away

There's no public transport to these parts but many of the bike crews servicing the Otago Central Rail Trail provide shuttles, and many accommodation providers can pick you up from the trail if you enquire in advance.

Alexandra

POP 4800

Unless you've come especially for the Easter Bunny Hunt or the springtime Blossom Festival and NZ Merino Shearing Championships, the main reason to visit unassuming Alexandra is mountain biking. It's the biggest Otago Central Rail Trail (p118) settlement by far, offering more eating and sleeping options than the rest of the one-horse (or fewer) towns on the route. It's also the start of the new Roxburgh Gorge Trail.

Alex, as it's known to the locals, marks the southeastern corner of the Central Otago wine region. Of the dozen wineries in the vicinity, only a handful are open for tastings. These are detailed on the *Central Otago Wine Map*, available from the i-SITE.

Sights & Activities

Central Stories MUSEUM
(☑ 03-448 6230; www.centralstories.com; 21 Centennial Ave; by donation; ☺ 10am-4pm) Central Otago's history of gold mining, winemaking, fruit growing and sheep farming is covered in this excellent regional museum and gallery, which shares a building with the i-SITE.

Clutha River Cruises BOATING
(☑ 0800 258 842; www.clutharivercruises.co.nz; boat ramp, Dunorling St; adult/child $95/55; ☺ 2.30pm Oct-May) Explore the scenery and history of the region on a 2½-hour heritage cruise. The same company runs the jetboat transfer for cyclists on the **Roxburgh Gorge Trail** (www.cluthagold.co.nz; suggested track maintenance donation per person $10).

Sleeping & Eating

Asure Avenue Motel MOTEL $$
(☑ 03-448 6919; www.avenue-motel.co.nz; 117 Centennial Ave; units from $142; ℗ 🛜) The pick of the motels on the main drag, these clean, modern units have all the mod cons – and some have full kitchens, too. Studio, one- and two-bedroom apartments are available.

★ Courthouse Cafe & Larder CAFE $
(☑ 03-448 7818; www.packingshedcompany.com; 8 Centennial Ave; mains $11-23; ☺ 6.30am-4.30pm Mon-Fri, 8am-4pm Sat) Fairy lights and botanical displays dispel any lingering austerity in this stone courthouse building, dating from 1878. The counter groans under the weight of an array of baked goods (cakes, doughnuts, croissants and more), which compete with gourmet brunch and lunch options – and if Jack's rolled ice cream happens to be on the menu when you visit, you'd best save room!

Information

Pick up a free map of town from the **Alexandra i-SITE** (☑ 03-262 7999; www.centralotagonz.com; 21 Centennial Ave; ☺ 9am-5pm; 🛜).

ALEXANDRA TO MILTON ON SH8

Heading south from Alexandra, SH8 winds along rugged, rock-strewn hills above the Clutha River as it passes Central Otago's famous orchards. In season (roughly December to March) roadside fruit stalls sell just-picked stone fruit, cherries and berries. En route there's a scattering of small towns, many dating from gold-rush days.

Thirteen kilometres south of Alexandra, the historic **Speargrass Inn** (☑03-449 2192; www.speargrassinn.co.nz; 1300 Fruitlands Roxburgh Rd, SH8, Fruitlands; r $180; ☺cafe 8.30am-4pm Sat-Thu, 8.30am-late Fri, closed May-Sep; ☎) has three handsome rooms in a block out the back, set in attractive gardens. The original 1869 building houses a charming cafe (mains $18 to $26). It's an excellent place to stop for coffee and cake or a more substantial meal.

Further south, the Clutha broadens into **Lake Roxburgh**, with a large hydroelectric power station at its terminus, before rushing past Roxburgh itself. Call into the friendly **i-SITE** (☑03-446 8920; www.centralotagonz.com; 120 Scotland St; ☺9am-5pm daily Nov-Apr, Mon-Fri May-Oct) for information on mountain biking, water sports and seasonal fruit-picking work in the surrounding apple and stone-fruit orchards.

Before you leave Roxburgh, drop into **Jimmy's Pies** (☑03-446 9012; www.jimmyspies.co.nz; 143 Scotland St; pies $4-6.50; ☺7.30am-5pm Mon-Fri), renowned across the South Island since 1959. If you're at a loss to which of the 20 different varieties of pies to choose, try the apricot chicken – you're in orchard country, after all.

Continuing south from Roxburgh, the road passes through **Lawrence** and the **Manuka Gorge Scenic Reserve**, a picturesque route through wooded hills and gullies. SH8 joins SH1 near Milton.

ℹ Getting There & Away

Alexandra lies on SH8, around 2½ hours' drive from Dunedin and 1¼ hours from Queenstown.

Atomic Shuttles (☑03-349 0697; www.atomictravel.co.nz) A daily bus heads to/from Dunedin ($40, three hours), Roxburgh ($20, 30 minutes), Cromwell ($20, 30 minutes) and Queenstown ($30, 1¾ hours).

Catch-a-Bus (☑03-449 2024; www.trailjourneys.co.nz) Door to door shuttles to Cromwell ($25, 30 minutes), Clyde ($15, 10 minutes), Ranfurly ($43, one hour), Middlemarch ($55, two hours) and Dunedin ($56, 3¼ hours).

InterCity (☑03-471 7143; www.intercity.co.nz) Coaches head to/from Dunedin (from $22, three hours), Roxburgh (from $14, 34 minutes), Clyde (from $10, nine minutes), Cromwell (from $11, 24 minutes) and Queenstown (from $14, 1½ hours).

Clyde

POP 1010

More charming than his buddy Alex, 8km down the road, Clyde looks more like a 19th-century gold-rush film set than a real town. Set on the banks of the emerald-green Clutha River, Clyde retains a friendly, small-town feel, even when holidaymakers arrive in numbers over summer. It's also the trailhead of the Otago Central Rail Trail (p118).

◉ Sights & Activities

Pick up a copy of *Walk Around Historic Clyde* from the Alexandra i-SITE (p144). The **Alexandra–Clyde 150th Anniversary Walk** (12.8km, three hours one way) is a riverside track that's fairly flat, with ample resting spots and shade.

Clyde Historical Museums MUSEUM
(5 Blyth St; by donation; ☺2-5pm Tue-Sun) This volunteer-run local museum showcases Māori and Victorian exhibits, and traces the construction of the Clyde Dam. You can also peep into the old council chambers. A second building, housed in the Herb Factory complex at 12 Fraser St, was closed for renovations when we visited.

🛏 Sleeping & Eating

Dunstan House B&B $$
(☑03-449 2295; www.dunstanhouse.co.nz; 29 Sunderland St; s/d without bathroom from $110/130, d/ste with bathroom from $190/260; ☺Oct-Apr; ☎) This restored late-Victorian balconied inn has lovely bar and lounge areas, and stylish rooms decorated in period style. The less expensive rooms share bathrooms but are just as comfortable and atmospheric.

Postmaster's House B&B $$
(☑03-449 2488; www.postofficecafeclyde.co.nz; 4 Blyth St; d with/without bathroom $125/95; P ☎)

Antique furnishings are dotted around the large and lovely rooms in this pretty stone cottage. Two of the three rooms share a bathroom; the third has its own.

★ **Oliver's** B&B $$$
(📋 03-449 2600; www.oliverscentralotago.co.nz; Holloway Rd; r/ste from $235/535; 🅿🛜) 🍴 Oliver's fills an 1860s merchant's house and stone stables with luxurious rooms decked out with old maps, heritage furniture and claw-foot baths. Most of the rooms open onto a secluded garden courtyard.

★ **Oliver's** MODERN NZ $$
(📋 03-449 2805; www.oliverscentralotago.co.nz; 34 Sunderland St; mains lunch $21-26, dinner $26-41; ⊙ restaurant noon-2pm & 6pm-late, bar noon-late) Housed in a gold-rush era general store, this classy complex incorporates a craft brewery, bar and bakery-cafe within its venerable stone walls. The restaurant shifts gears from on-trend cafe fare at lunchtime to a bistro showcasing the best local, seasonal produce in the evenings, with dishes like smoked rabbit and barley risotto or roast lamb rump.

ⓘ Getting There & Away

Catch-a-Bus (📋 03-449 2150; www.trailjourneys.co.nz; ⊙ Oct-Apr) Door-to-door shuttles to/from Cromwell ($25, 20 minutes), Alexandra ($15, 10 minutes), Ranfurly ($43, 1½ hours), Middlemarch ($55, 2½ hours) and Dunedin ($56, 3½ hours) during the main cycling season.

InterCity (📋 03-471 7143; www.intercity.co.nz) Coaches head to/from Dunedin (from $22, three hours), Roxburgh (from $14, 45 minutes), Alexandra (from $10, nine minutes), Cromwell (from $10, 14 minutes) and Queenstown (from $14, 1½ hours).

Cromwell

POP 4150

Cromwell has a charming lakeside historic precinct, a great weekly farmers market and perhaps the South Island's most over-the-top 'big thing' – a selection of giant fruit by the highway, representing the area's extensive fruit-growing industry.

It's also at the very heart of the prestigious Central Otago wine region (www.cowa.org.nz), known for its extraordinarily good pinot noir and, to a lesser extent, riesling, pinot gris and chardonnay. The Cromwell Basin – which stretches from Bannockburn, 5km southwest of Cromwell, to north of Lake Dunstan – accounts for over 70% of Central Otago's total wine production. Pick up the *Central Otago Wine Map* for details of upwards of 50 local wineries.

⊙ Sights

Cromwell Heritage Precinct HISTORIC BUILDING
(www.cromwellheritageprecinct.co.nz; Melmore Tce) When the Clyde Dam was completed in 1992 it flooded Cromwell's historic town centre, 280 homes, six farms and 17 orchards. Many historic buildings were disassembled before the flooding and have since been rebuilt in a pedestrianised precinct beside Lake Dunstan. While some have been set up as period museum pieces (stables and the like), others house a few good cafes, galleries and some interesting shops. In summer the area plays host to an excellent weekly **farmers market** (www.cromwellheritageprecinct.co.nz; ⊙ 9am-1pm Sun).

🏃 Activities & Tours

Highlands Motorsport Park ADVENTURE SPORTS
(📋 03-445 4052; www.highlands.co.nz; cnr SH6 & Sandflat Rd; ⊙ 10am-5pm) Transformed from a paddock into a top-notch 4km racing circuit in just 18 months, this revheads' paradise hosted its first major event in 2013. The action isn't reserved just for the professionals, with various high-octane experiences on offer, along with an excellent museum.

Budding speed freaks can start out on the **go-karts** ($45 per 10 minutes) before taking a 200km/h ride in the **Highlands Taxi** ($129 for up to four people), completing three laps of the circuit as a passenger in a **Porsche GT3** ($295), or having a go at the wheel of a **V8 muscle car** ($395).

If you'd prefer a less racy experience, the **National Motorsport Museum** (adult/child $25/10) showcases racing cars and displays about Kiwi legends such as Bruce McLaren, Possum Bourne, Emma Gilmour and Scott Dixon. Family groups can opt for the **Jurassic Safari Adventure**, a trip in a safari van through a forest inhabited by dinosaurs ($99 per family including museum entry). There's also free **minigolf** and a good cafe.

Goldfields Jet ADVENTURE
(📋 03-445 1038; www.goldfieldsjet.co.nz; SH6; adult/child $115/59; ⊙ 9am-5pm) Zip through the Kawarau Gorge on a 40-minute jetboat ride.

Central Otago Motorcycle Hire TOURS
(📋 03-445 4487; www.comotorcyclehire.co.nz; 271 Bannockburn Rd; per day from $185) The sinuous, hilly roads of Central Otago are perfect for two wheels. This crew hires out motorbikes and advises on improbably scenic routes. It

> **WORTH A TRIP**
>
> ## WINING & DINING IN BANNOCKBURN
>
> **Carrick** (☑ 03-445 3480; www.carrick.co.nz; Cairnmuir Rd, Bannockburn; ☺ 11am-5pm) A dozen or so Bannockburn wineries are open to the public; several offer notable dining. Carrick is one of the best, with an art-filled restaurant opening out on to a terrace and lush lawns, and a view of the Carrick mountains. The seasonal menu (including excellent share platters) is a pleasurable complement to the wine range, which includes an intense, spicy pinot noir – the flagship drop – as well as a toasty chardonnay and citrusy aromatic varietals.
>
> **Mt Difficulty** (☑ 03-445 3445; www.mtdifficulty.co.nz; 73 Felton Rd, Bannockburn; mains $34-39; ☺ tastings 10.30am-4.30pm, restaurant noon-4pm) As well as making our favourite NZ pinot noir, Mt Difficulty is a lovely spot for a leisurely lunch looking down over the valley. There are large wine-friendly platters to share, but save room for the decadent desserts.
>
> **Black Rabbit Kitchen & Bar** (☑ 03-445 1553; 430a Bannockburn Rd, Bannockburn; mains $23-28; ☺ 8am-6pm Sun-Thu, till late Fri & Sat) A welcome addition to the tiny hamlet of Bannockburn, this rustic chic cafe-bar offers great brunches, good coffee, an extensive wine list and a sunny deck on which you can happily while away the afternoon.
>
> **Bannockburn Hotel** (☑ 03-445 0615; www.bannockburnhotel.com; 420 Bannockburn Rd, Bannockburn; mains $22-29; ☺ 4-10pm Tue-Wed, from noon Thu-Sun) A refurbishment has turned this historic watering hole into a stylish modern pub with a tapas-inspired menu and a wine list longer than your arm. It's 5km out of town, but it operates a free courtesy bus.

also offers guided trail-bike tours (from $195) and extended road tours (from $575).

⚡ Festivals & Events

Highlands Festival of Speed SPORTS
(www.highlands.co.nz; ☺ Apr) Two days of classic motor racing, held in early April.

Highlands 101 SPORTS
(www.highlands.co.nz/highlands 501; ☺ Nov) A weekend-long motorsports festival at Highlands Park, culminating in a 101-lap endurance race.

🛏 Sleeping & Eating

Carrick Lodge MOTEL $$
(☑ 03-445 4519; www.carricklodge.co.nz; 10 Barry Ave; units $140-220; P ☎) One of Cromwell's more stylish motels, Carrick has spacious, modern units and is just a short stroll from the main shopping complex. Executive units have spa baths and views over the golf course.

★ Burn Cottage Retreat B&B, COTTAGE $$$
(☑ 03-445 3050; www.burncottageretreat.co.nz; 168 Burn Cottage Rd; cottage $235-265; P ☎) Set among walnut trees and gardens 3km northwest of Cromwell, this peaceful retreat has three luxurious, self-contained cottages with spacious kitchens and modern bathrooms.

Grain & Seed Café CAFE $
(Melmore Tce; meals $10-14; ☺ 9am-4pm) Set in a beautiful stone building that was once Jolly's Grain Store, this cafe serves up tasty

muffins and big, inexpensive meals. Grab an outside table beside the lake for great views.

ⓘ Information

Cromwell i-SITE (☑ 03-445 0212; www.centralotagonz.com; 2d The Mall; ☺ 9am-7pm Jan-Mar, to 5pm Apr-Dec) Stocks the *Walk Cromwell* brochure, covering local cycling and walking trails, including the nearby gold-rush ghost town of Bendigo

ⓘ Getting There & Away

Atomic Shuttles (p145) Daily buses head to/from Queenstown ($15, 1¼ hours), Alexandra ($20, 30 minutes), Roxburgh ($30, 1½ hours), Dunedin ($35, 3½ hours) and Christchurch ($40, 6¼ hours).

Catch-a-Bus (p146) Door-to-door shuttles to Clyde ($25, 20 minutes), Alexandra ($25, 30 minutes), Ranfurly ($52, 1¾ hours), Middlemarch ($59, 2¾ hours) and Dunedin ($60, 3¾ hours) during the main cycling season.

InterCity (p146) Coaches to Queenstown (from $11, one hour, four daily), Fox Glacier (from $44, 6¼ hours, one daily), Christchurch (from $51, 7¼ hours, two daily), Alexandra (from $12, 24 minutes, two daily) and Dunedin (from $22, 3½ hours).

Naked Bus (https://nakedbus.com) Buses from Queenstown (one hour) and Wanaka (45 minutes) stop in Cromwell before continuing to Omarama (1¼ hours), Lake Tekapo (three hours) and Christchurch (7½ hours). Prices vary.

Ritchies (☑ 03-443 9120; www.alpineconnexions.co.nz) Scheduled shuttles to/from Wanaka ($22, 45 minutes), Queenstown Airport ($22, one hour) and Queenstown CBD ($22, 1¼ hours).

Fiordland & Southland

Best Places to Eat

➡ Kepler's (p185)

➡ Batch (p167)

➡ Louie's (p167)

➡ Elegance at 148 on Elles (p167)

➡ Whistling Frog Cafe & Bar (p159)

Best Places to Stay

➡ Te Anau Lodge (p185)

➡ Newhaven Holiday Park (p158)

➡ Southern Comfort Backpackers (p166)

➡ Bushy Point Fernbirds (p166)

Why Go?

Brace yourself for sublime scenery on a breathtaking scale.

Fiordland National Park's mountains, forests and mirror-smooth waters hold visitors in thrall. Framed by kilometre-high cliffs, Milford Sound was clawed away by glaciers over millennia. Leading here is the Milford Hwy, which reveals a magnificent alpine view at every bend. Shying away from attention is Doubtful Sound, the pristine 'place of silence' (which leaves many admiring visitors speechless, too).

From here, a chain of towns characterised by friendliness and fresh seafood is strung along the Southern Scenic Route. The road snakes through Southland to the Catlins, where meadows roll to golden bays and sawtooth cliffs are speckled with dozing seals.

Then there's the end of the line – Stewart Island/Rakiura, an isolated isle home to seafarers and a flock of rare birds, including New Zealand's beloved icon, the kiwi.

When to Go

➡ Visit from December to April for the best chance of settled weather in Fiordland's notoriously fickle climate (although chances are, you'll still see rain!).

➡ Late October to late April is the Great Walks season for the Milford, Kepler, Routeburn and Rakiura Tracks – book in advance if you want to hike these popular routes.

➡ Stewart Island/Rakiura's changeable weather can bring four seasons in a day, at any time of year. But the temperature is mild: winter (June to August) averages around 10°C and summer (December to February) 16.5–18°C, with highs in the mid-20s.

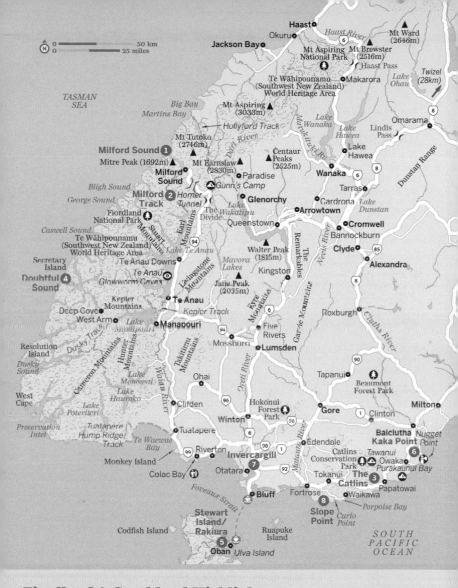

Fiordland & Southland Highlights

1 **Milford Sound** (p190)
Being overwhelmed by your first glimpse of Mitre Peak rising from the fjord's waters.

2 **Milford Track** (p152)
Tramping through a World Heritage wilderness.

3 **Catlins Waterfalls** (p157) Feeling the mist from forest waterfalls on road trips through Owaka and Papatowai.

4 **Doubtful Sound** (p181)
Embracing silence on this remote cruise.

5 **Stewart Island/Rakiura** (p169) Savouring solitude on NZ's 'third island', a haven for bird life.

6 **Kaka Point** (p156)
Squinting at yellow-eyed penguins or watching sea lions on the rock-studded coast.

7 **Invercargill** (p164)
Embracing your inner petrol-head at transport-themed museums before sampling the dining scene.

8 **Slope Point** (p160)
Tramping to sea-ravaged cliffs at the South Island's southernmost point.

DAY TRIPS FROM TE ANAU

MILFORD SOUND

In a country full of 'wow' sights, Milford Sound is perhaps the wow-inducing of all of them. The drive itself is spectacular, along the jaw-droppingly beautiful Milford Hwy. Leave early to beat the tour buses and then take your time to enjoy the many scenic stops on the way back. The must-do experience is a cruise out along the sound.

☆ Best Things to See/Do/Eat

◉ **Mitre Peak** Towering over the entrance to the Sound, this striking mountain is one of the most recognisable sights in all of New Zealand. (p190)

🜚 **Kayaking** Getting out on the water offers one of the best perspectives of Milford Sound. Kayak tours are suitable for total beginners and often include a paddle to the trailhead of the Milford Track for a short walk. (p190)

✖ **Mirror Lakes picnic** With nearly a million visitors a year, you'd think that Milford Sound would be able to muster a half-decent cafe. Instead, have lunch on your boat or pack a picnic to enjoy at this highly scenic spot on the way home. (p187)

☆ How to Get There

Car Fill up with petrol at Te Anau and allow 2½ hours for the drive along the gorgeous Milford Hwy.

Bus Numerous coaches, shuttles and tour buses depart from Te Anau.

DOUBTFUL SOUND

One of NZ's largest fjords, Doubtful Sound is a remarkable juxtaposition of steely, clear waters and towering peaks. It doesn't take much rain for waterfalls to sprout in profusion, some hundreds of metres high.

☆ Best Things to See/Do/Eat

◉ **Remote Wilderness** The mountainous southwest corner of NZ is largely uninhabited and unspoilt, representing a landscape so unique that it has been declared a World Heritage Area. The effort to get here demonstrates how remote a place this really is. A cruise along the fjord reveals a vast expanse of dense, inaccessible forest where humans rarely, if ever, set foot. (p181)

🜚 **Doubtful Sound Kayak** Like with Milford Sound, the majesty of the fjord is even more awe-inspiring from water level. Day paddles are suitable for beginners or pros. (p182)

✖ **The Church** Manapouri has a couple of good eating options, the best of which is this pub-style bistro housed in an old church. (p181)

☆ How to Get There

Car Getting to Doubtful Sound requires a drive to Manapouri, a boat ride across the lake and then a 40-minute bus ride to the edge of the Sound itself.

Bus Plenty of tour buses depart from Te Anau.

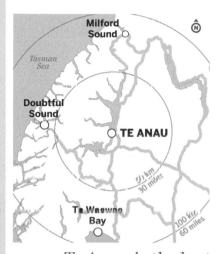

TE WAEWAE BAY

There's a definite ends-of-the-earth feel to this wild bay, where the Southern Alps fall into the ocean and waves roll in from the Antarctic. If it's a scorching hot day the frigid waters here will cool you off quick-smart. Neighbouring Colac Bay is a popular spot for hardy Southland surfers.

☆ Best Things to See/Do/Eat

◉ McCracken's Rest Stop at this wind-battered lookout for extraordinary views of mountains, sand and sea, and keep your eyes peeled for whales and dolphins. Afterwards, take a stroll along the driftwood-strewn beach. (p175)

⚓ Jetboating Get out into the wilderness on a whole-day jetboat tour along the exceedingly remote Wairaurahiri River, departing from Lake Hauroko (reached by 32km of mostly unsealed road; look for the Lillburn Valley Rd turn-off near Clifden). Tours include guided forest walks. (p180)

✗ Orepuki Beach Cafe Down the far end of Te Waewae Bay, set back from Gemstone Beach, this excellent cafe is a surprising find for such an out-of-the-way location. (p175)

☆ How to Get There

Car Te Waewae is due south of Te Anau via SH94 and SH99; allow around 80 minutes for the drive.

Bus Buses aren't practical for a day trip, so you'll need your own car.

Te Anau is the best staging point for trips to unmissable Milford Sound, plus a very good base for visiting neighbouring Doubtful Sound and the south coast.

TRAMPING IN SOUTHLAND

MILFORD TRACK

START GLADE WHARF
END SANDFLY POINT
DURATION 4 DAYS
DISTANCE 53.5KM
DIFFICULTY MODERATE

Routinely touted as 'the finest walk in the world', the Milford is an absolute stunner, complete with rainforest, deep glaciated valleys, a glorious alpine pass surrounded by towering peaks and powerful waterfalls, including the legendary **Sutherland Falls**, one of the loftiest in the world. All these account for its popularity: almost 7500 trampers complete the 54km-long track each summer.

During the Great Walks season (late October to April), you need to book your huts in advance ($70) and the track can only be walked in one direction. Bookings open sometime between February and May and fill up quickly – keep an eye on www.doc.govt.nz/milfordtrack for the online booking date. You must stay at **Clinton Hut** the first night, despite it being only one hour from the start of the track, and you must complete the trip in the prescribed three nights and four days. This is perfectly acceptable if the weather is kind, but when the weather turns sour you'll still have to push on across the alpine **Mackinnon Pass** and may miss some rather spectacular views. It's all down to the luck of the draw.

DOC advises against tackling the Milford Track between early May and late October because of the significant risk of avalanches and floods, and the fact that bridges at risk of avalanche are removed. It's wet, very cold, and snow conceals trail markers. If you're a well-equipped tramping pro considering the Milford Track out of season, get DOC advice on weather conditions. During this low season, huts revert to the 'serviced' category ($15), and restrictions on walking the track in four days are removed.

The track starts at **Glade Wharf**, at the head of Lake Te Anau, accessible by a 1½-hour boat trip from Te Anau Downs, itself 29km from Te Anau on the road to Milford Sound. It finishes at **Sandfly Point**, a 15-minute boat

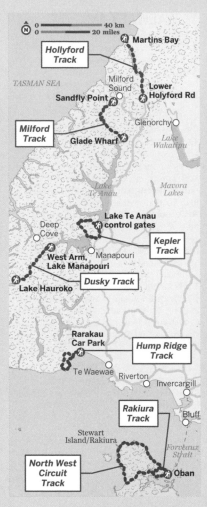

trip from Milford Sound village, from where you can return by road to Te Anau, around two hours away. You will be given options to book this connecting transport online, at the same time as you book your hut tickets.

Tracknet (p186) offers transport from Queenstown and Te Anau to meet the boats at Te Anau Downs and Milford Sound. There

The deep-green deep south, a still-untamed outdoor treasure, is home to some of NZ's most famous tracks including three of its Great Walks.

are other options for transport to and from the track, including a float-plane hop from Te Anau to Glade Wharf with **Wings & Water** (p183). Fiordland i-SITE and the Fiordland National Park Visitor Centre can advise on options to best suit you. **Safer Parking** (☑03-249 7198; www.saferparking.co.nz; 48 Caswell Rd; per day per motorbike/car/motorhome $4/9/10) is a good option for stashing your vehicle while you hike.

An alternative is to book a guided hike package through **Ultimate Hikes** (☑03-450 1940, 0800 659 255; www.ultimatehikes.co.nz; 5-day tramps incl food dm/s/d $2295/3330/5390; ⊙ Nov–mid-Apr) ✐, which includes transfers and private en-suite rooms in comfortable lodges with all meals included.

HOLLYFORD TRACK

START LOWER HOLLYFORD RD
END MARTINS BAY
DURATION 5 DAYS (ONE WAY)
DISTANCE 56.8KM
DIFFICULTY MODERATE

The four- to five-day (each way), 56km Hollyford Track is an easy to moderate tramp through the lower Hollyford – the longest valley in Fiordland National Park – to remote Martins Bay. Track upgrades and improved transport services, combined with the fact that it's a low-level hike achievable year-round (weather permitting), have resulted in more trampers discovering the splendid mountain and lake vistas, forest, extensive bird life and magical coast that make the Hollyford so special. Even so, the track averages only 4000 trampers a year, making it a good option for those in search of solitude.

The track is basically one way (unless combined with the super-challenging 88km Pyke–Big Bay Route). The majority of trampers turn tail and retrace their steps, or fly out from the airstrip at Martins Bay. Allow some time in the bay to view a seal colony and get a sneaky peek at a penguin, if you're lucky. This will more than make up for some of the most demonic sandflies in NZ.

Trampers have the use of six DOC huts on the track, ranging from serviced ($15) to standard ($5). Camping ($5) is permitted next to the huts, although sandflies will prevent this from being remotely enjoyable. Tickets should be obtained in advance.

Tracknet (p186) and **Trips & Tramps** (p183) both run shuttles to the Hollyford trailhead. Nine kilometres (two hours' walk) shy of the trailhead is **Gunn's Camp** (p191), a good bolthole before or after the feat, with car storage available.

Fly Fiordland (☑0800 359 346; www.flyfiordland.com; 52 Town Centre; up to 4 passengers $620) flies between Te Anau and the Martins Bay airstrip.

Ngāi Tahu–owned **Hollyford Track** (☑03-442 3000; www.hollyfordtrack.com; adult/child from $1895/1495; ⊙late Oct–late Apr) ✐ leads small-group (less than 16 people) three-day guided trips on the Hollyford staying at private huts/lodges. The journey is shortened with a jetboat trip down the river and Lake McKerrow on day two, and ends with a scenic flight to Milford Sound.

KEPLER TRACK

START/END LAKE TE ANAU CONTROL
GATES
DURATION 4 DAYS
DISTANCE 60.1KM
DIFFICULTY MODERATE

Opened in 1988, the Kepler is one of NZ's best-planned tracks and now one of its most popular. The route takes the form of a moderately strenuous 60km loop beginning and ending at the Waiau River control gates at the southern end of Lake Te Anau. It features an all-day tramp across the mountaintops taking in incredible panoramas of the lake, the Jackson Peaks and the Kepler Mountains. Along the way it traverses rocky ridges, tussock lands and peaceful beech forest.

The route can be covered in four days, staying in the three huts, although it is possible to reduce the tramp to three days by continuing past Moturau Hut and leaving the track at the **Rainbow Reach swing bridge**.

However, spending a night at **Moturau Hut** on the shore of Lake Manapouri is an ideal way to end this tramp. The track can be walked in either direction, although the most popular is Luxmore–Iris Burn–Moturau.

This is a heavily weather-dependent track at any time of year and the alpine sections require a good level of fitness. Parts of the track may be hazardous or impassible in winter. DOC recommends tackling this route between late October and April – and strongly advises against attempting it between early May and late October.

The Kepler is officially a Great Walk and you must obtain a Great Walk pass for the huts; it pays to book well in advance. In the low season (inadvisable for all but the most experienced NZ trampers) the huts revert to the 'serviced' category. There are campsites at **Brod Bay** and **Iris Burn**.

Conveniently, the track begins under an hour's walk from the **Fiordland National Park Visitor Centre** (p186), via the lakeside track alongside the Manapouri–Te Anau Rd (SH95). There's a car park and shelter near the control gates. **Tracknet** (p186) and **Topline Tours** (p181) both run shuttles to and from both the control gates and Rainbow Reach trailheads.

Kepler Water Taxi (p183) offers morning boat services across Lake Te Anau to Brod Bay, slicing 1½ hours off the first day's tramp.

DUSKY TRACK
START LAKE HAUROKO
END WEST ARM, LAKE MANAPOURI
DURATION 8 TO 10 DAYS
DISTANCE 84KM
DIFFICULTY ADVANCED

This challenging track begins (or ends) on the northern shores of dark, brooding Lake Hauroko, the deepest lake in NZ (462m). An epic journey, it only suits trampers at the top of their game: you'll wobble across three-wire bridges and wade through mud. Book a boat with Tuatapere-based **Lake Hauroko Tours** (☑0800 376 174, 03-225 5677; www.duskytrack.co.nz; track transport $99; ☺Nov-Apr) to access the trailhead (Mondays and Thursdays scheduled, other days by arrangement). **Trips & Tramps** (p183) offers transport ($50 per head) from Te Anau to Clifden Suspension Bridge, 12km north of Tuatapere, timed to meet boats near their launching point for the Dusky Track trailhead.

Ferns on the Hollyford Track (p153)

HUMP RIDGE TRACK
START/END RARAKAU CAR PARK
DURATION 3 DAYS
DISTANCE 62KM
DIFFICULTY MODERATE

This track is rich in natural and cultural history, from coastal and alpine scenery to the relics of a historic timber town. The tramping days are long (up to nine hours on the first two days, ascending 890m on the first) and the terrain suits intermediate-level trampers. There's bird life aplenty, and the chance to see Hector's dolphins on the lonely windswept coast. En route the path crosses a number of towering historic wooden viaducts, including NZ's highest.

To hike the track you need to book through the **Hump Ridge Track Information Centre** (p180). Packages include transport to the trailhead (19km from Tuatapere) and comfortable lodge accommodation. The tramp is possible year-round and operates in three seasonal bands, priced accordingly (from $175), with guided tramps also available. Advance bookings are essential.

Tramping the Kepler Track (p153)

NARUEDOM YAEMPONGSA / SHUTTERSTOCK ©

RAKIURA TRACK

START/END OBAN, STEWART ISLAND
DURATION 3 DAYS
DISTANCE 39KM
DIFFICULTY MODERATE

Another of NZ's Great Walks, the 32km, three-day Rakiura Track is a peaceful and leisurely loop that sidles around beautiful beaches before climbing over a 250m-high forested ridge and traversing the sheltered shores of **Paterson Inlet/Whaka ā Te Wera**. It passes sites of historical interest, including Māori sites and sawmilling relics, and introduces many common sea and forest birds.

Rakiura Track is 32km long, but adding in the road sections at either end bumps it up to 39km, conveniently forming a circuit from Oban. It's a well-defined loop requiring a moderate level of fitness, suitable for tramping year-round. Being a Great Walk, it has been gravelled to eliminate most of the mud for which the island is infamous.

There are two Great Walk huts ($22 to $24) en route, which need to be booked in advance. Camping ($6) is permitted at the 'standard' campsites near the huts, and also at Māori Beach.

NORTH WEST CIRCUIT TRACK

START/END OBAN, STEWART ISLAND
DURATION 9 TO 11 DAYS
DISTANCE 125KM
DIFFICULTY ADVANCED

The North West Circuit Track is Stewart Island/Rakiura's legendary tramp, a demanding coastal epic around a remote coastline featuring isolated beaches, sand dunes, birds galore and miles of mud. It's 125km, and takes nine to 11 days, although there are several options for shortening it involving boats and planes.

There are well-spaced huts along the way, all of which are 'standard' ($5) except for two Great Walk Huts ($22 to $24), which must be booked in advance. A North West Circuit Pass ($35), available at the national park visitor centre, provides for a night in each of the 'standard' huts.

Locator beacons are advised and be sure to call into DOC for up-to-date information and to purchase the essential topographical maps. You should also register your intentions at **AdventureSmart** (www.adventuresmart.org.nz) as this is no easy walk in the park.

THE CATLINS

The Catlins' meandering roads thread together a medley of pretty-as-a-picture landscapes. Bypassed entirely by SH1, this southeasterly swathe of the South Island is a road-tripper's dream. Narrow winding roads weave past golden-sand bays, zip through bucolic meadows and trace boulder-studded coast, while gravelly detours expose you to startled sheep and even more startled farmers. Eventful drives are part of the fun of reaching beauty spots like Roaring Bay, moodily monochromatic Purakaunui Falls (p157) and forlorn Waipapā Lighthouse (p160). But numerous natural stunners – like Lake Wilkie (p159) and Nugget Point – are only a short, flat walk from the car park. Too easy.

Over centuries, semi-nomadic Māori came to the Catlins to make canoes from local timber. In the 19th century, European whalers and sealers arrived (the region is named after a whaling captain). Though increasingly popular with visitors, the sparse Catlins retain a faraway feel – especially when an Antarctic southerly blasts in...

ℹ Information

Get maps and local tips at the small **Owaka Museum & Catlins Information Centre** (p157) and the even smaller **Waikawa Museum &**

ESSENTIAL SOUTHLAND

Eat Bluff oysters, a New Zealand gourmet obsession, followed by Stewart Island salmon, whitebait and blue cod.

Drink Hokonui Moonshine Whisky (p161) in Gore or a sheep's milk flat white at Invercargill's Blue River Dairy (p167).

Read poems by Hone Tuwhare (1922–2008), who drew inspiration from the landscapes of the Catlins.

Listen to roaring surf in Te Waewae, the crackle of static on road trips (radio signal is patchy), and dead silence in Doubtful Sound.

Watch *The World's Fastest Indian* (Roger Donaldson, 2005), to understand Invercargill's devotion to the legacy of Burt Munro.

Go online www.fiordland.org.nz, https://southlandnz.com

Information Centre (☑ 03-246 8464; waikawamuseum@hyper.net.nz; 604 Niagara–Waikawa Rd; museum admission by donation; ☺10am-5pm). En route to the Catlins, you can also grab lots of info from the i-SITEs in Invercargill and **Balclutha** (☑ 03-418 0388; www.cluthanz.com; 4 Clyde St, Balclutha; ☺8.30am-5pm Mon-Fri, 9.30am-3pm Sat & Sun).

For further information, see www.catlins.org.nz and www.catlins-nz.com.

ℹ Getting There & Away

There is no public transport in the Catlins area so you'll need your own vehicle to get around. From Invercargill you can reach the westerly end of the Catlins, Fortrose, on a 45km drive. From Dunedin, it's an 80km drive southwest to Balclutha, the Catlins' easterly gateway town.

Kaka Point & Around

The township might be sedate but the views at Kaka Point, 23km east of Owaka, are among the most mesmerising in the Catlins. The primary draws of this small coastal community are Nugget Point, a remarkable rock-studded peninsular shoreline, and Roaring Bay, where (with good timing) you can spot yellow-eyed penguins (hoiho). A much more common sight are sea lions and fur seals, which you'll see basking on beaches and camouflaging themselves among the rocks.

◉ Sights

★ Nugget Point   NATURAL FEATURE
(off Nugget Point Rd) Reach one of the South Island's most jaw-dropping coastal lookouts via the 900m Nugget Point (Tokatā) walkway. Wave-thrashed cliffs give way abruptly to sapphire waters dotted with toothy islets known as the Nuggets. The track to the lighthouse is dotted with poetic placards, and you can spot seals and sea lions lolling below. Look out for bird life, such as soaring titi (muttonbird) and spoonbills huddling in the lee of the breeze.

It's 9km south of Kaka Point township, just past the Roaring Bay car park.

Roaring Bay   VIEWPOINT
(Nugget Point Rd) Your best chance of spotting rare yellow-eyed penguins (hoiho) is from a hide at Roaring Bay, 8km south of Kaka Point's main drag. The hide is accessible throughout daylight hours but suggested viewing times are posted on a noticeboard at the car park. Penguin behaviour changes

The Catlins

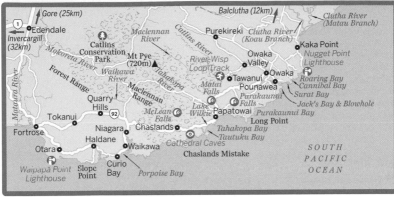

seasonally but times are usually before 7am or after 3pm or 4pm; ask locally or at your guesthouse.

Don't linger outside the hide and obey all warning signs: as you can see, penguins lead a precarious existence. If no penguins waddle into sight, console yourself with the majestic views of cliffs and rolling surf.

Sleeping

Nugget Lodge RENTAL HOUSE $$
(✓03-412 8783; www.nuggetlodge.co.nz; 367 The Nuggets Rd, Kaka Point; units for 1/2 people $140/190, additional person $30; 🛜) It's hard to imagine a lovelier outlook than the one from these two modern units, gazing from a seaside knoll midway between Kaka Point and Nugget Point. One has a balcony, the other a private garden, and if you're lucky you might spy a couple of resident sea lions lolling on the beach below.

Owaka & Around

The Catlins' main town is an ideal base for exploring the region. Ruggedly rocky Kaka Point is 24km east by road, while in the other direction lustrous waterfalls like Purakaunui are a short drive away. Languid Owaka township may be tiny but it has a top-quality museum and a supermarket and petrol station (no vain boast in these parts).

Four kilometres southeast of Owaka town is **Pounawea**, a beautiful hamlet on the edge of the Catlins River Estuary. Just across the inlet is **Surat Bay**, notable for the sea lions that lie around the beach between here and **Cannibal Bay**, an hour's beach-walk away.

Sights

★**Purakaunui Falls** WATERFALL
(Purakaunui Falls Rd) If you only see one waterfall in the Catlins, make it this magnificent cascade down three tiers of jet-black rock. It's an easy 15-minute clamber to reach the falls from the small parking area.

Purakaunui Falls are almost equidistant between Owaka and Papatowai (respectively 15km and 12km by road).

**Owaka Museum &
Catlins Information Centre** MUSEUM
(✓info centre 03-415 8371, museum 03-415 8323; www.owakamuseum.org.nz; 10 Campbell St, Owaka; museum adult/child $5/free; ☺9.30am-4.30pm Mon-Fri, 10am-4pm Sat & Sun) Vaguely canoe-shaped in honour of the town name (Owaka means 'place of the canoe'), this state-of-the-art museum is a pleasant surprise. Salty tales of shipwrecks are well explained in short video presentations, Māori and settler stories grippingly displayed, and an interesting array of artefacts exhibited. It doubles as the main information centre for the Catlins.

Activities

Catlins River–Wisp Loop Track TRAMPING
(www.doc.govt.nz) This 24km loop comprises two 12km sections: the low-level, well-formed Catlins River Walk (five to six hours), and the Wisp Loop Walk (four to five hours), a higher-altitude tramp with a side trip to Rocky Knoll boasting great views and subalpine vegetation.

The routes can be walked in either direction in one long day, divided over two days, or split into shorter sections accessed via various entry/exit points. The main access is via Catlins Valley Road, south of Owaka.

Catlins Horse Riding
HORSE RIDING

(☑ 027 629 2904; www.catlinshorseriding.co.nz; 41 Newhaven Rd, Owaka; 1/2/3hr rides $70/110/150) Explore the idiosyncratic coastline and landscapes on four legs. Learners' treks and the full gallop available, and trips are tailored to your level of experience. Full safety briefing (and glorious coastal views) included. Book ahead. Full-day treks also available (per person $230 to $260).

🛏 Sleeping

★Newhaven Holiday Park
HOLIDAY PARK $

(☑ 03-415 8834; www.newhavenholiday.com; 324 Newhaven Rd, Surat Bay; unpowered/powered sites from $35/40, units from $70, with bathroom from $110; 🐾) This exemplary holiday park has a choice of cabins and self-contained units and bags of camping space set among low hills at the entrance to Surat Bay. Communal bathrooms are improbably fragrant, the kitchen's well equipped and there's a merry village atmosphere throughout. A little footpath leads down to the beach for easy seal-spotting, too.

Split Level
HOSTEL $

(☑ 03-415 8868; www.thesplitlevel.co.nz; 9 Waikawa Rd, Owaka; dm $33, d with/without bathroom $82/74, tr with bathroom $99; 🐾) Very much like staying at a mate's house, this tidy two-level home has a comfortable lounge with a large TV and leather couches, and a well-equipped kitchen. Dorm rooms are spotless and there are en suites for those who want privacy but the perks of a sociable hostel setting.

Pounawea Grove Motel
MOTEL $$

(☑ 03-415 8339; www.pounaweagrove.co.nz; 5 Ocean Grove, Pounawea; d or tw $140; 🐾) More sophisticated than the average motel, Pounawea Grove has a boutique feel thanks to its roomy units with sharp, modern bathrooms and plush textiles. Throw in a warm welcome and the bucolic estuary setting, and a relaxing stay is almost guaranteed.

Kepplestone by the Sea
APARTMENT $$

(☑ 03-415 8134; www.kepplestonebythesea.iowners.net; 9 Surat Bay Rd, Surat Bay; units incl breakfast $120; 🐾) Esther and Jack are your welcoming hosts to these two self-contained cabins, kitted out with every comfort a traveller could require. Each includes a fully equipped kitchen, couches and comfy beds with myriad blankets for the chilly nights, plus a breakfast box for you to self-cater in the morning.

Papatowai & Around

Nature shows off some of her best angles at Papatowai, which is perched at a meeting of forest, sea and the Tahakopa River. The leafy village has barely 40 inhabitants but swells with holidaymakers in summer, drawn by a languid vibe and glittering views of waterfalls and golden bays. Adding to the low-key delight, tracks to beauty spots are easy peasy: Matai or McLean Falls are reached by an easy tramp, and walkers of all levels can idle around lustrous Lake Wilkie.

A couple of days in Papatowai satisfies most visitors. You'll soon find yourself drawn east to gorgeous Purakaunui Falls (along the road to Owaka) and the jagged coast of Kaka Point, or west to the wild surf of Curio Bay.

◉ Sights & Activities

Matai & Horseshoe Falls
WATERFALL

(Papatowai Hwy, Caberfeidh) Two falls for the price of one! A fork in the road leads you, on the left, to the graceful drop of Matai Falls, while stairs to the right bring you to water tumbling down the moss-clad U-shaped wall of Horseshoe Falls. Allow 40 minutes to walk to both waterfalls and back.

The waterfall walkway is signposted off the highway 8km north of Papatowai town.

Lost Gypsy Gallery
GALLERY

(☑ 021 122 8102; www.thelostgypsy.com; 2532 Papatowai Hwy; gallery admission $5; ⊙ 10am-5pm Thu-Tue mid-Oct–Apr) Fashioned from remaindered bits and bobs, artist Blair Somerville's intricately crafted automata are wonderfully irreverent. The bamboozling collection inside a converted bus (free entry) is a teaser for the carnival of creations through the gate (young children not allowed, sorry...). The buzz, bong and bright lights of the organ are bound to tickle your ribs. Espresso caravan and wi-fi on site.

Florence Hill Lookout VIEWPOINT
(Chaslands Hwy) Three kilometres southwest of Papatowai, a short gravel road leads to sweeping Tautuku Bay, which can be viewed from on high at the Florence Hill Lookout. The glow isn't your imagination, it's the quartz content of the sand.

Lake Wilkie Walkway WALKING
(Chaslands Hwy) It's well worth a half-hour walk to see this dazzling mirror lake, created during an ice age. Moss-scented pathways are lined with panels explaining the lake's ecosystem, and boardwalks take you right onto the water. If you're pressed for time but want a photo, it's a 10-minute return walk to a lookout over the water.

The walkway is signposted off the highway, less than 5km southwest of Papatowai.

Cathedral Caves CAVE
(www.cathedralcaves.co.nz; 1069 Chaslands Hwy; adult/child $5/1; ☺Nov-May) Cutting back into cliffs right on the beach, the huge, arched Cathedral Caves were carved out of the limestone by 160 million years of waves. Named for their acoustic properties, they are only accessible for two hours at either side of low tide (tide timetables are posted on the website, at the highway turn-off and at visitor information centres) – and even then they can be closed at short notice if the conditions are deemed dangerous.

If you're happy to wade, you can walk in one entrance and out the other.

From SH92 it's 2km to the car park, then a peaceful 15-minute forest walk down to the beach and a further 25 minutes on foot to the caves.

McLean Falls WATERFALL
(off Rewcastle Rd, Chaslands) A lovely walk along wooden walkways and fern-fringed tracks brings you to the attractive McLean Falls, named for an early 20th-century settler renowned for his sheep-shearing abilities. Allow 40 minutes to walk to the falls and back.

DON'T MISS

SOUTHERN SCENIC ROUTE

The Southern Scenic Route skirts lonesome beaches, forest-clad lakes and awe-inspiring lookout points, cutting a lazy arc from Queenstown to Te Anau, Manapouri, Tuatapere, Riverton and Invercargill. From Invercargill it continues east and then north through the Catlins to Dunedin. Yes, there are more direct routes than this 610km meander, but we can't think of a better excuse to dawdle through the South Island. See www.southernscenicroute.co.nz or pick up the free *Southern Scenic Route* map to join all the dots.

🛏 Sleeping & Eating

Hilltop LODGE $
(☑03-415 8028; 77 Tahakopa Valley Rd, Papatowai; d with/without bathroom $110/100) High on a hill 1.5km out of town, with native forest at the back door and surrounded by a sheep farm, these two shipshape cottages command spectacular views of the Tahakopa Valley and coast. Rent by the room or the whole house; the en suite double is the pick of a very nice bunch.

Catlins Kiwi Holiday Park HOLIDAY PARK $$
(Whistling Frog Holiday Resort; ☑03-415 8338; www.catlinskiwiholidaypark.com; 9 Rewcastle Rd, Chaslands; sites from $46, units with/without bathroom from $165/110; ☏) This modern holiday park offers personality-packed accommodation ranging from cute cabins to smart family motels. Tenters share good communal amenities with the 'Kiwiana' cabins.

★ Mohua Park COTTAGE $$$
(☑03-415 8613; www.catlinsmohuapark.co.nz; 744 Catlins Valley Rd, Tawanui; cottages $225; ☏) 🗲 Situated on the edge of a peaceful 14-hectare nature reserve (7km off the highway), these four spacious self-contained cottages offer peace, quiet and privacy. Instead of TV, you'll watch birds flitting through the forest on your doorstep and sigh at views of rolling hills.

★ Whistling Frog Cafe & Bar CAFE $$
(☑03-415 8338; www.whistlingfrogcafe.com; 9 Rewcastle Rd, Chaslands; mains $18-23; ☺8.30am-9.30pm Nov-Mar, 10am-6pm Apr-Oct; ☏) Colourful and fun, the Frog is the best dining option in the Catlins, offering craft beer on tap and crowd-pleasing meals,

NIAGARA FALLS

Located in a former Victorian school-house, this excellent **cafe** (☑ 03-246 8577; www.niagarafallscafe.co.nz; 256 Niagara–Waikawa Rd, Niagara; mains $14-22; ⏱ 11am-late Dec-Mar, to 4pm Thu-Mon Apr-Nov; 📶 ♿) puts the emphasis on local produce. Free-range eggs, Stewart Island salmon and tasty lamb burgers feature on the fulsome menu (usually with a serve of homegrown vegetables), while sticky date puddings and exceptional brownies beckon from the dessert board.

often garnished with flowers from the garden. We're talking seafood chowder, wood-fired pizza, gourmet burgers, craft-beer-battered blue cod, and vegie feeds like risotto and big salads. Excellent coffee and breakfast spreads, too. Ribbit!

Curio Bay & Around

Chasing sun and surf, droves of holiday-makers descend on Curio Bay in summer. For beach-lovers the focal point is Porpoise Bay, a reliably wave-lashed arc of sand and arguably the best swimming beach in the Catlins. Blue penguins nest in the dunes and in summer (December to February) Hector's dolphins come here to rear their young.

Nearby, other natural curiosities merit a visit: a Jurassic-age forest lies just south in Curio Bay while 15km west is the trailhead for a short walk to Slope Point, South Island's most southerly point.

Curio Bay is whisper-quiet in winter (June to August). Regardless of the season, it's handy to bring food provisions and a full tank of fuel along this sparse stretch of coast.

◎ Sights & Activities

★ Slope Point   LANDMARK
(Slope Point Rd, Haldane) South Island's true southerly point lies not in Bluff, as many mistakenly believe, but at the end of a 20-minute tramp through cliff-side meadows. From the trailhead, walk towards the sea and veer left along the fencing; a humble signpost marks this spectacular spot where blackened rocks tumble into turquoise sea while waves smash and swirl below.

Petrified Forest   NATURAL FEATURE
(Curio Bay) Marvel at the rare phenomenon of fossilised forest, extending south of Curio Bay. Preserved by silica in the ashy floodwaters that submerged these Jurassic-era trees, craggy stumps create a dramatic contrast with the frothing waves. The petrified forest is visible for around four hours either side of low tide.

Yellow-eyed penguins waddle ashore here an hour or so before sunset. Do the right thing and keep your distance.

Waipapā Lighthouse   LIGHTHOUSE
(Waipapā Lighthouse Rd, Otara) **FREE** Standing on a desolate but beautiful point surrounded by farmland, this 13.4m-high lighthouse was built after the SS *Tararua* disaster, an 1881 shipwreck that claimed 131 lives. The lighthouse was built three years later, to avert future tragedy on these rocky shores. The beach below is home to fur seals and sea lions (keep a safe distance). The turn-off to Waipapā Point is at Otara, 12km south-east of Fortrose.

Fortrose Cliffs   NATURAL FEATURE
(Fortrose) For those who appreciate stomach-flutteringly steep lookout points, the Fortrose Cliffs are a worthy photo-op on a drive between Invercargill and the Catlins. They're 2km south of Fortrose township.

Catlins Surf   SURFING
(☑ 03-246 8552; www.catlins-surf.co.nz; 601 Curio Bay Rd; 2hr lesson $60, full gear hire per 3½hr/day $45/65) Based at the Curio Bay Holiday Park, this surf school offers lessons on Porpoise Bay, much to the amusement of any passing dolphins. If you're already confident on the waves, you can hire a board, wet suit (very necessary) and flippers. Owner Nick also offers stand-up paddle boarding tuition ($75, 2½ hours).

🛏 Sleeping

Slope Point Accommodation   GUESTHOUSE $
(☑ 03-246 8420; www.slopepoint.co.nz; 164 Slope Point Rd, Slope Point; tent sites from $15, powered sites $30, d with/without bathroom $90/50; 📶) In the midst of a working farm 4km north of Slope Point, this family-run accommodation plunges you into the rhythms of rural life: calf-feeding time, scampering pets, and kids eager to introduce you to their favourite lamb. Double rooms and self-contained units are cosy and modern, while grassy

tent pitches and gravel campervan sites will satisfy campers.

Lazy Dolphin Lodge   HOSTEL $
(☑03-246 8579; www.lazydolphinlodge.co.nz; 529 Curio Bay Rd; dm/r without bathroom $40/90; @🛜) This perfect hybrid of seaside holiday home and hostel has light-filled bedrooms sporting cheerful linen. There are two kitchens and lounges, but you'll want to hang out upstairs on the deck overlooking Porpoise Bay. A path at the rear of the property leads directly to the beach.

Curio Bay Accommodation   APARTMENT $$
(☑03-246 8797; www.curiobay.co.nz; 521a Curio Bay Rd; apt from $190) Three plush units are on offer here – one apartment attached to the hosts' house, and two similar units down the road. All are self-contained, decorated in rustic, beachy style, with big windows and sun-drenched decks right next to the beach. There's also an old-fashioned Kiwi bach, sleeping up to six people.

❶ Getting There & Away

There is no public transport to Curio Bay. The area's western entry point is Fortrose, a 45km drive east from Invercargill; the eastern end of the region is its focal point, Curio and Porpoise Bays, 4km south of Waikawa. A 9km section of the road between Haldane and Curio Bay is unsealed.

CENTRAL SOUTHLAND

Sandwiched between world-famous Fiordland National Park and the scene-stealing Catlins, Central Southland is often forgotten about by travellers. But its peaceful farmland and savage coast form a memorable contrast, while its seam of small-town quirk is heaps of fun.

There's Gore, with a proud history of moonshine distilling; oyster-mad Bluff; and Tuatapere, as famous for challenging tramping trails as it is for sausages. Invercargill, the closest thing to a city slicker in Central Southland, has a long-standing revhead culture and a slew of impressive museums dedicated to classic cars, fast bikes and big diggers. Confused? This is a region where departing from the beaten track is inevitable and going local reaps big rewards.

Gore

POP 12,033

Gore struts to its own beat. The town declares itself New Zealand's 'home of country music', and when it isn't strumming its way through the **Gold Guitar Awards** (www.gold guitars.co.nz; ⊙ early Jun) it celebrates moonshine-distilling history, vintage aircraft and local art with a trio of distinctive museums. If small-town quirk plucks at your heart (or guitar) strings, Gore makes a crowd-pleasing stopover between Fiordland and the Catlins (66km northeast of Invercargill).

⦿ Sights & Activities

Eastern Southland Gallery   GALLERY
(☑03-208 9907; www.facebook.com/eastern southlandgallery; 14 Hokonui Dr; ⊙10am-4.30pm Mon-Fri, 1-4pm Sat & Sun) **FREE** Nicknamed the 'Goreggenheim', this gallery has an impressive treasury of contemporary New Zealand art, including a large Ralph Hotere collection, as well as fascinating indigenous folk art from West Africa and Australia. It's worth breaking up a road trip in Gore purely to step inside this attractive brick building; allow an hour to sidle between hefty Congolese statues, Ivory Coast masks and uplifting temporary exhibitions of local art.

Hokonui Heritage Centre   MUSEUM
(☑03-208 7032; 16 Hokonui Dr; ⊙8.30am-5pm Mon-Fri, 9.30am-4pm Sat, 1-4pm Sun) **FREE** The Hokonui Heritage Centre incorporates the Gore Visitor Centre, the Gore Historical Museum and the **Hokonui Moonshine Museum** (☑03-208 9907; www.hokonuiwhiskey.com; adult/child $5/free). Together they celebrate

---

SOUTHLAND MUST-EATS

Bluff oysters Succulent bivalves are eaten with gusto from late March to late August.

Wild Fiordland venison Far-roaming game scoffed as steaks, sausages and pies.

Stewart Island salmon Mouthwatering smoked fish from the ends of the Earth.

Southland cheese roll White bread oozing melted cheese; toasted then gobbled quickly.

Swedes Southland claims to grow the sweetest root vegies in NZ.

VENTURA / SHUTTERSTOCK ©

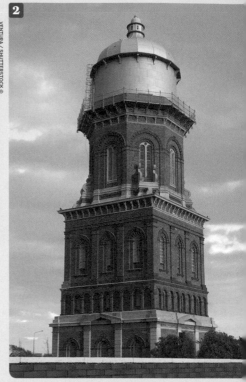

1. Cardrona Hotel (p234), Cardrona
New Zealand's most photographed pub is a gold-rush relic from 1863 with a palpable sense of history.

2. Water Tower (p164), Invercargill
At almost 43m high, this is perhaps Invercargill's most recognisable landmark.

3. Milford Sound (p190)
Glacier-carved cliffs meet indigo water at this spectacular natural attraction.

4. Kepler Track (p183)
This four-day tramp is one of NZ's best-planned and most popular. .

the town's proud history of fishing, farming and illegal distilleries.

The historical museum exhibits a more-intriguing-than-average collection, ranging from a taxidermied mollymawk bird to grandfather clocks and sparkling antiques, alongside tender homages to local passions such as angling and country music.

✖ Eating

Thomas Green   GASTROPUB $$

(☑ 03-208 9295; www.thethomasgreen.co.nz; cnr SH94 & Medway St; mains $16-36; ☺ 10am-11pm) Set in a restored 1906 building, modish Thomas Green is a cut above the average gastropub. It's named after the 'father of Gore', a jack-of-all-trades industrialist who helped build up the town. The menu is refined rather than rugged: medium-rare lamb strip loin, plum-stuffed chicken, and a choice of classy desserts.

❶ Getting There & Away

Gore is a 66km drive northeast of Invercargill. Most buses on the Te Anau–Dunedin–Christchurch, Invercargill–Queenstown and Invercargill–Dunedin routes stop in Gore.

Invercargill

POP 51,700

Don't underestimate Invercargill. Sure, it usually serves as a pit stop between Fiordland and the Catlins (or en route to Stewart Island/Rakiura), but its combination of motor-sport mania, historic buildings and friendly folk might win you over.

Invercargill has long been a revhead's heaven, thanks in part to local legend Burt Munro, who claimed an overland speed world record by motorcycle, but now there's a trio of motoring museums and attractions. A craft brewery and a scattering of good restaurants might also lengthen your stay in this slow-burner of a city.

❂ Sights

The streets of Invercargill are home to many 19th-century buildings. Eighteen landmarks are described in the *Invercargill Heritage Trail* brochure while the *Short Walks* brochure details various walks in and around the town; get both from the i-SITE (p168).

★ Bill Richardson Transport World   MUSEUM

(☑ 03-217 0199; www.transportworld.co.nz; 491 Tay St; adult/child $25/15; ☺ 10am-5pm; ❶) A king-

dom of shiny chrome lies beyond the doors of Transport World, touted as the largest private automotive museum on the planet. Across 15,000 sq metres of warehouse space you'll find classic cars, hulking tractors and vintage petrol pumps (even the bathrooms are on theme). Kids' play areas, a miniature movie theatre, displays of fashions of yesteryear and a great cafe round out Transport World as a crowd-pleaser, rather than just one for the petrol-heads.

Revved up for more? Smaller museum **Classic Motorcycle Mecca** (Map p165; ☑ 03-217 0199; www.transportworld.co.nz; 25 Tay St; adult/child $20/10; ☺ 10am-5pm) holds a collection of bikes, while Dig This (p166) puts you behind the controls of a bulldozer to dig ditches and stack tyres.

A 'Turbo Pass' (adult/child $40/20) grants access to both Transport World and Classic Motorcycle Mecca.

Water Tower   LANDMARK

(Map p165; Queens Dr) Built in 1889, this elegant brick-clad structure resembles a lighthouse more than it does a water tower. Almost 43m high, it was built to supply the city with ready water in the event of a fire.

Though it's Invercargill's most recognisable landmark, visits inside are off-limits for the foreseeable future because of safety concerns.

Queens Park   PARK

(Map p165; Gala St; ❶) Half-wild, half-tamed Queens Park encompasses a whopping 80 hectares, with various gardens themed from Japanese to native NZ plant life. There are also ponds, playgrounds, farm animals, aviaries and attractive landmarks to linger by, including a rotunda and 'Wonderland Castle'.

Southland Museum & Art Gallery   MUSEUM

(Map p165; ☑ 03-219 9069; www.southlandmuseum. com; Queens Park, 108 Gala St; ☺ 9am-5pm Mon-Fri, from 10am Sat & Sun) FREE Adjoining the local visitor centre in a big white pyramid (flashes of the Louvre?), Invercargill's cultural hub has permanent displays on Southland's natural and human history, recounting plenty of maritime exploits. The museum's rock stars are undoubtedly the tuatara, NZ's unique lizard-like reptiles, unchanged for 220 million years. Slow-moving patriarch Henry, more than 110 years old, holds a world record for living in captivity for more than 46 years.

Invercargill Brewery   BREWERY

(Map p165; ☑ 03-214 5070; www.invercargillbrew ery.co.nz; 72 Leet St; tours per person $25; ☺ 10am-

Invercargill

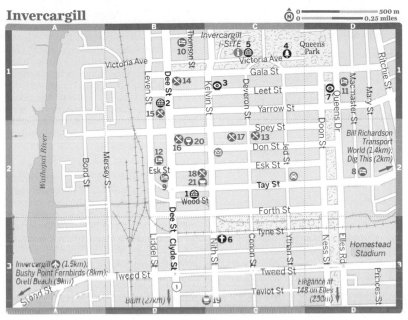

Invercargill

◉ Sights

🛏 Sleeping

⊗ Eating

☻ Drinking & Nightlife

6pm Mon-Sat) Helmed by a former rugby pro, Invercargill Brewery has grown from a passion project into Southland's best brewery. Rock up for a 45-minute tour at 1pm on weekdays (including tastings) or to stock up on wheat beer, honey pilsner or cider at the bottle shop. Our favourites are the crisp B.man Pilsner and the chocolatey Pitch Black stout.

E Hayes & Sons MUSEUM
(Map p165; ☎03-218 2059; www.ehayes.co.nz; 168 Dee St; ⊙7.30am-5.30pm Mon-Fri, 10am-4pm Sat & Sun) FREE Hardware shops aren't usually a must-see, but this one holds a piece of motoring history. In among the aisles of bolts, barbecues and brooms in this classic art-deco building are more than 100 items of motoring memorabilia, including the actual motorbike on which the late Burt Munro broke the world speed record (as immortalised in the 2005 film *The World's Fastest Indian*, starring Sir Anthony Hopkins).

St Mary's Basilica BASILICA
(Map p165; ☎03-218 4123; 65 Tyne St; ⊙8am-5pm) This broad-domed Roman Catholic basilica, open since 1905, is one of Invercargill's most elegant landmarks, and a standout

against the low-rise skyline. It's worth peeping inside to admire design features such as the intricate rose window.

Anderson Park PARK
(www.invercargillpublicartgallery.nz/the-house; McIvor Rd, Waikiwi; ☺ gardens 8am-dusk; 🖭) Stretching over 24 hectares, this beautiful park includes landscaped gardens fringed by an expanse of native bush, plus a children's playground and duck pond. Sadly the centrepiece, an elegant 1925 Georgian-style mansion, is off-limits to visitors while it undergoes earthquake-strengthening work.

🏃 Activities

Oreti Beach, 10km to the southwest of town, invites brisk walks and bike rides along its 26km stretch of sand. **Sandy Point**, which buts out on to the Oreti River, is good terrain for bird-watchers.

Dig This AMUSEMENT PARK
(☑ 03-217 0199; www.transportworld.co.nz; 84 Otepuni Ave; ☺ 9am-6pm Wed-Sun; 🖭) Want to commandeer industrial machinery to crush cars, dig ditches and flip tyres? Of course you do! This hands-on offshoot of Bill Richardson Transport World (p164) puts you behind the controls of bulldozers and excavators. Smashing up a vehicle costs $180, and kids aged 4 and up can take a turn operating big machines from $20 (don't worry, it's supervised).

🛏 Sleeping

★ **Southern Comfort Backpackers** HOSTEL $
(Map p165; ☑ 03-218 3838; www.southerncomfortbackpackers.com; 30 Thomson St, Avenal; dm/d from $32/72; 🖭) With a mix of snug and swish, this large Victorian house has a lounge with fireplace, fully equipped kitchen and peaceful gardens. Adding to the perks are two free bikes, laundry and a herb garden where you can pluck your own garnish. A restful package, just five minutes' walk from town.

Invercargill Top 10 HOLIDAY PARK $
(☑ 0800 486 873, 03-215 9032; www.invercargilltop10.co.nz; 77 McIvor Rd, Waikiwi; campervan sites from $42, units $105, d without bathroom $80; 🖭) 🖉 You know what to expect from this well-run holiday park chain: backpacker dorms, modern motels and plenty of grassy camping space, always with well-tended communal kitchens, laundry facilities and lounges. It's 6.5km north of town.

★ **Bushy Point Fernbirds** B&B $$
(☑ 03-213 1302; www.fernbirds.co.nz; 197 Grant Rd, Otatara; s/d incl breakfast $160/170) 🖉 A haven for the ornithologically inclined, this 25-year-old guesthouse is tucked into a private forest and wetland reserve. Rates include a guided walk between 600-year-old trees with the affable hosts, who point out bird life (including fernbirds, of course) along the way. Fernbirds only hosts one group at a time, lending this ecofriendly hideaway an exclusive air. Advance bookings only.

Bella Vista MOTEL $$
(Map p165; ☑ 03-217 9799; www.bellavista.co.nz; 240 Tay St; units from $125; 🖭) Friendly hosts, reasonable prices and tidy, well-equipped units put this modern, two-level place near the top of Invercargill's competitive motel pack. Units range from cosy studios with tea- and toast-making facilities to two-bedroom apartments with full kitchens (from $165).

Continental breakfast costs an extra $13.50 per person.

Victoria Railway Hotel HOTEL $$
(Map p165; ☑ 03-218 1281, 0800 777 557; www.hotelinvercargill.com; cnr Leven & Esk Sts; r $145-195; 🖭) This beautifully restored 1896 building is awash with nostalgia. With old portraits and an old-fashioned bar, the dining area feels like a snapshot of more genteel times, amplified by kind, personalised service. The 11 rooms aren't as stately as the common areas, though comfy beds, crimson drapes and sloped ceilings are refined enough to encourage dreams of a grander past.

Tower Lodge Motel MOTEL $$
(Map p165; ☑ 03-217 6729; www.towerlodgemotel.co.nz; 119 Queens Dr; units from $130; 🖭) 🖉 Across a busy road from Invercargill's ornate Victorian water tower, units at this crowd-pleasing motel have nicely furnished kitchens and bathrooms, and two-thirds of them have a spa bath. Two-bedroom units also feature roomy dining areas (our fave is number 18 for its direct water-tower views).

Quest Apartments APARTMENT $$$
(Map p165; ☑ 03-211 3966; www.questapartments.co.nz; 10 Dee St; apt $144-269; 🖭) The vibe is business more than pleasure, but serviced apartments from this accommodation chain have perfectly kitted-out studios and apartments (good cotton bedsheets, trim kitchens, modern bathrooms) within easy walking distance of Dee Street's food and drink scene. A

sweet, central choice for a city break, especially if you don't have your own car.

Eating

Seriously Good Chocolate Company CAFE $
(Map p165; ☑03-218 8060; www.seriously goodchocolate.nz; 147 Spey St; cheese rolls $4.80; ☺8am-4.30pm Mon-Fri, 9.30am-1.30pm Sat) Pick up logs of rocky road, salted caramel nibbles and bacon-flavoured chocolate at this sweet little cafe, which prides itself on featuring local ingredients and flavours. It's as good for edible gifts as it is for a breakfast of espresso and egg-and-bacon pie.

Colonial Bakery BAKERY $
(Map p165; ☑03-218 2376; 25a Gala St; pies $4.70; ☺7am-5pm Tue-Fri, 7.30am-3pm Sat) Chipper service and buttery pastry characterise this grab-and-go bakery. Homemade pies steal the show, with classic steak-and-kidney sitting temptingly next to chicken, Camembert and cranberry pies. Euro-goods such as baguettes, croissants and seedy Swiss-style breads nudge their way into a line of Kiwi classics, including the Southland cheese roll

★ Batch CAFE $$
(Map p165; ☑03-214 6357; 173 Spey St; mains $13-20; ☺7am-4pm Mon-Fri, from 8am Sat & Sun; 🖵🍴) Large shared tables, a relaxed beachy ambience, and top-notch coffee and smoothies give this cafe its reputation as Southland's best. Delicious counter food includes bagels, generously crammed rolls, cheese scones and great salads, along with full-blown brunches and cakes that are little works of art. There's a smallish wine and beer list, too.

★ Louie's MODERN NZ $$
(Map p165; ☑03-214 2913; www.facebook.com/pg/LouiesRestaurant; 142 Dee St; tapas $13-16, mains $29-32; ☺5.30pm-late Wed-Sat) Part tapas and cocktail bar, part chic fusion eatery, Louie's is a great place to while away an evening, snuggled into a sofa or a fireside nook. The seasonally changing menu veers from creative tapas (venison tacos, muttonbird, mussels with lime and chilli) to more substantial mains. Slow-cooked pork, locally sourced blue cod, magnificent steaks...you can't go wrong.

Rocks MODERN NZ $$
(Map p165; ☑03-218 7597; www.shop5rocks.com; Courtville Pl, 101 Dee St; mains lunch $18-23, dinner $28-41; ☺10am-2pm & 5pm-late Tue-Fri, 11am-2pm & 5pm-late Sat; 🖵) Tucked away in a shopping arcade, this reliable bistro with chirpy service plates up popcorn squid, slow-roasted

pork with fennel, and a smattering of Italian-inspired pasta and risotto dishes. Caramel croissants and orange-liqueur-poached pears with blue cheese feature on the attention-grabbing dessert menu.

Suzie Q TAPAS $$
(Map p165; ☑03-218 8322; www.suzieq.co.nz; 16 Kelvin St; tapas $9-22, set menus $38-49; ☺5.30-10.30pm Tue-Sun) Pretty ceramics, a warm terracotta colour scheme and a European soundtrack establish Suzie's Iberian tone. The wine list is Kiwi-dominated with a few splashes of Spain, while the formidable food menu of sharing plates mixes Europe and Asia with aplomb: pork *bao*, venison in port, and Israeli salad. We liked the wholesomely crunchy polenta bites and chorizo-crumbed scallops.

Elegance at 148 on Elles FRENCH, BRITISH $$$
(☑03-216 1000; 148 Elles Rd, Georgetown; mains $28-38; ☺6-11pm Mon-Sat) Welcome to 1984, and we mean that in a completely affectionate way. Elegance is the sort of old fashioned, up market, regional restaurant where the menu is vaguely French, vaguely British, and you can be guaranteed of a perfectly cooked piece of venison served on a bed of creamy mash.

🍷 Drinking & Nightlife

Blue River Dairy CAFE
(Map p165; ☑03-211 5150; www.blueriverdairy. co.nz; 111 Nith St; ☺10am-2pm Tue-Sat) Only sheep's milk could make an expertly poured flat white even silkier. Also on sale at this pocket-sized dairy shop and cafe are cheeses, including tangy cheddar and tasty halloumi, all made from Southland sheep's milk.

Zookeepers Cafe CAFE
(Map p165; ☑03-218 3373; www.facebook.com/pg/zookeeperscafe; 50 Tay St; ☺7am-10pm Tue-Sat, to 5pm Sun, to 8pm Mon) Parrot-design sofas and flying swordfish provide the distinctive animal-themed backdrop to this Invercargill institution. Stop by in the daytime for coffee and a satisfying menu of Caesar salads and BLTs, or for the open-mic night each Thursday at 7.30pm.

Tillermans Music Lounge BAR, CLUB
(Map p165; ☑03-218 9240; www.facebook.com/tillermans.invercargill; 16 Don St; ☺11pm-3.30am Fri & Sat) The saviour of Southland's live-music scene, Mr Tillerman's venue hosts everything from thrash to flash, with a battered old dance floor to show for it. Visit the fun downstairs Vinyl Bar, which is open from 8pm, to find out what's coming up.

ℹ Information

Invercargill i-SITE (Map p165; ☑ 03-211 0895; www.invercargillnz.com; Queens Park, 108 Gala St; ⊙ 8.30am-5pm Mon-Fri, to 4pm Sat & Sun) Sharing the Southland Museum pyramid, the i-SITE can help with general enquiries and is a godsend if you're stuck for Stewart Island/Rakiura or Catlins accommodation options.

ℹ Getting There & Away

AIR

Air New Zealand (www.airnewzealand.com) Flights link Invercargill to Christchurch (from $159) and Wellington (from $208) multiple times per day.

Stewart Island Flights (☑ 03-218 9129; www. stewartislandflights.com) Connects Invercargill to Stewart Island/Rakiura three times a day year-round.

BUS

Buses leave from the **Invercargill i-SITE** (p168), where you can also book your tickets.

Catch-a-Bus South (☑ 03-214 4014, 24hr 027 449 7994; www.catchabussouth.co.nz) Offers scheduled shuttle services at least daily to Bluff ($22, 35 minutes), Queenstown and Queenstown Airport ($60, 3–3¼ hours), Gore ($28, 1½ hours) and Dunedin ($57 to $60, 3½ hours). Bookings essential; reserve by 4pm on the day before you travel.

InterCity (☑ Dunedin 03-471 7143; www.inter city.co.nz) Direct coaches to and from Gore ($1 to $13, one hour, two daily), Queenstown Airport ($49, 3½ hours, daily) and Queenstown (from $38, 3¾ hours, daily).

Naked Bus (https://nakedbus.com) Twice daily buses to and from Gore ($1 to $13, 50 minutes, two daily), Dunedin (from $24, 3½ hours) and Queenstown (from $35, 3¾ hours).

ℹ Getting Around

Invercargill Airport (☑ 03-218 6920; www. invercargillairport.co.nz; 106 Airport Ave) is 3km west of central Invercargill. The door-to-door **Executive Car Service** (☑ 03-214 3434; https://executivecarservice.co.nz) costs around $15 from the city centre; more for residential pick-up. By taxi it's around $20; try **Blue Star Taxis** (Map p165; ☑ 03-217 7777; www.bluestartaxis.co.nz; 158 Tay St).

Bluff

POP 1794

Mention Bluff to any New Zealander and we bet they'll think of oysters. Bluff is Invercargill's port, windswept and more than a little bleak, located at the end of a protruding strip of land, 27km south of the city. Bluff's bulging bivalves are among the South Island's most prized produce, guzzled with gusto between March and August, and feted with a festival (p169) in May.

Outside oyster season, the main reason folk come here is to catch the ferry to Stewart Island/Rakiura, catch some maritime nostalgia at the museum, or pose for photos beside the Stirling Point signpost.

◉ Sights

Bluff Maritime Museum   MUSEUM
(☑ 03-212 7534; 241 Foreshore Rd; adult/child $3/1; ⊙ 10am-3.30pm Mon-Fri year-round, plus 12.30-4.30pm Sat & Sun Oct-Apr; ♿) Salty tales whisper from the portholes, driftwood and barnacle-clung planks displayed at Bluff's small museum. The best part is clambering aboard the *Monica* and posing at the control of this 1909 oystering ship, though steam and pump engines (which clank to action at the touch of a button) come a close second.

The museum also houses interesting displays on Bluff history and on the annual titi (muttonbird) harvest, an important tradition for local Māori.

Bluff Hill   HILL
(Flagstaff Rd) A steep sealed road leads up to the top of 265m Bluff Hill (Motupōhue), where a path spirals up to a lookout. Various walking tracks head up here, including the Foveaux Walkway to Stirling Point and Ocean Beach. If the wind isn't threatening to sweep you off your feet, stop to read the information panels along the way.

Stirling Point   LANDMARK
(off SH1) Posing for a photo beside the Stirling Point signpost is a quintessential Bluff experience. Distances to Wellington, London and New York are indicated by the many-branched sign, though the oft-quoted myth that this is the southernmost point of the South Island has no basis in fact. But let's not let such details get in the way of a glorious sea view.

✖ Eating

Oyster Cove   SEAFOOD $$
(☑ 03-212 8855; www.oystercove.co.nz; 8 Ward Pde; half-dozen oysters $39, mains $18-40; ⊙ 11am-7.30pm; ☎) Floor-to-ceiling windows offer spectacular sea views from this swish restaurant by Stirling Point's signpost. Renowned Bluff oysters and Stewart Island mussels dressed in coconut grace a menu

saltier than the view (with a few lamb and salad options too). Pricey but worth it.

ⓘ Getting There & Away

Catch-a-Bus South (☑ 03-479 9960; www.catchabussouth.co.nz) Offers scheduled shuttle services to Invercargill ($22, 30 minutes, four daily), Gore ($44, two hours, one or two daily) and Dunedin ($75, four hours, one or two daily). With prior notice, daily buses from Invercargill to Queenstown Airport ($75, 3½ hours) and Queenstown ($70, 3¾ hours) can include pick-up in Bluff.

Stewart Island Experience (☑ 03-212 7660; www.stewartislandexperience.co.nz) Runs a shuttle between Bluff and Invercargill connecting with its Stewart Island/Rakiura ferry. Transfers from Te Anau and Queenstown to Bluff are available from late October to late April. It also offers secure vehicle storage by the ferry terminal ($10 for 24 hours).

Stewart Island (Rakiura)

POP 378

If you make the short but extremely rewarding trip to Stewart Island/Rakiura you'll have one up on most New Zealanders, many of whom maintain a curiosity about the country's 'third island' without ever going there.

Travellers who make the effort are rewarded with a warm welcome from both the local Kiwis and the local kiwi. This is arguably the best place to spy the country's shy, feathered icon in the wild. Don't be surprised if the close-knit community of islanders quickly knows who you are – especially if you mingle over a beer at NZ's southernmost pub in **Oban**, the island's only settlement.

Stewart Island/Rakiura offers plenty of outdoor adventures including kayaking and tramping. A major impetus for such excursions is bird life. The island is a bird sanctuary of international repute, and even amateur spotters will be distracted by the squawking, singing and flitting of feathery flocks.

History

Stewart Island's Māori name is Rakiura (Glowing Skies), and you only need to catch a glimpse of a spectacular blood-red sunset or the aurora australis to see why. According to myth, New Zealand was hauled up from the ocean by Māui, who said, 'Let us go out of sight of land, far out in the open sea, and when we have quite lost sight of land, then let the anchor be dropped'. The North Island was the fish that Māui caught,

---

BLUFF OYSTERS

Bluff oysters are in huge demand from the minute they come into season (late March to late August). Top restaurants as far away as Auckland compete to be the first to add them to their menus. As oysters go, they're whoppers. Don't expect to be able to slurp one down in a dainty gulp – these beasts take some chewing. If you want to know what all the fuss is about, you can buy fresh or battered Bluff oysters when they're in season from **Fowlers Oysters** (☑ 03-212 8792; www.facebook.com/fowlersoysters; Ocean Beach Rd; half-dozen cooked $14.50, dozen raw from $24; ⊙ 9am-7pm Mar-Aug), on the left-hand side as you head into town. Up by the signpost for Stirling Point (p168) is Oyster Cove (p168), where you can guzzle oysters while admiring sea views through floor-to-ceiling windows. Or time your visit for the annual **Bluff Oyster & Food Festival** (www.bluffoysterfest.co.nz; ⊛ May) in May.

---

the South Island his canoe and Rakiura was the anchor – Te Punga o te Waka o Māui.

There is evidence that parts of Rakiura were occupied by moa (bird) hunters as early as the 13th century. The tītī (muttonbird) on adjacent islands were an important seasonal food source for the southern Māori.

The first European visitor was Captain Cook. Sailing around the eastern, southern and western coasts in 1770 he mistook it for the bottom end of the South Island and named it South Cape. In 1809 the sealing vessel *Pegasus* circumnavigated Rakiura and named it after its first officer, William Stewart.

In June 1864 Stewart and the adjacent islets were bought from local Māori for £6000. Early industries were sealing, timber-milling, fish-curing and shipbuilding, with a short-lived gold rush towards the end of the 19th century. Today the island's economy is dependent on tourism and fishing.

⊙ Sights

Rakiura Museum MUSEUM
(Map p172; ☑ 03-219 1221; www.rakiuramuseum.co.nz; 9 Ayr St, Halfmoon Bay; adult/child $2/50c; ⊙ 10am-1.30pm Mon-Sat, noon-2pm Sun Oct-Apr, shorter hrs May-Sep) Historic photographs are the stars of this small museum focused on

Stewart Island/Rakiura (North)

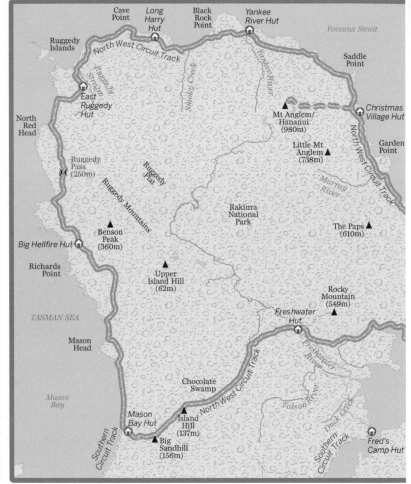

local natural and human history, and featuring Māori artefacts, whaling gear and more.

Big plans are in the works for a revamped, state-of-the-art Rakiura Museum in a new location. The new museum was slated to open at the end of 2018 or early 2019.

★**Ulva Island**　　　　WILDLIFE RESERVE
A tiny paradise covering only 269 hectares, Ulva Island/Te Wharawhara is a great place to see lots of native NZ birds. Established as a bird sanctuary in 1922, it remains one of Stewart Island/Rakiura's wildest corners. The island was declared rat-free in 1997 and

three years later was chosen as the site to release endangered South Island saddlebacks.

Today the air is bristling with birdsong, which can be appreciated on walking tracks in the island's northwest as detailed in *Ulva: Self-Guided Tour* ($2), available from the Rakiura National Park Visitor Centre (p174). Many paths intersect amid beautiful stands of rimu, miro, totara and rata. Any water-taxi company will run you to the island from Stewart Island's Golden Bay wharf, with scheduled services offered by **Ulva Island Ferry** (☑ 03-219 1013; return adult/

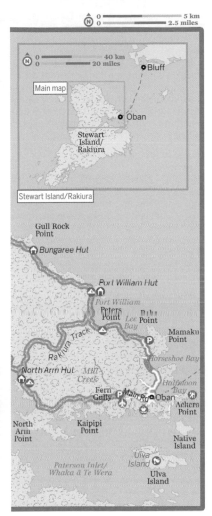

Stewart Island/Rakiura

child $20/10; ⊗departs 9am, noon, 4pm, returns
12.15pm, 2.15pm, 4.15pm, 6pm). To get the most
out of Ulva Island, go on a tour with Ulva's
Guided Walks (p171).

🏃 Activities

Rakiura National Park protects 85% of the
island, making it a paradise for trampers and bird-watchers. There are plenty of
tracks on which to explore the wilderness,
ranging from short, easy tracks, accessible
on foot from Oban, to the epic North West
Circuit, one of NZ's most isolated backcountry tramps.

Walking

Observation Rock　　　　　WALKING
(Map p172) This short, sharp 15-minute
climb through Oban's backstreets reaches
the Observation Rock lookout where there
are panoramic views of Paterson Inlet, Mt
Anglem and Rakeahua. The track is clearly marked from the end of Leonard Rd, off
Ayr St.

Ackers Point　　　　　WALKING
This three-hour return walk features an amble around the bay to a bushy track passing
the historic 1835 **Stone House** at **Harrold
Bay** before reaching **Ackers Point Lighthouse**, where there are wide views of Foveaux Strait and the chance to see blue penguins and a titi (muttonbird) colony.

Fishing

If you haven't ever sea-fished, or just fancy
it, this is the place, for NZ boasts no better
fisherfolk. Oh, and the answer to the question of swimming is definitely 'yes': yes, it
is possible, and yes, you will probably freeze
solid.

Lo-Loma Fishing Charters　　　FISHING
(☏ 027 393 8362, 03-219 1141; www.loloma.co.nz;
adult/child $100/50) Join Squizzy Squires on the
Lo-Loma for a fun hand-lining fishing trip.

👉 Tours

Numerous operators offer guided tours:
walking, driving, boating and by air, most
focusing on wildlife with history slotted in.
Independent walkers have plenty to choose
from; visit Rakiura National Park Visitor
Centre (p174) for details on local tramps,
long and short, and huts along the way.
The trails in DOC's *Stewart Island/Rakiu-
ra Short Walks* pamphlet ($2) would keep
you busy for several days, and a bit less if
you hire a bike from the Red Shed (p174) to
fast-track the road sections. Longer tramps
can also be shortened and indeed enhanced
via an air hop with **Stewart Island Flights**
(☏ 03-218 9129; www.stewartislandflights.co.nz;
Elgin Tce, Oban; adult/child one way $125/80,
return $215/130), which offers the fulfilling
day-long Coast to Coast cross-island hike.

Ulva's Guided Walks　　　　WALKING
(☏ 027 688 1332, 03-219 1216; www.ulva.co.nz)
Focused firmly on birding and guided by
expert naturalists, these excellent half-day
tours ($130; transport included) explore
Ulva Island. Book at the **Stewart Island
Gift Shop** (Map p172; ☏ 03-219 1453; www.

FIORDLAND & SOUTHLAND STEWART ISLAND (RAKIURA)

Oban

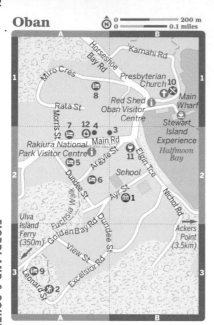

▲ (N) 0 — 200 m
0 — 0.1 miles

Oban

◎ Sights
1 Rakiura Museum B2

✪ Activities, Courses & Tours
2 Observation Rock A3
3 Rakiura Charters & Water Taxi B2
4 Ruggedy Range Wilderness
   Experience A2

🛏 Sleeping
5 Bay Motel A2
6 Bunkers Backpackers A2
7 Jo & Andy's B&B A2
8 Kaka Retreat A1
9 Observation Rock Lodge A3

✪ Eating
10 Church Hill Restaurant &
    Oyster Bar B1

🍷 Drinking & Nightlife
11 South Sea Hotel B2

🛍 Shopping
12 Stewart Island Gift Shop A2

facebook.com/StewartIslandGiftShop; 20 Main Rd, Oban; ⊙ 10.30am-5pm, reduced hours in winter). If you're a mad-keen twitcher, look for the Birding Bonanza trip ($480) on Ulva's website.

Aihe Eco Charters & Water Taxi   BOATING
(☑ 027 478 4433, 03-219 1066; www.aihe.co.nz) 🕊 Scenic and nature-spotting cruises with in-depth commentary. Options include wildlife-spotting cruises around Paterson Inlet ($75 per person for an hour; $130 for 2½ hours), or cruise-and-walk packages to the old Norwegian Whalers' Base ($95 per person for two hours; $140 for three hours). Minimum group numbers apply, usually two to four people depending on the tour.

**Ruggedy Range Wilderness
Experience**   ECOTOUR
(Map p172; ☑ 03-219 1066, 0274 784 433; www.ruggedyrange.com; 14 Main Rd, Oban) 🕊 Nature-guide Furhana runs small-group guided walks, including 'bird and forest' trips to Ulva Island (half/full day $135/255); overnight trips to see kiwi in the wild (adult/child from $825/695); and a three-day guided wilderness walk where your packs are ferried to huts along the route ($1050).

Rakiura Charters & Water Taxi   BOATING
(Map p172; ☑ 0800 725 487, 03-219 1487; www.rakiuracharters.co.nz; 10 Main Rd, Oban; adult/child from $100/70) The most popular outing on the *Rakiura Suzy* is the half-day cruise that stops in at the historic Whalers' Base. Trips can be tailored to suit timing and interests, such as wildlife-spotting and tramping.

🛏 Sleeping

Finding accommodation can be difficult, especially in the low season when many places shut down. Booking ahead is highly recommended. The island has many holiday homes, which are often good value and offer the benefit of self-catering, which is especially handy if you do a spot of fishing. (Note that many impose a two-night minimum stay or charge a surcharge for one night.)

Jo & Andy's B&B   B&B **$**
(Map p172; ☑ 03-219 1230; jriksem@gmail.com; 22 Main Rd, Oban; s $65, d & tw $95; @ 🛜) A great option for budget travellers, this cosy blue home squeezes in twin, double and single rooms that share bathroom facilities. A big breakfast of muesli, fruit and eggs prepares you for the most active of days. Jo is splendid company and there are hundreds of books if the weather packs up. Two-night minimum stay.

Bunkers Backpackers   HOSTEL **$**
(Map p172; ☑ 027 738 1796; www.bunkersbackpackers.co.nz; 15 Argyle St, Oban; dm/d $34/80; ⊙ closed mid-Apr–mid-Oct; 🛜) A converted

STEWART ISLAND FLORA & FAUNA

With an absence of mustelids (ferrets, stoats and weasels) and large areas of intact forest, Stewart Island/Rakiura has one of the largest and most diverse bird populations of anywhere in NZ. Even in the streets of Oban the air resonates with birds such as tui, bellbirds and kaka, which share their island home with weka, kakariki, fernbirds, robins and Rakiura tokoeka/kiwi. There are also plenty of shore- and seabirds, including dotterels, shags, mollymawks, prions, petrels and albatross, as well as the titi (muttonbird), which is seen in large numbers during breeding season. Ask locals about the evening parade of penguins on cliffs near the wharf; and *please* – don't feed the birds. It's bad for them.

Exotic animals include two species of deer, the red and the Virginia (whitetail), introduced in the early 20th century, as were brushtail possums, which are now numerous throughout the island and destructive to the native bush. Stewart Island/Rakiura also has NZ fur seals, NZ sea lions and elephant seals dawdling on its beaches and rocky shores.

Beech, the tree that dominates much of NZ, is absent from Stewart Island/Rakiura. The predominant lowland bush is podocarp (conifer) forest, with tall rimu, miro and totara forming the canopy. Because of mild winters, frequent rainfall and porous soil, most of the island is a lush forest, thick with vines and carpeted in deep green ferns and mosses.

wooden villa houses Stewart Island/Rakiura's best hostel option, which is somewhat squeezed but offers the benefits of a cosy lounge, sunny garden, inner-village location and friendly vibe. Perks include a barbecue area, hammocks and board games.

Bay Motel MOTEL **$$**
(Map p172; ☑ 03-219 1119; www.baymotel.co.nz; 9 Dundee St, Oban; units from $180; ☜) This hillside motel offers spacious, comfortable units with lots of light and harbour views. Some rooms have spa baths, all have kitchens and two are wheelchair-accessible. When you've exhausted the island's bustling after-dark scene, Sky TV's on hand for on-tap entertainment.

★ Observation Rock Lodge B&B **$$$**
(Map p172; ☑ 03-219 1444; www.observationrock lodge.co.nz; 7 Leonard St, Oban; r with/without bathroom $395/195; ☜) Secluded in bird-filled bush and angled for sea, sunset and aurora views, Annett and Phil's lodge has three stylish, luxurious rooms with private decks and a shared lounge. Guided activities, a sauna, a hot tub and Annett's gourmet dinners are included in the deluxe package ($780) or by arrangement as additions to the standard B&B rate.

Kaka Retreat MOTEL **$$$**
(Map p172; ☑ 03-219 1252; www.kakaretreat.co.nz; 7 Miro Cres; units from $230; ☜) ✎ These studio units are among the island's best, with plush interiors, flash bathrooms and private verandas, although kitchen facilities are scant. Two older-style but smart fully self-contained cottages offer good value for up to six people.

✗ Eating & Drinking

Church Hill Restaurant & Oyster Bar MODERN NZ **$$$**
(Map p172; ☑ 03-219 1123; www.churchhill.co.nz; 36 Kamahi Rd, Oban; mains $30-40, ☺ 5.00pm late daily Sep-May) During summer this heritage villa's sunny deck provides hilltop views, and in cooler months you can get cosy inside beside the open fire. Big on local seafood, highlights include oysters, crayfish and salmon, prepared in refined modern style, followed by excellent desserts. Bookings advisable.

South Sea Hotel PUB
(Map p172; ☑ 03-219 1059; www.stewart-island. co.nz; 26 Elgin Tce, Oban; ☺ 7am-9pm; ☜) Welcome to one of NZ's classic pubs, complete with stellar cod and chips, beer by the quart, a reliable cafe (mains $15 to $33) and plenty of friendly banter in the public bar. Great at any time of day (or night), and the Sunday-night quiz offers an unforgettable slice of island life. Basic rooms are available, too.

ⓘ Information

INTERNET ACCESS
Free wi-fi is available on Ayr St and at most accommodation.

MONEY
Stewart Island/Rakiura has no banks. In the Four Square supermarket there's an ATM, which has a mind of its own; credit cards are accepted for most activities.

SPOTTING A KIWI

Stewart Island/Rakiura is one of the few places on earth where you can spot a kiwi in the wild – and certainly the only place you're likely to see them in daylight. The bird has been around for 70 million years and is related to the now-extinct moa. Brown feathers camouflage the kiwi against its bush surroundings and a largely nocturnal lifestyle means spying one in the wild is a challenge.

As big as a barnyard chicken, with a population estimated to number around 13,000 birds, the Stewart Island/Rakiura brown kiwi (*Apteryx australis lawryi*, also known as the tokoeka) is larger in size, longer in the beak and thicker in the legs than its northern cousins. It is also the only kiwi active during daylight hours, and birds may be seen around sunrise and sunset foraging in grassed areas and on beaches, where they mine sandhoppers under washed-up kelp. If you spot one, keep silent, and stay still and away. The birds' poor eyesight and single-mindedness in searching for food will often lead them to bump right into you.

Organised tours are your best bet for a sighting. Given the island's fickle weather – with tours sometimes cancelled – allow a few nights here if you're desperate for an encounter. Otherwise, it's sometimes possible to spot the birds in and around Oban itself. Head to the bushy fringes of the rugby field after sundown and you might get lucky.

TOURIST INFORMATION

The best place for information is the **Invercargill i-SITE** (p168) back on the mainland.

Rakiura National Park Visitor Centre (Map p172; ☑ 03-219 0009; www.doc.govt.nz; 15 Main Rd, Oban; ⊘ 8am-5pm Dec-Mar, 8.30am-4.30pm Mon-Fri, 9am-4pm Apr-May & Oct-Nov, 8.30am-4.30pm Mon-Fri, 10am-2pm Sat & Sun Jun-Sep) Stop in to obtain information on walking tracks, as well as hut bookings and passes, topographical maps, locator beacons, books and a few tramping essentials, such as insect repellent and wool socks. Information displays introduce Stewart Island/Rakiura's flora and fauna, while a video library provides entertainment and education (a good rainy-day Plan B). Register your intentions here via AdventureSmart (www.adventuresmart.org.nz), so there is a record of your tramping plans if you get into trouble along the way.

Red Shed Oban Visitor Centre (Map p172; ☑ 0800 000 511, 03-219 0056; www.stewartislandexperience.co.nz; 12 Elgin Tce, Oban; ⊘7.30am-6.30pm Oct-Apr, 8am-5pm May-Sep) Conveniently located next to the wharf, this Stewart Island Experience booking office can hook you up with nearly everything on and around the island, including accommodation, guided tours, boat trips, bikes and hire cars.

ⓘ Getting There & Away

We've heard the island's arrival options summarised as a choice between 10 minutes of terror and an hour of torture. Usually the flights aren't all that scary, but the boat journey can certainly be challenging to the stomach on a rough day.

AIR

Stewart Island Flights (p171) Flies between the island and Invercargill three times daily, with good standby and over-60 discounts. The price includes transfers between the island airport and its office on the Oban waterfront.

BOAT

Stewart Island Experience (Map p172; ☑ 0800 000 511, 03-212 7660; www.stewartislandexperience.co.nz; Main Wharf, Oban; adult/child one way $79/40, return $139/40) The passenger-only ferry runs between Bluff and Oban up to four times daily (reduced in winter, June to August). Book a few days ahead in summer (December to February). The crossing takes one hour and can be a rough ride. The company also runs a shuttle between Bluff and Invercargill (adult/child $24/12), with pick-ups and drop-offs in Invercargill at the i-SITE, Tuatara Backpackers and Invercargill Airport.

Vehicles can be stored in a secure car park at Bluff for an additional cost.

ⓘ Getting Around

Roads on the island are limited to Oban and the bays surrounding it. **Stewart Island Experience** offers car and scooter hire from the **Red Shed**.

Water taxis offer pick-ups and drop-offs for trips to Ulva Island and to remote parts of the main island – a handy service for trampers. Operators include **Aihe Eco Charters & Water Taxi** (p172), **Ulva Island Ferry** (p170) and **Rakiura Charters & Water Taxi** (p172).

Riverton

POP 1430

Quiet little Riverton (in Māori, Aparima) is worth a detour for its dreamy bay views and gripping museum of local history. If near-Antarctic swimming takes your fancy, the long, broad sands of **Taramea Bay** are good for a dip; otherwise we suggest a stroll along **Palmerston St**, studded with cafes and 19th-century buildings. Riverton makes a good lunch stop if you're driving the Southern Scenic Route, or a pleasantly laid-back day trip from Invercargill, 38km east.

⊙ Sights

★**Te Hikoi Southern Journey**   MUSEUM
(✈️ 03-234 8260; www.tehikoi.co.nz; 172 Palmerston St; adult/child $8/free; ☺ 10am-4pm Apr-Sep, to 5pm Oct-Mar) Oh, that all small-town museums could be this good! This riveting museum starts with a 16 minute film dramatising key events in the region's history, including the arrival of the first European seal hunters (fiercely met by the local Māori). Legends behind the landscape are entertainingly told, as are anecdotes about characters from cabbage-tree rum distillers to the first recorded Pākehā (white European) Māori, James Caddell.

✖️ Eating

Postmaster Bakery   CAFE $
(✈️ 03-234 8153; http://postmasterbakery.simplesite.com; 166 Palmerston St; baked goods from $4.50; ☺ 7.30am-4pm; 🛜) Inside the charming 1911 post office, find great pies, frittatas and the best custard squares for miles. The soups change daily, full breakfasts ($16) are huge and there's sushi from October to March.

★**Beach House**   MODERN NZ $$
(✈️ 03-234 8274; http://beachhouseriverton.co.nz; 126 Rocks Hwy; mains lunch $17-32, dinner $27-39; ☺ 10am-10pm Wed-Sun, to 4pm Mon & Tue; 🛜🅿️) Looking over Taramea Bay, Beach House is a stylish, comfortable cafe famous for seafood, especially its creamy chowder studded with juicy mussels and hunks of salmon. On a sunny day with a warm breeze wafting off Foveaux Strait, the outside tables are a must. The other 90% of the time, retire inside to admire the view through the windows.

ℹ️ Information

Te Hikoi Southern Journey The local museum doubles as a helpful information centre and accommodation booking service.

ℹ️ BOOKING SERVICES

Invercargill i-SITE (p168) and the **Red Shed Oban Visitor Centre** (p174) can help you book holiday-home rentals on the island. See also www.stewartisland.co.nz.

ℹ️ Getting There & Away

Riverton is on SH99, the section of the Southern Scenic Route between Tuatapere (47km) and Invercargill (36km). There are no public transport connections.

Te Waewae & Colac Bays

Between Tuatapere and Riverton on SH99, a section of the Southern Scenic Route, these long, moody bays set a steely glare towards Antarctica. Colac Bay has a small but dedicated following among hardy surfers, but most travellers simply stop for a brisk dip or beach stroll before continuing the drive.

Driving west to east along SH99, pause at **McCracken's Rest** (SH99), the most impressive lookout point along the Southern Scenic Route. Admire views of wind-lashed Te Waewae Bay (and, if you're lucky, Hector's dolphins and southern right whales). Seven kilometres further, stroll along the sparkly sands at Orepuki, aka **Gemstone Beach**, before continuing a further 4km towards **Monkey Island** (off SH99, Orepuki), a former Māori whaling lookout.

If you're travelling from the east, driving this stretch of SH99 provides a glimpse of the snowcapped Southern Alps descending into the sea, framing the western end of the bay.

✖️ Eating

★**Orepuki Beach Cafe**   CAFE $$
(✈️ 03-234 5211; www.facebook.com/pg/orepukibeachcafe; cnr Dudley St & Stafford St (SH99), Orepuki; mains $19-29; ☺ 9am-5pm Sun-Thu, to 11pm Fri & Sat; 🅿️) What's this? A beacon of gastronomic hope, beaming out good vibes and delicious aromas along a desolate stretch of highway? This chipper cafe has soups, samosas, risottos and a rack of homemade cakes. Bigger feeds, like salmon fettuccine and lamb with plum sauce, have a sprinkling of sophistication, but the atmosphere is pure seaside charm.

FIORDLAND & SOUTHLAND RIVERTON

The South Island's Birds

New Zealand may lack for mammals, but that's conversely created a unique population of birds – a number of species are flightless, having had no need to take to the air to avoid predators. Check out the excellent Digital Encyclopedia of New Zealand Birds (www.nzbirdsonline.org.nz), and tune up on bird calls at the Department of Conservation website (www.doc.govt.nz/nature/native-animals/birds).

1. Silvereye/Tauhou
One of NZ's most prevalent birds, this small, agile creature is easily recognised by its white eye-ring and inclination to sing.

2. New Zealand Pigeon/Kereru
If you can hear heavy wingbeats overhead, it'll be the kereru. New Zealand's handsome native pigeon is widespread through the country and fond of powerlines and branches.

3. Bellbird/Korimako
Sounding less like a bell and more like Adele, this enchanting songbird sounds big but is a small, green slip of a thing, fond of nectar and found on both islands.

4. Fantail/Piwakawaka
This little charmer will entrance you up close, but in truth it cares not a jot about you, merely the insects you displace.

5. Grey Warbler/Riroriro
New Zealand's most widely distributed endemic bird species is also one of its smallest. Tending to hide in dense vegetation, the featherweight affirms its presence by warbling its jolly head off.

6. Woodhen/Weka
Often mistaken by visitors as a kiwi, this large flightless bird has a keen nose for lunch crumbs and will often appear at well-frequented picnic spots.

7. Pukeko
Looking like a smooth blue chicken with a red forehead, this bird is often seen pecking about in paddocks or crossing the road in front of high-speed traffic. It's territorial, highly social and easily recognised.

8. Paradise Shelduck
This colourful, conspicuous and honking waterfowl could be mistaken for a small goose as it hangs out in wild wetlands, river flats, sportsfields and other open grassed areas.

9. Rifleman/Tititipounamu
NZ's smallest bird, this hyperactive forest dweller produces a characteristic 'wing-flicking' while moving through the canopy and foraging up and down tree trunks.

10. Kiwi
A national icon with an onomatopoeic name, at least for the male, which cries 'kiwi!' The females make an ugly sound, a bit like someone with a sore throat. There are five different species.

11. South Island Robin
Inhabiting forest and scrub, the South Island robin (like its North Island cousin) stands leggy and erect, sings loud and long, and will often approach very closely.

12. Tomtit/Miromiro
Widespread inhabitant of forest and shrubland, the tomtit is often reclusive and hard to see, but occasionally moves in for a closer look.

13. Kea
Resident only in the South Island, this is the world's only true alpine parrot. Kea appear innately curious, but this is simply a pretence to peck destructively at your possessions.

14. Falcon/Karearea
The NZ falcon is a magpie-sized bird of prey found in both forest and open habitats such as tussocklands and roughly grazed hill country.

15. Kaka
This screechy parrot flaps boldly across the sky and settles in a wide variety of native forest, including podocarp and beech forest.

16. Tui
Common throughout town and country, the 'parson bird' is metallic bluey-green with white throat tufts. Sometimes tuneful, and sometimes cacophonous, it is always an aerobatic flapper.

17. Morepork/Ruru
You may not see this small, nocturnal owl, but you'll probably hear its 'more-pork' call and peculiar screeches. If you're lucky it may eyeball you from a low branch in both native and exotic forests.

18. Blue Duck/Whio
Mostly confined to clear, fast-flowing rivers in the mountains, this darling little bird issues a shrill 'whio' whistle above the noise of turbulent waters.

19. Kakariki
Also known as the red- or yellow-crowned parakeet and now reasonably rare on the mainland, this bird will most likely be seen in tall forest.

Tuatapere

POP 558

Formerly a timber-milling town, sleepy Tuatapere is gently shaken awake by trampers who pass through before embarking on the Hump Ridge or Dusky Tracks. The town's early woodcutters were very efficient, so only a remnant of a once-large tract of native podocarp (conifer) forest remains.

Still capitalising on a 1988 victory in a sausage-making competition, Tuatapere styles itself as New Zealand's sausage capital – scoff some snags, ride the rapids of the Waiau River by jetboat, and you'll do this low-slung town justice.

◎ Sights & Activities

Wilderness is never far away in Tuatapere. The town is the base for the Hump Ridge Track (p154), conceived and built by the local community, and opened in 2001. Trampers can also embark on the tough, 84km Dusky Track (p154) from here. If you prefer a refreshing, less strenuous adventure, Tuatapere is a hub for jetboating trips on the Wairaurahiri River.

Clifden Suspension Bridge   BRIDGE
Spanning the Waiau River about 12km north of Tuatapere, this suspension bridge, completed in 1899, is the longest of its kind in NZ. Its 15m-high concrete towers cut an imposing silhouette and the serene setting, information panels and picnic table invite a pit stop.

⛵ Tours

Lake Hauroko drains into the Tasman Sea from its southern end via the Wairaurahiri River. Two local jetboat operators – **W-Jet** (☑03-225 5677, 0800 376 174; www.wjet.co.nz; 1260 Clifden Hwy; tours adult/child from $249/149) and **Wairaurahiri Wilderness Jet** (☑0800 270 556; www.river-jet.co.nz; 17 Main Street, Otautau; day tours from $230) – offer thrill-seeking rides along the forest-shrouded river packaged into day-long excursions that include a nature-spotting walk and a barbecue.

🍴 Eating

Last Light Lodge   CAFE $$
(☑03-226 6667; www.lastlightlodge.com; 2 Clifden Hwy; mains $12-25; ☺7am-late; ☜) Attached to a fairly ordinary holiday park, this friendly cafe stands out for its homemade cookies, pies and truffles, smoothies thick enough to hold up a straw and a good all-day selection of food: fish and chips, *panini*, chicken curry and plenty more. The deck is a fine place to tackle a beer in fair weather.

ℹ️ Information

Tuatapere Hump Ridge Track Information Centre (☑0800 486 774, 03-226 6739; www.humpridgetrack.co.nz; 31 Orawia Rd; ☺7.30am-6pm Nov-Mar, limited hours Apr-Oct) Assists with local information, Hump Ridge hut passes and transport. Call ahead if you're passing through between April and October.

ℹ️ Getting There & Away

Buses must be booked through the **Tuatapere Hump Ridge Track Information Centre** (p180); with demand, services go to/from Queenstown ($95, three hours), Te Anau ($50, 1½ hours) and Invercargill ($60, one hour).

FIORDLAND

If you picture New Zealand, it might just be Fiordland National Park that flashes into your mind's eye. Part of the Te Wāhipounamu (Southwest New Zealand) World Heritage Area, this formidable tract of mountains and forest spanning 26,000 sq km has deeply recessed sounds (technically fiords) that spider inland from the Tasman Sea.

Some of the South Island's most iconic destinations are here. Along the world-famous Milford Hwy, views of mountains and mirror lakes are only surpassed in beauty by the road's end point, Milford Sound. Here, granite giants cast reflections in waters where dolphins and penguins frolic. Even more secluded is Doubtful Sound: the Māori-named 'place of silence' is teeming with wildlife; it's larger than Milford Sound, but much less visited.

Cruises enter the watery wilderness but walkers can delve deepest into Fiordland either on the multiday Milford, Kepler and Hollyford Tracks or shorter walks, easily reached from the highway.

Manapouri

POP 400

Manapouri, 20km south of Te Anau, is the jumping-off point for cruises to Doubtful Sound. Most visitors head straight to the boat harbour for the ferry to the West Arm of Lake Manapouri, known to early Māori as Roto Ua or 'rainy lake', and later as Moturau, the 'many island lake'.

But little Manapouri has a few tricks up its sleeve. The town can't compete with Te Anau's abundance of restaurants and motels but it has mountain-backed lake views easily as lovely as those enjoyed by its bigger, more popular sibling. At 440m, Lake Manapouri is the second-deepest lake in New Zealand. And with far fewer overnight visitors than Te Anau, you can enjoy the spectacular sunsets all to yourself.

🏃 Activities

By crossing the Waiau River at Pearl Harbour (p182) you can embark on day walks as detailed in DOC's *Fiordland Day Walks* brochure. A classic circuit with glimmering lake views (and occasional steep parts) is the **Circle Track** (3½ hours), which can be extended to **Hope Arm** (five to six hours return). You can cross the river aboard a hired row boat or water taxi from **Adventure Manapouri** (☑03-249 8070, 021 925 577; www.adventuromanapouri.co.nz; row boat hire per day $40, water taxi per person return $20), which also offers guided walks and fishing tours.

Running between the northern entrance to Manapouri township and Pearl Harbour, the one-hour **Frasers Beach** walk offers picnic and swimming spots as well as fantastic views across the lake.

🛏️ Sleeping & Eating

Possum Lodge   HOLIDAY PARK $
(☑03-249 6623; www.possumlodge.co.nz; 13 Murrell Ave; campervan sites $34-39, dm $25, units with/without bathroom $110/59; ☎) Nestled into forest by the lake, Possum Lodge is old-fashioned in the best kind of way. Hospitable hosts preside over basic cabins, time-worn motel units, enviably green campervan sites, laundry facilities and a fully equipped kitchen. Peace, quiet and a short walk to the riverbank: what more could you need? Oh that's right, unlimited wi-fi...done.

The Church   PUB FOOD $$
(☑03-249 6001; www.facebook.com/pg/mana pouri.co.nz; 23 Waiau St; mains $17-25; ⊙11am-10pm Sun-Thu, to midnight Fri & Sat) No need to head up to Te Anau for a satisfying feed and a few beers, hurrah! Plates heavy with steaks, burgers and butter chicken are hauled to tables in this converted church building, now a merry pub with exceptionally welcoming staff.

ⓘ Getting There & Away

Topline Tours (☑03-249 8059; www.topline tours.co.nz; 32 Caswell Rd) Offers year-round shuttles between Te Anau and Manapouri ($20).

Tracknet (p186) One daily bus to/from Te Anau ($25, 30 minutes) from November to April, and on demand at other times of the year.

Doubtful Sound

Remote Doubtful Sound is humbling in size and beauty. Carved by glaciers, it's one of New Zealand's largest fiords – almost three times the length of more popular Milford. Boats gliding through this maze of forested valleys have good chances of encountering fur seals and Fiordland penguins. Aside from haunting birdsong, Doubtful Sound deserves its Māori name, Patea, the 'place of silence'.

Until relatively recently, Doubtful Sound was isolated from all but intrepid explorers. Even Captain Cook only observed it from off the coast in 1770, because he was 'doubtful' whether winds would be sufficient to blow the ship back to sea. Access improved when the road over Wilmot Pass opened in 1959 to facilitate construction of West Arm power station.

Boat and coach transfers from Manapouri to Deep Cove are easily organised through tour operators, but time-consuming enough to deter some travellers...ideal for those who want to enjoy the silence.

🧭 Tours

Day cruises allow about three hours on the water (once you've factored in transport time to the sound). Overnight cruises are pricey but preferable; they include meals plus the option of fishing and kayaking, depending on the weather.

★ Real Journeys   CRUISE
(☑0800 656 501; www.realjourneys.co.nz) 🦭 A family-run tourism trailblazer, Real Journeys is ecofriendly, and just plain friendly. One-day 'wilderness cruises' (adult/child from $250/65) include a three-hour journey aboard a modern catamaran with a specialist nature guide. The overnight cruise, which runs from September to May, is aboard the *Fiordland Navigator*, which sleeps 70 in en suite cabins (quad-share per adult/child from $419/210, single/double from $1171/1338).

Fiordland Expeditions   CRUISE
(☑0508 888 656, 03-249 9005; www.fiord landexpeditions.co.nz; dm/s/d/tr from $645/

1340/1420/2130; 🖌) A classy operator offering overnight cruises on the *Tutoko II* (maximum 14 passengers). It's a standard Doubtful Sound program plus fishing for your dinner and a welcome drink of bubbly. Fiordland Expeditions also operates cruises in winter (June to August), if more time on the water (a full two days) and absolute tranquillity appeal.

Deep Cove Charters   CRUISE
(🖉 03-249 6828; https://doubtfulsoundcruise. nz; s $550, cabins tw/d $1300/1400) Overnight cruises on board the *Seafinn* (maximum 12 passengers) run by home-grown crew who nimbly tailor the cruise to the day's weather and wildlife-spotting conditions. There are options to kayak and fish but they had us at 'crayfish lunch and venison supper included'.

Doubtful Sound Kayak   KAYAKING
(🖉 03-249 7777, 0800 452 9257; www.fiordlandad venture.co.nz; day tours $299; ⊙ Oct-Apr) Runs day trips to Doubtful Sound, including four hours paddling time, suitable for beginners or seasoned kayakers.

❶ Getting There & Away

Getting to Doubtful Sound involves boarding a boat at **Pearl Harbour** (Waiau St, Manapouri) in Manapouri for a one-hour trip to West Arm power station, followed by a 22km (40-minute) drive over Wilmot Pass to Deep Cove (permanent population: two), where you hop aboard a boat for your cruise on the sound. Manapouri is the easiest place to base yourself, although Te Anau (20km) and Queenstown (170km) pick-ups are readily organised through the cruise-boat operators.

Te Anau

POP 1911

Picturesque Te Anau is the main gateway to Milford Sound and three Great Walks: the Milford, Kepler and Routeburn Tracks. Far

from being a humdrum stopover, Te Anau is stunning in its own right. The township borders Lake Te Anau, New Zealand's second-largest lake, whose glacier-gouged fiords spider into secluded forest on its western shore. To the east are the pastoral areas of central Southland, while west across Lake Te Anau lie the rugged mountains of Fiordland.

Te Anau is popular with fly-by sightseers and long-haul trampers alike. This has encouraged a sizeable accommodation scene and a decent array of places to eat. While Te Anau doesn't party nearly as hard as effervescent Queenstown, there are plenty of places to sink a few beers – which taste all the better after a long day of tramping, kayaking or driving the unforgettable Milford Hwy.

⦿ Sights

Punanga Manu o Te Anau   BIRD SANCTUARY
(Te Anau Bird Sanctuary; www.doc.govt.nz; Te Anau–Manapouri Rd; ⊙ dawn-dusk) `FREE` By the lake, this set of outdoor aviaries offers a chance to see native bird species difficult to spot in the wild, including the precious icon of Fiordland, the extremely rare takahe. Arrive for the feeding time of this royal-blue flightless bird at 9.30am (October to March) or 10.30am (April to September).

Te Anau Glowworm Caves   CAVE
(🖉 0800 656 501; www.realjourneys.co.nz; adult/ child $83/22) Stare up at constellations of glowworms on an underground boat ride. Once present only in Māori legends, this 200m-long cave system was rediscovered in 1948. Its sculpted rocks, waterfalls and whirlpools are impressive by themselves, but the bluish sparkle of glowworms, peculiar territorial larvae who lure prey with their come-hither lights, is the main draw.

Reach the caves on a 2¼-hour guided tour with **Real Journeys** (Map p184; 🖉 0800 656 501;

---

❶ WHICH CRUISE: MILFORD OR DOUBTFUL SOUND?

Both Milford and Doubtful Sound can be experienced in a single day, most easily from Te Anau. Both have overnight cruises to fully immerse you in natural beauty, but if your time in Fiordland is short, consider the following.

Milford Sound Popular, two-hour cruises of iconic fiord views, a straightforward day trip from Te Anau where the scenic drive is part of the fun. Allow 2¼ to three hours' car or coach transfer time from Te Anau each way. Doable on a (very long) day from Queenstown.

Doubtful Sound Rewarding precisely because it's remote, a three-hour cruise on Doubtful Sound takes up a full day because of transfer times by boat and coach from Manapouri (20km south of Te Anau). An easy day trip from Te Anau; if you're travelling from further afield, it's best to stay in Te Anau or Manapouri the night before.

www.realjourneys.co.nz; 85 Lakefront Dr; ⊙ 7.30am-8.30pm Sep-May, 8am-7pm Jun-Aug) ⏹, via a lake cruise, a walkway and a short boat ride. Tours depart from its Lakefront Dr office.

Activities

Te Anau is primarily a way to access the great wilderness of Te Wāhipounamu (Southwest New Zealand) World Heritage Area, which boasts such crowd-pullers as Milford Sound. However, there's plenty to keep you occupied around the town itself, as well as out on the water and in the air.

Walking

Te Anau's **Lakeside Track** makes for a very pleasant stroll or cycle in either direction – north to the marina and around to the Upukerora River (about an hour return), or south past the Fiordland National Park Visitor Centre and on to the control gates and start of the Kepler Track (50 minutes).

Day tramps in the national park are readily accessible from Te Anau. **Kepler Water Taxi** (Map p184; ☑ 027 249 8365, 03-249 8361; www.keplerwatertaxi.co.nz; one way $25) and **Fiordland Outdoors** (☑ 0800 347 4538; www.fiordlandoutdoors.co.nz) can scoot you over to Brod Bay, from where you can walk back along the Lakeside Track to Te Anau (two to three hours). During summer, **Trips & Tramps** (☑ 03-249 7081, 0800 305 807; www.tripsandtramps.com) offers small-group, guided day hikes on the Kepler and Routeburn, among other tracks (as well as shuttles to and from trailheads). Real Journeys (p181) runs guided day hikes (adult/child $195/127, November to mid-April) along an 11km stretch of the Milford Track. Various day walks can also be completed by linking with regular bus services run by Tracknet (p186).

For self-guided adventures, pick up DOC's *Fiordland National Park Day Walks* brochure ($2) from the Fiordland i-SITE (p186) or Fiordland National Park Visitor Centre (p186), or download it at www.doc.govt.nz.

Boating

Fiordland Jet ADVENTURE SPORTS
(Map p184; ☑ 0800 253 826; www.fjet.nz; 84 Lakefront Dr; adult/child $139/70) Thrilling 90-minute jetboating trips on the Upper Waiau River (in *Lord of the Rings*, the River Anduin), zipping between mountain-backed beech forest, with commentary on the area's natural (and fictional) highlights.

MAVORA LAKES CONSERVATION PARK

Within the Snowdon State Forest, this **conservation park's** (www.doc.govt.nz; Centre Hill Rd) huge golden meadows sit alongside two lakes – North and South Mavora – fringed by forest and towered over by the impressive Thomson and Livingstone Mountains, whose peaks rise to more than 1600m. Trampers can overnight at **Mavora Lakes Campsite** (adult/child $8/4), an unpowered 60-site camping space in a sublime setting in the heart of the park. The campsite is the starting point of the four-day, 50km Mavora–Greenstone Walkway.

Tours

Fiordland Tours TOURS
(Map p184; ☑ 0800 247 249; www.fiordlandtours.co.nz; 208 Milford Rd; adult/child from $149/69) Runs small-group bus and Milford Sound cruise tours (15 passengers or less), departing from Te Anau and stopping at scenic points along the way. It also provides track transport and guided day walks on the Kepler Track.

Southern Lakes Helicopters SCENIC FLIGHTS
(Map p184; ☑ 03-249 7167; www.southernlakeshelicopters.co.nz; Lakefront Dr) Offering flights over Te Anau for 30 minutes ($240) and longer trips with landings over Doubtful, Dusky and Milford Sounds (from $685), this operator's quarter-century of experience in Fiordland will reassure nervous flyers.

Wings & Water SCENIC FLIGHTS
(Map p184; ☑ 03-249 7405; www.wingsandwater.co.nz; Lakefront Dr) Take a scenic 20-minute flight over the Kepler Track (adult/child $225/130), or soar over Dusky, Doubtful and Milford Sounds (from $349/210) on longer joyrides of 40 minutes or more.

🛏 Sleeping

⭐ **Te Anau Lakefront Backpackers** HOSTEL $
(Map p184; ☑ 03-249 7713, 0800 200 074; www.teanaubackpackers.co.nz; 48-50 Lakefront Dr; tent sites $20, dm $35, d with/without bathroom from $98/88; 🖥) Tidy dorm and private rooms with a lakefront location hoist this backpackers to the top spot among Te Anau's budget beds. Gaze at the lake through huge windows, let the staff fill your brain with local

Te Anau

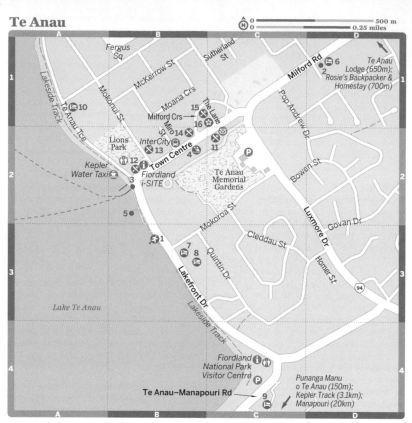

Te Anau

tips, or snooze in a game- and book-filled lounge with Dexter, the adopted house cat.

Rosie's Backpacker & Homestay HOSTEL $
(☎ 03-249 8431; www.rosiesbackpackers.co.nz; 23 Tom Plato Dr; dm/d $36/84; ☺ closed Jun & Jul; ☎) Guests become part of the family in this smart, intimate home-stay, a short walk north of the town centre in a wood-beamed house the hosts built themselves. It's not flash, but if you're feeling homesick and pining for a singalong around a piano, chances are you'll love it. If you'd rather keep to yourself or party all night, look elsewhere.

FIORDLAND & SOUTHLAND TE ANAU

Te Anau Lakeview Kiwi
Holiday Park & Motels HOLIDAY PARK $
(Map p184; ☑ 03-249 7457, 0800 483 262; www.te anauholidaypark.co.nz; 77 Te Anau–Manapouri Rd; unpowered/powered sites $23/24, dm/s/d without bathroom $35/40/80, units $125-306; @ ᐧ) This 9-hectare grassy lakeside holiday park has plenty of space to pitch your tent or park your van. It also has a wide range of accommodation from basic dorms through to tidy cabins and the rather swanky Marakura two-bedroom motel units with enviable lake and mountain views. Friendly staff will hook you up with local activities and transport.

Te Anau Top 10 HOLIDAY PARK $$
(Map p184; ☑ 03-249 7462, 0800 249 746; www. teanautop10.co.nz; 128 Te Anau Tce; powered sites from $50, cabins without bathroom $62-99, units with bathroom $150-236; @ ᐧ) Accommodation at this lakefront holiday park covers all budgets: motel units have slate-grey decor and compact kitchens, while private tent sites and well-priced cabins share modern kitchen facilities and bathrooms. Lake-facing hot tubs, a playground, bike hire and barbecue area are perfect when the sun's out, while a games room and sauna provide wet-weather distractions for parents and kids alike.

Keiko's Cottages B&B $$
(Map p184; ☑ 03-249 9248; www.keikos.co.nz; 228 Milford Rd; d from $175; ☺ closed Jun-Aug; ᐧ) Surrounded by Japanese-style flower gardens, complete with babbling water features and fish pond, Keiko's self-contained cottages are private, comfortable and decorated with feminine flair. The welcome is ebullient and breakfast ($30 per person) poses a difficult choice: Kiwi-style or a full Japanese banquet? The spa and sauna are worthy extras. Wi-fi vouchers cost extra.

★ Te Anau Lodge B&B $$$
(☑ 03-249 7477; www.teanaulodge.com; 52 Howden St; with breakfast s $225-350, d $250-375, tr $300-400; ᐧ) In a sea of functional but fusty motels, Te Anau's former Sisters of Mercy Convent distinguishes itself with unique history. Each chamber carries a whisper of its previous function, from the elegant 'Music Room' to the lavish 'Mother Superior'. Sip complimentary wine in a fireside chesterfield, collapse on a king-size bed, then awaken to an ample continental breakfast.

Radfords on the Lake MOTEL $$$
(Map p184; ☑ 03-249 9186; www.radfords onthelake.co.nz; 56 Lakefront Dr; 2-/4-person units from $299/499; ᐧ) ◆ Radfords isn't your bog-standard motel, as you've probably guessed by the grand-sounding name and commensurate prices. Set on manicured lawns across from the lake, this angular complex offers 14 pearly white units over two levels, all angled towards the view. They all have kitchens and five have spa baths.

✖ Eating

★ Sandfly Cafe CAFE $
(Map p184; ☑ 03-249 9529; 9 The Lane; mains $7-20; ☺ 7am-4.30pm; ᐧ) As popular with locals as travellers, Sandfly serves the town's best espresso alongside breakfasts, light meals of pasta or club sandwiches, and an impressive rack of sweet treats from caramel slices to berry friands (almond-flour cakes). Sun yourself on the lawn, or try to get maximum mileage out of the free 15 minutes of wi-fi.

Miles Better Pies FAST FOOD $
(Map p184; ☑ 03-249 9044; www.milesbetter pies.co.nz; 19 Town Centre; pies $5-6.50; ☺ 6am-6pm Oct-May, to 3pm Jun-Sep) The bumper selection here includes venison, lamb and mint, and fruit pies. There are a few pavement tables, but sitting and munching beside the lake is nicer.

Ristorante Paradiso ITALIAN $$
(Pizzeria da Toni; Map p184; ☑ 03-249 4305; www. paradisopizzeria.co.nz; 1 Milford Cres; mains $20-29; ☺ 4-9pm; ◆) Wood-fired pizzas with simple, high-quality toppings and homemade pastas are the stars of the show at this surprisingly authentic Italian restaurant. Red-gingham tablecloths and the odd splash of Italian art don't quite transport you to Rome but the marinara sauce comes close.

★ Kepler's SOUTH AMERICAN $$$
(Map p184; ☑ 03-249 7909; 90 Town Centre; mains $29-40; ☺ 5-9pm) Mountains of crayfish, mouth-watering ceviche and perfectly seared steaks are whisked to tables at this efficient but friendly family-run place. South American flair permeates the menu (quinoa-crusted orange roughy, Chilean malbec); we suggest the whopping roast lamb with a generous pour of merlot.

Redcliff Cafe MODERN NZ $$$
(Map p184; ☑ 03-249 7431; www.theredcliff.co.nz; 12 Mokonui St; mains $38-41; ☺ 4-10pm) Housed in a replica settler's cottage, relaxed Redcliff offers well-executed locally sourced food amid nostalgic decor (think old photos and antique sewing machines). We liked the

succulent slow-roasted pork and wild hare on barley risotto, but Redcliff is just as good for a drink in the antique bar (or the adjoining outdoor terrace, which catches the sun).

Live music on Friday nights in summer (December to February). One vegie meal choice daily.

🍷 Drinking & Entertainment

Black Dog Bar BAR
(Map p184; 03-249 9089; www.blackdogbar. co.nz; 7 The Lane; ⏱10am-late; 🛜) Cocktails, Kiwi-style tapas, a smooth soundtrack and plump black sofas by an open fire...they all conspire to make Black Dog the most sophisticated watering hole in Te Anau. It's attached to the Fiordland Cinema (p186),

Fiordland Cinema CINEMA
(Map p184; 03 249 8844; www.fiordlandcinema. co.nz; 7 The Lane; 🛜) In between regular showings of the excellent *Ata Whenua/ Fiordland on Film* (adult/child $10/5), essentially a 32-minute advertisement for Fiordland scenery, Fiordland Cinema serves as the local movie house.

ℹ Information

Fiordland i-SITE (Map p184; 03-249 8900; www.fiordland.org.nz; 19 Town Centre; ⏱8.30am-8pm Dec-Mar, to 5.30pm Apr-Nov) The official information centre, offering activity, accommodation and transport bookings.
Fiordland Medical Centre (03-249 7007; 25 Luxmore Dr; ⏱8am-5.30pm Mon-Fri, 9am-noon Sat, 10-10.30am & 5-5.30pm Sun) If you need medical help after hours, the centre's number will give the details of an on-call GP.
Fiordland National Park Visitor Centre (DOC; Map p184; 03-249 7924; www.doc.govt.nz; cnr Lakefront Dr & Te Anau–Manapouri Rd; ⏱8.30am-4.30pm) Can assist with Great Walks bookings, general hut tickets and information, with the bonus of a natural-history display and a shop stocking tramping supplies and essential topographical maps for backcountry trips.

ℹ Getting There & Away

InterCity (Map p184; 03-442 4922; www. intercity.co.nz; Miro St) Services to Milford Sound ($22 to $44, three hours, two to three daily) and Queenstown ($21 to $49, 3¼ hours, four daily), and daily morning buses to Gore ($20 to $40, 1¾ hours), Dunedin ($25 to $49, 4½ hours) and Christchurch ($31 to $81, 11 hours). Buses depart from a stop on Miro St, at the Town Centre end.
Naked Bus (https://nakedbus.com) Has daily bus services to Queenstown (from $30, 2¾

hours) and one daily morning bus to Milford Sound (from $32, 2¼ hours). Services depart from **Te Anau Lakeview Kiwi Holiday Park** (p185).
Topline Tours (p181) Offers year-round shuttles between Te Anau and Manapouri ($20), and, from November to March, transfers from Te Anau to the Kepler Track trailheads at the control gates ($5) and the Rainbow Reach swing bridge ($8).
Tracknet (0800 483 262; www.tracknet. net) From November to April Te Anau–based Tracknet has at least three daily scheduled buses to/from Te Anau Downs ($28, 30 minutes), the Divide ($41, 1¼ hours) and Milford Sound ($53, 2¼ hours), one bus to/from Manapouri ($25, 30 minutes) and four daily to Queenstown ($47, 2¾ hours). In winter, services are by demand. Buses depart from near the **Te Anau Lakeview Kiwi Holiday Park** (p185).

Milford Highway

Sometimes the journey is the destination, and that's certainly true of the 119km stretch of road between Te Anau and Milford Sound (SH94). The Milford Hwy offers the most easily accessible experience of Fiordland in all its diversity, taking in expanses of beautiful beech forest, gentle river valleys, mirror-like lakes, exquisite alpine scenery and ending at arguably New Zealand's most breathtaking vista, Milford Sound.

The journey should take about 2½ hours each way, but expect to spend time dawdling along walking trails and maxing out your camera's memory card. Most travellers embark on the Milford Hwy as a day trip from Te Anau, with a cruise on Milford Sound to break up the return journey. But the prospect of longer tramps or camping beneath jagged mountains might entice you to stay.

👁 Sights & Activities

Leaving Te Anau north along the Milford Hwy (SH94), the road meanders through rolling farmland atop the lateral moraine of the glacier that once gouged out Lake Te Anau. At the 29km mark it passes **Te Anau Downs**, where boats for the Milford Track depart. From here, an easy 45-minute return walk leads through forest to **Lake Mistletoe**, a small glacier-formed lake.

The road then heads into the **Eglinton Valley**, at first pocketed with sheepy pasture, then reaching deeper wilderness immersion as it crosses into Fiordland National Park: knobby peaks, thick beech forest, lupin-lined river banks and grassy meadows.

Just past the **Mackay Creek Campsite** (at 51km) are the **Eglinton Flats**, a wide-open space exposing truly epic views of Pyramid Peak (2295m) and Ngatimamoe Peak (2164m). The most popular roadside stop is **Mirror Lakes** (at 58km). A short boardwalk (five minutes' walk) overlooks glassy waters, their surface interrupted by occasional mallards. If you're lucky enough to stop by on a calm, clear day, the lakes perfectly reflect the mountains across the valley.

At the 77km mark, after an enchanting stretch of forest-framed road, is **Cascade Creek** and **Lake Gunn**. This area was known to Māori as O Tapara, and a stopover for parties heading to Anita Bay in search of *pounamu* (greenstone). The bewitching **Lake Gunn Nature Walk** (45 minutes return) loops through tall red beech forest. Moss-clung logs and a chorus of birdsong create a fairy-tale atmosphere, and side tracks lead to quiet lakeside beaches.

At 84km you pass across the **Divide**, the lowest east–west pass in the Southern Alps; from here the highway narrows and weaves. The roadside shelter is used by trampers finishing or starting the Routeburn or Greenstone and Caples Tracks. From here you can embark on a marvellous three-hour return walk along the the the start of the Routeburn, climbing up through beech forest to the alpine tussockland of **Key Summit**. On a good day the views of the Humboldt and Darran Mountains are sure to knock your socks off, and the nature walk around the boggy tops and stunted beech is a great excuse to linger.

From the Divide, the road falls into the beech forest of the Hollyford Valley (stop at **Pop's View** for a great outlook…if you can get a parking space). The road climbs through a cascade-tastic valley to the **Homer Tunnel**, 101km from Te Anau and framed by a high-walled, ice-carved amphitheatre. Begun as a relief project in the 1930s and completed in 1953, the tunnel is one way (traffic lights direct vehicle flow – patience required). Dark, rough-hewn and dripping with water, the 1270m-long tunnel emerges at the head of the spectacular **Cleddau Valley**. Any spare 'wows' might pop out about

ℹ **MILFORD HIGHWAY CHECKLIST**

➡ Set your alarm clock. Aim to leave Te Anau early (by 8am), or later in the morning (11am), to avoid the tour buses heading for midday sound cruises.

➡ Fill up with petrol in Te Anau. Also note that chains must be carried on icy or avalanche-risk days from May to November (there will be signs on the road); these can be hired from most service stations in Te Anau.

➡ Read up. Pick up DOC's *Fiordland National Park Day Walks* brochure ($2) from Fiordland i-SITE (p186) or Fiordland National Park Visitor Centre (p186), or download it at www.doc.govt. nz. Otherwise you risk zooming past the loveliest spots.

➡ Allow loads of time. The trip takes two to 2½ hours if you drive straight through, but take time to pull off the road and explore the many view points and nature walks along the way.

now. Kea (alpine parrots) hang around the tunnel entrance looking for food from tourists, but don't feed them as it's bad for their health.

About 10km before Milford Sound, the wheelchair- and pram-friendly **Chasm Walk** (20 minutes return) affords staggering views over the churning Cleddau River. Pebbles caught in its frenetic currents have hollowed boulders into shapes reminiscent of a Salvador Dalí scene. Along the final 9km to Milford Sound, watch for glimpses of Mt Tutoko (2723m), Fiordland's highest peak, above the beech forest.

🛌 Sleeping

There are eight basic DOC campsites (per adult/child $8/4) along the highway. All are scenic but also popular with sandflies. If you prefer four walls to canvas or campervans, find more robust accommodation at **Knob's Flat** (☑03-249 9122; www.knobsflat. co.nz; 6178 SH94; unpowered tent or campervan sites per adult/child $20/10, d $130-150), or reserve a frontier-feel cabin at Gunn's Camp (p191). Otherwise, you're better off returning to the abundant accommodation choices in Te Anau, 119km south.

TOMAS PAVELKA / SHUTTERSTOCK ©

1. Macetown (p225)
Some 15km north of Arrowtown, this gold-rush ghost town is an isolated and evocative destination.

2. Walking Franz Josef Glacier (p249)
A guided hike amid the stunning blue ice may be one of your most memorable South Island experiences.

3. Skyline Gondola, Queenstown (p202)
Enjoy access to a restaurant, activities and more – including stunning views of the city's surroundings.

4. Pancake Rocks, Punakaiki & Paparoa National Park (p264)
Striking limestone formations and a surging sea.

ⓘ MILFORD HIGHWAY TIPS

The majority of drivers along the Milford Hwy's 119km length are sightseers. Be on the lookout for cars decelerating suddenly, drifting across the centre line or parking dangerously. Allow plenty of time for your journey and leave adequate space between cars to avoid annoyance at fellow drivers (or worse).

Milford Sound

POP 120

The pot of gold at the end of Milford Hwy (SH94) is sublime Milford Sound (Piopiotahi). Rising above the fiord's indigo water is Mitre Peak (Rahotu), the deserved focal point of millions of photographs. Tapering to a cloud-piercing summit, the 1692m-high mountain appears sculpted by a divine hand.

In truth, it's the action of glaciers that carved these razor-edge cliffs. Scoured into the bare rock are pathways from tree avalanches, where entangled roots dragged whole forests down into darkly glittering water. When rain comes (and that's often), dozens of temporary waterfalls curtain the cliffs. Stirling and Lady Bowen Falls gush on in fine weather, with rainbows bouncing from their mists when sunlight strikes just right.

By 2019, Milford Sound will receive an estimated one million annual visitors – an almighty challenge to keep its beauty pristine. But out on the water, all human activity – cruise ships, divers, kayakers – seems dwarfed into insignificance.

🏃 Activities

Rosco's Milford Kayaks KAYAKING
(Map p184; ☑ 0800 476 726, 03-249 8500; www.roscosmilfordkayaks.com; 72 Town Centre, Te Anau; trips $99-199; ⊙ Nov-Apr) Rosco, a colourful character seasoned by decades of kayaking experience, leads guided tandem-kayak trips such as the 'Morning Glory' ($199), a challenging paddle the full length of the fiord to Anita Bay, and the 'Stirling Sunriser' ($195), which ventures beneath the 151m-high Stirling Falls. Beginners can take it easy on a two-hour paddle on the sound ($109).

Descend Scubadiving DIVING
(☑ 027 337 2363; www.descend.co.nz; dives incl gear $345) Black coral, more than 150 species of fish, the possibility of dolphins...

Milford Sound is as beautiful underwater as is it above. Descend's six-hour trips offer a sampler of both realms: cruising on Milford Sound in a 7m catamaran and two dives along the way. There are excursions for experienced divers and novices. Transport, equipment, hot drinks and snacks included.

Tours

Fiordland's most accessible experience is a cruise on Milford Sound, usually lasting 90 minutes or more. Numerous companies have booking desks in the flash cruise terminal, a 10-minute walk from the main car park, but it's always wiser to book ahead.

Each cruise company claims to be quieter, smaller, bigger, cheaper or in some way preferable to the rest. What really makes a difference is timing. Most bus tours aim for 1pm sailings, so if you avoid that time of day there will be fewer people on the boat, fewer boats on the water and fewer buses on the road.

If you're particularly keen on wildlife, opt for a cruise with a nature guide on board. These are usually a few minutes longer than the standard 'scenic' cruises, and often on smaller boats. Most companies offer coach transfers from Te Anau for an additional cost. Day trips from Queenstown make for a very long 13-hour day.

Arrive 20 minutes before departure. All cruises visit the mouth of the sound, just 15km from the wharf, poking their prows into the choppy waves of the Tasman Sea. Shorter cruises visit fewer en route 'highlights', which include Bowen Falls, Mitre Peak, Anita Bay and Stirling Falls.

Only visitable on trips run by Southern Discoveries and Mitre Peak Cruises (p191), **Milford Discovery Centre** (www.southerndiscoveries.co.nz; Harrison Cove; adult/child $36/18; ⊙ 9am-4pm), New Zealand's only floating underwater observatory, showcases interactive displays on the natural environment of the fiord. The centre offers a chance to view corals, tube anemones and bottom-dwelling sea perch from 10m below the waterline.

★ Real Journeys BOATING
(☑ 03-249 7416, 0800 656 501; www.realjourneys.co.nz) 🛶 Milford's biggest and most venerable operator runs a popular 1¾-hour scenic cruise (adult/child from $76/22). More specialised is the 2½-hour nature cruise (adult/child from $88/22), which homes in on wildlife with commentary from a nature guide. Overnight cruises are also available, from

which you can kayak and take nature tours in small boats en route.

Overnight trips depart from the cruise terminal in the mid-afternoon and return around 9.30am the following day. The *Milford Wanderer,* modelled on an old trading scow, accommodates 36 passengers in two- and four-bunk cabins with shared bathrooms (dorm/single/double $339/681/778). The *Milford Mariner* sleeps 60 in more-upmarket single ($803) or double ($918) en suite cabins. Cheaper prices apply from April through to September; food included but coach transport from Te Anau is extra.

Gilded with a long list of awards since it was founded in 1954, Real Journeys continues to be involved in local conservation efforts, from its minimal-impact cruises to fundraisers and charitable donations.

Cruise Milford BOATING
(📞 0800 645 367; www.cruisemilfordnz.com; adult/child from $95/18; ⏰ 10.45am, 12.45pm & 2.45pm) Offering a more personal touch than some of the big-boat tours, Cruise Milford's smaller vessels head out three times a day on 1¾-hour cruises, divulging great info from tectonics to wildlife.

Go Orange BOATING
(📞 03-442 7340, 0800 505 504; www.goorange. co.nz; adult/child from $45/15; ⏰ 9am, 12.30pm & 3pm) These low-cost two-hour cruises along the full length of Milford Sound include a complimentary breakfast, lunch or snack.

Mitre Peak Cruises BOATING
(📞 03-249 8110, 0800 744 633; www.mitrepeak. com; adult/child from $70/17) Two-hour cruises in smallish boats (maximum capacity 75), allowing closer views of waterfalls and wildlife than larger vessels. The 4.30pm cruise is a good choice because many larger boats are heading back at this time.

🛏 Sleeping

⭐ **Milford Sound Lodge** LODGE **$$$**
(📞 03-249 8071; www.milfordlodge.com; SH94; powered campervan sites $60, dm $40, chalets $415-465; 🛜) Alongside the Cleddau River, 1.5km from the Milford hub, this lodge feels simultaneously rustic and chic. Luxurious chalets have the wow factor, with either jaw-on-the-floor mountain views or a river-side setting, while the forest-clad campervan area and clean, no-frills dorm rooms (sleeping five to 11 people) suit smaller budgets. Book far in advance for November to April.

OFF THE BEATEN TRACK

DETOUR: HUMBOLDT FALLS & GUNN'S CAMP

Three kilometres north of the Divide, look out for a northeasterly detour off SH94. Follow the unsealed road (leading to the Hollyford Track) for 8km to reach **Gunn's Camp**. Blow dust off antique agricultural implements in the **museum** (Hollyford Rd; adult/child $2/free; ⏰ hours vary), or consider an **overnight stay** (www.gunnscamp.org.nz; Hollyford Rd; unpowered tent/campervan sites per person from $15, cabins $70, bed linen extra $7.50) in an unvarnished cabin, heated by a wood-fired stove. A further 9km northeast of here begins the Hollyford Track, where you will find the track to **Humboldt Falls** (off Hollyford Rd) (30 minutes' return). It's an easy 1.2km tramp through rainforest to a viewing platform where you can spy this distant 275m-high cascade.

🛈 Information

It's better to book a cruise in advance (and essential if you want an overnight cruise or a cruise-and-kayak combo). Otherwise, head straight to the cruise terminal to find booking desks for all the tour operators.

Although it's run by Southern Discoveries, the **Discover Milford Sound Information Centre** (📞 03-249 7931; www.southerndiscoveries. co.nz; SH94; ⏰ 8am-4pm) near Milford's main car park sells tickets for most of the tour and cruise companies, as well as for scenic flights and InterCity buses. There's also a mediocre cafe attached.

🛈 Getting There & Away

InterCity (p186) Runs twice-daily bus services to Milford Sound from Te Anau ($22 to $44, three hours) and Queenstown (from $44, six hours), onto which you can add a cruise or scenic flight when you book.

Naked Bus (p186) Runs daily morning buses from Te Anau to Milford Sound (from $32, 2¼ hours) and coach-and-cruise packages from Queenstown (from $111).

Tracknet (p186) From November to April Te Anau–based Tracknet has at least three daily scheduled buses to/from Te Anau Downs ($28, 30 minutes), the Divide ($41, 1¼ hours) and Milford Sound ($53, 2¼ hours). In winter (June to August), services are by demand.

Queenstown & Wanaka

Best Places to Eat

➡ Bespoke Kitchen (p213)

➡ Chop Shop (p224)

➡ Kai Whakapai (p231)

➡ Kika (p232)

➡ Public Kitchen & Bar (p213)

Best Places to Stay

➡ EcoScapes (p220)

➡ Hidden Lodge (p212)

➡ Wanaka Bakpaka (p230)

➡ Lime Tree Lodge (p231)

➡ YHA Queenstown Lakefront (p210)

Why Go?

Few people come to Queenstown to wind down. The self-styled 'adventure capital of the world' is a place where visitors come to throw their inhibitions out the window...and throw themselves out of planes and off mountain tops and bridges.

The region has a cinematic backdrop of mountains and lakes and a smattering of valley towns just as enticing as Queenstown itself. Wanaka may resemble Queenstown – lakeside setting, a fringe of mountains, a lengthy menu of adventures – but it runs at a less frenetic pace. Glenorchy is even more sedate, and yet it's the final stop for many on their way into arguably the finest alpine tramping terrain in NZ. History makes its home in gold-rush Arrowtown, where the main-street facades still hint at past glory. Settle in for dinner and a drink after the crowds disperse – the following day there'll be plenty more opportunities to dive back into Queenstown's action-packed whirlwind.

When to Go

➡ The fine and settled summer weather from January to March is the perfect backdrop to Queenstown's active menu of adventure sports and outdoor exploration. March also brings the Gibbston Wine & Food Festival to Queenstown Gardens.

➡ Gold returns to Arrowtown in autumn (March to May) with a vivid display of colour in the turning of the leaves.

➡ In late June the Queenstown Winter Festival celebrates the coming of the ski season. From June to August, the slopes of the four ski fields surrounding Queenstown and Wanaka are flush with skiers and snowboarders.

➡ The winter play season ends in a flourish from late August with Queenstown's Gay Ski Week and the Remarkables Ice & Mixed Festival.

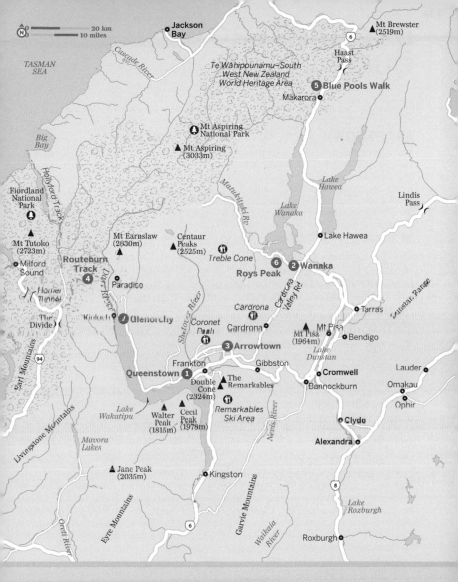

Queenstown & Wanaka Highlights

1 Queenstown (p200)
Taking the leap into any number of once-in-a-lifetime activities in this paradise for thrillseekers.

2 Wanaka (p225) Scaling a waterfall *via ferrata* before dining among the lakeside town's bevy of eateries.

3 Arrowtown (p221) Spending a day in a lower gear strolling this historic gold-rush town before discovering a couple of very chic bars.

4 Routeburn Track (p196) Tramping high into the mountains on arguably the greatest of NZ's Great Walks.

5 Blue Pools Walk (p234) Taking a short stroll to a luminous bloom of river colour just outside Makarora.

6 Roys Peak (p227) Snapping *that* photo and summiting this mountain with views over Lake Wanaka.

7 Glenorchy (p219) Discovering Paradise around the corner at one of NZ's most enticing tramping bases.

DAY TRIPS FROM QUEENSTOWN

ARROWTOWN

Transport yourself to the gold-rush era in this pretty little town lined with heritage buildings. We suspect there's less mud and rather more gift shops than would have greeted the initial prospectors, but if gentrification brings with it the quality selection of eateries that Arrowtown now boasts, we're certainly not complaining.

☆ Best Things to See/Do/Eat

◉ **Lakes District Museum & Gallery** Learn all about the gold rush and the town's early Chinese immigrants, and then hire a pan and have a go at panning for gold on the picturesque Arrow River which runs through the town. (p221)

🚲 **Arrow River Bridges Ride** Excellent bike-hire outlets will get you kitted out in style for a two-wheeled expedition along this scenic cycling trail. You can even arrange to be collected at the other end. (p221)

✖ **Chop Shop** You'll be spoilt for choice in Arrowtown, but our pick of the day-time options is this eccentric cafe tucked away above the shops. (p224)

☆ How to Get There

Car By car, it takes just over 20 minutes to reach Arrowtown. Make it a loop trip: head out along Gorge Rd and through Arthurs Point, then return alongside Lake Hayes and SH6.

Bus Catch the number 11 bus to Frankton and change to the number 10.

GLENORCHY

It's more about the journey than the destination on this wonderful day trip, tracing the edge of Lake Wakatipu to its northernmost point. The remote little town of Glenorchy sits at the head of a gorgeous river valley, surrounded by forest-draped mountains. It's the gateway to some of New Zealand's best wilderness walks.

☆ Best Things to See/Do/Eat

◉ **Glenorchy Lagoon** From the township, take an hour-long walk around this bewitching lagoon. Boardwalks will keep your feet dry on the swampy parts, and there are lots of opportunities for moody water-and-mountain photos. (p219)

🚲 **Routeburn Flats** The Routeburn Track is arguably NZ's best long-distance hike but, if you don't have three days to spare, get a taste for it on a three-hour hike along the end section. The trailhead is a 30-minute drive north of Glenorchy. (p219)

✖ **Queenie's Dumplings** There's not a lot to Glenorchy, so the presence of this authentic dumpling house comes as a very pleasant surprise. (p220)

☆ How to Get There

Car Unless you tag along with one of the hiking shuttles, you'll need your own wheels to get here. Take your time meandering along the lakeside, stopping at the various little beaches and viewpoints as the mood takes you.

WANAKA

With a breathtakingly beautiful lake-and-mountain setting, Wanaka is deserving of a much longer stay – but if a day trip is the only option, then don't miss it. Set out early and turn it into a grand loop, climbing up through the Crown Range and Cardrona on the way there, and returning via Lake Dunstan, Cromwell and the Gibbston Valley.

☆ Best Things to See/Do/Eat

◉ National Transport & Toy Museum While Wanaka has an abundance of natural attractions, this fascinating, nostalgia-inducing museum is deserving of an hour of your precious day trip time. (p226)

🌲 Roys Peak If you've got energy to burn and time to spare, this five-hour (return) hike is a goodie. It's not an easy stroll though. For a shorter alternative, head up Mt Iron (90 minutes return), conveniently located on the edge of the township. (p227)

✕ Kika It's only open in the evening, so finish your day with Italian-inspired tapas at this outstanding restaurant. Otherwise head to its big sister, Francesca's Italian Kitchen, for an authentic trattoria-style lunch. (p232)

☆ How to Get There

Car In the absence of snow, the quickest route by car is the Crown Range Rd through Cardrona, which takes around an hour. Allow an additional 30 minutes for SH6 via Cromwell.

Bus Various buses head between Queenstown and Wanaka.

Queenstown, with its excellent accommodation, restaurants and nightlife, is the logical base for exploring the Lakes Region. It's a compact area: snow notwithstanding, you can reach Glenorchy in 40 minutes and Wanaka in around an hour.

TRAMPING AROUND QUEENSTOWN & WANAKA

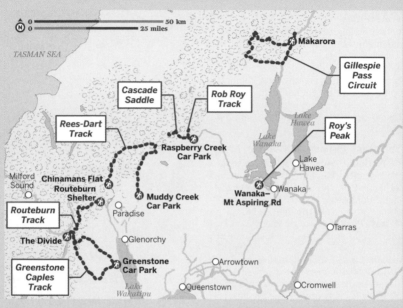

ROUTEBURN TRACK

START ROUTEBURN SHELTER
END THE DIVIDE
DURATION 3 DAYS
DISTANCE 32KM
DIFFICULTY MODERATE

Some trampers say the Routeburn Track is the greatest Great Walk of all. It's a high-level mountain route with fantastic views all the way – expansive panoramas of other ranges, and near-at-hand views of mirror-like tarns, waterfalls, fairy glades lined with plush moss, and gnarled trees with long, straggly, lichen beards.

The track can be started from either end. From the Routeburn Flats end, you'll walk along the top of **Routeburn Gorge** and then ascend past the impressive **Routeburn Falls**. Arriving at alpine **Lake Harris** is a awe-inspiring mountain moment, as is the moment you rise onto **Harris Saddle** with its vast view. From here, if you have any energy left, you can make a steep 1½- to two-hour detour up **Conical Hill**. On a clear day you can see waves breaking at Martins Bay, far away on the west coast, but it's not worth the climb on a cloudy or windy day. Shortly before you reach the Divide, a highly recommended one-hour detour heads up to the **Key Summit**, where there are views of the Hollyford Valley and the Eglinton and Greenstone Valleys.

During the Great Walks season (late October through April) you'll need to book ahead, which can be done online through **Great Walks Bookings** (☏ 0800 694 732; www.greatwalks.co.nz). You'll then need to call into the DOC visitor centre in either Queenstown or Te Anau to collect actual tickets, either the day before or on the day of departure. Outside of the season, bookings aren't required, but you'll still need to visit one of the DOC centres to purchase your hut and campsite tickets. There are four basic huts along the track: Routeburn Flats, Routeburn Falls, Lake Mackenzie and Lake Howden. Both the Routeburn Flats and Lake Mackenzie huts have camp-

At the quiet end of Lake Wakatipu some of New Zealand's finest mountain country awaits, but you barely need leave Wanaka for a memorable tramp.

sites nearby. The other option is to take a guided walk, staying at private lodges along the way, operated by **Ultimate Hikes** (p203).

The Routeburn Track remains open in winter, though traversing the alpine section after the snow falls is not recommended for casual hikers, as winter mountaineering skills are required. There are 32 avalanche paths across the section between Routeburn Falls and Lake Howden, and the avalanche risk continues through to spring. Always check conditions with DOC.

There are car parks at both ends of the track, but they're unattended, so don't leave any valuables in your vehicle. Track shuttles are plentiful, and many people arrange to get dropped at the Divide to start their walk after a Milford Sound tour, or alternatively time the end of their walk to catch one of the Milford Sound buses.

GREENSTONE CAPLES TRACKS

START/END GREENSTONE CAR PARK
DURATION 4 DAYS
DISTANCE 61KM
DIFFICULTY MODERATE

From the shores of large Lake Wakatipu, this scenic tramp circuits through the Caples and Greenstone Valleys, crossing the subalpine McKellar Saddle, where it almost intersects with the Routeburn Track.

The name of the Greenstone Valley hints at this valley's ancient use as a route for Māori to access the Dart Valley to collect highly prized *pounamu* (greenstone), though no Māori archaeological sites have been found in the Greenstone and Caples Valleys themselves. Europeans would later traverse the valleys in search of grazing sites, with farming commencing in the Caples in 1880. The Greenstone and Pass Burn were utilised as stock routes.

The Greenstone Valley is wide and open with tussock flats and beech forest. The Caples is narrower and more heavily forested,

interspersed with grassy clearings. Many trampers consider the Caples, with its park-like appearance, to be the more beautiful of the two.

The two tracks link at McKellar Saddle and again near Greenstone car park, where the road links to Glenorchy and on to Queenstown.Trampers can choose to walk just one track in one direction (joining the end of the Routeburn Track down to the Divide), or traverse both as a there-and-back journey of four days. Routeburn trampers planning to continue on the Greenstone can easily walk from Lake Mackenzie Hut to McKellar Hut, which takes around five to seven hours.

REES-DART TRACK

START MUDDY CREEK CAR PARK
END CHINAMANS FLAT
DURATION 4 DAYS
DISTANCE 63KM
DIFFICULTY MODERATE TO DEMANDING

The Rees Dart Track connects two splendid schist-lined valleys shaped by glaciation. The relatively small Dart Glacier was once part of an enormous system that terminated at Kingston, 135km away at the southern end of Lake Wakatipu.

As this tramp winds up one valley and back down the other, it takes in a variety of scenery, such as meadows of flowering herbs and mighty bluffs and moraine walls.

Pinched between the Routeburn Track and Cascade Saddle, the Rees-Dart has become a popular tramp, but it is longer and definitely more challenging than either the Routeburn or Greenstone Caples, and has several stream crossings, which can be hazardous in heavy rain or snowmelt.

The most common approach to the tramp is to head up the Rees Valley and return down the Dart – this is the easiest direction in which to climb **Rees Saddle**. Plan an extra night at **Dart Hut** if you want to include a day trip to **Dart Glacier** or even on to Cascade Saddle (p198).

CASCADE SADDLE

START/END RASPBERRY CREEK CAR PARK
DURATION 3 DAYS
DISTANCE 30KM
DIFFICULTY DEMANDING

Cascade Saddle is one of the most beautiful and dramatic of all the passes that trampers can reach in New Zealand. Pinched between the West Matukituki and Dart Valleys, it's a very steep and demanding climb. On a fine day, the rewards are as numerous as the mountains you can see from atop the alpine pass, including an eyeball-to-eyeball view of Tititea/Mt Aspiring.

Cascade Saddle can also be reached from Dart Hut (p197) on the Rees-Dart Track, providing an enticing opportunity for a four-day tramp, crossing the pass from the West Matukituki Valley and exiting along the Dart Valley. The easiest approach is from the West Matukituki.

The West Matukituki is tramping royalty in the South Island, and it's worth building in a couple of extra days to explore upstream to **Liverpool Hut**, and take a detour out to **Rob Roy Glacier**. You could easily while away a decent week based at **Aspiring Hut**, branching out on day walks and soaking up the spectacular mountain scenes.

Be warned: Cascade Saddle is a difficult climb, partially smothered in super-slippery snow grass, and trampers have fallen to their deaths here. It should not be attempted by inexperienced trampers, or in adverse conditions. If you have any doubts, seek advice from the warden in Aspiring Hut, who will have current weather forecasts on hand.

ROB ROY TRACK

START/END RASPBERRY CREEK CAR PARK
DURATION 3–4 HOURS
DISTANCE 10KM
DIFFICULTY EASY TO MODERATE

It's not uncommon to hear this short tramp, into a side pocket of the Matukituki Valley, described as the finest day walk in the South Island, and it's not difficult to see why. Few tracks provide such large-scale mountain scenery in such a short time frame, with the tramp beginning along the Matukituki Valley before climbing 400m through beech forest into a high and dramatic enclosure of mountains and glaciers.

The mix of beech forest and the clear blue water of Rob Roy Stream creates a bit of a fantasyland, before it all peels back to reveal the sort of mountain scene you might expect to find only after days of wilderness tramping.

Pay careful heed to the avalanche advisories in winter or spring, as the track beyond the lower lookout is susceptible to them.

GILLESPIE PASS CIRCUIT

START/END MAKARORA
DURATION 3 DAYS
DISTANCE 58KM
DIFFICULTY MODERATE TO DEMANDING

Located in the northern reaches of Mt Aspiring National Park, this popular tramp offers outstanding mountain scenery – some

View of Lake Wanaka from the Roy's Peak track.

would say it rivals both the Matukituki and Glenorchy area tramps.

There is plenty to see and enjoy along this route, including valleys filled with silver beech (tawhai), and alpine tussock fields alive with grasshoppers, black butterflies, buttercups and mountain daisies. The bird life you might encounter includes the fantail, tomtit and rifleman, as well as the mohua (yellowhead) and the parakeet known as the kakariki.

The tramp, which should only be undertaken by experienced parties, is best approached from the Young Valley to the Wilkin Valley, the easiest way to cross Gillespie Pass. This also makes for a thrilling finish if you choose, as many do, to eschew the final four to five hours' walking in favour of a jetboat ride.

It is recommended that you carry a tent, as huts are often overcrowded in summer.

ROY'S PEAK
START/END WANAKA–MT ASPIRING RD
DURATION 5–6 HOURS
DISTANCE 16KM
DIFFICULTY MODERATE

If you've seen any one photo of Lake Wanaka (other than of *that* tree), it's likely to have been taken from the Roys Peak Track, which provides one of the most photogenic vantage points in NZ. In the kindest of descriptions, the climb to Roys Peak is a grind, ascending 1220m from near the lakeshore to the antenna-tipped summit, but oh, those views...it's truly a spectacular tramp.

Those very views have made this an extremely popular track, though many hikers aspire only to reach the ridge, about three-quarters of the way up, from where the famous 'selfie with Lake Wanaka' moment bombards Instagram.

QUEENSTOWN

POP 12,500

Queenstown is as much a verb as a noun, a place of doing that likes to spruik itself as the 'adventure capital of the world'. It's famously the birthplace of bungy jumping, and the list of adventures you can throw yourself into here is encyclopedic – from alpine heliskiing to zip-lining. It's rare that a visitor leaves without having tried something that ups their heart rate, but to pigeonhole Queenstown as just a playground is to overlook its cosmopolitan dining and arts scene, its fine vineyards, and the diverse range of bars that can make evenings as fun-filled as the days.

Leap, lunge or luge here, but also find time to simply sit at the lakeside and watch the ever-dynamic play of light on the Remarkables and Lake Wakatipu, creating one of the most beautiful and dramatic natural scenes in NZ.

Expect big crowds, especially in summer and winter, but also big experiences.

History

The Queenstown region was deserted when the first British people arrived in the mid-1850s, although there is evidence of previous Māori settlement. Sheep farmers came first, but after two shearers discovered gold on the banks of the Shotover River in 1862, a deluge of prospectors followed.

Within a year the settlement was a mining town with streets, permanent buildings and a population of several thousand. It was declared 'fit for a queen' by the NZ government; hence Queenstown was born. Lake Wakatipu was the principal means of transport, and at the height of the boom there were four paddle steamers and 30 other craft plying the waters.

By 1900 the gold had petered out and the population was a mere 190. It wasn't until the 1950s that Queenstown became a popular holiday destination.

◉ Sights

Lake Wakatipu   LAKE

(Map p204) Shaped like a cartoon lightning bolt, Lake Wakatipu is NZ's third-largest lake. It reaches a depth of 379m, meaning the lake bed actually sits below sea level. Five rivers flow into it but only one (the Kawarau) flows out, making it prone to sometimes dramatic floods. The lake can be experienced at any number of speeds: the classic TSS Earnslaw (p207) steamboat trip, a spin with KJet (p206), the water taxi (p218), below decks in the Underwater Observatory (p202), or a shark's-eye view with **Hydro Attack** (Map p208; ☑0508 493 762; www.hydroattack.co.nz; Lapsley Butson Wharf; $149; ⊙9am-6pm Nov-Mar, 10am-4.30pm Apr-Oct).

If the water looks clean, that's because it is. Scientists have rated it as 99.9% pure – you're better off dipping your glass in the lake than buying bottled water. It's also very cold. That beach by Marine Pde may look tempting on a scorching day, but trust us – you won't want to splash about for long in water that hovers around 10°C year-round. Because cold water increases the risk of drowning, local bylaws require the wearing of life jackets in all boats under 6m, including kayaks, on the lake (and all of the district's lakes).

Māori tradition sees the lake's shape as the burnt outline of the evil giant Matau sleeping with his knees drawn up. Local lad Matakauri set fire to the bed of bracken on which the giant slept in order to rescue his beloved Manata, a chief's daughter who was kidnapped by the giant. The fat from Matau's body created a fire so intense that it burnt a hole deep into the ground.

ESSENTIAL QUEENSTOWN & WANAKA

Eat outdoors in the lingering summer dusk at the string of lakeside restaurants in both Queenstown and Wanaka.

Drink microbrews from near and far at Smiths Craft Beer House (p215) and Atlas Beer Cafe (p215).

Read *Creative Landscape Photography I* (2014) by Queenstown-based photographers Mike Langford and Jackie Ranken, a guide to capturing outdoor scenes, focusing on local destinations.

Listen to the silence as you kayak blissfully around Glenorchy and Kinloch.

Watch *Top of the Lake*, the Jane Campion–directed TV series set around Glenorchy.

Go online www.queenstownnz.co.nz, www.lakewanaka.co.nz

Queenstown Region

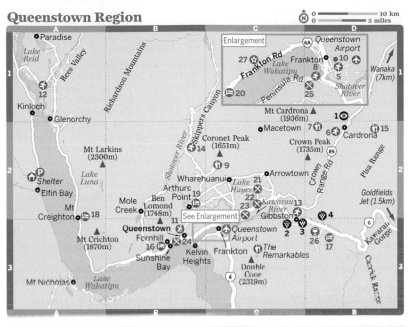

Queenstown Region

Queenstown Gardens PARK
(Map p204; Park St) Set on its own tongue of land framing Queenstown Bay, this pretty park is the perfect city escape right within the city. Laid out in 1876, it features an 18-'hole' **frisbee golf course** (Map p204; www.queenstowndiscgolf.co.nz; Queenstown Gardens)

FREE, an **ice-skating rink** (Map p204; ☏ 03-441 8000; www.queenstownicearena.co.nz; 29 Park St; entry incl skate hire $19; ⊙ 10am-5pm mid-Apr–mid-Oct), skate park, lawn-bowls club, tennis courts, mature exotic trees (including large sequoias and some fab monkey puzzles by the rotunda) and a rose garden. To stroll a loop around the peninsula and gardens should take about 30 minutes.

Underwater Observatory   VIEWPOINT

(Map p208; ☑03-442 6142; www.kjet.co.nz; Marine Pde; adult/child $10/5; ⊘8.30am-dusk) Six windows showcase life under the lake in this reverse aquarium (the people are behind glass) beneath the KJet office. Large brown trout abound, and look out for freshwater eels and scaup ducks, which dive past the windows – especially when the coin-operated food-release box is triggered. A KJet trip (p206) gets you free entry.

St Peter's Anglican Church   CHURCH

(Map p208; ☑03-442 8391; www.stpeters.co.nz; 2 Church St) This pretty stone building (1932) has colourful stained glass and an impressive gilded and painted organ. Take a look at the eagle-shaped cedar lectern, carved and donated in 1874 by John Ah Tong, a Chinese immigrant.

Kiwi Birdlife Park   ZOO

(Map p204; ☑03-442 8059; www.kiwibird.co.nz; Brecon St; adult/child $49/24; ⊘9am-5pm, shows 11am, 1.30pm & 4pm) These two hectares are home to 10,000 native plants, tuatara and scores of birds, including kiwi, kea, NZ falcons, parakeets and extremely rare black stilts. Stroll around the aviaries, watch the conservation show and tiptoe quietly into the darkened kiwi houses. Kiwi feedings take place five times a day.

Skyline Gondola   CABLE CAR

(Map p204; ☑03-441 0101; www.skyline.co.nz; Brecon St; adult/child return $35/22; ⊘9am-9pm) Hop aboard for some fantastic views as the gondola squeezes through pine forest to its grandstand location 400m above Queenstown. At the top there's the inevitable cafe, restaurant, souvenir shop and observation deck, as well as the Queenstown Bike Park (p205), Skyline Luge (p207), **Ledge Bungy** (Map p204; ☑0800 286 4958; www.bungy.co.nz; adult/child $195/145), **Ledge Swing** (Map p204; ☑0800 286 4958; www.bungy.co.nz; adult/child $160/110) and Ziptrek Ecotours (p206). At night there are Māori culture shows from **Kiwi Haka** (Map p204; ☑03-441 0101; www.skyline.co.nz; Skyline; adult/child incl gondola $77/52) and stargazing tours (including gondola, adult/child $93/49).

Walking trails include the **Skyline Loop track** through the Douglas firs (30 minutes return). The energetic (or frugal) can forgo the gondola and hike to the top on the **Tiki Trail** (Map p204), while the popular Ben Lomond Track (p203) climbs on another 940m.

 ## Activities

Head to Shotover St to get a handle on the baffling array of activities on offer in Queenstown. This street, particularly the two blocks between Stanley and Brecon Sts, is wall-to-wall with adventure-tour operators selling their products, interspersed with travel agencies and 'information centres' hawking the very same products. Adding to the confusion is the fact that some stores change their name from summer to winter, while some tour operators list street addresses that are primarily their pick-up points rather than distinct shopfronts for the business.

If you're planning on tackling several activities, various combination tickets are available, including those offered by **Queenstown Combos** (Map p208; ☑03-442 7318; www.combos.co.nz; The Station, cnr Shotover & Camp Sts).

Skiing

Queenstown has two excellent ski fields: The Remarkables (p203) and Coronet Peak (p203). If you fancy a change of scenery, there's also Cardrona Alpine Resort (p233) and Treble Cone (p228) near Wanaka. Coronet Peak is the only field to offer night skiing, which is an experience not to be missed if you strike a starry night. Roads around Queenstown become almost commuter-busy on ski mornings and evenings, so taking the NZSki Snowline Express (p218) can mean one less vehicle holding up the show.

The ski season generally lasts from around June to September. In winter, shops throughout Queenstown are full of ski gear for purchase and hire; Outside Sports (p207) and **Small Planet Outdoors** (Map p208; ☑03-442 5397; www.smallplanetsports.com; 15-17 Shotover St; ⊘9am-7pm Oct-May, 8am-9pm Jun-Sep) are reliable options.

Even outside of the main ski season, heliskiing is an option for serious, cashed-up skiers; try **Harris Mountains Heli-Ski** (Map p208; ☑03-442 6722; www.heliski.co.nz; The Station, cnr Shotover & Camp Sts; from $990), **Alpine Heliski** (Map p208; ☑03-441 2300; www.alpineheliski.com; 37 Shotover St; 3-8 runs $940-1340; ⊘Jul-Sep) or **Southern Lakes Heliski** (Map p208; ☑03-442 6222; www.heliskinz.com; Torpedo 7, 20 Athol St; from $1050).

Coronet Peak
SKIING

(Map p42; ☑03-442 4620; www.nzski.com; Coronet Peak Rd; daily lift pass adult/child $119/55) New Zealand's oldest commercial ski field, opened in 1947, offers excellent skiing and snowboarding for all levels thanks to its treeless slopes and multimillion-dollar snow-making system. It's also the only one to offer night skiing, staying open until 9pm on Fridays and Saturdays at the peak of the season (and on Wednesdays through July).

The Remarkables
SKIING

(Map p201; ☑03-442 4615; www.nzski.com; daily lift pass adult/child $119/55) Remarkable by name, and remarkable visually, too, this ski field across the lake from Queenstown has a good smattering of intermediate, advanced and beginner runs. The access road is rough, but shuttles from Queenstown head here during the ski season, so you don't have to worry about driving yourself.

Tramping

DOC publishes a dedicated *Wakatipu Walks* brochure, as well as the *Head of Lake Wakatipu* brochure, which covers trails closer to Glenorchy. Between them, they outline more than 60 day walks in the area, including Ben Lomond (p203), Queenstown Hill (p203) and the Tiki Trail (p202). They can be downloaded from the DOC website (www.doc.govt.nz), or picked up from DOC's Queenstown visitor centre (p217).

Ben Lomond Track
TRAMPING

(Map p204; www.doc.govt.nz) The popular track to Ben Lomond (1748m, six to eight hours return) culminates in probably the best accessible view in the area. From the top gondola station, the track climbs almost 1000m, and past Ben Lomond Saddle it gets pretty steep and rocky, but the views offered here are quite incredible, stretching over Lake Wakatipu and as far as Tititea/Mt Aspiring.

Snow and ice can make it even more difficult, so in winter, check at the DOC visitor centre (p217) before setting out.

Queenstown Hill/Te Tapunui
Time Walk
TRAMPING

(Map p204) Ascend 500m to the summit of Queenstown Hill/Te Tapunui for a 360-degree view over the lake and along the Remarkables. The walk takes around three hours return. Access is from Belfast Tce.

Ultimate Hikes
TRAMPING

(Map p208; ☑03-450 1940; www.ultimatehikes.co.nz; The Station, Duke St entrance; ⊙Nov-Apr) 🏃 If you like your adventure with a little comfort, Ultimate Hikes offers three-day guided tramps on the Routeburn (from $1375) and Milford (from $2130) Tracks, staying in its own well-appointed private lodges. It also runs day walks on both tracks (from $179) and a couple of combinations of tracks. Prices include transfers from Queenstown, meals and accommodation.

Guided Walks New Zealand
TRAMPING

(Map p201; ☑03-442 3000; www.nzwalks.com; unit 29, 159 Gorge Rd) Guided walks ranging from half-day nature walks near Queenstown (adult/child $109/69) to a day on the Routeburn Track ($199/140) and the full three-day Hollyford Track (from $1895/1495). Also offers snowshoeing in winter.

Cycling

Since the opening of the Queenstown Bike Park (p205) in 2011, Queenstown has been entrenched as a bona fide international destination for mountain bikers. Your best bets for hiring serious wheels in the bike park are **Vertigo Bikes** (Map p208; ☑03-442 8378; www.vertigobikes.co.nz; 4 Brecon St;

> ### WATCH THIS CYCLING SPACE
>
> The backbone of the cycling network in this region is the Queenstown Trail, a series of five routes that radiate out like spokes from Queenstown, providing 120km of traffic-free riding. But plans are afoot to connect the Queenstown Trail to the popular Otago Central Rail Trail (p118), creating an interlinked network of more than 500km of trails – effectively you will be able to cycle almost from Dunedin to Queenstown entirely on bike trails.
>
> The $26-million project will involve building 35km of trail from Gibbston through the Kawarau Gorge to Cromwell, with another 35km of new trail linking Cromwell to Clyde, where it will connect to the rail trail. A spur trail will also be built from Cromwell to Wanaka, providing a full cycling link between Queenstown and Wanaka. The project is expected to be completed around 2021.

Queenstown

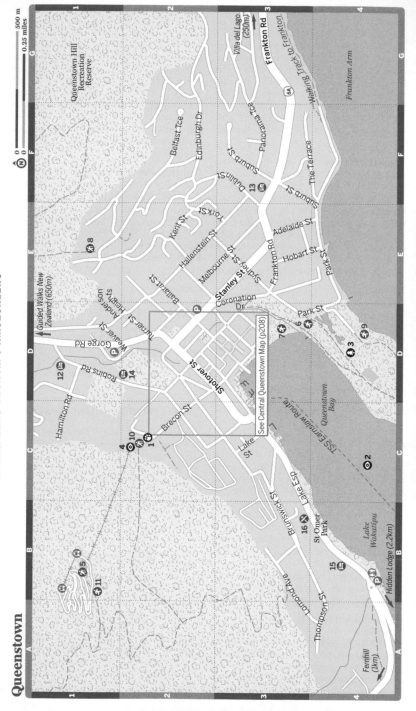

Queenstown Hill Recreation Reserve

Guided Walks New Zealand (650m)

Villa del Lago (250m)

Frankton Rd

Walking Track to Frankton

Frankton Arm

Belfast Tce

Edinburgh Dr

Panorama Tce

The Terrace

Suburb St

Dublin St

13

Suburb St

Kent St

York St

Adelaide St

Hallenstein St

Melbourne St

Sydney St

Frankton Rd

Hobart St

Park St

Ballarat St

Anderson Heights

Turner St

Weaver St

Gorge Rd

Robins Rd

Hamilton Rd

12

14

8

Stanley St

Coronation Dr

P

Park St

6

7

9

3

See Central Queenstown Map (p208)

Shotover St

Brecon St

4

10

1

Lake St

TSS Earnslaw Route

Queenstown Bay

2

Brunswick St

Lake Esp

St Omer Park

16

Lomond Ave

Thompson St

15

Lake Wakatipu

Hidden Lodge (2.2km)

P

Fernhill (1km)

500 m
0.25 miles
N

Queenstown

rental half/full day from $39/59; ⊙8am-7pm) and Outside Sports (p207).

The **Queenstown Trail** links five scenic cycling routes that radiate out like spokes to Arrowtown, Gibbston, Jack's Point, Lake Hayes and along the shores of Lake Wakatipu – 120km of trails in total. The trail is suitable for cyclists of all levels. Bike-hire places such as **ChargeAbout** (Map p201; ☑03-442 6376; http://chargeabout. co.nz; Hilton Hotel, 79 Peninsula Rd, Kelvin Heights; ebike half/full day $79/119; ⊙10am-5pm) and Arrowtown Bike Hire (p222) typically offer packages that include shuttle-bus pick-ups from Gibbston – ride one way, sip a few wines and get a designated driver for the return trip.

Queenstown Bike Park   MOUNTAIN BIKING
(Map p204; ☑03-441 0101; www.skyline.co.nz; Skyline Gondola; half/full day incl gondola $70/95; ⊙Sep-May) More than 30 different trails – from easy (green) to extreme (double black) – radiate out from the top of the Skyline Gondola. Once you've descended the 400m of vertical, simply jump on the gondola and do it all over again. The best trail for novice riders is the 6km-long **Hammy's Track**, which is studded with lake views and picnic spots.

Bungy, Swings & Zip-lines
**Shotover Canyon
Swing & Fox**   ADVENTURE SPORTS
(Map p208; ☑03-442 6990; www.canyonswing. co.nz; 34 Shotover St; swing $229, fox $169, swing & fox combo $299) ✦ Pick from any number of jump styles – backwards, in a chair, upside down – and then leap from a 109m cliff

above the Shotover River, with 60m of free fall and a wild swing across the canyon at 150km/h. The Canyon Fox, new in 2016, can have you whizzing across the Shotover Canyon, more than 180m above the river.

AJ Hackett Bungy   BUNGY JUMPING
(Map p208; ☑0800 286 4958, 03-450 1300; www.bungy.co.nz; The Station, cnr Camp & Shotover Sts) The bungy originator now offers jumps from three sites in the Queenstown area, with giant swings available at two of them. It all started at the historic 1880 **Kawarau Bridge** (Map p201; ☑0800 286 4958; www.bungy.co.nz; Gibbston Hwy; adult/child $195/145), 23km from Queenstown, which became the world's first commercial bungy site in 1988. The 43m leap has you plunging towards the river, and is the only bungy site in the region to offer tandem jumps.

The Kawarau Bridge site also features the **Kawarau Zipride** (Map p201; ☑0800 286 4958; www.bungy.co.nz; Gibbston Hwy; adult/ child $50/40, 3-/5-ride pack $105/150), a zipline (flying fox) along the riverbank that reaches speeds of 60km/h. Multi-ride packs can be split between groups, making it a far cheaper alternative to the bungy.

The closest options to Queenstown are the Ledge Bungy (p202) and Ledge Swing (p202), set just beneath the top station of the Skyline Gondola. The drop is 47m, but it's 400m above town. In winter you can even leap into the dark.

Last but most airy is the **Nevis Bungy** (Map p208; ☑0800 286 4958; www.bungy.co.nz; The Station, cnr Camp & Shotover Sts; $275), the highest leap in New Zealand. From Queenstown, 4WD buses will transport you onto private farmland where you can jump from a specially constructed pod, 134m above the Nevis River. The **Nevis Swing** (Map p208; ☑0800 286 4958; www.bungy.co.nz; solo $195, tandem per person $175) starts 160m above the river and cuts a 300m arc across the canyon on a rope longer than a rugby field – yes, it's the world's biggest swing.

If you're keen to try more than one AJ Hackett experience, enquire about the range of combo tickets.

Ziptrek Ecotours
ADVENTURE SPORTS

(Map p204; ☑03-441 2102; www.ziptrek.co.nz; Skyline Gondola) ✈ Incorporating a series of zip-lines (flying foxes), this thrill-ride takes you whirring through the forest canopy, from treetop platform to treetop platform, high above Queenstown. Choose from the two-hour four-line Moa tour (adult/child $139/89) or the gnarlier and faster three-hour six-line Kea option ($189/139); both end back at the base of the gondola.

Jetboating

Shotover Jet
BOATING

(☑03-442 8570; www.shotoverjet.com; Gorge Rd, Arthurs Point; adult/child $145/75) ✈ Half-hour jetboat trips through the narrow Shotover Canyon, with lots of thrilling 360-degree spins and reaching speeds of 85km/h.

Skippers Canyon Jet
BOATING

(Map p201; ☑03-442 9434; www.skipperscanyonjet.co.nz; Skippers Rd; adult/child $145/85) ✈ A 30-minute jetboat blast through the remote and hard-to-access Skippers Canyon, among the narrowest gorges on the Shotover River. Trips pick up from Queenstown, taking around three hours in total.

KJet
BOATING

(Map p208; ☑03-442 6142; www.kjet.co.nz; adult/child $129/69) Skim, skid and spin around Lake Wakatipu and the Kawarau and Lower Shotover Rivers on these one-hour trips, leaving from the main town pier.

Rafting & Riverboarding

Queenstown Rafting
RAFTING

(Map p208; ☑03-442 9792; www.queenstownrafting.co.nz; 35 Shotover St; rafting/helirafting $229/339) ✈ Rafts year-round on the churning Shotover River (Grades III to V) and calmer Kawarau River (Grades II to III). Half-day trips give you two to three hours on the water. Helirafting trips are an exciting alternative, and there are multiday trips on the Landsborough River. Rafters must be at least 13 years old and weigh more than 40kg.

Family Adventures
RAFTING

(Map p208; ☑03-442 8836; www.familyadventures.co.nz; adult/child $189/120; ☺Oct-Apr; ⚐) Gentle (Grades I to II) rafting trips on the Shotover River, suitable for children aged three years and older. Trips depart from Browns Ski Shop (39 Shotover St).

Serious Fun Riverboarding
ADVENTURE SPORTS

(Map p208; ☑03-442 5262; http://riverboarding.co.nz; 37 Shotover St; from $225) Steer buoyant sledges or bodyboards on the rapids and whirlpools of the Kawarau River.

FIXING THE KNOTS

After days of adventure and activity, your body might well be craving a break in the pace. Here's our pick of the best ways to slow down and recharge in Queenstown.

➡ Visit **Onsen Hot Pools** (☑03-442 5707; www.onsen.co.nz; 160 Arthurs Point Rd, Arthurs Point; 1/2/3/4 people $75/95/129/152; ☺10am-11pm), which has private Japanese-style hot tubs with mountain views. Book ahead and one will be warmed up for you.

➡ Let the goodness come to you with in-room massage and spa treatments with the **Mobile Massage Company** (Map p208; ☑0800 426 161; 2c Shotover St; 1hr from $125; ☺9am-9pm).

➡ Check into **Hush Spa** (Map p208; ☑03-442 9656; www.hushspa.co.nz; 1st fl, 32 Rees St; 30/60min massage from $70/129; ☺9am-6pm Fri-Mon, to 9pm Tue-Thu) for a massage or pedicure.

➡ Make the short trek to Millbrook near Arrowtown, where the **Spa at Millbrook** (p223) is regularly rated as NZ's best spa.

➡ Catch a water taxi across the lake to **Eforea Spa at Hilton** (Map p201; ☑03-450 9416; www.queenstownhilton.com; 79 Peninsula Rd, Kelvin Heights; treatments from $70; ☺9am-8pm).

RAINY DAY OPTIONS

Book in for a Japanese-style spa experience at **Onsen Hot Pools** (p206) in Queenstown, or head to Arrowtown for a movie at the delightful **Dorothy Browns** (p225) cinema. If you're holed up in Wanaka, **Cinema Paradiso** (p232) and **Ruby's** (p232) are equally cool. Other all-weather attractions in Wanaka include **Puzzling World** (p227), **Warbirds & Wheels** (p227) and you could easily spend a whole day at the excellent **National Transport & Toy Museum** (p226). You can always wet your insides as well at **Chard Farm** (p216), **Gibbston Valley** (p216) and **Peregrine** (p216) wineries in the Gibbston Valley, **Rippon** (p227) and **Archangel** (p227) in Wanaka, or the **Cardrona Distillery & Museum** (p233).

Skydiving, Paragliding & Parasailing

NZone ADVENTURE SPORTS
(Map p208; ☑ 03-442 5867; www.nzoneskydive. co.nz; 35 Shotover St; from $299) Jump out of a perfectly good airplane from 9000, 12,000 or 15,000ft...in tandem with someone who actually knows what they're doing.

GForce Paragliding PARAGLIDING
(Map p204; ☑ 03 441 8581; www.nzgforce.com; incl gondola $219) Tandem paragliding from the top of the gondola (9am departures are $20 cheaper).

Queenstown Paraflights ADVENTURE SPORTS
(Map p208; ☑ 03-441 2242; www.paraflights. co.nz; solo $159, tandem/triple per person $129/99) Take a solo, tandem or triple paraflight, zipping along 200m above the lake, pulled behind a boat. Departs from the town pier.

Other Activities

If you've heard it can be done, it's likely that it can be done in Queenstown. Short of us writing an activities encyclopedia, check in at the i-SITE (p217) if you're interested in the likes of golf, minigolf, sailing or diving.

Climbing Queenstown CLIMBING
(Map p208; ☑ 027 477 9393; www.climbing queenstown.com; 9 Shotover St; from $179) Rock-climbing, mountaineering and guided tramping and snowshoeing trips in the Remarkables. Trips depart from (and can be booked at) **Outside Sports** (Map p208; ☑ 03-441 0074; www.outsidesports.co.nz; 9 Shotover St; ⊗ 8.30am-8pm).

Skyline Luge ADVENTURE SPORTS
(Map p204; ☑ 03-441 0101; www.skyline.co.nz; Skyline Gondola; 2/3/5 rides incl gondola adult $49/52/56, child $37/42/46; ⊗ from 10am, closing times vary btwn 6pm & 9pm) 🐾 Ride the gondola to the top, then hop on a three-wheeled cart to ride 800m of track. Your first run

must be on the easy Blue Track then you're allowed to advance to the Red Track, with its banked corners and tunnel. Children must be over 135cm in height to ride the Red Track.

🚩 Tours

Lake Cruise

TSS Earnslaw BOATING
(Map p208; ☑ 0800 656 501; www.realjourneys. co.nz; Steamer Wharf, Beach St) The stately, steam-powered TSS Earnslaw was built in the same year as the *Titanic* (but with infinitely better results). Climb aboard for the standard 1½-hour Lake Wakatipu tour (adult/child $65/22), or take a 3½-hour excursion to the high-country Walter Peak Farm for $80/22 where there are sheepdog and shearing demonstrations.

Winery Tours

Most winery tours include cellar door stops in the Gibbston, Bannockburn and Cromwell Basin subregions.

New Zealand Wine Tours WINE
(☑ 0800 666 778; www.nzwinetours.co.nz; from $235) Small-group (maximum seven people) or private winery tours, including lunch – platter, degustation or à la carte, depending on the tour – and an 'aroma room' experience.

Appellation Central Wine Tours WINE
(☑ 03-442 0246; www.appellationcentral.co.nz; tours $199-265) Take a tipple at four or five wineries in Gibbston, Bannockburn and Cromwell, including platter lunches at a winery restaurant.

Driving Tours

Nomad Safaris DRIVING
(Map p208; ☑ 03-442 6699; www.nomad safaris.co.nz; 37 Shotover St; adult/child from $185/90) Runs 4WD tours into hard-to-

Central Queenstown

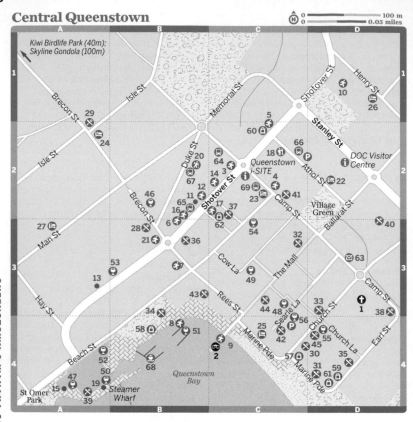

get-to backcountry destinations such as Skippers Canyon and Macetown, as well as a trip through Middle-Earth locations around Glenorchy and the Wakatipu Basin. You can also quad-bike through a sheep station on Queenstown Hill ($245).

Off Road Adventures DRIVING
(Map p208; ☑ 03-442 7858; www.offroad.co.nz; 61a Shotover St) Exciting off-road trips by quad bike (from $199) or dirt bike (from $289), with exclusive access to a 4500-hectare property along the Kawarau River and Nevis Range.

Scenic Flights

Air Milford SCENIC FLIGHTS
(Map p201; ☑ 03-442 2351; www.airmilford.co.nz; 3 Tex Smith Lane, Queenstown Airport) Options include a Milford Sound flyover (adult/child $440/265), a fly-cruise-fly combo (from $510/305), and longer flights to

Doubtful Sound (summer only) and Aoraki/Mt Cook.

Glenorchy Air SCENIC FLIGHTS
(Map p201; ☑ 03-442 2207; www.glenorchyair.co.nz; Queenstown Airport, Frankton) Scenic trips from Queenstown or Glenorchy include a Milford Sound fly-cruise-fly option (adult/child from $460/295), an Aoraki/Mt Cook flyover ($655/375) and a couple of *Lord of the Rings*–themed flights (from $395/195).

Over The Top SCENIC FLIGHTS
(Map p201; ☑ 03-442 2233; www.flynz.co.nz; 10 Tex Smith Lane, Frankton) Offers a range of helicopter flights, from a picnic on a peak near town (per person $770) to a flight to a high-country sheep station (from $4400), to an Ultimate Milford flight with four landings (from $7400). From July to October it offers heliskiing.

Central Queenstown

QUEENSTOWN & WANAKA QUEENSTOWN

Milford Sound Tours

Day trips from Queenstown to Milford Sound via Te Anau take 12 to 13 hours, including a two-hour cruise on the sound. Bus-cruise-flight options are also available, as is pick-up from the Routeburn Track trailhead at the Divide. It's a long day in the saddle, so you might consider visiting Milford from Te Anau. Another way to speed things up are plane or helicopter sightseeing flights to Milford. A number of these offer landings at Milford Sound with cruise options.

BBQ Bus TOURS
(☏ 03-442 1045; http://bbqbus.co.nz; adult/child $220/110) Small-group bus tours to Milford

QUEENSTOWN WITH CHILDREN

While Queenstown is brimming with activities, some of them have age restrictions that may exclude the youngest in your group. Nevertheless, you shouldn't have any trouble keeping the littlies busy.

All-age attractions include the **Kiwi Birdlife Park** (p202) and lake cruises on the **TSS Earnslaw** (p207). The small ones in your group will love watching the duck dives from the **Underwater Observatory** (p202). There's a good beachside **playground** (Map p204; 🚸) near the entrance to the **Queenstown Gardens** (p201) on Marine Pde. Also in the gardens, **Queenstown Ice Arena** (p201) is great for a rainy day, and a round of **Frisbee golf** (p201) will easily fill in a couple of hours. The **Skyline Gondola** (p202) offers a slow-moving activity with a dizzying view. Small children can also ride the **luge** (p207) with an adult, but need to be at least 110cm in height to go it alone on the scenic or intermediate track. Children over 10 years of age (and taller than 135cm) can hurtle down the advanced track alone.

For a high that will make sugar rushes seem passé, a surprising number of activities cater to little daredevils. Children need only weigh more than 20kg to take a tandem ride with **Queenstown Paraflights** (p207), while those over 12 years and 60kg can skim along alone. **Family Adventures** (p206) runs gentle rafting trips suitable for three-year-olds. The shark-shaped **Hydro Attack** (p200) will thrill kids – there's a minimum age of six and your child must be able to travel without you as there's only room for one passenger. Under-fives can ride on the **Shotover Jet** (p206) for free, provided they're over 1m in height, and six-year-olds can tackle the zip-lines with **Ziptrek Ecotours** (p206). If your 10-year-old is fearless enough (and weighs more than 35kg), he or she can bungy or swing at any of the **AJ Hackett Bungy** (p205) jumps, except the Nevis Bungy (minimum age 13, minimum weight 45kg). Children as young as eight can tackle the **Kawarau Zipride** (p205), though eight- and nine-year-olds must ride tandem with an adult. **Canyoning Queenstown** (Map p208; ☎03-441 3003; www.canyoning.co.nz; 39 Camp St) has a dedicated 'Via Ferrata Family' climbing route, suitable for children aged 10 and over.

Outside Sports (p207) hires out bikes suitable for children aged seven and above, with child seats and tag-alongs also available. **Vertigo Bikes** (p203) also hires out kids' mountain bikes. **ChargeAbout** (p205) has e-bikes suitable for 10-year-olds, with toddler trailers for hire if you have a younger crew.

For more ideas and information, including details of local babysitters, visit the **i-SITE** (p217) or www.kidzgo.co.nz.

Sound (maximum 15 people), including a barbecue lunch followed by a cruise. Te Anau drop-offs and pick-ups are $40 cheaper.

Real Journeys TOURS
(Map p208; ☎0800 656 501; www.realjourneys.co.nz; Steamer Wharf, Beach St) 🍴 Runs a host of trips, including the TSS Earnslaw (p207) cruises and activities at Walter Peak Farm, as well as day and overnight tours to Milford and Doubtful Sounds.

🎉 Festivals & Events

Queenstown Winter Festival SPORTS
(www.winterfestival.co.nz; ⊗ Jun) Four days of wacky ski and snowboard activities, live music, comedy, fireworks, a community carnival, parade, ball and plenty of frigid frivolity in late June.

Gay Ski Week LGBT
(www.gayskiweekqt.com; ⊗ Aug/Sep) The South Island's biggest and best gay-and-lesbian event, held in late August/early September.

🛏 Sleeping

🛏 Central Queenstown

★**YHA Queenstown Lakefront** HOSTEL $
(Map p204; ☎03-442 8413; www.yha.co.nz; 88-90 Lake Esplanade; dm/s/d without bathroom from $30/80/102; P🖤) 🍴 This large lakefront hostel, fresh from a refit in 2017, has basic but neat-as-a-pin bunkrooms and an industrial-sized kitchen with window benches to absorb the view. The TV room is filled with beanbags and there are even a couple of massage chairs in the lounge.

Lakeview suites get a shared balcony (and some traffic noise).

Adventure Queenstown Hostel   HOSTEL $
(Map p208; ☑ 03-409 0862; www.aqhostel.co.nz; 36 Camp St; dm with/without bathroom $34/32, d from $110; @ 🛜) Run by experienced travellers (as the photos displayed throughout testify), this central hostel has spotless dorms, a modern kitchen (complete with bread-maker) and balconies that are like a window onto the city. Free stuff includes use of bikes, frisbees and even GoPros. Private rooms have en suite bathrooms, as do some of the dorms.

Adventure Q2 Hostel   HOSTEL $
(Map p208; ☑ 03-409 0862; http://adventureq2.co.nz; 5 Athol St; dm with/without bathroom from $35/33, d from $115; 🛜) Opened in 2016, this sister hostel to Adventure Queenstown Hostel (p211) is pretty much its twin (complete with the ski hire, free GoPro hire etc), but with sturdier bunks, disabled access bathrooms and an elevator in case you're tired of lugging around that rock-heavy backpack.

Haka Lodge   HOSTEL $
(Map p208; ☑ 03-442 4970; www.hakalodge.com; 6 Henry St; dm/r without bathroom from $33/99, apt $229; P 🛜) Part of a small Kiwi chain of higher-brow hostels, the warren-like Haka has cosy dorms with solid bunks that include large lockable storage chests, privacy curtains, personal lights and electrical sockets. There's a one-bedroom apartment attached, with its own kitchen, spacious lounge, laundry facilities and private deck where you can watch paragliders swirl down from the gondola.

★ Creeksyde Queenstown Holiday Park & Motels   HOLIDAY PARK $$
(Map p204; ☑ 03-442 9447; www.camp.co.nz; 54 Robins Rd; sites from $55, d without bathroom from $83, units from $139; P 🛜) 🌊 In a garden setting, this pretty and extremely well-kept holiday park has accommodation ranging from small tent sites along the creek to fully self-contained motel units. It claims to be the 'world's first environmentally certified holiday park' and a number of the powered sites were switched to solar power in 2017.

Lomond Lodge   MOTEL $$
(Map p208; ☑ 03-442 8235; www.lomondlodge.com; 33 Man St; d from $145; P 🛜) This midrange motel on the fringe of the town centre has small but smartly designed rooms with a newly landscaped, sunny terrace and barbecue area out back. It's worth plumping for one of the upstairs Lakeview rooms ($220), which come with lookout-worthy balconies.

Queenstown Motel Apartments   MOTEL $$
(Map p204; ☑ 03-442 6095; www.qma.co.nz; 62 Frankton Rd; units $145-225; P 🛜) This well-run, sunlit spot is like two distinct properties in one – smallish and cheaper new-er units at the front and cheaper 1970s-style units (with newly renovated bathrooms) lined along the back. It has good views across the lake to Cecil Peak and Walter Peak. No children under 18.

Dairy   BOUTIQUE HOTEL $$$
(Map p208; ☑ 03-442 5164; www.thedairy.co.nz; cnr Brecon & Isle Sts; r from $439; P 🛜) Its dining room was once a corner store, but the Dairy is now a luxury B&B with 13 rooms packed with classy touches such as designer bed linen, silk cushions and luxurious mohair rugs. Rates include cooked breakfasts and complimentary NZ bubbly on arrival. There are discounts in winter.

Eichardt's Private Hotel   BOUTIQUE HOTEL $$$
(Map p208; ☑ 03-441 0450; www.eichardts.com; Marine Pde; apt/ste from $1200/1500; 🛜) Dating from 1867, this restored hotel enjoys an absolute lakefront location. Each of the five giant suites – lake view or mountain view – has a fireplace, king-sized bed, heated floor, lake-sized bathtub and views. Four nearby apartments are equally luxurious.

Queenstown Park Boutique Hotel   BOUTIQUE HOTEL $$$
(Map p204; ☑ 03-441 8441; www.queenstownpark.co.nz; 21 Robins Rd; r from $380; P 🛜) 🌊 White curtains billow over beds decked out in luxurious linen at this very chic 19-room hotel. The 'Remarkables' rooms overlook a park, to the namesake mountain range (there aren't any lake views), while the 'Gondola' rooms are smaller but have courtyards or balconies. All have kitchenettes, and there's free wine and nibbles during 'canapé hour' (6pm to 7pm).

🛏 Surrounds

Queenstown Top 10 Holiday Park   HOLIDAY PARK $
(Map p201; ☑ 03-442 9306; www.qtowntop10.co.nz; 70 Arthurs Point Rd, Arthurs Point; sites

from $48, units with/without bathroom from $95/85; ⓟ🛜) 🧭 High above the Shotover River, this relatively small and extremely neat park with better-than-the-norm motel units is 10 minutes' drive from the hustle and bustle of Queenstown. There's bike storage, a ski drying room and a complimentary shuttle bus into town. Fall out of your campervan straight onto the famous Shotover Jet.

⭐**Little Paradise Lodge**   LODGE $$
(Map p201; ☑03-442 6196; www.littleparadise. co.nz; Glenorchy–Queenstown Rd, Mt Creighton; s/d $90/140, units $180; ⓟ) This isolated and peaceful lodge, almost midway between Queenstown and Glenorchy, is a whimsical gem. From the toilet-cistern aquariums (complete with fish) to the huge garden with 3000 roses, monkey puzzle trees and the Swiss owner's own sculptural work, you won't have seen a place like it. There are two rooms in the main house and a unit out the back.

⭐**Hidden Lodge**   B&B $$$
(Map p201; ☑03-442 6636; www.hidden lodgequeenstown.co.nz; 28 Evergreen Pl, Sunshine Bay; r from $395; ⓟ@🛜) The well-named Hidden Lodge is literally the last place west in Queenstown. Tucked away in Sunshine Bay, it has enormous rooms, unfettered lake and mountain views, complimentary beer and wine and a new outdoor hot tub. A quiet escape that is indeed a hidden gem.

Villa del Lago   APARTMENT $$$
(Map p201; ☑03-442 5727; www.villadellago. co.nz; 249 Frankton Rd, Queenstown East; apt from $360; ⓟ🛜) Clinging to the slopes between the highway and the lake, these spacious one- to three-bedroom apartments have lake-facing terraces, incredible views and all the mod cons, including full kitchens, laundries and gas fires. The water taxi (p218) can stop at the private jetty, or you can walk along the lake to Queenstown in 25 minutes.

✖ Eating

✖ Central Queenstown

Fergbaker   BAKERY $
(Map p208; 40 Shotover St; items $5-10; ☺6.30am-4.30am) The sweeter sister of Fergburger (p213) bakes all manner of tempting treats – and though most things look tasty with 3am beer goggles on, it withstands the daylight test admirably. Goodies include inventive pies (venison and portobello mushroom) and breads (pinot, fig and cranberry), filled rolls and a sugary wealth of sweet treats. If you're after gelato, call into Mrs Ferg next door.

Taco Medic   FAST FOOD $
(Map p208; ☑03-442 8174; www.tacomedic. co.nz; 3 Searle Lane; tacos $7; ☺11am-10pm) Taco Medic began life as a food truck, but has put on the handbrake to become a stylishly simple bolthole eatery. Cosy up to the bar and choose from seven tacos made with local free-farmed meats and a changing fish-of-the-day taco. The food truck, parked now at the airport, also still rolls them out.

Caribe Latin Kitchen   MEXICAN $
(Map p208; ☑03-442 6658; www.caribelat inkitchen.com; 36 Ballarat St; mains $8-15) One of the mall's more characterful and colourful restaurants, Caribe is a small nook dishing out quality tacos, quesadillas and burritos stuffed fuller than a piñata. The tiled decor plays to a Day of the Dead theme, and the few tables are brighter than a Mexican sun. Excellent value.

Erik's Fish & Chips   FISH & CHIPS $
(Map p208; ☑03-441 3474; www.eriksfishand chips.co.nz; 12 Earl St; fish $5-10; ☺noon-9pm) A pair of food trucks squeezed into a laneway between buildings – order your hoki, dory or blue cod from one, and eat inside the other. Ever fancied a deep-fried kiwifruit to finish your meal? You've come to the right place...

Habebes   MIDDLE EASTERN $
(Map p208; ☑03-442 9861; www.habebes.co.nz; Plaza Arcade, 30 Shotover St; meals $8-17; ☺8am-5pm; 🧭) Middle Eastern–inspired kebabs, salads and wraps are the go. Soups and yummy pies (try the chicken, kumara and mushroom one) break the mould.

Empanada Kitchen   FAST FOOD $
(Map p208; ☑021 0279 2109; www.theempanada kitchen.com; 60 Beach St; empanadas $5.50; ☺10am-5pm) Yes, this little hole-in-the-wall kiosk is built into a public toilet, but that's far from a statement about its food. The empanadas are absolutely delicious, with flavours that change daily and include savoury and sweet options.

Rehab   HEALTH FOOD $

(Map p208; ☑03-442 5294; www.therehabstory.com; 33 Camp St; bowls $12-14; ☺8.30am-8pm Mon-Fri, 9am-7pm Sat & Sun; ☎☑) If the hard living of Queenstown is wearing you out, pop into Rehab for a Buddha bowl, miso and edamame broth bowl, kale and cashew wrap, or something from its raw bakery – instant recovery in a bowl of locally sourced ingredients.

★ **Public Kitchen & Bar**   MODERN NZ $$

(Map p208; ☑03-442 5969; www.publickitchen.co.nz; Steamer Wharf, Beach St; dishes $12-46; ☺11am-late; ☎) You can't eat closer to the water than at this excellent lakefront eatery where local is law: Cardrona lamb, Fiordland wild venison, Geraldine pork, South Island fish. Grab a group and order a selection of plates of varying sizes from the menu. The meaty dishes, in particular, are excellent.

★ **Bespoke Kitchen**   CAFE $$

(Map p208; ☑03-409 0552; www.bespokekitchen.co.nz; 9 Isle St; mains $11-19; ☺8am-5pm; ☎) Occupying a light-filled corner site near the gondola, Bespoke delivers everything you'd expect of a smart Kiwi cafe. It has a good selection of counter food, beautifully presented cooked options, a range of outside seating in sight of the mountains and, of course, great coffee. In 2015, within six months of opening, it was named NZ's cafe of the year.

Blue Kanu   MODERN NZ $$

(Map p208; ☑03-442 6060; www.bluekanu.co.nz; 16 Church St; mains $28-38; ☺4pm-late) Disproving the rule that all tiki houses are inherently tacky, Blue Kanu serves up a food style it calls 'Polynesian' – *bibimbap* in one hand, fried chicken pineapple buns in the other. It's relaxed and personable, capable of making you feel like a regular in minutes. The marriage of the Polynesian decor and the chopsticks sounds impossible to pull off, but it works.

Vudu Cafe & Larder   CAFE $$

(Map p208; ☑03-441 8370; www.vudu.co.nz; 16 Rees St; breakfast $15-23, lunch $19-23; ☺7.30am-6pm) Excellent home-style baking combines with great coffee and the sort of breakfasts that make bacon and eggs seem very passé (try the French-toast pudding) at this ever-popular cafe. Admire the huge photo of a far less populated Queenstown from an inside table, or head outside to

---

① QUEENSTOWN ON A BUDGET

➡ Play **frisbee golf** (p201) for free in Queenstown Gardens.

➡ Shun the gondola and hike to a view on **Queenstown Hill** (p203) or the **Tiki Trail** (p202); for a free and full day out to Queenstowns' finest view, continue along the **Ben Lomond Track** (p203).

➡ Fuel up at **Fergbaker** (p212), **Taco Medic** (p212), **Empanada Kitchen** (p212) or **Caribe Latin Kitchen** (p212).

➡ Skip an organised lake tour and ride the **water taxi** (p218) across to Kelvin Heights.

---

graze by the lake. Service can be slow, but that's the weight of numbers.

Yonder   CAFE $$

(Map p208; ☑03-409 0994; www.yonderqt.co.nz; 14 Church St; brunch $9-23; ☺7.30am-late; ☎) With a menu inspired by 'the things we've loved around our travels', this new cafe brings to the table a cosmopolitan assortment of dishes: bacon butties, kimchi bowls, tuna poke bowls. There are power points and USB ports by many of the indoor tables, but when the sun's out you'll want to be on the outdoor patio.

Eichardt's Bar   TAPAS $$

(Map p208; www.eichardts.com; Marine Pde; breakfast $12-18, tapas $8-13; ☺7.30am-late) Elegant without being stuffy, the small bar attached to Eichardt's Private Hotel (p211) is a wonderful refuge from the buzz of the streets. Tapas is the main food focus, and though the selection isn't particularly Spanish (think caramelised gnocchi or grilled brushcetta), it is particularly delicious.

Fergburger   BURGERS $$

(Map p208; ☑03-441 1232; www.fergburger.com; 42 Shotover St; burgers $12-19; ☺8am-5am) Who knew a burger joint could ever be a destination restaurant? Such are the queues at Fergburger that it often looks like an All Blacks scrum out the front. The burgers are as tasty and satisfying as ever, but the wait can be horrendous and the menu has more choices than the place has seats.

QUEENSTOWN & WANAKA QUEENSTOWN

Devil Burger BURGERS $$
(Map p208; ✆03-442 4666; www.devilburger.
com; 5/11 Church St; burgers $10-20; ⊗10am-
4am; 🥗) If gluttony is a sin, this Devil is
doing its job, with 20 burgers coming in
sizes regular and large. Wraps include the
hangover-busting 'Walk of Shame', which is
basically a rolled-up full-cooked breakfast.
It gives Fergburger a run for its bun, even if
purely for the lack of queues.

Winnie's PIZZA $$
(Map p208; ✆03-442 8635; www.winnies.co.nz;
1st fl, 7 Ballarat St; mains $20-37; ⊗noon-late;
🕾) It's a Tardis-like journey leaving the
mall and finding Winnie's – part pizza joint
and part bar, looking a little like a '50s diner with a drinking habit. Pizzas come in
various accents – Moroccan, Mexican, Chinese – along with burgers, nachos, chicken
wings and salads. Whatever the blurring of
genres, it's undeniably fun and alive.

On balmy nights the roof opens up and
the party continues into the wee smalls.

Halo Forbidden Bite CAFE $$
(Map p208; ✆03-441 1411; www.haloforbidden
bite.co.nz; 1 Earl St; breakfast $14-24, mains $14-
36; ⊗6am-9pm; 🕾) Pitching itself as both
heavenly and devilish, the Forbidden Bite
is a stylish, sunny place that effortlessly
blurs the line between breakfast, lunch and
dinner. The breakfast burrito will set you
up for a day's adventuring. There's almost
as much seating outside as inside.

Bella Cucina ITALIAN $$
(Map p208; ✆03-442 6762; www.bellacucina.
co.nz; 6 Brecon St; mains $25-29; ⊗5pm-late)
Settle into one of Queenstown's cosiest dining rooms and tuck into simple food done
just right. Fresh pasta and risotto are highlights, while the rustic wood-fired pizza is
perfect for sharing. The pasta is made in-
house daily.

Rata MODERN NZ $$$
(Map p208; ✆03-442 9393; www.ratadining.
co.nz; 43 Ballarat St; mains $35-44, 2-/3-course
lunch $28/38; ⊗noon-late) After gaining
Michelin stars for restaurants in London,
New York and LA, chef-owner Josh Emett
now wields his exceptional but surprisingly
unflashy cooking back home in this upmar-
ket but informal back-lane eatery. Native
bush, edging the windows and in a large-
scale photographic mural, sets the scene for
a short menu showcasing the best seasonal
NZ produce.

Botswana Butchery MODERN NZ $$$
(Map p208; ✆03-442 6994; www.botswana
butchery.co.nz; 17 Marine Pde; lunch mains $17-34,
dinner $35-55; ⊗noon-late) Named as one of
NZ's top 100 restaurants in 2017, this swish
lakefront place is one of the flag-bearers
of Queenstown high-end dining. Despite
that, it doesn't come across as too sniffy,
especially at lunch when prices drop and a
casual air pervades. Evenings are predominantly but not exclusively meaty – a 1.4kg
cut of Cardrona lamb, anyone?

Bazaar
Interactive Marketplace MODERN NZ $$$
(Map p204; ✆03-450 1336; https://bazaar
restaurant.co.nz; 6th fl, Rydges Lakeland Resort,
38-54 Lake Esplanade; breakfast $34, dinner $79;
⊗6-10am & 6-10pm) From one of the loftiest
perches along the lakeshore, this new res-
taurant features a series of 'stations' where
chefs turn out the likes of Asian noodles,
seafood, wood-fired pizzas and grills, as
well as stations of charcuterie and cheese.
It's the perfect spot to watch life on the lake
begin or end for the day.

🍴 Surrounds

VKnow MODERN NZ $$
(Map p201; ✆03-442 5444; www.vknow.co.nz;
155 Fernhill Rd, Fernhill; pizza $19-30, mains $30-
36; ⊗5.30pm-late) The name might sound
like a silly something you'd come up with
during a drunken night on the said *vino*,
but this restaurant will reward the short
trek out to Fernhill. The menu showcases
local venison and blue cod, while pizzas
err on the elaborate side – smoked salmon,
cream cheese and lemon aioli, perhaps?

Wakatipu Grill EUROPEAN $$$
(Map p201; ✆03-450 9400; www.queenstown
hilton.com; Hilton Queenstown, Peninsula Rd, Kel-
vin Heights; mains $28-47; ⊗6-10.30am Mon-Fri,
6-11am Sat & Sun, 6-9.30pm daily) The Hilton
sprawls along the lakeside by the Kawarau
River outlet, and part of the fun of visiting
its signature restaurant is the water-taxi
(p218) ride. As the name implies, there's
always a decent selection of steak on the
menu, but much more besides, including
locally sourced fish and lamb.

Gantley's MODERN NZ $$$
(✆03-442 8999; www.gantleys.co.nz; 172 Ar-
thurs Point Rd, Arthurs Point; 2-/3-course dinner
$65/75, 6-/8-course degustation $95/130, with
paired wines $160/215; ⊗6-10pm) Gantley's

French-influenced menu and highly regarded wine list justify the 7km journey from Queenstown. The atmospheric dining experience is showcased in a stone-and-timber building, built in 1863 as a wayside inn and surrounded by beautiful gardens. The degustation options are the menu's centrepiece. Reservations are essential, and free pick-up from Queenstown is available by arrangement.

♟ Drinking & Entertainment

Pick up a copy of *The Source* (www.source mag.nz), a free monthly publication with articles and details of goings-on around Queenstown.

★ Zephyr   BAR
(Map p208; ☑03-409 0852; www.facebook.com/zephyrqt; Searle Lane; ⊙7pm-4am) Queenstown's coolest indie rock bar is located – as all such places should be – in a dark, grungy, concrete-floored space off a back lane. There's a popular pool table and live bands on Wednesday nights. Beer comes only in bottles, and there's a permanently rockin' soundtrack.

★ Atlas Beer Cafe   BAR
(Map p208; ☑03-442 5995; www.atlasbeercafe.com; Steamer Wharf, Beach St; ⊙10am-late) There are usually around 20 beers on tap at this pint-sized lakefront bar, headlined by brews from Dunedin's Emerson's Brewery and Queenstown's Altitude. There are tasting paddles (with tasting notes) with four beers of your choice available. It serves excellent cooked breakfasts ($10 to $20) and simple substantial fare such as steaks, burgers and chicken parmigiana ($20).

★ Smiths Craft Beer House   CRAFT BEER
(Map p208; ☑03-409 2337; www.smithscraftbeer.co.nz; 53 Shotover St; ⊙noon-late) It's back to basics in everything but the taps, with bare concrete floors and industrial tables and chairs, but up to 20 creative craft beers on tap. The folks behind the bar will chat brews as long as you'll listen, and there's a menu (mains $17 to $20) of burgers and po'boys to mop up the suds.

1789   LOUNGE
(Map p208; ☑03-450 0045; www.sofitel-queenstown.com; 8 Duke St; ⊙4pm-midnight Sun-Thu, to 1am Fri & Sat) Tucked into a corner of the Sofitel, this velvet-smooth new jazz lounge is named for the French Revolution, with a bloody colour scheme to suit. There are around 350 wines by the bottle and 50 by the glass, live jazz sessions on Friday and Saturday evenings and jazz piano on Wednesday and Sunday.

Bunker   COCKTAIL BAR
(Map p208; ☑03-441 8030; www.thebunker.co.nz; 14 Cow Lane; ⊙5pm-4am) Bunkered upstairs rather than down, this chichi little bar clearly fancies itself the kind of place that Sean Connery's James Bond might frequent, if the decor is anything to go by. Best of all is the outside terrace, with couches, a fire in winter and a projector screening classic movies onto the wall of a neighbouring building.

Vinyl Underground   CLUB
(Map p208; www.facebook.com/Vinylundergroundqt; 12 Church St; ⊙8pm late) Enter the underworld, or at least the space under the World Bar (p215), to find the heartbeat of Queenstown's nightlife. Inside the concrete bunker – the bar alone must weigh several tonnes – projectors screen dance clips onto a faux brick wall, and DJs spin from 10pm. There's a pool table in the back room.

World Bar   BAR
(Map p208; ☑03-450 0008; www.theworldbar.co.nz; 12 Church St; ⊙11.30am-2.30am) Queenstown's legendary party hub before it was destroyed by fire in 2013, the World Bar is well and truly getting its groove back. Decor swings between degrees of eclectic, from the mounted moose head with halo,

---

MĀORI QUEENSTOWN & WANAKA

The same transition, from moa hunter to Waitaha, to Ngāti Māmoe to Ngāi Tahu rule, took place here as in other parts of the South Island. Lake Wakatipu is shrouded in legend, and sites to its north were highly valued sources of *pounamu* (greenstone).

The Ngāi Tahu *iwi* (tribe) owns **Shotover Jet** (p206), **Dart Stables** (p349), **Guided Walks New Zealand** (p203) and **Dart River Wilderness Jet** (p220), the last of which offers a cultural component with its excursions. Other cultural insights are offered by **Kiwi Haka** (p202), which performs nightly atop the gondola in Queenstown.

GIBBSTON VALLEY

Queenstown's adrenaline junkies might be happiest dangling off a giant rubber band, but as they're plunging towards the Kawarau River, they might not realise they're in the heart of Gibbston, one of Central Otago's main wine subregions, accounting for around 20% of plantings.

Strung along Gibbston Hwy (SH6) is an interesting and beautiful selection of vineyards. Almost opposite the Kawarau Bridge, a precipitous 2km gravel road leads to **Chard Farm** (Map p201; ☏03-442 6110; www.chardfarm.co.nz; Chard Rd, Gibbston; ⊙10am-5pm Mon-Fri, 11am-5pm Sat & Sun), the most picturesque of the wineries. A further 1km along SH6 is **Gibbston Valley** (Map p201; ☏03-442 6910; www.gibbstonvalley.com; 1820 Gibbston Hwy/SH6, Gibbston; ⊙10am-5pm), the area's oldest commercial winery. As well as tastings, it has a restaurant, cheesery, tours of NZ's largest wine cave and bike hire. It also operates its own bus from Queenstown – you could always take the bus and then hire a bike to get between cellar doors.

Another 3km along SH6, **Peregrine** (Map p201; ☏03-442 4000; www.peregrinewines. co.nz; 2127 Gibbston Hwy/SH6, Gibbston; ⊙11am-5pm) has an impressive, award-winning cellar door – a bunker-like building with a roof reminiscent of a falcon's wing in flight. As well as tastings, you can take a stroll through the adjoining barrel room.

The **Gibbston River Trail**, part of the Queenstown Trail, is a walking and cycling track that follows the Kawarau River for 11km from the Kawarau Bridge, passing all of the wineries. From Peregrine, walkers (but not cyclists) can swing onto the **Peregrine Loop** (one hour, 2.7km), which crosses over old mining works on 11 timber and two steel bridges, one of which passes through the branches of a willow tree. A 30-minute loop track from Waitiri Creek Wines heads to **Big Beach** on the Kawarau River, with views of Nevis Bluff.

While you're in the area, be sure to call into the rustic **Gibbston Tavern** (Map p201; ☏03-409 0508; www.gibbstontavern.co.nz; 8 Coalpit Rd, Gibbston; ⊙11am-8pm), just off the highway past Peregrine. It stocks Gibbston wines, fires up good pizzas and has a small art gallery.

If you're keen to explore the valley's wineries without needing to contemplate a drive afterwards, consider staying among the vines in **Kinross Cottages** (Map p201; ☏0800 131 101; www.kinrosscottages.co.nz; 2300 Gibbston Hwy/SH6, Gibbston; r $275-325; 🕸), where the heritage-looking cottages are a front for modern, luxurious studio rooms. It has its own cellar door, representing five Central Otago vineyards, plus a general store with good meals.

Ask at the **Queenstown i-SITE** (p217) for maps and information about touring the area.

to the cocktails that come in teapots. The food's good, there are regular DJs and the outdoor area is prime real estate on balmy afternoons and evenings.

Bardeaux   WINE BAR
(Map p208; ☏03-442 8284; www.goodgroup. co.nz; Eureka Arcade, Searle Lane; ⊙4pm-4am) This small, cavelike wine bar is all class. Under a low ceiling are plush leather armchairs and a fireplace made from Central Otago schist. Whisky is king here, but the wine list is extraordinary, especially if you're keen to drop $4500 on a bottle once in your life. It's surprisingly relaxed for a place with such lofty tastes.

Pub on Wharf   PUB
(Map p208; ☏03-441 2155; www.pubonwharf. co.nz; 88 Beach St; ⊙10am-late) Ubercool interior design combines with handsome woodwork and lighting fit for a hipster hideaway, with fake sheep heads to remind you that you're still in NZ. Mac's beers on tap, scrummy nibbles and a decent wine list make this a great place to settle in for the evening. There's live music nightly and comedy occasionally.

Little Blackwood   COCKTAIL BAR
(Map p208; ☏03-441 8066; www.littleblack wood.com; Steamer Wharf, Beach St; ⊙3pm-1am) Its constituent parts sound kitsch and quirky – subway tiles on the walls behind

the bar, barmen dressed in stripy shirts looking like old-fashioned sailor boys – and yet Little Blackwood is surprisingly chic. The cocktails are good, too.

Perky's BAR
(Map p208; ☑ 021 664 043; www.facebook.com/perkysqueenstown; main town pier; ☺ noon-late) That hint of wobbliness you feel isn't the alcohol (yet), it's the fact that you're drinking at NZ's only floating bar and coffee shop. It's on an old sailing boat that used to do lake tours, but is now nosed up at the lakeshore. It has a good small selection of local wine, but we've had better coffee.

The Winery WINE BAR
(Map p208; ☑ 03-409 2226; www.thewinery.co.nz; 14 Beach St; ☺ 10.30am-late) Ignore the uninspiring location and settle in for a journey around NZ wine. Load up cash on a smartcard and then help yourself to tasting pours or glasses of more than 80 NZ wines dispensed through an automated gas-closure system. There's also a whisky corner, and cheese and salami platters are available. Wines are arranged by varietals along the walls.

Sherwood LIVE MUSIC
(Map p201; ☑ 03-450 1090; www.sherwoodqueenstown.nz; 554 Frankton Rd) The faux-Tudor architecture might have you expecting lutes and folk ballads, but the Sherwood is Queenstown's go-to spot for visiting musos. Many of NZ's bigger names have performed here; check the website for coming gigs.

🛍 Shopping

★ **Romer Gallery** PHOTOGRAPHY
(Map p208; ☑ 021 171 1771; www.romer-gallery.com; 15 Earl St; ☺ 8.30am-5pm) Stunning gallery of large-format, perspex-finished NZ landscapes from renowned Queenstown-based photographer Stephan Romer. Images are up to $15,000 a pop, but they display a rare beauty.

Vesta ARTS & CRAFTS
(Map p208; ☑ 03-442 5687; www.vestadesign.co.nz; 19 Marine Pde; ☺ 10am-5.30pm) Arguably Queenstown's most interesting store, inside inarguably the town's oldest building. Vesta sells a collection of prints, glassware, jewellery and homewares as fascinating as the original wallpaper and the floorboards warped by time in the 1864 wooden cottage.

Walk in Wardrobe CLOTHING
(Map p208; ☑ 03-409 0190; www.thewalkinwardrobe.co.nz; Beech Tree Arcade, 34 Shotover St; ☺ 10am-6pm Tue & Wed, to 8.30pm Thu-Mon) Benefitting from travellers lightening their suitcases before jetting out, this 'preloved fashion boutique' is a great place to hunt for bargain designer duds. Womenswear fills most of the racks.

Artbay Gallery ART
(Map p208; ☑ 03-442 9090; www.artbay.co.nz; 13 Marine Pde; ☺ 10am-9pm) Occupying an attractive 1863-built Freemason's Hall on the lakefront, Artbay is always an interesting place to peruse, even if you don't have $10,000 to drop on a painting. It showcases the work of contemporary NZ artists, most of whom have a connection to the region.

Creative Queenstown
Arts & Crafts Market MARKET
(Map p208; www.queenstownmarket.com; Earnslaw Park; ☺ 9am-4.30pm Sat Nov-Apr, 9.30am-3.30pm May-Oct) Gifts and souvenirs crafted from around the South Island; on the lakefront beside Steamer Wharf.

❶ Information

In 2016 Queenstown introduced free wi-fi in four town-centre locations: the Village Green, Earnslaw Park, Beach St and the Mall.

DOC Visitor Centre (Map p208; ☑ 03-442 7935; www.doc.govt.nz; 50 Stanley St; ☺ 8.30am-4.30pm) Head here to pick up Routeburn Track bookings and backcountry hut passes. Posts weather and tramper alerts, has good day-walk advice and sells maps.

Queenstown i-SITE (Map p208; ☑ 03-442 4100; www.queenstownisite.co.nz; cnr Shotover & Camp Sts; ☺ 8.30am-8pm) Friendly and informative despite being perpetually frantic, the saintly staff here can help with bookings and information on Queenstown, Gibbston, Arrowtown and Glenorchy.

❶ Getting There & Away

AIR

Air New Zealand (☑ 0800 737 000; www.airnewzealand.co.nz) flies direct to Queenstown from Auckland, Wellington and Christchurch. **Jetstar** (☑ 0800 800 995; www.jetstar.com) also flies the Auckland route.

Various airlines offer direct flights to Queenstown from Sydney, Melbourne, Brisbane and the Gold Coast in Australia.

BUS

Most buses and shuttles stop on Athol St or opposite the i-SITE; check when you book.

Atomic Travel (Map p208; ☎03-349 0697; www.atomictravel.co.nz) Daily (except Tuesday) bus to and from Cromwell ($15, one hour), Omarama ($35, 2¼ hours), Twizel ($30, 3¼ hours), Tekapo ($45, four hours) and Christchurch ($55, 7¼ hours).

Catch-a-Bus South (☎03-479 9960; www.catchabussouth.co.nz) Door-to-door daily bus from Invercargill ($60, 3¼ hours) and Bluff ($75, 3¾ hours), heading via Gore ($61, 2½ hours) three times a week.

InterCity (Map p208; ☎03-442 4922; www.intercity.co.nz) Daily coaches to/from Wanaka (from $17, 1¾ hours), Franz Josef (from $62, eight hours), Dunedin (from $26, 4¼ hours), Invercargill (from $49, 2½ hours) and Christchurch (from $55, 8½ to 11½ hours).

Naked Bus (Map p208; https://nakedbus.com) Buses daily to Wanaka (from $17, 1¾ hours), Cromwell (from $11, one hour), Te Anau (from $10, 2½ hours), Franz Josef (from $62, eight hours) and Christchurch (from $55, 8½ hours).

Ritchies (Map p208; ☎03-443 9120; www.alpineconnexions.co.nz) Buses head to/from Dunedin ($50, 4½ hours, daily), with stops at towns along the route on request.

Ritchies Connectabus Wanaka (Map p208; ☎0800 405 066; www.connectabus.com;) Heads to/from Wanaka five times daily ($35, two hours). Does hotel pick-ups and has free wi-fi on board.

HIKERS' & SKIERS' TRANSPORT

Buckley Track Transport (☎03-442 8215; www.buckleytracktransport.nz) Shuttles between Queenstown and the Routeburn and Greenstone & Caples Tracks, as well as Te Anau Downs (for the Milford Track).

EasyHike (☎027 370 7019; www.easyhike.co.nz) Offers a car-relocation service for the Milford, Routeburn and Kepler Tracks, dropping you at the start and shifting your car to the end. It can also kit you out entirely for the hike, offering a range of packages up to a 'Premium' service that includes booking your hut tickets, track transport, backpack, food, rain gear, cooking pots and first-aid kit.

Glenorchy Journeys (☎03-409 0800; www.glenorchyjourneys.co.nz) Shuttles from Queenstown and Glenorchy to the Routeburn, Greenstone & Caples and Rees-Dart Tracks.

Info & Track (Map p208; ☎03-442 9708; www.infotrack.co.nz; 37 Shotover St; ⏱7.30am-9pm) During the Great Walks season, this agency provides transfers to the trailheads of the Routeburn, Greenstone & Caples and Rees-Dart Tracks. In winter it morphs into Info & Snow and heads to the Cardrona, Coronet Peak, Remarkables and Treble Cone ski fields instead.

Kiwi Discovery (Map p208; ☎03-442 7340; www.kiwidiscovery.com; 37 Camp St) Offers trailhead transport for the Milford, Routeburn and Kepler Tracks. In winter it runs buses to the four ski fields around the area.

NZSki Snowline Express (Map p208; www.nzski.com) During the ski season shuttles depart from outside the Snow Centre on Duke St every 20 minutes from 8am until 11.30am (noon for Coronet Peak), heading to both Coronet Peak and the Remarkables (return $20). Buses return as they fill up, from 1.30pm onwards. They also leave on the hour from 4pm to 7pm for night skiing at Coronet Peak, returning on the half-hour from 5.30pm to 9.30pm.

Trackhopper (☎021-187 7732; www.trackhopper.co.nz) Offers a handy car-relocation service for the Routeburn, Milford, Greenstone and Rees-Dart Tracks, driving you to one end of the track and leaving your car for you at the other. Prices start from $160, plus fuel.

Tracknet (Map p208; ☎03-249 7777; www.tracknet.net) This Te Anau–based outfit offers Queenstown connections to the Routeburn, Greenstone Caples, Kepler, Hollyford and Milford Tracks throughout the Great Walks season. Its Invercargill bus service can connect with transport to the Rakiura Track on Stewart Island. Charter transport to trailheads during winter can also be arranged.

Getting Around

TO/FROM THE AIRPORT

Queenstown Airport (ZQN; Map p201; ☎03-450 9031; www.queenstownairport.co.nz; Sir Henry Wrigley Dr, Frankton) is 7km east of the town centre. **Blue Bubble Taxis** (☎0800 228 294; www.queenstown.bluebubbletaxi.co.nz) and **Green Cabs** (☎0800 464 7336; www.greencabs.co.nz) charge around $45 to $50 for trips between the airport and town.

Ritchies Connectabus (p218) has an airport service that runs every 15 minutes to Queenstown ($12), while also running four times daily to Cromwell ($22, one hour) and Wanaka ($35, 1½ hours).

Super Shuttle (Map p201; ☎0800 748 885; www.supershuttle.co.nz) runs a door-to-door shuttle service from Queenstown Airport to the city ($20).

BOAT

Water taxis (Map p208; ☎03-441 1124; www.queenstownwatertaxis.co.nz; Steamer Wharf, Beach St; ⏱10am-9.30pm Sun-Thu, to 10.30pm Fri & Sat) zip across the lake from near Steamer Wharf to the Hilton Hotel (and requested stops in between) on the Kelvin Peninsula (adult/child $10/5). Pay the driver on the boat in cash.

BUS

Ritchies Connectabus (Map p208; ☑ 03-441 4471; www.connectabus.com) has various colour-coded routes, reaching Sunshine Bay, Fernhill, Arthurs Point, Frankton and Arrowtown. A day pass (adult/child $33/17) allows travel on the entire network. Pick up a route map and timetable from the **i-SITE** (p217). Buses leave from beside the clock tower on Camp St.

AROUND QUEENSTOWN

Glenorchy

POP 360

Perhaps best known as the gateway to the Routeburn Track, Glenorchy sits on a rare shelf of flat land at the head of Lake Wakatipu. The small town is a great option if you want to be beside the lake and the mountains but prefer to stay once removed from the bustle and bluster of Queenstown. The tramping around Glenorchy is sensational, and the town is also a base for horse treks, jetboat rides, helicopter flights and skydives. It's Queenstown on sedatives.

There's often a sense of déjà vu when you arrive in Glenorchy, with areas around the town featuring heavily in the *Lord of the Rings* trilogy, as well as being the setting for Jane Campion's *Top of the Lake* BBC series.

The town centre sits slightly back from the lake, so be sure to wander down to the wharf, where the Humboldt Mountains rise from the opposite shore.

🏃 Activities

Shuttles from Queenstown to the Routeburn, Rees-Dart and Greenstone & Caples Tracks pass through Glenorchy; you can be picked up here along the way. Other activities on offer include farm tours, fly-fishing and guided photography tours; enquire at the Queenstown i-SITE (p217) or the Glenorchy Information Centre & Store (p220).

Tramping

DOC's *Head of Lake Wakatipu* and *Wakatipu Walks* brochures detail more

THE ROAD TO PARADISE

Road signs in Glenorchy promote the town as the 'Gateway to Paradise' and it is...literally. Paradise lies around 15km north of Glenorchy, near the start of the Dart Track.

The road from Glenorchy to Paradise, which is unsealed from the Kinloch turn-off, heads up the broad Rees Valley, edging along the foot of the Richardson Range. Approaching Paradise it cuts through a beautiful section of beech forest on the shores of Diamond Lake before fording the River Jordan – how's that for a biblical entrance to paradise! – and arriving at Paradise. There's not much here (ok, there's pretty much nothing here); it's just paddocks. But it sure is pretty!

than 60 day walks in the area. Both brochures can be downloaded from the DOC website (www.doc.govt.nz). Two of the best short tracks are the **Routeburn Flats** (three hours), which follows the first section of the Routeburn Track, and **Lake Sylvan** (one hour, 40 minutes).

Another good wander, especially if you like your birds, is the **Glenorchy Walkway**, which starts in the town centre and loops around Glenorchy lagoon, switching to boardwalks for the swampy bits. It's split into the Southern Circuit (30 minutes) and the Northern Circuit (one hour) and there are plenty of seats along the way, well positioned for views over the water to the mountains.

Before setting out on any longer tramps, call into DOC's Queenstown visitor centre (p217) for the latest track conditions and to purchase detailed maps. Another good resource is Lonely Planet's *Hiking & Tramping in New Zealand*.

For track snacks or meals, stock up on groceries in Queenstown, though you'll also find a small selection of trail-perfect fodder at **Mrs Woolly's General Store** (64 Oban St; ⊙10am-5.30pm). Track transport is at a premium during the Great Walks season (late October to April), so try to book in advance.

👉 Tours

Heli Glenorchy   SCENIC FLIGHTS
(☑0800 435 449; www.heliglenorchy.co.nz; 35 Mull St) It takes the best part of a day to

OFF THE BEATEN TRACK

KINLOCH

Just 3km from Glenorchy, but 26km by road, **Kinloch Lodge** (☑ 03-442 4900; www. kinlochlodge.co.nz; Kinloch Rd, Kinloch; dm $39, d with/without bathroom from $175/115; 🛜) is the perfect escape if getting away from it all to Glenorchy isn't getting away from it all enough. The wonderfully remote 1868 lodge has small rooms with shared bathrooms, while rooms in the YHA-associated hostel are comfy and colourful. The open-air hot tub has cracking mountain and lake views.

The lodge also has mountain bikes for hire, offers guided kayaking (one/two hours $50/95) and provides transfers to the Routeburn ($27) and Greenstone & Caples Tracks ($22).

The cafe-bar (mains $18 to $29) is open year-round for breakfast, lunch and dinner. From Wednesday to Sunday there's a three-course chef's-menu dinner that changes every week.

Opened in 2017, the twin contemporary cabins of **EcoScapes** (☑ 03-442 4900; http:// ecoscapes.nz; Kinloch Rd, Kinloch; r $395; 🛜) are in utter contrast to the historic Kinloch Lodge next door. Built using passive design, they feature blonde woods, ultra-modern furnishings and feel almost like a city apartment plonked into the wilderness.

drive from Glenorchy to Milford Sound, but it's only 15 minutes by helicopter. Heli Glenorchy has a three-hour Milford Sound heli-cruise-heli package ($825) and a wilderness drop-off so that you can walk the last few kilometres of the Milford Track to Giant's Gate Falls before being whisked back over the mountains ($865).

Private Discovery Tours   DRIVING
(☑ 03-442 2299; www.privatediscoverytours. co.nz; half/full day from $190/350) A range of 4WD tours, including exclusive access to Mt Earnslaw Station, a high-country sheep property in a remote valley between Mts Earnslaw and Alfred, complete with Middle-Earth movie locations. Prices include pick-up from Queenstown. Also runs a couple of day-walk tours.

High Country Horses   HORSE RIDING
(Map p201; ☑ 03-442 9915; www.high-country-horses.co.nz; 243 Priory Rd) Has more equine options than the Auckland Cup, from tootling around Glenorchy on a 30-minute carriage ride (adult/child $50/25) to an overnight 'Around the Mountain' trek ($675).

Dart River Wilderness Jet   BOATING
(☑ 03-442 9992; www.dartriver.co.nz; 45 Mull St; adult/child from $249/139) The only jetboat operator on the Dart River, with trips including a 30-minute walk through the rainforest. Also offers jetboat rides combined with a river descent in an inflatable three-seater 'funyak' (departs 8.45am, adult/child from $339/239). Prices include

Queenstown pick-ups, which depart an hour before each trip.

🛏 Sleeping & Eating

Glenorchy Lake House   B&B $$$
(☑ 03-442 4900; www.glenorchylakehouse.co.nz; Mull St; r $295, house from $495; 🛜) 🍃 The well-named Lake House (it's the closest place in town to the lake) is a boutique B&B attached to the excellent Trading Post cafe. The two guest bedrooms are decked out with Egyptian cotton sheets and flatscreen TVs and there's an outdoor spa in which to soak away the rigours of a day's tramping.

Queenie's Dumplings   DUMPLINGS $
(☑ 03-442 6070; http://queeniesdumplings. wixsite.com/queeniesdumplings; 27 Mull St; 9 dumplings $13.50, noodle soup $15; ⏰ 11am-4pm) Where else would you expect to find an authentic little dumpling joint than far-flung, rural Glenorchy? Choose from seven types of dumplings, or a handful of noodle soups.

Glenorchy Cafe   CAFE $$
(GYC; ☑ 03-442 9978; 25 Mull St; mains $12-20; ⏰ 10am-4.30pm Sun-Fri, to 1.30am Sat) Grab a sunny table out the back of this cute little cottage and tuck into cooked breakfasts, sandwiches and soup. Head inside on Saturday night to partake in pizza and beer underneath the oddball light fixtures.

ⓘ Information

Glenorchy Information Centre & Store
(☑ 03-409 2049; www.glenorchy-nz.co.nz;

42-50 Mull St; ⊘8.30am-9pm) Attached to the Glenorchy Hotel, this little shop is a good source of weather and track information. Fishing rods and mountain bikes can be hired, and it sells tramping supplies, including gas canisters and a good selection of maps. It also has a bottle shop, bless it.

❶ Getting There & Away

Glenorchy lies at the head of Lake Wakatipu, a scenic 40-minute (46km) drive northwest from Queenstown, winding around bluffs and coves with sweeping views over the lake and its frame of mountains. There are no bus services, but there are trampers' shuttles (p218) during the Great Walks season (late October to April). Shuttles pick up from the Glenorchy Hotel, which offers free parking to trampers.

Arrowtown

POP 2450

Beloved by day-trippers from Queenstown, exceedingly quaint, Arrowtown sprang up in the 1860s following the discovery of gold in the Arrow River. Today its pretty, tree-lined avenues retain more than 60 of their original gold-rush buildings, and history is so ingrained here that even the golf course wraps around the ruined cottages and relics of the town's gold-mining heyday. But don't be fooled by the rustic facades; Arrowtown has a thriving contemporary scene, with chic modern dining, a cool cinema and a couple of drinking dens to rival the finest in Queenstown.

The pace in Arrowtown is very different to that of Queenstown, just 20km away. Strolling Buckingham St, with its gold-era facades, is the major activity here; when you need something more, there are gentle bike rides along the valleys, or an expanding network of walks along the Arrow River and Bush Creek.

◉ Sights

Chinese Settlement HISTORIC SITE
(Map p222; Buckingham St; ⊘24hr) FREE
Strung along the creek, near the site of Arrowtown's first gold find, is NZ's best example of an early Chinese settlement. Interpretive signs explain the lives of Chinese miners during and after the gold rush (the last resident died in 1932), while restored huts and the only remaining Chinese store in the southern goldfields make the story more tangible. Subjected to significant racism, the Chinese often had little choice but

to rework old tailings rather than seek new claims.

Lakes District Museum & Gallery MUSEUM
(Map p222; ☑03-442 1824; www.museumqueen stown.com; 49 Buckingham St; adult/child $10/3; ⊘8.30am-5pm) Exhibits cover the gold-rush era and the early days of Chinese settlement around Arrowtown. Kids are kept engaged by the likes of a 'Crack the Code' game they can play as you wander the exhibits. You can also hire pans ($3) here to try your luck panning for gold on the Arrow River; you're more likely to find some traces if you head away from the town centre.

St Patrick's Catholic Church CHURCH
(Map p222; www.stjosephsqueenstown.co.nz; 7 Hertford St) Apart from its impressive Star of David–shaped rose window, this 1874 stone Gothic Revival church, built from local schist rock, wouldn't be worth noting if it weren't for its connection to Australia's only Catholic saint. Acclaimed educator St Mary of the Cross, aka Mary McKillop (1842–1909), founded a convent in the tiny 1870s miners cottage next door. There are interesting displays about the saint in the church and in the restored cottage.

Arrowtown Gaol HISTORIC BUILDING
(Map p222; Cardigan St) FREE With the gold rushes came lawlessness. Arrowtown's prisoners were originally manacled to logs, but in 1876 this schist jail, now surrounded by homes, was constructed. The building was used as a jail as recently as 1987 when two men were held here for drunkenness. The jail is locked, but you can grab the key (after paying a $5 deposit) from the visitor information centre (p225).

🏃 Activities & Tours

The information centre stocks a *Cycling & Walking Trail* brochure ($1) outlining some excellent tracks in the area. One particularly good cycling route is the **Arrow River Bridges Ride** (12km) from Arrowtown to the Kawarau Bridge, which traverses various purpose-built suspension bridges and a tunnel cut under the highway. If you have more time and energy, you can connect onto the Gibbston River Trail at the Kawarau Bridge to cycle past a string of cellar doors.

Local walks range from hour-long strolls along Bush Creek and the Arrow River to a

Arrowtown

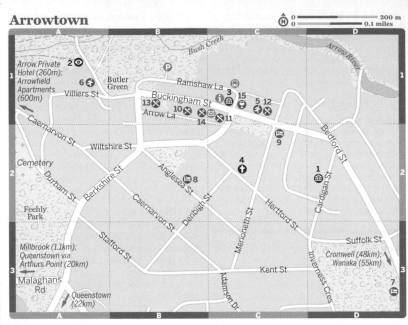

Arrowtown

◎ Sights
1 Arrowtown Gaol	D2
2 Chinese Settlement	A1
3 Lakes District Museum & Gallery	C1
4 St Patrick's Catholic Church	C2

◎ Activities, Courses & Tours
5 Arrowtown Bike Hire	C1
Arrowtown Time Walks	(see 3)
6 Dudley's Cottage	A1
Queenstown Bike Tours	(see 6)

◎ Sleeping
7 Arrowtown Holiday Park	D3
8 Arrowtown Lodge	B2

9 Shades of Arrowtown	C2

◎ Eating
10 Chop Shop	B1
11 La Rumbla	C1
12 Provisions	C1
13 Saffron	B1
14 Slow Cuts	B1

◎ Drinking & Nightlife
Blue Door	(see 13)
15 Fork & Tap	C1

◎ Entertainment
Dorothy Browns	(see 13)

climb along the **Big Hill Trail** (12km, five to six hours) that meets the Arrow River closer to Macetown.

Arrowtown Bike Hire CYCLING
(Map p222; ☑ 0800 224 473; www.arrowtown bikehire.co.nz; 59 Buckingham St; half-/full-day hire $42/55, e-bikes $80/120; ⊙ 8.30am-5.30pm daily Sep-Apr, Tue-Sat May-Aug) Hires out bikes (including e-bikes) and provides great advice about local trails. If you fancy tackling the 16km Arrow River Bridges ride through to the Gibbston wineries, the

company will collect you, your companions and your bikes for $79. Multiday hires are also available, and bikes can be delivered to your Arrowtown accommodation. Find the entrance on Romans Lane.

Queenstown Bike Tours CYCLING
(Map p222; ☑ 03-442 0339; www.queenstown biketours.co.nz; Dudley's Cottage, 4 Buckingham St; half/full day $45/55) From straightforward bike hire to a Gibbston Wine Tour package ($195, September to April only) that includes bike hire, lunch in Gibbston,

tastings at four vineyards and return transport to Arrowtown to save you wobbling back. E-bikes available.

Dudley's Cottage OUTDOORS
(Map p222; ☑ 03-409 8162; www.dudleyscottage nz.com; 4 Buckingham St; ☉ 9am-5pm) Call into this historic cottage for a gold-panning lesson ($10, plus an extra $5 if you're keen to hire a pan and give it a go). If you've already got golden skills, hire a pan and shovel ($6) or sluice box ($35) and head out on your own.

Arrowtown Time Walks WALKING
(Map p222; ☑ 021 782 278; www.arrowtown timewalks.com; adult/child $20/12) Guided walks (1½ hours) depart from the museum on demand, tracing a path through Arrowtown's golden past, pointing out places of interest along the way and delving into gold-rush history. Book through the website, or in person at the museum (p221).

🛏 Sleeping

Arrowtown Holiday Park HOLIDAY PARK $
(Map p222; ☑ 03-442 1876; www.arrowtownhol idaypark.co.nz; 12 Centennial Ave; sites/units from $42/135, r without bathroom $69) Close to the town centre, this small holiday park offers a cul-de-sac of en suite cabins and a gleaming amenities block with coin-operated showers. When it's not booked up by school groups, budget travellers can get a room in Oregon Lodge – each room has two sets of bunks and shares the communal kitchen and bathrooms.

Arrowtown Lodge B&B $$
(Map p222; ☑ 03-442 1101; www.arrowtown lodge.co.nz; 7 Anglesea St; r/cottage $195/395; ☎) From the outside, the guest rooms look like heritage cottages, but inside they're cosy and modern, with en suite bathrooms. There are three rooms, including a large cottage that has its own separate outdoor living space and spa. A continental breakfast is provided, and Buckingham St is a two-minute walk from the lodge's back entrance.

Shades of Arrowtown MOTEL $$
(Map p222; ☑ 03-442 1613; www.shadesofarrow town.co.nz; cnr Buckingham & Merioneth Sts; units from $150; ☎) Tall shady trees and a garden setting give these stylish bungalow-type cottages a relaxed air. Some have full kitchens and spa baths. The two-bedroom, self-contained cottage is good value if you're travelling with the whole clan.

Arrowtown Motel Apartments MOTEL $$
(☑ 03-442 1833; www.arrowtownmotel.co.nz; 48 Adamson Dr; units from $150; ☎) This child of the 1980s goes better on the inside than the outside, with spacious units with colourful feature walls, soft furnishings and interesting art. It's on a suburban road, facing onto a reserve, so peace and quiet is all but assured.

Arrowfield Apartments RENTAL HOUSE $$$
(☑ 03-442 0012; www.arrowfield.co.nz; 115 Essex Ave, Butel Park; houses from $250; ☎ ⊞) Lining a quiet crescent in a new development at Arrowtown's edge, these 10 spacious townhouses, identical in all but colour, have internal garages, full kitchens, underfloor heating, gas fires and three bedrooms. Bedroom doors can be locked off for a smaller, cheaper rental.

Arrow Private Hotel BOUTIQUE HOTEL $$$
(☑ 021 414 141; www.thearrow.co.nz; 63 Manse Rd; ste from $305; ☎) Five understated but luxurious suites feature at this modern property on Arrowtown's outskirts. Accommodation is chic and contemporary with huge picture windows showcasing the surrounding countryside. The suites are framed around an old stone cottage that has an open fire, armchairs and a selection of spirits and local wines. The Queenstown Trail goes right by the door.

Millbrook Resort RESORT $$$
(☑ 03-441 7000; www.millbrook.co.nz; Malaghans Rd; r from $265; ☎ ⊞) 🐾 Further from Arrowtown in aesthetics than kilometres, this massive manicured resort is a town unto itself. Rooms range from studios to luxury homes overlooking the fairways of the resort's golf course, which has been rated among the top 10 courses in NZ. At the end of the day, take your pick from four restaurants, or relax at the **spa** (☑ 03-441 7017; www.millbrook.co.nz; Malaghans Rd; treatments from $79).

🍴 Eating

Slow Cuts RIBS, BURGERS $
(Map p222; ☑ 03-442 0066; 46-50 Buckingham St; mains $11-14; ☉ noon-9pm) From the *amigas* at La Rumbla (p224) comes Slow Cuts, dishing up fast food in slow motion. There are rotisserie chickens, burgers, ribs,

LAKE HAYES

Around 14,000 years ago, little Lake Hayes was joined to the Frankton Arm of Lake Wakatipu. Now it sits in quiet isolation, its often-mirror-perfect reflections of the surrounding hills and mountains leading some to claim it as the most photographed lake in New Zealand. It's a great place for an easy stroll, with the 8km, bike-friendly **Lake Hayes Walkway** looping right around it. Allow two to three hours to walk it.

North of the lake, **Akarua Wines & Kitchen by Artisan** (Map p201; ☑ 03-442 1090; http://akaruaandartisan.co.nz; 265 Arrowtown–Lake Hayes Rd; mains $22-33; ⊙ 9am-5pm) features a restaurant inside a cottage originally built as offices for a flour mill, and a cellar door in a shipping container. The most enticing option if the sun's out, however, will be the beanbags in the garden. Lunch comes as individual serves, shared plates or a platter.

On the lake's eastern flank is **Amisfield Bistro & Cellar Door** (Map p201; ☑ 03-442 0556; www.amisfield.co.nz; 10 Lake Hayes Rd; 3-/5-course menu $75/95; ⊙ cellar door 10am-6pm, restaurant noon-8pm), a match for any of the wineries in nearby Gibbston, though it's the bistro that's the real showstopper. In 2017 it was named as one of NZ's top 100 restaurants, so you can feel reassured leaving yourself in the hands of the chefs when you order – there's no menu; you simply pick three or five courses and await whatever the chefs decide. Wine tastings are free if you purchase a bottle, or $10 otherwise.

Hidden in a natural depression across the highway, south of the lake, is **Lake Hayes Estate**, established in the 1990s as a more affordable, less touristy residential option to Queenstown. It's worth dropping by for a bite at **Graze** (Map p201; ☑ 03-441 4074; www.grazenz.co.nz; 1 Onslow Rd, Lake Hayes Estate; brunch $13-25, dinner $20-34; ⊙ 7.30am-5pm Mon, to late Tue-Sun; 🐾), an unexpectedly stylish cafe-bar at the heart of the estate. Its offerings run the gamut from morning coffee to dinner, to a beer from its own attached microbrewery.

Lake Hayes is 4km south of Arrowtown, on the road to Frankton.

smashed fries and a good small list of local wines.

★Chop Shop
CAFE **$$**

(Map p222; ☑ 03-442 1116; www.facebook.com/thechopshopfoodmerchants; 7 Arrow Lane; mains $20-30; ⊙ 8am-3pm) Perhaps the tables are a little tightly packed, and the open kitchen does take up half the space, but we're splitting hairs. This place is uniformly fabulous (and uniformly popular) – from the internationally inspired menu (pork dumplings, Turkish eggs, smoked pork-hock hash) to the interesting decor (pressed-tin bar, cool wallpaper, chandeliers made from bicycle wheels and chains). Great coffee, too.

La Rumbla
TAPAS **$$**

(Map p222; ☑ 03-442 0509; www.facebook.com/larumbla.arrowtown; 54 Buckingham St; tapas $11-24; ⊙ 4pm-late Tue-Sun) Tucked behind the post office, this little gem does a brilliant job of bringing the bold flavours and late-dining habits of Spain to sleepy little Arrowtown. Local produce is showcased in tasty bites on an ever-changing menu, and

the cocktail list goes long and strong in the evening.

Provisions
CAFE **$$**

(Map p222; ☑ 03-442 0714; www.provisionsofarrowtown.co.nz; 65 Buckingham St; mains $13-24; ⊙ 8am-4pm; 🐾) In a strip of old miners' cottages, this cute cafe serves up inventive creations – the likes of spiced sole tortillas or poached eggs on rosti. Everything is baked on-site, including bread, bagels and the deservedly famous sticky buns.

Saffron
MODERN NZ **$$$**

(Map p222; ☑ 03-442 0131; www.saffronrestaurant.co.nz; 18 Buckingham St; lunch $18-29, dinner $25-49; ⊙ noon-3pm & 6pm-late) Walking into Saffron is like stepping out of town, with its formal, clean-lined setting providing a contrast to Buckingham St's gunslinger appearance. Expect lamb, wild boar and fish, with both the portions and the soundtrack having a bit more spunk than you might expect from the setting.

MACETOWN

Macetown, 15km north of Arrowtown, is a gold-rush ghost town, built in the 1860s but abandoned by the 1930s. Many of its buildings have been restored, creating an isolated and evocative destination. It's reached along a rugged, flood-prone road (the original miners' wagon track) that crosses the Arrow River more than 25 times.

Don't even think about taking your hire car here. A much more sensible option is the 4WD tour offered by Nomad Safaris (p207), which also includes gold panning in the Arrow River. Or you can hike to Macetown from Arrowtown (15km each way, three to four hours one way), but it's particularly tricky in winter and spring; check with the information centre about conditions before heading out. An alternative route (four to five hours each way) climbs over Big Hill, avoiding many of the river crossings. This track climbs above 1000m, however, so shouldn't be attempted if the weather forecast isn't looking good.

The road to Macetown is sometimes touted as a mountain-biking route, but it's for experienced riders only, with steep drop-offs and almost no mobile-phone coverage if you do get into trouble.

Drinking & Entertainment

★ **Blue Door** BAR
(Map p222, ☑ 03-442 0415; www.facebook.com/TheBlueDoorBar; 18 Buckingham St; ⊙ 4pm-late; 🔊) The only indications that you've arrived are the unmarked blue doors – push them open and it's as though you've stepped into a prohibition-era speakeasy. The cool little bar has a formidable wine list and enough rustic ambience to keep you mellow for the evening. Low ceilings, an open fire and abundant candles create an intimate setting.

Fork & Tap PUB
(Map p222; ☑ 03-442 1860; www.theforkandtap.co.nz; 51 Buckingham St; ⊙ 11am-11pm) Built as a bank in the 1870s, Fork and Tap's currency is now craft beer, with up to 19 suds on tap. Add in good food, including shared meat and cheese platters, and a large sunny, kid-friendly back garden, and you have the pick of Arrowtown's pubs. Grab a tasting paddle of four 150mL beers of your choice for $14.

There's Irish music every Wednesday night, and live music in the garden on summer Sunday evenings.

Dorothy Browns CINEMA
(Map p222; ☑ 03-442 1964; www.dorothybrowns.com; 18 Buckingham St; adult/child $18.50/15) This is what a cinema should be like: wide, ultra-comfortable seating with fine local wine, cheese boards and olives available to accompany the mostly art-house films on offer. Most screenings in the main theatre

have an intermission – the perfect opportunity to tuck into a tub of gourmet ice cream.

Information

Arrowtown Visitor Information Centre (Map p222, ☑ 03-442 1824, www.arrowtown.com; 49 Buckingham St; ⊙ 8.30am-5pm) Shares premises with the Lake District Museum and Gallery.

Getting There & Away

Ritchies Connectabus (Map p222; ☑ 03-441 4471; www.connectabus.com) runs regular services from around 7am to 10pm on its route 10 from Frankton to Arrowtown ($15). From Queenstown, you'll need to catch a bus 11 to Frankton and change there.

WANAKA

POP 6480

So long described as Queenstown's smaller and more demure sibling, Wanaka now feels grown up enough to have moved out of home and asserted its own identity.

What it does share with Queenstown is the fact that they're both lake and mountain towns bristling with outdoors and adventure opportunities. Wanaka's list of adventure options is impressive by almost any measure, except against the Queenstown ruler. The breadth and selection of adventures here might not be as comprehensive, but the lakefront is more natural and less developed – complete with a day-at-the-beach feel on sunny days – and the town centre has a more soulful atmosphere.

Wanaka

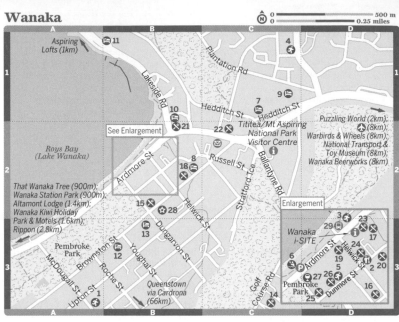

Wanaka

Despite constant growth – in both size and costs – Wanaka retains a fairly laid-back, small-town atmosphere. Days are invariably active here, but evenings are an invitation into a wave of new eateries and some truly quirky bars.

◉ Sights

★ National Transport & Toy Museum
MUSEUM

(☏03-443 8765; www.nttmuseumwanaka.co.nz; 891 Wanaka–Luggate Hwy/SH6; adult/child $18/5; ⊙8.30am-5pm; 🚗) Mixing Smurfs with Studebakers and Skidoos (and an authentic MiG jet fighter flown by the Polish Air Force) is this completely eclectic and absorbing collection of more than 60,000 items. Suitably, it's as jumbled as a toy box, making it all a bit of a treasure hunt, but it's a nostalgic journey even if you're only young enough to remember as far back as the Sylvanian Families.

That Wanaka Tree NATURAL FEATURE
One of the true stars of the Instagram age is this lakeshore tree that's now almost as famous as Wanaka itself. Once used as a fence post, it provides a classically photogenic prop to the mountains and Ruby Island behind. If you are here for the Instagram moment, come at dawn, when reflections are typically at their best.

Wanaka Station Park PARK
Wanaka Station Park is a piece of Wanaka that existed before Wanaka did. This remnant of the sheep station that once covered the town area and beyond is a beautiful, well-hidden park space with trees far more impressive (just less photogenic) than That Wanaka Tree nearby – giant sequoias, Himalayan cedars, a large walnut tree, an enormous rhododendron hedge and the station's surviving orchard, with pears and apples that are free for picking.

Rippon WINERY
(☑03-443 8084; www.rippon.co.nz; 246 Mt Aspiring Rd; ☺11am-5pm) It's worth raising a glass to the view alone at Rippon since the Tuscan-styled cellar door has surely the finest winery view in NZ. Free tastings take in five varieties. To save fights over who's going to be the designated driver, take a 2km stroll there along the lakeside Glendhu Bay Track, heading up the side trail to Rippon.

Puzzling World AMUSEMENT PARK
(☑03-443 7489; www.puzzlingworld.com; 188 Wanaka–Luggate Hwy/SH84; adult/child $20/14, Great Maze only $16/12; ☺8.30am-5.30pm; 🖶) A 3D Great Maze and lots of fascinating brain-bending visual illusions to keep people of all ages bemused, bothered and bewildered. Even the cafe tables come equipped with puzzles. It's en route to Cromwell, 2km from town.

Warbirds & Wheels MUSEUM
(www.warbirdsandwheels.com; 11 Lloyd Dunn Ave, Wanaka Airport; adult/child $20/5; ☺9am-5pm) Dedicated to NZ combat pilots, the aircraft they flew and the sacrifices they made, this museum features a replica of a Hawker Hurricane, a de Havilland FB5 Vampire and twin rows of gleaming classic cars – pride of place goes to the 1934 Duesenberg Model J, described as the finest car ever made in the USA. There's a retro diner attached.

Archangel WINERY
(☑03-443 4347; http://archangelwines.co.nz; 68 Queensberry Tce, Queensberry) Take a step up the social ladder with a visit not to a cellar door, but to a wine lounge at this stylish, boutique, 23-hectare vineyard 15 minutes' drive from Wanaka. Book ahead for the gourmet wine-tasting experience (from $35) and you'll not only get to sample Archangel's wines and local cheeses, but you'll also hear the fateful wartime story behind the winery's name.

🏃 Activities

Wanaka might not have bridges to leap off, but you could still bottle the adrenaline here. For powder monkeys it's the gateway to the Treble Cone (p229), Cardrona (p229), Snow Farm (p233) and Harris Mountains (p202) ski areas, and it's the last stop before Tititea/Mt Aspiring National Park for those in hiking boots.

Tramping

For walks close to town, including various lakeside wanders, download DOC's *Wanaka Outdoor Pursuits* brochure from its website (www.doc.govt.nz). **Roys Peak** is usually Wanaka's tramp *du jour*, though you can get lofty views with far less effort atop **Mt Iron** (527m, 1½ hours return) – it's a rather grandiose name for what's really just a hill.

For something low-level, the **Glendhu Bay Track** bobbles along the western shore of Lake Wanaka, passing That Wanaka Tree (p227) and Rippon (p227) before rolling into Glendhu Bay after three to four hours on foot. It's also a good track for a gentle mountain-bike ride.

Mountain Biking

Hundreds of kilometres of tracks and trails in the region are open to mountain bikers. Download DOC's *Wanaka Outdoor Pursuits* brochure, which describes a range of mountain-bike rides, including the popular **Deans Bank Track** (12km).

One particularly scenic route is the **Newcastle Track** (12km), which follows the

WORTH A TRIP

LAKE HAWEA

People looking to escape the bright lights of Queenstown typically gravitate to Wanaka; those looking to escape the slightly less bright lights of Wanaka come to Lake Hawea.

This small town, 15km north of Wanaka, is strung along the southern shore of its 141-sq-km namesake. Separated from Lake Wanaka by a narrow strip of land called the Neck, the blue-grey Lake Hawea (with an average water temperature of just 9°C) is 35km long and 410m deep. It's particularly popular with fisherfolk looking to do battle with its trout and landlocked salmon. The lake was raised 20m in 1958 when it was dammed to facilitate the power stations downriver.

There's little here, but that's the town's appeal.

raging blue waters of the Clutha River from Albert Town to the Red Bridge on Kane Rd. You can make it a 30km loop by joining the **Upper Clutha River Track** at Luggate.

The **Glendhu Bay Track** provides easy riding along the shore of Lake Wanaka, while a local favourite is **Sticky Forest**, with around 30km of purpose-built trails through pine forest.

Bike hire is easy to find in town – try **Outside Sports** (Map p226; ☑03-443 7966; www.outsidesports.co.nz; 17/23 Dunmore St; half/full day from $30/50; ☺bike hire 9am-6pm) for a quality dual-suspension or downhill mountain bike, or if you prefer the boost of an e-bike, head to **Good Rotations** (Map p226; ☑03-443 4349; www.goodrotations.co; 34 Anderson Rd; half/full day from $45/89; ☺11am-5pm Tue-Fri).

Rock Climbing & Mountaineering

Excellent rock climbing can be found at Hospital Flat, around 20km from Wanaka towards Tititea/Mt Aspiring National Park, and the adjoining Diamond Lake Conservation Area.

Aspiring Guides   ADVENTURE SPORTS
(Map p226; ☑03-443 9422; www.aspiringguides.com; 58 McDougall St) This crew offers a multitude of adventure options, including guided tramping on around a dozen wilderness routes, mountaineering and ice-climbing

courses, guided ascents of Tititea/Mt Aspiring and Aoraki/Mt Cook, and off-piste ski trips (one- to five-day backcountry expeditions).

Other Activities

Treble Cone   SKIING
(☑03-443 1406; www.treblecone.com; daily lift pass adult/child $110/55) The highest and largest of the region's ski areas, spectacular Treble Cone delivers powder with panoramas. Its steep slopes are suitable for intermediate to advanced skiers, with a beginners area that includes free lift access. There's around 700m of vertical, as well as numerous half-pipes and a terrain park for snowboarding.

★**Wildwire Wanaka**   ADVENTURE SPORTS
(☑027 430 1332; www.wildwire.co.nz) The Italian world of *via ferrata* – climbing using the likes of iron rungs, plank bridges and cables – arrives in Wanaka, scaling the cliffs beside (and sometimes across) Twin Falls. Make the half-day climb partway up the falls ($249), or go the whole hog on Lord of the Rungs ($595), the world's highest waterfall *via ferrata,* with a helicopter flight back down.

Deep Canyon   ADVENTURE SPORTS
(Map p226; ☑03-443 7922; www.deepcanyon.co.nz; 100 Ardmore St; from $240; ☺Oct-Apr) Climb, walk, leap, zip-line and abseil your way through narrow, wild gorges – 10 options on offer, from novice to 'oh God'.

Pioneer Rafting   RAFTING
(☑03-443 1246; www.ecoraft.co.nz; by donation) ✐ Raft on the high-volume Clutha, with Grade II to III rapids, incorporating a spot of gold panning and bird-watching. The operation is based on non-commercial principles – you don't pay for the trip per se, you donate a sum of money of your choosing towards Pioneer Rafting's river conservation projects.

Skydive Wanaka   SKYDIVING
(☑03-443 7207; www.skydivewanaka.com; 14 Mustang Lane, Wanaka Airport; from $229) Grab some airtime, jumping from 9000ft, 12,000ft, or going the whole banana with a 15,000ft leap and 60 seconds of free fall.

Paddle Wanaka   KAYAKING
(Map p226; ☑0800 926 925; www.paddlewanaka.co.nz; Ardmore St; ☺9am-6pm Oct-Easter) Offers kayaks ($20 per hour) and stand-up paddle boards (SUP, $20 per hour) for hire

and guided paddle-powered tours of the lake (half/full day $135/275) and the rapids of the Clutha River (half day $189). For something unique, how about a heli-SUP trip to a remote mountain lake?

Wanaka River Journeys   ADVENTURE SPORTS
(☑ 03-443 4416; www.wanakariverjourneys.co.nz; adult/child from $185/120) 🍃 Combination walk (50 minutes) and jetboat ride in the gorgeous Matukituki Valley. Also offers packrafting and heli-jetboating.

🛈 Tours

Scenic Flights

Classic Flights   SCENIC FLIGHTS
(☑ 03-443 4043; www.classicflights.co.nz; Spitfire Lane, Wanaka Airport; from $249) Sightseeing flights in a vintage Tiger Moth or Waco biplane. 'Biggles' goggles, leather helmet and flowing silk scarf provided to complete the moment.

U Fly   SCENIC FLIGHTS
(☑ 03-445 4005; www.u-flywanaka.co.nz; 8 Spitfire Lane, Wanaka Airport; from $199) The name doesn't lie...you'll be flying the plane on a scenic flight over Lake Wanaka or into Tititea/Mt Aspiring National Park. Don't fret; there are dual controls ready for the real pilot to take over at a moment's notice they're not completely insane.

Aspiring Helicopters   SCENIC FLIGHTS
(☑ 03-443 7152; www.aspiringhelicopters.co.nz; Cattle Flat Station, 2211 Mt Aspiring Rd) A range of flight options, from a 20-minute buzz over Lake Wanaka ($185) to a three-hour flight to Milford Sound ($1250), choppering along the sound's length and making four landings.

Wanaka Helicopters   SCENIC FLIGHTS
(☑ 03-443 1085; www.wanakahelicopters.co.nz; 6 Lloyd Dunn Ave, Wanaka Airport) Options range from 10-minute tasters ($99) to two-hour-plus trips to Milford Sound (from $995).

Southern Alps Air   SCENIC FLIGHTS
(☑ 03-443 4385, 0800 345 666; www.southernalpsair.co.nz; 12 Lloyd Dunn Ave, Wanaka Airport) Flights over Aoraki/Mt Cook, taking in Tasman, Fox and Franz Josef Glaciers (adult/child $485/320), along with Milford Sound flyovers ($455/300), Milford fly-cruise combos ($540/355) and whirls over Tititea/Mt Aspiring and Lake Wanaka ($290/200).

Alpine Helicopters   SCENIC FLIGHTS
(☑ 03-443 4000; www.alpineheli.co.nz; 10 Lloyd Dunn Ave, Wanaka Airport) Options range from a 20-minute flight over Wanaka with a hilltop landing ($230), to the half-day Fiordland Heli Traverse ($2490), which includes multiple landings and a remote alpine picnic.

Other Tours

Eco Wanaka Adventures   OUTDOORS
(☑ 03-443 2869; www.ecowanaka.co.nz) 🍃 Trips include a full-day walk to the Rob Roy Glacier ($275), a four-hour cruise and walk on Mou Waho Island ($225) to find a lake within a lake, and a full-day cruise-4WD combo ($454). Also offers helihikes.

Wanaka Bike Tours   CYCLING
(☑ 03-443 6363; www.wanakabiketours.co.nz; from $199) Guided trips along the shores of Lake Hawea, the Clutha River bike trail, or into the mountains above Lake Wanaka. Also has helibiking options.

Ridgeline Adventures   DRIVING
(☑ 0800 234 000; www.ridgeline.co.nz) 🍃 Choose from a range of 4WD explorations, be it a 'safari' through farming country ($229), a 4WD/jetboat/helicopter combo ($846), or a drive to a romantic dinner for two on a remote hilltop overlooking Lake Wanaka ($375).

Funny French Cars   DRIVING
(☑ 027 386 6932; www.funnyfrenchcars.co.nz) Ride in a classic 2CV Citroën around local wineries (from $165), or tour scenic highlights of Wanaka (from $99).

🎉 Festivals & Events

TUKI   MUSIC
(www.tukifestival.nz; ⊕ Feb) New incarnation of the former Rippon Festival, moving up the road to Glendhu Bay in 2018, but featuring the same ilk of big-name Kiwi bands and musicians. It's held every second year, in even-numbered years.

Warbirds over Wanaka   AIR SHOW
(☑ 0800 496 920, 03-443 8619; www.warbirdsoverwanaka.com; Wanaka Airport; adult/child 1 day from $70/15, 3 days from $190/35) Held every second Easter (in even-numbered years), this incredibly popular international airshow attracts upwards of 50,000 people.

🛏 Sleeping

★ Wanaka Bakpaka
HOSTEL $

(Map p226; ☑ 03-443 7837; www.wanakabakpaka.
co.nz; 117 Lakeside Rd; dm $31, d with/without
bathroom $92/74; P@🛜) The only lake-
side hostel in town delivers million-dollar
views at backpacker prices. Amenities are
top-shelf and it's worth paying a bit extra
for the en suite double with the gorgeous
views, though you can also just lap it all
up from the wide lounge windows. There
are bikes for hire and the hot-water bottles
come free.

YHA Wanaka
HOSTEL $

(Map p226; ☑ 03-443 1880; www.yha.co.nz; 94
Brownston St; dm $30-38, d with/without bath-
room from $108/93; @🛜) 🖉 This Wanaka
stalwart is older than many of its guests,
and it's mellowed comfortably with age. It
has a mix of dorms and private rooms, but
best of all are the large lounge, with com-
manding lake and mountain views, and the
quiet reading room. The giant topo map in
the lounge is great for planning tramps.

Wanaka Kiwi
Holiday Park & Motels
HOLIDAY PARK $

(☑ 03-443 7766; www.wanakakiwiholidaypark.nz;
263 Studholme Rd North; campsites $25-27, units
with/without bathroom from $124/80; P🛜)
This charming and relaxing campground
is tucked under Roys Peak, with grassy ter-
raced sites for tents and campervans, lots
of trees and pretty views. Facilities include
a barbecue area with heaters, and free unlimited wi-fi, plus spa pool and sauna ($5).
Older-style motel units have all been renovated, and the newest budget cabins are
warm and cosy with wooden floors.

Altamont Lodge
LODGE $

(☑ 03-443 8864; www.altamontlodge.co.nz; 121
Mt Aspiring Rd; s/d $79/99; 🛜) At the quiet
end of town, Altamont is like a hostel for
grown-ups. There are no dorms but the tidy
little rooms share spotless bathrooms and a
spacious, well-equipped kitchen. Pine-lined
walls give it a ski-lodge ambience, while
the spa pool and roaring fire in the lounge
with its views of Roys Peak will warm you
up post-slopes.

Criffel Peak View
B&B $$

(Map p226; ☑ 03-443 5511; www.criffel
peakview.co.nz; 98 Hedditch St; s/d/apt from
$140/170/280; P🛜) Situated in a quiet cul-
de-sac, this excellent B&B has three rooms

sharing a large lounge with a log fire and a
sunny wisteria-draped deck. The charming
hostesses live in a separate house behind,
which also has a self-contained two-bed-
room apartment attached.

Wanaka View Motel
MOTEL $$

(Map p226; ☑ 03-443 7480; www.wanakaview
motel.co.nz; 122 Brownston St; apts $135-255;
P🛜) The refurbished Wanaka View has
five apartments with spa baths and full
kitchens squeezed tightly into a house
block. The largest has three bedrooms and
most have lake views. There's also a comfortable studio unit tucked around the
back, which is cheaper but doesn't have a
kitchen or view.

Archway Motels
MOTEL $$

(Map p226; ☑ 03-443 7698; www.archwaymotels.
co.nz; 64 Hedditch St; units/chalets from
$135/155; 🛜) Classically old-school motel
with clean and spacious units and chalets,
a short uphill walk from the town centre.
Cedar hot tubs with mountain views give
this place an extra edge. Also has two large
self-contained caravans ($125) on site.

Asure Brookvale Motel
MOTEL $$

(Map p226; ☑ 03-443 8333; www.brookvale.co.nz;
35 Brownston St; d from $135; 🛜🏊) The patios
at this old-fashioned concrete-block motel
open onto a grassy lawn edged by a gently
flowing creek. It also has a barbecue, hot
tub and plunge pool.

★ Lakeside
APARTMENT $$$

(Map p226; ☑ 03-443 0188; www.lakesidewana
ka.co.nz; 9 Lakeside Rd; apt from $295; 🛜🏊)
Luxuriate in a modern apartment in a
prime position overlooking the lake, right
by the town centre. All 23 apartments have
three bedrooms, but can be rented with
only one or two bedrooms open. The swim-
ming pool is a relative rarity in these parts,
and if you hire ski gear through the website
it can be delivered to your door.

★ Aspiring Lofts
B&B $$$

(☑ 03-443 7856; www.aspiringlofts.co.nz; 42
Manuka Cres; s/d $220/240; 🛜) Perched on
a rise overlooking the lake, this modern
house has two upmarket rooms in the loft
above the garage. Each has its own private
balcony to make the most of the views – sit
out at night in winter and you can watch
the lights as Treble Cone is groomed. You
can also stargaze through the roof of the
bathroom.

★ **Lime Tree Lodge**   LODGE **$$$**
(☑03-443 7305; www.limetreelodge.co.nz; 672 Ballantyne Rd; d $395-595; P 🛜 🏊) Quietly removed from town, this intimate lodge has four luxury rooms and two suites. Outside there's a pool, spa, tennis court and pitch-and-putt golf, while the lodge is centred on an inviting living area with open kitchen where the in-house chef prepares meals. There are pre-dinner drinks with the owners – former local sheep-station owners – each night.

Alpine View Lodge   B&B **$$$**
(☑03-443 7111; www.alpineviewlodge.co.nz; 23 Studholme Rd South; d from $195, cottage $290; 🛜) In a peaceful rural setting on the edge of town, this excellent lodge has three B&B rooms, one of which has its own private deck with mountain views. Little extras include homemade shortbread in the rooms and a hot tub. Alternatively, you can opt for the fully self-contained two-bedroom cottage, which opens onto the garden.

🍴 Eating

Red Star   BURGERS **$**
(Map p226; ☑03-443 9322; https://redstar burgerbar.mobi2go.com; 26 Ardmore St; burgers $12-17; ⊘11.30am-9pm) The burger menu is exhaustive and inventive – beef, chicken, venison, fish and veggie burgers on crunchy toasted buns. Grab a seat on the terrace and sip on a craft beer with your craft burger.

Charlie Brown   CRÊPES **$**
(Map p226; www.charliebrowncrepes.co.nz; 28 Dungarvon St; crêpes $6-11; ⊘9am-9pm, shorter hours off-season) Started by a Frenchman in 2016 and taken over by, well, another Frenchman a year later, this retro caravan purveys French crêpes and savoury galettes, with a permanent menu and a seasonal specials board. Grab a crêpe before you head into Cinema Paradiso (p232) – it's right across the road.

Yohei   JAPANESE **$**
(Map p226; ☑03-443 4222; Spencer House, 31 Dunmore St; mains $9-15; ⊘9am-5.30pm; 🛜 🍴) Tucked away in a shopping arcade, this relaxed eatery does interesting local spins on sushi (feta and sun-dried tomato, anyone?), Japanese curries, noodles and superlative juices and smoothies.

★ **Kai Whakapai**   CAFE **$$**
(Map p226; ☑03-443 7795; cnr Helwick & Ardmore Sts; mains $19-26; ⊘7am-11pm; 🍴) As Wanaka as *that* tree, this local institution is where the town seems to congregate on a sunny evening for a liquid sundowner over excellent pizza or salad. Locally brewed craft beers are on tap and there are Central Otago wines as well.

★ **Francesca's Italian Kitchen**   ITALIAN **$$**
(Map p226; ☑03-443 5599; www.fransitalian. co.nz; 93 Ardmore St; mains $20-32; ⊘noon-3pm & 5pm-late) Pretty much the matriarch of Wanaka eateries, the perennially busy and cavernous Francesca's has the big flavours and easy conviviality of an authentic Italian family trattoria. Even simple things such as pizza, pasta and polenta chips are exceptional. It also runs a **pizza food truck** (Map p226; ☑0800 4647 4992; www.francescaspizzas. com; Brownston St; pizza $10-20; ⊘4-9pm) on Brownston St.

Landing   MODERN NZ **$$$**
(Map p226; ☑03-443 5099; www.thelanding lakewanaka.co.nz; 1st fl, 80 Ardmore St; mains $26-35; ⊘5pm-late Tue-Sun) Looking over the lake from an upstairs perch, the Landing is a stylish place where both menus and views change with the seasons. Expect local meats and fish served in innovative ways. The wine list is strong on Central Otago drops, and there's typically a Wanaka craft beer on tap.

Relishes Cafe   CAFE **$$**
(Map p226; ☑03-443 9018; www.relishescafe. co.nz; 99 Ardmore St; brunch $8.50-19, breakfast $11-22, dinner $33-36; ⊘7am-10pm) A cafe by day with good breakfast and lunch options, this place transforms into a sophisticated restaurant with a fine wine list at night. Central Otago wines take centre stage.

Federal Diner   CAFE **$$**
(Map p226; ☑03-443 5152; www.federaldiner. co.nz; 47 Helwick St; breakfast $10-19, mains $22-40; ⊘7am-4pm Mon & Tue, to 9pm Wed-Sun; 🛜) When it's this hidden away and still this popular, you know to expect good things. This cosmopolitan cafe delivers robust breakfasts, excellent coffee, legendary scones, gourmet sandwiches and salads. In the evenings the menu shifts to substantial dishes such as baked gnocchi and slow-roasted lamb shoulder.

Ritual
CAFE **$$**

(Map p226; ☑03-443 6662; 18 Helwick St; mains $11-25; ⊗9am-5pm; 🐾) A classic 21st-century Kiwi cafe, Ritual is smart but not too trendy, and filled to the gills with delicious food. The counter positively groans under the weight of tasty salads, slices and scones.

★Kika
TAPAS **$$$**

(Map p226; ☑03-443 6535; http://kika.nz; 2 Dunmore St; plates $12-55; ⊗5.30pm-late) The baby sister to Francesca's (p231) has grown up fast, vaulting within just a year of opening to become the only Wanaka eatery named among New Zealand's top 100 restaurants in 2017. It's a Mediterranean mix of modern Italian food, served tapas-style in a casual dining space. Unsure what to choose? Let the chefs decide with the Just Feed Me menu ($62).

White House Restaurant & Bar
MEDITERRANEAN **$$$**

(Map p226; ☑03-443 9595; 33 Dunmore St; mains $25-45; ⊗4-10.30pm Tue-Sat) This curious restaurant is, well, yeah, in a house – a white one – looking as though someone dropped a casual eatery into the lounge room of an art-deco home. The ever-changing menu ranges through a selection of bruschetta and the likes of lamb with puy lentils, or linguine with surf clams.

Bistro Gentil
FRENCH **$$$**

(Map p226; ☑03-443 2299; www.bistrogentil. co.nz; 76a Golf Course Rd; mains $42-44; ⊗6pm-late Tue-Sat) Far removed from the madding crowd, with fabulous NZ art and delicious modern French cuisine, Gentil ticks plenty of boxes for a memorable night out. The self-serve wine machine feels a little too vending machine, but with dishes such as coffee-rubbed pork tenderloin and Cardrona lamb with hazelnut and rosemary jus, it's easy to forgive.

🍷 Drinking & Nightlife

Lalaland
COCKTAIL BAR

(Map p226; ☑03-443 4911; www.facebook.com/ Lalalandwanaka; 1st fl, 99 Ardmore St; ⊗4pm-2.30am) Before Ryan Gosling and Emma Stone popularised the term, there was already this Lalaland in Wanaka. Sink into a comfy chair at the little, low-lit palace/bordello, where bar staff concoct elixirs to suit every mood. The lake view might be better at other upstairs Ardmore St bars, but can they top this playlist or cocktail list? Entry via the rear stairs.

Gin & Raspberry
COCKTAIL BAR

(Map p226; ☑03-443 4216; www.ginandraspberry.co.nz; 1st fl, 155 Ardmore St; ⊗3pm-late) If you're in the swing for bling, this lush bar is like stepping into a Baz Luhrmann film set. Among the gilded mirrors, grand piano (yes, you can ask to play it) and purple mood lighting, classic movies provide a backdrop to classic cocktails (including various martinis). The gin collection is impressive and the deck is the perfect sunset perch.

☆ Entertainment

Ruby's
CINEMA

(☑03-443 6901; www.rubyscinema.co.nz; 50 Cardrona Valley Rd; adult/child $19/13) How very Wanaka that an art-house cinema should adjoin an indoor climbing wall. Channelling a lush New York or Shanghai vibe, Ruby's has a whiff of cinema's glory days. Watch a movie from a reclining leather chair with a warming blanket over your knees, or just chill in the red-velvet lounge with local craft beers and wine or classic cocktails.

Cinema Paradiso
CINEMA

(Map p226; ☑03-443 1505; www.paradiso.net.nz; 72 Brownston St; adult/child $15/9.50) Sprawl on a comfy couch, or recline in a dentist's chair or an old Morris Minor at this Wanaka institution, screening the best of Hollywood and art-house flicks. At intermission head to the lobby for freshly baked cookies (simply follow your nose), though the homemade ice cream is just as enticing.

ℹ Information

MEDICAL SERVICES

Wanaka Medical Centre (☑03-443 0710; www.wanakamedical.co.nz; 23 Cardrona Valley Rd; ⊗9am-6pm Mon-Fri) is the place to go if you need to patch up any adventure mishaps.

TOURIST INFORMATION

Tititea/Mt Aspiring National Park Visitor Centre (Map p226; ☑03-443 7660; www. doc.govt.nz; cnr Ardmore St & Ballantyne Rd; ⊗8.30am-5pm daily Nov-Apr, Mon-Sat May-Oct) In an A-framed building on the edge of the town centre, this DOC office takes hut bookings and offers advice on tracks and conditions. Be sure to call in before undertaking any wilderness tramps.

Wanaka i-SITE (Map p226; ☑03-443 1233; www.lakewanaka.co.nz; 103 Ardmore St;

⊙ 8am-7pm summer, to 5pm winter) Lakefront office that's ever helpful, but always busy.

ℹ Getting There & Away

Queenstown is Wanaka's main transport link to the outside world, but bus services do range out from here to Dunedin and up the West Coast.

InterCity (Map p226; ☑ 03-442 4922; www. intercity.co.nz) Coaches depart from outside the **Log Cabin** on the lakefront, with daily services to Cromwell (from $10, 35 minutes), Queenstown (from $17, two hours), Lake Hawea (from $10, 20 minutes), Makarora (from $12, 1½ hours) and Franz Josef (from $43, six hours).

Naked Bus (Map p226; https://nakedbus. com) Services to Queenstown (from $17, two hours), Cromwell (from $10, 35 minutes) and Franz Josef (from $43, six hours).

Ritchies (Map p226; ☑ 03-443 9120; www. alpinecoachlines.co.nz) Links Wanaka with Dunedin ($50, four hours), transferring to an InterCity coach at Cromwell.

Ritchies Connectabus Wanaka (Map p226; ☑ 0800 405 066; www.connectabus.com) Heads to/from Queenstown five times daily ($35, two hours) via Cromwell ($22, 45 minutes) and Queenstown Airport. Free wi fi on board. Call ahead for a hotel pick-up.

ℹ Getting Around

Adventure Rentals (☑ 03-443 6050; www. adventurerentals.co.nz; 51 Brownston St) hires cars and 4WDs (the latter is the best option if you're heading to Tititea/Mt Aspiring National Park), while **Yello** (☑ 03-443 5555; www.yello.co.nz) operates taxis and scheduled winter shuttles to Cardrona and Treble Cone ski fields ($35 return). Bikes can be hired from **Outside Sports** (p228) or **Good Rotations** (p228).

AROUND WANAKA

Cardrona

Gouged between the Crown and Criffel Ranges, the cute settlement of Cardrona reached its zenith in the 1870s at the height of the gold rush, when its population numbered more than 1000. Today it's effectively a ski field balanced atop a pub, albeit perhaps the most recognisable and evocative pub in New Zealand.

Cardrona wakes with a jolt for the ski season, but even if you're not here for powder, it's well worth a visit. Drink in the views and the beer, take a horse ride through the open tussock country, be slightly bemused at the bra fence and understand that a distillery rightly belongs here since the landscape is so reminiscent of the Scottish Highlands.

◉ Sights & Activities

Cardrona Distillery & Museum   DISTILLERY
(Map p201; ☑ 03-443 1393; www.cardronadistillery.com; 2125 Cardrona Valley Rd; tours $25; ⊙ 9.30am-5pm) Matching the ever-so-Scottish setting is this single-malt distillery. Enter past the fence of bras (Bra-drona!) and you'll find the beautiful cellar door inside a building of local schist rock. Have a sip of the orange liqueur and award-winning gin, or take the 75-minute distillery tour, which leaves on the hour from 10am to 3pm. You probably won't want to hang around waiting for the whisky to be ready – the first release is due in 2025.

Cardrona Alpine Resort   SKIING
(Map p201; ☑ 03-443 8880, snow report 03-443 7007; www.cardrona.com; Cardrona Skifield Access Rd; daily lift passes adult/child Jul & Aug $110/60, Jun, Sep & Oct $99/50; ⊙ 8.30am-4pm Jun-Oct) Well organised and professional, this 345-hectare ski field offers runs to suit all abilities (25% beginners, 25% intermediate, 30% advanced, 20% expert) at elevations ranging from 1670m to 1860m. Cardrona has several high-capacity chairlifts (including a new Chondola in 2017), beginners' tows and extreme snowboard terrain.

Buses run from Wanaka and Queenstown during ski season.

In summer, the mountain bikers take over. The **Cardrona Peak to Pub**, from the ski fields to the Cardrona Hotel, is a classic NZ ride with 1270m of descent – the resort runs shuttles back up the mountain.

Snow Farm   SKIING
(Map p42; ☑ 03-443 7542; www.snowfarmnz.com; Snow Farm Access Rd; day trail pass adult/child $40/20, snowshoe day trail pass $20/10; ♿) In winter this is home to fantastic cross-country skiing and snowshoeing, with 55km of groomed ski trails and 24km of snowshoe trails. Lessons and ski hire are available.

The Cardrona   HORSE RIDING
(Map p201; ☑ 03-443 1228; www.thecardrona. co.nz; 2125 Cardrona Valley Rd) Guided horse

rides through the Cardrona Valley, including a High Country Pub ride ($149) that'll have you tying up at the Cardrona Hotel hitching rail for a beer. Also runs quad-bike tours and winter snowmobiling trips onto the Pisa Range.

**Backcountry
Saddle Expeditions** HORSE RIDING
(Map p201; ☑ 03-443 8151; www.backcountry saddles.co.nz; 2416 Cardrona Valley Rd; adult/child $90/70) Two-hour horse treks across Mt Cardrona Station on Appaloosa horses. Also now runs quad-bike tours ($149).

🛏 Sleeping & Drinking

Waiorau Homestead B&B $$$
(Map p201; ☑ 03-443 2225; www.waiorauhome stead.co.nz; 2127 Cardrona Valley Rd; r from $250; 🛜🌊) Tucked away in a private bucolic nook near the Snow Farm, this lovely stone house, fringed by an old stand of conifers, has deep verandas and three luxurious guest bedrooms, each with their own bathroom. Rates include a full cooked breakfast. Enquire about the cheaper self-contained cabin ($170 to $190); the owners usually rent it on Airbnb.

Cardrona Hotel PUB
(☑ 03-443 8153; www.cardronahotel.co.nz; 2310 Cardrona Valley Rd; 🛜) The wood-panelled facade looks like a film set, but it's the real deal – NZ's most photographed pub is a gold-rush relic from 1863. The sense of history is palpable (note the exposed mine shaft over which the pub was built) and things get busy in the après-ski thawing hours.

The meals are good (mains $23 to $36) and there are 16 lovingly restored rooms ($195) if you want to stay the night.

ℹ Getting There & Away

There are no scheduled bus services to Cardrona, but winter ski shuttles are offered by **Yello** (p233) and **Ridgeline Adventures** (p229) in Wanaka, and **Kiwi Discovery** (p218) in Queenstown.

The 45km drive from Queenstown to Cardrona along the Crown Range Rd is one of the South Island's most scenic drives. Topping out at 1076m, it's the highest sealed road in NZ. There are some great places to stop and ogle the view, particularly at the Queenstown end of the road. However, the road is narrow and winding, and needs to be tackled with care in poor weather. In winter it's sometimes closed after heavy snows, and you'll often need snow chains for your tyres.

Makarora

POP 40

Just 20km from Haast Pass, where the West Coast begins its wild ways, remote Makarora is very much a last frontier – and it certainly feels like it. Traffic to and from the West Coast rolls through, but then Makarora settles back to silence.

🏃 Activities

The most popular short hike in this secluded area is the vibrant Blue Pools Walk (p234). **Haast Pass Lookout Track** (one hour return, 3.5km) offers great views from above the bush line. If you really want the upstairs view, the **Mt Shrimpton Track** climbs high onto the McKerrow Range (five hours return to the bush line, 6km); the track begins just a few hundred metres north of the Makarora Tourist Centre.

Longer tramps go deep into the valleys that radiate through the mountains around Makarora, but shouldn't be undertaken lightly. Changeable alpine and river conditions mean you must be well prepared; consult with DOC before heading off. Call in to the Tititea/Mt Aspiring National Park visitor centre (p232) in Wanaka to check conditions and routes before undertaking any wilderness tramps.

⭐ **Blue Pools Walk** TRAMPING
Far and away the most popular walk in the Makarora area is the 750m (30-minute return) track to the luminously blue pools at the point where the Makarora and Blue Rivers converge. The water is so clear you can see the trout seemingly suspended in it. The trailhead is around 8km north of the Makarora Tourist Centre.

Wilkin Valley Track TRAMPING
The Wilkin Valley Track starts from SH6 and heads along the Wilkin River to Kerin Forks Hut (four to five hours, 15km). Another day's walk up the valley will bring you to Top Forks Hut (six to eight hours, 15km), from where the picturesque Lakes Diana, Lucidus and Castalia (one hour, 1½ hours and three hours respectively) can be reached.

Siberia Experience   ADVENTURE

(☑03-443 4385; www.siberiaexperience.co.nz; Makarora Tourist Centre, 5944 Haast Pass-Makarora Rd/SH6; adult/child $395/299) This thrill-seeking extravaganza combines a 25-minute scenic flight, a three-hour tramp through a remote valley and a half-hour jetboat trip down the Wilkin and Makarora Rivers in Tititea/Mt Aspiring National Park.

🛏 Sleeping

The **Makarora Tourist Centre** (☑03-443 8372; www.makarora.co.nz; 5944 Haast Pass-Makarora Rd/SH6; ☺summer 8am-late, winter 9am-5.30pm; 🐕) can accommodate enough people to turn the place into a town – 160 beds plus camping. It has dorms, cabins and self-contained A-frame chalets. The nearest DOC camping grounds (adult/child $8/4) are on SH6 at **Cameron Flat**, 9km north of Makarora, and at **Boundary Creek**, 15km south of Makarora on the northern shores of Lake Wanaka.

ⓘ Getting There & Away

InterCity (☑03-442 4922; www.intercity. co.nz) has daily coaches to/from Queenstown (from $24, 3½ hours), Cromwell (from $19, 2¼ hours), Wanaka (from $12, 1½ hours), Lake Hawea (from $10, 1¼ hours) and Franz Josef (from $36, 4¾ hours).

The West Coast

Best Places to Eat

➡ Snake Bite Brewery (p251)

➡ Aurora (p257)

➡ Lake Matheson Cafe (p246)

➡ Ramble + Ritual (p257)

Best Places to Stay

➡ Theatre Royal Hotel (p259)

➡ Rough & Tumble Lodge (p268)

➡ Drifting Sands (p256)

➡ Te Waonui Forest Retreat (p251)

➡ Bazil's Hostel (p267)

Why Go?

Nowhere is solitude sweeter than on the West Coast. A few marvels pull big crowds – like Franz Josef and Fox Glaciers, and the magnificent Pancake Rocks – but you'll need jet-boats, helicopter rides and tramping trails to explore its inner realms. Hemmed in by the Southern Alps and the savage Tasman Sea, the West Coast forms almost 9% of the land area of New Zealand (NZ) but contains less than 1% of its population.

Nineteenth-century European settlers in this region faced great hardships as fortunes built on gold, coal and timber wavered. A chain of ghost towns and forlorn pioneer cemeteries were left in their wake, and only the hardiest remained. Present-day Coasters exhibit the same grit, softened with ironic humour and unquestioning hospitality. Time spent in these indomitable communities will have you spinning yarns of the wild West Coast long into the future.

When to Go

➡ December through February is peak season, so book accommodation at least a couple of months ahead during this period.

➡ The shoulder months of October/November and March/April are increasingly busy, particularly around Punakaiki, Hokitika and the Glaciers.

➡ The West Coast has plenty of sunshine but serious rainfall (in places, up to 5m annually).

➡ May to September has fewer crowds and cheaper accommodation; though mild (for NZ), it's reliably rainy.

➡ All year round, backcountry trampers should check conditions with local DOC (Department of Conservation) office staff. Rivers are treacherous and snow hangs around longer than you think.

The West Coast Highlights

1 Glacier Country (p243) Soaring above Franz Josef and Fox Glaciers before a guided walk on glistening ice.

2 The Great Coast Road (p263) Admiring salt-licked beaches and the dramatic Pancake Rocks along an unforgettable 100km drive.

3 Hokitika Gorge (p256) Gawping at vibrant turquoise waters from a lofty swing bridge.

4 Gold-Rush History (p266) Delving into the past on the Old Ghost Road, or in mining towns like Reefton.

5 Oparara Basin (p269) Craning your neck at limestone formations girded by dense forest.

6 Buller River (p272) Getting wet 'n' wild taking on this mighty river's rapids.

7 West Coast Wilderness Trail (p256) Enjoying equal measures of views and history by bike or on foot.

8 Okarito (p252) Kayaking through rainforest channels before joining a kiwi-spotting walk.

9 Hokitika (p257) Hunting out authentic local *pounamu* in working studios.

10 Waiatoto River (p242) Jetboating deep into Haast's World Heritage wilderness.

DAY TRIPS FROM WESTPORT

KARAMEA

As far north as the coastal road will take you before you hit the wilderness of Kahurangi National Park, little Karamea is wonderfully remote. There's not much to the village itself, but it's a terrific launching point for some sublime back-to-nature walks.

☆ Best Things to See/Do/Eat

◉ **Scotts Beach** It's hugely dangerous and definitely not recommended for swimming, but this deserted beach is a good target for an hour's walk along the beloved Heaphy Track, one of NZ's 'Great Walks'. If you're happy just to look from afar, stop at the lookout 30 minutes along the trail. (p268)

🥾 **Oparara Basin hike** Hidden within Kahurangi National Park, this spectacular valley is reached by a 45-minute walk from the end of a rough, unsealed road. The effort is rewarded by views of magnificent limestone arches, the largest of which is 200m long and 37m high. (p269)

🍽 **Karamea Village Hotel** Eateries are thin on the ground but this friendly pub is a good place for a simple meal and some banter with the locals. (p270)

☆ How to Get There

Car Heading north from Westport on SH67, you'll reach Karamea in less than an hour and a half.
Shuttle Various shuttle companies provide track transport.

PUNAKAIKI

This famous stopping point on the Great Coast Road between Westport and Greymouth is renowned for it's layered limestone stacks. It's also the gateway to Paparoa National Park, a 380-sq-km expanse of mountainous wilderness.

☆ Best Things to See/Do/Eat

◉ **Pancake Rocks** Looking like they sound, these towers of layered limestone front a wild stretch of coast which the surf batters constantly. (p264)

🥾 **Punakaiki–Porari Loop** Allow 3½ hours for this loop walk up a limestone river gorge and through mature rainforest in Paparoa National Park. Stop for a picnic by the Porarari River before crossing the ridge and returning along the Punakaiki River. (p264)

🍽 **Pancake Rocks Cafe** If looking at those rocks left you craving pancakes, here's where you'll get them. Before 11am they serve good breakfasts ranging from bagels to German sausage fry-ups, and the conservatory area – all wooden benches and fairy lights – is a pleasant spot for a drink around sundown. (p265)

☆ How to Get There

Car Take the Great Coast Road (SH6) south from Westport and you'll reach Punakaiki in less than an hour.
Bus Coaches stop here, but there's usually only a couple a day in each direction.

REEFTON

Mining is a big part of the West Coast psyche to this day, although coal has long since replaced the gold which built towns like Reefton. The handsome set of Victorian-era buildings that remains is the legacy of those crusty prospectors of yesteryear that poured in during and after the big 1870 goldrush.

☆ Best Things to See/Do/Eat

๏ Waiuta Not all gold-mining towns were as lucky as Reefton, as is demonstrated by a stroll around the bare bones of this fascinating ghost town, 37m to the south. (p271)

🚶 Reefton Walks The *Walks and Tracks of Reefton* leaflet lists heritage walks around the town itself, along with longer tracks into the vast Victoria Forest Park which surrounds it. If you want to fill half a day, tackle the five-hour return Murray Creek Track. (p271)

✕ Future Dough Co. On a sunny day, this bakery's outdoor tables are a great spot to survey the action along Reefton's high street. Settle in for a coffee and slice. (p271)

☆ How to Get There

Car Follow the Buller River along SH67 and SH6, and then branch off south onto SH69 (Reefton Hwy) which follows the Inangahua River.

Bus There's a daily bus service but it isn't a practical day-trip option.

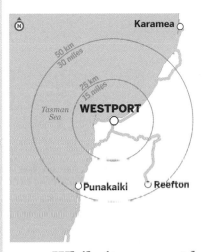

While it may not be New Zealand's most exciting town, Westport is a great base for exploring the wild nature and gold-mining heritage of the northern reaches of the West Coast.

TRAMPING ON THE WEST COAST

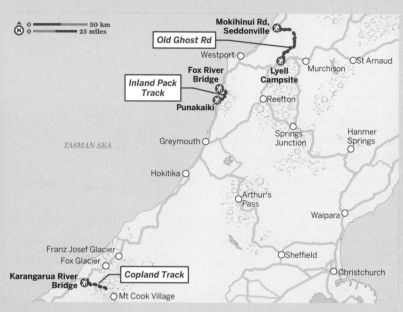

OLD GHOST ROAD

START LYELL CAMPSITE
END MOKIHINUI RD, SEDDONVILLE
DURATION 5 DAYS
DISTANCE 85KM
DIFFICULTY MODERATE

One of the gnarliest of NZ's cycling and tramping trails, the Old Ghost Road follows a historic miners' track that was started in the 1870s but never finished as the gold rush petered out. Following a painstaking, volunteer-led build, the gruelling track now traverses native forests, tussock tops, river flats and valleys.

The southern trailhead is at Lyell, 50 minutes' drive (62km) east of Westport along the scenic Buller Gorge (SH6). The DOC campsite and day walks here have long been popular, with visitors drawn in by readily accessible historic sites, including a graveyard secreted in the bush. The northern trailhead is at Seddonville, 45 minutes' drive (50km) north of Westport off SH67, from where the track sidles along the steep-sided and utterly stunning Mokihinui River. Joining the two ends is an alpine section, with entrancing views from sunrise to sunset.

The track is dual use, but favours walkers (allow five days). For advanced mountain bikers who can handle narrow trails and plenty of jolts, it is pretty much the Holy Grail, completed in two to four days, preferably from Lyell to Seddonville. The four huts along the way need to be booked in advance on the Old Ghost Road website (www.oldghostroad.org.nz), which also details a range of other ways to experience the track other than an end-to-end ride or hike. Day trips from either end are a rewarding, flexible way in, particularly from the West Coast end via the inimitable **Rough & Tumble Lodge** (p268).

Being a long and remote track through wild terrain, conditions can change quickly, so check the trail website for status. Westport's **Buller Adventures** (☑ 0508 486 877; www.bulleradventures.com; 193 Palmerston

Take a walk on the wild side, literally. The West Coast is one of the most dynamic tramping regions in New Zealand, with an emerging network of tracks.

St), **Habitat Sports** (p266) and **Hike n Bike Shuttle** (☑ 027 446 7876; www.hikenbikeshuttle.co.nz; shuttle from $40) provide bike and equipment hire, shuttles and other related services.

INLAND PACK TRACK

START PUNAKAIKI
END FOX RIVER BRIDGE
DURATION 2 DAYS
DISTANCE 25KM
DIFFICULTY MODERATE

This track explores Paparoa National Park's otherwise hidden treasures, including valleys lined with nikau palms and spectacular limestone formations. A major highlight is spending a night at the Ballroom Overhang, one of the largest rock bivvies in NZ.

While there are no alpine passes to negotiate, nor any excruciating climbs above the bushline, the tramp is no easy stroll. There is plenty of mud to contend with, and numerous river crossings. It is suitable for well-equipped trampers with solid route-finding skills.

Dilemma Creek flows through a gorge so steep and narrow that trampers just walk down the middle of it. Occasionally you can follow a gravel bank, but much of the tramp involves sloshing from one pool to the next. When water levels are normal the stream rarely rises above your knees, and if it's a hot, sunny day this can be the most pleasant segment of the trip, but during heavy rain and flooding you should avoid this track at all costs. If the forecast is poor, wait another day or move down the coast to find another tramp. To be trapped by rising rivers with no tent makes for a very long night.

The track can be tramped in either direction, but starting at Punakaiki makes navigating the Fox River bed much easier.

COPLAND TRACK

START/END KARANGARUA RIVER BRIDGE
DURATION 2 DAYS
DISTANCE 36KM
DIFFICULTY EASY TO MODERATE

This tramp up the Copland Valley to Welcome Flat Hut is a popular overnight return trip for visitors to the Glacier Region. It offers a window into Westland Tai Poutini's spectacular forest, river and mountain scenery, while natural hot pools at Welcome Flat are an added attraction for foot-weary adventurers.

The forests of the Copland Valley are visually dominated by a healthy canopy of southern rata, which makes for a spectacular sight during the summer flowering season. The forest gives way at higher altitudes to the upper montane vegetation of tree daisies and Dracophyllums, which in turn give way to the truly alpine habitats of tussock grasslands and native herbs.

Regular possum control has been undertaken since the mid-1980s and as a result the forest damage is significantly less than in the neighbouring Karangarua Valley, which has extensive canopy dieback. The only real drawback of this tramp is that you must eventually turn around and backtrack to SH6.

WESTLAND

Bookended by Mt Aspiring National Park to its south and the rugged Great Coast Road to its north, Westland is one of New Zealand's most thinly populated regions.

Amid this tapestry of farmland and rainforest, the most remarkable (and famous) features are Franz Josef and Fox Glaciers. Though currently in retreat, these frosty monoliths framed by granite cliffs hook thousands of adventure-seekers, many of whom stick around for pulse-thudding pursuits like mountain biking the West Coast Wilderness Trail, tramping the Copland Track, soaring above national parks by helicopter, or tiptoeing through the bush on kiwi-spotting walks.

There's culture, too, if you like it quaint and low-key: gold-rush sights in Ross, jade-carving classes in Hokitika and art galleries in lonely locales all provide brain fodder for days when you want to hang up your tramping boots.

Haast

POP 240

A small township at the yawning mouth of the Haast River, Haast acts as a springboard to forests, sand dunes, craggy coast and tree-knotted lakes. Only in 1965 was Haast linked to the rest of the West Coast Hwy and the untouched feel endures. It's a handy stop for filling the tank and tummy if you're travelling between Otago and the West Coast glaciers, but we'd recommend sticking around at least long enough for a river cruise and one blazing sunset.

If you're heading north, check your fuel gauge as Haast petrol station is the last one before Fox Glacier.

ESSENTIAL WEST COAST

Eat Fish and chips, sitting near the beach at sunset.

Drink The only roast on the coast, organic and fair trade Kawatiri Coffee.

Read Eleanor Catton's 2013 Man Booker Prize–winning novel, *The Luminaries*, set around Hokitika.

Listen to Karamea's laid-back community radio station on 107.5FM.

Go online www.westcoast.co.nz

◉ Sights & Activities

Haast's main selling point is its frontier location, but plenty of hikes hereabouts are easy, hour-long affairs. Explore with the help of the free Haast Visitor Map (www.haastnz.com) or DOC's brochure *Walks and Activities in the Haast Area* ($2 from the visitor centre (p243), or downloadable online). The best way to plunge into Haast's wilderness is through **Waiatoto River Safaris** (☑ 0800 538 723, 03-750 0780; www.riversafaris.co.nz; 1975 Haast-Jackson Bay Rd, Hannahs Clearing; adult/child $199/139; ⊙ trips 10am, 1pm & 4pm Nov-Mar, 11am Apr-Oct) ⏀, a mix of bird-watching, untrammelled forest views and juddering jetboat thrills.

Lake Moeraki   LAKE
Alongside the highway and within the bounds of the World Heritage wilderness, Lake Moeraki is an undeveloped and tranquil spot to contemplate the forested, mountainous surroundings. There's no trail all the way around, but there are plenty of lake beaches where you can park and ponder.

Knights Point   VIEWPOINT
Admire expansive views of boulder-studded sea from this roadside lookout. A granite column commemorates the opening of this section of coastal highway in 1965. It's an easy pull-over off the highway, 5km south of Lake Moeraki.

★ Ship Creek   WALKING
(www.doc.govt.nz) Two contrasting walks begin at Ship Creek, 15km north of Haast, each with interesting interpretive panels. Stroll sand dunes, stunted forest and driftwood-strewn beaches on the **Dune Lake Walk** (30 minutes return), before embarking on the enchanting **Kahikatea Swamp Forest Walk** (20 minutes return), along boardwalks that hover above glistening marshland (the bird-watching's superb).

🛏 Sleeping & Eating

Haast River
Motels & Holiday Park   HOLIDAY PARK, MOTEL $$
(☑ 03-750 0020, 0800 624 847; www.haastrivermotels.co.nz; 52 Haast Pass Hwy (SH6), Haast township; sites $44-48, d $128, units $155-232; 🛜) Easy-going staff, a reasonable free wi-fi allowance (500MB), and roomy motel units with dive-in beds. This holiday park ticks a lot of boxes. Campervan guests are kept happy with on-site facilities like a laundry,

HAAST PASS HIGHWAY

The 145km road careening between the West Coast and Central Otago is a spectacular drive. It takes roughly 2½ hours from Haast to Wanaka, but allow more time to drive this Southern Alpine saddle if you want to stop at lookouts and waterfall trails.

Heading inland from Haast, the highway (SH6) snakes alongside the Haast River, crossing the boundary into Mt Aspiring National Park. The further you go, the narrower the river valley becomes, until the road clambers around sheer-sided valley walls streaked with waterfalls and scarred by rock slips. Princely sums are involved in keeping this highway clear, and even so it sets plenty of traps for unwary drivers. Stop at signposted lookouts and short walkways to admire the scenery, such as small, graceful **Fantail Falls** (10 minutes return) and aptly named **Thunder Creek Falls** (one hour return). These are detailed in DOC's booklet *Walks along the Haast Highway* ($2), but sufficient detail is provided at the trailheads. The highway tops out at the 563m mark, shortly after which you will reach food and fuel at Makarora. Hello Otago!

Early Māori travelled this route in their quest for *pounamu*, naming it Tioripātea, meaning 'Clear Path'. Northern chief Te Puoho led troops across the pass in 1836 to raid southern tribes. German geologist Julius von Haast led a party of Europeans across in 1863 – hence the name of the pass, river and township – but evidence suggests that Scottish prospector Charles Cameron may have pipped Haast at the post. It was clearly no mean feat: the terrain is such that the Haast Pass Hwy wasn't opened until as late as 1965.

a games room, and a book and DVD filled lounge surveyed by mounted deer heads.

⭐**Wilderness Lodge**
Lake Moeraki   LODGE $$$
(☑ 03-750 0881; www.wildernesslodge.co.nz; SH6, Lake Moeraki; s $520-770, d $840-1240, incl breakfast & dinner; ☎) 🏊 At the southern end of Lake Moeraki, 31km north of Haast, you'll find one of NZ's best nature lodges. In a verdant setting on the edge of the Moeraki River, it offers comfortable rooms and four-course dinners, but the real delights are the outdoor activities, such as kayak trips and coastal walks, guided by people with conservation in their blood.

Hard Antler   PUB FOOD $$
(☑ 03-750 0034; Marks Rd, Haast township; mains $14-30; ☺11am-late) Antlers and a wall of fame of local fishing folk establishes the hunting-lodge vibe of Haast's best boozer. Service is gruff but meaty main courses (venison stew, burgers and tasty grilled blue cod) are served all day. Vegetarians, we hope you like nachos.

🛈 Information

DOC Haast Visitor Centre (☑ 03-750 0809; www.doc.govt.nz; cnr SH6 & Jackson Bay Rd; ☺9am-6pm Nov-Mar, to 4.30pm Apr-Oct) Wall-to-wall regional information and free screenings of Haast landscape film *Edge of*

Wilderness. With outdoor water features and a brimming museum, it's more attractive than the average info centre. Sells insect repellent.

General regional information and visitor services listings can be found on www.haastnz.com.

🛈 Getting There & Away

Naked Bus (☑ 09-979 1616; https://nakedbus. com) and **Intercity** (☑ 03-365 1113; www.intercity.co.nz) buses stop on Marks Rd (opposite Wilderness Accommodation) on their daily runs from Queenstown ($36, 4¾ hours) to Franz Josef and Fox Glaciers (from $23, 3½ hours).

Westland Tai Poutini National Park

With colossal mountains, forests and glaciers, Westland Tai Poutini National Park clobbers visitors with its mind-bending proportions. Reaching from the West Coast to the razor peaks of the Southern Alps, the park's supreme attractions are twin glaciers Franz Josef and Fox, served by townships 23km apart. Out of more than 60 glaciers in the park, only these two are easily accessible.

The glaciers are the most majestic handiwork of the West Coast's ample precipitation. Snowfall in the glaciers' broad accumulation zones fuses into clear ice at 20m depth, and then creeps down the steep valleys. Nowhere

JACKSON BAY

Most travellers drive northeast from Haast Junction towards epic Fox and Franz Josef Glaciers, but the road less travelled makes an interesting detour. Steering southwest, 45km from Haast, find the pocket-sized outpost of Jackson Bay, towered over by the Southern Alps. There's no through road: this fishing hamlet is truly the end of the line.

Farms here stand testament to some of the hardiest souls who ever attempted settlement in New Zealand. Migrants arrived in 1875 under a doomed settlement scheme, their farming and timber-milling aspirations shattered by never-ending rain and the lack of a wharf, not built until 1938. Until the 1950s, the only way to reach Haast overland was via bush tracks from Hokitika and Wanaka. Supplies came by an infrequent coastal shipping service.

Unless you're in the market for whitebait, present-day Jackson Bay has few attractions other than a couple of lovely and lonely walking trails.

Near Okuru, 10km west of Haast, is the **Hapuka Estuary Walk** (20 minutes return), a winding boardwalk that loops through a sleepy wildlife sanctuary with good interpretation panels en route.

The road continues west to Arawhata Bridge, where a turn-off leads to the **Lake Ellery Track** (www.doc.govt.nz), 3.5km south along an unsealed road. A one-hour round trip takes you through mossy beech forest to a lookout over peaceful Lake Ellery. There's not much besides a picnic bench when you arrive, but you'll likely have it to yourself.

From the end of Jackson Bay Rd begins the **Wharekai Te Kou Walk** (www.doc.govt. nz), 40 minutes return, to Ocean Beach, a tiny bay with some interesting rock formations. The muddy three- to four-hour **Smoothwater Bay Track**, following an old pioneers' track, also begins nearby.

else at this latitude do glaciers descend so close to the ocean.

But the glaciers are as fragile as they are amazing to behold. Rising temperatures have beaten the glaciers into retreat, reducing opportunities to view them on foot and clanging a death knell for their long-term future if climate change continues unchecked.

History

During the last ice age (around 15,000 to 20,000 years ago) Westland's twin glaciers reached the sea. In the ensuing thaw they may have crawled back even further than their current positions, but around the 14th century a mini ice age caused them to advance to their greatest modern-era extent around 1750, and the terminal moraines from this time are still visible.

Fox Glacier

POP 400

Descending from the brooding Southern Alps, impassable Fox Glacier seems to flow steadily, ominously towards the township below. But in this fragile landscape it's the glacier that's at risk: despite hints of advance in recent years, this 12km glacier

(named for former New Zealand PM Sir William Fox) has been steadily retreating over the past century.

Compared with the glacier, the eponymous township isn't nearly so dramatic. Surrounded by farmland, its cafes and tour operators are strung along the main road, along with dozens of motels catering to visiting crowds that descend between November and March. Most are here to helihike or embark on scenic flights, but flying weather is never guaranteed on the turbulent West Coast. Fortunately Fox Glacier has tramping trails, skydiving and remnants of pioneers past to keep you busy while waiting for skies to clear.

🏃 Activities

Independent Walks

⭐**Lake Matheson**   TRAMPING
(www.doc.govt.nz) The famous 'mirror lake' can be found about 6km down Cook Flat Rd. Wandering slowly (as you should), it will take 1½ hours to complete the circuit. The best time to visit is early morning, or when the sun is low in the late afternoon, although the presence of the Lake Matheson Cafe (p246) means that any time is a good time.

Fox Glacier & Village

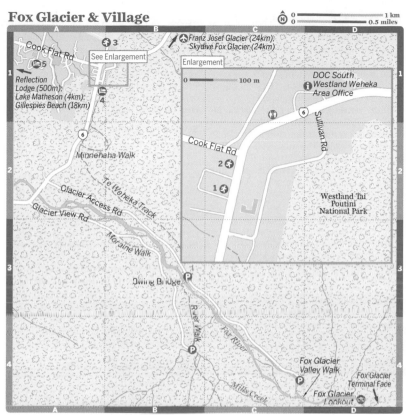

Gillespies Beach   TRAMPING

(www.doc.govt.nz) Follow Cook Flat Rd for its full 21km (final 12km unsealed) to remote Gillespies Beach, a wind-blasted length of slate-grey sand and shingle near an old mining settlement. Interesting walks from here include a 30-minute, partly sheltered circuit to a rusting gold dredge from 1932, and a 3½-hour return walk to **Galway Beach**, a seal hang-out. Don't disturb them.

Five-hundred metres shy of the beach, signposted from the road, is an eerie miners' cemetery, reached by a five-minute walk.

There's a basic, eight-site DOC campground by the beach.

Glacier Walks & Helihikes

The only way on to the ice is by taking a helihiking trip, run by the superb Fox Glacier Guiding (p246). Independent walks offer a chance to explore the valley – raw and staggeringly beautiful even in its ice-less lower reaches – and get as close to the glacier's

Fox Glacier & Village

◉ Activities, Courses & Tours

1 Fox Glacier Guiding	C2
2 Helicopter Line	C2
3 Skydive Fox Glacier	B1

◉ Sleeping

4 Fox Glacier Lodge	A1
5 Fox Glacier Top 10 Holiday Park	A1

terminal face as safety allows. They're also good options if unstable weather is keeping helicopters grounded.

It's 1.5km from Fox Village to the glacier turn-off, and a further 2km to the car park, which you can reach under your own steam via **Te Weheka Walkway/Cycleway**, a pleasant rainforest trail starting just south of the Bella Vista motel. It's 2½ hours return on foot, or an hour by bike (leave your bikes at the car park – you can't cycle on the glacier walkways). Hire bikes from **Fox**

Glacier Lodge (Map p245; ☑ 0800 369 800, 03-751 0888; www.foxglacierlodge.com; 41 Sullivan Rd; unpowered/powered sites $30/40, d $175-235; ☜) for $5 per hour for $15 for half a day.

From the car park, the terminal-face viewpoint is around 40 minutes' walk, depending on current conditions. Obey all signs: this place is dangerously dynamic.

Short return walks near the glacier include the half-hour **Moraine Walk** (over a major 18th-century advance) and 20-minute **Minnehaha Walk**. The fully accessible **River Walk Lookout Track** (20 minutes return) starts from the Glacier View Rd car park and allows people of all abilities the chance to view the glacier.

Pick up a copy of DOC's excellent *Glacier Region Walks* booklet ($2, or download at www.doc.govt.nz/Documents/parks-and-recreation/tracks-and-walks/west-coast/glacier-region-walks.pdf), which provides maps and illuminating background reading.

★ **Fox Glacier Guiding** ADVENTURE SPORTS
(Map p245; ☑ 03-751 0825, 0800 111 600; www.foxguides.co.nz; 44 Main Rd) Locally run Fox Glacier Guiding fosters a friendly, unhurried atmosphere on small-group helihikes (equipment provided). A five-minute helicopter ride whooshes you onto the ice for an unstrenuous four-hour tramp (adult/child $450/425), or more demanding eight-hour tramp (adult $699). Scrambling through little ice caves, peering into crevasses and sipping glacial meltwater included with the animated commentary. Age restrictions vary by trip.

Skydiving & Aerial Sightseeing

Short heliflights (10 to 20 minutes) offer a spectacular vantage point over Fox Glacier with a snow landing up top. On a longer flight (30 to 50 minutes) you can also enjoy sky-high sightseeing over Franz Josef Glacier and Aoraki/Mt Cook. Ten-minute joy flights cost from around $120, but we recommend 20 minutes or more in the air (from $245). Children are admitted, though age restrictions vary; expect to pay around 70% of the adult price. Shop around: most operators are situated on the main road in Fox Glacier village.

Skydive Fox Glacier SKYDIVING
(Map p245; ☑ 03-751 0080, 0800 751 0080; www.skydivefox.co.nz; Fox Glacier Airfield, SH6) Eye-popping scenery abounds on leaps from 16,500ft ($399), 13,000ft ($299) or 9000ft ($249)…between 30 and 65 seconds of freefall, depending on height. The airfield is three minutes' walk from the village centre.

Helicopter Line SCENIC FLIGHTS
(Map p245; ☑ 0800 807 767, 03-751 0767; www.helicopter.co.nz; cnr SH6 & Cook Flat Rd; 20-50min flights $245-640) Whisking travellers to giddy heights since 1986, this well-established operator has a big menu of scenic flight options. The 50-minute flight taking in Aoraki/Mt Cook and Tasman Glacier (NZ's longest glacier) is noteworthy for the comparatively long amount of time spent in the air.

🛏 Sleeping & Eating

★ **Fox Glacier**
Top 10 Holiday Park HOLIDAY PARK $
(Map p245; ☑ 03-751 0821, 0800 154 366; www.fghp.co.nz; Kerr Rd; sites $45-52, cabins from $75, units $144-280; ☜) Inspiring mountain views and ample amenities lift this reliable chain holiday park above its local competition. Grassy tent and hard campervan sites access a quality communal kitchen and dining room, and trim cabins (no private bathroom) and upscale self-contained units offer extra comfort. A spa pool, playground with trampoline and double-seater fun bikes pile on the family fun factor.

Reflection Lodge B&B $$$
(☑ 03-751 0707; www.reflectionlodge.co.nz; 141 Cook Flat Rd; d incl breakfast $230; ☜) The gregarious hosts of this ski-lodge-style B&B go the extra mile to make your stay a memorable one. Blooming gardens complete with alpine views and a Monet-like pond seal the deal.

★ **Lake Matheson Cafe** MODERN NZ $$
(☑ 03-751 0878; www.lakematheson.com; Lake Matheson Rd; breakfast & lunch $10-21, dinner $29-35; ☺ 8am-late Nov-Mar, to 3pm Apr-Oct)

ⓘ GLACIER SAFETY

The only way to get close to or on to the ice safely is with a guided tour. Both glacier terminal faces are roped off to prevent people being caught in icefalls and river surges, which can flood the valleys in a matter of minutes. Obey warning signs and stay out of roped-off areas (even if you see guides leading walkers that way…they know where to tread safely, you don't).

GLACIERS FOR DUMMIES

Hashtag a few of these suckers into your social media posts and make yourself look like a #geologist #geek.

Ablation zone Where the glacier melts.

Accumulation zone Where the ice and snow collects.

Bergschrund A large crevasse in the ice near the glacier's starting point.

Blue ice As the accumulation zone (névé) snow is compressed by subsequent snowfalls, it becomes firn and then blue ice.

Calving The process of ice breaking away from the glacier terminal face.

Crevasse A crack in the glacial ice formed by the stress of competing forces.

Firn Partly compressed snow en route to becoming blue ice.

Glacial flour Finely ground rock particles in the milky rivers flowing off glaciers.

Icefall When a glacier descends so steeply that the upper ice breaks into a jumble of ice blocks.

Kettle lake A lake formed by the melt of an area of isolated dead ice.

Moraine Walls of debris formed at the glacier's sides (lateral moraine) or end (terminal moraine).

Névé Snowfield area where firn is formed.

Seracs Ice pinnacles formed, like crevasses, by the glacier rolling over obstacles.

Terminus The final ice face at the bottom of the glacier.

Next to Lake Matheson, this cafe does everything right: sharp architecture that maximises inspiring mountain views, strong coffee, craft beers and upmarket fare. Bratwurst breakfasts are a good prelude to rambling the lake, the pizzas are heaped with seasonal ingredients, and seafood risotto is topped with salmon sourced down the road in Paringa.

ℹ Information

MEDICAL SERVICES

Fox Glacier Health Centre (☑ 03-751 0836, 24hr 0800 794 325; SH6) Clinic opening hours are displayed at the centre, or ring the 0800 number for 24-hour assistance.

TOURIST INFORMATION

DOC South Westland Weheka Area Office (Map p245; ☑ 03-751 0807; SH6; ⊙10am-2pm Mon-Fri) This is no longer a general visitor-information centre, but has the usual DOC information and hut tickets, with weather and track updates posted on the board outside.

Activity operators and accommodation providers are slick at providing information (and usually a booking service for transport and activities elsewhere), but you can also find info online at www.glaciercountry.co.nz. Ask your accommodation provider about transport bookings, or try **Fox Glacier Guiding** (p246), which also offers postal and currency-exchange services.

ℹ Getting There & Away

Direct **InterCity** (p243) and **Naked Bus** (p243) services along SH6 trundle through Fox Glacier once a day, heading south to Haast (from $20, 2½ hours) and north to Hokitika ($53, 3¼ hours) and Greymouth ($61, 4½ hours), stopping at Franz Josef ($10, 40 minutes) on the way. Book ahead for fares as low as $1. A direct daily bus also reaches Queenstown (from $59, 7¾ hours). For Nelson or Christchurch, transfer in Greymouth.

Most buses stop outside the **Fox Glacier Guiding** (p246) building.

If you're heading south along the coast, **Fox Glacier Motors** (☑ 03-751 0823; 52 Main Rd (SH6)) is your last chance for fuel before Haast, 120km away.

Franz Josef Glacier

POP 441

Franz Josef's cloak of ice once flowed from the mountains right to the sea. Following millennia of gradual retreat, the glacier is now 19km inland and accessible only by helicopter. Swarms of small aircraft from Franz Josef Glacier village, 5km north, lift

Franz Josef Glacier & Village

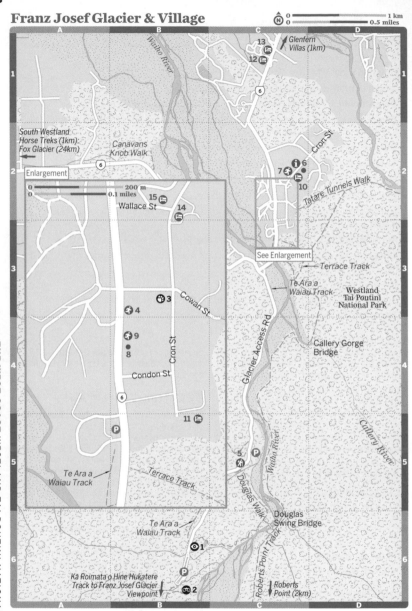

visitors to views of sparkling ice and toothy mountains. Many land on the glacier to lead groups to blue-tinged caves and crevasses. A glacier experience is the crowning moment for thousands of annual visitors, but walking trails, hot pools, and adventure sports

from quad biking to clay target shooting keep adrenaline pulsing.

Geologist Julius von Haast led the first European expedition here in 1865, and named the glacier after the Austrian emperor. The dismal forecast of a rainier, warmer

Franz Josef Glacier & Village

future spells more shrinkage for Franz Josef, whose trimlines (strips of vegetation on the valley walls) mark out decades of dramatic glacial retreat.

⊙ Sights

West Coast Wildlife Centre WILDLIFE RESERVE (Map p248; ☑03-752 0600; www.wildkiwi.co.nz; cnr Cron & Cowan Sts; day pass adult/child/family $38/20/85, incl backstage pass $58/35/145; ⊗8am-5pm) ✹ The purpose of this feel-good attraction is breeding two of the world's rarest kiwi – the rowi and the Haast tokoeka. The entry fee is well worthwhile by the time you've viewed the conservation, glacier and heritage displays, hung out with kiwi in their ferny enclosure, and met the five resident tuatara (native reptiles). The backstage pass into the incubating and rearing area is a rare opportunity to learn how a species can be brought back from the brink of extinction.

⊼ Activities

Independent Walks

A series of walks start from the glacier car park, 5km from the village. **Sentinel Rock** (Map p248; 20 minutes return) reveals either impressive views of the glacier valley or a mysterious panorama swallowed by mist and cloud. **Kā Roimata o Hine Hukatere Track** (1½ hours return), the main glacier valley walk, leads you to the best permissible view of the terminal face.

Other walks include the **Douglas Walk** (one hour return), off the Glacier Access Rd, which passes moraine piled up by the glacier's advance in 1750, and **Peters Pool** (Map p248), a small kettle lake. The **Terrace Track** (30 minutes return) is an easy amble over bushy terraces behind the village,

with Waiho River views. Two good rainforest walks, **Callery Gorge Walk** and **Tatare Tunnels** (both around 1½ hours return), start from Cowan St – bring a torch for the latter.

Much more challenging walks, such as the five-hour **Roberts Point Track** and eight-hour **Alex Knob Track** (Map p248), are detailed along with all the others, in DOC's excellent *Glacier Region Walks* booklet ($2, or download at www.doc.govt.nz/Documents/parks-and-recreation/tracks-and-walks/west-coast/glacier-region-walks.pdf), which provides maps and illuminating background reading.

A rewarding alternative to driving to the glacier car park is the richly rainforested **Te Ara a Waiau Walkway/Cycleway**, starting from near the fire station at the south end of town. It's a one-hour walk (each way) or half that by bicycle. Leave your bikes at the car park – you can't cycle on the glacier walkways. When we passed through, bike hire wasn't easy to come by and folks were recommending rental from Fox Glacier Lodge (p246; per hour/half-day $5/15), 24km south. Ask in the i-SITE (p252) for the latest.

Guided Walks & Helihikes

Franz Josef Glacier Guides (Map p248; ☑03-752 0763, 0800 484 337; www.franzjosefglacier.com; 63 Cron St) runs small group walks with experienced guides (boots, jackets and equipment supplied). With dazzling blue ice, photo ops in ice caves, and helicopter rides to and from the ice, this might be one of your most memorable experiences in NZ. The standard trip involves three hours of guided rambling on the ice ($459); the daring can seize an ice pick for a five-hour ice-climbing tour (adults only, $575). If you don't need to

ℹ️ HELIHIKES: FOX OR FRANZ?

If skies are blue and choppers are flying, seize the chance to helihike either glacier. Weather changes quickly, sometimes grounding aircraft for days and inflicting tourist heartbreak. Franz Josef is the more popular of the two glaciers, its steepness intensifying the drama of crevasses and ice formations, while Fox is longer and faster-moving (not that you'll notice). The two major operators offering helihikes on the glaciers have primo standards on safety and technical expertise. More popular **Franz Josef Glacier Guides** (p249) is a well-oiled machine, while family-run **Fox Glacier Guiding** (p246) prides itself on a friendly, personalised experience. They're comparable on price (around $450 for a helihike with three hours on the ice) and both offer photo-ops in the famous blue ice caves (though Franz' caves are bigger).

get on the ice, choose a three-hour guided valley walk (adult/child $75/65). **Glacier Valley Eco Tours** (Map p248; ☎ 0800 925 586; www.glaciervalley.co.nz; 22 Main Rd; adult/child $75/37.50) 🌿 offers a similar experience, a 3½-hour ramble by the river and into native forest. Conservation-focused commentary on local flora and geological forces enlivens the journey, which is rewarded by a steaming cuppa sipped in view of the glacier face.

Skydiving & Aerial Sightseeing

Forget sandflies and mozzies, the buzzing you're hearing is a swarm of small aircraft. The most affordable scenic flights involve 10 or 12 minutes in the air above Franz Josef Glacier (around $120 to $165) but it's worth paying for 20 minutes or more to get a snow landing or to view both Franz Josef and Fox Glaciers (from $245). Pricier, 40-minute flights enjoy the most eye-popping views (around $370 to $460), swooping around Aoraki/Mt Cook. Fares for children under 12 years usually cost around 70% of the adult price. Shop around: most operators are situated on the main road.

Skydive Franz SKYDIVING
(Map p248; ☎ 03-752 0714, 0800 458 677; www.skydivefranz.co.nz; Main Rd) Claiming NZ's highest jump (19,000ft, 80 to 90 seconds freefall; $559), this company also offers

16,500ft for $419, 13,000ft for $319 and 9000ft for $249. With Aoraki/Mt Cook in your sights, this could be the most scenic jump you ever do.

Air Safaris SCENIC FLIGHTS
(Map p248; ☎ 0800 723 274, 03-752 0716; www.airsafaris.co.nz; Main Rd) Franz' only fixed-wing flyer offers 50-minute 'grand traverse' ($370) flights that expose breathtaking views of Franz Josef and Fox Glaciers, Aoraki/Mt Cook, and far-flung valleys, lakes and waterways en route. Charge your camera.

Glacier Helicopters SCENIC FLIGHTS
(Map p248; ☎ 03-752 0755, 0800 800 732; www.glacierhelicopters.co.nz; Main Rd; 20-40min flights $245-460) This reliable operator has been running scenic flights since 1970. Shorter flights take you to one of the glaciers, while the 40-minute option reaches both, as well as soaring to spectacular views of Aoraki/Mt Cook. There's a brief snow landing on each trip.

Other Activities

⭐ **Glacier Country Kayaks** KAYAKING
(Map p248; ☎ 03-752 0230, 0800 423 262; www.glacierkayaks.com; 64 Cron St; 3hr kayak adult/child $115/70) Enjoy a change of pace from chopper rides and sheer-faced glaciers on a guided kayak trip on Lake Mapourika (10km north of Franz). The 'kayak classic' is three hours of bird-spotting and mountain views, plus a short bush walk. The summer-only 'sunset classic' ($125) is at the golden hour (no cameras, but guides snap pictures and share them for free).

Glacier Hot Pools HOT SPRINGS
(Map p248; ☎ 03-752 0099; www.glacierhotpools.co.nz; 63 Cron St; adult/child $28/24; ⊙ 11am-9pm, last entry 8pm) Cleverly set into a pretty rainforest on the edge of town, this stylish and well-maintained outdoor hotpool complex is perfect après-hike or on a rainy day. Private pools also available, and hour-long massages cost from $140.

Franz Josef Clay Target Shooting OUTDOORS
(☎ 03-752 0288; www.franzjosefclayshooting.co.nz; per person $110-130; ⊙ by arrangement) Lock your sights onto clay discs hurtling through the air, before obliterating them into smithereens...sound like fun? This clay target operator offers exhilarating two-hour shoot-'em-ups. Tours include transfers to and from the range, 6km south of Franz Josef township, plus training and a com-

prehensive safety briefing. Book at least a day or two ahead, by phone or through the i-SITE (p252).

🛌 Sleeping

Franz Josef Glacier YHA HOSTEL $
(Map p248; ☑03-752 0754; www.yha.co.nz; 2-4 Cron St; dm from $32, d with/without bathroom from $150/125; ☎) Functional and friendly, the YHA has warm, spacious communal areas, family rooms, a large free sauna, and a booking desk for transport and activities. It has 103 beds, but you'll still need to book ahead.

Franz Josef
Top 10 Holiday Park HOLIDAY PARK $
(Map p248; ☑0800 467 8975, 03-752 0735; www.franzjoseftop10.co.nz; 2902 Franz Josef Hwy; sites $45-47, cabins $78-83, units $128-160; ☎) With such voluminous sleeping options, this spacious holiday park has no room for frills. Tents and motorhomes enjoy free-draining grassy sites away from the road, while travellers who prefer four walls can choose good-value cabins (sharing the well-maintained bathroom and kitchen areas) or trim self-contained units. It's 1.5km north of the township.

Rainforest Retreat HOSTEL, HOLIDAY PARK $$
(Map p248; ☑03-752 0220, 0800 873 346; www.rainforestretreat.co.nz; 46 Cron St; sites $39-48, dm $30-39, d $69-220; ☎) Options abound in these forested grounds: en suite doubles, self-contained units and dorm rooms that sleep between four and six (four-bed 'flashpacker' rooms are worth the higher rate). Campervan sites are nestled in native bush, the backpacker lodge brims with tour-bus custom, and you may have to fight for a spot in the gigantic hot tub, touted as NZ's largest.

58 on Cron MOTEL $$
(Map p248; ☑0800 662 766, 03-752 0627; www.58oncron.co.nz; 58 Cron St; d $175-245; ☎) Guests staying in these 16 comfortable motel units, from petite doubles to family suites that sleep six, enjoy sweet service and a barbecue area. Bonus: you won't forget the motel's address.

⭐ Te Waonui Forest Retreat HOTEL $$$
(Map p248; ☑0800 696 963, 03-752 0555; www.tewaonui.co.nz; 3 Wallace St; d incl breakfast & dinner from $749; ☺Sep-Apr; @☎) 🌱 Luxurious Te Waonui is filled with design flourishes that evoke the land: twinkly lights suggest glowworms, coal-black walls nod to the mining past, and local stone provides an earthy backdrop. Beyond the gorgeous, greenery-facing rooms, the prime draws are the five-course degustation dinner (included in the price) and the nightly Māori cultural show.

⭐ Glenfern Villas APARTMENT $$$
(☑0800 453 633, 03-752 0054; www.glenfern.co.nz; SH6; d $265-299; ☎) Forming something of a tiny, elite village 3km north of town, Glenfern's one- and two-bedroom villas are equipped with every comfort from quality beds to plump couches, gleaming kitchenettes and private decks where you can listen to birdsong. Book well ahead.

Holly Homestead B&B $$$
(Map p248; ☑03-752 0299; www.hollyhomestead.co.nz; SH6; d incl breakfast $285-395; ☎) This jasmine-draped B&B stays true to its 1926 beginnings with an old-fashioned welcome and freshly baked bread for breakfast. Choose from three characterful en-suite rooms or a suite, all of which share a classy lounge and a deck perfect for that sundowner. Children over 12 years welcome.

🍴 Eating & Drinking

⭐ Snake Bite Brewery ASIAN, FUSION $$
(Map p248; ☑03-752 0234; www.snakebite.co.nz; 28 Main Rd; mains $18-25; ☺7.30am-10.30pm) Snake Bite's motley Asian meals awaken tastebuds after their long slumber through the West Coast's lamb-and-whitebait menus. Choices include nasi goreng (fried rice), Thai- and Malaysian-style curries and salads of calamari and carrot that zing with fresh lime. Try the mussel fritters with wasabi

> **FRANZ JOSEF ON THE MOVE**
>
> A town built on top of a fault line can't just up and leave. Or can it? A fault line slices right through Franz Josef, and fears of future earthquake damage and flooding from the ever-rising Waiho River have prompted regional council members to consider a lift and shift: moving the township 10km north. Building an earthquake-resistant town next to Lake Mapourika has its appeal, though the price-tag – an estimated $600m at last count – has sent town planners scrambling for alternatives.

RESIDENT WILDLIFE

Diverse and often unique habitats are huddled into more than 1300 sq km of the national park. Endangered bird species include kakariki, kaka and kea (parrots) and rowi (Okarito brown kiwi). Also scampering through these forests are red deer, chamois and tahr, an introduced goat-antelope.

mayo. Between courses, glug craft beers on tap or 'snakebite' (a mix of cider and beer).

Monsoon BAR
(Map p248; ☑ 03-752 0220; www.monsoonbar. co.nz; 46 Cron St; mains $15-33; ⊗ 11am-11pm) Sip drinks in the sunshine or within the cosy, chalet-style bar of the Rainforest Retreat (p251), usually packed to the rafters with a sociable crowd of travellers. Bar snacks, burgers and posh pizzas (like chorizo and prawn) ensure you needn't move from your comfy spot by the fire.

❶ Information

Franz Josef Health Centre (☑ appointment booking 0800 7943 2584, direct 03-752 0700; 97 Cron St; ⊗ 8.30am-6pm Mon-Fri) South Westland's main medical centre. After hours, calls connect to a local nurse.

Westland Tai Poutini National Park Visitor Centre & i-SITE (Map p248; ☑ 03-752 0360; www.doc.govt.nz; 69 Cron St; ⊗ 8.30am-6pm Dec-Feb, to 5pm Mar-Nov) Regional DOC office with good exhibits, weather information and track updates; the i-SITE (Map p248; ☑ 0800 354 748; www.glaciercountry.co.nz; 63 Cron St; ⊗ 8.30am-6pm) desk books major nationwide transport except the Interislander.

❶ Getting There & Away

Direct **InterCity** (p243) and **Naked Bus** (p243) services along SH6 pass through once daily, northwards to Hokitika ($29, 2½ hours) and Greymouth (around $29, four hours) and south to Haast (from $23, 3¼ hours), stopping at Fox Glacier ($10, 40 minutes) on the way. Book ahead for fares as low as $1. A direct daily bus also reaches Queenstown (from $62, 8½ hours). For Nelson or Christchurch, change services in Greymouth.

Book at the **i-SITE** or **YHA** (p251). The bus stop is opposite the Fern Grove Four Square supermarket.

After hours, there's a a 24-hour diesel and petrol pump at **Glacier Motors** (☑ 03-752 0725; Main Rd; ⊗ 8am-7.30pm).

❶ Getting Around

Glacier Shuttles & Charters (☑ 0800 999 739) runs scheduled shuttle services to the glacier car park (return trip $12.50). You can also charter return transport to Lake Matheson, Okarito or Fox Glacier ($55 per person, minimum two people).

Okarito

POP 30

Huddled against a lagoon, the seaside hamlet of Okarito has a restorative air. Barely 10km from SH6, Okarito Lagoon is the largest unmodified wetland in NZ. More than 76 bird species preen and glide among its waterways, including gossamer-winged kōtuku (white heron). Hiding out in the forest are rowi kiwi, the rarest species of NZ's iconic land-bird – for a great chance of seeing one in the wild, hook up with the South Island's only licensed kiwi-tour operator, based in the village.

Okarito has no shops, limited visitor facilities and patchy phone reception, so stock up and book before you arrive.

❇ Activities & Tours

From a car park on the Strand you can begin the easy **Wetland Walk** (20 minutes), a longer mission along the **Three Mile Pack Track** (three hours, with the coastal return route tide dependent, so check in with the locals for tide times), and a jolly good puff up to **Okarito Trig** (1½ hours return), which rewards the effort with spectacular Southern Alps and Okarito Lagoon views (weather contingent).

★ **Okarito Kiwi Tours** WILDLIFE
(☑ 03-753 4330; www.okaritokiwitours.co.nz; 53 The Strand; 3-5hr tours $75) ✐ Spotting the rare kiwi in Okarito's tangle of native forest isn't easy, but bird-whisperer Ian has a 98% success rate for his small-group evening tours. Patience, tiptoeing and fine weather are essential. If you have your heart set on a kiwi encounter, book ahead and be within reach of Okarito for a couple of nights, in case of poor weather.

★ **Okarito Kayaks** KAYAKING
(☑ 03-753 4014, 0800 652 748; www.okarito.co.nz; 1 The Strand; kayak rental half-/full day $65/75; ⊗ hours vary) This hands-on operator hires out kayaks for paddles across Okarito's

shallow lagoon, in the company of strutting waterfowl and beneath a breathtaking mountainscape. Personalised guided kayaking trips (from $100) are ideal for getting to know the landscape; otherwise honest advice on weather, tides and paddling routes are gamely offered.

Okarito Boat Eco Tours WILDLIFE
(☑03-753 4223; www.okaritoboattours.co.nz; 31 Wharf St; ☺late Oct-May) Runs bird-spotting lagoon tours, the most fruitful of which is the 'early bird' ($80, 1½ hrs, 7.30am). The popular two-hour 'ecotour' offers deeper insights into this remarkable natural area ($90, 9am and 11.30am), or there's an afternoon 'wetlands tour' ($70, 2.30pm) if you aren't a morning person. Book at least 24 hours in advance.

🛏 Sleeping

Code Time Lodge APARTMENT $$
(☑021 037 2031; www.codetimelodge.co.nz; 8 Albert St; apt $150-250; ☎) Driftwood decorations and soft colour schemes impart a dreamy air to the Code Time Lodge, whose two roomy, self-contained apartments (kitchen included) are kept toasty by log-burning stoves.

❶ Getting There & Away

Okarito is 10km north off SH6 between Franz Josef and Whataroa. You'll need your own wheels to get there.

Whataroa

POP 288

Though it looks humdrum, Whataroa is a gateway to rare natural wonders. Strung out along the SH6, 30km north of Franz Josef Glacier, this nondescript town is the departure point for tours of NZ's only nesting site for the kōtuku (white heron). Their wings as delicately pretty as a bridal veil, these rare birds hold a special significance for Māori, who treasure their feathers and use 'kōtuku' as a compliment describing seldom-seen guests. When the birds roost between late September and February, White Heron Sanctuary Tours (p253) offers exclusive access to a viewing hide.

🐆 Tours

★ **White Heron Sanctuary Tours** WILDLIFE
(☑03-753 4120, 0800 523 456; www.whiteheron tours.co.nz; Main Rd; adult/child $150/75; ☺tours late Sep-Feb) 🌿 The sight of scores of rare kōtuku (white heron) nesting, nuzzling and soaring over the water is sheer delight, whether you're a bird-watcher or along for the ride. This operator offers the only excursion to the nests in Waitangi-Roto Nature Reserve near Whataroa. The 2½-hour tour involves a gentle jetboat ride and short boardwalk to the viewing hide. Book ahead.

Alpine Fault Tours OUTDOORS
(☑03 753 4236, 0800 556 244; http://alpinefault tours.co.nz; 70 Main Rd (SH6); adult/child $50/20; ☺by arrangement) Stand astride two tectonic plates, marvelling at Mother Nature's might, on a two-hour fault line tour. The experience is geared towards tourists as much as geology buffs: small groups are bussed to an area 10km from Whataroa where the Australian and Pacific plates meet, with engaging commentary on the forces that created the Southern Alps. Book ahead.

Glacier Country Scenic Flights SCENIC FLIGHTS
(☑0800 423 463, 03-753 4096; www.glacier adventures.co.nz; cnr SH6 & Scally Rd; flights $225-525) Offers a range of scenic flights and helihikes, lifting off from Whataroa Valley. These guys give you more mountain-gawping for your buck than many of the operators flying from the glacier townships, with optional snow landings.

❶ Getting There & Away

This stretch of SH6 is serviced once daily by **InterCity** (p243) or **Naked Bus** (p243) services. Northwards they go to Ross (1¼ hours), Hokitika (two hours) and Greymouth (3¼ hours), and southwards to Fox and Franz Josef Glaciers (30 minutes and 1¼ hours respectively). Full fares are around $29 to $45 but book online for cheaper advance tickets.

Ross

POP 297

When folks sensed gold in these hills in the mid-1860s, the township of Ross was hurriedly established. It soon ballooned to 2500 people and reached giddy heights of fame with the discovery of the 'Honourable Roddy' gold nugget, weighing in at nearly 3kg.

It's the start or finish point of the West Coast Wilderness Trail (p256), but gold-rush history makes Ross an entertaining stopoff along drives between Hokitika and the West Coast glacier towns.

◉ Sights

The **Water Race Walk** (one hour return) starts near the **heritage centre** (☑03-755 4077; 4 Aylmer St; $2; ⊙9am-4pm Dec-Mar, to 2pm Apr-Nov), passing old gold diggings, caves, tunnels and a cemetery. Hire a gold pan ($10) from the centre and head to Jones Creek to look for Roddy's great, great grand-nuggets.

⊨ Sleeping & Drinking

Top 10 Holiday Park
Ross Beach   HOLIDAY PARK $

(☑03-429 8277, 021 428 566; https://rossbeach top10.co.nz; 145 Ross Beach Rd; site unpowered/powered $40/50, dm $35, pod with/without bathroom from $125/99; 🛜) Three kilometres north of Ross by the beach, this holiday park plants guests in the midst of six windswept acres overlooking the Tasman Sea. There's plenty of space for tents and motorhomes, as well as a neat amenities block with a kitchen and laundry. We adore the converted shipping containers, upcycled into chic, self-contained pods.

Empire Hotel   PUB

(☑03-755 4005; 19 Aylmer St; ⊙10am-late) Nostalgia wafts from every brightly painted beam of the Empire Hotel. Since 1866, West Coasters have huddled inside the pub, amid yellowing photographs and dusty antiques, to spin yarns of yesteryear and swap gossip about whitebaiting locations. Breathe in the authenticity, along with a whiff of woodsmoke, over a pint and a bowl of chowder (mains $10 to $30).

❶ Getting There & Away

This stretch of SH6 is serviced once daily by **InterCity** (p243)/**Naked Bus** (p243) services. Heading north, they connect you directly to Hokitika (30 minutes) and Greymouth (1¾ hours), and south to Fox and Franz Josef Glaciers (2¼–2¾ hours). Full fares are around $29-45 but book online to score cheap advance tickets.

Hokitika

POP 3078

This sweet seaside town has a glint in its eye: indigenous *pounamu* (greenstone), carved and buffed to a shine by a thriving community of local artists. Shopping for greenstone, glassware, textiles and other home-grown crafts inspires droves of visitors to dawdle along Hokitika's streets, which are dotted with grand buildings from its 1860s gold-rush days.

Radiant sunsets and a glowworm dell add extra sparkle to this coastal idyll, though many visitors prefer to work up a sweat: Hokitika accesses the West Coast Wilderness Trail as well as view-laden tramps at Lakes Kaniere and Mahinapua.

◉ Sights

Sunset Point   VIEWPOINT

(Map p255; Gibson Quay) A visit to stunning Sunset Point is a quintessential Hokitika experience: watch the day's light fade away, observe whitebaiters casting nets, munch fish and chips, or stroll around the quayside shipwreck memorial.

Hokitika Museum   MUSEUM

(Map p255; www.hokitikamuseum.co.nz; 17 Hamilton St; gold coin donation; ⊙10am-5pm Nov-Mar, 10am-2pm Apr-Oct) When we visited, most of the Hokitika Museum's excellent collection was inaccessible while the imposing Carnegie Building (1908) awaited assessment about its earthquake-strengthening needs. A small array of displays on jade, town history and whitebait fishing remained free to view. When it's restored to its former glory, expect to find it packed with intelligently curated exhibitions presented in a clear, modern style.

National Kiwi Centre   BIRD SANCTUARY

(Map p255; ☑03-755 5251; www.thenationalkiwi centre.co.nz; 64 Tancred St; adult/child $24/12; ⊙9am-5pm Dec-Feb, to 4.30pm Mar-Nov; 🎡) Tiptoe through the darkened kiwi house to watch these iconic birds rummage for tasty insects, or stare a tuatara – a reptile unchanged for 225 million years – in its beady eyes. Time your visit for eel feeding time (three times a day, usually 10am, noon and 3pm) when you can hold out scraps of meat for these slithery critters to grab from a pair of tongs (or, shudder, your bare hands).

Glowworm Dell   NATURAL FEATURE

(SH6) At nightfall, bring a torch (or grope your way) into this grotto on the northern edge of town, signposted off the SH6. The dell is an easy opportunity to glimpse legions of glowworms (aka fungus gnat larvae), which emit an other-worldly blue light. An information panel at the entrance will further illuminate your way.

Hokitika

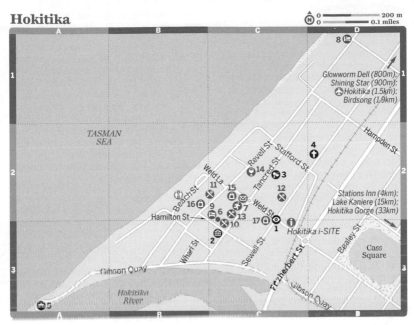

Glowworm Dell (800m);
Shining Star (900m);
Hokitika (1.5km);
Birdsong (1.9km)

TASMAN
SEA

Stations Inn (4km);
Lake Kaniere (15km);
Hokitika Gorge (33km)

Hamilton St

Hokitika i-SITE

Cass
Square

Gibson Quay

Hokitika
River

Lake Mahinapua   LAKE
(www.doc.govt.nz; SH6, Ruatapu) Serene Lake
Mahinapua and its diverse forests lie 10km
south of Hokitika. The scenic reserve, ga-
zetted in 1907, has a picnic area and DOC
campsite that bask in mountain views,
and the shallow, lagoon-fed water is warm
enough for a paddle. There are several short
walks (an hour return or less) signposted
along the shore.

The starting point of the **Mahinapua
Walkway** is 8km south of Hokitika. It's an
easy four- to five-hour return walk following
an old logging tramway.

Lake Kaniere   LAKE
(www.doc.govt.nz) Lying at the heart of a
7000-hectare scenic reserve, beautiful Lake
Kaniere is 8km long, 2km wide, 195m deep,
and freezing cold (as you'll discover if you
swim). You may prefer to camp or picnic
at **Hans Bay** (www.doc.govt.nz; Hans Bay Rd,
Lake Kaniere; sites per adult/child $8/4), peer
at **Dorothy Creek Falls** (4km south of the
campground), or undertake one of numerous walks, ranging from the 15-minute **Canoe Cove Walk** to the seven-hour return
gut-buster up **Mt Tuhua**. It's 20km southeast of central Hokitika.

WORTH A TRIP

HOKITIKA GORGE

Water this turquoise doesn't come easy. Half a million years of glacial movement sculpted the porcelain-white ravine of **Hokitika Gorge** (www.doc. govt.nz) ; the rock 'flour' ground over millennia intensifies the water's dazzling hue. A lookout at the swingbridge is only 10 minutes' walk from the car park, but you'll want to spend a full hour admiring and photographing the scene (until the sandflies chase you away). It's a scenic 35km drive south of Hokitika, well signposted from Stafford St (past the dairy factory).

The historic **Kaniere Water Race Walkway** (3½ hours one way) forms part of the West Coast Wilderness Trail.

Activities

Hokitika is a great base for walking and cycling. Download DOC's brochure *Walks in the Hokitika Area*, and visit **Hokitika Cycles & Sports World** (Map p255; ☑ 03-755 8662; www.hokitikasportsworld.co.nz; 33 Tancred St; bike rental per day $55; ⏰ 9am-5pm) for bike rental and advice on tracks, including the West Coast Wilderness Trail.

West Coast Wilderness Trail   CYCLING
(www.westcoastwildernesstrail.co.nz) One of 22 NZ Cycle Trails (www.nzcycletrail.com), the 136km West Coast Wilderness Trail stretches from Greymouth to Ross, following goldrush trails, reservoirs, old tramways and railway lines, forging new routes cross-country. Suitable for intermediate riders, the trail reveals dense rainforest, glacial rivers, lakes and wetlands, and views from the snow-capped mountains of the Southern Alps to the wild Tasman Sea.

The trail is gently graded most of the way, and although the full shebang takes a good four days by bike, it can easily be sliced up into sections of various lengths, catering to every ability and area of interest. Novice riders can tackle the fairly easy 'Big Day Out' from Kawhaka to Kaniere, which takes in major highlights over seven hours, or a four-hour ride following Kumara's gold trails.

Bike hire, transport and advice are available from the major setting-off points. In Hokitika, contact **Wilderness Trail Shuttle** (☑ 03-755 5042, 021 263 3299; www.wildernesstrail

shuttle.co.nz) and in Greymouth Trail Transport (p262).

West Coast Treetops Walkway   OUTDOORS
(☑ 0508 8733 8677, 03-755 5052; www.treetopsnz. com; 1128 Woodstock-Rimu Rd; adult/child $38/15; ⏰ 9am-5pm Oct-Mar, 9am-4pm Apr-Sep) Visitors strolling along this wobbly steel walkway, 450m long and 20m off the ground, can enjoy an unusual perspective on the canopy of native trees, featuring many old rimu and kamahi. The highlight is the 40m-high tower, from which extend views across Lake Mahinapua, the Southern Alps and Tasman Sea. Wheelchair-friendly.

Bonz 'N' Stonz   ART
(Map p255; www.bonz-n-stonz.co.nz; 16 Hamilton St; carving per hour $30, full-day bone/jade workshop $80/180) Design, carve and polish your own *pounamu* (greenstone), bone or paua (shellfish) masterpiece, with tutelage from Steve. Prices vary with materials and design complexity. Bookings recommended, and 'laughter therapy' included in the price.

Festivals & Events

Driftwood & Sand   ART
(Hokitika Beach; ⏰ Jan) Free spirits and budding artists transform flotsam and jetsam into sculptures on Hokitika Beach during this three-day, volunteer-led festival. Participants range from beginners to pros, and accordingly their creations span the full spectrum from enigmatic to delightfully daft.

★**Wildfoods Festival**   FOOD & DRINK
(www.wildfoods.co.nz; ⏰ Mar) Finding the West Coast's seafood scene a little samey? Give your tastebuds the equivalent of a defibrillator shock at this one-day festival of daredevil eating in early March. Fish eyes, pigs' ears and huhu beetle grubs usually grace the menu. Don't worry, there are local and international food stands to expunge the lingering taste of blood casserole...

Sleeping

★**Drifting Sands**   B&B $
(Map p255; ☑ 021 0266 5154; www.driftingsands. nz; 197 Revell St; d & tr $99-125, f $200; ☎) Natural tones and textures, upcycled furniture and hip vibes make this boutique beachside guesthouse a winner on style and location. Heightening the feel-good factor, there's a lounge warmed by a log burner and fresh bread every morning, plus free bike hire. One night isn't enough.

Birdsong HOSTEL **$**

(☑ 03-755 7179; www.birdsong.co.nz; 124 Kumara Junction Hwy; dm $34, s/d with shared bathroom $69/85, d with private bathroom $119, all incl breakfast; ☜) Sigh at sea views from the shared lounge and kitchen of this adorable hostel, 2.5km north of town. Rooms are themed around native bird life, hosts welcome guests with wit, and our only gripe is that bathrooms could be bigger (with better privacy than saloon-style doors).

Shining Star HOLIDAY PARK, MOTEL **$$**

(☑ 03-755 8921; 16 Richards Dr; sites per adult/child $20/10, d $119-149, f $185; ☜) Attractive and versatile beachside spot with everything from camping to log-lined cabins facing the sea. Kids will love the menagerie, including pigs and alpacas straight from Dr Doolittle's appointment book. Parents might prefer the spa or sauna ($15).

Teichelmann's B&B B&B **$$$**

(Map p255; ☑ 03-755 8232; www.teichelmanns. nz; 20 Hamilton St; s/d incl breakfast $235-280; ☜) Once home to surgeon, mountaineer and professional beard-cultivator Ebenezer Teichelmann, this B&B holds on to its venerable history but adds first-rate hospitality and splashes of complimentary port. Its six rooms each have an airy, restorative ambience, replete with great beds, quality cotton sheets and private bathrooms; the best enjoy fern-filled garden views. For added privacy, request self-contained Teichy's Cottage.

✖️ Eating & Drinking

★ Ramble + Ritual CAFE **$**

(Map p255; ☑ 03-755 6347; 51 Sewell St; snacks $3-8, meals $8-15; ☺ 7.30am-4pm Mon-Fri; ☞) Tucked away near the **Clock Tower** (Map p255; cnr Weld & Sewell Sts), this gallery-cum-cafe is a stylish spot to linger while hobnobbing with friendly staff and punters. Let's see, will it be a Gruyère and mushroom slice, superfood salad, or a ginger oaty munched in between gulps of super-strength coffee?

Sweet Alice's Fudge Kitchen SWEETS **$**

(Map p255; ☑ 03-755 5359; 27 Tancred St; fudge per slice $7; ☺ 10am-5pm) Treat yourself with a slice of Alice's handmade fudge, real fruit ice cream or a bag of boiled lollies – or maybe all three. Jars of kiwifruit jam allow you to stash a little sweetness for later.

★ Aurora MODERN NZ **$$**

(Map p255; ☑ 03-755 8319; http://aurorahoki. co.nz; 19 Tancred St; breakfast $10, mains $18-40; ☺ 8am-11pm) Breakfast egg-and-bacon ciabattas, Thai-style mussels, mid-afternoon tapas, desserts crowned with rich ice cream... from morning until closing time, everything at Aurora is beautifully plated and served with cheer.

Fat Pipi PIZZA **$$**

(Map p255; www.fatpipi.co.nz; 89 Revell St; pizzas $20-30; ☺ noon-2.30pm Wed-Sun, 5-9pm daily; ☞) Purists might balk at flavour combos like smoked chicken and apricot, but Fat Pipi bakes Hokitika's best pizza. There are versions for veggies and gluten-free diners, and garlicky whitebait pizza adds a local twist. Sweet tooth? Try dessert pizza heaped with blueberry, caramel and crumble. Enjoy it in the garden bar, or grab a takeaway and nibble at Sunset Point (p254).

Stations Inn Restaurant MODERN NZ **$$$**

(☑ 03-755 5499; www.stationsinnhokitika.co.nz; 11 Blue Spur Rd; mains $32-42; ☺ 6-10pm Tue-Sun) Pub food with added flair fills plates at the Stations Inn, adjoining the eponymous **motel** (d $170-300; ☜) 4km from Hokitika. Pork belly, lamb and other meaty fare are joined by at least one vegie option, served in a swish antique-feel bar and dining room. Book ahead.

West Coast Wine Bar WINE BAR

(Map p255; www.westcoastwine.co.nz; 108 Revell St; ☺ 4pm-late Wed-Sat) Upping Hoki's sophistication factor, this weeny joint packs a fridge full of fine wine and craft beer. Sip it in the hidden-away back garden, laden with murals and dangling antlers.

🛍 Shopping

Hokitika has a buzzing arts and crafts scene centred on carving and polishing *pounamu* into ornaments and jewellery. Be aware that some galleries sell jade imported from Europe and Asia, so ask before you buy.

> **REQUIRED READING**
>
> Sticking around in Hokitika for a while? Good, then you'll have time to read 800-page mystery *The Luminaries* by Eleanor Catton, a 2013 Man Booker Prize–winning novel set in Hokitika's gold-rush era.

Along for the ride are woodworkers, textile weavers and glass-blowers, all represented at classy boutiques in the centre of town.

Hokitika Craft Gallery   ARTS & CRAFTS
(Map p255; ☑ 03-755 8802; www.hokitikacraft gallery.co.nz; 25 Tancred St; ⊗ 9.30am-5pm) The town's best one-stop shop, this co-op showcases a wide range of local work, including *pounamu* (greenstone), jewellery, flax handbags, hand-coloured silk scarves, ceramics and woodwork.

Waewae Pounamu   ARTS & CRAFTS
(Map p255; ☑ 03-755 8304; www.waewae pounamu.co.nz; 39 Weld St; 8am-5pm) This stronghold of NZ *pounamu* (greenstone) displays traditional and contemporary designs in its main-road gallery-boutique.

Hokitika Glass Studio   ARTS & CRAFTS
(Map p255; ☑ 03-755 7775; www.hokitikaglass. co.nz; 9 Weld St; ⊗ 8.30am-5pm) Art and souvenirs from garish to glorious: glass eggs, multicoloured bowls and animal ornaments. And yes, they secure these fragile objects in oodles of protective wrapping. Watch the blowers at the furnace on weekdays.

Tectonic Jade   ARTS & CRAFTS
(Map p255; ☑ 03-755 6644; www.tectonicjade.com; 67 Revell St; ⊗ 9am-5pm) If you like your jade art and jewellery with a side-order of spirituality, the lustrous *pounamu* (greenstone) carved by local artist Rex Scott will leave you entranced.

❶ Information

Hokitika i-SITE (Map p255; ☑ 03-755 6166; www.hokitika.org; 36 Weld St; ⊗ 8.30am-5pm Mon-Fri, 10am-4pm Sat & Sun) One of NZ's best i-SITEs offers extensive bookings, including all bus services. Also holds DOC info, although you'll need to book online or at DOC Visitor Centres further afield. See also www. westcoastnz.com.

MĀORI WEST COAST

Early Māori forged paths through to the alps' mountains and river valleys to the West Coast in search of highly prized *pounamu* (greenstone), which they carved into tools, weapons and adornments. Admire and buy classy carvings created by town artists or polish your own stone at **Bonz 'N' Stonz** (p256).

Westland Medical Centre (☑ 03-755 8180; www.westlandmedical.co.nz; 54a Sewell St; ⊗ 8am-4.45pm Mon & Wed-Fri, 9am-4.45pm Tue) Call ahead for appointments, or use the after-hours phone service (24 hours). In urgent cases, use the weekend walk-in service at 10am and 5pm.

❶ Getting There & Away

AIR

Hokitika Airport (www.hokitikaairport.co.nz; Airport Dr, off Tudor St) is 1.5km east of the town centre. **Air New Zealand** (www.air-newzealand.com) has two flights most days to/from Christchurch.

BUS

One **InterCity** (p243)/**Naked Bus** (p243) service leaves from the Kiwi Centre on Tancred St, then outside the i-SITE, daily for Greymouth (around $15, 45 minutes) and Fox and Franz Josef Glaciers (from $29, two to 2½ hours). For Nelson (from $42, seven hours), change buses in Greymouth. For Christchurch, bus to Greymouth and take the **TranzAlpine** (p260).

❶ Getting Around

Greymouth's branch of **NZ Rent-a-Car** (☑ 03-768 0379; www.nzrentacar.co.nz; 170 Tainui St) can arrange vehicle pick-up/drop-off at Hokitika Airport.

Hokitika Taxis (☑ 03-755 5075)

Kumara

POP 309

Once upon a time, folks piled into Kumara's two theatres, waltzing until dawn and roaring with delight at travelling circus acts that passed through this gold-rush town. But with the glittering 1880s long faded into memory, only a threadbare settlement remains, near the western end of Arthur's Pass (30km south of Greymouth). Thanks to local enthusiasm for Kumara's boom time, display panels around town tell stories of feisty figures from history while the Theatre Royal Hotel (p259) and other converted period properties offer a glimpse of life in the gold-flecked past.

In recent times Kumara's main claim to fame is as a supporter of the multisport **Coast to Coast race** (www.coasttocoast.co.nz). Held each February, the strong, the brave and the totally knackered run, cycle and kayak a total of 243km all the way across the mountains to Christchurch, with top competitors dusting it off in just under 11 hours.

Sights

Don't expect big-ticket attractions, but Kumara has a couple of ramble-worthy sights where you can stretch your legs. There's a **glowworm dell** in the bush behind the Theatre Royal's miners cottages. Some 800m south of town, off the highway, you'll find a **historic swimming pool** from the 1930s; it was once New Zealand's largest, though little but overgrown walls remain today.

Sleeping & Eating

★ Theatre Royal Hotel HOTEL $$$
(☑03-736 9277; www.theatreroyalhotel.co.nz; 81 Seddon St, SH73, Kumara; d from $180; 🛜) Themed around colourful figures from Kumara's past, rooms at the beautifully restored Theatre Royal Hotel are reason enough to stay in town. We especially loved the feminine flourishes of Barbara Weldon's room, honouring a former lady of the night (good soundproofing). Motel-style miners cottages ($200 to $280), sleeping up to four, are brand new but have vintage finishes such as clawfoot tubs.

The opulence continues in the hotel's apartments (from $239): have a full-on Marie Antoinette fantasy in the boutique apartments (complete with four-poster beds) or bed down in the old Bank of New Zealand building (gold was once weighed in what's now the bathroom).

Stop for game specials or afternoon tea in the Theatre Royal's **restaurant** (lunch mains $16-25, dinner mains $22-33; ⏰11am-8pm Sun-Thu, to late Fri & Sat), whose adjoining bar is a great spot for a yarn with the locals.

Getting There & Away

West Coast Shuttle (☑027 492 7000, 03-768 0028; www.westcoastshuttle.co.nz) passes through Kumara (not to be confused with Kumara Junction, close to the coast) on its daily service from Christchurch to Greymouth ($55, 3½ hours) – but most travellers arrive by car or bike.

GREY DISTRICT

Bookending the magnificent alpine highway across Arthur's Pass and sitting roughly halfway along the West Coast road, Greymouth and its surrounds are more of a transit point than a destination.

The largest town, Greymouth (to the Māori 'Māwhera', wide river mouth), is big

GREENSTONE SYMBOLS

The West Coast has a thriving community of artists sourcing *pounamu* (greenstone) and carving it into sculptures and jewellery, particularly in Hokitika and Greymouth. It's considered luckier to buy greenstone for others, rather than yourself, and a few recurring shapes carry distinctive meanings.

Koru Whirl reminiscent of a fern shoot, signifying the life journey: creation, growth and travel.

Toki A rectangular shape harking to traditional Māori tools; a symbol of courage and strength.

Pikorua Contemporary 'twist' design symbolising the continuity of bonds between family or friends.

Hei matau Curved fish hook design with a variety of meanings: health, safe travel and prosperity.

on services but light on attractions, though the classy brewery and historic village Shantytown (p260) merit a visit. Inland, Kumara is a common stop-off for cyclists on the West Coast Wilderness Trail, Lake Brunner is a soothing getaway for fishing or bird-watching, and remote Blackball is firmly in trampers' eyelines as a starting point for the Pike29 Memorial Track, a 45km 'Great Walk' destined to open in 2019. Even by NZ's standards, the Greymouth region is a standout for friendliness; its down-to-earth folks might be reason enough to dawdle here before you travel on.

Greymouth

POP 13,371 (DISTRICT)

Greymouth is the largest town on the West Coast and the region's 'Big Smoke'. For locals it's a refuelling and shopping pit stop, for travellers it's a noteworthy portal to tramping trails. Arriving on a dreary day, it's no mystery why Greymouth, crouched at the mouth of the imaginatively named Grey River, is sometimes the butt of jokes. But with gold-mining history, a scattering of jade shops, and worthy walks in its surrounds, it pays to look beyond the grey.

Greymouth

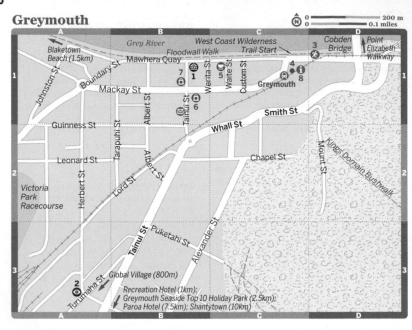

Greymouth

⊙ Sights

Shantytown   MUSEUM
(☏ 03-762 6634; www.shantytown.co.nz; Rutherglen Rd, Paroa; adult/child/family $33/16/78; ⊙ 8.30am-5pm; ⊞) Good fun for kids and young-of-heart travellers, Shantytown is a recreated 1860s gold-mining town, 10km south of Greymouth. Peer inside a church, workshops and gory hospital (shield the kids' eyes), all painstakingly crafted to evoke the spirit of the era. Take cheesy souvenir pics in period costume and try gold-panning, but the highlight is a steam-train ride into the bush (five to seven daily).

Monteith's Brewing Co   BREWERY
(Map p260; ☏ 03-768 4149; www.monteiths.co.nz; cnr Turumaha & Herbert Sts; guided tour $25; ⊙ tours 4 daily, tasting room & bar 11am-8pm May-Oct, to 9pm Nov-Mar) The original Monteith's brewhouse is brand HQ: glossy and a wee bit corporate, but it delivers a high-quality experience. Plan ahead for one of four daily guided tours (25 minutes, including generous samples) or DIY in the industrial-chic tasting room and bar, complete with roaring fire.

Left Bank Art Gallery   GALLERY
(Map p260; ☏ 03-768 0038; www.leftbankarts.org.nz; 1 Tainui St; admission by donation; ⊙ 10.30am-4pm Tue-Fri, 11am-2pm Sat) A former bank houses contemporary NZ jade carvings, prints, paintings, photographs and ceramics within its almost century-old walls.

🏃 Activities

★ TranzAlpine   RAIL
(Map p260; ☏ 04-495 0775, 0800 872 467; www.greatjourneysofnz.co.nz; one way adult/child from $119/83) The *TranzAlpine* is one of the world's great train journeys. It traverses the

Southern Alps between Christchurch and Greymouth, through Arthur's Pass National Park, from the Pacific Ocean to the Tasman Sea. Dramatic landscapes span its 223km length, from the flat, alluvial Canterbury Plains, through alpine gorges, an 8.5km tunnel, beech-forested river valleys and a lake fringed with cabbage trees.

Point Elizabeth Walkway WALKING
(www.doc.govt.nz) Accessible from Dommett Esplanade in Cobden, 6km north of Greymouth, this enjoyable walkway (three hours return) skirts around a richly forested headland in the shadow of the Rapahoe Range to an impressive ocean lookout, before continuing on to the northern trailhead at Rapahoe (11km from Greymouth) – small town, big beach, friendly local pub.

If you want a shorter walk, it's 45 minutes to the ocean lookout (one-way).

Floodwall Walk WALKING
(Map p260) Once subject to serious flooding, Greymouth hasn't experienced a deluge since the building of this floodwall, masterminded after a flood in 1988. Take a 10-minute riverside stroll along Mawhera Quay, the start of the West Coast Wilderness Trail (p256), or stretch your legs by pressing on for the full hour-long route.

The hour-long walk takes in the fishing boat harbour, Blaketown Beach and breakwater – a great place to experience the power of the ocean and savour a famous West Coast sunset.

Coal Creek Falls Track TRAMPING
(Ballance St, Runanga) A 30-minute bushwalk through mixed beech-podocarp forest leads to a broad waterfall tumbling into a swimmable pool. The trail starts in Runanga, 8km north of Greymouth.

🛏 Sleeping

★ Global Village HOSTEL $
(☑03-768 7272; www.globalvillagebackpackers.co.nz; 42 Cowper St; dm/d $32/80; @🛜) Collages of African and Asian art on its walls, and a passionate traveller vibe at its core. Global Village also has free kayaks – the Lake Karoro wetlands reserve is a short walk away – and mountain bikes for guests, and relaxation comes easy with a spa, sauna, barbecue and fire pit.

Paroa Hotel HOTEL $$
(☑03-762 6860, 0800 762 6860; www.paroa.co.nz; 508 Main South Rd, Paroa; units $149-300; 🛜) A

family affair since 1954, from kitchen to reception, the venerable Paroa has benefitted from a makeover. Sizeable units with great beds are decorated in fetching monochrome and share a garden. The hotel's warm service continues inside the noteworthy bar and restaurant. It's opposite the Shantytown turn-off.

🍴 Eating & Drinking

Recreation Hotel BISTRO $$
(☑03-768 5154; www.rechotel.co.nz; 68 High St; mains $17-26; ⊙11am-late) A strong local following fronts up to 'the Rec' for its smart public bar serving good pub grub, such as a daily roast, burgers and local fish and chips amid pool tables and the TAB.

DP1 Cafe CAFE
(Map p260; 104 Mawhera Quay; ⊙8am-5pm Mon-Fri, 9am-5pm Sat & Sun; 🛜) A stalwart of the Greymouth cafe scene, this quayside java joint is awash in local artwork. Hip clientele and friendly staff make it an excellent place to mingle (while sipping the best espresso in town). Swing in for the $6 morning muffin and coffee special, or a caramel slice at any other hour.

🛍 Shopping

Nimmo Gallery & Store ARTS & CRAFTS
(Map p260; ☑03-768 6499; https://nimmophoto.co.nz; 102 Mackay St; ⊙9am-5pm Mon-Sat) Ostensibly the gallery of local landscape photographer Stewart Nimmo, this friendly space overflows with cracking souvenirs (with more handicrafts and clothing sold in the courtyard out back). Honeyed beauty products, postcards, clothing, sheep-themed goodies, they've got it all.

Shades of Jade JEWELLERY
(Map p260; ☑03-768 0794; www.shadesofjade.co.nz; 22 Tainui St; ⊙9am-5pm Mon-Fri, 10am-2pm Sat & Sun) Browse some of the prettiest jade creations we've seen along the West Coast, and get the inside scoop on local beaches where you can hunt out a stone of your own.

ℹ Information

Grey Base Hospital (☑03-769 7400; High St)
Greymouth i-SITE (Map p260; ☑03-768 7080, 0800 767 080; www.westcoasttravel.co.nz; 164 Mackay St, Greymouth Train Station; ⊙9am-5pm Mon-Fri, 10am-4pm Sat & Sun; 🛜) The helpful crew at the train station can assist with all manner of advice and bookings, including those for DOC huts and walks. See also www.westcoastnz.com.

ℹ Getting There & Away

BUS

All buses stop outside the train station. **Inter-City** (p243) has daily buses north to Westport (from $21, 2¼ hours) and Nelson (from $40, six hours), and south to Franz Josef and Fox Glaciers (around $30, 3½ hours). **Naked Bus** (p243) runs the same route. Both companies offer connections to destinations further afield.

Atomic Travel (📞 03-349 0697; www.atomic travel.co.nz) runs daily between Greymouth and Christchurch, as does **West Coast Shuttle** (p259) – the fare is around $50.

Combined with the **i-SITE** (p261) in the train station, the **West Coast Travel Centre** (Map p260; 📞 03-768 7080; www.westcoasttravel. co.nz; 164 Mackay St, Greymouth Train Station; ⊙9am-5pm Mon-Fri, 10am-4pm Sat & Sun; 🛜) books local and national transport, and offers luggage storage.

TRAIN

TranzAlpine (p260) This view-laden train connection to Christchurch leaves Greymouth daily at 2.05pm.

ℹ Getting Around

CAR

Several car-hire company desks are located within the train station including **NZ Rent-a-Car** (p258).

TAXI & SHUTTLE

Greymouth Taxis (📞 03-768 7078) A taxi to Shantytown will cost you around $35 (one way).

Trail Transport (📞 03-768 6618; www.trail transport.co.nz; bike hire per day from $50, shuttle transport $28-65) Bike rental and shuttle transport focusing on the West Coast Wilderness Trail.

Lake Brunner

Expect your pulse to slow almost as soon as you arrive at Lake Brunner. Named for England-born explorer Thomas Brunner, this 40 sq km expanse of sapphire water lies 35km southeast of Greymouth. The lake is large but main settlement Moana (on its northern shore) is minuscule; nonetheless it brims with accommodation options to suit the families and trout-fishing enthusiasts drawn to this sedate spot.

Brunner is a scenic place to idle away a day or two strolling lakeside tracks, fishing or bird-watching. Book ahead in summer (and note that it's whisper-quiet in winter).

🏃 Activities

One of many lakes in the area, Brunner is a tranquil spot for bush walks, bird-spotting and various water sports, including boating and fishing. Indeed, the local boast is that the lake and Arnold River are 'where the trout die of old age', which suggests this is a largely untouched spot for you to dangle a line. Greymouth i-SITE (p261) can hook you up with a guide.

🛏 Sleeping & Eating

Lake Brunner
Country Motel   MOTEL, CAMPGROUND $
(📞 03-738 0144; www.lakebrunnermotel.co.nz; 2014 Arnold Valley Rd; sites $35-40, cabins $65-75, cottages d $130-155; 🛜) Birdsong, flower beds and 6 acres of greenery...feeling relaxed yet? At this motel and campground, 2km from Lake Brunner, choose from powered and unpowered sites, and plain, unvarnished cabins, all of which share bathrooms and kitchen facilities. More plush are the self-contained cottages, complete with floral trimmings and nice bathrooms.

Stationhouse Cafe   CAFE $
(📞 03-738 0158; www.lakebrunner.net; 40 Koe St, Moana; snacks from $4, mains from $15; ⊙9.30am-10pm) It's one of the only shows in town but luckily the Stationhouse, dating to 1901, is a winner. The cafe serves fruit smoothies, savoury muffins as well as indulgent baked goods, along with a sizeable menu of fish, meat and veggie main courses. In good weather, grab a spot on the deck for views of the water and Mt Alexander.

ℹ Getting There & Away

Reach Lake Brunner via the SH7 turn-off at Stillwater, a journey of 36km from Greymouth. It can also be reached from the south via Kumara Junction. The *TranzAlpine* train pulls into Moana train station daily on its way between Christchurch and Greymouth. **Atomic Travel** (p262) shuttles also pass through daily on the same journey.

Blackball

POP 330

Ramshackle Blackball is a shadow of its mining glory days, but this spirited town offers more than meets the eye. Around 25km upriver of Greymouth, Blackball was established in 1866 to service gold diggers;

coal mining kicked in between 1890 and 1964. The National Federation of Labour (a trade union) was conceived here, born from influential strikes in 1908 and 1913.

Blackball remains fiercely proud of its trade union history – just check out the old posters in **Formerly the Blackball Hilton** (✆ 03-732 4705, 0800 425 225; www.blackballhilton.co.nz; 26 Hart St; s/d incl breakfast $55/110; ☎). This century-old hotel is a major talking point: it changed its name to avoid a legal battle with a certain hotel chain. Another claim to fame is **Blackball Salami Co** (✆ 03-732 4111; www.blackballsalami.co.nz; 11 Hilton St; salami packs from $9; ⊙ 8am 4pm Mon-Fri, 9am-2pm Sat), whose smoky meats are renowned up and down the West Coast.

Sleepy Blackball is likely to be stirred up by the opening of the Pike29 Memorial Track (probably in 2019), which will bring a new influx of trampers.

⚡ Activities

Croesus Track TRAMPING
(www.doc.govt.nz) Following an old mining track from the late 19th century, the Croesus is an 18km, one- to two-day trail that suits experienced trampers. The track links inland Blackball with coastal Barrytown, crossing the Paparoa Ranges (climbing as high as 1km above sea level) and passing historic relics of the mining glory days.

From 2019, the Croesus Track will link to a new Great Walk, the Pike29 Memorial Track, a two- to three-day walking trail between Blackball and Punakaiki.

ⓘ Getting There & Away

It's half an hour's drive east (25km) to Blackball from Greymouth on the West Coast Hwy (SH7); you'll need your own wheels.

Barrytown & Around

The southernmost stretch of the Great Coast Road, between Punakaiki and Greymouth, carves a path between rocky bays and the steep, bushy Paparoa Ranges. Sleepy, sparsely populated Barrytown is the main settlement along this section of the SH6, but expansive views provide an excuse to stop and take it all in. Set out on a clear day and you can see as far as the Southern Alps.

THE GREAT COAST ROAD

One hundred kilometres of salty vistas line the road between Westport and Greymouth. One of New Zealand's most beautiful drives, the Great Coast Road meanders past foaming surf and shingle beaches on one side, and forbidding, overhanging cliffs on the other. The best-known stop along this inspiring stretch of SH6 is Punakaiki's geologically fascinating **Pancake Rocks** (p264). But there are numerous wind-whipped lookouts where you can pull over to gaze at waves smashing against haggard turrets of stone.

Fill up in Westport or Greymouth if you're low on petrol and cash.

⚡ Activities

Book ahead to forge your own blade from hot steel with **Barrytown Knifemaking** (✆ 03-731 1053, 0800 256 433; www.barrytownknifemaking.com; 2662 SH6, Barrytown; classes $160; ⊙ Tue-Sun by arrangement), 17km south of Punakaiki. Day-long courses feature a sandwich lunch, axe-throwing and a stream of entertainingly bad jokes from Steve, friendly host and knife-making expert. Fifteen kilometres south is Rapahoe, a tiny seaside settlement. Here you'll find the northern trailhead for the **Point Elizabeth Walkway** (p261), an enjoyable 1¾-hour tramp to wind-battered cliffs, rewarded by a panoramic lookout.

🛏 Sleeping

★ **Breakers** B&B $$$
(✆ 03-762 7743; www.breakers.co.nz; 1367 SH6, Nine Mile Creek, Rapahoe; d incl breakfast $275-385; ☎) Crafted to tug at the heart strings of surfers and beach bunnies, every room at Breakers has a sea view and easy access down to the shore. Tucked into a hillside nook 14km north of Greymouth, all four self-contained units are tasteful and modern, with decks for sighing over the sunset.

ⓘ Getting There & Away

InterCity (p243) and **Naked Bus** (p243) services ply this leg of the Great Coast Road once a day, stopping at Barrytown on their way between Westport (from $17, 1¾ hours) and Greymouth (from $10, 20 minutes), via Punakaiki (from $10, 15 minutes).

BULLER REGION

Forest and coast unite in dramatic form in the Buller Region. This northwesterly expanse of the South Island is a promised land for trampers. Trails wend riverside through primeval forest, some accessing geological marvels like the Oparara Arch.

Gold was found in the Buller River in the mid-19th century, and coal mining scorched the landscape soon after. Mining history is carefully conserved in main towns Westport and Reefton, though agriculture and tourism are the Buller Region's prime moneymakers today. Mining history makes a pleasant diversion, if you need a breather from muddy trails, white-water rafting, and kayaking tannin-stained waterways.

Punakaiki & Paparoa National Park

Located midway between Westport and Greymouth is Punakaiki, a small settlement beside the rugged 38,000-hectare Paparoa National Park. Most visitors come for a quick squiz at the Pancake Rocks, layers of limestone that resemble stacked crepes. But these are just one feature of the impressive, boulder-sprinkled shoreline. Pebble beaches (keep an eye out for greenstone) are kissed by spectacular sunsets and there are some riveting walking trails into the national park.

◎ Sights

Paparoa National Park is blessed with high cliffs and empty beaches, a dramatic mountain range, crazy limestone river valleys, diverse flora, and a profusion of bird life, including weka and the Westland petrel, a rare sea bird that nests only here.

★ **Pancake Rocks**　　　NATURAL FEATURE
(www.doc.govt.nz; SH6) Punakaiki's claim to fame is Dolomite Point, where a layering-weathering process called stylobedding has carved the limestone into what looks like piles of thick pancakes. Aim for high tide (tide timetables are posted at the visitor centre (p265); hope that it coincides with sunset) when the sea surges into caverns and booms menacingly through blowholes. See it on a wild day and be reminded that Mother Nature really is the boss.

Allow 20 minutes for the straightforward walk, which loops from the highway out to the rocks and blowholes (or 40 minutes if you want to take photos). Parts of the trail are suitable for wheelchair access.

🏃 Activities

Tramps around Punakaiki include the **Truman Track** (30 minutes return) and the **Punakaiki–Porari Loop** (3½ hours), which goes up the spectacular limestone Pororari River gorge before popping over a hill and coming down the bouldery Punakaiki River to rejoin the highway.

Surefooted types can embark on the **Fox River Cave Walk** (three hours return), 12km north of Punakaiki and open to amateur explorers. BYO torch and sturdy shoes.

The Paparoa National Park Visitor Centre (p265) has free maps detailing other tramps in the area. Note that many of Paparoa's inland walks are susceptible to river flooding so it is vital that you obtain updates from the centre before you depart, and always heed warning signs and roped-off trails.

Punakaiki Horse Treks　　　HORSE RIDING
(✆03-731 1839, 021 264 2600; www.pancake-rocks.co.nz; SH6, Punakaiki; 2½hr ride $180; ⊙mid-Oct–early May) Trek through the beautiful Punakaiki Valley right onto the beach on these guided horseback tours, suitable for all experience levels. Private rides start at $220 (minimum two people).

🛌 Sleeping

★ **Punakaiki Beach Hostel**　　　HOSTEL $
(✆03-731 1852; www.punakaikibeachhostel.co.nz; 4 Webb St; sites per person $22, dm/d $32/89; 🐾) The ambience is laid-back but Punakaiki Beach is efficiently run. This spick-and-span 24-bed hostel has all the amenities a traveller could need, from laundry to a shared kitchen to staff who smile because they mean it. Comfy dorm rooms aside, the en-suite bus ($140) is the most novel stay, but cutesy Sunset Cottage ($150) is also worth a splurge.

Te Nikau Retreat　　　HOSTEL $
(✆03-731 1111; www.tenikauretreat.co.nz; 19 Hartmount Pl; dm $32, d $85-110, cabins $120-210; 🐾) 🌿 Checking in to Te Nikau feels instantly restorative. Kindly staff establish a relaxing tone, and charming wooden lodges (dorms and private cabins) are tucked into rainforest, a short walk from the beach. Our favourite is tiny Stargazer: it's little more than a double bed in a low hut but glass roof panels

allow you to count constellations on clear nights.

Punakaiki Beachfront Motels MOTEL **$$**
(✆03-731 1008; www.punakaikibeachfrontmotels.co.nz; Mabel St; d $120-200; ☎) Six classy, wood-accented motel units are sandwiched between cliff and sea, with private access to a wind-blown pebble beach. Larger groups (up to nine) can rent a two-storey, four-bedroom holiday home ($210–300). The setting feels pleasingly remote, but it's only 500m respectively from Pancake Rocks to the south and the **Punakaiki Tavern** (✆03-731 1188; SH6; breakfasts $6-26, mains $20-40; ☺8am-late; ☎) to the north.

Hydrangea Cottages COTTAGE **$$$**
(✆03-731 1839; www.pancake-rocks.co.nz; SH6; cottages $245-485; ☎) On a hillside overlooking the Tasman, these six standalone and mostly self-contained cottages are built from salvaged timber and stone. Each is distinct, like 'Miro' with splashes of colour and bright tiles, and two-storey 'Nikau' with a private, sea-facing deck. Occasional quirks like outdoor bathtubs add to the charm. It's 800m south of Pancake Rocks and the visitor centre.

✖ Eating

Fox River Market MARKET **$**
(Fox River; ☺8am-noon Sun) In summer, a food and craft market unfolds in a jaw-dropping location beneath overhanging cliffs 12km north of Punakaiki (follow signs to Fox River car park). Offerings vary by vendor but you can expect Thai food, freshly baked cakes, and take-home treats like smoked cheese and kiwifruit relish. Ask locally about seasonal start dates.

Pancake Rocks Cafe CAFE **$$**
(✆03-731 1122; www.pancakerockscafe.com; 4300 Coast Rd (SH6), Punakaiki; mains $10-26; ☺8am-5pm, to 10pm Dec-Feb; ✎) Almost inevitably, pancakes are the pride of the cafe opposite the Pancake Rocks trail, heaped with bacon, berries, cream and other tasty toppings. Even better are the pizzas, from whitebait to four cheese (with a few good veggie options, too). Time a visit for summer open-mic nights from 6pm on Fridays.

ℹ Information

Paparoa National Park Visitor Centre (✆03-731 1895; www.doc.govt.nz; SH6, Punakaiki; ☺9am-5pm Oct-Nov, to 6pm Dec-Mar, to 4.30pm Apr-Sep) Across the road from the Pancake Rocks walkway, the visitor centre has information on the national park and track conditions, and handles bookings for some local attractions and accommodation, including hut tickets.

Punakaiki Promotions (www.punakaiki.co.nz) Online directory of accommodation, activities and tide times.

ℹ Getting There & Away

InterCity (p243) and **Naked Bus** (p243) services travel daily north to Westport (from $16, one hour), and south to Greymouth (from $11, 45 minutes) and Fox Glacier (from $37, 5½ hours). Buses stop long enough for passengers to admire the Pancake Rocks.

Charleston & Around

The northernmost section of the Great Coast Road plies gold-mining history, dreamy coast and quiet farmland on its way between Westport and Punakaiki's Pancake Rocks. Roughly midway is Charleston, an 1860s gold-rush boom town that once boasted 80 hotels, three breweries and hundreds of thirsty gold-diggers staking claims along the Nile River. There's not much left now except a motel, camping ground, a clutch of local houses, and the brilliant Underworld Adventures, with whom you can explore some utterly amazing hidden treasures.

South of Charleston is where the Great Coast Road becomes truly enthralling, with a series of dramatic bays. Drive as slowly as the traffic behind you will allow.

◉ Sights & Activities

Mitchells Gully Gold Mine HISTORIC SITE
(✆03-789 6257; http://mitchellsgullygoldmine.co.nz; SH6, Charleston; adult/child $10/free; ☺9am-4pm) For a true taste of the region's gold-mining past, swing into Mitchells Gully Gold Mine, 3km north of Charleston. You'll get a friendly primer on the 1860s mining days and then explore mining tunnels and railway tracks on a pleasant, 40-minute bush walk, goggling at Charleston's last remaining waterwheel and stamping battery along the way.

If you're staying in the area, reserve a spot on a night-time glowworm tour (adult/child $25/5).

Underworld Adventures CAVING
(✆03-788 8168, 0800 116 686; www.caverafting.com; SH6, Charleston) Glow with the flow

on black-water rafting trips deep into glowworm-filled Nile River Caves (adult/child $185/150, four hours). This friendly Charleston-based operator also runs cave excursions without rafting (adult/child $120/87.50). Short on time? Take the rainforest train ride (adult/child $25/20), a 1½-hour return journey departing two or three times daily. The centre and its cafe are 26km south of Westport.

Kids aged 10 and over can raft, while the cave tours suit anyone who can walk on slippery surfaces for a couple of hours.

The Adventure Caving trip ($350, five hours) includes a 40m abseil into Te Tahi cave system, with rock squeezes, waterfalls, prehistoric fossils and trippy cave formations.

🛏 Sleeping

Beaconstone Eco Lodge HOSTEL **$**
(☑027 3341136; www.beaconstoneecolodge.co.nz; Birds Ferry Rd, SH6; dm $40, d & tw $96-104; ☺ Oct-Apr; 🖀) 🏝 Set on 42 serene hectares, 9km north of Charleston, this solar-powered, energy-efficient lodge is both eco- and guest-friendly. Fashioned from sustainably sourced native timber and featuring comfy beds and a laid-back communal area, the lodge's style is Americana cool meets West Coast charm. Bush walks lead right from the doorstep. Book ahead.

❶ Getting There & Away

InterCity (p243) and **Naked Bus** (p243) services ply this leg of the Great Coast Road once a day, stopping at Charleston on their way between Westport (from $10, 25 minutes) and Greymouth (from $16, two hours), via Punakaiki (around $13, 40 minutes).

Westport & Around

POP 4035

The 'capital' of the northern West Coast is Westport. The town's fortunes have waxed and waned on coal mining, but in the current climate it sits quietly stoked up on various industries, including dairy and, increasingly, tourism. It boasts respectable hospitality and visitor services, and makes a good base for exploring the fascinating coast north to Denniston, Charming Creek, Karamea and the Heaphy Track.

◎ Sights

The most riveting sights are beyond Westport's city walls, particularly heading north on SH67, which passes **Granity**, **Ngakawau** (home to the well named Charming Creek) and **Hector**, where stands a monument to Hector's dolphins, NZ's smallest, although you'll be lucky to see them unless your timing is impeccable. It's also worth poking around **Seddonville**, a small bush town on the Mokihinui River. This small dot on the map is about to get slightly bigger, being the northern trailhead for the thrilling **Old Ghost Road** (www.oldghostroad.org.nz).

Coaltown Museum MUSEUM
(www.coaltown.co.nz; 123 Palmerston St; adult/child $10/2; ☺9am-5pm Mon-Fri, 10am-4pm Sat & Sun) Westport's 'black gold' is paid homage at this remarkably interesting museum, adjoining the i-SITE. A replica mine, well-scripted display panels and an excellent selection of photographs and pioneer ephemera allow for an informative trip into the coal-blackened past. Best of all are the Denniston displays, including a whopping brake drum and panels explaining the daily tribulations of miners.

Denniston Plateau HISTORIC SITE
(www.doc.govt.nz; Denniston Rd) Six hundred metres above sea level, Denniston was once NZ's largest coal town, with 1500 residents in 1911. By 1981 there were eight. Its claim to fame was the fantastically steep Denniston Incline, which hurtled laden wagons down a 45-degree hillside. Display panels bring the plateau's history to life and trails provide a direct route into the past: the **Town Walk** (40 minutes) loops around the old township while the **Bridle Path** (5½ hours return) follows old coal transportation routes.

The turn-off to Denniston is 16km north of Westport at Waimangaroa. Denniston is another nine winding kilometres inland from there.

Look out for DOC's Westport brochure detailing five tramps around the Denniston plateau; the eager can read Jenny Pattrick's evocative novels set in these parts, like *The Denniston Rose*.

🏃 Activities

Westport is good for a stroll – the i-SITE (p268) can direct you to the **Millennium Walkway** and **North Beach Reserve**. The most exciting excursion hereabouts is cave rafting with Underworld Adventures (p265) in Charleston, although mountain biking is gaining momentum as a popular pastime among local and visiting backcountry adventurers. The folk at **Habitat Sports** (☑ 03-788 8002; www.habitatsports.co.nz; 234 Palmerston St, Westport; bike rental from $35; ⊙ 9am-5pm Mon-Fri, 9am-1pm Sat) offer bike rental, maps and advice.

★ **Cape Foulwind Walkway**   WALKING
(www.doc.govt.nz) Screaming gulls and rasping waves are the soundtrack to tramps around Cape Foulwind (45 minutes to one hour each way), as wind-battered a walk as its name promises. The trail traverses buttercup-speckled farmland, which carpets the coastal hills between Omau and Tauranga Bay. Towards the southern end is the seal colony where – depending on the season – up to 200 fur seals loll on the rocks. Further north the walkway passes a replica astrolabe (a navigational aid) and lighthouse.

Abel Tasman was the first European to sight the Cape, in 1642, naming it Clyppygen Hoek (Rocky Point). However, his name was eclipsed by James Cook in 1770, who clearly found it less than pleasing.

Cape Foulwind is well signposted from Westport. It's 13km to Lighthouse Rd at Omau, where the welcoming **Star Tavern** (☑ 03-789 6923; 6 Lighthouse Rd, Cape Foulwind; meals $9-30; ⊙ 4pm-late Mon-Fri, noon-late Sat & Sun) signals the walkway's northern end. The southern end is 16km from town at Tauranga Bay, popular with surfers who dodge its rocky edges.

Charming Creek Walkway   TRAMPING, CYCLING
(www.doc.govt.nz) Starting from either Ngakawau (30km north of Westport), or near Seddonville, a few kilometres further on, this is one of the best day walks on the coast, taking around six hours return. Following an old coal line through the Ngakawau River Gorge, it features rusty relics galore, tunnels, a suspension bridge and waterfall, and lots of interesting plants and geological formations.

Ask a local about transport if you don't want to walk it both ways. The trail is dual use, if you'd prefer to tackle it by mountain bike.

🛏 Sleeping & Eating

★ **Bazil's Hostel**   HOSTEL $
(☑ 03-789 6410; www.bazils.com; 54 Russell St, Westport; dm $32, d with/without bathroom $110/72; 🛜) Mural-painted Bazil's has homey, well-maintained dorm and private rooms in a sociable setting. It's managed by worldly types who offer surfing lessons

(three hours $80; board and suit hire per day $45), rainforest SUP trips, and social activities aplenty. So do you want the yoga class ($8), something from the pizza oven ($10), or a little of both?

★ **Old Slaughterhouse**   HOSTEL $
(☑ 027 529 7640, 03-782 8333; www.oldslaughter house.co.nz; SH67, Hector; tent sites $22, dm/s/d $40/70/88; ⊙ Oct-Jun) 🌿 Perched on a hillside 32km north of Westport, this lodge and chalets gaze across epic views of the Tasman Sea. Powered largely by a waterwheel, the central lodge has a roomy lounge, shared kitchen, reading nooks and a deck where you can luxuriate in the lack of wi-fi. A steep, 10-minute walk from the car park bolsters its off-the-grid charm.

Carters Beach
Top 10 Holiday Park   HOLIDAY PARK, MOTEL $
(☑ 03-789 8002, 050 893 7876; www.top10west port.co.nz; 57 Marine Pde, Carters Beach; unpowered/powered site from $20/47, units $72-215; 🖥🛜) Right on Carters Beach and located 4km from Westport and 12km to Tauranga Bay, this tidy complex has pleasant sites as well as comfortable cabins and motel units. It's a good option for tourers seeking a peaceful stop-off with a swim (or on foul-weather days, a games room and playground to distract the kids).

Archer House   B&B $$
(☑ 0800 789 877, 03-789 8778; www.archerhouse. co.nz; 75 Queen St, Westport; d incl breakfast $195-245; 🛜) This beautiful 1880s heritage building, formerly the home of a goldfields trader, has original features galore. There are three individually decorated rooms (each one a work of art) with private bathrooms and three tastefully attired lounges in which to swirl a glass of complimentary wine while admiring English stained glass, Moroccan lights, tiled fireplaces and the flourishing garden.

Miners on Sea   CABIN, APARTMENT $$
(☑ 03-782 6646; www.minersonsea.co.nz; 117 Torea St (SH6), Granity; pods d/tr $85/100, chalets $195-245) This place knows what bikers passing through Granity need: serviceable and clean 'pod' rooms (with shared kitchen and bathroom facilities), and adjoining **Tommyknockers** (snacks from $4, mains $18-39; ⊙ 11am-8pm) for easy-to-reach booze and food. More upmarket are the modern, self-contained studio chalets: fireplaces, gleaming bathrooms and marine-themed trimmings that

THE WEST COAST WESTPORT & AROUND

befit their sea-facing location. Breakfast platters cost $17.

Omau Settlers Lodge MOTEL **$$**
(☑03-789 5200; www.omausettlerslodge.co.nz; cnr Cape Foulwind & Omau Rds, Cape Foulwind; d incl breakfast $145-175; ☎) Relaxation is the mantra at this faultless motel near Cape Foulwind. Beds are plump, bathrooms are glossy and fragrant, plus there's a hot tub surrounded by bush. Chatty hosts Karen and Lee offer superb service, and lay out a satisfying continental breakfast. Ask nicely and you might get a lift to the end of Cape Foulwind Walkway.

★ Rough & Tumble Lodge LODGE **$$$**
(☑03-782 1337; www.roughandtumble.co.nz; Mokihinui Rd, Seddonville; d incl continental breakfast $210, extra person $50; ☎) 🐾 With invigorating views of river and bush, this luxe tramping lodge sits at the West Coast end of the Old Ghost Road, at a bend in the Mokihinui River. Its five split-level quad rooms have silver birch banisters, posh bathrooms and verdant views. Bonus: profits are poured back into the maintenance of the walking track.

PR's Cafe CAFE **$**
(☑03-789 7779; 124 Palmerston St, Westport; mains $10-20; ⊙7am-4.30pm Mon-Fri, to 3pm Sat & Sun; ☎) Westport's sharpest cafe has a cabinet full of sandwiches and pastries, and a counter groaning under the weight of cakes (Dutch apple, banoffee pie) and cookies. An all-day menu delivers carefully composed meals such as salmon omelette oozing with dill aioli, spanakopita, and fish and chips.

ℹ Information

Buller Hospital (☑03-788 9030; Cobden St, Westport; ⊙24hr)

DOC Westport Office (☑03-788 8008; www. doc.govt.nz; 72 Russell St, Westport; ⊙8-11am & 2-4.30pm Mon-Fri) DOC bookings and information can be gained from the **i-SITE** (☑03-789 6658; www.buller.co.nz; 123 Palmerston St, Westport; ⊙9am-5pm Mon-Fri, 10am-4pm Sat & Sun; ☎). For curly questions visit this field office.

Westport i-SITE (☑03-789 6658; www. buller.co.nz; 123 Palmerston St, Westport; ⊙9am-5pm Mon-Fri, 10am-4pm Sat & Sun; ☎) Information on local tracks, walkways, tours, accommodation and transport. Self-help terminal for DOC information and hut/track bookings. See also www.westcoastnz.com.

ℹ Getting There & Away

AIR

Sounds Air (☑0800 505 005, 03-520 3080; www.soundsair.com) has two to three flights daily to/from Wellington.

BUS

East West Coaches (☑03-789 6251; www. eastwestcoaches.co.nz) Operates a service through to Christchurch, via Reefton and the Lewis Pass, every day except Saturday, departing from the Caltex petrol station.

InterCity (p243) buses reach Nelson (from $36, 3½ hours) and Greymouth (from $21, 2¼ hours). Change in Greymouth for Franz Josef or Fox Glacier (from $39, six hours). Similar prices on the same routes are available through **Naked Bus** (p243). Buses leave from the **i-SITE** (p268).

Karamea Express (p270) Links Westport and Karamea ($35, two hours, Monday to Friday May to September, plus Saturday from October to April). It also services Kohaihai twice daily during peak summer, and other times on demand. Wangapeka transport is also available.

Trek Express (☑027 222 1872, 0800 128 735; www.trekexpress.co.nz) Passes through Westport on its frequent high-season tramper transport link between Nelson and the Wangapeka/Heaphy Tracks.

ℹ Getting Around

Buller Taxis (☑03-789 6900) can take you to/from the airport (around $25).

Karamea & Around

POP 575

Friendly tramping hub Karamea is colourful, pint-sized, and perched by the enticing wilderness of Kahurangi National Park. As the beginning (or end) point of the Heaphy and Wangapeka Tracks, it's common to see trampers gearing up for adventure (or shuffling wearily to the pub). You can delve into the national park on much shorter walks, in particular around the 35-million-year-old Oparara Basin, whose rainforest hides limestone caverns and natural rock arches.

Driving north from Westport, Karamea is 98 scenic (and petrol station–free) kilometres along SH67 (fill your tank before you set out).

◉ Sights

★ Scotts Beach BEACH
It's almost an hour's walk each way from Kohaihai over the hill to Scotts Beach – a wild,

empty shoreline shrouded in mist, awash in foamy waves, strewn with driftwood and backed by nikau palm forest. Wander in wonder, but don't even think about dipping a toe in – there are dangerous currents at work here.

About 30 minutes into the trail, you can detour to a lookout over the beach if you don't want to tramp the whole distance.

🏃 Activities

The outdoor wonderland of nikau palms, moss-clad forests and stunning shores is the prime reason to visit Karamea. Trampers can launch into the Heaphy Track (p270) or embark on trails around the imposing Oparara Basin. Flexible and friendly **Karamea Outdoor Adventures** (☑03-782 6181; www.karameaadventures.co.nz; Bridge St, Karamea; guided kayak/riverbug trips from $70, 2hr biking trips from $35) offers guided and freedom kayaking and riverbug trips, plus mountain bike hire, horse treks and caving.

Never swim at Karamea's beaches, where currents are wild and waves smash the shore. If you must dip a toe in some water, ask at the information centre about freshwater swimming spots like river holes.

Tramping

Hats off to the Karamea community who established the very pleasant **Karamea Estuary Walkway**, a long-as-you-like stroll bordering the estuary and Karamea River. The adjacent beach can be reached via Flagstaff Rd, north of town. Both feature plenty of bird life and are best walked at sunset. The Karamea Information & Resource Centre (p270) has various maps, including the free *Karamea* brochure, which details other walks such as **Big Rimu** (one hour return to a whopping tree) and the **Zig Zag** (one hour return), which accesses lookouts over peaceful farmland.

Longer walks around Karamea include the **Fenian Walk** (four hours return, bring a torch) leading to **Cavern Creek Cave**, **Tunnel Cave** and **Adams Flat**, where there's a replica gold-miner's hut; and the first leg of the **Wangapeka Track** to Belltown Hut. The Wangapeka Track is a four-to-six-day backcountry trip suitable for highly experienced trampers only.

★ Oparara Basin · · · · · · · · · · TRAMPING

Lying within Kahurangi National Park, the Oparara Basin is a hidden valley concealing limestone arches and caves within a thick forest of massive, moss-laden trees. The valley's signature sight is the 200m-long, 37m-high **Oparara Arch**, spanning the picturesque Oparara River, tannin-stained a fetching shade of caramel, which wends alongside the easy walkway (45 minutes return). The main car park, a 25km drive northeast of Karamea (very rough and narrow in places) is the trailhead for walks of various lengths, and there are excellent information panels here, too.

At the cave mouth of the Oparara Arch walk, some trampers continue uphill for lofty views but it's steep and treacherous (especially after rain), so we advise against it.

The smaller but no less stunning **Moria Gate Arch** (43m long, 19m high) is reached via a simply divine forest loop walk (1½ hours), which also passes the **Mirror Tarn** (itself 15 minutes from the car park).

Just a 10-minute walk from the second car park are the **Crazy Paving and Box Canyon Caves**. Take your torch to enter a world of weird subterranean shapes and rare, leggy spiders. Spiders, caves, darkness...sound like fun!

Beyond this point are the superb **Honeycomb Hill Caves and Arch**, accessible only by guided tours (three-/five-/eight-hour tours $95/150/240) run by the Karamea Information & Resource Centre (p270). Ask about other guided tours of the area, and also about transport for the **Oparara Valley Track**, a rewarding five-hour independent tramp through ancient forest, along the river, popping out at the **Fenian Walk** car park.

To drive to the valley from Karamea, travel 10km along the main road north and turn off at McCallum's Mill Rd, where signposts will direct you a further 14km up and over into the valley along a road that is winding, gravel, rough in places and sometimes steep. Don't attempt it with a campervan.

🛏 Sleeping & Eating

Karamea Farm Baches · · · · · · · · · CABIN $
(☑03-782 6838; www.karameafarmbaches.com; 17 Wharf Rd, Karamea; d/tr/q $99/129/157; 🛜) 🌿 These seven 1960s self-contained baches push reuse and recycle to the limit, from period wallpaper and grandma's carpet to organic vegetables grown on site. Light on luxury but brimming with old-school charm.

Rongo Dinner, Bed & Breakfast · · · B&B $$
(☑03-782 6667; http://rongo.nz; 130 Waverley St, Karamea; half-board s/d $90/180; 🛜) 🌿 Rongo's rainbow-coloured exterior draws you in,

THE WEST COAST KARAMEA & AROUND

DON'T MISS

HEAPHY TRACK DAY WALK

The West Coast road ends 14km from Karamea at **Kohaihai**, the western trailhead (and most commonly, the finish point) of the Heaphy Track, where there's also a **DOC campsite** (www.doc.govt.nz; Kahurangi National Park; sites per adult/child $8/4). A day walk or overnight stay can readily be had from here. Walk to **Scotts Beach** (p268; two hours return), or go as far as the fabulous new Heaphy Hut (five hours) and stay a night or two before returning.

This section can also be mountain-biked, as can the whole track (two to three days) from May to September; ask at Westport's **Habitat Sports** (p266) for bike hire and details.

Helicopter Charter Karamea (☑ 03-782 6111; www.helicharterkaramea.com; 78 Aerodrome Rd, Karamea) offers flights through to the northern trailhead in Golden Bay: up to six passengers $1450; up to five passengers with mountain bikes $1600. (Ask about other drop-off/pick-ups, including the Old Ghost Road.)

while its free-spirited vibe lengthens your stay. Formerly a backpacker hostel, Rongo retains a slouchy, neo-hippie ethos but these days wows guests with zero-kilometre cuisine whipped up by a French chef (breakfasts and dinners included in the price).

Last Resort LODGE $$
(☑ 0800 505 042, 03-782 6617; www.lastresortkaramea.co.nz; 71 Waverley St, Karamea; dm $37, r for 2/3/4 guests with private bathroom $107/127/147, studio from $130; 🛜) Enclosed by greenery some 600m west of Market Cross, this rambling resort suits most budgets, with a choice of rooms with and without private bathrooms. At the posher end of the price range are self-contained two-bedroom cottages (from $155) complete with spa tub. Bonus points for laundry facilities and a comfy communal lounge with TV and tea-making.

The attached **cafe** (snacks from $4, mains $15-30; ⊙ 7.30am-11pm) is the best place in town for a feed.

Karamea Village Hotel PUB FOOD $$
(☑ 03-782 6800; www.karameahotel.co.nz; cnr Waverley St & Wharf Rd, Karamea; meals $15-34; ⊙ 11am-11pm) Here lie simple pleasures and warm hospitality: a game of pool, a pint of ale, and a choice of roast dinners, nachos and beer-battered whitebait, to a soundtrack of local gossip and dinging pokie machines.

ⓘ Information

Karamea Information & Resource Centre
(☑ 03-782 6652; www.karameainfo.co.nz; Market Cross; ⊙ 9am-5pm Mon-Fri, 10am-1pm Sat & Sun, shorter hours May-Dec) This excellent, community-owned centre has the local low-down, internet access, maps and DOC hut tickets. It also doubles as the petrol station.

ⓘ Getting There & Away

Karamea Express (☑ 03-782 6757; info@karamea-express.co.nz) links Karamea and Westport ($35, two hours, Monday to Friday May to September, plus Saturday from October to April). On Mondays and Saturdays, this service connects to a shuttle to Kohaihai ($20). Wangapeka transport is also available. Bookings essential – services are by demand outside peak season.

Heaphy Bus (☑ 0800 128 735, 03-540 2042; www.theheaphybus.co.nz), based in Nelson, services both ends of the Heaphy Track, as well as the Wangapeka.

Fly from Karamea to Takaka with **Helicopter Charter Karamea** (p270), **Golden Bay Air** (☑ 0800 588 885; www.goldenbayair.co.nz) or **Adventure Flights Golden Bay** (☑ 0800 150 338, 03-525 6167; www.adventureflightsgoldenbay.co.nz; from $185) starting from $150 per person, then tramp back on the Heaphy Track; contact the **Karamea Information & Resource Centre** (p270) for details.

Based at **Rongo** (p269), **Karamea Connections** (☑ 03-782 6667; www.karameaconnections.co.nz) runs track and town transport, including services to Heaphy, Wangapeka, Oparara Basin and Westport on demand. Fares vary by group number and destination; for a group of four going from Karamea to the Oparara Basin (with a later pick-up at the Fenian Track), you can expect to pay $25 per head ($10 extra for bikes).

Reefton

POP 1026

In Reefton town, nostalgia permeates every period building and forlorn mining hut. Reefton's gold-mining hey-day is never far from mind, with museums dedicated to the gold rush and a ghost town, 23km south, dating to this lost era. Early adoption of the electricity grid and street lighting gave Reefton its tag line 'the town of light', but these days it's the great outdoors that shines brightest. Reefton is a good base for mountain biking, tramping and rafting, if the good ol' days aren't enough of an enticer to swing by.

◉ Sights

With loads of crusty, century-old buildings situated within a 200m radius, Reefton is well worth a stroll. To find out who lived where and why, undertake the short **Heritage Walk** outlined in the *Historic Reefton* leaflet, available from the Reefton i-SITE (p271).

Waiuta   GHOST TOWN
(www.waiuta.org.nz; off SH7) Remote Waiuta is one of the West Coast's most famous ghost towns. Spread over a square kilometre or so of plateau, this once-burgeoning gold town was abandoned in 1951 after the mineshaft collapsed. Waiuta grew quickly after a gold discovery in 1905 but these days the forest-shrouded settlement is reduced to a big old rusty boiler, an overgrown swimming pool, stranded brick chimneys and the odd intact cottage, which face off against Mother Nature who has sent in the strangleweed.

Drive 23km south of Reefton on SH7 to the signposted turn-off from where it's another 17km, the last half of which is unsealed, winding and narrow in places (keep your headlights on). Ask at Reefton's i-SITE (p271) for information and maps or consult the DOC website.

Bearded Mining Company   HISTORIC BUILDING
(Broadway; admission by donation; ⊙9am-2pm) Looking like a ZZ Top tribute band, the straight-talkin', wispy-bearded fellas at this recreated high-street mining hut introduce you to taxidermied animals, and rollick your socks off with tales tall and true about the good ol' mining days. If you're lucky, you'll be served a cuppa from the billy along with local tips galore.

🏃 Activities

Pick up the *Walks and Tracks of Reefton* leaflet detailing the **Golden Fleece Walk** (15 minutes), **Powerhouse Walk** (25 minutes) and other easy strolls.

Surrounding Reefton is the 206,000-hectare **Victoria Forest Park** (NZ's largest forest park), which sports hidden historic sites, such as the old goldfields around

Blacks Point. Starting at Blacks Point, the enjoyable **Murray Creek Track** is a five-hour return trip. A number of walks, from 90 minutes to three hours, begin in or around the ghost town of Waiuta, 23km south of Reefton.

Longer tramps in the Forest Park include the three-day **Kirwans** or two-day **Big River Track**, both of which can be traversed on a mountain bike. Pick up the free *Reefton Mountain Biking ('the best riding in history')* leaflet for more information; bikes can be hired from **Reefton Sports Centre** (☑03-732 8593; 56 Broadway; bike rental per day $30; ⊙9am-5pm Mon-Fri, 10am-1pm Sat, 11am-2pm Sun), where you can also enquire about legendary trout fishing in the environs.

🛏 Sleeping & Eating

★**Reef Cottage B&B**   B&B $$
(☑03-732 8440; www.reefcottage.co.nz; 51-55 Broadway; d incl breakfast $150-170; 🐾) Enjoy total immersion into olde worlde Reefton at this converted 1887 solicitor's office. Compact rooms are furnished in period style, with modern touches like swish bathrooms and a well-equipped guest kitchen. In our favourite room, a burglar-proof money vault has been converted into the bathroom – privacy guaranteed! There's extra elbow room in the communal lounge and garden, too.

Future Dough Co.   BAKERY $$
(☑03-732 8497; www.thefuturedoughco.co.nz; 31 Broadway; snacks $3-8, meals $13-20; ⊙8am-5pm) This wooden-floored tea room gets by far the most daytime traffic in Reefton, whether for a fresh loaf and homemade shortbread, or a bigger feed of sausage breakfasts, toasties and whitebait lunches. But we're here for the seriously good coffee and jammy, cinnamon-dusted Linzer slice.

ℹ Information

Reefton i-SITE (☑03-732 8391; www.reefton. co.nz; 67-69 Broadway; ⊙9.30am-5pm Mon-Fri, 9.30am-2pm Sat, 9.30am-1pm Sun) Helpful staff, and a compact recreation of the Quartzopolis Mine (gold coin entry). There's internet at the adjoining library, and the building doubles as the postal agency and ATM.

ℹ Getting There & Away

East West Coaches (p268) stops in Reefton every day except Saturday on the run between Westport ($20, 1¼ hours) and Christchurch ($60, four hours).

Murchison & Buller Gorge

POP 492

In Murchison, tumbling river rapids add freshness to the air and forested hills beckon bushwalkers. This humble township, 125km southwest of Nelson and 95km east of Westport, lies on the 'Four Rivers Plain'. The mightiest waterway is the Buller, running alongside Murchison, whose class II-IV rapids have made Murchison hugely popular with experienced rafters, as well as those testing the waters for the first time (some jetboat operators have trips to suit kids... and risk-averse grown-ups).

Unless you have a passion for small-town history and antiques, Murchison itself won't excite you. But a day or two spent rafting or tramping here is a satisfying, adrenaline-drenched way to break up journeys between Nelson and the West Coast.

🏃 Activities & Tours

Ask at the Murchison Information Centre (p273) about local walks, such as the **Skyline Walk**, a 90-minute tramp through fern-filled beech and podocarp forest, and the **Johnson Creek Track**, a two-hour circuit through pine forest to the 'big slip', formed during the 1929 earthquake. Staff can also hook you up with mountain-bike hire and trout-fishing guides.

★ Wild Rivers Rafting　　　　RAFTING
(☑ 0508 467 238, 03-789 8953; www.wildrivers rafting.co.nz; 2hr rafting adult/child $160/85) White-water rafting with Bruce and Marty on the particularly exciting Earthquake

Rapids section of the beautiful Buller River (good luck with 'gunslinger' and the 'pop-up toaster'!).

Ultimate Descents　　　　RAFTING
(☑ 03-523 9899, 0800 748 377; www.rivers.co.nz; 38 Waller St; ⊕) Murchison-based outfit offering white-water rafting and kayaking trips on the Buller, including the classic grade III-IV gorge trip ($160), and gentler family excursions (adult/child $130/100) suitable for kids aged five or more.

Buller Canyon Jet　　　　ADVENTURE SPORTS
(☑ 03-523 9883; www.bullercanyonjet.co.nz; adult/child $110/70; ⊕ Sep-May; ⊕) Launching from the whopping 110m Buller Gorge Swingbridge (p272) is one of NZ's most scenic and best-value jetboat trips – 40 minutes of ripping through the beautiful Buller with a good-humoured captain.

Buller Gorge Swingbridge　　　ADVENTURE SPORTS
(☑ 0800 285 537; www.bullergorge.co.nz; SH6; bridge crossing adult/child $10/5; ⊕ 8am-7pm Dec-Apr, 9am-5.30pm May-Nov; ⊕) About 15km west of Murchison is NZ's longest swingbridge (110m), across which lie short bushwalks taking in the White Creek Faultline, epicentre of the 1929 earthquake, and former gold-mining sites. Alternatively, ride the 160m Cometline Flying Fox, either seated (adult/child $30/15) or forward-facing 'Supaman' style (adult $60).

Natural Flames Experience　　　TOURS
(☑ 0800 687 244, 027 698 7244; www.natural flames.co.nz; 34 Waller St; adult/child $95/65) Who would have thought oil-drilling history would be a high point of your trip? This

---

WHITEBAIT FEVER

If you visit the West Coast between September and mid-November, you're sure to catch a whiff of whitebait fever. The West Coast is gripped by an annual craze for tiny, transparent fish, and netting buckets of whitebait is an all-consuming, highly competitive passion. Firstly there's money in it (from $60 to $70 per kilo along the coast, and much more elsewhere), then there's the satisfaction of netting more than your neighbours. Riverbanks bustle with baiters from Karamea to Haast, but ask a whitebaiter if they're catching much and they'll likely say no...to throw you off the scent of their best whitebaiting spots.

In season you'll see whitebait sold from backdoors and served in cafes and restaurants. They mostly surface in a pattie, made best with just an egg, and accompanied by a wedge of lemon or perhaps mint sauce. We've seen them topping pizzas and salads, too.

Whitebait are the young of native fish, including inanga, kokopu, smelt and eels. Conservationists say they shouldn't be eaten at all, with some species threatened or in decline. The DOC applies stiff penalties for anyone breaching their rules on whitebaiting season and the size of nets, and they urge locals to keep their catch small.

informative half-day 4WD and bushwalking tour through verdant valleys, beech forest and capped oil wells arrives at a hot spot where natural gas seeping out of the ground has been burning since 1922. Boil a billy on the flames and cook pancakes before returning to civilisation.

🛏 Sleeping

Lazy Cow   HOSTEL **$**
(☑ 03-523 9451; www.lazycow.co.nz; 37 Waller St; dm $32-35, d & tw $90-110; 🛜) It's easy to be a lazy cow here, with all the comforts of home in a stress-free, small-scale package. Four-bed dorms and private rooms all have electric blankets and guests are welcomed with free muffins or cake, which you can enjoy in the backyard or cosy lounge.

Riversong Cottages   COTTAGE **$$**
(☑ 03-523 9011; www.riversong.co.nz; 30 Fairfax St; studio $110, unit from $180; 🛜) Boutique studio and two-bedroom units open out to a big, grassy yard and vegetable garden at this relaxed and refined set-up, and hosts Arran and Alonia offer service with a personal touch.

Murchison Lodge   B&B **$$**
(☑ 021 27 27 228, 03-523 9196; www.murchison lodge.co.nz; 15 Grey St; d $170-240; 🛜) This quality B&B surrounded by extensive gardens and paddocks is a short walk from the Buller River. Attractive timber features and charming hosts add to the comfortable feel. A hearty breakfast, home baking and plenty of local information are complimentary.

🍴 Eating

Sweet Dreams   BAKERY **$**
(☑ 03-523 9742; www.facebook.com/sweetdreams frenchbakery; 52 Fairfax St; pastries from $4; ⊘ 8.30am-3pm Wed-Sun) An authentic French bakery in Murchison? *Mais oui!* Macarons, croissants and proper French bread brim from the shelves of candy-coloured Sweet Dreams. Come early, the shop closes when the day's stock has been eaten.

★**Cow Shed**   PIZZA **$$**
(☑ 03-523 9523; http://lazycow.co.nz/eating; 37 Waller St; mains $18-24; ⊘ 5-9pm Mon-Fri; 🖉) In the garage of the Lazy Cow (p273) backpackers, the cute Cow Shed restaurant is a deservedly popular option for its crisp, generously topped pizzas served in intimate surrounds. There's a daily non-pizza option (lasagna, enchiladas), tangy dressed side-salads, Italy-inflected desserts and takeaway for those who can't get a table. Gluten-free options available.

🛍 Shopping

Dust & Rust   ANTIQUES
(☑ 03-523 9300; www.dustandrust.nz; 35 Fairfax St; ⊘ 10am-5pm Dec-Feb, 10am-5pm Thu-Mon Sep-Nov & Mar-May, closed Jun-Aug) Rummage an ever-changing array of vintage cars, foreign number-plates, hubcaps, 1970s kitchenware and vintage clothing at this impressive archive of curios. They're all originals – dust and rust comes included in the price.

ℹ Information

Murchison Information Centre (☑ 03-523 9350; www.visitmurchison.nz; 47 Waller St; ⊘ 10am-5pm daily Dec-Mar, 10am-4pm Mon-Fri Apr & Oct-Nov, closed May-Sep) Activity and hotel bookings plus bags of local info.

ℹ Getting There & Away

Daily **Intercity** (p243) and **Naked Bus** (p243) services travelling from Picton ($47, three hours) and Nelson (from $29, two hours) pass through Murchison, with one continuing to Westport (from $24, 1½ hours) on the West Coast. During the peak tramping season **Trek Express** (p268) passes through, between Nelson and the Wangapeka/Heaphy Tracks.

Buses stop at Beechwoods Cafe on Waller St.

Nelson & Marlborough

Best Places to Eat

➜ Arbour (p315)

➜ Hopgood's (p286)

➜ Rock Ferry (p315)

➜ Cod & Lobster (p285)

➜ Boat Shed Cafe (p290)

Best Places to Stay

➜ Hopewell (p305)

➜ Bay of Many Coves Resort (p306)

➜ Lemon Tree Lodge (p321)

➜ Zatori Retreat (p301)

➜ St Leonards (p313)

Why Go?

For many travellers, Marlborough and Nelson will be their introduction to what South Islanders refer to as the 'Mainland'. Having left windy Wellington, and made a white-knuckled crossing of Cook Strait, folk are often surprised to find the sun shining and the temperature 10°C warmer.

These top-of-the-South neighbours have much in common beyond an amenable climate: both boast renowned coastal holiday spots, particularly the Marlborough Sounds, Abel Tasman National Park and Kaikoura. There are two other national parks (Kahurangi and Nelson Lakes) amid more mountain ranges than you can poke a Leki stick at.

The two regions also have an abundance of produce, from game and seafood to summer fruits, and most famously the grapes that work their way into the wine glasses of the world's finest restaurants. Keep your penknife and picnic set at the ready.

When to Go

➜ The forecast is good: Marlborough and Nelson soak up some of New Zealand's sunniest weather, with January and February the warmest months when daytime temperatures average 22°C.

➜ July is the coldest, averaging 12°C. However, the top of the South sees some wonderful winter weather, with frosty mornings often giving way to sparklingly clear skies and T-shirt temperatures.

➜ The rumours are true: it *is* wetter and more windswept the closer you get to the West Coast.

➜ From around Christmas to mid-February, the top of the South teems with Kiwi holidaymakers, so plan ahead during this time and be prepared to jostle for position with a load of jandal (flip-flop)–wearing families.

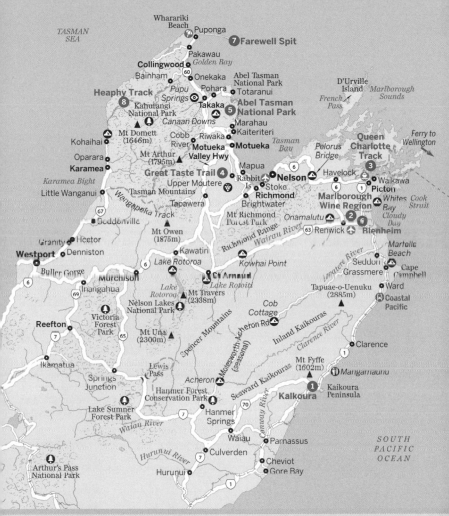

Nelson & Marlborough Highlights

1 **Kaikoura** (p316) Getting up close to wildlife, including whales, seals, dolphins and albatrosses.

2 **Marlborough Wine Region** (p314) Nosing your way through the wineries.

3 **Queen Charlotte Track** (p279) Tramping or biking in the Marlborough Sounds.

4 **Great Taste Trail** (p289) Eating and drinking your way along this popular cycle trail.

5 **Abel Tasman National Park** (p294) Kayaking or tramping in this postcard-perfect park.

6 **Omaka Aviation Heritage Centre** (p311)

Getting blown away at one of New Zealand's best museums.

7 **Farewell Spit** (p302) Driving through a dunescape with gannets and godwits for company.

8 **Heaphy Track** (p280) Reaching the wild West Coast on foot, crossing through Kahurangi National Park.

DAY TRIPS FROM NELSON

MARLBOROUGH SOUNDS

The deeply indented watery tentacles of the Marlborough Sounds are the defining feature of the South Island's northeastern tip. You can get a decent taster by car but for the full feast you'll need to get out on the water. From Nelson, the closest access point is Havelock, although a greater range of tours depart from Picton.

☆ Best Things to See/Do/Eat

◉ **Motuara Island** Sitting near the very end of Queen Charlotte Sound, this little island is an important predator-free refuge for native birds. It's most easily visited on a tour from Picton. (p303)

🌿 **Pelorus Eco Adventures** Recreate the barrel scene from *The Hobbit* – albeit in an inflatable kayak – paddling on the same stretch of the Pelorus River that they used in the movie. There are a few rapids and lovely views of forest and waterfalls. (p305)

✗ **Picton Village Bakkerij** Stock up for a picnic or stop for lunch at this excellent Dutch-owned bakery. (p310)

☆ How to Get There

Car From Nelson, head east on SH6. It takes about an hour to reach Havelock, gateway to Pelorus Sound, and an additional 45 minutes to get to Picton on Queen Charlotte Sound. Buses are infrequent.

BLENHEIM

Blenheim is a pretty but unassuming little country town that has come to prominence as the gateway to the world-famous Marlborough Wine Region. Draw straws to decide on a sober driver and then embark on a day filled with wine, food and heritage planes.

☆ Best Things to See/Do/Eat

◉ **Omaka Aviation Heritage Centre** Check out Sir Peter Jackson's own collection of WWI and WWII aircraft, dramatically displayed amongst wartime scenes in this groundbreaking museum. There's also a classic car museum next door. (p311)

🌿 **Wine Tasting** Marlborough is NZ's most prestigious wine region, with its signature sauvignon blanc gracing tables from Timaru to Timbuktu. Find out what all the fuss is about, touring some of the 35 wineries with public tasting rooms. Big names include Cloudy Bay, Spy Valley, Huia, St Clair Estate, Brancott Estate and Te Whare Ra. (p314)

✗ **Arbour** Fine wines and fine dining go hand in hand, and the Marlborough countryside is dotted with excellent restaurants. Our pick is upmarket Arbour near Renwick. (p315)

☆ How to Get There

Car It takes just over an hour and a half to drive to Blenheim from Nelson, heading east on SH6. There are buses but they're not frequent.

ABEL TASMAN NATIONAL PARK

The outstanding beaches of the Abel Tasman National Park lie just across the bay from Nelson. The consummate experience is a multiday hike or kayak along the coast, but you can get a good teaser on a day trip.

☆ Best Things to See/Do/Eat

🥾 **Abel Tasman Coast Track** Clearly you're not going to be able to walk all 60km in a day, but starting from Marahau you'll be able to wander to some gorgeous golden-sand beaches before it's time to turn back. (p279)

🥾 **Kayaking Tour** Numerous companies offering guided sea-kayaking trips along the Abel Tasman Coast, most of which depart from Marahau. It's also possible to hire kayaks for self-guided explorations, although you're best to paddle with a companion. (p296)

🍴 **Boat Shed Cafe** On the way or back, take a detour to little Mapua for a meal or a beer with a view at this waterside cafe. The gourmet cheeseburgers are excellent. (p290)

☆ How to Get There

Car From Nelson it takes around an hour to reach Marahau by car. Head southwest on SH6 and turn right onto SH60 just past Richmond. Shortly after Riwaka turn off onto the windy Riwaka-Sandy Bay Rd.

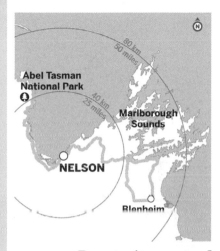

Due to its central location and proximity to the Marlborough Sounds and three extraordinary national parks, the city of Nelson makes a great base for exploring this region.

TRAMPING IN NELSON & MARLBOROUGH

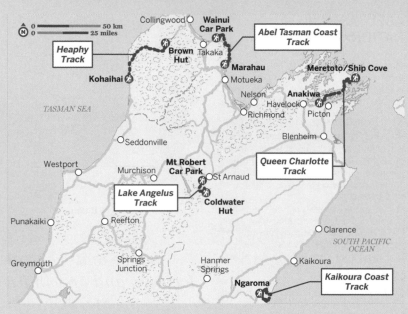

KAIKOURA COAST TRACK

START/END NGAROMA
DURATION 2 DAYS
DISTANCE 26KM
DIFFICULTY EASY TO MODERATE

In 1994 adjoining farms along the Kaikoura coast were searching for a way to diversify their activities while preserving, even expanding, their large areas of native forest and bush. Taking a cue from the Banks Track, the country's first private track, just down the coast, the farmers/landowners formed one of their own, opening up their farms and homes to a small number of trampers each day.

Kaikoura Coast Track is a two-day tramp that has you traversing tussock tops and skirting the Pacific Ocean, keeping an eye out for marine wildlife. A large part of the experience, however, is the farms themselves, Medina and Ngaroma – scattering sheep as you cut through a paddock, stopping to watch sheepdogs round up a flock, and sipping lemonade made from freshly squeezed, home-grown lemons. It's a tramp through remote and rural NZ, with your hosts each night being the families who work the farms. For many that's as intriguing as the view from Skull Peak. The track fee includes both comfortable accommodation and the transport of your luggage and food. That means every night you can enjoy a hot shower and a soft bed, and pack along a few steaks and a bottle of good NZ wine. Without having to haul a backpack, the climbs are easily accomplished by most trampers, and you can then recover with a bit of luxury at night before setting out the next day.

The number of trampers on the track is limited to 10 per day, so bookings are essential if you have particular dates you want to walk. The cost is $200 per person (students $180), which includes transfers of luggage, accommodation and secured parking. Book through **Kaikoura Coast Track** (☎ 03-319 2715; www.kaikouratrack.co.nz; 356 Conway Flat Rd, Ngaroma).

Welcome to the sunny side! This end of the South Island has more sunshine hours than any other, which means long, sun-baked days that are perfect for tramping.

QUEEN CHARLOTTE TRACK

START MERETOTO/SHIP COVE
END ANAKIWA
DURATION 4 DAYS
DISTANCE 71KM
DIFFICULTY MODERATE

The hugely popular, meandering Queen Charlotte Track offers gorgeous coastal scenery on its way from historic Meretoto/Ship Cove to Anakiwa, passing through a mixture of privately owned land and DOC reserves. The coastal forest is lush, and from the ridges there are regular views into either Queen Charlotte or Kenepuru Sounds.

Queen Charlotte is a well-defined track, suitable for people of most fitness levels. It can be completed in three to five days, and can be walked in either direction, though Meretoto/Ship Cove is the usual (and recommended) starting point. This is mainly because it's easier to arrange a boat from Picton to Meretoto/Ship Cove than the reverse. It can also be walked in sections by hopping aboard numerous boat services. A good two-day tramp is from Meretoto/Ship Cove to Punga Cove (27km), while recommended day walks include the sections from Mistletoe Bay to Anakiwa (12.5km), or from Meretoto/Ship Cove to Furneaux Lodge (15km).

You can also turn the tramp into a multisport outing by combining sections of hiking with kayaking or mountain biking. In 2013 the track was opened to cyclists, though they're forbidden from riding the section between Meretoto/Ship Cove and Kenepuru Saddle from 1 December to the end of February.

Six DOC camping grounds are dotted along the route, while other accommodation ranges from old-fashioned home-stays to luxury waterfront lodges. This is one of the enduring appeals of the track – the chance to spend the day tramping, then enjoy a hot shower and a cold beer at the end of it. Boat operators will also happily transport your pack along the track for you as a packhorse-type service. At first it seems decadent...then it just seems welcome.

The district council, DOC and private landowners manage the track as a partnership. The private landowners are members of the Queen Charlotte Track Land Cooperative (www.qctlc.com). They require each track user to purchase and display a pass for the private-land sections between Kenepuru Saddle and Bottle Bay (a one-day pass costs $10, while the $18 pass covers you for up to five consecutive days). Passes can be purchased from various accommodation providers and boat operators near the track, and from the Picton or Blenheim i-SITEs.

ABEL TASMAN COAST TRACK

START MARAHAU
END WAINUI CAR PARK
DURATION 5 DAYS
DISTANCE 60KM
DIFFICULTY EASY

Think of it as a beach holiday on foot. Arguably the most beautiful of the Great Walks, the Abel Tasman Coast Track is a seductive combination of reliably pleasant weather, sparkling seas, golden sand, quintessential NZ coastal forest and hidden surprises with intriguing names such as Cleopatra's Pool. Pretty sure we have your attention now...

You're not alone. Such is the pulling power of this track that it now attracts more than 43,000 trampers and kayakers each year who stay at least one night in the park. By way of comparison, the next most popular Great Walk is the Routeburn Track, which draws around 17,000.

Another attraction is the terrain, for this is not a typical, rugged New Zealand track. It is better serviced than any other track in the country: well cut, well graded and well marked. It's almost impossible to get lost and can be tramped in a pair of running shoes. Leaving the boots behind is a bonus, as you'll probably get your feet wet –

indeed, you'll probably want to get your feet wet.

This is a track with long stretches of beach walking and crazy tides to work around. The tidal ranges in the park are among the greatest in the country – up to a staggering 6m. At Awaroa Bay you have no choice but to plan on crossing at low tide. Tide times are published on the the DOC website (www.doc.govt.nz), and also displayed at DOC's Nelson Visitor Centre and regional i-SITEs. It's important to consult these at the time of planning your trip, as the times of the tides will affect the huts or campsites that you use and the direction in which you walk the track.

The tramp finishes at a car park near Wainui Bay, though most people extend their hike beyond Wainui by returning to Totaranui via the Gibbs Hill Track to pick up the water taxis back to Marahau or Kaiteriteri. You could always just stop at Totaranui the first time you walk through, but by continuing north you will discover the most dramatic view point (Separation Point), the least-crowded hut (Whariwharangi) and some of the best beaches (Anapai and Mutton Cove) in the park.

The entire tramp takes only three to five days, although with water-taxi transport you can convert it into an almost endless array of options, particularly if you combine it with a kayak leg. Note, however, that kayaks aren't available from within the park and have to be brought in and out from Marahau/Kaiteriteri each day. If you plan to combine a tramp with kayaking, you should arrange the logistics with a kayak hire company before you book huts or campsites to ensure everything aligns.

If you can only spare a couple of days to tramp here, a deservedly popular option is the loop around the northern end of the park, hiking the Coast Track from Totaranui, passing Anapai and Mutton Cove, overnighting at Whariwharangi Hut then returning to Totaranui via the Gibbs Hill Track. This will give you a slice of the park's best features (beaches, seals, coastal scenery) and will be far less crowded than any other segment.

Those wishing to explore the interior of the national park might like to consider the Inland Track, a tougher and much less frequented path taking three days. It can be combined with the Coast Track to form a five- to six-day loop.

TOBIN AKEHURST /SHUTTERSTOCK ©

Abel Tasman Coast Track

HEAPHY TRACK

START BROWN HUT
END KOHAIHAI
DURATION 5 DAYS
DISTANCE 78.5KM
DIFFICULTY MODERATE

The Heaphy Track is one of the most popular tracks in the country. A Great Walk in every sense, it traverses diverse terrain – dense native forest, the mystical Gouland Downs, secluded river valleys, and beaches dusted in salt spray and fringed by nikau palms.

Although quite long, the Heaphy is well cut and benched, making it easier than any other extended tramp found in Kahurangi National Park. That said, you may still find it arduous, particularly in unfavourable weather.

Walking from east to west most of the climbing is done on the first day, and the scenic beach walk is saved for the end, a fitting and invigorating grand finale.

The track is open to mountain bikers between May and October. Factoring in distance, remoteness and the possibility of bad weather, this epic journey is only suited to well-equipped cyclists with advanced riding skills. A good port of call for more

Kaikoura Coast Track (p278)

information is the **Quiet Revolution Cycle Shop** (p298) in Takaka.

A strong tramper could walk the Heaphy in three days, but most people take four or five days. For a detailed track description, see DOC's *Heaphy Track* brochure.

LAKE ANGELUS TRACK

START MT ROBERT CAR PARK
END COLDWATER HUT
DURATION 2 DAYS
DISTANCE 21.5KM
DIFFICULTY MODERATE

Despite its relatively short length, this tramp rates as one of the best in the country, showcasing all that's good about Nelson Lakes National Park. In fine weather, the walk along Robert Ridge is spectacular – seldom do tramps afford such an extended period across such open tops. The views will blow your socks off, as they will again as you descend into the extraordinary Lake Angelus basin (1650m) and Angelus Hut, which is a good base for short forays to the ridge above the lake and to Mt Angelus. A two-night stay at Angelus Hut is highly desirable.

Angelus Hut is an alpine hut and weather conditions can change rapidly. Snow, frost and freezing winds can occur even in midsummer, so visitors should be well equipped when attempting this tramp.

NELSON

POP 46,440

Dishing up a winning combination of beautiful surroundings, sophisticated art and culinary scenes, and lashings of sunshine, Nelson is hailed as one of New Zealand's most 'liveable' cities. In summer it fills up with local and international visitors, who lap up its diverse offerings.

◉ Sights

★ Tahuna Beach
BEACH

Nelson's primo playground takes the form of an epic sandy beach (with lifeguards in summer) backed by dunes, and a large grassy parkland with a playground, an espresso cart, a hydroslide, bumper boats, a roller-skating rink, a model railway, and an adjacent restaurant strip. Weekends can get very busy!

★ World of WearableArt & Classic Cars Museum
MUSEUM

(WOW; ☑ 03-547 4573; www.wowcars.co.nz; 1 Cadillac Way; adult/child $24/10; ☺ 10am-5pm) Nelson is the birthplace of NZ's most inspiring fashion show, the annual World of WearableArt Awards. You can see 70 or so current and past entries in this museum's several sensory-overloading galleries, including a glow-in-the-dark room. Look out for the 'Bizarre Bras'.

ESSENTIAL NELSON & MARLBOROUGH

....

Eat amid the vines at Marlborough's excellent vineyard restaurants.

Drink pale ale infused with local Riwaka hops at Hop Federation (p292).

Read *How to Have a Beer* (2017) by Alice Galletly.

Listen to the dawn chorus in Nelson Lakes National Park (p288).

Watch the horizon to spot whales around Kaikoura.

Celebrate at the Marlborough Wine & Food Festival (☑ 03-577 9299; www.wine-marlborough-festival.co.nz; tickets $62; ☺ mid-Feb).

Go green at Lochmara (p303) learning about its eco-protection programs.

Go online www.marlboroughnz.com, www.nelsonnz.com, www.kaikoura.co.nz

---

More car than bra? Under the same roof are more than 100 mint-condition classic cars and motorbikes. Exhibits change, but may include a 1959 pink Cadillac, a yellow 1950 Bullet Nose Studebaker convertible and a BMW bubble car.

Christ Church Cathedral
CHURCH

(Map p284; www.nelsoncathedral.org; Trafalgar Sq; ☺ 9am-6pm) **FREE** The enduring symbol of Nelson, the art-deco Christ Church Cathedral lords it over the city from the top of Trafalgar St. The best time to visit is during the 10am and 7pm Sunday services when you can hear the organist and the choir in song.

Nelson Provincial Museum
MUSEUM

(Map p284; ☑ 03-548 9588; www.nelsonmuseum.co.nz; cnr Trafalgar & Hardy Sts; adult/child $5/3; ☺ 10am-5pm Mon-Fri, to 4.30pm Sat & Sun) This modern museum space is filled with cultural heritage and natural history exhibits that have a regional bias, as well as regular touring exhibitions (for which admission fees vary). It also features a great rooftop garden.

Suter Art Gallery
GALLERY

(Map p284; www.thesuter.org.nz; 208 Bridge St; ☺ 9.30am-4.30pm) **FREE** Adjacent to Queen's Gardens (p282), Nelson's public art gallery presents changing exhibitions, floor talks, musical and theatrical performances, and films. The Suter reopened after a fabulous redevelopment in late 2016 and now features an arthouse cinema and a great riverside cafe. Check the website to find out what's on.

Queen's Gardens
GARDENS

(Map p284; Bridge St) Immerse yourself in around 125 years of botanical history in this ornamental garden, which commemorates the 50th jubilee of Queen Victoria's coronation. Great for a picnic or lawny lie-down.

Botanical Reserve
PARK

(Milton St) Walking tracks ascend Botanical Hill, where a spire proclaims the **Centre of New Zealand**. NZ's first-ever rugby match was played at the foot of the hill on 14 May 1870: Nelson Rugby Football Club trounced the lily-livered players from Nelson College 2-0.

Founders Heritage Park
MUSEUM

(☑ 03-548 2649; www.founderspark.co.nz; 87 Atawhai Dr; adult/child/family $7/5/15; ☺ 10am-4.30pm) Two kilometres from the city centre, this park comprises a replica historic village with a museum, gallery displays, and artisan products such as chocolate and clothing. It makes for a fascinating wander, which you can augment with a visit to the on-site **Park Life Brewery** (☑03-548 4638; www.facebook. com/parklifebrewing; ⊙9am-4.30pm Mon-Fri, to 5.30pm Sat & Sun). Check its Facebook page for occasional Food Truck Fridays from 5pm (late October to Easter).

McCashin's Brewery   BREWERY
(☑03-547 5357; www.mccashins.co.nz; 660 Main Rd, Stoke; ⊙7am-6pm Mon-Wed, 7am-10pm Thu & Fri, 9am-10pm Sat, 9am-8pm Sun) A groundbreaker in the new era of craft brewing in NZ, which started way back in the 1980s. Visit the historic cider factory for a tasting, cafe meal or tour.

🏃 Activities

Walking & Cycling

There's plenty of walking and cycling to be enjoyed in and around the town, for which the i-SITE (p287) has maps. The classic walk from town is to the **Centre of NZ** atop the Botanical Reserve (p282), if you enjoy that then ask about the **Grampians**.

Nelson has two of the New Zealand Cycle Trail's 23 Great Rides: **Dun Mountain Trail** (www.heartofbiking.org.nz), an awesome but challenging one-day ride ranging over the hills to the south of the city; and the Great Taste Trail (p289) offering a blissfully flat meander through beautiful countryside dotted with wine, food and art stops.

Gentle Cycling Company   CYCLING
(☑03-929 5652, 0800 932 453; www.gentle cycling.co.nz; 411 Nayland Rd, Stoke; day tours from $95) Self-guided cycle tours along the Great Taste Trail, with drop-ins (and tastings) at wineries, breweries, cafes and occasional galleries. Bike hire (from $30) and shuttles also available.

Other Activities

Nelson is a great place for adrenaline activities, with plenty of action in summer, particularly around the rather divine Tahuna Beach (p282). Tandem paragliding costs around $180, introductory kitesurfing starts at $150, and paddle-board hire is around $20 per hour.

Cable Bay Kayaks   KAYAKING
(☑03-391 0010; www.cablebaykayaks.co.nz; Cable Bay Rd, Hira; half-/full-day guided trips $90/150) Fifteen minutes' drive from Nelson city, Greig and the team offer richly rewarding guided sea-kayaking trips exploring the

local coastline, where you'll likely meet local marine life (snorkelling gear on board helps). You might even enter a cave.

Moana SUP   WATER SPORTS
(☑027 656 0268; www.moananzsup.co.nz; lessons from $70) Learn SUP with the guys at Moana, or hire a board if you're already enlightened.

Nelson Paragliding   PARAGLIDING
(☑03-544 1182; www.nelsonparagliding.co.nz; Ngawhatu Recreation Ground, Stoke; tandem paragliding $220) Get high in the sky over Tahunanui with Nelson Paragliding.

Kite Surf Nelson   KITESURFING
(☑0800 548 363; www.kitesurfnelson.co.nz; lessons from $175) Learn to kite surf at Tahunanui, or hire a stand-up paddle board.

👉 Tours

Nelson Tours & Travel   TOURS
(☑027 237 5007, 0800 222 373; www.nelsontours andtravel.co.nz) CJ and crew run various small-group, flexible tours honing in on Nelson's wine, craft beer, art and scenic highlights. The five-hour 'Best of Both Worlds' ($140) tour includes beer, wine and lunch at the heritage Moutere Inn. Day tours of Marlborough wineries also available ($250).

🎉 Festivals & Events

For current info on Nelson's active events program, visit www.itson.co.nz.

Nelson Jazz Festival   MUSIC
(www.nelsonjazzfest.co.nz; ⊙Jan) More scoo-be-doo-bop events over a week in January than you can shake a leg at. Features local and national acts.

🛏 Sleeping

Prince Albert   HOSTEL $
(Map p284; ☑0800 867 3529, 03-548 8477; www. theprincealbert.co.nz; 113 Nile St; dm $27-29, s/d/ tw $50/85/85; 🛜) A five-minute walk from the city centre, this lively, well-run backpackers has roomy en-suite dorms surrounding a sunny courtyard. Private rooms are upstairs in the main building, which also houses an English-style pub where guests can meet the locals and refuel with a good-value meal.

Bug Backpackers   HOSTEL $
(☑03-539 4227; www.thebug.co.nz; 226 Vanguard St; dm $26-29, d $69-95; @🛜) A buzzy hostel about 15-minutes' walk from town, occupying a converted villa, a modern building

Central Nelson

next door and a self-contained unit sleeping up to four. The VW-themed Bug boasts an unashamedly bold colour scheme, a homey backyard and jovial owners. Free bikes, wi-fi and pick-ups/drop-offs.

Tasman Bay Backpackers　　HOSTEL **$**
(☑0800 222 572, 03-548 7950; www.tasmanbay backpackers.co.nz; 10 Weka St; sites from $20, dm $28-30, d $76-88; @ 🛜) This well-designed, friendly hostel has airy communal spaces with a 100% Kiwi music soundtrack, hypercoloured rooms, a sunny outdoor deck and a well-used hammock. Good freebies: wi-fi, decent bikes, breakfast during winter, and chocolate pudding and ice cream year-round.

Sussex House　　B&B **$$**
(☑03-548 9972; www.sussex.co.nz; 238 Bridge St; d $170-190, tr $180; 🛜) In a relatively quiet riverside spot, only a five-minute walk to town, this creaky old lady dates back to around

1880. The five tastefully decorated rooms feature upmarket bedding, period-piece furniture and en-suite bathrooms, except one room that has a private bathroom down the hall. Enjoy local fruit at breakfast in the grand dining room.

Te Maunga House　　B&B **$$**
(☑021 201 2461; www.nelsoncityaccommodation. co.nz; 15 Dorothy Annie Way; s $80-100, d $125-140; ☺closed May-Oct; 🛜) Aptly named (The Mountain), this grand old family home has exceptional views and a well-travelled host. Two doubles and a twin have a homey feel with comfy beds and their own bathrooms. Your hearty breakfast can be walked off up and down *that* hill, a very steep 10-minute climb with an extra five minutes to town.

Cedar Grove Motor Lodge　　MOTEL **$$**
(Map p284; ☑03-545 1133; www.cedargrove.co.nz; cnr Trafalgar & Grove Sts; d $160-210; 🛜) A big old cedar landmark, this smart, modern block of

Central Nelson

spacious apartments is just a three-minute walk to town. Its range of studios and doubles are plush and elegant, with full cooking facilities.

Palazzo Motor Lodge   MOTEL $$$
(Map p284; ☑03-545 8171, 0800 472 5293; www.palazzomotorlodge.co.nz; 159 Rutherford St; d $210-335; ☎) This modern, Italian-tinged motor lodge offers stylish studios and one- and two-room apartments featuring enviable kitchens with decent cooking equipment, classy glassware and a dishwasher. Its comfort and convenient location easily atone for the odd bit of dubious art.

🍴 Eating

Nelson has a lively cafe scene and a varied array of restaurants. Self-caterers should steer resolutely towards the fruitful **Nelson Market** (Map p284; ☑03-546 6454; www.nelsonmarket.co.nz; Montgomery Sq; ⊙8am-1pm Sat) on Saturday and the Wednesday **farmers market** (☑022 010 2776; www.nelsonfarmersmarket.org.nz; Maitai Blvd, Paru Paru Rd; ⊙8am-2pm Wed). Trafalgar St beneath the cathedral has the city's best restaurants and pleasant outdoor seating, while there's everything from Vietnamese and Korean flavours to Spanish tapas on Hardy St west of Trafalgar.

Falafel Gourmet   MIDDLE EASTERN $
(Map p284; ☑03-545 6220; 195 Hardy St; meals $11-19; ⊙10am-4pm Mon-Sat; ☑) A cranking joint dishing out the best kebabs for miles around. They're healthy, too!

Stefano's   PIZZA $
(Map p284; ☑03-546 7630; www.pizzeria.co.nz; 91 Trafalgar St; pizzas $8-33; ⊙noon-2pm & 4.30-9pm; ☑) Located upstairs in the **State Cinemas** (Map p284; ☑03-548 3885; www.statecinemas.co.nz; tickets $16.50) complex, this Italian-run joint turns out the town's best pizza. Thin, crispy, authentic and delicious, with some variations a veritable bargain. Wash it down with a beer and chase it with a creamy dessert.

Swedish Bakery & Cafe   BAKERY $
(Map p284; ☑03-546 8685; www.facebook.com/TheSwedishBakeryandCafe; 54 Bridge St; snacks $3-8; ⊙8am-3pm Tue-Fri, to 1.30pm Sat) Delicious breads, pastries, cakes and small chocolate treats from the resident Scandinavian baker. Freshly filled rolls and croissants are delicious too. Take your goodies away or eat in the bijou cafe.

★ Cod & Lobster   SEAFOOD, BISTRO $$
(Map p284; ☑03-546 4300; www.codandlobster.com; 300 Trafalgar St; mains $22-36; ⊙11am-11pm) Stellar cocktails and NZ's biggest selection of gin make Cod & Lobster's corner bar an essential destination, but this heritage space also serves up excellent food. Unsurprisingly, seafood is the main focus, so enliven your palate with Bloody Mary oyster shooters before moving on to Louisiana-style prawns with spicy sausage or the good-value seafood platter ($40 for two people).

A concise selection of steak, chicken and vegetarian dishes is available, but it's the briny-fresh catch of the day you're really here for.

Urban Oyster
MODERN NZ $$

(Map p284; ☑03-546 7861; www.urbaneatery. co.nz; 278 Hardy St; dishes $11-27; ⊙4pm-late Mon, 11am-late Tue-Sat) Slurp oysters from the shell, or revitalise with sashimi and ceviche, then sate your cravings with street-food dishes such as kung pao Sichuan fried chicken or smoked-pork empanadas with charcoal shrimp mayo. Black butchers' tiles, edgy artwork and a fine wine list all bolster this metropolitan experience, and craft beers come courtesy of Golden Bear Brewing in nearby Mapua.

DeVille
CAFE $$

(Map p284; ☑03-545 6911; www.devillecafe.co.nz; 22 New St; meals $12-21; ⊙8am-4pm Mon-Sat, 9am-3pm Sun; ☑) Most of DeVille's tables lie in its sweet walled courtyard, a hidden boho oasis in the inner city and the perfect place for a meal or morning tea. The food's good and local – from fresh baking to a chorizo-burrito brunch, Caesar salad and proper burgers, washed down with regional wines and beers. Open late for live music Fridays in summer.

Morri Street Cafe
CAFE $$

(Map p284; ☑03-548 8110; www.morrison streetcafe.co.nz; 244 Hardy St; mains $11-21; ⊙7.30am-3.30pm Mon-Fri, 8.30am-4pm Sat & Sun; ☑) Shared tables, colourful local art and a quieter atrium at the back all combine to make Morri Street a top place for a leisurely breakfast or lunch. You may have to share

---

IN PURSUIT OF HOPPINESS

The Nelson region lays claim to the title of craft-brewing capital of New Zealand. World-class hops have been grown here since the 1840s, and around a dozen breweries are spread between Nelson and Golden Bay.

Pick up a copy of the *Nelson Craft Beer Trail* map (available from the i-SITE (p287) and other outlets, and online at www.craftbrewingcapital.co.nz) and wind your way between brewers and pubs. Top picks for a tipple include **Free House** and the **Craft Beer Depot** in Nelson, **Hop Federation** (p292) in Riwaka, and the Townshend Brewery at Motueka's **Toad Hall** (p292).

---

the buzzy space with a few locals having impromptu business meetings, but it's a price worth paying for dishes including Moroccan eggs and a good pulled-pork burger.

Indian Café
INDIAN $$

(Map p284; ☑03-548 4089; www.theindian cafe.com; 94 Collingwood St; mains $13-20; ⊙noon-2pm Mon-Fri, 5pm-late daily; ☑) This saffron-coloured Edwardian villa houses an Indian restaurant that keeps the bhajis raised with impressive interpretations of Anglo-Indian standards such as chicken tandoori, rogan josh and beef Madras. Share the mixed platter to start, then mop up your mains with one of 10 different breads.

★Hopgood's
MODERN NZ $$$

(Map p284; ☑03-545 7191; www.hopgoods.co.nz; 284 Trafalgar St; mains $36-39; ⊙5.30pm-late Mon-Sat) Tongue-and-groove-lined Hopgood's is perfect for a romantic dinner or holiday treat. The food is decadent but skilfully prepared but unfussy, allowing quality local ingredients to shine. Try the duck breast with chestnut polenta or the lamb rump with a mint and caper dressing. The five-course tasting menu ($95) affords the full Hopgood's experience. Desirable, predominantly Kiwi wine list. Bookings advisable.

Drinking & Entertainment

Craft Beer Depot
CRAFT BEER

(Map p284; ☑03-548 2126; www.craftbeerdepot. nz; 70 Achilles Ave; ⊙noon-9pm Tue-Thu, to 10pm Fri & Sat, to 8pm Sun) Concealed behind the bus station, Craft Beer Depot is a rustic and loads-of-fun showcase of the best of NZ craft beer. Ten taps dispense brews from around the country, and a back room has plenty more bottled beers. Foosball, old sofas and occasional Friday and Saturday food trucks combine with some of the most beer-savvy bartenders in NZ.

Free House
CRAFT BEER

(Map p284; ☑03-548 9391; www.freehouse.co.nz; 95 Collingwood St; ⊙3-11pm Mon-Fri, noon-11pm Sat & Sun) Tastefully converted from its original more reverent purpose, this former church is now home to an excellent, oft-changing selection of NZ craft beers. Munch on Brazilian-influenced bar snacks on the outside deck, and visit on a Friday or Saturday afternoon from noon to 6pm to browse the racks of vinyl at the Free House's excellent Family Jewels Records pop-up store.

Rhythm & Brown
BAR

(Map p284; ☑03-546 6319; www.facebook.com/rhythmandbrown.nz; 19 New St; ☺4pm-late Tue-Sat) Nelson's slinkiest late-night drinking den, where classy cocktails, fine wines and craft beer flow from behind the bar and sweet vinyl tunes drift from the speakers. Regular Saturday-night microgigs in a compact, groovy space.

Theatre Royal
THEATRE

(Map p284; ☑03-548 3840; www.theatreroyalnelson.co.nz; 78 Rutherford St; ☺box office 10am-4pm Mon-Fri) State-of-the-art theatre in a charmingly restored heritage building. This 'grand old lady of Nelson' boasts a full program of local and touring drama, dance and musical productions. Visit the website for the current program and bookings (or book online at www.ticketdirect.co.nz), or visit the box office.

🛍 Shopping

Nelson has an inordinate number of galleries, most of which are listed in the *Art & Crafts Nelson City* brochure (with walking trail map) available from the i-SITE. A fruitful wander can be had by starting at the woolly **Fibre Spectrum** (Map p284; ☑03-548 1939; www.fibrespectrum.co.nz; 280 Trafalgar St; ☺9am-5pm Mon-Fri, 9.30am-2.30pm Sat), before moving on to *The Lord of the Rings* jeweller **Jens Hansen** (Map p284; ☑03-548 0640; www.jenshansen.com; 320 Trafalgar Sq; ☺9am-5pm Mon-Fri, to 2pm Sat year-round, 10am-1pm Sun late Oct-Easter) and glass-blower **Flamedaisy** (Map p284, ☑03-548 4475; www.flamedaisy.co.nz; 324 Trafalgar Sq; ☺10am-4pm Mon-Sat) nearby. Other interesting local creations can be found at the Nelson Market (p285) on Saturday.

ℹ Information

After Hours & Duty Doctors (☑03-546 8881; 98 Waimea Rd; ☺8am-10pm)

Nelson Hospital (☑03-546 1800; www.nmdhb.govt.nz; Waimea Rd)

Nelson i-SITE (Map p284; ☑03-548 2304; www.nelsonnz.com, cnr Trafalgar & Halifax Sts; ☺9am-5pm Mon-Fri, to 4pm Sat & Sun) An efficient centre complete with DOC information desk for the low-down on national parks and walks (including the Abel Tasman and Heaphy tracks).

ℹ Getting There & Away

Book Abel Tasman Coachlines, InterCity, KiwiRail Scenic and Interisland ferry services at the **Nelson SBL Travel Centre** (Map p284; ☑03-548 1539; www.nelsoncoachlines.co.nz; 27 Bridge St; ☺7am-5.15pm Mon-Fri) or the **i-SITE**.

AIR

Nelson Airport is 5km southwest of town, near Tahunanui Beach. A taxi from there to town will cost around $30 or **Super Shuttle** (☑0800 748 885, 03-547 5782; www.supershuttle.co.nz) offers door-to-door service for around $20.

Air New Zealand (☑0800 737 000; www.airnewzealand.co.nz) Direct flights to/from Wellington, Auckland and Christchurch.

Air2There (☑0800 777 000, 04-904 5133; www.air2there.com) Flies to/from Paraparaumu.

Jetstar (☑09-975 9426, 0800 800 995; www.jetstar.com) Flies to/from Auckland and Wellington.

Originair (☑0800 380 380; www.originair.co.nz) To/from Palmerston North.

Soundsair (☑0800 505 005, 03-520 3080; www.soundsair.com) To/from Wellington and Paraparaumu.

BUS

Abel Tasman Coachlines (☑03-548 0285; www.abeltasmantravel.co.nz) operates bus services to Motueka ($14, one hour), and Kaiteriteri and Marahau (both $21, two hours). These services also connect with **Golden Bay Coachlines** (☑03-525 8352; www.gbcoachlines.co.nz) services for Takaka and around. Transport to/from the three national parks is provided by **Trek Express** (☑027 222 1872, 0800 128 735; www.trekexpress.co.nz).

InterCity (Map p284; ☑03-548 1538; www.intercity.co.nz; Bridge St) runs from Nelson to most key South Island destinations including Picton ($23, two hours), Kaikoura ($52, 3½ hours) and Greymouth ($40, six hours).

ℹ Getting Around

BICYCLE

Bikes are available for hire from **Nelson Cycle Hire & Tours** (☑03-539 4193; www.nelsoncyclehire.co.nz; Nelson Airport; bike hire per day $45), among many other cycle tour companies.

BUS

Nelson Suburban Bus Lines (SBL; Map p284; ☑03-548 3290; www.nbus.co.nz; 27 Bridge St) operates NBUS local services from the **Central Bus Stop** (Map p284; Wakatu Lane) between Nelson and Richmond via Tahunanui and Bishopdale until about 7pm weekdays and 4.30pm on weekends. It also runs the **Late Late Bus** (Map p284; www.nbus.co.nz; Trafalgar St; ☺hourly 10pm-3am Fri & Sat) from Nelson to Richmond via Tahunanui on Friday and Saturday nights, departing from the Westpac Bank on Trafalgar St. Maximum fare for these services is $4.

TAXI

Nelson City Taxis (☑ 03-548 8225; www.nelsontaxis.co.nz)

Sun City Taxis (Map p284; ☑ 03-548 2666; www.suncitytaxis.co.nz)

TASMAN DISTRICT

This Tasman District is centred upon Tasman Bay. It stretches north to Golden Bay and Farewell Spit, and south to Nelson Lakes. It's not hard to see why it's such a popular travel destination for international and domestic travellers alike: not only does it boast three national parks (Kahurangi, Nelson Lakes and Abel Tasman), it can also satisfy nearly every other whim, from food, wine and beer, art, craft and festivals, to that most precious of pastimes for which the region is well known: lazing about in the sunshine.

Nelson Lakes National Park

Nelson Lakes National Park surrounds two lakes – Rotoiti and Rotoroa – fringed by sweet-smelling beech forest with a backdrop of greywacke mountains. Located at the northern end of the Southern Alps, and with a dramatic glacier-carved landscape, it's an awe-inspiring place to get up on high.

Part of the park, east of Lake Rotoiti, is classed as a 'mainland island' where a conservation scheme aims to eradicate introduced pests (rats, possums and stoats), and regenerate native flora and fauna. It offers excellent tramping, including short walks, lake scenery and one or two sandflies... The park is flush with bird life, and famous for brown-trout fishing.

The human hub of the Nelson Lakes region is the small, low-key village of **St Arnaud**.

🏃 Activities

Many spectacular walks allow you to appreciate this rugged landscape, but before you tackle them, stop by the DOC Nelson Lakes Visitor Centre (p289) for maps, track/weather updates and to pay your hut or camping fees.

There are two fantastic day hikes to be had. The five-hour **Mt Robert Circuit Track** starts at Mt Robert car park, a short drive away from St Arnaud, serviced by Nelson Lakes Shuttles (p289), and circumnavigates the mountain. The optional side trip along

Robert Ridge offers staggering views into the heart of the national park. Alternatively, the **St Arnaud Range Track** (five hours return), on the east side of the lake, climbs steadily to the ridge line adjacent to Parachute Rocks. Both tracks are strenuous, but reward with jaw-dropping vistas of glaciated valleys, arête peaks and Lake Rotoiti. Only attempt these tramps in fine weather. At other times they are both pointless (no views) and dangerous.

There are also plenty of shorter (and flatter) walks from Lake Rotoiti's Kerr Bay and the road end at Lake Rotoroa. These and the longer day tramps are described in DOC's *Walks in Nelson Lakes National Park* pamphlet ($2).

The fit and well-equipped can embark upon longer hikes such as the Lake Angelus Track (p281).

🛌 Sleeping

Travers-Sabine Lodge HOSTEL $
(☑ 03-521 1887; www.nelsonlakes.co.nz; Main Rd, St Arnaud; dm/d $32/75; 🛜) This hostel is a great base for outdoor adventure – being a short walk to Lake Rotoiti – inexpensive, clean and comfortable. It also has particularly cheerful Technicolor linen in the dorms, doubles and family room. The owners are experienced adventurers themselves, so tips come as standard; tramping equipment available for hire.

Kerr Bay DOC Campsite CAMPGROUND $
(www.doc.govt.nz; unpowered/powered sites per person $18/21) Near the Lake Rotoiti shore, the hugely popular Kerr Bay campsite has powered sites, toilets, hot showers, a laundry and a kitchen shelter. It's an inspiring base for your adventures, but do book in advance. Overflow camping is available around at DOC's **West Bay Campsite** (☑ 03-521 1806; www.doc.govt.nz; adult/child $13/6.50; ⊘ mid-Dec–Apr), which is more basic.

★ Alpine Lodge LODGE $$
(☑ 03-521 1869; www.alpinelodge.co.nz; Main Rd, St Arnaud; d $180-229; @🛜) Family owned and a consistent performer, this large lodge complex offers a range of accommodation, the pick of which is the split-level doubles with mezzanine bedroom and spa. If nothing else, go for the inviting in-house restaurant – a snug affair sporting an open fire, mountain views, good food (meals $15 to $32, takeaway pizza $20) and local beer.

GREAT TASTE TRAIL

In a stroke of genius inspired by great weather and easy topography, the Tasman region has developed one of New Zealand's most popular cycle trails. Why is it so popular? Because no other is so frequently punctuated by stops for food, wine, craft beer and art, as it passes through a range of landscapes from bucolic countryside to estuary boardwalk.

The 174km **Great Taste Trail** (www.heartofbiking.org.nz) stretches from Nelson to Kaiteriteri, with plans afoot to propel it further inland. While it can certainly be ridden in full in a few days, stopping at accommodation en route, it is even more easily ridden as day trips of various lengths. Mapua is a great place to set off from, with bike hire from **Wheelie Fantastic** (☑ 03-543 2245; www.wheeliefantastic.co.nz; 151 Aranui Rd, Mapua; self-guided tours from $65, bike hire per day from $50) or **Trail Journeys** (Map p284; ☑ 03-540 3095, 0800 292 538; www.trailjourneysnelson.co.nz; 37-39 Halifax St; full-day tours from $89) and a ferry ride over to the trails of **Rabbit Island** (p290). The trail also passes through thrilling **Kaiteriteri Mountain Bike Park** (www.kaiteriterimtbpark.org.nz).

Nelson's many other cycle-tour and bike-hire companies can get you out on the trail, with bike drops and pick-ups.

Nelson Lakes Motels   MOTEL **$$**
(☑ 03-521 1887; www.nelsonlakes.co.nz; Main Rd, St Arnaud; d $135-155, q $145-155, ☺) These log cabins and newer board-and-batten units offer all the creature comforts, including kitchenettes and Sky TV. Bigger units have full kitchens and sleep up to six.

ℹ Information

DOC Nelson Lakes Visitor Centre (☑ 03-521 1806; www.doc.govt.nz; View Rd; ☺ 8am-4.30pm, to 5pm Dec-Apr) Happily proffers park information (weather, activities) and hut passes, plus displays on park ecology and history.

ℹ Getting There & Away

Nelson Lakes Shuttles (☑ 027 222 1872, 03-540 2042; www.nelsonlakesshuttles.co.nz) runs a weekly scheduled service between Nelson and the national park from December to February (Tuesday at 10am; $45), and on-demand the rest of the year. The service returns to Nelson at 11am on Fridays from December to February. It will also collect/drop off at Kawatiri Junction on SH63 to meet other bus services heading between Nelson and the West Coast, and offers services from St Arnaud through to Picton, Kaikoura, Hanmer Springs and other top-of-the-South destinations on demand. Try also **Trek Express** (p287), which regularly plies such routes.

ℹ Getting Around

Rotoiti Water Taxis (☑ 021 702 278; www.rotoitiwatertaxis.co.nz; Kerr Bay) runs to/from Kerr Bay and West Bay to the southern end of Lake Rotoiti (three/four passengers $100/120). Kayaks, canoes and rowing boats can be hired from $50 per half-day; fishing

trips and scenic lake cruises are available by arrangement.

Ruby Coast & Moutere Hills

From Richmond, south of Nelson, there are two routes to Motueka: the quicker, busier route along the Ruby Coast, and the inland route through the Moutere Hills. If you're making a round trip from Nelson, drive one route out, and the other on the way back.

The two highways aren't particularly far apart, and the whole area can be explored by bicycle on the Great Taste Trail (p289), so named for the many wineries and other culinary (and art) stops along the way. The *Nelson Wine Guide* pamphlet (www.wine nelson.co.nz) will help you find them. Other useful resources for this area are the *Nelson Art Guide* and *Nelson's Creative Pathways* pamphlets.

◉ Sights

The Ruby Coast route begins on SH60 and skirts around Waimea Inlet before diverting along the well signposted **Ruby Coast Scenic Route**. Although this is the quickest way to get from Nelson to Motueka (around a 45-minute drive), there are various distractions waiting to slow you down. Major attractions include Rabbit Island (p290) recreation reserve, and **Mapua**, near the mouth of the Waimea River, home to arty shops and eateries.

The inland **Moutere Highway** (signposted at Appleby on SH60) is a pleasant alternative traversing gently rolling countryside dotted with farms, orchards and lifestyle blocks. Visitor attractions are fewer and further between, but it's a scenic and fruitful drive, particularly in high summer when roadside stalls are laden with fresh produce. The main settlement along the way is **Upper Moutere**. First settled by German immigrants and originally named Sarau, today it's a sleepy hamlet with a couple of notable stops. Look for the *Moutere Artisans* trail guide (www.moutereartisans.co.nz).

Rabbit Island/Moturoa　　　BEACH, FOREST
(☉dawn-dusk) Around 9km from Richmond on SH60 is the signposted turn-off to Rabbit Island/Moturoa, a recreation reserve offering estuary views from many angles, sandy beaches and quiet pine forest trails forming part of the Great Taste Trail (p289). The bridge to the island closes at sunset; overnight stays are not allowed.

Höglund Art Glass　　　GALLERY
(☑03-544 6500; www.hoglundartglass.com; 52 Lansdowne Rd, Appleby; ☉10am-5pm) Ola, Marie and their associates work the furnace to produce internationally acclaimed glass art. The process is amazing to watch, and the results beautiful to view in the gallery. Their jewellery and penguins make memorable souvenirs if their signature vases are too heavy to take home.

Neudorf Vineyards　　　WINERY
(☑03-543 2643; www.neudorf.co.nz; 138 Neudorf Rd, Upper Moutere; ☉11am-5pm Oct-Apr, Mon-Fri May, Jun & Sep, closed Jul & Aug) 🍴 Sitting pretty in Upper Moutere with views across the grapes to the mountains of Kahurangi National Park, bijou Neudorf produces gorgeous wines including seductive pinot noir and some of NZ's finest chardonnay.

Seifried　　　WINERY
(☑03-544 5599; www.seifried.co.nz; cnr SH60 & Redwood Rd, Appleby; ☉10am-4pm) Situated at the SH60 Rabbit Island/Moturoa turn-off, Seifried is one of the region's biggest wineries, and is home to a pleasant garden restaurant and the delicious Sweet Agnes riesling.

✖ Eating & Drinking

Smokehouse　　　FISH & CHIPS $
(☑0800 540 2280; www.smokehouse.co.nz; Mapua Wharf, Mapua; fish & chips $8-12; ☉11am-8pm) Visit this Mapua institution to order fish and chips and eat them on the wharf while the gulls eye off your crispy bits. Get some delicious wood-smoked fish and pâté to go.

★**Boat Shed Cafe**　　　MODERN NZ $$
(☑03-540 2656; www.boatshedcafe.co.nz/mapua; 33 Toru St, Mapua; shared plates $15-20, mains $31; ☉10.30am-late; 🍴) 🍴 Look past the slightly odd location – the cafe's waterfront pavilion is reached by travelling through the Mapua Leisure Park – and focus on views of nearby Rabbit Island (p290) and a menu combining diverse international influences. Flavours include Vietnamese beef tartare, fish carpaccio and one of the South Island's best gourmet cheeseburgers, and the surprising drinks list is exceedingly local.

Jester House　　　CAFE $$
(☑03-526 6742; www.jesterhouse.co.nz; 320 Aporo Rd, Tasman; meals $16-21; ☉9am-4.30pm) Long-standing Jester House is reason alone to take this coastal detour, as much for its tame eels as for the peaceful sculpture gardens that encourage you to linger over lunch. A short, simple menu puts a few twists into staples (venison burger, lavender shortbread), and there are local beers and wines. It's 8km to Mapua or Motueka.

Moutere Inn　　　PUB
(☑03-543 2759; www.moutereinn.co.nz; 1406 Moutere Hwy, Upper Moutere; ☉noon-8pm Mon & Tue, to 9pm Wed & Sun, to 11pm Thu-Sat) Reputedly NZ's oldest pub, complete with retro decor, the Moutere Inn is a welcoming establishment serving thoughtful meals ($13 to $32; homemade burgers, potato gnocchi) and predominantly local and NZ craft beer. Sit in the sunshine with a beer-tasting platter, or settle in on music nights with a folksy bent. Rooms are available if you need to rest your head.

❶ Getting There & Away

InterCity (p287) buses service Nelson and Motueka, but to access the Ruby Coast and Moutere Hills you'll need your own transport. Biking the Great Taste Trail (p289) is a good way of exploring.

Motueka

POP 7600

Motueka (pronounced mott-oo-ecka, meaning 'Island of Weka') is a bustling agricultural hub, and a great base from which to explore the Nelson region. It has vital amenities, ample accommodation, cafes and roadside fruit stalls, all in a beautiful river and estuary setting. Stock up here if you're en route to Golden Bay or the Abel Tasman and Kahurangi National Parks. Tasty distractions before you leave town include local craft beers and ciders served in a leafy garden cafe, and an excellent Sunday morning farmers market. Airborne thrill seekers are spoilt for choice.

◉ Sights & Activities

While most of Mot's drawcards are out of town, there are a few attractions worth checking out, the buzziest of which is the active aerodrome, home to some of the country's best skydiving. It's a good place to soak up some sun and views, and watch a few folks drop in.

While you might not realise it from the high street, Motueka is just a stone's throw from the sea. Eyeball the waters (with birds and saltwater baths) along the **estuary walkway**, which can also be cycled; hire bikes from the **Bike Shed** (Map p291; ☑ 03-929 8607; www.motuekabikeshed.co.nz; 132 High St; half-/full-day hire from $30/40). Follow your nose or obtain a town map from the i-SITE (p292), where you can also get the *Motueka Art Walk* pamphlet detailing sculptures, murals and occasional peculiarities around town.

Motueka District Museum MUSEUM
(Map p291; ☑ 03-528 7660; www.motuekadistrictmuseum.org.nz; 140 High St; by donation; ☺10am-3pm Mon-Fri, to 2pm Sat & Sun Dec-Mar, closed Tue & Sat Apr-Nov) An interesting collection of regional artefacts, housed in a dear old school building.

★ Skydive Abel Tasman ADVENTURE SPORTS
(☑ 03-528 4091, 0800 422 899; www.skydive.co.nz; Motueka Aerodrome, 60 College St; jumps 13,000/16,500ft $319/409) Move over, Taupo: we've jumped both and think Mot takes the cake. Presumably so do the many sports jumpers who favour this drop zone, some of whom you may see rocketing in. Photo and video packages are extra. Excellent spectating from the front lawn.

🛏 Sleeping

Motueka Top 10 Holiday Park HOLIDAY PARK $
(Map p291; ☑ 03-528 7189; www.motuekatop10.co.nz; 10 Fearon St; sites from $40, cabins $65-150, units & motels $165-457; @ 🎧 🖥 ☀) 🅿 Close to town and the Great Taste Trail, this place is packed with grassy, green charm – check out those lofty kahikatea trees! Shipshape

Motueka
△ Ⓝ 0 ─── 200 m
      0 ─── 0.1 miles

Motueka

◉ Sights
1 Motueka District Museum B2

☀ Activities, Courses & Tours
2 Bike Shed A2

🛏 Sleeping
3 Avalon Manor Motel A3
4 Equestrian Lodge Motel B3
5 Laughing Kiwi A3
6 Motueka Top 10 Holiday Park B1

✕ Eating
7 Motueka Sunday Market B2
8 Precinct Dining Co A2

⊖ Drinking & Nightlife
9 Sprig & Fern B2

communal amenities include a swimming pool, spa and jumping pillow, and there are ample accommodation options from smart new cabins to an apartment sleeping up to 11. On-site bike hire, plus local advice and bookings freely offered.

Laughing Kiwi HOSTEL $
(Map p291; ☑ 03-528 9229; www.laughingkiwi.co.nz; 310 High St; dm $29, d with/without bathroom $76/68; 🎧) Compact, low-key YHA hostel

WORTH A TRIP

RIWAKA

Hop Federation (☑ 03-528 0486; www.
hopfederation.co.nz; 483 Main Rd, Riwaka;
☺ 11am-6pm) Pop in for tastings and fill
a flagon to go at this teeny-weeny but
terrific craft brewery 5km from Mot. A
mixed sampler pack of four different
brews ($15) is good value. Our pick of
the ales is the Red IPA. And note the
cherry stall across the road.

Eden's Edge Lodge (☑ 03-528
4242; www.edensedge.co.nz; 137 Lodder
Lane, Riwaka; d/tw/tr with bathroom
$120/120/150; 🛜) Surrounded by farm-
land 4km from Motueka, this lodge's
facilities include smart rooms and
relaxed communal areas. Breakfast
is included – with organic eggs from
the owners' hens – and there are fresh
herbs aplenty in the garden for cooking
up in the spotless kitchen. Hire a bike
for nearby beer, ice-cream and coffee
stops along the Great Taste Trail.

with rooms spread between an old villa and a
purpose-built backpacker lodge with a smart
kitchen/lounge. The self-contained bach is a
good option for groups of up to four ($180).

Equestrian Lodge Motel   MOTEL $$
(Map p291; ☑ 0800 668 782, 03-528 9369; www.
equestrianlodge.co.nz; Avalon Ct; d $148-178, q
$199-255; 🛜🏊) No horses, no lodge, but no
matter. This excellent motel complex is close
to town (off Tudor St) and features expan-
sive lawns, rose gardens, and a heated pool
and spa alongside a series of continually re-
freshed units. Cheerful owners will hook you
up with local activities.

Avalon Manor Motel   MOTEL $$
(Map p291; ☑ 03-528 8320, 0800 282 566; www.
avalonmotels.co.nz; 314 High St; d $150-225; 🛜)
Prominent L-shaped motel with spacious
rooms, five-minutes' walk from the town
centre. All rooms have a contemporary vibe,
with cooking facilities, while the sumptuous
studios have king-size beds and large flat-
screen TVs. There's also a guest barbecue, a
laundry and views of Mt Arthur.

🍴 Eating & Drinking

Motueka Sunday Market   MARKET $
(Map p291; Wallace St; ☺ 8am-1pm Sun) On Sundays the car park behind the i-SITE fills up
with trestle tables for the Motueka Sunday
Market, with produce, jewellery, buskers,
arts, crafts and grilled Argentinean treats
from Via La Vaca.

★**Toad Hall**   CAFE $$
(☑ 03-528 6456; www.toadhallmotueka.co.nz; 502
High St; mains $16-23; ☺ 8am-5pm Easter-Oct,
8am-6pm Mon & Tue, to 10pm Wed-Sun Oct-Easter)
This fantastic cafe serves excellent breakfast
and lunch dishes (think potato hashcakes
and pork-belly burgers). Also on offer are
smoothies, juices, baked goods, pies and se-
lected groceries. Look forward to live music
and pizza on Friday and Saturday nights in
summer. Have a drink at its new tap room,
with beers and ciders brewed on site by
Townshend Brewery.

Precinct Dining Co   CAFE $$
(Map p291; ☑ 03-528 5332; www.precinctdining.
com; 108 High St; breakfast & lunch mains $10-18,
dinner mains $24-30; ☺ 9am-3pm Mon, 9am-late
Tue-Sat) At the northern end of town, Precinct Dining Co is a relaxed and versatile
slice of well-priced cosmopolitan cool. Kick
off with eggs Benedict and pea-and-chorizo
smash for brunch, before returning at dinner for fish with local Golden Bay clams or a
rustic pumpkin risotto with toasted walnuts.
Good coffee and a savvy drinks list seal the
deal.

Sprig & Fern   CRAFT BEER
(Map p291; ☑ 03-528 4684; www.sprigandfern.
co.nz; Wallace St; ☺ 2pm-late) A member of
the local Sprig & Fern brewery family, this
backstreet tavern is the pick of Motueka's
drinking holes. Small and pleasant, with two
courtyards, it offers 20 hand-pulled brews,
simple food (pizza, platters and an awesome
burger; meals $15 to $25) and occasional
live music.

🛈 Information

Motueka i-SITE (Map p291; ☑ 03-528 6543;
www.motuekaisite.co.nz; 20 Wallace St; ☺ 9am-
4.30pm Mon-Fri, to 4pm Sat & Sun) An excellent
centre with helpful staff who handle bookings
from Cape Reinga to Bluff and provide local
national-park expertise and necessaries. DOC
information and bookings are also available.

🛈 Getting There & Away

Bus services depart from **Motueka i-SITE**. **Abel
Tasman Coachlines** (p287) runs daily from
Nelson, where you can connect to other South
Island destinations via **InterCity** (☑ 03-365
1113; www.intercity.co.nz), to Motueka (one

hour), Kaiteriteri (25 minutes) and Marahau (30 minutes). These services connect with **Golden Bay Coachlines** (p287) services to Takaka (1¼ hours) and other Golden Bay destinations including Totaranui in Abel Tasman National Park, Collingwood, and on to the Heaphy Track trailhead. Note that from May to September all buses run less frequently.

Kaiteriteri

POP 790

Known simply as 'Kaiteri', this seaside hamlet 13km from Motueka is the most popular resort town in the area. During the summer holidays its golden swimming beach feels more like Noumea than New Zealand, with more towels than sand. Consider yourself warned. Kaiteri is also a major departure point for Abel Tasman National Park transport, although Marahau is the main base.

🛏 Sleeping & Eating

Torlesse Coastal Motels   MOTEL $$

(📞 03-527 0003; www.torlessemotels.co.nz; 8 Kotare Pl, Little Kaiteriteri Beach; d $100-210, q $200-350; 🐾) Just 200m from Little Kaiteriteri Beach (around the corner from the main beach) is this congregation of roomy hillside units with pitched ceilings, full kitchens and laundries. Most have water views, and there's a ferny barbecue area and spa.

Kai   BISTRO $$

(📞 03-527 8507; www.experiencekaiteriteri.co.nz; cnr Inlet & Sandy Bay Rds; mains $15-33, shared platters $18-32; ⊙ 7.30am-9pm, reduced hours Apr-Nov) Formerly called Shoreline, this cafe-restaurant near the beach has re-emerged as Kai, a modern and stylish bistro. Breakfast and lunch options include buttermilk pancakes and bagels with salmon, while dinner is (slightly) more formal with fish, beef and lamb dishes. Erratic winter hours, but the adjacent **Goneburger** booth is usually open to dispense burgers, wraps and coffee to holidaying families.

❶ Getting There & Away

Kaiteriteri is serviced by **Abel Tasman Coachlines** (p287). Services include Motueka ($11, 20 minutes) and Nelson ($21, 90 minutes).

Trail Journeys (📞 03-548 0093; www.trailjourneysnelson.co.nz; 3 Kaiteriteri-Sandy Bay Rd) offers bike rental and advice on negotiating the Great Taste Trail (p289). It also has mountain bikes to rent for the nearby **Kaiteriteri Mountain Bike Park** (p289).

Marahau

POP 120

Just up the coast from Kaiteriteri and 18km north of Motueka, Marahau is the main gateway to Abel Tasman National Park. It's less of a town, more of a procession of holiday homes and tourist businesses.

🏃 Activities

Abel Tasman Horse Trekking   HORSE RIDING

(📞 03-527 8232; https://abeltasmanhorsetrekking.co.nz; Ocean View Chalets, 305 Sandy Bay-Marahau Rd; 2hr ride per person $95) If you're in an equine state of mind, head here for the chance to belt along the beach on four legs. Offers two-hour beach rides (for those 12 years and older), with training for newbie riders. Younger ones can be led around a paddock on a pony for 30 minutes ($35) after helping to brush and saddle up their mount.

🛏 Sleeping

Barn   HOSTEL $

(📞 03-527 8043; www.barn.co.nz; 14 Harvey Rd; unpowered/powered sites per person $20/22, dm $32, d & tw $89; @🐾) This backpackers has hit its straps with comfortable dorms, a toilet block and a grassy camping field added to a mix of microcabins, alfresco kitchens and barbecue areas. The barn itself is the hub – the communal kitchen and lounge area are good for socialising, as is the central deck, which has a fireplace. Activity bookings and secure parking available.

Abel Tasman Lodge   MOTEL $$

(📞 03-527 8250; www.abeltasmanlodge.co.nz; 295 Sandy Bay-Marahau Rd; d $145-195, q $200-260; @🐾) 🖉 Enjoy halcyon days in this renovated arc of 15 studios and self-contained units with groovy styling and cathedral ceilings, opening onto landscaped gardens. There's also a communal kitchen for self-caterers, plus spa and sauna. Cuckoos, tui and bellbirds squawk and warble in the bushy surrounds, and some of the cool interior decor is styled after local bird life.

Ocean View Chalets   CHALET $$

(📞 03-527 8232; www.accommodationabeltasman.co.nz; 305 Sandy Bay-Marahau Rd; d $145-245, q $299; 🐾) On a leafy hillside affording plenty of privacy, these cheerful, cypress-lined chalets are 300m from the Coast Track with views out to Fisherman Island. All except the cheapest studios are self-contained; breakfast and packed lunches available.

✖ Eating

Fat Tui BURGERS $
(☑03-527 8420; cnr Marahau-Sandy Bay & Marahau Valley Rds; burgers $14-17; ⊘noon-8pm late
Oct-Easter, Wed-Sun May-late Oct) Everyone's
heard about this bird, based in a caravan
that ain't rollin' anywhere fast. It serves su-
perlative burgers, such as the Cowpat (beef),
the Ewe Beaut (lamb) and Roots, Shoots &
Leaves (vegie). Fish and chips, and coffee, too.

Hooked CAFE $$
(☑03-527 8576; www.hookedonmarahau.co.nz;
229 Marahau-Sandy Bay Rd; lunch $15-20, dinner
$26-32; ⊘8am-10pm Dec-Mar, 8-11am & 3-10pm
Oct, Nov & Apr) This popular place reels them
in, so dinner reservations are recommend-
ed. The art-bedecked interior opens on to
an outdoor terrace with distracting views.
Lunch centres on salads and seafood, while
the dinner menu boasts fresh fish of the day
– ask if bluenose is available – green-lipped
mussels and NZ lamb shanks. Pop in for
happy hour drinks from 4pm to 6pm.

Park Cafe CAFE $$
(☑03-527 8270; www.parkcafe.co.nz; Harvey Rd;
lunch $12-22, dinner $17-36; ⊘8am-late mid-Sep–
May; ☑) At the Coast Track trailhead, this
breezy cafe is perfect for fuelling up or re-
storing the waistline. High-calorie options
include the big breakfast, burgers and cakes,
but there are also seafood and salad options
plus wood-fired pizza Wednesday through
Saturday evenings. Enjoy in the room with a
view or the sunny courtyard garden. Check
Facebook for occasional live music listings.

❶ Getting There & Away

Marahau is serviced by **Abel Tasman Coachlines** (p287). Services include Motueka ($11, 30
minutes) and Nelson ($21, two hours).

Abel Tasman National Park

Coastal Abel Tasman National Park blankets
the northern end of a range of marble and
limestone hills that extend from Kahurangi
National Park. Various tracks in the park
include an inland route, although the Coast
Track (p274) is what everyone is here for –
it's New Zealand's most popular Great Walk.

Even if you're not keen on tackling the
walk, kayaking or cruising amid Abel Tasman's hidden coves and beaches is accessible to all visitors.

☞ Tours

Tour companies usually offer free Motueka
pick-up/drop-off, with Nelson pick-up available at extra cost.

★ Abel Tasman Canyons ADVENTURE
(☑03-528 9800, 0800 863 472; www.abeltasman
canyons.co.nz; Motueka; full-day trips $269) Few
Abel Tasman visitors see the Torrent River,
but here's your chance to journey down its
staggeringly beautiful granite-lined canyon,
via a fun-filled combination of swimming,
sliding, abseiling, zip-lining and big leaps
into jewel-like pools. Other trips explore Kahurangi National Park and Richmond Forest
Park, and combo adventures including kayaking or sky diving are also available.

Wilsons Abel Tasman OUTDOORS
(☑03-528 2027, 0800 223 582; www.abeltasman.
co.nz; 409 High St, Motueka; walk/kayak from
$62/90) This long-standing, family owned
operator offers an impressive array of cruises, walking, kayaking and combo tours.
Overnight stays are available at Wilsons'
lodges in pretty Awaroa and Torrent Bay for
guided-tour guests.

Offers an Explorer Pass for unlimited boat
travel on three days over a seven-day period
(adult/child $150/75).

🛏 Sleeping

Along the Abel Tasman Coast Track are four
Great Walk huts ($38) with bunks, heating,
flush toilets and limited lighting, but no
cooking facilities. There are also 19 designated Great Walk campsites ($15). An interest-
ing alternative is Aquapackers, a catamaran
moored permanently in Anchorage Bay.

Anchorage Campsite CAMPGROUND $
(www.doc.govt.nz; adult/child $15/free) One of
the most popular campsites in Abel Tasman
National Park, beside Anchorage's lovely
sandy beach.

Totaranui Campsite CAMPGROUND $
(☑03-528 8083; www.doc.govt.nz; Oct-Apr $15,
May-Sep $10) An extremely popular facility
with a whopping capacity (850 campers)
and a splendid setting next to the beach
backed by some of the best bush in the park.
A staffed DOC office has interpretive displays, flush toilets, cold showers and a public
phone. Note there's a one-night limit here.

Aquapackers HOSTEL $$
(☑0800 430 744; www.aquapackers.co.nz; An-
chorage; dm/d $85/245; ⊘closed May-Sep) The

Abel Tasman National Park

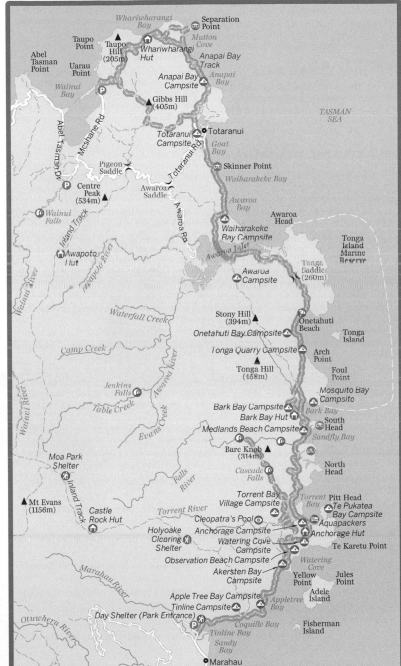

specially converted 13m *Catarac* (catamaran), moored permanently in Anchorage Bay, provides unusual but buoyant backpacker accommodation for 22. Facilities are basic but decent; prices include bedding, dinner and breakfast. Bookings essential.

ⓘ Getting There & Away

The closest big town to Abel Tasman is Motueka, with nearby Marahau the southern gateway. Although Wainui is the official northern trailhead for the Coast Track, it is more common to finish

in Totaranui, either skipping the northernmost section or looping back to Totaranui over Gibbs Hill Track. All gateways are serviced by either **Abel Tasman Coachlines** (p287) and **Golden Bay Coachlines** (p287).

ⓘ Getting Around

Once you hit the park, it is easy to get to/from any point on the Coast Track via the numerous tour companies and water-taxi operators offering scheduled and on-demand services, either from Kaiteriteri or Marahau. Typical one-way prices

---

PADDLING THE ABEL TASMAN

The Abel Tasman Coast Track has long been tramping territory, but its coastal beauty makes it an equally seductive spot for sea kayaking, which can easily be combined with walking and camping.

A variety of professional outfits are able to float you out on the water, and the possibilities and permutations for guided or freedom trips are vast. You can kayak from half a day up to three days, camping, or staying in DOC huts, bachs, even a **floating backpackers** (p294), either fully catered or self-catering. You can kayak one day, camp overnight then walk back, or walk further into the park and catch a water taxi back.

Most operators offer similar trips at similar prices. Marahau is the main base, but trips also depart from Kaiteriteri. There are numerous day-trip options, including guided trips often departing Marahau and taking in bird-filled Adele Island (around $200). There are also various multiday guided trips, with three days a common option, costing anything from $260 to $750 depending on accommodation and other inclusions.

Freedom rentals (double-kayak and equipment hire) are around $75/115 per person for one/two days; all depart from Marahau with the exception of **Golden Bay Kayaks** (☑03-525 9095; www.goldenbaykayaks.co.nz; 29 Cornwall Pl, Tata Beach; half-day guided tours adult/child from $85/50, freedom hire from $55; ⚐), which is based at Tata Beach in Golden Bay.

Instruction is given to everyone, and most tour companies have a minimum age of either eight or 14 depending on the trip. None allow solo hires. Camping gear is usually provided on overnight trips; if you're disappearing into the park for a few days, most operators provide free car parking.

November to Easter is the busiest time, with December to February the absolute peak. You can, however, paddle all year round, with winter offering its own rewards; the weather is surprisingly amenable, the seals are more playful, and there's more bird life and less haze.

Following are the main players in this competitive market (shop around):

Abel Tasman Kayaks (☑0800 732 529, 03-527 8022; www.abeltasmankayaks.co.nz; Main Rd, Marahau; guided tours from $150)

Kahu Kayaks (☑0800 300 101, 03-527 8300; www.kahukayaks.co.nz; 11 Marahau Valley Rd; self-guided/guided tours from $75/215)

Kaiteriteri Kayaks (☑0800 252 925, 03-527 8383; www.seakayak.co.nz; Kaiteriteri Beach; ⊙ adult/child from $80/60)

Marahau Sea Kayaks (☑0800 529 257, 03-527 8176; www.msk.co.nz; Abel Tasman Centre, Franklin St, Marahau; tours from $150)

R&R Kayaks (☑0508 223 224; www.rrkayaks.co.nz; 279 Sandy Bay-Marahau Rd; tours from $135)

Sea Kayak Company (☑0508 252 925, 03-528 7251; www.seakayaknz.co.nz; 506 High St, Motueka; tours from $85)

Tasman Bay Sea Kayaking (☑0800 827 525; www.tasmanbayseakayaking.co.nz; Harvey Rd, Marahau; tours from $110)

Wilsons Abel Tasman (p294)

from either Marahau or Kaiteriteri: Anchorage and Torrent Bay ($37), Bark Bay ($42), Awaroa ($47) and Totaranui ($49). Getting around on the water is best accomplished with **Abel Tasman Aqua Taxi** (☑ 03-527 8083, 0800 278 282; www.aquataxi.co.nz; Marahau-Sandy Bay Rd, Marahau) or **Marahau Water Taxis** (☑ 03-527 8176, 0800 808 018; www.marahauwatertaxis.co.nz; Abel Tasman Centre, Franklin St, Marahau).

Takaka Hill

Takaka Hill (791m) butts in between Tasman Bay and Golden Bay. It looks pretty bushy but closer inspection reveals a remarkable marble landscape formed by millions of years of erosion. Its smooth beauty is revealed on the one-hour drive over the hill road (SH60), a steep, winding route punctuated by spectacular lookout points and a smattering of other interesting stops.

Just before the summit is the turn-off to Canaan Downs Scenic Reserve, reached at the end of an 11km gravel road. This area stars in both *The Lord of the Rings* and *The Hobbit* movies, but **Harwoods Hole** is the most famous feature here. It's one of the largest *tomo* (caves) in the country at 357m deep and 70m wide, with a 176m vertical drop. It's a 30-minute walk from the car park. Allow us to state the obvious: the cave is off limits to all but the most experienced cavers.

◉ Sights & Activities

Harwood Lookout on the SH60 affords tantalising views down the Takaka River Valley to Takaka and Golden Bay.

Mountain bikers with intermediate-level skills can venture along a couple of loop tracks, or head all the way down to Takaka via the titillating **Rameka Track**. Also close to the top, the **Takaka Hill Walkway** is a three-hour loop through marble karst rock formations, native forest and farmland. For more walks, see DOC's brochure *Walks in Golden Bay*.

Ngarua Caves   CAVE
(☑ 03-528 8093; www.ngaruacaves.co.nz; SH60; adult/child $20/8; ⊙45min tours hourly 10am-4pm Oct-Apr, phone ahead other months) Just below the summit of Takaka Hill (literally) are the Ngarua Caves, a rock-solid attraction, where you can see myriad subterranean delights including moa bones. Access is restricted to tours – you can't go solo spelunking.

🛏 Sleeping

Resurgence   LODGE $$$
(☑ 03-528 4664; www.resurgence.co.nz; 574 Riwaka Valley Rd; d lodge from $695, chalets from $595; ◉🛈🛜🏊) 🍴 Choose a luxurious en-suite lodge room or a self-contained chalet at this magical green retreat. It's a 15-minute drive from Abel Tasman National Park, and a 30-minute walk from the picturesque source of the Riwaka River. Lodge rates include aperitifs and a four-course dinner as well as breakfast; chalet rates are for B&B, with dinner an extra $120.

❶ Getting There & Away

If you don't have your own wheels, you can bus over Takaka Hill between Motueka and Takaka with **Golden Bay Coachlines** (p287).

Takaka

POP 1240

Boasting New Zealand's highest concentration of yoga pants, dreadlocks and bare feet in the high street, Takaka is a lovable little town and the last 'big' centre before the road west ends at Farewell Spit (p302). You'll find most things you need here, and a few things you don't, but we all have an unworn tie-dyed tank top in our wardrobe, don't we?

Beyond the town's past and present as a bit of a hippie enclave, an interesting new arts cooperative and Takaka's very own distillery (p299) are adding a more contemporary and diverse sheen.

◉ Sights

Golden Bay Museum   MUSEUM
(www.goldenbaymuseum.org.nz; 73 Commercial St; by donation; ⊙10am-4pm Mon-Fri, to 1pm Sat & Sun) This small museum's standout exhibits include a diorama depicting Abel Tasman's 1642 landing, and some dubious human taxidermy. Ask about the albatross, and look out for the whale skeleton currently on the cards – it's to be installed in the renovated room at the front.

Grove Scenic Reserve   VIEWPOINT
(www.doc.govt.nz) Around a 10-minute drive from Takaka (signposted down Clifton Rd), you will find this crazy limestone maze punctuated by gnarled old rata trees. The walkway takes around 10 minutes and passes an impressive lookout.

NELSON & MARLBOROUGH TAKAKA HILL

AWAROA BAY: THE PEOPLE'S BEACH

When the 800m arc of Awaroa Bay in the northern reaches of Abel Tasman National Park was offered for sale by a private owner in late 2015, there was concern overseas buyers could secure the sheltered slice of paradise. But following a few chats over a few beers on Christmas Day 2015, up stepped two proud South Islanders to rally the public of NZ and instigate the biggest crowd-funding campaign the country has ever seen.

Against the threat of offshore purchasers winning the tender for the 7 hectares of coastal perfection, Duane Major and Adam Gard'ner – both regular summertime visitors to the bays and coves of Abel Tasman National Park – launched a campaign on the NZ crowdfunding website, Givealittle, to secure the beach for all New Zealanders.

By the time the tender deadline was reached on 15 February 2016, 29,239 private donors had raised $2,259,923, and, along with significant corporate donations and $350,000 from the NZ government, the winning tender of more than $2.8 million was reached.

Less than five months later, on 10 July 2016, Awaroa Bay was officially incorporated into Abel Tasman National Park. With its now-protected status, there are ongoing efforts to restore the beach's sand dune ecosystem, and native plant species are being repopulated to improve the natural habitat for coastal birds, including oystercatchers, dotterel and godwits.

Rawhiti Cave   CAVE

(www.doc.govt.nz) The ultimate in geological eye-candy around these parts are the phytokarst features of Rawhiti Cave, a 15-minute drive from Takaka (reached via Motupipi, turning right into Glenview Rd, then left into Packard Rd and following the signs). The rugged two-hour-return walk (steep in places; dangerous in the wet) may well leave you speechless (although we managed 'monster', 'fangs' and even 'Sarlacc').

🏃 Activities

Pupu Hydro Walkway   TRAMPING

(www.doc.govt.nz; Pupu Valley Rd) This enjoyable two-hour circuit follows an old water race through beech forest, past engineering and gold-mining relics to the restored (and operational) Pupu Hydro Powerhouse, built in 1929. It's 9km from Takaka at the end of Pupu Valley Rd; just follow the signs at the Te Waikoropupū Springs (p299) junction.

Quiet Revolution Cycle Shop   CYCLING

(☑ 03-525 9555; www.quietrevolution.co.nz; 11 Commercial St; bike hire per day $30-65; ⏰ 9am-5pm Mon-Fri, to 12.30pm Sat) You'll get personal service at this most proper of bike shops. Town- and mountain-bike hire, plus topnotch servicing and sales. Local ride maps and a car relocation service for the Heaphy Track in winter, too.

Golden Bay Air   SCENIC FLIGHTS

(☑ 03-525 8725, 0800 588 885; www.goldenbayair. co.nz; Takaka Airfield, SH60) Offering scenic and charter flights around Golden Bay and surrounds.

Adventure Flights Golden Bay   SCENIC FLIGHTS

(☑ 0800 150 338, 03-525 6167; www.adventure flightsgoldenbay.co.nz; Takaka Airfield, SH60; from $40) Look forward to scenic and charter flights in the area around Golden Bay.

🛏️ Sleeping & Eating

Golden Bay Kiwi Holiday Park   HOLIDAY PARK $

(☑ 03-525 9742; www.goldenbayholidaypark.co.nz; 99 Tukurua Rd, Tukurua; unpowered/powered sites $43/47, d cabins from $98; @ 🛜) Eighteen kilometres north of Takaka with a quiet beach right out front, this gem of a park has acres of grass, graceful shade trees and hedgerows, easily atoning for tight communal facilities. There are tidy, family friendly cabins for budget travellers, and luxury beach houses sleeping up to four ($195 to $315).

Kiwiana   HOSTEL $

(☑ 0800 805 494, 03-525 7676; www.kiwianaback packers.co.nz; 73 Motupipi St; tent sites per person $24, dm $30, s/d $55/70; @ 🛜) Beyond the welcoming garden is a cute cottage where rooms are named after classic Kiwiana (the jandal, Buzzy Bee...). The garage has been converted into a convivial lounge, with wood-fired stove, table tennis, pool table, music, books and games; free bikes for guest use.

Golden Bay Motel   MOTEL $$

(☑ 0800 401 212, 03-525 9428; www.golden baymotel.co.nz; 132 Commercial St; d $125-160; 🛜) It's golden, alright: check out the paint job. Inside, the decor's a bit daggy, but it's spacious, cheap and cheerful, and there are improvements afoot. The clincher is the big garden at the rear.

★ **Adrift**   COTTAGE $$$

(✆ 03-525 8353; www.adrift.co.nz; 53 Tukurua Rd, Tukurua; d $378-585; 🐾) ✈ Adrift on a bed of beachside bliss is what you'll be in one of these five cottages dotted within landscaped grounds, right on the beach. Tuck into your breakfast hamper, then self-cater in the fully equipped kitchen, dine on the sunny deck, or soak in the spa bath. A minimum two-night stay usually applies. Also available is a stylish studio.

Dangerous Kitchen   CAFE $$

(✆ 03-525 8686; www.thedangerouskitchen.co.nz; 46a Commercial St; mains $13-30; ◷ 9am-8.30pm Mon-Sat; 🐾) ✈ DK serves largely healthy, good-value fare such as felafel, pizza, bean burritos, pasta, great baking and juices as well as local wines and craft beer. It's mellow and musical, with a sunny courtyard out back and people-watching out front. Check out the quirky, Instagram-worthy mural near the entrance, and ask about occasional live music.

🍷 **Drinking & Entertainment**

★ **Mussel Inn**   PUB

(✆ 03-525 9241; www.musselinn.co.nz; 1259 SH60, Onekaka; all-day snacks $5-19, dinner $24-30; ◷ 11am-late, closed mid-Jul–mid-Sep) You will find one of NZ's most beloved brewery-taverns halfway between Takaka and Collingwood. The Mussel Inn is rustic NZ at its most genuine, complete with creaking timbers, a rambling beer garden with a brazier, regular music and other events, and hearty, homemade food. Try the signature 'Captain Cooker', a brown beer brewed naturally with manuka.

Dancing Sands Distillery   DISTILLERY

(✆ 03-525 9899; www.dancingsands.com; 46a Commercial St; ◷ 10am-4pm Mon-Sat) ✈ Here's a surprise – an award-winning distillery tucked down a laneway off Takaka's main street. Its Sacred Spring gin is crafted from water from the same aquifer that feeds the pristine waters of the nearby Pupū Springs, and variations include NZ's first barrel-aged gin, and gin flavoured with chocolate or saffron. Other standout Dancing Sands tipples include rum and vodka.

Roots Bar   BAR

(✆ 03-525 9592; www.rootsbar.co.nz; 1 Commercial St; ◷ 2pm-late Tue-Sun; 🐾) ✈ This popular dance-music-focused joint has a quality sound system, lively evenings and a garden bar with eclectic Bay residents lending colour. Tasman and Marlborough craft beers

---

WORTH A TRIP

TE WAIKOROPUPŪ SPRINGS

These **springs** (www.doc.govt.nz) are the largest freshwater springs in the southern hemisphere and some of the clearest in the world. 'Pupū Springs' is a colourful little lake refreshed with around 14,000L of water per second surging from underground vents. From Takaka, head 4km northwest on SH60 and follow the signs inland for 3km from Waitapu Bridge. There are illuminating information panels at the car park and a 30-minute forest loop taking in the waters, which are sacred and therefore off limits.

---

go well with an interesting snacks menu – think wild venison burgers, wild goat and smoked eel bruschetta – from a local who's returned home after cooking in the big smoke for 18 years.

Village Theatre   CINEMA

(✆ 03-525 8453; www.villagetheatre.org.nz; 32 Commercial St; tickets adult/child $14/8) Demonstrating, yet again, provincial NZ's commitment to quality viewing.

🛍 **Shopping**

Shopping in Takaka is a highlight if you enjoy festival chic and homespun art and craft. To extend your arty ambles, look for the free *Arts in Golden Bay* and *Arts Trail* pamphlets. Galleries along Takaka's main street are also worthy of attention.

ℹ **Information**

Golden Bay Area DOC Office (✆ 03-525 8026; www.doc.govt.nz; 62 Commercial St; ◷ 1-3pm Mon-Fri) Information on Abel Tasman and Kahurangi National Parks, the Heaphy Track, Farewell Spit and Cobb Valley. Sells hut passes.

Golden Bay Visitor Centre (✆ 03-525 9136; www.goldenbaynz.co.nz; Willow St; ◷ 10am-3pm Mon-Fri, to 2pm Sat) A friendly little centre with all the necessary information, including the exemplary free visitor map. Bookings and DOC passes.

ℹ **Getting There & Away**

Golden Bay Air (p298) flies at least once and up to four times daily between Wellington and Takaka (one way adult/child from $169/129).

Golden Bay Coachlines (p287) departs from Takaka and runs through to Collingwood ($21,

WORTH A TRIP

ANATOKI SALMON

Visit **Anatoki Salmon** (📞 0800 262 865, 03-525 7251; www.anatokisalmon.co.nz; 230 McCallum Rd; 🚗) for your chance to catch a salmon and have it smoked for lunch or prepared as super-fresh sashimi. Rods and instructions are provided, but the fish pretty well catch themselves anyway. Other attractions beyond fishing include hand-feeding tame eels, a petting zoo for the kids and minigolf. There's no entrance fee, but expect to pay around $35 to $55 for your salmon.

Salmon snacks and platters ($16 to $32) are also available at Anatoki's cafe.

25 minutes), the Heaphy Track ($35, one hour), Totaranui ($24, one hour), and over to Motueka ($28, 1¼ hours) and Nelson ($38, 2¼ hours).

Pohara

POP 550

About 10km northeast of Takaka is pint-sized Pohara, a beachy village with a population that quadruples over summer. It has more flash holiday homes than other parts of Golden Bay, but an agreeable air persists nonetheless, aided by decent food and lodging, and a beach that at low tide is as big as Heathrow's runway.

Pohara lies close to the northern gateway of Abel Tasman National Park. The largely unsealed road into the park passes **Tarakohe Harbour** (Pohara's working port), followed by **Ligar Bay**. It's worth climbing to the Abel Tasman lookout as you pass by.

🏃 Activities

The next settlement along from Pohara is **Tata Beach**, where Golden Bay Kayaks (p296) offers kayaks and stand-up paddle boards for hire, as well as guided trips into Abel Tasman National Park.

Signposted from the Totaranui Rd at Wainui Bay is a leafy one-hour return walk to the best cascade in the bay: **Wainui Falls**.

🛏 Sleeping

Pohara Beach
Top 10 Holiday Park   HOLIDAY PARK **$**
(📞 0800 764 272, 03-525 9500; www.pohara beach.com; 809 Abel Tasman Dr; sites $49, cabins & units $81-169; @🛜) Lining grassy parkland

between the dunes and the main road, this place is in prime position for some beach time. Sites are nice and there are some beaut cabins, but be warned – this is a favourite spot for NZ holidaymakers so it goes a bit mental in high summer. General store and takeaway on site.

★ **Sans Souci Inn**   LODGE **$$**
(📞 03-525 8663; www.sanssouciinn.co.nz; 11 Richmond Rd; s/d $95/120, units from $160; ⊘ closed Jul–mid-Sep; 🛜) 🌿 Sans Souci means 'no worries' in French, and this will be your mantra too after staying in one of the seven Mediterranean-flavoured, mud-brick rooms. Guests share a plant-filled, mosaic bathroom with composting toilets, and an airy lounge and kitchen that open onto a semitropical courtyard. Dinner in the restaurant is highly recommended (bookings essential; mains $35 to $37); breakfast by request.

Ratanui   LODGE **$$$**
(📞 03-525 7998; www.ratanuilodge.com; 818 Abel Tasman Dr; d from $235; @🛜🏊) A romantic haven close to the beach, this boutique lodge is styled with Victorian panache. It features myriad sensual stimulants such as perfumed rose gardens, a swimming pool, a spa, a massage service, cocktails and a candelabra-lit restaurant showcasing local produce (open to the public; bookings required). Free bikes, too.

❶ Getting There & Away

Golden Bay Coachlines (p287) runs daily from Takaka to Pohara ($17, 15 minutes) on the way to Totaranui.

Collingwood & Around

POP 240

Far-flung Collingwood is the last town in Golden Bay, and has a real end-of-the-line vibe. It's busy in summer, though for most people it's simply a launch pad for the Heaphy Track (p280) or Farewell Spit (p302).

◉ Sights

Collingwood Museum   MUSEUM
(Tasman St; by donation; ⊘ 10am-6pm) The Collingwood Museum fills a tiny, unstaffed corridor with a quirky collection of saddlery, Māori artefacts, moa bones, shells and old typewriters.

Next door, the **Aorere Centre** has an on-rotation slide show featuring the works of the pioneer photographer Fred Tyree.

🛏 Sleeping & Eating

★Innlet Backpackers & Cottages HOSTEL $
(☑03-524 8040, 027 970 8397; www.theinnlet.
co.nz; 839 Collingwood-Puponga Rd, Pakawau;
dm/s/d $35/69/80, cabins from $95; ⊘closed
Jun-Aug; 🐕) 🍂 This leafy charmer is 10km
from Collingwood on the way to Farewell
Spit (p302). The main house has elegant
backpacker rooms, and there are self-contained options including a cottage sleeping
six. Enjoy the garden, explore the local area
on a bike or in a kayak, or venture out for a
tramp on the property. Check the website for
occasional three-night specials.

Somerset House HOSTEL $
(☑03-524 8624; www.backpackerscollingwood.
co.nz; 10 Gibbs Rd; dm/s/d incl breakfast
$32/50/78; ⊘closed May-Oct; @🐕) A small,
low-key hostel in a bright, historic building on a hill with views from the deck. Get
tramping advice from the charming owners,
who offer track transport, free bikes and
kayaks, freshly baked bread for breakfast,
and your fourth night's stay free.

★Zatori Retreat LODGE, HOSTEL $$
(☑03-524 8692; www.zatori.co.nz; 2321 Taka-
ka-Collingwood Rd; s/d/f with shared bathroom
$60/120/210, ste with breakfast $229-399; 🐕)
🍂 This former maternity hospital has been
transformed into a stylish and relaxing retreat. Chic suites are arrayed around a spacious lounge area enlivened with colourful
artworks from Asia, and looking out onto
brilliant views of Farewell Spit (p302). A separate wing houses rooms with shared bathrooms for budget travellers. Massage services, kayaks and paddle boards are available,
and there's a restaurant-bar.

Many of the restaurant's ingredients are
sourced from Zatori's own gardens and orchards, and over summer an in-house chef
crafts seasonal daily menus with an organic
and wholefood bent. A great wine and craft
beer list means guests don't have to be *too*
virtuous.

ℹ Getting There & Away

Golden Bay Coachlines (p287) runs twice
daily from Takaka to Collingwood ($21, 25
minutes).

Kahurangi National Park

Kahurangi – 'blue skies' in one of several
translations – is the second largest of New

Zealand's national parks, and also one of its
most diverse. Its most eye-catching features
are geological, ranging from windswept
beaches and sea cliffs to earthquake-shat-
tered slopes and moraine-dammed lakes,
and the smooth, strange karst forms of the
interior tableland.

Around 85% of the 4520 sq km park is
forested, and more than 50% of NZ's plant
species can be found here, including more
than 80% of its alpine plant species. Among
the park's 60 bird species are great spotted
kiwi, kea, kaka and whio (blue duck). There
are creepy cave weta, weird beetles and a
huge, leggy spider, but there's also a majestic and ancient snail known as Powelliphan-
ta – something of a flag bearer for the park's
animal kingdom. If you like a field trip filled
with the new and strange, Kahurangi National Park will certainly satisfy.

🏃 Activities & Tours

The best-known tramp in Kahurangi is the
Heaphy Track (p280). The more challenging
Wangapeka is not as well known, but many
consider it a more enjoyable tramp. Taking
about five days, the track starts 25km south of
Karamea at Little Wanganui and runs 52km
east to Rolling River near Tapawera. There's a
chain of huts along the track.

The Heaphy and Wangapeka, however,
are just one part of a 650km network of
tracks that includes excellent full-day and
overnight tramps such as those in the **Cobb
Valley** and **Mt Arthur/Tablelands**. See
www.doc.govt.nz for detailed information
on all Kahurangi tracks.

🛏 Sleeping

Seven designated Great Walk huts ($34) lie
along the Heaphy Track, which have bunks
and kitchen areas, heating, flush toilets and
washbasins with cold water. Most but not all
have gas rings; a couple have lighting. There
are also nine Great Walk campsites ($14),
plus the beachside **Kohaihai Campsite**
(www.doc.govt.nz; per person $8) at the West
Coast trailhead. The two day shelters are
just that; overnight stays are not permitted.

ℹ Getting There & Away

The two road ends of the Heaphy Track are an
almost unfathomable distance apart: 463km
to be precise. From Takaka, you can get to the
Heaphy Track (via Collingwood) with **Golden
Bay Coachlines** (p287; $35, 9.15am, one hour)
from December to March.

OFF THE BEATEN TRACK

CAPE FAREWELL & FAREWELL SPIT

Bleak, exposed and positively sci-fi, **Farewell Spit** is a wetland of international importance and renowned bird sanctuary – the summer home of thousands of migratory waders, notably the godwit, Caspian tern and Australasian gannet. Walkers can explore the first 4km of the spit via a network of tracks (see DOC's *Farewell Spit & Puponga Farm Park* brochure; $2 or downloadable from www.doc.govt.nz). Beyond that point access is limited to trips with the brilliant Farewell Spit Eco Tours (p302), scheduled according to tides.

The spit's 35km beach features colossal, crescent-shaped dunes, from where panoramic views extend across Golden Bay and a vast low-tide salt marsh.

At the foot of the spit is a hilltop visitor-centre-cum-cafe – a convenient spot to write a postcard over a coffee, especially on an inclement day.

Wharariki Beach Remote, desolate Wharariki Beach is along an unsealed road, then a 20-minute walk from the car park over farmland (part of the DOC-administered Puponga Farm Park). It's a wild introduction to the West Coast, with mighty dune formations, looming rock islets and a seal colony at its eastern end (look out for seals in the stream on the walk here). As inviting as a swim may seem, there are strong undertows – what the sea wants, the sea shall have...

Cape Farewell Horse Treks (☑ 03-524 8031; www.horsetreksnz.com; McGowan St, Puponga; treks from $80) Befitting a frontier, this is the place to saddle up: Cape Farewell Horse Treks is en route to Wharariki Beach (p302). Treks in this wind-blown country range from 1½ hours (to Pillar Point) to three hours (to Wharariki Beach), with longer (including overnight) trips by arrangement.

Farewell Spit Eco Tours (☑ 03-524 8257, 0800 808 257; www.farewellspit.com; 6 Tasman St, Collingwood; tours $130-165) Operating for more than 70 years and featuring expert, knowledgable guides, this company runs memorable tours ranging from two to 6½ hours. Departing from Collingwood, tours take in the spit (p302), the lighthouse and up to 20 species of bird, which may include gannets and godwits. Expect ripping yarns aplenty.

The Kohaihai trailhead is 15km from the small town of Karamea. **Karamea Express** (☑ 03-782 6757; info@karamea-express.co.nz; Heaphy Track trailhead transport per person $20) departs from the shelter at 1pm and 2pm for Karamea from October to the end of April. Booking ahead is essential. **Karamea Connections** (☑ 03-782 6767; www.karameaconnections. co.nz) offers on-demand pick-ups.

Heaphy Bus (☑ 0800 128 735, 0272 221 872; www.theheaphybus.co.nz) offers a round-trip shuttle service – drop-off at Brown Hut and pickup from Kohaihai ($160) – and other on-demand local track transport.

Heaphy Track Help (☑ 03-525 9576; www. heaphytrackhelp.co.nz) offers car relocations (around $300, depending on the direction and time), food drops, shuttles and advice.

Adventure Flights Golden Bay (p298) will fly you back to Takaka from Karamea (or vice versa) for $240 to $265 per person (up to five people). **Golden Bay Air** (☑ 0800 588 885; www.golden bayair.co.nz) flies the same route ($149 to $179 per person), as does **Helicopter Charter Karamea** (p270), which will take up to six passengers for $1400. With five passengers and mountain bikes the cost is $1600.

MARLBOROUGH DISTRICT

Picton is the gateway to the South Island and the launching point for Marlborough Sounds exploration. A cork's pop south of Picton is Blenheim and its world-famous wineries, and further south still is Kaikoura, the whale-watching mecca. Highlights of this region include negotiating the famed Queen Charlotte Track by tramping or mountain biking, and discovering the many hidden bays and coves of the Marlborough Sounds by boat. Relaxing over a glass of local sauvignon blanc is recommended at the end of a busy day.

History

Long before Abel Tasman sheltered on the east coast of D'Urville Island in 1642 (more than 100 years before James Cook blew through in 1770), Māori knew the Marlborough area as Te Tau Ihu o Te Waka a Māui (the prow of Māui's canoe). It was Cook who named Queen Charlotte Sound; his reports made the area the best-known sheltered anchorage in the southern hemisphere. In 1827

French navigator Jules Dumont d'Urville discovered the narrow strait now known as French Pass. His officers named the island just to the north in his honour. In that year a whaling station was established at Te Awaiti in Tory Channel, which brought about the first permanent European settlement in the district.

Marlborough Sounds

The Marlborough Sounds are a maze of peaks, bays, beaches and watery reaches, formed when the sea flooded deep river valleys after the last ice age. They are very convoluted: Pelorus Sound, for example, is 42km long but has 379km of shoreline.

Many spectacular locations can be reached by car. The wiggly 35km route along **Queen Charlotte Drive** from Picton to Havelock is a great Sounds snapshot, but if you have a spare day, head out to **French Pass** (or even **D'Urville Island**) for some big-picture framing of the Outer Sounds. Roads are predominantly narrow and occasionally unsealed; allow plenty of driving time and keep your wits about you.

There are loads of tramping, kayaking, boating and biking opportunities, and there's diving as well – notably the wreck of the *Mikhail Lermontov*, a Russian cruise ship that sank in Port Gore in 1986.

Sights & Activities

Kenepuru & Pelorus Sounds

Kenepuru and Pelorus Sounds, to the west of Queen Charlotte Sound, are less populous and therefore offer fewer traveller services, including transport. There's some cracking scenery, however, and those with time to spare will be well rewarded by their explorations.

Havelock is the hub of this area, the western bookend of the 35km Queen Charlotte Drive (Picton being the eastern one) and the self-proclaimed 'Greenshell Mussel Capital of the World'. While hardly the most rock-and-roll of New Zealand towns, Havelock offers most necessities, including accommodation, fuel and food.

It's worth a trip to the **Cullen Point Lookout**, a 10-minute drive from Havelock along the Queen Charlotte Drive. A short walk leads up and around a headland overlooking Havelock, the surrounding valleys and Pelorus Sound.

Havelock Museum   MUSEUM
(www.peloruspeople.org.nz; Main St, Havelock; ⊙10am-4pm) FREE This cute, locally focused museum presents old pioneering tales in a contemporary, easily digestible style.

Nydia Track   TRAMPING
(Map p304; www.doc.govt.nz) The Nydia Track (27km, 10 hours) starts at Kaiuma Bay and ends at Duncan Bay (or vice versa). You'll need water and road transport to complete the journey; Havelock's **Blue Moon Lodge** (☑0800 252 663, 03-574 2212; www.bluemoonhavelock.co.nz; 48 Main Rd, Havelock; dm $33, r with/without bathroom from $96/82; @🎧) ✈ runs a shuttle to Duncan Bay.

Around halfway along is beautiful Nydia Bay, where there's a **DOC campsite** (Map p304; www.doc.govt.nz; adult/child $6/3) and **Nydia Lodge** (Map p304; ☑03-520 3002; www.doc.govt.nz; Nydia Bay; dm $15, minimum charge $60), an unhosted 50-bed lodge. Also in Nydia Bay, **On the Track Lodge** (Map p304; ☑03-579 8411; www.onthetracklodge.nz; Nydia Bay; dm $60, s $90-120, d $140-180) ✈ is a tranquil, eco-focused affair offering everything from packed lunches to evening meals and a hot tub.

Queen Charlotte Sound

One of New Zealand's classic walks – and now one of its Great Rides, too – the meandering, 70km Queen Charlotte Track (p279) offers gorgeous coastal scenery on its way from historic Ship Cove to Anakiwa, passing through a mixture of privately owned land and DOC reserves. Access depends on the cooperation of local landowners; respect their property by utilising designated campsites and toilets, and carrying out your rubbish. Your purchase of the Track Pass ($10 to $18), available from the Picton i-SITE (p310) and track-related businesses, provides the co-op with the means to maintain and enhance the experience for all.

Motuara Island   WILDLIFE RESERVE
(Map p304; www.doc.govt.nz; Queen Charlotte Sound) ✈ This DOC-managed, predator-free island reserve is chock-full of rare NZ birds including Okarito kiwi (rowi), native pigeons (kereru), saddleback (tieke) and king shags. You can get here by water taxi and with tour operators working out of Picton.

Lochmara   BAY
(Map p304; ☑03-573 4554; www.lochmara.co.nz; Lochmara Bay; day trips from $40) ✈ Also an excellent lodge (p306), Lochmara can be

Marlborough Sounds

visited as a day trip by water taxi from Picton. Activities include kayaking, cruising, walking and a forest-clad flying fox, and it's possible to learn about the various wildlife protection and conservation projects at the lodge. Highlights include hand-feeding stingrays, eels and endangered kakariki parakeets, and checking out Lochmara's new underwater observatory.

👉 Tours

★ Wilderness Guides   TOURS
(Map p308; ☎ 0800 266 266, 03-573 5432; www. wildernessguidesnz.com; Town Wharf, Picton; 1-day guided trips from $130, kayak/bike hire per day $60) Host of the popular and flexible one- to three-day 'multisport' trips (kayak/ tramp/cycle) plus many other guided and independent biking, tramping and kayaking tours, including a remote Ship Cove paddle. Mountain bikes and kayaks for hire, too.

Cougar Line   TOURS
(Map p308; ☎ 03-573 7925, 0800 504 090; www. cougarline.co.nz; Town Wharf, Picton; track round trips $105, cruises from $85) Queen Charlotte Track transport, plus various half- and full-day cruise/walk trips, including the rather special (and flexible) eco-cruise to Motuara Island (p303) and a day walk from Resolution Bay to Furneaux Lodge.

Marlborough Sounds
Adventure Company   TOURS
(Map p308; ☎ 03-573 6078, 0800 283 283; www. marlboroughsounds.co.nz; Town Wharf, Picton; half-/5-day guided packages $95/2420, kayak hire per half day from $40) Bike-tramp-kayak trips, with options to suit every inclination and interest. Bikes, kayaks and camping equipment are also available for rent. Trip durations range from half days to five days, and the popular Kayak & Hike option combines one day of kayaking, one day of tramping and an overnight stay in the Sounds.

Marlborough Sounds

Beachcomber Cruises TOURS
(Map p308; ☑ 03-573 6175, 0800 624 526; www.
beachcombercruises.co.nz; Town Wharf, Picton;
mail runs $101, cruises from $85, track round trips
$103) Two- to eight-hour cruise adventures,
including the classic 'Magic Mail Run', plus
walking, biking and resort lunch options
and round-trip track transport.

E-Ko Tours TOURS
(Map p308; ☑ 03-573 8040, 0800 945 354; www.
e-ko.nz; Town Wharf, Picton; dolphin swimming/
viewing $165/135) Half-day 'swim with dol-
phins' trips, and various other wildlife tours
including trips to Motuara Island (p303).
Tours are cheaper if you don't want to get in
the water with the wildlife.

Sea Kayak Adventures KAYAKING, BIKING
(Map p304; ☑ 03-574 2765, 0800 262 5492; www.
nzseakayaking.com; cnr Queen Charlotte Dr &
Anakiwa Rd; half-/1-day guided paddles $90/125)
Guided and 'guided then go' kayaking with
bike/hike options around Queen Charlotte,
Kenepuru and Pelorus Sounds. Also offers

kayak and mountain-bike rental (half/full
day $40/60).

Pelorus Eco Adventures KAYAKING
(☑ 03-574 2211, 0800 252 663; www.kayak-newzea
land.com; Blue Moon Lodge, 48 Main Rd, Havelock;
per person $180) Float in an inflatable kayak
on scenic Pelorus River, star of the barrel
scene in *The Hobbit*. Wend your way down
exhilarating rapids, through crystal-clear
pools and past native forest and waterfalls.
No experience required; minimum two people. Tours last around four to five hours.

Pelorus Mail Boat CRUISE
(☑ 03-574 1088; www.themailboat.co.nz; Jetty 1,
Havelock Marina; adult/child $128/free; ⊙ departs
9.30am Nov-Apr, Tue, Thu & Fri May-Oct) Popular
full-day boat cruise through the far reaches of
Pelorus Sound on a genuine NZ Post delivery
run. Bookings essential; BYO lunch. Picton
and Blenheim pick-up and drop-off available.

🛏 Sleeping

Some Sounds sleeping options are accessi
ble only by boat and are deliciously isolated,
but the most popular are those on (or just
off) the Queen Charlotte Track. Some places
close over winter; call ahead to check.

There are over 30 DOC camping grounds
throughout the Sounds (many accessible
only by boat), providing water and toilet facilities but not much else.

🛏 Kenepuru & Pelorus Sounds

★**Hopewell** LODGE $$
(Map p304; ☑ 03-573 4341; www.hopewell.co.nz;
7204 Kenepuru Rd, Double Bay; dm/cottages
$40/240, d with/without bathroom $150/110;
@ 🖥) Beloved of travellers, remote Hopewell
sits waterside surrounded by native bush.
Savour the long, winding drive to get there,
or take a water taxi from Te Mahia ($25).
Stay a couple of days, so you can chill out
or enjoy the roll-call of activities: mountain
biking, kayaking, sailing, fishing, eating
gourmet pizza, soaking in the outdoor hot
tub and more.

Havelock Garden Motels MOTEL $$
(☑ 03-574 2387; www.gardenmotels.com; 71 Main
Rd, Havelock; d $125-160; 🖥) Set in a large,
graceful garden complete with dear old trees
and blooms galore, these 1960s units have
been tastefully revamped to offer homey
comforts. Local activities are happily booked
for you.

WORTH A TRIP

PELORUS BRIDGE SCENIC RESERVE

A peaky pocket of deep, green forest tucked between paddocks of bog-standard pasture, 18km west of Havelock, this scenic reserve contains one of the last stands of river-flat forest in Marlborough. It survived only because a town planned in 1865 didn't get off the ground by 1912, by which time obliterative logging made this little remnant look precious. Visitors can explore its many tracks, admire the historic bridge, take a dip in the limpid Pelorus River (alluring enough to star in Peter Jackson's *The Hobbit*), and partake in some home baking at the cafe. The fortunate few can stay overnight in DOC's small but perfectly formed **Pelorus Bridge Campground** (☑ 03-571 6019; www.doc.govt.nz; Pelorus Bridge, SH6; unpowered/powered sites per person $9/18), with its snazzy facilities building. Come sundown keep an eye out for long-tailed bats – the reserve is home to one of the last remaining populations in Marlborough.

🛏 Queen Charlotte Sound

A complete list of sleeping and eating options can be found in the official Queen Charlotte Track Directory (www.qctrack.co.nz).

Anakiwa 401 HOSTEL $
(Map p304; ☑ 03-574 1388; www.anakiwa401.co.nz; 401 Anakiwa Rd; s/q $75/200, d $100-120; 🛜) At the southern end of the track, this former schoolhouse is a soothing spot to rest and reflect. There are two doubles (one with en suite), one twin and a beachy self-contained unit. Jocular owners will have you jumping off the jetty for joy and enjoying espresso and ice cream from their green caravan (open afternoons). Free bikes and kayaks.

Smiths Farm Holiday Park HOLIDAY PARK $
(Map p304; ☑ 03-574 2806; www.smithsfarm. co.nz; 1419 Queen Charlotte Dr, Linkwater; campsites per person from $18, cabins $65, units $115-150; @🛜) 🦮 Located on the aptly named Linkwater flat between Queen Charlotte and Pelorus, friendly Smiths makes a handy base camp for the track and beyond. Well-kept cabins and motel units face out onto the bushy hillside, while livestock nibble around the lush camping lawns. Short walks extend to a waterfall and magical glow-worm dell.

Mistletoe Bay HOLIDAY PARK $
(Map p304; ☑ 03-573 4048; www.mistletoebay. co.nz; Onahau Bay; campsites adult/child $16/10, dm/d $40/80, linen $7.50; 🛜) 🦮 Surrounded by bushy hills, Mistletoe Bay offers attractive camping with no-frills facilities. There are also eight modern cabins ($140) sleeping up to six, plus a bunkhouse and modern shared kitchen. Environmental sustainability abounds, as does the opportunity to jump off the jetty, kayak in the bay, or tramp the Queen Charlotte Track.

⭐ **Te Mahia Bay Resort** RESORT $$
(Map p304; ☑ 03-573 4089; www.temahia.co.nz; 63 Te Mahia Rd; d $160-258; 🛜) This lovely low-key resort is within cooee (shouting distance) of the Queen Charlotte Track in a picturesque bay on Kenepuru Sound. It has a range of delightful rooms-with-a-view, our pick of which are the great-value heritage units. The on-site shop has precooked meals, pizza, cakes, coffee and camping supplies (wine!), plus there is kayak hire and massage.

Lochmara Lodge RESORT $$
(Map p304; ☑ 03-573 4554, 0800 562 462; www. lochmaralodge.co.nz; Lochmara Bay; units $99-300; 🛜) 🦮 Set in lush surroundings, this arty eco-retreat can either be reached via the Queen Charlotte Track or from Picton aboard the lodge's water taxi ($30 one way). There are en-suite doubles, units and chalets, an excellent cafe and restaurant, plus a bathhouse for spa and massage services. Recent additions are Lochmara's (p303) wildlife conservation activities and an interesting underwater observatory.

⭐ **Bay of Many Coves Resort** RESORT $$$
(Map p304; ☑ 0800 579 9771, 03-579 9771; www.bayofmanycoves.co.nz; Bay of Many Coves; 1-/2-/3-bedroom apt $860/1090/1435; 🛜🏊) These stylish and secluded apartments feature all mod cons and private balconies overlooking the water. As well as upmarket cuisine, there are various indulgences such as massage, a spa and a hot tub. Kayaking and bush walks are also on the cards, as are adventures in the Sounds organised by the charming, hands-on owners and staff.

Mahana Lodge LODGE $$$
(Map p304; ☑ 03-579 8373; www.mahanalodge. co.nz; Camp Bay, Endeavour Inlet; d $250; ☺ closed

Jun-Aug) 🌱 This beautiful property features a pretty waterside lawn and purpose-built lodge with four en-suite doubles. Ecofriendly initiatives include bush regeneration, pest trapping and an organic veggie garden. In fact, feel-good factors abound: free kayaks, home baking and a blooming conservatory where prearranged evening meals are served (three courses $75).

ℹ Information

Havelock i-SITE (☎ 03-577 8080; www.marl boroughnz.com; 61 Main Rd, Havelock; ⊗ 9am-4.30pm Sep-May) This helpful wee visitor centre shares its home with the **Eyes On Nature** museum, chock-full of frighteningly lifelike, full-size replicas of birds, fish and other critters.

For a complete list of visitor services, visit www.pelorusnz.co.nz, which covers Havelock, Kenepuru and Pelorus Sounds, and the extremities of French Pass and D'Urville Island.

ℹ Getting There & Away

BOAT

The Marlborough Sounds are most commonly explored from Picton, where boat operators congregate at the centrally located Town Wharf. They offer everything from lodge transfers to cruises taking in sites such as Ship Cove and **Motuara Island** (p303) bird sanctuary, to round-trip Queen Charlotte Track transport and pack transfers that allow trampers to walk without a heavy burden. Bikes and kayaks can also be transported.

BUS

InterCity (p292) runs daily buses from Picton to Havelock via Blenheim ($17, one hour), and from Havelock to Nelson ($17, 1¼ hours). Buses depart from near the **Havelock i-SITE**.

ℹ Getting Around

Sounds travel is invariably quicker by boat (for example, Punga Cove from Picton by car takes two to three hours, but just 45 minutes by boat). Fortunately, an armada of vessels offer scheduled and on-demand boat services, with the bulk operating out of Picton for the Queen Charlotte Sound, and some from Havelock for Kenepuru and Pelorus Sounds.

Options to get around include **Arrow Water Taxis** (Map p308; ☎ 03-573 8229, 027 444 4689; www.arrowwatertaxis.co.nz; Town Wharf, Picton), a **float plane** (Map p308; ☎ 021 704 248, 03-573 9012; www.nz-scenic-flights. co.nz; Ferry Terminal, Picton; flights from $110) service, **Kenepuru Water Taxi** (Map p304; ☎ 03-573 4344, 021 132 3261; www.kenepuru.co.nz; 7170 Kenepuru Rd, Raetihi), **Pelorus Sound**

ℹ QUEEN CHARLOTTE TRACK INFORMATION

The best place to get track information and advice is **Picton i-SITE** (p310), which also handles bookings for transport and accommodation. Also see the Queen Charlotte Track website (www. qctrack.co.nz) and the Queen Charlotte Track Land Cooperative website (www. qctlc.com).

Water Taxi (☎ 0508 4283 5625, 027 444 2852; www.pelorussoundwatertaxis.co.nz; Pier C, Havelock Marina) and **Picton Water Taxis** (Map p308; ☎ 03-573 7853, 027 227 0284; www. pictonwatertaxis.co.nz; Waterfront, cnr London Quay & Wellington St, Picton).

Picton

POP 4360

Half asleep in winter, but hyperactive in summer (with up to eight fully laden ferry arrivals per day), boaty Picton clusters around a deep gulch at the head of Queen Charlotte Sound. It's the main traveller port for the South Island, and the best base for tackling the Marlborough Sounds and Queen Charlotte Track. Over the last few years this little town has really bloomed, and offers visitors plenty of reasons to linger even after the obvious attractions are knocked off the list.

◉ Sights

Edwin Fox Maritime Museum   MUSEUM
(Map p308; ☎ 03-573 6868; www.edwinfoxsociety. co.nz; Dunbar Wharf; adult/child $15/5; ⊗ 9am-5pm) Purportedly the world's ninth-oldest surviving wooden ship, the *Edwin Fox* was built near Calcutta and launched in 1853. During its chequered career it carried troops to the Crimean War, convicts to Australia and immigrants to NZ. This museum has maritime exhibits, including this venerable old dear.

Eco World Aquarium   AQUARIUM
(Map p308; ☎ 03-573 6030; www.ecoworldnz. co.nz; Dunbar Wharf; adult/child/family $24/12/67; ⊗ 9.30am-7.30pm) 🌱 The primary purpose of this centre is animal rehabilitation: all sorts of critters come here for fix-ups and rest-ups, and the odd bit of hanky-panky! Special specimens include NZ's 'living dinosaur' – the tuatara – as well as blue penguins, geckos

Picton

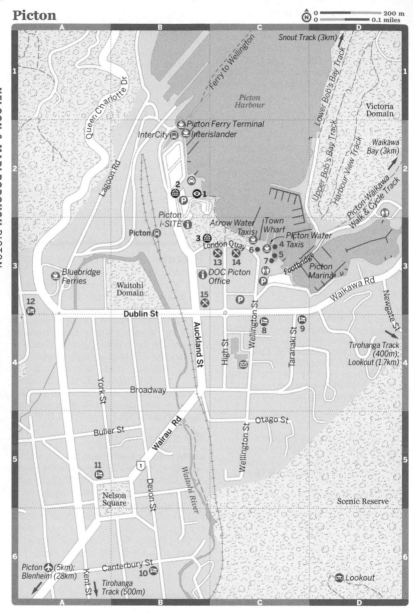

Ferry to Wellington

Snout Track (3km)

Picton Harbour

Lower Bob's Bay Track

Victoria Domain

Queen Charlotte Dr

Upper Bob's Bay Track

Waikawa Bay (3km)

Picton Ferry Terminal
InterCity
Interislander

Harbour View Track

Lagoon Rd

Picton-Waikawa Walk & Cycle Track

2

P

1

Picton i-SITE

Arrow Water Taxis

Town Wharf

Picton Water Taxis

Picton

3

London Quay

6

4

5

Footbridge

Picton Marina

13

14

7

Bluebridge Ferries

Waikawa Rd

DOC Picton Office

Waitohi Domain

15

P

Newgate St

12

Dublin St

8

9

Tirohanga Track (400m); Lookout (1.7km)

High St

Wellington St

Taranaki St

Auckland St

Broadway

York St

Otago St

Buller St

Wairau Rd

Wellington St

Waitohi River

11

1

Devon St

Nelson Square

Scenic Reserve

Picton ✈ (5km);
Blenheim (28km)

Canterbury St

10

Kent St

Tirohanga Track (500m)

Lookout

---

and giant weta. Fish-feeding time (11am and 2pm) is a splashy spectacle. Sharing the ageing building is the **Picton Cinema** (Map p308; ☎03-573 6030; www.pictoncinemas.co.nz; Dunbar Wharf; tickets adult/child $16/11), screening mainstream and edgy flicks.

Picton Museum   MUSEUM

(Map p308; ☎03-573 8283; www.pictonmuseum-newzealand.com; London Quay; adult/child $5/1; ⊙10am-4pm) If you dig local history – whaling, sailing and the 1964 Roller Skating Champs – this will float your boat. The

Picton

◎ Sights
1 Eco World Aquarium B2
2 Edwin Fox Maritime Museum B2
3 Picton Museum B3

◎ Activities, Courses & Tours
4 Beachcomber Cruises C3
5 Cougar Line C3
6 E-Ko Tours C3
7 Marlborough Sounds
   Adventure Company C3
   Wilderness Guides .... (see 6)

◎ Sleeping
8 Gables B&B C4
9 Harbour View Motel C4
10 Jugglers Rest B6
11 Sequoia Lodge Backpackers A5
12 Tombstone Backpackers A3

◎ Eating
13 Café Cortado C3
14 Le Café C3
15 Picton Village Bakkerij B3

◎ Entertainment
   Picton Cinema .... (see 1)

photo displays are well worth a look, especially for five bucks.

🏃 Activities & Tours

The town has some very pleasant walks. A free i-SITE map details many of these, including an easy 1km track to **Bob's Bay**. The **Snout Track** (three hours return) continues along the ridge offering superb water views. Climbing a hill behind the town, the **Tirohanga Track** is a two-hour leg-stretching loop offering the best view in the house.

Escape to Marlborough   TOURS
(☑ 0800 6937 2273; www.escapetomarlborough. co.nz; adult/child $69.50/15.50; ⊗ 8am-6pm) Hop-on, hop-off bus services running at hourly intervals and linking Picton and Blenheim, stopping at 18 key attractions, vineyards and breweries. There are two routes, both taking eight hours in full, and it's possible to change onto the other service en route. Direct transport to Blenheim or Blenheim airport and bespoke wine tours are also offered.

🛏 Sleeping

★ Jugglers Rest   HOSTEL $
(Map p308; ☑ 03-573 5570; www.jugglersrest.com; 8 Canterbury St; dm $33, d $75-85; ⊗ closed Jun-

Sep; @ 🛜) 🍃 Jocular hosts keep all their balls in the air at this well-run, ecofriendly, bunk-free backpackers. Peacefully located a 10-minute walk from town, or even less on a free bike. Cheery gardens are a good place to socialise with fellow travellers, especially during the occasional circus-skills shows.

Buccaneer Lodge   LODGE $
(Map p304; ☑ 03-573 5002; www.buccaneerlodge. co.nz; 314 Waikawa Rd, Waikawa; d $110; 🛜) This Waikawa Bay lodge offers four redecorated en-suite rooms, some with expansive views of the Sounds from the 1st-floor balcony. Town transfers, bike hire and home-baked bread come courtesy of kindly owners Mel and Phil. A smaller downstairs room ($80) is also available.

Tombstone Backpackers   HOSTEL $
(Map p308; ☑ 03-573 7116; www.tombstonebp. co.nz; 16 Gravesend Pl; dm $31-36, d with/without bathroom $91/84, apt $120; @ 🛜) Rest in peace in a smart dorm, double room or self-contained apartment. Also on offer are a spa overlooking the harbour, free breakfast, a sunny reading room, table tennis, free internet, ferry pick-up and drop-off...the list goes on.

Sequoia Lodge Backpackers   HOSTEL $
(Map p308; ☑ 0800 222 257, 03-573 8399; www.se quoialodge.co.nz; 3a Nelson Sq; dm $29-31, d with/without bathroom $84/74; 🛜) This well-managed backpackers in a colourful Victorian house is a little out of the centre, but has bonuses including free wi-fi, hammocks, barbecues, a hot tub and nightly chocolate pudding. Complimentary breakfast May to October. In the special Netflix room, you can fire up your video-on-demand content of choice. Family rooms are good for groups (from $100 for three people).

Gables B&B   B&B $$
(Map p308; ☑ 03-573 6772; www.thegables.co.nz; 20 Waikawa Rd; d $175-195, units $230; @ 🛜) This historic B&B (once home to Picton's mayor) has three individually styled rooms in the main house and two homey self-contained units out the back. Lovely hosts show good humour (ask about the Muffin Club) and provide excellent local advice.

Harbour View Motel   MOTEL $$
(Map p308; ☑ 03-573 6259, 0800 101 133; www. harbourviewpicton.co.nz; 30 Waikawa Rd; d $140-240; 🛜) Its elevated position means this motel commands good views of Picton's

mast-filled harbour from its smart, self-contained studios with timber decks.

Bay Vista Waterfront Motel
MOTEL $$

(Map p304; ☑03-573 6733; www.bayvistapicton.co.nz; 303 Waikawa Rd, Waikawa; d $160-220; 🐾) This smart motel enjoys an enviable position on Waikawa foreshore, with views down Queen Charlotte Sound. All units have their own patio and share a big, lush lawn. Located 4km from Picton (courtesy transfer available).

Whatamonga Homestay
HOMESTAY $$$

(Map p304; ☑03-573 7192; www.whsl.co.nz; 425 Port Underwood Rd; d incl breakfast $360-390; 🐾🐾) Follow Waikawa Rd, which becomes Port Underwood Rd, for 8km and you'll bump into this classy waterside option – two self-contained units with king-sized beds and balconies with magic views. Two other rooms under the main house share a bathroom. Free kayaks, dinghies and fishing gear are available. Minimum two-night stay.

🍴 Eating

Picton Village Bakkerij
BAKERY $

(Map p308; ☑03-573 7082; www.facebook.com/PictonVillageBakery; cnr Auckland & Dublin Sts; bakery items $2-8; ⊙6am-4pm Mon-Fri, to 3.30pm Sat; 🐾) Dutch owners bake trays of European goodies here, including interesting breads, filled rolls, cakes and custardy, tarty treats. The savoury pies are very good – ask if the chicken, chilli and cream cheese one is available (trust us, it's a winning combination). An excellent stop before or after the ferry, or to stock a packed lunch.

Café Cortado
CAFE $$

(Map p308; ☑03-573 5630; www.cafecortado.co.nz; cnr High St & London Quay; mains $17-35; ⊙8am-late Nov-Apr, 8am-late Wed-Sun May-Oct) Pleasant corner cafe and bar with views of the harbour through the foreshore's pohutukawa and palms. This consistent performer turns out fish dishes, homemade cheeseburgers and decent pizza. There's a surprisingly eclectic selection of local Marlborough wines and a few craft beers on tap. Kick off with the breakfast burrito and come back for a dinner of beer-battered blue cod.

Le Café
CAFE $$

(Map p308; ☑03-573 5588; www.lecafepicton.co.nz; London Quay; breakfast & lunch $14-25, dinner $24-30; ⊙7.30am-8pm Sun-Thu, to late Fri & Sat; 🐾) A spot perennially popular for its quayside location, dependable food

and Havana coffee. The likes of salami sandwiches and sweets are in the cabinet, while a good antipasto platter, generous pasta dishes, local mussels, and lamb and fish dishes feature à la carte. The laid-back atmosphere, craft beer and occasional live gigs make this a good evening hang-out.

ℹ️ Information

DOC Picton Office (Map p308; ☑03-520 3002; www.doc.govt.nz; 14 Auckland St; ⊙9am-4.30pm Mon-Fri) This Department of Conservation office is largely a field office and offers only hut and camp tickets and local tramping information.

Picton i-SITE (Map p308; ☑03-520 3113; www.marlboroughnz.com; foreshore; ⊙8am-5pm) All vital tourist guff including maps, Queen Charlotte Track information, lockers and transport bookings. Dedicated DOC counter.

Picton Library (67 High St; ⊙8am-5pm Mon-Fri, 10am-1pm Sat; 🐾) has free wi-fi.

ℹ️ Getting There & Away

AIR

Soundsair (☑0800 505 005, 03-520 3080; www.soundsair.co.nz; 10 London Quay; ⊙7.30am-5.30pm Mon-Thu & Sat, to 7pm Fri, 9am-7pm Sun) flies between Picton and Wellington (adult/child from $99/89); a shuttle bus to/from the airstrip at Koromiko is available.

BOAT

There are two operators crossing Cook Strait between Picton and Wellington, and although all ferries leave from more or less the same place, each has its own terminal. The main transport hub (with car-rental depots) is at the **Interislander Terminal** (Map p308; Auckland St), which also has a cafe and internet facilities.

Bluebridge Ferries (Map p308; ☑0800 844 844, 04-471 6188; www.bluebridge.co.nz; adult/child to Wellington from $53/27; 🐾) crossings take just over three hours, and the company has up to four sailings in each direction daily. Cars cost from $120 and campervans from $155. The sleeper service arrives in Picton at 6am.

Interislander (Map p308; ☑0800 802 802; www.interislander.co.nz; Interislander Ferry Terminal, Auckland St; adult/child to Wellington from $52/32) crossings take just over three hours; there are up to six sailings in each direction daily. Cars are priced from $121, campervans (up to 5.5m) from $153, motorbikes $56, bicycles $15.

Local transport for the Queen Charlotte Track is provided by a wide range of water-based transport options based in Picton.

BUS

Buses serving Picton depart from the **Interislander** (p310) ferry terminal or the nearby **i-SITE** (p310).

InterCity (Map p308; ☑ 03-365 1113; www.intercity.co.nz; outside Interislander Ferry Terminal, Auckland St) runs south to Christchurch twice daily ($56, 5½ hours) via Blenheim ($12, 30 minutes) and Kaikoura ($21, 2½ hours), with connections to Dunedin, Queenstown and Invercargill. Services also run to/from Nelson ($23, 2¼ hours), with connections to Motueka and the West Coast. At least one bus daily on each of these routes connects with a Wellington ferry service.

Escape to Marlborough (p309) runs hourly services linking Picton to Blenheim ($12.50) and Blenheim airport ($17.50). A good local shuttle company is **Marlborough Sounds Shuttles** (☑ 03-573 7122; www.marlborough soundsshuttles.co.nz).

CAR

Renting a car in Picton is easy and competitively priced (as low as $50 per day), with numerous rental companies based at the **Interislander** (p310) ferry terminal and many others within a short walk. **Ace** (☑ 03-573 8939; www.acerentalcars.co.nz; Interislander Ferry Terminal) and **Omega** (☑ 03-573 5580; www.omega-rentalcars.com; 1 Lagoon Rd) are reliable local operators. Most agencies allow drop-offs in Christchurch; if you're planning to drive to the North Island, most companies suggest you leave your car at Picton and pick up another one in Wellington after crossing Cook Strait.

TRAIN

KiwiRail Scenic (☑ 0800 872 467; www.greatjourneysofnz.co.nz) runs the *Coastal Pacific* service daily each way between Picton and Christchurch via Blenheim and Kaikoura connecting with the **Interislander** (p310) ferry. Note this service was suspended following the November 2016 Kaikoura earthquake, but was planned to be back up and running in late 2018. Check KiwiRail's website (www.kiwirail.co.nz) for the latest update.

ⓘ Getting Around

Shuttle services around town and beyond are offered by **A1 Picton Shuttles** (☑ 022 018 8472; www.a1pictonshuttles.co.nz).

Blenheim

POP 31,300

Blenheim is an agricultural town 29km south of Picton on the pretty Wairau Plains between the Wither Hills and the Richmond Ranges. The last decade or so has seen town beautification projects, the maturation of the wine industry and the addition of a landmark museum significantly increase the town's appeal to visitors.

Check out the new riverside development, including compact parks, walkways and a pedestrian footbridge, on the northeastern edge of the town centre.

◉ Sights

★Omaka Aviation Heritage Centre   MUSEUM

(Map p312; ☑ 03-579 1305; www.omaka.org.nz; 79 Aerodrome Rd, Omaka; adult/child/family both exhibitions $30/16/99; ☺ 9am-5pm Dec-Mar, 10am-5pm Apr-Nov) This exceptionally brilliant museum houses film-director Peter Jackson's collection of original and replica Great War aircraft, brought to life in a series of dioramas that depict dramatic wartime scenes, such as the death of the Red Baron. A new wing houses Dangerous Skies, a WWII collection. Vintage biplane flights are available (10/20 minutes, $250/380 for one or two people).

A cafe and shop are on site, and next door is **Omaka Classic Cars** (Map p312; ☑ 03-577 9419; www.omakaclassiccars.co.nz; Aerodrome Rd, Omaka; adult/child $15/free; ☺ 10am-4pm), which houses more than 100 vehicles dating from the '50s to the '80s.

Marlborough Museum   MUSEUM

(Map p312; ☑ 03-578 1712; www.marlborough museum.org.nz; 26 Arthur Baker Pl, off New Renwick Rd; adult/child $10/5; ☺ 10am-4pm) Besides a replica street scene, vintage mechanicals and well-presented historical displays, there's the Wine Exhibition, for those looking to cap off their vineyard experiences.

Pollard Park   PARK

(Map p312; Parker St) Ten minutes' walk from town, this 25-hectare park boasts beautiful blooming and scented gardens, a playground, tennis courts, croquet and a nine-hole golf course. It's pretty as a picture when lit up on summer evenings. Five minutes away, on the way to or from town, is the extensive **Taylor River Reserve**, a lovely place for a stroll.

🏃 Activities & Tours

Wither Hills Farm Park   WALKING

(Map p312) In a town as flat as a pancake, this hilly 11-sq-km park provides welcome relief, offering over 60km of walking and mountain-biking trails with grand views across the

Marlborough Wine Region

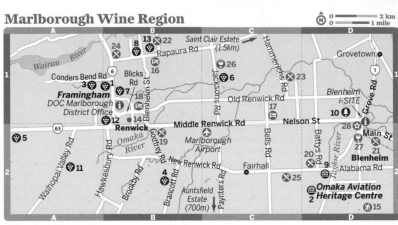

Wairau Valley and out to Cloudy Bay. Pick up a map from the i-SITE (p313) or check the information panels at the many entrances including Redwood St and Taylor Pass Rd.

★**Driftwood Eco-Tours**   KAYAKING, ECOTOUR
(☑03-577 7651; www.driftwoodecotours.co.nz; 749 Dillons Point Rd; kayak & 4WD tours $200) Go on a kayak or 4WD tour for fascinating natural history on and around the ecologically and historically significant Wairau Lagoon, 10 minutes' drive from Blenheim. Rare birds and the muppetty royal spoonbill may well be spotted. The semi self-contained 'Retreat' provides accommodation for up to four (double/quad $250/450), while the 'tree-house' offers accommodation for up to three (double/triple $200/250).

🛏 Sleeping

Watson's Way Lodge   LODGE $
(Map p312; ☑03-572 8228; www.watsonsway lodge.com; 56 High St, Renwick; tents/campervans $15/18, dm $30, d & tw $88-99; ⊘closed Aug & Sep; @🛜) This traveller-focused lodge has spick-and-span en-suite rooms in a sweetly converted bungalow with a full kitchen and comfy lounge. There are also spacious leafy gardens dotted with fruit trees and hammocks, an outdoor claw-foot bath, bikes for hire (guest/public rate $18/28 per day) and local information aplenty.

★ **St Leonards** COTTAGE $$
(Map p312; ☑ 03-577 8328; www.stleonards.co.nz;
18 St Leonards Rd; d incl breakfast $150-340; ☕ ⚙)
Tucked into the 4.5-acre grounds of an 1886
homestead, these five stylish and rustic cot-
tages offer privacy and a reason to stay put.
Each is unique in its layout and perspective
on the gardens and vines. Our pick is the
capacious and cosy Woolshed, exuding agri-
cultural chic. Resident sheep, chickens and
deer await your attention.

Olde Mill House B&B $$
(Map p312; ☑ 03-572 8458; www.oldemillhouse.
co.nz; 9 Wilson St, Renwick; d $175-195; ☕) On an
elevated section in otherwise flat Renwick,
this charming old house is a treat. New
owners are keeping standards high at this
welcoming B&B infused with stately decor,
and home-grown fruit and homemade jams
and pickles are offered for breakfast. Free
bikes, an outdoor spa and gardens make
this a tip top choice in the heart of the wine
country.

Marlborough Vintners Hotel HOTEL $$$
(Map p312; ☑ 0800 684 190, 03-572 5094; www.
mvh.co.nz; 190 Rapaura Rd; d from $315; ☕) ✦
Sixteen architecturally designed suites make
the most of valley views and boast wet-room
bathrooms and abstract art. The stylish re-
ception building has a bar and restaurant
opening out on to a cherry orchard and or-
ganic veggie garden.

✕ Eating

★ **Burleigh** DELI $
(Map p312; ☑ 03-579 2531; www.facebook.com/the
burleighnz; 72 New Renwick Rd; pies $6;
☺ 7.30am-3pm Mon-Fri, 9am-1pm Sat) The hum-
ble pie rises to stratospheric heights at this
fabulous deli; try the sweet pork-belly or
savoury steak and blue cheese, or perhaps
both. Fresh-filled baguettes, local sausage,
French cheeses and great coffee also make
tempting appearances. Avoid the lunch-
time rush.

Gramado's BRAZILIAN $$
(Map p312; ☑ 03-579 1192; www.gramadosres
taurant.com; 74 Main St; mains $28-40; ☺ 4pm-
late Tue-Sat) Injecting a little Latin American flair into the Blenheim dining scene,
Gramado's is a fun place to tuck into unashamedly hearty meals such as lamb *assa-
do*, feijoada (smoky pork and bean stew)
and Brazilian-spiced fish. Kick things off
with a caipirinha, of course.

♀ Drinking & Entertainment

Scotch Wine Bar WINE BAR
(Map p312; ☑ 03-579 1176; www.scotchbar.co.nz;
24-26 Maxwell Rd; ☺ 4pm-late) A versatile and
sociable spot in central Blenheim, Scotch offers local wines, craft beer on tap and shared
plates ($18 to $30), including spiced lamb
and hummus, and steamed buns crammed
with Japanese-style fried chicken. Pop next
door and buy wine from a stellar selection,
including many local Marlborough tipples,
either to be enjoyed in the bar or at home.

Moa Brewing Company CRAFT BEER
(Map p312; ☑ 03-572 5146; www.moabeer.com; 258
Jacksons Rd, Rapaura; tastings $8; ☺ 11am-5pm)
Take a break from wine-tasting at Moa's laid-
back beer-tasting room amid Rapaura's rural
vineyards. You won't find any flightless moa
roaming around, but there's still plenty of other bird life in the gardens. Food trucks often
rock up Friday to Sunday, and there's usually
a few seasonal brews on tap. Travelling beer
geeks should try Moa's excellent sour beers.

Dodson Street CRAFT BEER
(☑ 03-577 8348; www.dodsonstreet.co.nz; 1 Dodson
St; ☺ 11am-11pm) Pub and garden with a beer-
hall ambience and suitably Teutonic menu
(mains $17 to $27) featuring pork knuckle,
bratwurst and schnitzel (its pizza and burgers are also good). The stars of the show are
the 24 taps pouring quality, ever-changing
craft beer from around Marlborough and the
rest of NZ. A tasting of five brews is $10.

ASB Theatre THEATRE
(Map p312; ☑ 03-520 8558; www.asbtheatre.com;
42a Alfred St) Opened in 2016, this modern
theatre presents a wide program of concerts
and performances. Check the website to see
what's on.

❶ Information

Blenheim i-SITE (☑ 03-577 8080; www.marl
boroughnz.com; Railway Station, 8 Sinclair St;
☺ 9am-5pm Mon-Fri, to 3pm Sat, 10am-3pm
Sun) Information on Marlborough and beyond.
Wine-trail maps and bookings for everything
under the sun.

Wairau Hospital (☑ 03-520 9999; www.
nmdhb.govt.nz; Hospital Rd)

❶ Getting There & Away

AIR

Marlborough Airport (www.marlboroughair
port.co.nz; Tancred Cres, Woodbourne) is 6km
west of town on Middle Renwick Rd.

Air New Zealand (☑ 0800 747 000; www.air newzealand.co.nz) has flights to/from Wellington and Auckland with onward connections. **Sound-sair** (p310) connects Blenheim with Wellington, Paraparaumu, Napier and Kaikoura.

BUS

InterCity (p292) buses run daily from the Blenheim **i-SITE** (p313) to Picton (from $10, 30 minutes) and Nelson (from $22, 1¾ hours).

MARLBOROUGH WINERIES

Marlborough is NZ's vinous colossus, producing around three-quarters of the country's wine. At last count, there were 244 sq km of vines planted – that's more than 28,000 rugby pitches! Sunny days and cool nights create the perfect conditions for cool-climate grapes: world-famous sauvignon blanc, top-notch pinot noir, and notable chardonnay, riesling, gewürztraminer, pinot gris and bubbly. Drifting between tasting rooms and dining among the vines is a quintessential South Island experience.

A Taste of the Tastings

Around 35 wineries are open to the public. Our picks provide a range of high-quality cellar-door experiences, with most being open from around 10.30am till 4.30pm (some scale back operations in winter). Wineries may charge a small fee for tasting, normally refunded if you purchase a bottle. Pick up a copy of the *Marlborough Wine Trail* map from **Blenheim i-SITE** (p313), also available online at www.wine-marlborough.co.nz. If your time is limited, pop into **Wino's** (☑ 03-578 4196; www.winos.co.nz; 49 Grove Rd; ⊘ 10am-7pm Sun-Thu, to 8pm Fri & Sat) in Blenheim, a one-stop shop for some of Marlborough's finer and less common drops.

Saint Clair Estate (☑ 03-570 5280; www.saintclair.co.nz; 13 Selmes Rd, Rapaura; ⊘ 9am-5pm Nov-Apr, 11am-4pm May-Oct) Prepare to be blown away by the Pioneer Block and Reserve range sauvignon blanc and pinot noir. There's a decent cafe on site, and the adjacent Pataka deli offers cheese-tasting and local gourmet products.

Framingham (Map p312; ☑ 03-572 8884; www.framingham.co.nz; 19 Conders Bend Rd, Renwick; ⊘ 10.30am-4.30pm) Consistent, quality wines including exceptional riesling and stellar stickies.

Yealands Estate (☑ 03-575 7618; www.yealandsestate.co.nz; cnr Seaview & Reserve Rds, Seddon; ⊘ 10am-4.30pm) Zero-carbon winemaking on a grand scale at this space-age winery near Seddon. A 7km self-drive vineyard tour includes spectacular views over the vineyard towards Cook St. If you're lucky, you'll see Yealands' compact babydoll sheep grazing between the vines. They're handy at keeping the grass down, but not tall enough to augment their diet with the grapes ripening above them.

Te Whare Ra (Map p312; ☑ 03-572 8581; www.twrwines.co.nz; 56 Anglesea St, Renwick; ⊘ 11am-4pm Mon-Fri Nov–mid-Mar) Compact, hands-on winery creating gorgeous sauvignon blanc, riesling, gewürztraminer and pinot gris.

Cloudy Bay (Map p312; ☑ 03-520 9147; www.cloudybay.co.nz; 230 Jacksons Rd; ⊘ 10am-4pm) Globally coveted sauvignon blanc, bubbly and pinot noir, plus Jack's Raw Bar (December through April) for shucked oysters and clams. Decadent.

Spy Valley Wines (Map p312; ☑ 03-572 6207; www.spyvalleywine.co.nz; 37 Lake Timara Rd, Waihopai Valley; ⊘ 10.30am-4.30pm mid-Oct to mid-May, 10.30am-4.30pm Mon-Fri mid-May to mid-Oct) Stylish, edgy architecture features at this espionage-themed winery with drops in the top echelons. Memorable merchandise.

Huia (Map p312; ☑ 03-572 8326; www.huiavineyards.com; 22 Boyces Rd; ⊘ 10am-5pm Nov-Mar) Sustainable, small-scale family winemaking and a personable cellar-door experience. Delectable dry-style gewürztraminer.

Brancott Estate Heritage Centre (Map p312; ☑ 03-520 6975; www.brancottestate.com; 180 Brancott Rd; ⊘ 10am-4.30pm) Ubermodern cellar door and restaurant complex atop a hillock overlooking one of the original sauvignon blanc vineyards.

Clos Henri Vineyard (Map p312; ☑ 03-572 7293; www.clos-henri.com; 639 State Hwy 63, RD1; ⊘ 10am-4pm Mon-Fri Oct-Apr) French winemaking meets Marlborough terroir with *très bon* results. A beautifully restored local country church houses the cellar door.

Buses also head down south to Christchurch (from $41, six hours, four daily) via Kaikoura.

Naked Bus (☑ 0900 625 33; https://naked bus.com) sells bargain seats on some of the same services, and on its own buses on major routes.

 Getting Around

BICYCLE

Avantiplus (☑ 03-578 0433; www.bikemarlbor ough.co.nz; 61 Queen St; hire per half/full day

Forrest (Map p312; ☑ 03-572 9084; www.forrest.co.nz; 19 Blicks Rd; ⊙10am-4.30pm) Doctor-owners produce a range of fine vinous medicines, including a fab riesling.

Bladen (Map p312; ☑ 03-572 9417; www.bladen.co.nz; 83 Conders Bend Rd; ⊙11am-4.30pm late Oct-Apr) Bijou family winery that's big on charm.

Vines Village (Map p312; ☑ 03-579 5424; www.thevinesvillage.co.nz; 193 Rapaura Rd; ⊙10am-5pm) A conveniently located hub for bike hire, boutique shopping, wine tasting (Whitehaven) and cafe meals with a pretty vines outlook. Pop into Gourmet Collection for the best range of artisan food products from around the Marlborough and Tasman regions.

Wining & Dining

Arbour (Map p312; ☑ 03-572 7989; www.arbour.co.nz; 36 Godfrey Rd, Renwick; mains $37-39; ⊙5-11pm Tue-Sat Aug-Jun; ☑) Located in the thick of Renwick wine country, this elegant restaurant offers 'a taste of Marlborough' by focusing on local produce fashioned into contemporary, crowd-pleasing dishes. Settle in for a three-, four- or multiple-course à la carte offering ($75/85/99), or an end-of-the-day nibble and glass or two from the mesmerising wine list.

Wairau River Restaurant (Map p312; ☑ 03-572 9800; www.wairauriverwines.com; cnr Rapaura Rd & SH6, Renwick; mains $21-27; ⊙noon-3pm) Modishly modified mud-brick bistro with wide veranda and beautiful gardens with plenty of shade. Order the chilli salt prawns or the double-baked blue-cheese soufflé. Relaxing and thoroughly enjoyable.

Rock Ferry (Map p312; ☑ 03-579 6431; www.rockferry.co.nz; 130 Hammerichs Rd; mains $25-29; ⊙11.30am-3pm) Pleasant environment inside and out, with a slightly groovy edge. The compact summery menu – think miso-marinated salmon with an Asian slaw or the organic open steak sandwich topped with a creamy spinach and anchovy spread – is accompanied by wines from Marlborough and Otago. Leave room for dessert and coffee in the garden.

Wither Hills (Map p312; ☑ 03-520 8284; www.witherhills.co.nz; 211 New Renwick Rd; mains $27-30, platters $22-24; ⊙11am-4pm) Simple, well-executed food in a stylish space. Pull up a beanbag on the Hockneyesque lawns and enjoy confit duck, local king salmon, or a cheese and charcuterie platter, before climbing the ziggurat for impressive views across the Wairau.

Herzog Winery (Map p312; ☑ 03-572 8770; www.herzog.co.nz; 81 Jefferies Rd; bistro mains $22-32, 3-/5-/7-course degustation menu $94/125/155; ⊙bistro noon-2.30pm & 6-7.30pm, restaurant 7-10pm Wed-Sun Nov–mid-May) Dining at Herzog's cellar door offers two options. Select a three-, five- or seven-course degustation menu in the formal restaurant – wine matches are available – or order à la carte at the more casual garden bistro. South Island veal and salmon are given inspired treatment in the restaurant, while bistro highlights might include a seafood curry.

Wine Tours

Wine tours are generally conducted in a minibus, last between four and seven hours, take in four to seven wineries and range in price from $65 to $95 (with a few grand tours up to around $200 for the day, including a winery lunch).

Sounds Connection (☑ 03-573 8843, 0800 742 866; www.soundsconnection.co.nz; tours from $75) Wine-based excursions exploring the best of the area's wineries and vineyard restaurants. Also incorporating boat excursions on the Marlborough Sounds.

Bubbly Grape Wine Tours (☑ 027 672 2195, 0800 228 2253; www.bubblygrape.co.nz; tours $100-195) Three different tours including a gourmet lunch option.

Highlight Wine Tours (☑ 027 434 6451, 03-577 9046; www.highlightwinetours.co.nz; tours $115-130) Visit a chocolate factory, too. Custom tours available.

from $25/40; ⊙8am-5.30pm Mon-Fri, 10am-2pm Sat) rents bikes; extended hire and delivery by arrangement. **Bike2Wine** (Map p312; ✑0800 653 262, 03-572 8458; www.bike2wine.co.nz; 9 Wilson St, Renwick; standard/tandem per day $30/60, pick-ups from $10; ⊙10am-5.30pm) also rents bikes to explore nearby vineyards.

BUS

Shuttles around Blenheim and the wider Marlborough region are offered by **Blenheim Shuttles** (✑03-577 5277, 0800 577 527; www.blenheimshuttles.co.nz).

TAXI

Regular services are offered by **Marlborough Taxis** (✑03-577 5511).

KAIKOURA

POP 2080

Take SH1 129km southeast from Blenheim (or 180km north from Christchurch) and you'll encounter Kaikoura, a pretty peninsula town backed by the snow-capped Seaward Kaikoura Range. Few places in the world are home to such a variety of easily spottable wildlife: whales, dolphins, NZ fur seals, penguins, shearwaters, petrels and several species of albatross live in or pass by the area.

Marine animals are abundant here due to ocean-current and continental-shelf conditions: the seabed gradually slopes away from the land before plunging to more than 800m where the southerly current hits the continental shelf. This creates an upwelling of nutrients from the ocean floor into the feeding zone.

In November 2016, the Kaikoura region was struck by a severe magnitude 7.8 earthquake, but following the reestablishment of badly damaged transport links, the town is once again easily reached and an essential destination for visitors to New Zealand.

History

In Māori legend, Kaikoura Peninsula (Taumanu o Te Waka a Māui) was the seat where the demigod Māui placed his feet when he fished the North Island up from the depths. The area was heavily settled by Māori, with excavations showing that the area was a moa-hunter settlement about 800 to 1000 years ago. The name Kaikoura comes from 'kai' (food/eat) and 'koura' (crayfish).

James Cook sailed past the peninsula in 1770, but didn't land. His journal states that 57 Māori in four double-hulled canoes came towards the *Endeavour,* but 'would not be prevail'd upon to put along side'.

In 1828 Kaikoura's beachfront was the scene of a tremendous battle. A northern Ngāti Toa war party, led by chief Te Rauparaha, bore down on Kaikoura, killing or capturing several hundred of the local Ngāi Tahu tribe.

Europeans established a whaling station here in 1842, and the town remained a whaling centre until 1922, after which time farming and fishing sustained the community. It was in the 1980s that wildlife tours began to transform Kaikoura into a lively tourist town with excellent marine mammal viewing.

In November 2016, a powerful 7.8 magnitude earthquake struck the region, but following the reestablishment of vital transport links (in some cases ongoing into 2018), Kaikoura is again looking forward to a positive future.

◉ Sights

Kaikoura Museum MUSEUM
(Map p318; ✑03-319 7440; https://kaikouramuseum.co.nz; 96 West End; adult/child $12/6; ⊙10am-4pm) Housed in a modern building designed to resemble a crayfishing pot, the Kaikoura Museum is one of NZ's best provincial museums. The region's geology and natural and coastal histories are illuminated with well-curated exhibitions – highlights include the fossilised remains of a plesiosaur – and there are poignant displays on the November 2016 earthquake that struck the region. The 'New Normal' section consists of more than 30 individual 'mini exhibitions' about the earthquake's impact, contributed by local residents.

Fyffe House HISTORIC BUILDING
(Map p318; www.heritage.org.nz; 62 Avoca St; adult/child $10/free; ⊙10am-5pm Oct-Apr, to 4pm Thu-Mon May-Sep) Kaikoura's oldest surviving building, Fyffe House's whale-bone foundations were laid in 1844. Proudly positioned and fronted with a colourful garden, the little two-storey cottage offers a fascinating insight into the lives of colonial settlers. Interpretive displays are complemented by historic objects, while peeling wallpaper and the odd cobweb lend authenticity. Cute maritime-themed shop.

Point Kean Seal Colony WILDLIFE RESERVE
(Map p318) At the end of the peninsula, seals laze around on the rocks lapping up all the

attention. Give them a wide berth (10m), and never get between them and the sea – they will attack if they feel cornered and can move surprisingly fast. Since the uplift of the coastline during the 2016 earthquake, the seals have moved further from the road and car park, so keep a close eye on tides.

🏃 Activities

Walking

⭐**Kaikoura Peninsula Walkway** WALKING
(Map p318) Starting from town, this must-do three- to four-hour loop heads out to Point Kean, along the cliffs to South Bay, then back to town over the isthmus (or in reverse, of course). En route you'll see fur seals and red-billed seagull and shearwater colonies. Lookouts and interesting interpretive panels abound. Collect a map at the i-SITE (p322) or follow your nose.

The walkway is a good way to see the massive changes the 2016 earthquake made to the coastline and seabed.

Kaikoura Wilderness Walks TRAMPING
(☐0800 945 777, 03 319 6066; www.trailsofnewwilderness.co.nz; day walks $250-795) 🖈 A choice of three guided day walks through the privately owned Puhi Peaks Nature Reserve high in the Seaward Kaikoura range. Most accessible is the Valley of the Feathers walk (four hours), climbing to Totara Saddle and taking in views of the changes wrought on the landscape by the 2016 earthquake.

Water Sports

There's a safe swimming **beach** on the Esplanade, and a small surf break has been formed nearby following the 2016 earthquake. Decent **surfing** can be found around the area, particularly at **Mangamaunu Beach** (15km north of town), where there's a 500m point break. Water-sports gear hire and advice are available from Board Silly Surf & SUP Adventures (p317) and Coastal Sports (p322).

Clarence River Rafting RAFTING
(☐03-319 6993; www.clarenceriverrafting.co.nz; 1/3802 SH1, at Clarence Bridge; half-day trips adult/child $120/80) Raft the rapids of the Clarence River and experience the spectacular uplift and changes to the landscape following the 2016 Kaikoura earthquake. Half-day trips incorporate 2½ hours on the water, while longer journeys include a three- to five-day adventure with wilderness camping (adult/child $1400/900).

Based on SH1, 35km north of Kaikoura near the Clarence Bridge. Grade II; all gear provided.

Board Silly Surf & SUP Adventures SURFING
(☐027 418 8900, 0800 787 352; www.boardsilly.co.nz; 9 Hawthorne Rd, Mangamaunu; 3hr lessons $80, board & suit from $40) Get the low-down and transport, learn to surf or stand-up paddle board, and hire gear from Board Silly Surf & SUP Adventures.

Kaikoura Kayaks KAYAKING
(Map p318; ☐0800 452 456, 03-319 7118; www.kaikourakayaks.nz; 19 Killarney St; 3hr tours adult/child $99/70; ⏱tours 8.30am, 12.30pm & 4.30pm Nov-Apr, 9am & 1pm May-Oct; 🖈) Excellent, family friendly, guided sea-kayak tours to view fur seals and explore the peninsula's coastline. Kayak fishing and other on-demand trips available, plus freedom kayak and paddle-board hire. Ask about visiting Hope Springs, a sulphurous, bubbling section of the ocean that was discovered following the 2016 earthquake.

Seal Kayak Kaikoura KAYAKING
(Levi's Pedal Kayaks; Map p318; ☐027 261 0124, 0800 387 7325; www.sealkayakkaikoura.com; 2 Beach Rd; tours from $59) Sightseeing, seal encounters and fishing trips using pedal kayaks, which provide the option of propelling the craft either with your arms or legs.

Cycling

For town riding, hire bicycles from the i-SITE (p322) or Coastal Sports (p322). While you're there, ask about the Kowhai Trail to the foot of Mt Fyffe.

🚌 Tours

Wildlife tours are Kaikoura's speciality, particularly those involving whales (including sperm, pilot, killer, humpback and southern right), dolphins (Hector's, bottlenose and dusky – a particularly social species sometimes seen in the hundreds) and NZ fur seals. There's also plenty of bird life, including albatrosses and blue penguins. During summer, book your tour a few weeks ahead, and allow some leeway for lousy weather.

Wildlife Watching

Your choices are boat, plane or helicopter. Aerial options are shorter and pricier, but allow you to see the whole whale, as opposed to just a tail, flipper or spout.

Kaikoura

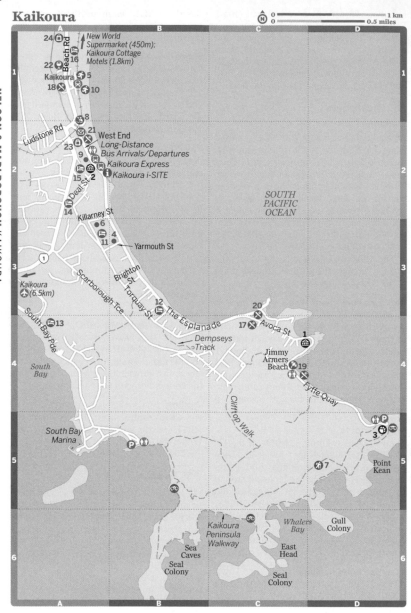

★**Albatross Encounter** BIRDWATCHING
(Map p318; ☑ 03-319 6777, 0800 733 365; www.
encounterkaikoura.co.nz; 96 Esplanade; adult/
child $125/60; ⊙ tours 9am & 1pm year-round,
plus 6am Nov-Apr) ✎ Even if you don't consider yourself a bird-nerd, you'll love this
close encounter with pelagic species such
as shearwaters, shags, mollymawks and
petrels. It's the various albatross species,
however, that steal the show. In a word:
awesome.

Kaikoura

Whale Watch Kaikoura WILDLIFE WATCHING
(Map p318; ☎0800 655 121, 03-319 6767; www.whalewatch.co.nz; Railway Station; 3½hr tours adult/child $150/60) 🦺 With knowledgeable guides and fascinating on-board animation, Kaikoura's biggest operator heads out on boat trips (with admirable frequency) in search of some of the big fellas. It'll refund 80% of your fare if no whales are sighted (success rate: 95%). If this trip is a must for you, allow a few days' flexibility in case the weather turns to custard.

Wings over Whales SCENIC FLIGHTS
(☎03-319 6580, 0800 226 629; www.whales.co.nz; 30min flights adult/child $180/75) Light-plane flights departing from Kaikoura Airport, 8km south of town on SH1. Spotting success rate: 95%.

Kaikoura Helicopters SCENIC FLIGHTS
(Map p318; ☎03-319 6609; www.worldofwhales.co.nz; Whaleway Station Rd; 15/60min flights $100/490) Reliable whale-spotting flights (standard tour 30 minutes, $220 each for three or more people), plus jaunts around the peninsula, Mt Fyffe and peaks beyond. Ask about flights taking in the area's spectacular post-earthquake landscapes from above.

South Pacific Whale Watch WHALE WATCHING
(Map p318; ☎0800 360 886; www.southpacificwhales.co.nz; 72 West End; per person $350-650) Offers a wide range of whale-watching and flightseeing trips by helicopter.

Seal Swim Kaikoura ECOTOUR
(Map p318; ☎03-319 6182, 0800 732 579; www.sealswimkaikoura.co.nz; 58 West End; adult/child $110/70, viewing $55/35, ☻Oct-May) 🦺 Take a (warmly wet-suited) swim with Kaikoura's healthy population of playful seals – including very cute pups – on two-hour guided snorkelling tours (by boat) run by the Chambers family.

Dolphin Encounter ECOTOUR
(Map p318; ☎0800 733 365, 03-319 6777; www.encounterkaikoura.co.nz; 96 Esplanade; swim adult/child $175/160, observation $95/50; ☻tours 8.30am & 12.30pm year-round, plus 5.30am Nov-Apr) 🦺 Claiming NZ's highest success rate (90%) for both locating and swimming with dolphins, this operator runs feel-good three-hour tours, which often encounter sizeable pods of sociable duskies – the classic Kaikoura treat.

Fishing
Fishing is a common obsession in Kaikoura, with local boaties angling for any excuse to go out for a little look-sea. It's a good opportunity to *kai koura* (eat crayfish). Trips start at around $70; the i-SITE (p322) has a full list of operators.

🛏 Sleeping

Albatross Backpacker Inn HOSTEL $
(Map p318; ☎0800 222 247, 03-319 6090; www.albatross-kaikoura.co.nz; 1 Torquay St; dm $34-36, tw/d/tr $79/84/105; ☎) 🦺 This arty backpackers resides in three sweet buildings, one

a former post office. It's colourful and close to the beach but sheltered from the breeze. As well as a laid-back lounge with musical instruments for jamming, there are decks and verandas to chill out on.

Sunrise Lodge
HOSTEL $

(Map p318; 03-319 7444; sunrisehostel@xtra. co.nz; 74 Beach Rd; dm $34-36, d $90;) In a modern house a short walk from good cafes and restaurants, Sunrise has spotless four- and six-bed dorms, doubles and sunny out- door chairs and tables.

SkyHi Hostel Lodge
GUESTHOUSE $

(Map p318; 03-319 5538; www.skyhi.nz; 11 Churchill St; s/d/tr $55/72/105;) More guesthouse than hostel, SkyHi combines simple but spotless rooms and shared bath- rooms with a modern kitchen, spacious guest lounge, and a conservatory with ex- cellent mountain and ocean views. Usually patrolled by the affable owner's friendly cat, the sunny garden and barbecue area is a great place to relax. Pick-ups from the i-SITE (p322) are available on request.

★Kaikoura Cottage Motels
MOTEL $$

(0800 526 882, 03-319 5599; www.kaikoura cottagemotels.co.nz; cnr Old Beach & Mill Rds; d $140-200;) This enclave of eight modern tourist flats looks mighty fine, surround- ed by attractive native plantings. Oriented for mountain views, the spick-and-span self-contained units sleep four between an open-plan studio-style living room and one private bedroom. Proud and lovely hosts seal the deal.

THE 2016 KAIKOURA EARTHQUAKE

Dubbed the 'Shaky Isles', New Zealand is no stranger to significant seismic activity, but the 7.8 magnitude earthquake that struck the Kaikoura region just after midnight on 14 November 2016 was one of the largest magnitude and longest duration quakes to strike the country since European settlement.

Fatalities were mercifully limited to two deaths in Kaikoura and nearby Mt Lyford, but the damage done to the landscape by the violent rupturing of multiple fault lines stretching north for 170km from North Canterbury was staggering. Huge gashes were torn through farmland, new lakes were formed overnight when rivers were dammed, and parts of NZ's South Island moved more than 5m closer to the North Island.

North of Kaikoura, sections of the coastline were uplifted by 8m, and around the town, former areas of the seabed are now starkly exposed after being violently thrust upwards by more than 2m. It's the kind of earth-shattering (literally) seismic activity that's seen world-leading earthquake experts descend on the region to observe and learn.

Up to 85 landslides also created havoc along SH1, the country's main road linking Kaikoura north to the interisland ferry port at Picton, and it was only in December 2017 that the road was reopened on a limited basis to the public. Railway lines were also badly damaged, and ongoing work through 2018 (and beyond) will be needed to repair impor- tant transport infrastructure damaged by the quake. Other roads linking Kaikoura to the rest of the country were also damaged, and in the immediate aftermath of the earth- quake, almost 1000 tourists visiting the town had to be evacuated either on NZ Defence Force aircraft or on the NZ Navy's HMNZS Canterbury.

Following the earthquake there were initial fears Kaikoura's famed marine mammals would abandon the location, but the nutrient-rich waters of the massive underwater canyon just off the coast have ensured whales and other species have returned and continue to visit in significant numbers.

Benefits of the massive post-quake reconstruction activity transforming the region have been a modern new boat marina at Kaikoura – the previous harbour was instantly made useless after the earthquake – and improved roads north to Picton and south to Christchurch. For active types, there's even a newly formed surf break right in the middle of Kaikoura township, and a spectacular new coastal cycleway north of town spanning around 60km from Clarence south to Mangamaunu. Future plans are to ex- tend this cycleway to link Blenheim and Christchurch.

Bay Cottages MOTEL $$
(Map p318; ☑0800 556 623, 03-319 7165; www.
baycottages.co.nz; 29a South Bay Pde; cottages
$120-200; ☜) Here's a great-value option in
South Bay, a few kilometres south of town.
Five cottages sleeping up to four all feature
a kitchen, lounge area and free Netflix. The
surrounding area is private and quiet. Vari-
ous walkways start in South Bay, and fishing
charters leave nearby from Kaikoura's new
harbour. A barbecue to cook your fish on is
also available.

★**Lemon Tree Lodge** B&B $$$
(Map p318; ☑03-319 7464; www.lemontree.co.nz;
31 Adelphi Tce; s $280, d $280-320; ☜) Enjoying
superb ocean and mountain views, Lemon Tree Lodge combines four charming
and stylish rooms in the main house with
two quiet and secluded garden units. Our
favourites are the Ocean View Suites with
expansive windows and private balconies
showcasing brilliant Pacific vistas. The
well-travelled and friendly owners have
plenty of great advice on how best to enjoy
the region.

Anchor Inn Motel MOTEL $$$
(Map p318; ☑03-319 5426; www.anchorinn.co.nz;
208 Esplanade; d $185-255; ☜) The Aussie
owners liked this Kaikoura motel so much
they bought it and moved here. The sharp
and spacious units are a pleasant 15-minute
walk from town and about 10 seconds from
the ocean. The motel reopened in December
2017 after a post-earthquake makeover.

Nikau Lodge B&B $$$
(Map p318; ☑03-319 6973; www.nikaulodge.com;
53 Deal St; d $220-280; @☜) New owners are
maintaining high standards at this beautiful
B&B high on the hill with grand-scale vistas.
Five en-suite rooms are plush and comfy,
with additional satisfaction arriving in the
form of cafe-quality breakfasts accompanied
by fresh local coffee. Good humour, home
baking, free wi-fi, complimentary drinks,
a hot tub and blooming gardens: you may
want to move in.

✖ Eating & Drinking

Hislops Wholefoods Cafe CAFE $$
(Map p318; ☑03-319 6971; www.hislops-whole
foods.co.nz; 33 Beach Rd; breakfast & lunch mains
$12-19, dinner mains $26-36; ☺8.30am-8pm
Wed-Sat, to 4pm Sun; ☑) ✔ Organic ingredi-
ents shine at this long-established Kaikou-
ra eatery. Come for breakfast on the shaded

deck and enjoy hotcakes with blueberries
or spicy harissa eggs, or book for dinner
and partner organic and biodynamic NZ
wines with the lamb salad or local seafood.
Throughout the day, homestyle baking
blurs the line between healthy and tasty,
and the coffee is always good.

Pier Hotel PUB FOOD $$
(Map p318; ☑03-319 5037; www.thepierhotel.
co.nz; 1 Avoca St; lunch $16-25, dinner $29-40;
☺11am-late) Situated in the town's primo
seaside spot, with panoramic views, the
historic Pier Hotel is a friendly and inviting
place for a drink and respectable pub grub,
including crayfish (half/whole $50/100).
Great outside area for sundowners with vistas of the Inland Kaikoura mountain range.
You'll find beers here from Kaikoura's two
craft breweries: Emporium Brewing and
the Kaikoura Brewing Company.

★**Green Dolphin** MODERN NZ $$$
(Map p318; ☑03-319 6666; www.greendolphin
kaikoura.co.nz; 12 Avoca St; mains $28-39; ☺5pm-
late) Kaikoura's consistent top-ender dishes
up high-quality local produce including sea-
food, beef, lamb and venison. There are also
lovely homemade pasta dishes. The hefty
drinks list demands attention, featuring ex-
citing aperitifs, craft beer from Three Boys
Brewery in Christchurch, interesting wines
and more. Booking ahead is definitely rec-
ommended. Ask for a window table to expe-
rience a sunlit Kaikoura dusk.

Zephyr BISTRO $$$
(Map p318; ☑03-319 6999; www.zephyr
restaurant.co.nz; 40 West End; mains $29-37;
☺5.30pm-late Tue-Sat, reduced hours Easter-late
Oct) ✔ Focusing on a concise and seasonal menu, Zephyr's modern dining room
is a good place to enjoy seafood chowder,
mushroom-crusted venison or local fish and
crayfish with a gourmet spin. The wine and
beer list is equally focused and well curated.

Emporium Brewing MICROBREWERY
(Map p318; ☑03-319 5897; www.emporiumbrew
ing.co.nz; 57a Beach Rd; ☺10am-8pm) Fill up
a takeaway rigger or buy bottles of Emporium's tasty brews at this simple taproom.
Our favourite is the award-winning Angry
Sky Red IPA. There's also an on-site minigolf
course. Check out the hole featuring the
'earthquake cows', three bovine locals that
were stranded precariously on a tiny 'island'
of farmland for three days following the
2016 earthquake.

CRAY CRAZY

Among all of Kaikoura's munificent marine life, the one species you just can't avoid is the crayfish, whose delicate flesh dominates local menus. Unfortunately (some say unnecessarily), it's pricey – at a restaurant you'll shell out around $50 for half a cray or up to $100 for the whole beast.

You can also buy fresh cooked or uncooked crays from **Cods & Crayfish** (Map p318; 03-319 7899; 81 Beach Rd; 8am-6pm), or from the iconic **Nins Bin** (SH1) and **Cay's Crays** (SH1), surf-side caravans around a 20-minute drive north of town. Note both Nins Bin and Cay's Crays were forced to close following the 2016 earthquake, but were expected to reopen when the SH1 north to Picton was repaired (works happening throughout 2018).

Alternatively, go out on a fishing tour, or simply head to the **Kaikoura Seafood BBQ** (Map p318; 027 376 3619; Fyffe Quay; items from $6; 11am-7pm Sun-Fri, to 3pm Sat, reduced hours late Oct-Easter) near the peninsula seal colony where cooked crays can be gobbled in the sunshine, by the sea.

🛍 Shopping

Coastal Sports　　　　SPORTS & OUTDOORS
(Map p318; 03-319 5028; www.coastalsports.
co.nz; 24 West End; 9am-5.30pm Mon-Sat,
10am-5pm Sun, extended hours late Oct-Easter)
The friendly folk at this great sports shop
can hook you up with hire bikes (half/full
day $30/40), surf gear (board and wetsuit
per day $40) and lots of local intel. There's
also a good selection of hiking and outdoor
gear.

ℹ Information

Kaikoura i-SITE (Map p318; 03-319 5641;
www.kaikoura.co.nz; West End; 9am-5pm
Mon-Fri, to 4pm Sat & Sun, extended hours
Dec-Mar) Helpful staff make tour, accommo-
dation and transport bookings, and help with
DOC-related matters.

ℹ Getting There & Away

InterCity (p292) buses have traditionally run
between Kaikoura and Nelson once daily (3¾
hours), and Picton (2¼ hours) and Christchurch
(from $26, 2¼ hours) twice daily. The **bus stop**
(Map p318) is next to the **i-SITE** (p322), and
you can get tickets and info inside.

Kaikoura Express (Map p318; 0800 500
929; www.kaikouraexpress.co.nz; adult one way/
return $35/60, child $30/50; the 'Red Bus') runs
a handy service (2¾ hours) linking Christchurch
and Kaikoura. Buses leave from the i-SITE.

ℹ Getting Around

Kaikoura Shuttles (03-319 6166; www.
kaikourashuttles.co.nz) will run you around the
local sights as well as to and from the airport.
It can also get you to the starting point of the
Kaikoura Coast Track (p278). For local car hire,
contact **Kaikoura Rentals** (03-319 3311;
www.kaikourarentals.co.nz; 94 Churchill St).

Understand the South Island

New Zealand Today

Despite a decade marred by disasters, including devastating earthquakes and mining and helicopter tragedies, New Zealand never loses its nerve. The country remains a titan on both the silver screen and the sports field, and change is coming in the world of politics...

Best on Film

Lord of the Rings trilogy (2001–03) Hobbits, dragons and magical rings – Tolkien's vision comes to life.
The Piano (1993) A piano and its owners arrive on a mid-19th-century West Coast beach.
Whale Rider (2002) Magical tale of family and heritage on the East Coast.
Once Were Warriors (1994) Brutal relationship dysfunction in South Auckland.
Boy (2010) Taika Waititi's bitter-sweet coming-of-age drama set in the Bay of Plenty.

Best in Print

The Luminaries (Eleanor Catton; 2013) Man Booker Prize winner: crime and intrigue on West Coast goldfields.
Mister Pip (Lloyd Jones; 2006) Tumult on Bougainville Island, intertwined with Dickens' *Great Expectations*.
Live Bodies (Maurice Gee; 1998) Post-WWII loss and redemption in NZ.
The 10pm Question (Kate de Goldi; 2009) Twelve-year-old Frankie grapples with life's big anxieties.
The Collected Stories of Katherine Mansfield (2006) Kathy's greatest hits.
The Wish Child (Catherine Chidgey; 2016) Harrowing, heartbreaking WWII novel; NZ Book Awards winner.

Jacinda Mania

In 2010 she was NZ's youngest sitting MP, by 2017 she was running the country. The swift rise of Jacinda Ardern has been touted as part of a global political shift. Ardern became the youngest ever Labour Party leader in 2017, only a few weeks ahead of the election that propelled her to the role of prime minister at the age of 37 – making her NZ's youngest PM for 150 years. Passionate about climate change, unabashedly feminist and an ardent supporter of gay rights, Ardern's ability to win support with her energetic style was dubbed 'Jacinda-mania'. The final polls gave Labour a less-than-maniacal 37% of the vote, but resulted in a coalition government led by Labour.

Ardern's articulacy and verve have seen her aligned with other youthful, socially progressive world leaders like Justin Trudeau and Emmanuel Macron, part of a youth-powered political sea change. But Ardern's style remains quintessentially Kiwi: unpretentious and accessible. When an Australian radio journalist sought to fact-check the correct pronunciation of Ardern's name in 2017, he was astonished to be connected with the PM directly, who explained the right pronunciation personally. It's 'AH-durn', if you're wondering.

Overseas Stampede

Being a dre\am destination isn't all it's cracked up to be, especially when tourist numbers boom and property investors swoop in. Aussie and Asian buyers are increasingly wise to NZ property – some seek holiday homes, others see the far-flung nation as a safe haven from global unrest and nuclear war. Cue a spiralling housing crisis, and the International Monetary Fund (IMF) ranking NZ's housing as the most unaffordable in the Organisation for Economic Co-operation and Development (OECD) in 2016.

The worst effects have been felt in Auckland, home to almost one-third of the country's population. Auckland has struggled to keep pace with demand for housing since the post-WWII housing boom, but in recent years rental rates and house prices have sprinted past local incomes, dashing dreams of home ownership and leaving more New Zealanders homeless. With house prices that grew by 75% within four years, oversubscribed Auckland was named one of the world's least affordable cities. There were signs of a slowdown at the end of 2017, but Auckland Council and the government have scrambled to plan more than 420,000 new dwellings, clamp down on foreign buyers and plug black holes in the construction sector – where a dearth of skilled tradespeople and monopolies on building supplies have helped contribute to eye-watering prices. With Auckland's population expected to increase by one million in the next 30 years, the fixes can't come swiftly enough.

International property purchasers aren't the only ones carving off a little too much of NZ. The issue of managing NZ's increasing number of visitors – now an annual 3.54 million – is high on the agenda, particularly from a conservation perspective. In response to the enormous popularity of the North Island's Tongariro Alpine Crossing, DOC has placed a time limit at the car park at the beginning of the track, forcing tourists to use traffic-reducing shuttle services. Meanwhile, tourism hubs like Te Anau, gateway to world-famous Milford Sound, are seeing their peak season start ever earlier, and local grumbles about the numbers of visitors on tramping tracks and roads are getting louder. A country beloved for being wild, green and beautiful faces the challenge of keeping it that way, in the face of a tourism stampede.

Never Forget

Kiwi battler spirit has been repeatedly pushed to its limits over the past decade. Christchurch's recovery from the 2010 and 2011 earthquakes suffered a setback when another quake hit in 2016, while earthquakes in Kaikoura in November 2016 rattled road and rail access until repairs were finished at the end of 2017. But NZ doesn't just rebuild, it reinvents: pop-up cafes and restaurants and a shipping-container mall showed how fast Christchurch could dust itself off after disaster. Ensuing years have allowed the bigger post-earthquake projects to take shape, including the Canterbury Earthquake National Memorial, unveiled in 2017.

Another notable memorial remembers the Pike River Disaster in 2010, in which a methane explosion claimed 29 lives – the country's worst mining accident in more than a century. Following the wishes of the families of the men killed in the accident, the site of the mine has been folded into Paparoa National Park and their memorial will be a new 'Great Walk', opening in 2018.

POPULATION: **4.83 MILLION**

AREA: **268,021 SQ KM**

GDP GROWTH: **4.1% (2016)**

INFLATION: **1.9% (2017)**

UNEMPLOYMENT: **4.8% (2017)**

if New Zealand were 100 people

65 would be European
15 would be Maori
12 would be Asian
7 would be Pacific Islanders
1 would be Other

where they live
(% of New Zealanders)

North Island 65
South Island 19
Australia 11
Rest of the World 4
Travelling 1

population per sq km

NEW ZEALAND AUSTRALIA USA

≈ 3 people

History

Historians continue to unravel New Zealand's early history, with much of what they discover confirming traditional Māori narratives. In less than a thousand years NZ produced two new peoples: the Polynesian Māori and European New Zealanders (also known by their Māori name, 'Pākehā'). New Zealand shares some of its history with the rest of Polynesia, and with other European settler societies. This cultural intermingling has created unique features along the way.

Māori Settlement

The first settlers of NZ were the Polynesian forebears of today's Māori. Archaeologists and anthropologists continue to search for the details, but the most widely accepted evidence suggests they arrived in the 13th century. The DNA of Polynesian rat bones found in NZ, dated to centuries earlier, has been written off as unreliable (and certainly not conclusive evidence of earlier settlement). Most historians now agree on 1280 as the Māori's likeliest arrival date. Scientists have sequenced the DNA of settlers buried at the Wairau Bar archaeological site on the South Island, and confirmed the settlers as originating from east Polynesia (though work is ongoing to pinpoint their origins more precisely). The genetic diversity of the buried settlers suggests a fairly large-scale settlement – a finding consistent with Māori narratives about numerous vessels reaching the islands.

Prime sites for first settlement were warm coastal gardens for the food plants brought from Polynesia (kumara or sweet potato, gourd, yam and taro); sources of stone for knives and adzes; and areas with abundant big game. New Zealand has no native land mammals apart from a few species of bat, but 'big game' is no exaggeration: the islands were home to a dozen species of moa (a large flightless bird) – the largest of which weighed up to 240kg, about twice the size of an ostrich – preyed upon by *Harpagornis moorei*, a whopping 15kg eagle that is now extinct. Other species of flightless birds and large sea mammals, such as fur seals, were easy game for hunters from small Pacific islands. The settlers spread far and fast, from the top of the North Island to the bottom of the South Island within the first 100 years. High-protein diets are likely to have boosted population growth.

TIMELINE	AD 1280	1500–1642	1642
	Based on evidence from archaeological digs, the most likely arrival date of east Polynesians in NZ, now known as Māori.	The 'classic period' of Māori culture, when weapon-making and artistic techniques were refined. Many remain cultural hallmarks to this day.	First European contact: Abel Tasman arrives on an expedition from the Dutch East Indies (Indonesia) but leaves in a hurry after a sea skirmish with Māori.

By about 1400, however, with big-game supply dwindling, Māori economics turned from big game to small game – forest birds and rats – and from hunting to farming and fishing. A good living could still be made, but it required detailed local knowledge, steady effort and complex communal organisation, hence the rise of the Māori tribes. Competition for resources increased, conflict did likewise, and this led to the building of increasingly sophisticated *pā* (fortified villages), complete with wells and food storage pits. Vestiges of *pā* earthworks can still be seen around the country (on the hilltops of Auckland, for example).

Around 1500 is considered the dawn of the 'classic period', when Māori developed a social structure and aesthetic that was truly distinct, rather than an offshoot of the parent Polynesian culture. Māori had no metals and no written language (and no alcoholic drinks or drugs). Traditional Māori culture from these times endures, including performance art like *kapa haka* (cultural dance) and unmistakeable visual art, notably woodcarving, weaponry and *pounamu* (greenstone) carving.

Spiritual life was similarly distinctive. Below Ranginui (sky father) and Papatūānuku (earth mother) were various gods of land, forest and sea, joined by deified ancestors over time. The mischievous demigod Māui was particularly important. In legend, he vanquished the sun and fished up the North Island before meeting his death between the thighs of the goddess Hine-nui-te-pō in an attempt to bring immortality to humankind.

Enter Europe

The first authenticated contact between Māori and European explorers took place in 1642. Seafarer Abel Tasman had just claimed Van Diemen's Land ('Tasmania') for the Dutch when rough winds steered his ships east, where he sighted New Zealand. Tasman's two ships were searching for southern

THE MORIORI MYTH

One of NZ's most persistent legends is that Māori found mainland NZ already occupied by a more peaceful and racially distinct Melanesian people, known as the Moriori, whom they exterminated. This myth has been regularly debunked by scholars since the 1920s, but somehow hangs on.

To complicate matters, there were real 'Moriori', and Māori did treat them badly. The real Moriori were the people of the Chatham Islands, a windswept group about 900km east of the mainland. They were, however, fully Polynesian, and descended from Māori – 'Moriori' was their version of the same word. Mainland Māori arrived in the Chathams in 1835, as a spin-off of the Musket Wars, killing some Moriori and enslaving the rest, but they did not exterminate them.

1769	1772	1790s	1818–45
European contact recommences with visits by James Cook and Jean de Surville. Despite violence, both manage to communicate with Māori. This time NZ's link with the outside world proves permanent.	Marion du Fresne's French expedition arrives; it stays for some weeks at the Bay of Islands. Relations with Māori start well, but a breach of Māori *tapu* (sacred law) leads to violence.	Whaling ships and sealing gangs arrive in the country. Relations are established with Māori, with Europeans depending on the contact for essentials, such as food, water and protection.	Intertribal Māori 'Musket Wars' take place: tribes acquire muskets and win bloody victories against tribes without them. The wars taper off, probably due to the equal distribution of weapons.

JAMES COOK'S ENDEAVOURS

Countless obelisks, faded plaques and graffiti-covered statues remember the renowned navigator James Cook (1728–79). It's impossible to travel the Pacific without encountering the captain's image and his controversial legacy in the lands he opened to the West.

Cook came from an extremely pinched and provincial background. The son of a day labourer in rural Yorkshire, he was born in a mud cottage, had little schooling and seemed destined for farm work. Instead, Cook went to sea as a teenager, worked his way up from coal-ship servant to naval officer, and attracted notice for his exceptional charts of Canada. But Cook remained a little-known second lieutenant until, in 1768, the Royal Navy chose him to command a daring voyage to the South Seas.

In a converted coal ship called *Endeavour*, Cook sailed to Tahiti and then became the first European to land in New Zealand and the east coast of Australia. While he was there, Cook sailed and mapped NZ's coastline in full – with impressive accuracy. The ship almost sank after striking the Great Barrier Reef, and 40% of the crew died from disease and accidents, but somehow the *Endeavour* arrived home in 1771. On a return voyage (1772–75), Cook became the first navigator to pierce the Antarctic Circle and circled the globe near its southernmost latitude, demolishing the ancient myth that a vast, populous and fertile continent surrounded the South Pole.

Cook's travels made an enormous contribution to world thought. During his voyages, Cook and his crew took astronomical measurements. Botanists accompanied him on his voyages, diligently recording and studying the flora they encountered. Cook was also remarkable for completing a round-the-world voyage without any of his crew dying of scurvy – adding 'nutrition' to his impressive roster of specialist subjects.

But these achievements exist beneath a long shadow. Cook's travels spurred colonisation of the Pacific and, within a few decades of his death, missionaries, whalers, traders and settlers began transforming (and often devastating) island cultures. As a result, many indigenous people now revile Cook as an imperialist villain who introduced disease, dispossession and other ills to the region (hence the frequent vandalising of Cook monuments). However, as islanders revive traditional crafts and practices, from tattooing to *tapa* (traditional barkcloth), they have turned to the art and writing of Cook and his men as a resource for cultural renewal. Significant geographical features in NZ bear his name, including Aoraki/Mt Cook, Cook Strait and Cook River, along with countless streets and hotels.

For good and ill, a Yorkshire farm boy remains one of the single most significant figures in shaping the modern Pacific.

land and anything valuable it might contain. Tasman was instructed to pretend to any natives he might meet 'that you are by no means eager for precious metals, so as to leave them ignorant of the value of the same'.

When Tasman's ships anchored in the bay, local Māori came out in their canoes to make the traditional challenge: friends or foes? The Dutch blew

1837	1840	1844	1858
European settlers introduce possums from Australia to NZ, creating a possum population boom that comes to threaten native flora and bird life.	Starting at Waitangi in the Bay of Islands on 6 February, around 500 chiefs countrywide sign the Treaty of Waitangi to 'settle' sovereignty once and for all. NZ becomes a nominal British colony.	Young Ngāpuhi chief Hōne Heke challenges British sovereignty, first by cutting down the British flag at Kororāreka (now Russell), then by sacking the town itself. The ensuing Northland war continues until 1846.	The Waikato chief Te Wherowhero is installed as the first Māori king.

their trumpets, unwittingly challenging back. When a boat was lowered to take a party between the two ships, it was attacked and four crewmen were killed. Having not even set foot on the land, Tasman sailed away and didn't return; nor did any other European for 127 years. But the Dutch did leave a name: 'Statenland', later changed to 'Nova Zeelandia' by cartographers.

Contact between Māori and Europeans was renewed in 1769, when English and French explorers arrived, under James Cook and Jean de Surville – Cook narrowly pipped the latter to the post, naming Doubtless Bay before the French party dropped anchor there. The first French exploration ended sourly, with mistrust between the ailing French seamen and Māori, one of whom they took prisoner (he died at sea). Bloody skirmishes took place during a second French expedition, led by Marc-Joseph Marion du Fresne, when cultural misunderstandings led to violent reprisals; later expeditions were more fruitful. Meanwhile Cook made two more visits between 1773 and 1777. Exploration continued, motivated by science, profit and political rivalry.

Unofficial visits, by whaling ships in the north and seal-hunting gangs in the south, began in the 1790s (though Māori living in New Zealand's interior remained largely unaffected). The first Christian missionaries established themselves in the Bay of Islands in 1814, followed by dozens of others – Anglican, Methodist and Catholic. Europe brought such things as pigs and potatoes, which benefited Māori and were even used as currency. Trade in flax and timber generated small European–Māori settlements by the 1820s. Surprisingly, the most numerous category of 'European' visitor was probably American. New England whaling ships favoured the Bay of Islands for rest and recreation, which meant sex and drink. Their favourite haunt, the little town of Kororāreka (now Russell), was known as 'Gomorrah, the scourge of the Pacific'. As a result, New England visitors today might well have distant relatives among the local Māori.

One or two dozen bloody clashes dot the history of Māori–European contact before 1840 but, given the number of visits, interracial conflict was modest. Europeans needed Māori protection, food and labour, and Māori came to need European articles, especially muskets. Whaling stations and mission stations were linked to local Māori groups by intermarriage, which helped keep the peace. Most warfare was between Māori and Māori: the terrible intertribal 'Musket Wars' of 1818–36. Because Northland had the majority of early contact with Europe, its Ngāpuhi tribe acquired muskets first. Under their great general Hongi Hika, Ngāpuhi then raided south, winning bloody victories against tribes without muskets. Once they acquired muskets, these tribes then saw off Ngāpuhi, but also raided further south in their turn. The domino effect continued to the far south of the South Island in 1836. The missionaries claimed that the Musket Wars then tapered off through their influence,

One of the first European women to settle in New Zealand was Charlotte Badger, a convict mutineer who fled to the Bay of Islands in 1806 and refused to return to European society.

Abel Tasman named NZ 'Statenland', assuming it was connected to Staten Island near Argentina. It was subsequently named after the province of Zeeland in Tasman's native Holland.

1860–69	1861	1863–64	1867
The Taranaki wars, starting with the controversial swindling of Māori land by the government at Waitara, and continuing with outrage over the confiscation of more land as a result.	Gold discovered in Otago by Gabriel Read, an Australian prospector. As a result, the population of Otago climbs from less than 13,000 to over 30,000 in six months.	Waikato Land War. Up to 5000 Māori resist an invasion mounted by 20,000 imperial, colonial and 'friendly' Māori troops. Despite surprising successes, Māori are defeated and much land is confiscated.	All Māori men (rather than individual landowners) are granted the right to vote.

but the restoration of the balance of power through the equal distribution of muskets was probably more important.

The Māori population for 1769 has been estimated at between 85,000 and 110,000. The Musket Wars killed perhaps 20,000, and new diseases (including typhoid, tuberculosis and venereal disease) did considerable damage, too. Fortunately NZ had the natural quarantine of distance: infected Europeans often recovered or died during the long voyage, and smallpox, for example, which devastated indigenous North Americans, never arrived. By 1840 Māori had been reduced to about 70,000, a decline of at least 20%. Māori bent under the weight of European contact, but they certainly did not break.

Growing Pains

Māori tribes valued the profit and prestige brought by the Pākehā and wanted both, along with protection from foreign powers. Accepting nominal British authority was the way to get them. James Busby was appointed New Zealand's first British Resident in 1833, though his powers were largely symbolic. Busby selected the country's first official flag and established the Declaration of the Independence of New Zealand. But he was too ineffectual to curb rampant colonisation.

By 1840 the British government was overcoming its reluctance to undertake potentially expensive intervention in NZ. The British were eager to secure their commercial interests and they also believed, wrongly but sincerely, that Māori could not handle the increasing scale of unofficial European contact. In 1840 the two peoples struck a deal, symbolised by the treaty first signed at Waitangi on 6 February that year. The Treaty of Waitangi now has a standing not dissimilar to that of the Constitution in the US, but is even more contested. The original problem was a discrepancy between British and Māori understandings of it. The English version promised Māori full equality as British subjects in return for complete rights of government. The Māori version also promised that Māori would retain their chieftainship, which implied local rights of government. The problem was not great at first, because the Māori version applied outside the small European settlements. But as those settlements grew, conflict brewed.

In 1840 there were only about 2000 Europeans in NZ, with the shanty town of Kororāreka as the capital and biggest settlement. By 1850 six new settlements had been formed, with 22,000 settlers between them. About half of these had arrived under the auspices of the New Zealand Company and its associates. The company was the brainchild of Edward Gibbon Wakefield, who also influenced the settlement of South Australia. Wakefield hoped to short-circuit the barbarous frontier phase of settlement with 'instant civilisation', but his success was limited. From the 1850s his settlers, who included a high proportion of upper-middle-class gentlefolk,

'I believe we were all glad to leave New Zealand. It is not a pleasant place. Amongst the natives there is absent that charming simplicity...and the greater part of the English are the very refuse of society.' Charles Darwin, writing about his 1835 visit to Kororāreka (Russell).

1868–72	1886–87	1893	1901
East Coast war. Te Kooti, having led an escape from his prison on the Chatham Islands, leads a holy guerrilla war in the Urewera region. He finally retreats to establish the Ringatū Church.	Tuwharetoa tribe gifts the mountains of Ruapehu, Ngauruhoe and Tongariro to the government to establish NZ's first national park.	NZ becomes the first country in the world to grant the vote to women, following a campaign led by Kate Sheppard, who petitioned the government for years.	New Zealand politely declines the invitation to join the new Commonwealth of Australia, but thanks for asking.

were swamped by succeeding waves of immigrants that continued to wash in until the 1880s. These people were part of the great British and Irish diaspora that also populated Australia and much of North America, but the NZ mix was distinctive. Lowland Scots settlers were more prominent in NZ than elsewhere, for example, with the possible exception of parts of Canada. New Zealand's Irish, even the Catholics, tended to come from the north of Ireland. New Zealand's English tended to come from the counties close to London. Small groups of Germans, Scandinavians and Chinese made their way in, though the last faced increasing racial prejudice from the 1880s, when the Pākehā population reached half a million.

Much of the mass immigration from the 1850s to the 1870s was assisted by the provincial and central governments, which also mounted large-scale public works schemes, especially in the 1870s under Julius Vogel. In 1876 Vogel abolished the provinces on the grounds that they were hampering his development efforts. The last imperial governor with substantial power was the talented but machiavellian George Grey, who ended his second governorship in 1868. Thereafter, the governors (governors-general from 1917) were largely just nominal heads of state; the head of government, the premier or prime minister, had more power. The central government, originally weaker than the provincial governments, the imperial governor and the Māori tribes, eventually exceeded the power of all three.

The Māori tribes did not go down without a fight. Indeed, their resistance was one of the most formidable ever mounted against European expansion. The first clash took place in 1843 in the Wairau Valley, now a wine-growing district. A posse of settlers set out to enforce the myth of British control, but encountered the reality of Māori control. Twenty-two settlers were killed, including Wakefield's brother, Arthur, along with about six Māori. In 1845 more serious fighting broke out in the Bay of Islands, when Hōne Heke sacked a British settlement. Heke and his ally Kawiti baffled three British punitive expeditions, using a modern variant of the traditional *pā* fortification. Vestiges of these innovative earthworks can still be seen at Ruapekapeka (south of Kawakawa). Governor Grey claimed victory in the north, but few were convinced at the time. Grey had more success in the south, where he arrested the formidable Ngāti Toa chief Te Rauparaha, who until then wielded great influence on both sides of Cook Strait. Pākehā were able to swamp the few Māori living on the South Island, but the fighting of the 1840s confirmed that the North Island at that time comprised a European fringe around an independent Māori heartland.

In the 1850s settler population and aspirations grew, and fighting broke out again in 1860. The wars burned on sporadically until 1872 over much of the North Island. In the early years the King Movement, seeking to establish a monarchy that would allow Māori to assume a more equal footing with the European settlers, was the backbone of resistance.

The Waitangi Treaty Grounds, where the Treaty of Waitangi was first signed in 1840, is now a tourist attraction for Kiwis and non-Kiwis alike. Each year on 6 February, Waitangi hosts treaty commemorations and protests.

'Kaore e mau te rongo – ake, ake!' (Peace never shall be made – never, never!) War chief Rewi Maniapoto in response to government troops at the battle of Orakau, 1864

HISTORY GROWING PAINS

1908	1914–18	1931	1935–49
NZ physicist Ernest Rutherford is awarded the Nobel Prize in chemistry for 'splitting the atom', investigating the disintegration of elements and the chemistry of radioactive substances.	NZ's contribution to WWI is staggering: for a country of just over one million people, about 100,000 NZ men serve overseas. Some 60,000 become casualties, mostly on the Western Front in France.	A massive earthquake in Napier and Hastings kills at least 256 people.	First Labour government in power, under Michael Savage. This government creates NZ's pioneering version of the welfare state, and also takes some independent initiatives in foreign policy.

THE NEW ZEALAND WARS

Starting in Northland and moving throughout the North Island, the New Zealand Wars had many complex causes, but *whenua* (land) was the one common factor. In these conflicts, also referred to as the Land Wars or Māori Wars, Māori fought both for and against the NZ government, on whose side stood the Imperial British Army, Australians and NZ's own Armed Constabulary. Land confiscations imposed on the Māori as punishment for involvement in these wars are still the source of conflict today, with the government struggling to finance compensation for what are now acknowledged to have been illegal seizures.

In later years some remarkable prophet-generals, notably Titokowaru and Te Kooti, took over. Most wars were small-scale, but the Waikato Land War of 1863–64 was not. This conflict, fought at the same time as the American Civil War, involved armoured steamships, ultra-modern heavy artillery, and 10 proud British regular regiments. Despite the odds, Māori forces won several battles, such as that at Gate Pā, near Tauranga, in 1864. But in the end they were ground down by European numbers and resources. Māori political, though not cultural, independence ebbed away in the last decades of the 19th century. It finally expired when police invaded its last sanctuary, the Urewera Mountains, in 1916.

From Golden Rush to Welfare State

From the 1850s to the 1880s, despite conflict with Māori, the Pākehā economy boomed. A gold rush on the South Island made Dunedin NZ's biggest town, and a young, mostly male population chased their fortunes on the West Coast. Fretting over the imbalance in this frontier society, the British tried to entice women to settle in NZ. Huge amounts of wool were exported and there were unwise levels of overseas borrowing for development of railways and roads. By 1886 the population reached a tipping point: the population of non-Māori people were mostly born in NZ. Many still considered Britain their distant home, but a new identity was taking shape.

Depression followed in 1879, when wool prices slipped and gold production thinned out. Unemployment pushed some of the working population to Australia, and many of those who stayed suffered miserable working conditions. There was still cause for optimism: NZ successfully exported frozen meat in 1882, raising hopes of a new backbone for the economy. Forests were enthusiastically cleared to make way for farmland.

In 1890 the Liberals, NZ's first organised political party, came to power. They stayed there until 1912, helped by a recovering economy. For decades, social reform movements such as the Woman's Christian Temperance Union (WCTU) had lobbied for women's freedom, and NZ became

Maurice Shadbolt's *Season of the Jew* (1987) is a semi-fictionalised story of bloody campaigns led by warrior Te Kooti against the British in Poverty Bay in the 1860s. Te Kooti and his followers compared themselves to the Israelites cast out of Egypt. For more about the NZ Wars, visit www.newzealand wars.co.nz.

1936	1939–45	1953	1973
NZ aviatrix Jean Batten becomes the first aviator to fly solo directly from Britain to NZ.	NZ troops back Britain and the Allied war effort during WWII; from 1942 as many as 45,000 American soldiers camp in NZ to guard against Japanese attack.	New Zealander Edmund Hillary, with Tenzing Norgay, 'knocks the bastard off'; the pair become the first men to reach the summit of Mt Everest.	Fledgling Kiwi prog-rockers Split Enz enter a TV talent quest...finishing second to last.

the first country in the world to give women the vote in 1893. (Another major WCTU push, for countrywide prohibition, didn't take off.) Old-age pensions were introduced in 1898 but these social leaps forward didn't bring universal good news. Pensions only applied for those falling within a very particular definition of 'good character', and the pension reforms deliberately excluded the population of Chinese settlers who had arrived to labour in the goldfields. Meanwhile, the Liberals were obtaining more and more Māori land for settlement. By now, the non-Māori population outnumbered the Māori by 17 to one.

Nation Building

New Zealand had backed Britain in the Boer War (1899–1902) and WWI (1914–18), with dramatic losses in WWI. However, the bravery of ANZAC (Australian and New Zealander Army Corps) forces in the failed Gallipoli campaign endures as a nation-building moment for NZ. In the 1930s NZ's experience of the Great Depression was as grim as any. The derelict farmhouses still seen in rural areas often date from this era. In 1935 a second reforming government took office, campaigning on a platform of social justice: the First Labour government, led by Australian-born Michael Joseph Savage. In WWII NZ formally declared war on Germany: 140,000 or so New Zealanders fought in Europe and the Middle East, while at home, women took on increasing roles in the labour force.

By the 1930s giant ships were regularly carrying frozen meat, cheese and butter, as well as wool, on regular voyages from NZ to Britain. As the NZ economy adapted to the feeding of London, cultural links were also enhanced. New Zealand children studied British history and literature, not their own. New Zealand's leading scientists and writers, such as Ernest Rutherford and Katherine Mansfield, gravitated to Britain. Average living standards in NZ were normally better than in Britain, as were the welfare and lower-level education systems. New Zealanders had access to British markets and culture, and they contributed their share to the latter as equals. The list of 'British' writers, academics, scientists, military leaders, publishers and the like who were actually New Zealanders is long.

New Zealand prided itself on its affluence, equality and social harmony. But it was also conformist, even puritanical. The 1953 Marlon Brando movie, *The Wild One*, was banned until 1977. Full Sunday trading was not allowed until 1989. Licensed restaurants hardly existed in 1960, nor did supermarkets or TV. Notoriously, from 1917 to 1967 pubs were obliged to shut at 6pm (which, ironically, paved the way for a culture of fast, heavy drinking before closing time). Yet puritanism was never the whole story. Opposition to Sunday trading stemmed not so much from belief in the sanctity of the sabbath, but from the belief that workers should have weekends, too. Six o'clock closing was a standing joke in rural areas.

Revered NZ Prime Minister (1893–1906) Richard 'King Dick' Seddon popularised the country's self-proclaimed nickname 'Godzone' with his famous final telegraph: 'Just leaving for God's own country'.

Scottish influence can still be felt in NZ, particularly in the south of the South Island. New Zealand has more Scottish pipe bands per capita than Scotland itself.

1974	1981	1985	1992
Pacific Island migrants who have outstayed visas (dubbed 'overstayers') are subjected to Dawn Raids (crackdowns by immigration police). These raids continue until the early 1980s.	Springbok rugby tour divides the nation. Many New Zealanders show a strong anti-apartheid stance by protesting the games. Other Kiwis feel that sport and politics should not mix, and support the tour.	*Rainbow Warrior* sunk in Auckland Harbour by French agents to prevent the Greenpeace protest ship from making its intended voyage to Moruroa, where the French government is conducting nuclear tests.	Government begins reparations for land confiscated in the NZ Wars, and confirms Māori fishing rights in the 'Sealord deal'. Major settlements of historical confiscation follow.

New Zealand's staunch anti-nuclear stance earned it the nickname 'The Mouse that Roared'.

There was always something of a Kiwi counterculture, even before imported countercultures took root from the 1960s onward.

In 1973 'Mother England' ran off and joined the budding EU. New Zealand was beginning to develop alternative markets to Britain, and alternative exports to wool, meat and dairy products. Wide-bodied jet aircraft were allowing the world and NZ to visit each other on an increasing scale. Women were beginning to penetrate first the upper reaches of the workforce and then the political sphere. Gay people came out of the closet, despite vigorous efforts by moral conservatives to push them back in. University-educated youths were becoming more numerous and more assertive.

THE BOMBING OF THE RAINBOW WARRIOR

On the morning of 10 July 1985, New Zealanders awoke to news reporting that a terrorist attack had killed a man in Auckland Harbour. The Greenpeace flagship *Rainbow Warrior* had been sunk at its anchorage at Marsden Wharf, where it was preparing to sail to Mururoa atoll near Tahiti to protest against French nuclear testing.

A tip-off from a Neighbourhood Watch group eventually led to the arrest of two French foreign intelligence service (DGSE) agents, posing as tourists. The agents had detonated two mines on the boat in staggered explosions – the first designed to cause the crew to evacuate and the second to sink her. However, after the initial evacuation, some of the crew returned to the vessel to investigate and document the attack. Greenpeace photographer Fernando Pereira was drowned below decks following the second explosion.

The arrested agents pleaded guilty to manslaughter and were sentenced to 10 years' imprisonment. In response, the French government threatened to embargo NZ goods from entering the European Economic Community – which would have crippled NZ's economy. A deal was struck whereby France paid $13 million to NZ and apologised, in return for the agents being delivered into French custody on a South Pacific atoll for three years. France eventually paid over $8 million to Greenpeace in reparation – and the bombers were quietly freed before their sentence was served.

Initially French President François Mitterrand denied any government involvement in the attack, but following an inquiry he eventually sacked his Defence Minister and the head of the DGSE, Admiral Pierre Lacoste. On the 20th anniversary of the attack, *Le Monde* newspaper published a report from Lacoste dating from 1986, declaring that the president had personally authorised the operation.

The bombing left a lasting impact on NZ, and French nuclear testing at Moruroa ceased for good in 1996. The wreck of the *Rainbow Warrior* was re-sunk near Northland's Cavalli Islands, where, today, it can be explored by divers. The masts were bought by the North Island's Dargaville Museum and overlook the town. The memory of Fernando Pereira endures in a peaceful bird hide in Thames, while a memorial to the boat sits atop a Māori *pā* (fortified village) site at Matauri Bay, north of the Bay of Islands.

1995	2004	2010	2011
Peter Blake and Russell Coutts win the America's Cup for NZ, sailing *Black Magic;* red socks become a matter of national pride.	Māori TV begins broadcasting – for the first time a channel committed to NZ content and the revitalisation of Māori language and culture hits the small screen.	A cave-in at Pike River coalmine on the South Island's West Coast kills 29 miners.	A severe earthquake strikes Christchurch, killing 185 people and badly damaging the central business district.

The Modern Age

From the 1930s, Māori experienced both a population explosion and massive urbanisation. Life expectancy was lengthening, the birth rate was high, and Māori were moving to cities for occupations formerly filled by Pākehā servicemen. Almost 80% of Māori were urban dwellers by 1986, a staggering reversal of the status quo that brought cultural displacement but simultaneously triggered a movement to strengthen pride in Māori identity. Immigration was broadening, too, first allowing in Pacific Islanders for their labour, and then (East) Asians for their money.

Then, in 1984, NZ's next great reforming government was elected – the Fourth Labour Government, led nominally by David Lange, and in fact by Roger Douglas, the Minister of Finance. This government adopted a more market-led economic policy (dubbed 'Rogernomics'), delighting the right, and an anti-nuclear foreign policy, delighting the left. New Zealand's numerous economic controls were dismantled with breakneck speed. Middle NZ was uneasy about the anti-nuclear policy, which threatened NZ's ANZUS alliance with Australia and the US. But in 1985 French spies sank the anti-nuclear protest ship *Rainbow Warrior* in Auckland Harbour, killing one crewman. The lukewarm American condemnation of the French act brought middle NZ in behind the anti-nuclear policy, which became associated with national independence. Other New Zealanders were uneasy about the market-based economic policy, but failed to come up with a convincing alternative. Revelling in their new freedom, NZ investors engaged in a frenzy of speculation, and suffered even more than the rest of the world from the economic crash of 1987.

From the 1990s, a change to points-based immigration was weaving an increasingly multicultural tapestry in NZ. Numbers of incoming Brits fell but new arrivals increased, particularly from Asia but also from North Africa, the Middle East and various European countries. By 2006 more than 9% of the population was Asian.

By 2017 NZ had a new face to show the world. Helmed by Jacinda Ardern, a coalition government was formed by Labour and NZ First, with support from the Green Party, New Zealand's third woman prime minister is faced with a balancing act between her governing parties while tackling the housing crisis and effecting bigger investment in education and health. It's no wonder that Ardern's ascendancy has been touted as the dawn of a new period of major reform.

In 2015 there was a public referendum to decide between five proposed designs for a new national flag, and the winner was a black-and blue-backed silver fern. During a second referendum in 2016, Kiwis decided that, on reflection, they preferred the original flag – if it ain't broke...

HISTORY THE MODERN AGE

The Ministry for Culture & Heritage's history website (www.nzhistory.net.nz) is an excellent source of info on NZ history

2011	**2013**	**2013**	**2015**
NZ hosts and wins the Rugby World Cup for just the second time; brave France succumbs 8-7 in the final.	New Zealand becomes one of just 15 countries in the world to legally recognise same-sex marriage.	Auckland teenager Ella Yelich-O'Connor, aka Lorde, hits No 1 on the US music charts with her mesmeric, chant-like tune 'Royals'.	New Zealand's beloved All Blacks win back-to-back Rugby World Cups in England, defeating arch-rivals Australia 34-17 in the final.

Environment

New Zealand's landforms have a diversity that you would expect to find across an entire continent: snow-dusted mountains, drowned glacial valleys, rainforests, dunelands and an otherworldly volcanic plateau. Straddling the boundary of two great colliding slabs of the earth's crust – the Pacific plate and the Indo-Australian plate – NZ is a plaything for nature's strongest forces.

The Land

New Zealand is a young country – its present shape is less than 10,000 years old. Having broken away from the supercontinent of Gondwanaland (which included Africa, Australia, Antarctica and South America) some 85 million years ago, it endured continual uplift and erosion, buckling and tearing, and the slow fall and rise of the sea as ice ages came and went.

Evidence of NZ's tumultuous past is everywhere. The South Island's mountainous spine – the 650km-long ranges of the Southern Alps – grew from the clash between plates at a rate of 20km over three million years; in geological terms, that's a sprint. Despite NZ's highest peak, Aoraki/Mt Cook, losing 10m from its summit overnight in a 1991 landslide (and a couple of dozen more metres to erosion), the Alps are overall believed to be some of the fastest-growing mountains in the world.

Volcanic New Zealand

New Zealand is one of the most spectacular places in the world to see geysers. On the North Island, Rotorua's short-lived Waimangu geyser, formed after the 1886 Mt Tarawera eruption, was once the world's largest, often gushing to a dizzying height of 400m.

The North Island's most impressive landscapes have been wrought by volcanoes. Auckland is built on an isthmus peppered by some 48 scoria cones (cinder cones, or volcanic vents). The city's biggest and most recently formed volcano, 600-year-old Rangitoto Island, is a short ferry ride from the downtown wharves. Some 300km further south, the classically shaped cone of snowcapped Mt Taranaki overlooks tranquil dairy pastures.

But the real volcanic heartland runs through the centre of the North Island, from the restless bulk of Mt Ruapehu in Tongariro National Park, northeast through the Rotorua lake district out to NZ's most active volcano, White Island, in the Bay of Plenty. Called the Taupo Volcanic Zone, this great 350km-long rift valley – part of a volcano chain known as the 'Pacific Ring of Fire' – has been the seat of massive eruptions that have left their mark on the country physically and culturally. The volcano that created Lake Taupo last erupted 1800 years ago in a display that was the most violent anywhere on the planet within the past 5000 years.

The South Island can also see some evidence of volcanism – if the remains of the old volcanoes of Banks Peninsula weren't there to repel the sea, the vast Canterbury Plains, built from alpine sediment washed down the rivers from the Alps, would have eroded long ago.

Earthquakes

Not for nothing has New Zealand been called 'the Shaky Isles'. Earthquakes are common, but most only rattle the glassware. A few have wrecked major towns. In 1931 an earthquake measuring 7.9 on the Richter scale levelled the Hawke's Bay city of Napier, causing huge damage and loss of life. Napier was rebuilt almost entirely in then-fashionable art-deco architectural style.

On the South Island, in September 2010 Christchurch was rocked by a magnitude 7.1 earthquake. Less than six months later, in February 2011, a magnitude 6.3 quake destroyed much of the city's historic heart and claimed 185 lives, making it the country's second-deadliest natural disaster. Then in November 2016 an earthquake measuring 7.8 on the Richter scale struck Kaikoura – further up the coast – resulting in two deaths and widespread damage to local infrastructure.

Flora & Fauna

New Zealand's long isolation has allowed it to become a veritable warehouse of unique and varied plants. Separation of NZ's landmass occurred before mammals appeared on the scene, leaving birds and insects to evolve in spectacular ways. As one of the last places on earth to be colonised by humans, NZ was for millennia a safe laboratory for risky evolutionary strategies. But the arrival of Māori, and later Europeans, brought new threats and sometimes extinction.

The now-extinct flightless moa, the largest of which grew to 3.5m tall and weighed over 200kg, browsed open grasslands much as cattle do today (skeletons can be seen at the Canterbury Museum and Otago Museum), while the smaller kiwi still ekes out a nocturnal living rummaging among forest leaf litter for insects and worms. One of the country's most ferocious-looking insects, the mouse-sized giant weta, meanwhile, has taken on a scavenging role that is elsewhere filled by rodents.

Many endemic creatures, including moa and the huia, an exquisite songbird, were driven to extinction, and the vast forests were cleared for their timber and to make way for agriculture. Destruction of habitat and the introduction of exotic animals and plants have taken a terrible environmental toll and New Zealanders are now fighting a rearguard battle to save what remains.

Birds & Bats

Pause in any NZ forest and listen: this country is aflutter with melodious feathered creatures. The country's first Polynesian settlers found little in the way of land mammals – just two species of bat – and most of NZ's present mammals are introduced species. New Zealand's birds generally aren't flashy, but they have an understated beauty that reveals itself in more delicate details: the lacy plumage of rare white heron (kōtuku), the bespectacled appearance of a silvereye or the golden frowns of Fiordland penguins.

The most beautiful songbird is the tui, a nectar-eater with an inventive repertoire that includes clicks, grunts and chuckles. Notable for the white throat feathers that stand out against its dark plumage, the tui often feeds on flax flowers in suburban gardens but is most at home in densely tangled forest ('bush' to New Zealanders). The bellbird (korimako) is also musical; it's common in both native and exotic forests everywhere except Northland (though it is more likely to be heard than seen).

NEW ZEALAND'S ANCIENT LIZARD

The largest native reptile in NZ is the tuatara, a crested lizard that can grow to 50cm long. Thought to be unchanged for more than 220 million years, these endearing creatures can live for up to a century. Meet them at Invercargill's **Southland Museum** (p164), Hokitika's **National Kiwi Centre** (p254), and other zoos and sanctuaries around NZ.

B Heather and H Robertson's *Field Guide to the Birds of New Zealand* is a comprehensive guide for bird-watchers and a model of helpfulness for anyone even casually interested in the country's remarkable bird life. Another good guide is *Birds of New Zealand: Locality Guide* by Stuart Chambers.

Its call is a series of liquid bell notes, most often sounded at dawn or dusk. Fantails (pīwakawaka) are also common on forest trails, swooping and jinking to catch insects stirred up by passing hikers.

At ground level, the most famous native bird is of course the kiwi, NZ's national emblem, with a rounded body and a long, distinctive bill with nostrils at the tip for sniffing out food. Sightings in the wild require patience and luck but numerous sanctuaries (p202) allow a peep of this iconic bird. Look out for other land birds like pukeko, elegant swamp-hens with blue plumage and bright-red beaks. They're readily seen along wetland margins and even on the sides of roads nearby – be warned, they have little road sense. Far rarer (though not dissimilar in appearance) is the takahe, a flightless bird thought extinct until a small colony was discovered in 1948. It's worth seeking them out at Te Anau's bird sanctuary (p182).

If you spend any time in the South Island high country, you are likely to spot the kea (unless it finds you first). A dark-green parrot with red underwings and a sense of mischief, its bold antics are a source of frustration and delight to New Zealanders, who crowned the kea 'Bird of the Year' in 2017. Kea are particularly common in car parks along the Milford Hwy, and in the West Coast's glacier country, where they hang out for food scraps or tear rubber from car windscreens (we've also seen them nibbling at ski bindings in winter sports resorts around Queenstown: consider yourself warned). Resist the urge to feed them, as it's hugely damaging to their health.

And what of the native bats? Populations of both short-tailed and long-tailed bats are declining at frightening speed, though Kahurangi National Park and Nelson are believed to be home to small populations. DOC (Department of Conservation) is hard at work protecting bats, including ambitious plans to resettle them on predator-free islands. If you spot a bat, count yourself lucky – and consider telling DOC.

Trees

No visitor to NZ (particularly Australians) can last long without hearing about the damage done to the bush by that bad-mannered Australian import, the brushtail possum. The long list of mammal pests introduced to

GLOWWORM MAGIC

Glowworms are the larvae of the fungus gnat. The larva glowworm has luminescent organs that produce a soft, greenish light. Living in a sort of hammock suspended from an overhang, it weaves sticky threads that trail down and catch unwary insects attracted by its light. When an insect flies towards the light it gets stuck in the threads – the glowworm just has to reel it in for a feed.

The larval stage lasts from six to nine months, depending on how much food the glowworm gets. When it has grown to about the size of a matchstick, it goes into a pupal stage, much like a cocoon. The adult fungus gnat emerges about two weeks later.

The adult insect doesn't live very long because it doesn't have a mouth. It emerges, mates, lays eggs and dies, all within about two or three days. The sticky eggs, laid in groups of 40 or 50, hatch in about three weeks to become larval glowworms.

Glowworms thrive in moist, dark caves but they can survive anywhere if they have the requisites of moisture, an overhang to suspend from and insects to eat. Waitomo is famous for its glowworms but you can see them in many other places around New Zealand, both in caves and outdoors.

When you come upon glowworms, don't touch their hammocks or hanging threads, try not to make loud noises and don't shine a light right on them. All of these things will cause them to dim their lights. It takes them a few hours to become bright again, during which time the grub will go hungry. The glowworms that shine most brightly are the hungriest.

NZ, whether accidentally or for a variety of misguided reasons, includes deer, rabbits, stoats, pigs and goats. But by far the most destructive is the possum. At their height, 70 million possums were chewing through millions of tonnes of foliage a year. Following efforts by DOC to control their numbers, the possum population has almost halved but they remain an enormous threat to native flora (and to birdlife – possums prey on chicks and eggs).

Among favoured possum food are colourful kowhai, a small-leaved tree growing to 11m, which in spring has drooping clusters of bright-yellow flowers (informally considered NZ's national flower); the pohutukawa, a beautiful coastal tree of the northern North Island that bursts into vivid red flower in December, earning the nickname 'Christmas tree'; and a similar crimson-flowered tree, the rata. Rata species are found on both islands; the northern rata starts life as a climber on a host tree (that it eventually chokes).

Native timber trees include the distinctive rimu (red pine) and the long-lived totara (favoured for Māori war canoes). NZ's perfect pine-growing conditions encouraged one of the country's most successful imports, *Pinus radiata,* which grow to maturity in 35 years (sometimes less).

You won't get far into the bush without coming across tree ferns. NZ has an impressive 200 species of fern and almost half grow nowhere else on the planet. Most easily recognised are the mamaku (black tree fern) – which grows to 20m and can be seen in damp gullies throughout the country – and the 10m-high ponga (silver tree fern) with its distinctive white underside. The silver fern is a national symbol and adorns sporting and corporate logos, as well as shop signs, clothing and jewellery.

Nature Guide to the New Zealand Forest by J Dawson and R Lucas is a beautifully photographed foray into NZ's forests, home to ancient species dating from the time of the dinosaurs.

ENVIRONMENT NATIONAL PARKS

National Parks

More than 85,000 sq km of NZ – almost one-third of the country – is protected and managed within parks and reserves. Almost every conceivable landscape is present: from mangrove-fringed inlets in the north to the snow-topped volcanoes of the Central Plateau, and from the forested fastness of the Urewera ranges in the east to the Southern Alps' majestic mountains, glaciers and fiords. The 13 national parks and more than 30 marine reserves and parks, along with numerous forest parks, offer huge scope for wilderness experiences, ranging from climbing, skiing and mountain biking to tramping, kayaking and trout fishing.

Three places are World Heritage Areas: NZ's Subantarctic Islands; Tongariro National Park (on the North Island); and Te Wāhipounamu (Southwest New Zealand), an amalgam of several national parks in southwest NZ that boast the world's finest surviving Gondwanaland plants and animals in their natural habitats.

Access to the country's wild places is relatively straightforward, though huts on walking tracks require passes and may need to be booked in advance. In practical terms, there is little difference for travellers between a national park and a forest park, though pets are generally not allowed in national parks without a permit. Disability assist dogs can be taken into dog-controlled areas without a permit. Camping is possible in all parks, but may be restricted to dedicated camping grounds – check with DOC first.

The Department of Conservation website (www. doc.govt.nz) has useful information on the country's national parks, tracks and walkways. It also lists backcountry huts and campsites.

Environmental Issues

New Zealand's reputation as an Eden, replete with pristine wilderness and ecofriendly practices, has been repeatedly placed under the microscope. The industry most visible to visitors, tourism, appears studded in green accolades, with environmental best practices employed in areas as broad as heating insulation in hotels to minimum-impact wildlife-watching. But mining, offshore oil and gas exploration, pollution, biodiversity loss, conservation funding cuts and questionable urban planning have provided endless hooks for bad-news stories.

Water quality is arguably the most serious environmental issue faced by New Zealanders. More than a quarter of the country's lakes and rivers have been deemed unsafe for swimming, and research from diverse sources confirms that the health of waterways is in decline. The primary culprit is 'dirty dairying' – cow effluent leaching into freshwater ecosystems, carrying with it high levels of nitrates, as well as bacteria and parasites such as *E. coli* and giardia. A 2017 report by the Ministry for the Environment and Statistics showed that nitrate levels in water were worsening at 55% of monitored river sites, and that urban waterways were in an especially dire state – with levels of harmful bacteria more than 20 times higher than in forest areas. A government push to make 90% of rivers and lakes swimmable by 2040 was met with initial scepticism about the metrics involved, but it's hoped that it will provide an impetus to make NZ's waterways worthy of the country's eco-conscious reputation.

Another ambitious initiative is Predator Free 2050, which aims to rid NZ of introduced animals that prey on native flora and fauna. The worst offenders are possums, stoats and rats, which eat swaths of forest and kill wildlife, particularly birds. Controversy rages at the Department of Conservation's (DOC) use of 1080 poison (sodium fluoroacetate) to control these pests, despite it being sanctioned by prominent environmental groups, such as Forest & Bird, as well as the Parliamentary Commissioner for the Environment. Vehement opposition to 1080 is expressed by such diverse camps as hunters and animal-rights activists, who cite detriments such as by-kill and the potential for poison passing into waterways. Proponents of its use argue that it's biodegradable and that aerial distribution of 1080 is the only cost-effective way to target predators across vast, inaccessible parts of NZ. Still, 'Ban 1080' signs remain common in rural communities and the controversy is likely to continue.

As well as its damaging impact on waterways, the $12 billion dairy industry – the country's biggest export earner – generates 48% of NZ's greenhouse gas emissions. Some farmers are cleaning up their act, lowering emissions through improved management of fertilisers and higher-quality feed, and major players DairyNZ and Fonterra have pledged support. But when it comes to contributing to climate change, the dairy industry isn't NZ's only dirty habit. New Zealand might be a nation of avid recyclers and solar-panel enthusiasts, but it also has the world's fourth-highest ratio of motor vehicles to people.

There have been fears about safeguarding the principal legislation governing the NZ environment, the 1991 Resource Management Act, in the face of proposed amendments. NGOs and community groups – ever-vigilant and already making major contributions to the welfare of NZ's environment – will find plenty to keep them occupied in coming years. But with eco-conscious Jacinda Ardern leading a coalition government from 2017, New Zealanders have reason to be hopeful of a greener future – Ardern has pledged an ambitious goal of reducing net greenhouse gas emissions to zero by 2050. More trains, 100% renewable energy sources and planting 100 million trees per year – goals worthy of NZ's clean, green reputation.

Travellers seeking sustainable tourism operators should look for businesses accredited with Qualmark (www. qualmark.co.nz) or those listed at Organic Explorer (www.organic explorer.co.nz).

Māori Culture

'Māori' once just meant 'common' or 'everyday', but Māori today are a diverse people. Some are engaged with traditional cultural networks and pursuits; others are occupied with adapting tradition and placing it into a dialogue with globalising culture.

People of the Land

Māori are New Zealand's *tangata whenua* (people of the land), and the Māori relationship with the land has developed over hundreds of years of occupation. Once a predominantly rural people, many Māori now live in urban centres, away from their traditional home base. But it's still common practice in formal settings to introduce oneself by referring to home: an ancestral mountain, river, sea or lake, or an ancestor.

The Māori concept of *whanaungatanga* – family relationships – is central to the culture: families spread out from the *whānau* (extended family) to the *hapū* (subtribe) and *iwi* (tribe) and even, in a sense, beyond the human world and into the natural and spiritual worlds.

If you're looking for a Māori experience in NZ you'll find it – in performance, in conversation, in an art gallery, on a tour...

The best way to learn about the relationship between the land and the *tangata whenua* (people of the land) is to get out there and start talking with Māori.

Māori Then

Some three millennia ago people began moving eastward into the Pacific, sailing against the prevailing winds and currents (hard to go out, easier to return safely). Some stopped at Tonga and Samoa, and others settled the small central East Polynesian tropical islands.

The Māori colonisation of Aotearoa began from an original homeland known to Māori as Hawaiki. Skilled navigators and sailors travelled across the Pacific, using many navigational tools – currents, winds, stars, birds and wave patterns – to guide their large, double-hulled ocean-going craft to a new land. The first of many was the great navigator Kupe, who arrived, the story goes, chasing a giant octopus named Muturangi. But the distinction of giving NZ its well-known Māori name – Aotearoa – goes to his wife, Kuramarotini, who cried out, '*He ao, he ao tea, he ao tea roa!*' (A cloud, a white cloud, a long white cloud!).

Kupe and his crew journeyed around the land, and many places around Cook Strait (between the North and South Islands) and the Hokianga in Northland still bear the names that the crew gave them and the marks of their passage. Kupe returned to Hawaiki, leaving from (and naming) Northland's Hokianga. He gave other seafarers valuable navigational information. And then the great *waka* (ocean-going craft) began to arrive.

Wikipedia has a good list of *iwi* websites and a map showing *iwi* distribution (www.wikipedia.org/wiki/list_of_iwi).

The *waka* that the first settlers arrived on, and their landing places, are immortalised in tribal histories. Well-known *waka* include *Tākitimu, Kurahaupō, Te Arawa, Mataatua, Tainui, Aotea* and *Tokomaru*. There are many others. Māori trace their genealogies back to those who arrived on the *waka* (and further back as well).

What would it have been like, making the transition from small tropical islands to a much larger, cooler land mass? Goodbye breadfruit,

HOW THE WORLD BEGAN

In the Māori story of creation, first there was the void, then the night, then Ranginui (sky father) and Papatūānuku (earth mother) came into being, embracing with their children nurtured between them. But nurturing became something else. Their children were stifled in the darkness of their embrace. Unable to stretch out to their full dimensions and struggling to see clearly in the darkness, their children tried to separate them. Tāwhirimātea, the god of winds, raged against them; Tūmatauenga, the god of war, assaulted them. Each god child in turn tried to separate them, but still Rangi and Papa pressed against each other. And then Tāne Mahuta, god of the great forests and of humanity, placed his feet against his father and his back against his mother and slowly, inexorably, began to move them apart. Then came the world of light, of demigods and humanity.

In this world of light Māui, the demigod ancestor, was cast out to sea at birth and was found floating in his mother's topknot. He was a shape-shifter, becoming a pigeon or a dog or an eel if it suited his purposes. He stole fire from the gods. Using his grandmother's jawbone, he bashed the sun so that it could only limp slowly across the sky, so that people would have enough time during the day to get things done (if only he would do it again!). Using the South Island as a canoe, he used the jawbone as a hook to fish up Te Ika-a-Māui (the fish of Māui) – the North Island. And, finally, he met his end trying to defeat death itself. The goddess of death, Hine-nui-te-pō, had obsidian teeth in her vagina (obsidian is a volcanic glass that has a razor edge when chipped). Māui attempted to reverse birth (and hence defeat death) by crawling into her birth canal to reach her heart as she slept. A small bird – a fantail – laughed at the absurd sight. Hine-nui-te-pō awoke, and crushed Māui to death between her thighs. Death one, humanity nil.

coconuts, paper mulberry; hello moa, fernroot, flax – and immense space (relatively speaking). New Zealand has more than 15,000km of coastline. Rarotonga, by way of contrast, has a little over 30km. There was land, lots of it, and flora and fauna that had developed more or less separately from the rest of the world for 80 million years. There was an untouched, massive fishery. There were great seaside mammalian convenience stores – seals and sea lions – as well as a fabulous array of birds.

The early settlers went on the move, pulled by love, trade opportunities and greater resources; pushed by disputes and threats to security. When they settled, Māori established *mana whenua* (regional authority), whether by military campaigns or by the peaceful methods of intermarriage and diplomacy. Looking over tribal history it's possible to see the many alliances, absorptions and extinctions that went on.

Histories were carried by the voice, in stories, songs and chants. Great stress was placed on accurate learning – after all, in an oral culture where people are the libraries, the past is always a generation or two away from oblivion.

Māori lived in *kainga* (small villages), which often had associated gardens. Housing was quite cosy by modern standards – often it was hard to stand upright while inside. From time to time people would leave their home base and go to harvest seasonal foods. When peaceful life was interrupted by conflict, the people would withdraw to *pā* (fortified villages).

And then Europeans began to arrive.

Kupe's passage is marked around NZ: he left his sails (Nga Ra o Kupe) near Cape Palliser as triangular land-forms; he named the two islands in Wellington Harbour Matiu and Makoro after his daughters; his blood stains the red rocks of Wellington's south coast.

Māori Today

Today's culture is marked by new developments in the arts, business, sport and politics. Many historical grievances still stand, but some *iwi* (Ngāi Tahu and Tainui, for example) have settled major historical grievances and are significant forces in the NZ economy. Māori have also addressed the decline in Māori language use by establishing *kōhanga reo*, *kura kaupapa Māori* and *wānanga* (Māori-language pre-schools, schools and universities). There is now a generation of people who speak Māori as a first language. There is a network of Māori radio stations, and Māori TV attracts a committed viewership. A recently revived Māori event is becoming more and more prominent – Matariki (Māori New Year). The constellation Matariki is also known as the Pleiades. It begins to rise above the horizon in late May or early June and its appearance traditionally signals a time for learning, planning and preparing as well as singing, dancing and celebrating. Watch out for talks and lectures, concerts, dinners and even formal balls.

Read Hirini Moko Mead's *Tikanga Māori*, Pat and Hiwi Tauroa's *Te Marae*, and Anne Salmond's *Hui* for detailed information on Māori customs.

Religion

Christian churches and denominations are prominent in the Māori world, including televangelists, mainstream churches for regular and occasional worship, and two major Māori churches (Ringatū and Rātana). But in the (non-Judeo-Christian) beginning there were the *atua Māori*, the Māori gods, and for many Māori the gods are a vital and relevant force still. It is common to greet the earth mother and sky father when speaking formally at a *marae* (meeting house). The gods are represented in art and carving, sung of in *waiata* (songs) and invoked through *karakia* (prayer and incantation) when a meeting house is opened, when a *waka* is launched, even (more simply) when a meal is served. They are spoken of in the *marae* and in wider Māori contexts. The traditional Māori creation story is well known and widely celebrated.

The Arts

There are many collections of Māori *taonga* (treasures) around the country. Canterbury Museum (p69) in Christchurch also has a good collection, while Te Hikoi Southern Journey (p175) in Riverton has riveting displays on early interactions between Māori and Pākehā.

You can stay up to date with what's happening in the Māori arts by listening to *iwi* stations (www.irirangi.net) or tuning into Māori TV (www.maoritelevision.com) for regular features on the Māori arts. Māori TV went to air in 2004, an emotional time for many Māori who could at last see their culture, their concerns and their language in a mass medium. Over 90% of content is NZ made, and programs are in both Māori and English; they're subtitled and accessible to everyone. If you want to really get a feel for the rhythm and metre of spoken Māori from the comfort of your own chair, switch to Te Reo (www.maoritelevision.com/tv/te-reo-channel), a Māori-language-only channel.

When we wrote this, production of Māori lifestyle magazine *Mana* (www.manaonline.co.nz) had stopped, but there were hopes of a relaunch down the line.

Māori legends are all around you as you tour NZ: Maui's *waka* became today's Southern Alps; a *taniwha* (legendary water being) formed Lake Waikaremoana in its death throes; and a rejected Mt Taranaki walked into exile from the central North Island mountain group, carving the Whanganui River.

Tā Moko

Tā moko is the Māori art of tattoo, traditionally worn by men on their faces, thighs and buttocks, and by women on their chins and lips. *Moko* were permanent grooves tapped into the skin using pigment (made from burnt caterpillar or kauri-gum soot) and bone chisels (fine, sharp combs for broad work, and straight blades for detailed work). Canterbury Museum (p69) in Christchurch has a display of traditional implements for *tā moko*.

The modern tattooist's gun is common now, but bone chisels are coming back into use for Māori who want to reconnect with tradition. Since the general renaissance in Māori culture in the 1960s, many artists have

MĀORI CULTURE RELIGION

See Ngahuia Te Awekotuku's book *Mau Moko: The World of Māori Tattoo* (2007) for a close-up of Māori body art, including powerful, beautiful images and an incisive commentary.

taken up *tā moko* and now many Māori wear *moko* with quiet pride and humility.

Can visitors get some work done? The art of *tā moko* is learned by, and inked upon, Māori people – but the term *kirituhi* (skin inscriptions) has arisen to describe Māori-motif-inspired modern tattoos that non-Māori can wear. *Kirituhi* can be profoundly meaningful and designed to fit the wearer's personal story, but there's an important line in the sand between *kirituhi* and *tā moko*.

Whakairo

Traditional Māori carving, with its intricate detailing and curved lines, can transport the viewer. It's quite amazing to consider that *whakairo* was done with stone tools, themselves painstakingly made, until the advent of iron (nails suddenly became very popular).

Some major traditional forms are *waka* (canoes), *pātaka* (storage buildings) and *wharenui* (meeting houses). Along the greenstone-rich West Coast, numerous workshop-boutiques double as galleries that showcase fine examples of modern *pounamu* carving (particularly in Hokitika). You can see sublime examples of traditional wood carving at Dunedin's Otago Museum (p131), including an impressive *waka taua* (war canoe).

The apex of carving today is the *whare whakairo* (carved meeting house). A commissioning group relates its history and ancestral stories to a carver, who then draws (sometimes quite loosely) on traditional motifs to interpret or embody the stories and ancestors in wood or composite fibreboard.

The biggest change in carving (as with most traditional arts) has been in the use of new mediums and tools. Rangi Kipa uses a high-density plastic to make his *hei tiki* (traditional pendants). You can check out his gallery at www.rangikipa.com.

Weaving

A conversation starter for your next New Zealand barbecue: would NZ's 2011 and 2015 Rugby World Cup–winning All Blacks teams have been as unstoppable without key Māori players such as Dan Carter, Piri Weepu, Nehe Milner-Skudder and Aaron Smith?

Weaving was an essential art that provided clothing, nets and cordage, footwear for rough country travel, mats to cover earthen floors, and *kete* (bags) to carry stuff in. Many woven items are beautiful as well as practical. Some were major works – *korowai* (cloaks) could take years to finish. Woven predominantly with flax and feathers, they are worn now on ceremonial occasions – a stunning sight.

Today, tradition is greatly respected, but not all traditions are necessarily followed. Flax was (and still is) the preferred medium for weaving. To get a strong fibre from flax leaves, weavers scraped away the leaves' flesh with a mussel shell, pounded it until it was soft, dyed it, then dried it. But contemporary weavers are using everything in their work: raffia, copper wire, rubber – even polar fleece and garden hoses!

The best way to experience weaving is to contact one of the many weavers running workshops. By learning the art, you'll appreciate the examples of weaving in museums even more. And if you want your own? Woven *kete* and backpacks have become fashion accessories and are on sale in most cities. Weaving is also found in dealer art galleries around the country.

Haka

Adrenalising, awe-inspiring and uplifting, the *haka* is not only a war dance – it is used to welcome visitors, honour achievement, express identity or to put forth very strong opinions.

Haka involve chanted words, vigorous body movements and *pūkana* (when performers distort their faces, eyes bulging with the whites showing, perhaps with tongue extended).

The well-known *haka* 'Ka Mate', performed by the All Blacks before rugby test matches, is credited to the cunning fighting chief Te Rauparaha. It celebrates his escape from death. Chased by enemies, he hid himself in a food pit. After his pursuers had left, a friendly chief named Te Whareangi (the 'hairy man' referred to in the *haka*), let him out; he climbed out into the sunshine and performed 'Ka Mate'.

VISITING MARAE (TRADITIONAL MEETING PLACES)

As you travel around NZ, you will see many *marae* complexes. Often *marae* are owned by a descent group. They are also owned by urban Māori groups, schools, universities and church groups, and they should only be visited by arrangement with the owners.

Marae complexes include a *wharenui* (meeting house), which often embodies an ancestor. Its ridge is the backbone, the rafters are ribs, and it shelters the descendants. There is a clear space in front of the *wharenui*, the *marae ātea*. Sometimes there are other buildings: a *wharekai* (dining hall); a toilet and shower block; perhaps even classrooms, play equipment and the like.

Hui (gatherings) are held at *marae*. Issues are discussed, classes conducted, milestones celebrated and the dead farewelled. Te reo Māori (the Māori language) is prominent, and sometimes the only language used.

Visitors sleep in the meeting house if a *hui* goes on for longer than a day. Mattresses are placed on the floor, someone may bring a guitar, and stories and jokes always go down well as the evening stretches out.

The Pōwhiri

If you visit a *marae* as part of an organised group, you'll be welcomed in a *pōwhiri* (welcoming ceremony).

Outside the *marae*, there may be a *wero* (challenge). Using *taiaha* (quarter-staff) moves, a warrior will approach the visitors and place a baton on the ground for a visitor to pick up, to demonstrate their peaceful intent.

There is a *karanga* (ceremonial call). A woman from the host group calls to the visitors and a woman from the visitors responds. Their long, high, falling calls begin to overlap and interweave and the visiting group walks on to the *marae ātea* (meeting house courtyard). It is then time for *whaikōrero* (speechmaking). The hosts welcome the visitors, the visitors respond. Speeches are capped off by a *waiata* (song), and the visitors' speakers present a *koha* (gift, usually an envelope of cash). The hosts then invite the visitors to *hariru* (shake hands) and *hongi*. Visitors and hosts are now united and will share light refreshments or a meal.

The Hongi

To perform the *hongi*, press forehead and nose together firmly, shake hands, and perhaps offer a greeting such as '*Kia ora*' or '*Tēnā koe*'. Some prefer one press (for two or three seconds, or longer), others prefer two shorter (press, release, press). Men and women sometimes kiss on one cheek. Some people mistakenly think the *hongi* is a pressing of noses only (awkward to aim!) or the rubbing of noses (even more awkward).

Tapu

Tapu (spiritual restrictions) and *mana* (power and prestige) are taken seriously in the Māori world. Sit on chairs or seating provided (never on tables), and walk around people, not over them. The *pōwhiri* is *tapu*, and mixing food and *tapu* is right up there on the offence-o-meter. Do eat and drink when invited to do so by your hosts. You needn't worry about starvation: an important Māori value is *manaakitanga* (kindness).

Depending on area, the *pōwhiri* has gender roles: women *karanga* (call), men *whaikōrero* (orate); women lead the way on to the *marae*, men sit on the *paepae* (the speakers' bench at the front). In a modern context, the debate around these roles continues.

COMMON MĀORI GEOGRAPHICAL TERMS

The following words form part of many Māori place names in New Zealand, and help you understand the meaning of these place names. For example, in Nelson Lakes National Park, Rotoroa is the Long (roa) Lake (roto) and Rotoiti is the Small (iti) Lake (roto).

a – of; **ara** – way, path or road; **awa** – river or valley; **iti** – small; **kai** – food; **kare** – rippling; **kati** – to shut or close; **makariri** – cold; **maunga** – mountain; **moana** – sea or lake; **motu** – island; **mutu** – finished, ended, over; **ngā** – the (plural); **nui** – big or great; **o** – of, place of...; **one** – beach, sand or mud; **pā** – fortified village; **poto** – short; **puke** – hill; **puna** – spring, hole, fountain; **rangi** – sky, heavens; **raro** – north; **roa** – long; **roto** – lake; **rua** – hole in the ground, two; **runga** – above; **tāhuna** – beach, sandbank; **tāne** – man; **tapu** – sacred, forbidden or taboo; **tata** – close to, dash against, twin islands; **te** – the (singular); **tonga** – south; **wāhine** – woman; **wai** – water; **waka** – canoe; **wera** – burnt or hot; **whanga** – harbour, bay or inlet; **whenua** – land or country

You can experience *haka* at various cultural performances, including Ko Tane (p72) at Willowbank in Christchurch and Kiwi Haka (p202) in Queenstown.

But the best displays of *haka* are at the national Te Matatini National Kapa Haka Festival (www.tematatini.co.nz), when NZ's top groups compete. It's held every two years.

Contemporary Visual Art

A distinctive feature of Māori visual art is the tension between traditional Māori ideas and modern artistic mediums and trends. Shane Cotton has produced a series of works that conversed with 19th-century painted meeting houses, which themselves departed from Māori carved houses. Kelcy Taratoa uses sci-fi, superheroes and pop-art imagery.

Of course, Māori motifs aren't necessarily the dominant features of work by Māori artists. Major NZ artist Ralph Hotere (1931–2013) was wary about being assigned any cultural, ethnic or genre label and his work confronted a broad range of political and social issues.

Contemporary Māori art is by no means only about painting. Many other artists use installations or digital formats – look out for work by Jacqueline Fraser, Peter Robinson and Lisa Reihana.

There are some great permanent exhibitions of Māori visual arts in the major centres. The Christchurch Art Gallery (p71) holds a particularly strong collection.

Theatre

Could heavy metal be the newest form of expressing Māori identity? Singing (and screaming) in Te Reo Māori, Waipu guitar trio Alien Weaponry thrash out songs that narrate the battles of their ancestors.

Powered by a wave of political activism, the 1970s saw the emergence of many Māori playwrights and plays, and theatre remains a prominent area of the Māori arts today. Māori theatre drew heavily on the traditions of the *marae*. Instead of dimming the lights and immediately beginning the performance, many Māori theatre groups began with a stylised *pōwhiri* (welcoming ceremony), had space for audience members to respond to the play, and ended with a *karakia* (prayer or incantation), or a farewell.

The Taki Rua company is an independent producer of Māori work for both children and adults and has been in existence for more than 30 years. As well as staging its shows in the major centres, it tours most of its work – check out its website (www.takirua.co.nz) for the current offerings. Māori drama is also often showcased at the professional theatres in the main centres. Look out for work by Hone Kouka, Briar Grace-Smith and Mitch Tawhi Thomas.

Contemporary Dance

Contemporary Māori dance often takes its inspiration from *kapa haka* (cultural dance) and traditional Māori imagery. The exploration of pre-European life also provides inspiration.

New Zealand's leading specifically Māori dance company is the Atamira Dance Collective (www.atamiradance.co.nz), which has been producing critically acclaimed, beautiful and challenging work since 2000. If that sounds too earnest, get acquainted with the work of musician and visual artist Mika Torotoro, who happily blends *kapa haka*, drag, opera, ballet and disco. You can check out clips of his work at www.mika.co.nz.

Cinema

Although there had already been successful Māori documentaries (*Patu!* and the *Tangata Whenua* series are brilliant), it wasn't until 1987 that NZ had its first fictional feature-length movie by a Māori writer and director, with Barry Barclay's *Ngati*. Mereta Mita was the first Māori woman to direct a fiction feature, with *Mauri* (1988). Both Mita and Barclay had highly political aims and ways of working, which involved a lengthy pre-production phase, during which they would consult with and seek direction from their *kaumātua* (elders). Films with significant Māori participation or control include the harrowing *Once Were Warriors* and the uplifting *Whale Rider*. Oscar-nominated Taika Waititi, of Te Whānau-ā-Apanui descent, wrote and directed *Eagle vs Shark* and *Boy*.

Literature

There are many novels and collections of short stories by Māori writers, and personal taste will govern your choices. Keri Hulme *(The Bone People, Stonefish)* and the South Island go together like a mass of whitebait bound in a frying pan by a single egg (ie very well). Other significant writers include Patricia Grace *(Potiki, Cousins, Dogside Story, Tu,)* Witi Ihimaera *(Pounamu, Pounamu; The Matriarch; Bulibasha; The Whale Rider)*, Alan Duff *(Once Were Warriors)*, James George *(Hummingbird, Ocean Roads)*, Paula Morris *(Rangatira, Queen of Beauty, Hibiscus Coast, Trendy but Casual)* and Kelly Ana Morey *(Bloom, Grace Is Gone)*. If poetry appeals, you can't go past the giant of Māori poetry in English, the late, lamented Hone Tuwhare *(Deep River Talk: Collected Poems)*, who famously sounds like he's at church and in the pub at the same time.

MĀORI CULTURE THE ARTS

The first NZ hip-hop song to become a hit was Dalvanius Prime's 'Poi E', which was sung entirely in Māori by the Patea Māori Club. It was the highest-selling single of 1984 in NZ.

The Arts

Māori music and art extends back to New Zealand's early, unrecorded history, but its motifs endure today in diverse forms. European settlers imported artistic styles from back home, but it took a century for postcolonial NZ to hone its distinctive artistic identity. In the first half of the 20th century it was writers and visual artists who led the charge, but in the decades that followed, music and movies catapulted the nation's creativity into the world's consciousness.

Literature

In 2013 New Zealanders rejoiced to hear that 28-year-old Eleanor Catton had become only the second NZ writer to ever win the Man Booker Prize, arguably the world's most prestigious award for literature, for her epic historical novel *The Luminaries,* set on the West Coast. Lloyd Jones had come close in 2007 when his novel *Mister Pip* was shortlisted, but it had been a long wait between drinks since Keri Hulme took the prize in 1985 for her haunting novel *The Bone People.*

Catton and Hulme continue in a proud line of NZ women writers, starting in the early 20th century with Katherine Mansfield. Mansfield's work began a Kiwi tradition in short fiction, and for years the standard was carried by novelist Janet Frame, whose dramatic life was depicted in Jane Campion's film of her autobiography, *An Angel at My Table.* Frame's novel *The Carpathians* won the Commonwealth Writers' Prize in 1989. A new author on New Zealanders' must-read lists is Catherine Chidgey, whose heart-rending novel *The Wish Child* (2016) won the country's top fiction prize at 2017's NZ Book Awards.

Less recognised internationally, Maurice Gee has gained the nation's annual top fiction gong six times, most recently with *Blindsight* in 2006. His much-loved children's novel *Under the Mountain* (1979) was made into a seminal NZ TV series in 1981, and then a major motion picture in 2009. In 2004 the adaptation of another of his novels, *In My Father's Den* (1972), won major awards at international film festivals.

The late Maurice Shadbolt also achieved much acclaim for his many novels, particularly those set during the New Zealand Wars. Try *Season of the Jew* (1987) or *The House of Strife* (1993).

MĀORI VOICES IN PRINT

Some of the most interesting and enjoyable NZ fiction voices belong to Māori writers, with Booker-winner Keri Hulme leading the way. Witi Ihimaera's novels give a wonderful insight into small-town Māori life on the East Coast – especially *Bulibasha* (1994) and *The Whale Rider* (1987), which was made into an acclaimed film. Patricia Grace's work is similarly filled with exquisitely told stories of rural *marae*-centred life: try *Mutuwhenua* (1978), *Potiki* (1986), *Dogside Story* (2001) or *Tu* (2004). *Chappy* (2015) is Grace's expansive tale of a prodigal son returning to NZ to untangle his cross-cultural heritage.

MIDDLE-EARTH TOURISM

Did the scenery of the epic film trilogies *Lord of the Rings (LOTR)* and *The Hobbit* lure you to Aotearoa? The North Island has most of the big-ticket filming locations but both islands have knowledgeable operators that can take you set-jetting on foot, on horseback or by 4WD. Dedicated enthusiasts can buy a copy of Ian Brodie's *The Lord of the Rings: Location Guidebook* for detail on filming locations and their GPS coordinates. Online, DOC has a useful primer (www.doc.govt.nz/lordoftherings).

Southern Alps, aka Misty Mountains Peter Jackson made the most of this untamed landscape, choosing Mt Cook Village as the setting for Minas Tirith. **Hassle Free Tours** (p77) offers a trip from Christchurch to the site of Edoras.

Takaka Hill Used for various scenes in both trilogies.

Pelorus River, Marlborough Sounds The setting for the barrel scene in *The Hobbit: The Desolation of Smaug*. Experience it on a kayaking trip with **Pelorus Eco Adventures** (p305).

Twizel OneRing Tours (☑0800 213 868, 03-435 0073; www.lordoftheringstour.com; cnr Ostler & Wairepo Sts) allows you to play dress-up at the sites of Laketown and the Battle of the Pelennor Fields.

Queenstown & Glenorchy Nomad Safaris (p207) and **Private Discovery Tours** (p220) offer a range of 4WD tours out of Queenstown, complete with Middle-earth movie locations. Glenorchy-based **Dart Stables** (☑03 442 5688, www.dartstables.com; Coll St) runs horse treks along a LOTR theme.

Te Anau Fangorn Forest, Silverlode and Nen Hithoel were set in **Mavora Lakes Conservation Park** (p183), while the Upper Waiau River became the River Anduin.

Cinema & TV

If you first became interested in New Zealand when watching it on the silver screen, you're in good company. Sir Peter Jackson's NZ-made *The Lord of the Rings* and *The Hobbit* trilogies were the best thing to happen to NZ tourism since Captain Cook.

Yet NZ cinema is hardly ever easygoing. In his BBC-funded documentary, *Cinema of Unease*, NZ actor Sam Neill described the country's film industry as producing bleak, haunted work. One need only watch Lee Tamahori's harrowing *Once Were Warriors* (1994) to see what he means.

The uniting factor in NZ film and TV is the landscape, which provides a haunting backdrop – arguably as much of a presence as the characters themselves. Jane Campion's *The Piano* (1993) and *Top of the Lake* (2013), Brad McGann's *In My Father's Den* (2004) and Jackson's *Heavenly Creatures* (1994) all use magically lush scenery to couch disturbing violence. It's a land-mysticism constantly bordering on the creepy.

Even when Kiwis do humour, it's as resolutely black as their rugby jerseys; check out Jackson's early splatter-fests and Taika Waititi's *Boy* (2010). Exporting NZ comedy hasn't been easy, yet the HBO-produced TV musical parody *Flight of the Conchords* – featuring a mumbling, bumbling Kiwi folk-singing duo trying to get a break in New York – found surprising international success. It's the Polynesian giggle-factor that seems likeliest to break down the bleak house of NZ cinema, with feel-good-through-and-through *Sione's Wedding* (2006) enjoying the biggest opening weekend of any NZ film at the time.

Also packaging offbeat NZ humour for an international audience, *Hunt for the Wilderpeople* (2016) and *What We Do in the Shadows* (2014) have propelled scriptwriter and director Taika Waititi to critical acclaim, while *Thor: Ragnarok* (2017) made him a household name – though

Jane Campion was the first Kiwi nominated as Best Director for the Academy Awards and Peter Jackson the first to win. *The Return of the King* won a mighty 11 Oscars in 2004.

The only Kiwi actors to have won an Oscar are Anna Paquin (for *The Piano*) and Russell Crowe (for *Gladiator*). Paquin was born in Canada but moved to NZ when she was four, while Crowe moved from NZ to Australia at the same age.

many argue that the director's star turn as a softly spoken rock creature is the movie's highlight.

New Zealanders have gone from never seeing themselves in international cinema to having whole cloned armies of Temuera Morrisons invading the universe in *Star Wars*. Familiar faces such as Cliff Curtis and Karl Urban seem to constantly pop up playing Mexican or Russian gangsters in action movies. Many of them got their start in long-running soap opera *Shortland Street*.

Visual Arts

The NZ 'can do' attitude extends to the visual arts. If you're visiting a local's home, don't be surprised to find one of the owner's paintings on the wall or one of their mate's sculptures in the back garden, pieced together out of bits of shell, driftwood and a length of the magical 'number 8 wire'.

This is symptomatic of a flourishing local art and crafts scene cultivated by lively tertiary courses churning out traditional carvers and weavers, jewellery-makers, and moulders of metal and glass. The larger cities have excellent dealer galleries representing interesting local artists working across all media.

Traditional Māori art has a distinctive visual style with well-developed motifs that have been embraced by NZ artists of every race. In the painting medium, these include the cool modernism of Gordon Walters and the more controversial pop-art approach of Dick Frizzell's *Tiki* series. Likewise, Pacific Island themes are common, particularly in Auckland; look out for the intricate, collage-like paintings of Niuean-born, Auckland-raised John Pule.

Charles Frederick Goldie painted a series of compelling, realist portraits of Māori, who were feared to be a dying race. Debate over the political propriety of Goldie's work raged for years, but its value is widely accepted now: not least because Māori themselves generally acknowledge and value them as ancestral representations. In 2016 Goldie's last work became the first NZ painting to be sold for more than $1 million.

Recalibrating the ways in which Pacific Islander and Māori people are depicted in art, Lisa Reihana wowed the Venice Biennale in 2017 with her multimedia work *In Pursuit of Venus*.

Depicting the Land

It's no surprise that in a nation so defined by its natural environment, landscape painting constituted the first post-European body of art. In the late 19th century, John Gully and Petrus van der Velden were among those to arrive and capture the drama of the land in paintings.

Colin McCahon is widely regarded to have been NZ's most important artist. Even where McCahon lurched into Catholic mysticism, his spirituality was rooted in geography. His brooding landscapes evoke the land's power but also its vulnerability. McCahon is widely quoted as describing his work as a depiction of NZ before its seas become cluttered with debris and the sky turns dark with soot.

Not all the best galleries are in Auckland, Wellington or Christchurch. Gore's Eastern Southland Gallery (p161) has an important and growing collection. Some of the most interesting galleries have a makeshift, multi-use vibe: part-gallery, part-museum of curios, part-cafe, designed for road trippers to pull over and marvel, like the Catlins' Lost Gypsy Gallery (p158), which showcases a bamboozling collection inside a bus.

Landscape photographers also capture the fierceness and fragility of NZ's terrain. It's worth detouring to a few of the country's resident photographers, many of whom have their own gallery (sometimes within, or adjoining, their own home). Westland is home to the gallery of exceptionally gifted photographer **Andris Apse** (☑021 884 618, 03-753 4241; www.andrisapse.com; 109 The Strand; ⊙hours vary) and to the **Petr Hlavacek Gallery** (☑03-753 4199; www.nzicescapes.com; 2811b SH6; ⊙9am-7pm Mon-Fri) FREE, which showcases some of NZ's finest landscape photography.

Music

New Zealand music began with the *waiata* (singing) developed by Māori following their arrival in the country. The main musical instruments were wind instruments made of bone or wood, the most well known of which is the *nguru* (also known as the 'nose flute'), while percussion was provided by chest- and thigh-slapping. These days, the liveliest place to see Māori music being performed is at *kapa haka* competitions in which groups compete with their own routines of traditional song and dance.

Classical

Early European immigrants brought their own styles of music and gave birth to local variants during the early 1900s. In the 1950s Douglas Lilburn became one of the first internationally recognised NZ classical composers. More recently the country has produced a number of world-renowned musicians in this field, including legendary opera singer Dame Kiri Te Kanawa, million-selling classic-to-pop singer Hayley Westenra, composer John Psathas (who created music for the 2004 Olympic Games) and composer/percussionist Gareth Farr (who also performs in drag under the name Lilith LaCroix).

Rock

New Zealand's most acclaimed rock exports are the revered indie label Flying Nun and the music of the Finn Brothers.

Started in 1981 by Christchurch record-store owner Roger Shepherd, many of Flying Nun's early groups came from Dunedin, where local musicians took the DIY attitude of punk but used it to produce a lo-fi indie-pop that received rave reviews from the likes of *NME* in the UK and *Rolling Stone* in the US. Many of the musicians from the Flying Nun scene still perform live to this day, including David Kilgour (from the Clean) and Shayne Carter (from the Straitjacket Fits, and subsequently Dimmer and the Adults).

Want something heavier? Hamilton heavy-metal act Devilskin's 2014 debut album hit the top spot on NZ's charts, as did their punchy 2016 follow-up *Be Like the River*. Beastwars, a rasping, trance-inducing sludge metal band from Wellington, is another stalwart of NZ's heavy-metal scene. Meanwhile, hitting the big leagues during tours of North America and Europe, technical death-metal band Ulcerate have risen to prominence as NZ's best-known extreme metal act. We're not worthy.

A wide range of cultural events are listed on www.eventfinda.co.nz. This is a good place to find out about concerts, classical music recitals and *kapa haka* performances. For more specific information on the NZ classical music scene, see www.sounz.org.nz.

THE BROTHERS FINN

There are certain tunes that all Kiwis can sing along to, given a beer and the opportunity. A surprising proportion of these were written by Tim and Neil Finn, many of which have been international hits. Tim Finn first came to prominence in the 1970s group Split Enz, who amassed a solid following in Australia, NZ and Canada before disbanding in 1985. Neil then formed Crowded House with two Australian musicians (Paul Hester and Nick Seymour) and one of their early singles, 'Don't Dream It's Over', hit number two on the US charts. Tim later did a brief spell in the band, during which the brothers wrote 'Weather with You' – a song that reached number seven on the UK charts, pushing their album *Woodface* to gold sales. Neil has also remained busy, organising a set of shows/releases under the name 7 Worlds Collide – a collaboration with well-known overseas musicians. Tim and Neil have both released a number of solo albums, as well as releasing material together as the Finn Brothers.

Reggae, Hip-Hop & Dance

The genres of music that have been adopted most enthusiastically by Māori and Polynesian New Zealanders have been reggae (in the 1970s) and hip-hop (in the 1980s), which has led to distinct local forms. In Wellington, a thriving jazz scene took on a reggae influence to create a host of groups that blended dub, roots and funky jazz – most notably Fat Freddy's Drop.

The local hip-hop scene has its heart in the suburbs of South Auckland, which have a high concentration of Māori and Pacific Island residents. This area is home to one of New Zealand's foremost hip-hop labels, Dawn Raid, which takes its name from the infamous 1970s early-morning house raids that police performed on Pacific Islanders suspected of outstaying their visas. Dawn Raid's most successful artist is Savage, who sold a million copies of his single 'Swing' after it was featured in the movie *Knocked Up*. Within New Zealand, the most well-known hip-hop acts are Scribe, Che Fu and Smashproof (whose song 'Brother' held number one on the NZ singles charts for 11 weeks).

Dance music gained a foothold in Christchurch in the 1990s, spawning dub/electronica outfit Salmonella Dub and its offshoot act, Tiki Taane. Drum 'n' bass remains popular locally and has spawned internationally renowned acts such as Concord Dawn and Shapeshifter.

For more on local hip-hop, pop and rock, check out www.thecorner. co.nz and the long-running www.muzic. net.nz.

Movers & Shakers

Since 2000, the NZ music scene has developed new vitality after the government convinced commercial radio stations to adopt a voluntary quota of 20% local music. This enabled commercially oriented musicians to develop solid careers. Rock groups such as Shihad, the Feelers and Opshop thrived in this environment, as have a set of soulful female solo artists: Bic Runga, Anika Moa and Brooke Fraser (daughter of All Black Bernie Fraser). New Zealand also produced two internationally acclaimed garage rock acts over this time: the Datsuns and the D4.

Current Kiwis garnering international recognition include the incredibly gifted songstress Kimbra (who sang on Gotye's global smash 'Somebody That I Used To Know'); indie electro-rockers the Naked and Famous; multitalented singer-songwriter Ladyhawke; the arty Lawrence Arabia; and the semipsychedelic Unknown Mortal Orchestra.

R&B singer Aaradhna made a splash with her album *Treble & Reverb*, which won Album of the Year at the 2013 New Zealand Music Awards. When the title track of her album *Brown Girl* was awarded a gong for 'best hip-hop' in 2016, she turned it down saying she'd been placed in the wrong musical category because of the colour of her skin.

The TV show *Popstars* originated in New Zealand, though the resulting group, TrueBliss, was short-lived. The series concept was then picked up in Australia, the UK and the US, inspiring the *Idols* series.

Good Lorde!

The biggest name in Kiwi music is Lorde, a singer-songwriter from Devonport on Auckland's North Shore. Known less regally to her friends as Ella Yelich-O'Connor, Lorde was 16 years old when she cracked the number-one spot on the US Billboard charts in 2013 with her magical, schoolyard-chant-evoking hit 'Royals' – the first NZ solo artist to top the American charts. 'Royals' then went on to win the Song of the Year Grammy in 2014. Her debut album *Pure Heroine* spawned a string of hits and sold millions of copies worldwide, while moody follow-up *Melodrama* instantly topped charts in NZ and the US upon its release in 2017.

Survival Guide

Directory A-Z

Accommodation

Book well in advance in peak times: from Christmas to late January, at Easter, and during winter (June to September) in snowy resort towns like Queenstown and Wanaka.

B&Bs The whole gamut, from luxury, antique-stuffed country houses to simple tea-and-toast operations in private homes.

Holiday Parks A top choice for camping or touring in a campervan, with myriad options from unpowered tent sites to family en suite cabins.

Hostels From beery, party-prone joints to classy, family-friendly 'flashpackers'.

Hotels From small-town pubs to slick global chain operations – with commensurate price ranges.

Motels Decent midrange motels on the outskirts of most towns.

Booking Services

Local visitor information centres around NZ provide reams of local accommodation information, sometimes in the form of folders detailing facilities and up-to-date prices; many can also make bookings on your behalf.

Lonely Planet (www.lonely planet.com/new-zealand/hotels) The full range of NZ accommodation, from hostels to hotels.

Automobile Association (www.aa.co.nz/travel) Online accommodation bookings (especially good for motels, B&Bs and holiday parks).

Jasons (www.jasons.co.nz) Long-running travel service with myriad online booking options.

New Zealand Bed & Breakfast (www.bnb.co.nz) The name says it all.

Bed & Breakfast New Zealand (www.bed-and-breakfast.co.nz) B&B and self-contained accommodation directory.

Rural Holidays NZ (www.ruralholidays.co.nz) Farm and homestay listings across NZ.

Book a Bach (www.bookabach.co.nz) Apartment and holiday-house bookings (and maybe even a bach or two!).

Holiday Houses (www.holiday houses.co.nz) Holiday-house rentals NZ-wide.

New Zealand Apartments (www.nzapartments.co.nz) Rental listings for upmarket apartments of all sizes.

B&Bs

Bed and breakfast (B&B) accommodation in NZ pops up in the middle of cities, in rural hamlets and on stretches of isolated coastline, with rooms on offer in everything from suburban bungalows to stately manors.

Breakfast may be 'continental' (a standard offering of cereal, toast and tea or coffee, or a heartier version with yoghurt, fruit, home-baked bread or muffins), or a stomach-loading cooked meal (eggs, bacon, sausages – though, with notice, vegetarians are increasingly being well catered for). Some B&B hosts may also cook dinner for guests and advertise dinner, bed and breakfast (DB&B) packages.

B&B tariffs are typically in the $120 to $200 bracket (per double), though some places cost upwards of $300 per double. Some hosts charge cheeky prices for what is, in essence, a bedroom in their home. Off-street parking is often a bonus in the big cities.

Camping & Holiday Parks

Campers and campervan drivers converge on NZ's hugely popular 'holiday parks', slumbering in powered and unpowered sites, cheap bunk rooms (dorm rooms), cabins (shared bathroom facilities) and self-contained units (often called

---

BOOK YOUR STAY ONLINE

For more accommodation reviews by Lonely Planet authors, check out http://lonelyplanet.com/new-zealand/hotels/. You'll find independent reviews, as well as recommendations on the best places to stay. Best of all, you can book online.

motels or tourist flats). Well-equipped communal kitchens, dining areas, games and TV rooms, and playgrounds often feature. In cities, holiday parks are usually a fair way from the action, but in smaller towns they can be impressively central or near lakes, beaches, rivers and forests.

The nightly cost of holiday-park tent sites is usually $15 to $20 per adult, with children charged half price; powered campervan sites can be anything from a couple of dollars more to around the $40 mark. Cabin/unit accommodation normally ranges from $70 to $120 per double. Unless noted otherwise, Lonely Planet lists campsite, campervan site, hut and cabin prices for two people.

DOC & FREEDOM CAMPING

A fantastic option for those in campervans is the 250-plus vehicle-accessible 'Conservation Campsites' run by the Department of Conservation (DOC; www.doc.govt. nz), with fees ranging from free (basic toilets and fresh water) to $21 per adult (flush toilets and showers). DOC publishes free brochures with detailed descriptions and instructions to find every campsite (even GPS coordinates). Pick up copies from DOC offices before you hit the road, or visit the website.

DOC also looks after hundreds of 'Backcountry Huts' and 'Backcountry Campsites', which can only be reached on foot. 'Great Walk' huts and campsites are also managed by DOC.

New Zealand is so photogenic, it's tempting to just pull off the road at a gorgeous viewpoint and camp the night. But never assume it's OK to camp somewhere: always ask a local or check with the local i-SITE visitor centre, DOC office or commercial campground. If you are 'freedom camping', treat the area

with respect. If your chosen campsite doesn't have toilet facilities and neither does your campervan, it's illegal for you to sleep there (your campervan must also have an on-board grey-water storage system). Legislation allows for $200 instant fines for camping in prohibited areas or improper disposal of waste (in cases where dumping waste could damage the environment, fees are up to $10,000). See www.camping.org.nz for more freedom-camping tips and consider downloading the free Campermate App (www.campermate.co.nz), which flags drinking-water sources, public toilets, freedom-camping spots and locals happy to rent their driveway to campervans.

Farmstays

Farmstays open the door to the agricultural side of NZ life, with visitors encouraged to get some dirt beneath their fingernails at orchards, and dairy, sheep and cattle farms. Costs can vary widely, with bed and breakfast generally costing $80 to $140. Some farms have separate cottages where you can fix your own food; others offer low-cost, shared, backpacker-style accommodation.

Farm Helpers in NZ (www.fhinz.co.nz) produces a booklet ($25) that lists around 350 NZ farms providing lodging in exchange for four to six hours' work per day.

WWOOFING

If you don't mind getting your hands dirty, an economical way of travelling around NZ involves doing some voluntary work as a member of the international **Willing Workers On Organic Farms** (WWOOF; ☏03-544 9890; www.wwoof.co.nz; ⊙9am-3pm Mon-Fri) scheme. Down on the farm, in exchange for a hard day's work, owners provide food, accommodation and some hands-on organic farming experience. Contact farm owners a week or two beforehand to arrange your stay, as you would for a hotel or hostel – don't turn up unannounced!

A one-year online membership costs $40 for an individual or a couple. A farm listing book, which is mailed to you, costs an extra $10 to $30, depending on where in the world your mailbox is. You should have a Working Holiday Visa when you visit NZ, as the immigration department considers WWOOFers to be working.

Hostels

New Zealand is packed to the rafters with backpacker hostels, both independent and part of large chains, ranging from small, homestay-style affairs with a handful of beds to refurbished hotels and towering modern structures in the big cities. Hostel bed prices listed by Lonely Planet are nonmember rates, usually $25 to $35 per night.

HOSTEL ORGANISATIONS

Budget Backpacker Hostels
(www.bbh.co.nz) A network of more than 160 hostels. Membership costs $45 for 12 months and entitles you to stay at member hostels at rates listed in the annual (free) BBH Backpacker Accommodation booklet. Nonmembers pay an extra $4 per night. Pick up a membership card from any member hostel or order one online ($50).

YHA New Zealand (www.yha. co.nz) Around 40 hostels in prime NZ locations. The YHA is part of the Hostelling International network (www.hihostels. com), so if you're already an HI member in your own country, membership entitles you to a discount at its NZ hostels. If you don't already have a home membership, you can join at major NZ YHA hostels or online for $25, valid for 12 months (it's free for under-18s). Nonmembers pay an extra $3 or more per night. Membership has other perks, such as discounts with some car-hire providers, travel insurers, DOC hut passes and more.

Base Backpackers (www.stayat base.com) Chain with hostels in Wanaka, Queenstown, Dunedin and Christchurch. Expect clean dorms, women-only areas and party opportunities aplenty. Offers a flexible 10-night 'Base Jumping' accommodation package for $289, bookable online.

VIP Backpackers (www.vip backpackers.com) International organisation affiliated with around 20 NZ hostels (not BBH or YHA), mainly in the cities and tourist hot spots. For around $61 (including postage) you'll receive a 12-month membership entitling you to a $1 discount off nightly accommodation and discounts with affiliated activity and tour providers. Join online or at VIP hostels.

Haka Lodge (www.hakalodge. com) A local chain on the way up, with snazzy hostels in Queenstown and Christchurch. Rates are comparable to other hostels around NZ, and quality is high. Tours are also available.

Climate

Christchurch

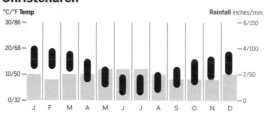

Nelson

Queenstown

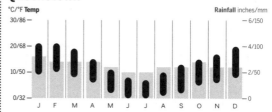

Pubs, Hotels & Motels

The least expensive form of NZ hotel accommodation is the humble pub. Some are full of character (and characters); others are grotty, ramshackle places that are best avoided (especially by women travelling solo). Check whether there's a band playing the night you're staying – you could be in for a sleepless night. In the cheapest pubs, singles/doubles might cost as little as $45/70 (with a shared bathroom down the hall); $70/90 is more common.

At the top end of the hotel scale are five-star international chains, resort complexes and architecturally splendorous boutique hotels, all of which charge a hefty premium for their mod cons, snappy service and/or historic opu-lence. We quote 'rack rates' (official advertised rates) for such places, but discounts and special deals often apply.

New Zealand's towns have a glut of nondescript low-rise motels and 'motor lodges', charging $90 to $200 for double rooms. These tend to be squat structures skulking by highways on the edges of towns. Most are modernish (though decor is often mired in the early 2000s or earlier) and have basic facilities, namely tea- and coffee-making equipment, fridge and TV. Prices vary with standard.

Rental Accommodation

The basic Kiwi holiday home is called a 'bach' (short for 'bachelor', as they were historically used by single men as hunting and fishing hideouts); in Otago and Southland they're known as 'cribs'. These are simple self-contained cottages that can be rented in rural and coastal areas, often in isolated locations, and sometimes include surf, fishing or other outdoor gear hire in the cost. Prices are typically $90 to $180 per night, which isn't bad for a whole house or self-contained bungalow. For more upmarket holiday houses, expect to pay anything from $180 to $400 per double.

Customs Regulations

For the low-down on what you can and can't bring into NZ, see the New Zealand Customs Service website (www.customs.govt.nz). Per-person duty free allowances.

➡ Three 1125ml (max) bottles of spirits or liqueur

➡ 4.5L of wine or beer

➡ 50 cigarettes, or 50g of tobacco or cigars

➡ Dutiable goods up to the value of $700

It's a good idea to declare any unusual medicines. Tramping gear (boots, tents etc) will be checked and may need to be cleaned before being allowed in. You must declare any plant or animal products (including anything made of wood), and food of any kind. Weapons and firearms are either prohibited or require a permit and safety testing. Don't take these rules lightly – noncompliance penalties will really hurt your hip pocket.

Discount Cards

The internationally recognised **International Student Identity Card** is produced by the ISIC Association (www.isic.org), and issued to full-time students aged 12 and over. It provides discounts on accommodation, transport and admission to attractions. The same folks also produce the **International Youth**

Travel Card, available to travellers aged under 31 who are not full-time students, with equivalent benefits to the ISIC. Also similar is the **International Teacher Identity Card**, available to teaching professionals. All three cards ($30 each) are available online at www.isiccard.co.nz, or from student travel companies like STA Travel.

The **New Zealand Card** (www.newzealandcard.com) is a $35 discount pass that'll score you between 5% and 50% off a range of accommodation, tours, sights and activities. Browse participating businesses before you buy. A **Budget Backpacker Hostels** (www.bbh.co.nz) membership card costs $45 and entitles you to discounts at BBH member hostels, usually shipping $4 off the price per night.

Travellers aged over 60 with some form of identification (eg an official seniors card from your home country) are often eligible for concession prices.

Electricity

To plug into the electricity supply (230V AC, 50Hz), use a three-pin adaptor (the same as in Australia; different to British three-pin adaptors).

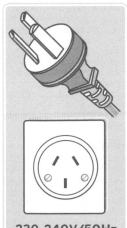

230-240V/50Hz

Food

New Zealand is a mighty fine place to wine and dine (p50). From country pubs to chic restaurants, the emphasis is on home-grown ingredients like lamb, seafood and venison, with a thriving vegetarian and vegan food scene to cleanse the palate. Dining choices depend on destination: you'll be spoilt for choice in Queenstown while little seaside towns might have just a bakery and pub to pick from.

Health

New Zealand poses minimal health risks to travellers. Diseases such as malaria and typhoid are unheard of, poisonous snakes and other dangerous animals are absent, and there are currently no dangerous insect-borne diseases. The biggest risks to travellers involve exploring the great outdoors: trampers must be clued in on rapidly changing weather and diligent about sharing any plans to visit remote areas; drivers must exert extreme caution on NZ's notoriously winding roads.

Before You Go
HEALTH INSURANCE

Health insurance is essential for all travellers. While health care in NZ is of a high quality and not overly expensive by international standards, considerable costs can be built up and repatriation is pricey.

If you don't have a health insurance plan that covers you for medical expenses incurred overseas, buy a travel insurance policy – see www.lonelyplanet.com/travel-insurance. Find out in advance if your insurance plan will make payments directly to providers or reimburse you later for overseas health expenditures. Check whether your policy covers the activities you're planning to do in NZ (eg rock climbing or winter sports) and whether there's a limit on the number of days of cover for the activity.

RECOMMENDED VACCINATIONS

New Zealand has no vaccination requirements for any traveller, but the World Health Organization recommends that all travellers should be covered for chickenpox, diphtheria, hepatitis B, measles, mumps, pertussis (whooping cough), polio, rubella, seasonal flu, tetanus and tuberculosis, regardless of their destination. Ask your doctor for an international certificate of vaccination (or 'the yellow booklet') in which they will list all the vaccinations you've received.

MEDICATIONS

Bring any prescribed medications for your trip in their original, clearly labelled containers. It is also wise to bring a signed and dated letter from your physician describing your medical conditions and medications (including generic names), and any requisite syringes or needles.

In New Zealand

AVAILABILITY & COST OF HEALTH CARE

New Zealand's public hospitals offer a high standard of care (free for residents). All travellers are covered for medical care resulting from accidents that occur while in NZ (eg motor-vehicle accidents or adventure-activity accidents) by the Accident Compensation Corporation (www.acc.co.nz). Costs

incurred due to treatment of a medical illness that occurs while in NZ will only be covered by travel insurance. For more details, see www.health.govt.nz.

The 24-hour **Healthline** (☑0800 611 116) offers health advice throughout NZ (free from local mobile phones or landlines). Interpreters are available.

INFECTIOUS DISEASES

Aside from the same sexually transferred infections that are found worldwide (take normal precautions), giardiasis is the main infectious disease to be aware of when travelling in NZ.

GIARDIASIS

The giardia parasite is widespread in NZ waterways: drinking untreated water from streams and lakes is not recommended. Using water filters and boiling or treating water with iodine are effective ways of preventing the disease. The parasite can also latch on to swimmers in rivers and lakes (try not to swallow water), or through contact with infected animals. Symptoms consist of diarrhoea, vomiting, stomach cramps, abdominal bloating and wind. Effective treatment is available (tinidazole or metronidazole).

HYPOTHERMIA

Hypothermia, a dangerous drop in body temperature, is a significant risk to travellers in NZ, especially during winter and year-round at altitude. Mountain ranges and/or strong winds produce a high chill factor, which can cause hypothermia even in

moderate temperatures. Early signs include the inability to perform fine movements (such as doing up buttons), shivering and a bad case of the 'umbles' (fumbles, mumbles, grumbles, stumbles).

To treat, minimise heat loss: remove wet clothing, add dry clothes with wind- and waterproof layers, and consume carbohydrates and water or warm liquids (not caffeine) to allow shivering to build the internal temperature. In severe hypothermia cases, shivering actually stops; this is a medical emergency requiring rapid evacuation in addition to the above measures.

SURF BEACHES

New Zealand has exceptional surf beaches. The power of the surf can fluctuate as a result of the varying slope of the seabed: rips and undertows are common, and drownings do happen. Check with local surf lifesaving organisations before jumping in the sea, always heed warning signs at beaches, and be realistic about your own limitations and expertise.

BITING INSECTS

Wear long, loose clothing and use an insect repellent containing 20% or more DEET to ward off sandflies and mosquitoes, which are particularly common in lake areas and tree-lined clearings on the South Island. Bites are intensely itchy, but fortunately don't spread disease.

TAP WATER

Tap water throughout New Zealand is generally safe to drink, and public taps with nondrinkable water tend to be labelled as such. However, water quality has faced pollution challenges in some places. Very occasionally, a warning may be issued that tap water must be boiled – your accommodation should inform you if this happens.

PHARMACEUTICALS

Over-the-counter medications are widely available in NZ through private chemists (pharmacies). These include painkillers, antihistamines, skincare products and sunscreen. Some medications, such as antibiotics, are only available via a prescription obtained from a general practitioner. Some varieties of the contraceptive pill can be bought at pharmacies without a prescription (provided the woman has been prescribed the pill within the last three years). If you take regular medications, bring an adequate supply and details of the generic name, as brand names differ from country to country.

Insurance

➡ A watertight travel-insurance policy covering theft, loss and medical problems is essential. Some policies specifically exclude designated 'dangerous activities', such as scuba diving, bungy jumping, whitewater rafting, skiing and even tramping. If you plan on doing any of these things (a distinct possibility in NZ!), make sure your policy covers you fully.

➡ It's worth mentioning that, under NZ law, you cannot sue for personal injury (other than exemplary damages). Instead, the country's Accident Compensation Corporation (www.acc.co.nz) administers an accident compensation scheme that provides accident insurance for NZ residents and visitors to the country, regardless of fault. This scheme, however, does not negate the necessity for your own comprehensive travel-insurance policy, as it doesn't cover you for such things as income loss, treatment at home or ongoing illness.

➡ Consider a policy that pays doctors or hospitals directly, rather than you paying on the spot and claiming later. If you have to claim later, keep all documentation. Some policies ask you to call (reverse charges) to a centre in your home country where an immediate assessment of your problem is made. Check that the policy covers ambulances and emergency medical evacuations by air.

➡ Worldwide travel insurance is available at www.lonelyplanet.com/travel-insurance. You can buy, extend and claim online anytime – even if you're already on the road.

Internet Access

Getting online in NZ is easy in all but remote locales. Expect abundant wi-fi in cafes and accommodation in big towns and cities, but thrifty download limits elsewhere.

Wireless Access

Wi-fi You'll be able to find wi-fi access around the country, from hotel rooms to pub beer gardens to hostel dorms. Usually you have to be a guest or customer to log in; you'll be issued with an access code. Sometimes it's free, sometimes there's a charge, often there's a limit on time or data.

Hotspots The country's main telecommunications company is Spark New Zealand (www.spark.co.nz), which has more than 1000 wireless hotspots around the country. You can purchase prepaid access cards or a prepaid number from the login page at any wireless hotspot using your credit card. See Spark's website for hotspot listings.

Equipment & ISPs If you've brought your tablet or laptop, consider buying a prepay USB modem (aka a 'dongle') with a local SIM card: both Spark and Vodafone (www.vodafone.co.nz) sell these from around $50.

Internet Cafes

There are fewer internet cafes around these days than there were two years ago, but you'll still find them in the bigger cities (frequented more by gamers than tourists). Access costs anywhere from $3 to $6 per hour.

Similarly, most hostels and holiday parks have done away with actual computers in favour of wi-fi. Most hotels, motels, B&Bs and holiday parks also offer wi-fi, sometimes for free, but usually for a small charge.

PRACTICALITIES

Newspapers Check out Christchurch's *The Press* (www.stuff.co.nz/the-press).

TV Watch one of the national government-owned TV stations – including TVNZ 1, TVNZ 2, Māori TV or the 100% Māori-language Te Reo.

Radio Tune in to Radio New Zealand (www.radionz.co.nz) for news, current affairs, classical and jazz. Radio Hauraki (www.hauraki.co.nz) cranks out rock.

DVDs Kiwi DVDs are encoded for Region 4, which includes Australia, the Pacific, Mexico, Central America, the Caribbean and South America.

Weights & measures New Zealand uses the metric system.

Smoking Like much of the Western world, smoking rates in NZ have been on the slide in recent decades. Smoking on public transport and in restaurants, cafes, bars and pubs is banned.

Legal Matters

If you are questioned or arrested by police, it's your right to ask why, to refrain from making a statement, and to consult a lawyer in private.

Plans are brewing for a referendum on whether personal use of cannabis should be decriminalised, but at the time of writing it was still illegal. Anyone caught carrying this or other illicit drugs will have the book thrown at them.

Drink-driving is a serious offence and remains a significant problem in NZ. The legal blood alcohol limit is 0.05% for drivers aged 20 years and over, and zero for those under 20.

LGBT Travellers

NZ has progressive laws protecting human rights: same-sex marriage and adoption by same-sex couples were legalised in 2013, while the legal minimum age for sex between consenting persons is 16. Generally speaking, Kiwis are fairly relaxed and accepting about homosexuality and gender fluidity, but that's not to say that homophobia doesn't exist. Rural communities tend to be more conservative; here public displays of affection should probably be avoided.

There are very few gay-focused venues in the South Island. The biggest event on the annual calendar is Queenstown's **Gay Ski Week** (www.gayskiweekqt.com; ⊙Aug/Sep).

Resources

There are loads of websites dedicated to gay and lesbian travel in NZ. Gay Tourism New Zealand (www.gaytourismnewzealand.com) is a starting point, with links to various sites. Other worthwhile websites include the following:

➡ www.gaynz.net.nz
➡ www.lesbian.net.nz
➡ www.gaystay.co.nz

Check out the nationwide monthly magazine *express* (www.gayexpress.co.nz) for the latest happenings, reviews and listings on the NZ gay scene. New Zealand Awaits (www.newzealand-awaits.com) is a local operator specialising in tours serving LGBT travellers.

Maps

New Zealand's **Automobile Association** (AA; ☐0800 500 444; www.aa.co.nz/travel) produces excellent city, town, regional, island and highway maps, available from its local offices. The AA also produces a detailed *New Zealand Road Atlas*. Other reliable country-wide atlases, available from visitor information centres and bookshops, are published by Hema and KiwiMaps.

Land Information New Zealand (www.linz.govt.nz) publishes several exhaustive map series, including street, country and holiday maps, national park and forest park maps, and topographical trampers' maps. Scan the larger bookshops, or try the nearest DOC office or visitor information centre for topo maps.

Online, log onto AA Maps (www.aamaps.co.nz) or Wises (www.wises.co.nz) to pinpoint exact NZ addresses.

Money

Credit cards are used for most purchases in NZ, and are accepted in most hotels and restaurants. ATMs are widely available in cities and larger towns.

ATMs & EFTPOS

Branches of the country's major banks across both islands have ATMs, but you won't find them everywhere (eg not in small towns).

Many NZ businesses use Eftpos (electronic funds transfer at point of sale), allowing you to use your bank card (credit or debit) to make

direct purchases and often withdraw cash as well. Eftpos is available practically everywhere: just like at an ATM, you'll need a PIN number.

Bank Accounts

You'll need to open a bank account if you want to work in NZ in any capacity (including working holiday scenarios) and it's best to do your homework before you arrive. Some banks, such as ANZ, allow you to apply before you arrive and activate the account at a branch when you get here (armed with the requisite ID, usually a passport, certified translation if applicable, and proof of NZ residence). Proof of address might involve using an identity verification service.

Credit Cards

Credit cards (Visa, MasterCard) are widely accepted for everything from a hostel bed to a bungy jump, and are pretty much essential for car hire. Credit cards can also be used for over-the-counter cash advances at banks and from ATMs, but be aware that such transactions incur charges. Diners Club and American Express cards are not as widely accepted.

Currency

New Zealand's currency is the NZ dollar, comprising 100 cents. There are 10c, 20c, 50c, $1 and $2 coins, and $5, $10, $20, $50 and $100 notes. Prices are often still marked in single cents and then rounded to the nearest 10c when you hand over your money.

Debit Cards

Debit cards enable you to draw money directly from your home bank account using ATMs, banks or Eftpos facilities. Any card connected to the international banking network (Cirrus, Maestro, Visa Plus and Eurocard) should work with your PIN. Fees will vary depending on your home bank; check before you leave. Alternatively, companies such as Travelex offer debit cards with set withdrawal fees and a balance you can top up from your personal bank account while on the road.

Money Changers

Changing foreign currency (and to a lesser extent old-fashioned travellers cheques) is usually no problem at NZ banks or at licensed money changers (eg Travelex) in major tourist areas, cities and airports.

Tipping

Tipping is completely optional in NZ.

Guides Your kayaking guide or tour group leader will happily accept tips; up to $10 is fine.

Restaurants The total on your bill is all you need to pay (though sometimes a service charge is factored in). If you like, reward good service with 5% to 10%

Taxis If you round up your fare, don't be surprised if the driver hands back your change.

Travellers Cheques

Amex, Travelex and other international brands of travellers cheques are a bit old hat these days, but they're still easily exchanged at banks and money changers. Present your passport for identification when cashing them; shop around for the best rates.

Opening Hours

Opening hours vary seasonally depending on where you are. Most places close on Christmas Day and Good Friday.

Banks 9am–4.30pm Monday to Friday, some also 9am–noon Saturday

Cafes 7am–4pm

Post Offices 8.30am–5pm Monday to Friday; larger branches also 9.30am–noon Saturday

Pubs & Bars noon–late ('late' varies by region, and by day)

Restaurants noon–2.30pm and 6.30pm–9pm

Shops & Businesses 9am–5.30pm Monday to Friday and 9am to noon or 5pm Saturday

Supermarkets 8am–7pm, often 9pm or later in cities

Post

The services offered by **New Zealand Post** (☏0800 501 501; www.nzpost.co.nz) are reliable and reasonably inexpensive. See the website for info on national and international zones and rates, plus post office (or 'post shop') locations.

Public Holidays

New Zealand's main public holidays:

New Year 1 and 2 January

Waitangi Day 6 February

Easter Good Friday and Easter Monday; March/April

Anzac Day 25 April

Queen's Birthday First Monday in June

Labour Day Fourth Monday in October

Christmas Day 25 December

Boxing Day 26 December

In addition, each NZ province has its own anniversary-day holiday. The dates

of these provincial holidays vary: when they fall on Friday to Sunday, they're usually observed the following Monday; if they fall on Tuesday to Thursday, they're held on the preceding Monday. To see an up-to-date list of provincial anniversaries during the year you travel, see www.govt.nz/browse/work/public-holidays-and-work/public-holidays-and-anniversary-dates.

School Holidays

The Christmas holiday season, from mid-December to late January, is part of the summer school vacation: expect transport and accommodation to be booked out in advance, and queues at tourist attractions. There are three shorter school-holiday periods during the year: from mid- to late April, early to mid- July, and late September to mid-October. For exact dates, see the Ministry of Education website (www.education.govt.nz).

Safe Travel

New Zealand is no more dangerous than other developed countries, but exert normal safety precautions, especially after dark on city streets and in remote areas.

GOVERNMENT TRAVEL ADVICE

The following government websites offer travel advisories and information on current hotspots:

Australian Department of Foreign Affairs & Trade (www.smarttraveller.gov.au)

British Foreign & Commonwealth Office (www.gov.uk/fco)

Dutch Ministry of Foreign Affairs (www.government.nl/ministries/ministry-of-foreign-affairs)

Foreign Affairs, Trade & Development Canada (www.international.gc.ca)

German Federal Foreign Office (www.auswaertiges-amt.de)

Japanese Ministry of Foreign Affairs (www.mofa.go.jp)

US Department of State (www.travel.state.gov)

➜ Kiwi roads are often made hazardous by map-distracted tourists, wide-cornering campervans and traffic-ignorant sheep.

➜ Major fault lines run the length of NZ, causing occasional earthquakes.

➜ Avoid leaving valuables in vehicles: theft is a problem, even in remote areas.

➜ New Zealand's climate is unpredictable: hypothermia is a risk in high-altitude areas.

➜ At the beach, beware of rips and undertows, which can drag swimmers out to sea.

➜ New Zealand's sandflies are an itchy annoyance. Use repellent in coastal and lakeside areas.

Telephone

New Zealand uses regional two-digit area codes for long-distance calls, which can be made from any payphone. If you're making a local call (ie to someone else in the same town), you don't need to dial the area code. But if you're dialling within a region (even if it's to a nearby town with the same area code), you do have to dial the area code.

To make international calls from NZ (which is possible on payphones), you need to dial the international access code ✒00, then the country code and the area code (without the initial '0'). So for a London number, for example, you'd dial ✒00-44-20, then the number. If dialling NZ from overseas, the country code is ✒64, followed by the appropriate area code minus the initial '0'.

Mobile Phones

European phones should work on NZ's network, but most American or Japanese phones will not. It's straightforward to buy a local SIM card and prepaid account at

outlets in airports and large towns (provided your mobile is unlocked).

Most NZ mobile phone numbers begin with the prefix 021, 022 or 027. Mobile phone coverage is good in cities and towns and most parts of the North Island, but can be patchy away from urban centres on the South Island.

If you want to bring your own phone and use a prepaid service with a local SIM card (rather than pay for expensive global roaming on your home network), Vodafone (www.vodafone.co.nz) is a practical option. Any Vodafone shop (in most major towns) will set you up with a NZ Travel SIM and a phone number (from around $30; valid for 30, 60 or 90 days). Top-ups can be purchased at newsagents, post offices and petrol stations all over the country.

Phone Hire New Zealand (www.phonehirenz.com) rents out mobiles, modems and GPS systems (from $3/10/7 per day).

Pay Phones

Local calls from payphones cost $1 for the first 15 minutes, and $0.20 per minute thereafter, though coin-operated payphones are scarce (and if you do find one, chances are the coin slot will be gummed up); you'll generally need a phonecard. Calls to mobile phones attract higher rates.

Phonecards

New Zealand has a wide range of phonecards available, which can be bought at hostels, newsagents and post offices for a fixed-dollar value (usually $5, $10, $20 and $50). These can be used with any public or private phone by dialling a toll-free access number and then the PIN number on the card. Shop around – rates vary from company to company.

Premium-Rate & Toll-Free Calls

Numbers starting with 0900 charge upwards of $1 per minute (more from mobiles). These numbers cannot be dialled from payphones, and sometimes not from prepaid mobile phones.

Toll-free numbers in NZ have the prefix 0800 or 0508, and can be called from anywhere in the country, though they may not be accessible from certain areas or from mobile phones. Numbers beginning with 0508, 0800 or 0900 cannot be dialled from outside NZ.

Time

New Zealand is 12 hours ahead of GMT/UTC and two hours ahead of Australian Eastern Standard Time. The Chathams are 45 minutes ahead of NZ's main islands.

In summer, NZ observes daylight saving time: clocks are wound forward by one hour on the last Sunday in September; clocks are wound back on the first Sunday of April.

Toilets

Toilets in NZ are sit-down Western style. Public toilets are plentiful, and are usually reasonably clean with working locks and plenty of toilet paper.

See www.toiletmap.co.nz for public-toilet locations around the country.

Tourist Information

Almost every Kiwi city or town seems to have a visitor information centre. The bigger centres stand united within the outstanding i-SITE network (www.newzealand. com/travel/i-sites) – more than 80 info centres affiliated with Tourism New Zealand. The i-SITE centres have trained staff, information on local activities and attractions, and free brochures and maps. Staff can also book activities, transport and accommodation.

Bear in mind that some information centres only promote accommodation and tour operators who are paying members of the local tourist association, and that sometimes staff aren't supposed to recommend one activity or accommodation provider over another.

There's also a network of Department of Conservation (DOC; www.doc.govt.nz) visitor centres to help you plan outdoor activities and make bookings (particularly for tramping tracks and huts).The DOC visitor centres – in national parks, regional centres and major cities – usually also have displays on local flora and fauna.

Travellers with Disabilities

Kiwi accommodation generally caters fairly well for travellers with disabilities, with most hostels, hotels and motels equipped with one or two wheelchair-accessible rooms. (B&Bs aren't required to have accessible rooms.) Many tourist attractions similarly provide wheelchair access, with wheelchairs often available. Most i-SITE visitor centres can advise on suitable attractions in the locality.

Tour operators with accessible vehicles operate from most major centres. Key cities are also serviced by 'kneeling' buses (buses that hydraulically stoop down to kerb level to allow easy access), and many taxi companies offer wheelchair-accessible vans. Large car-hire firms (Avis, Hertz etc) provide cars with hand controls at no extra charge (but advance notice is required). Air New Zealand is also very well equipped to accommodate travellers in wheelchairs.

Download Lonely Planet's free Accessible Travel guides from http://lptravel.to/AccessibleTravel.

Activities

Out and about, the DOC has been hard at work improving access to short walking tracks (and some of the longer ones). Tracks that are wheelchair accessible are categorised as 'easy access short walks': the Milford Foreshore Walk in Milford Sound is a prime example.

If cold-weather activity is more your thing, see Snow Sports NZ's page on adaptive winter sports: www.snowsports.co.nz/get-involved/adaptive-snow-sports.

Resources

Access4All (www.access4all.co.nz) Listings of accessible accommodation and activities around New Zealand.

Firstport (http://firstport.co.nz) Includes a high-level overview of transport in NZ, including mobility taxis and accessible public transport.

Mobility Parking (www.mobilityparking.org.nz) Apply for an overseas visitor mobility parking permit ($35 for 12 months) and have it posted to you before you even reach NZ.

Visas

Visa application forms are available from NZ diplomatic missions overseas, travel agents and **Immigration New Zealand** (☑09-914 4100, 0508 558 855; www.immigration.govt.nz). Immigration New Zealand has more than 25 offices overseas, including the US, UK and Australia; consult the website.

Visitor Visa

Citizens of Australia don't need a visa to visit NZ and can stay indefinitely (provided they have no criminal convictions). UK citizens don't need a visa either and can stay in the country for up to six months.

Citizens of another 58 countries that have visa-waiver agreements with NZ don't need a visa for stays of up to three months per visit, for no more than six months within any 12-month period, provided they have an onward ticket and sufficient funds to support their stay: see the website for details. Nations in this group include Canada, France, Germany, Ireland, Japan, the Netherlands, South Africa and the USA.

Citizens of other countries must obtain a visa before entering NZ. Visitor visas allow stays of up to nine months within an 18-month period, and cost $170 to $220, depending on where in the world the application is processed.

A visitor's visa can be extended from nine to 12 months, but if you get this extension you'll have to leave NZ after your 12-month stay has expired and wait another 12 months before you can come back. Applications are assessed on a case-by-case basis; you may need to provide proof of adequate funds to sustain you during your visit ($1000 per month) plus an onward ticket establishing your intent to leave. Apply for extensions at any Immigration New Zealand office – see the website (www.immigration.govt.nz) for locations.

Work Visa

It's illegal for foreign nationals to work in NZ on a visitor visa, except for Australian citizens or permanent residents, who can legally gain work without a visa or permit. If you're visiting NZ to find work, or you already have an employment offer, you'll need to apply for a work visa, which can be valid for up to three years, depending on your circumstance. You can apply for a work permit after you're in NZ, but its validity will be backdated to when you entered the country. The fee for a work visa can be anything upwards of $190, depending on where and how it's processed (paper or online) and the type of application.

Working Holiday Scheme

Eligible travellers who are only interested in short-term employment to supplement their travels can take part in one of NZ's working holiday schemes (WHS). Under these schemes citizens aged 18 to 30 (occasionally 35) from 44 countries – including France, Germany, Ireland, Japan, Malaysia, the Netherlands, Scandinavian countries and the USA – can apply for such a visa. For most nationalities the visa is valid for 12 months but citizens of Canada and the UK can work for up to 23 months. It's only issued to those seeking a genuine working holiday, not permanent work, so you're not supposed to work for one employer for more than three months.

Eligible nationals must apply for a WHS visa from within their own country. Applicants must have an onward ticket, a passport valid for at least three months from the date they will leave NZ and evidence of at least $350 in accessible funds for each month of their stay. The application fee is $165 and isn't refunded if your application is declined.

The rules vary for different nationalities, so make sure you read up on the specifics of your country's agreement with NZ at www.immigration. govt.nz.

Volunteering

New Zealand presents an array of active, outdoorsy volunteer opportunities for travellers to get some dirt under their fingernails and participate in conservation programs. These programs can include anything from tree planting and weed removal to track construction, habitat conservation and fencing.

Ask about local opportunities at any regional i-SITE visitor information centre, join one of the programs run by DOC (www.doc.govt.nz/getting-involved), or check out these online resources:

➡ www. conservationvolunteers. org.nz

➡ www.helpx.net

➡ www.nature.org.nz

➡ www.volunteeringnz. org.nz

➡ www.wwf.org.nz

Women Travellers

New Zealand is generally a very safe place for female travellers, although the usual sensible precautions apply (for both sexes): avoid walking alone at night; never hitchhike alone; and if you're out on the town, have a plan for how to get back to your accommodation safely. Sexual harassment is not a widely reported problem in NZ, but of course that doesn't mean it doesn't happen. See www.women-travel.co.nz for tours aimed at solo women.

Work

If you have been approved for a working holiday scheme (WHS) visa, there are a number of possibilities for temporary employment in NZ. Pay rates start at the minimum wage ($15.75 per hour, at the time of writing), but depend on the work. There's plenty of casual work around, mainly in agriculture (fruit picking, farming, wineries), hospitality (bar work, waiting tables) or at ski resorts. Office-based work can be found in IT, banking, finance and telemarketing. Register with a local office-work agency to get started.

Seasonal fruit picking, pruning and harvesting is prime short-term work for visitors. Kiwifruit and other fruit and veg are harvested from December to May (and other farming work is available outside that season). Fruit picking is physically taxing toil, working in the dirt under the hot sun – turnover of workers is high. You're usually paid by how much you pick (per bin, bucket or kilogram): if you stick with it for a while, you'll get faster and fitter and can actually make some reasonable cash. Prime South Island picking locations include Nelson (Golden Bay), Marlborough (around Blenheim) and Central Otago (Cromwell, Alexandra and Roxburgh).

Winter work at ski resorts and their service towns includes bartending, waiting, cleaning, ski-tow operation and, if you're properly qualified, ski or snowboard instructing.

Resources

Backpacker publications, hostel managers and other travellers are often good sources of info on local work possibilities. Base Backpackers (www.stayatbase.com/work) runs an employment service via its website, while the Notice Boards page on the Budget Backpacker Hostels website (www.bbh.co.nz) lists job vacancies in BBH hostels and a few other possibilities. Kiwi Careers (www.careers.govt.nz) lists professional opportunities in various fields (agriculture, creative, health, teaching, volunteer work and recruitment), while Seek (www.seek.co.nz) is one of the biggest NZ job-search networks, with thousands of jobs listed.

Try the following websites for seasonal work:

➡ www.backpackerboard. co.nz

➡ www.seasonalwork.co.nz

➡ www.seasonaljobs.co.nz

➡ www.picknz.co.nz

➡ www.pickingjobs.com

➡ www.pricktheworld.org

Income Tax

Death and taxes – no escape! For most travellers, Kiwi dollars earned in NZ will be subject to income tax, which is deducted from payments by employers – a process called Pay As You Earn (PAYE).

Income tax rates are 10.5% for annual salaries up to $14,000, then 17.5% up to $48,000, 30% up to $70,000, and 33% for higher incomes. A NZ Accident Compensation Corporation (ACC) scheme levy (around 1.5%) will also be deducted from your pay packet. Note that these rates tend to change slightly year to year.

If you visit NZ and work for a short time (eg on a working holiday scheme), you may qualify for a tax refund when you leave. Lodging a tax return before you leave NZ is the best way of securing a refund. For more info, see the Inland Revenue Department website (www.ird.govt.nz), or call 03-951 2020.

IRD Number

Travellers undertaking paid work in NZ (including working holidays) must first open a New Zealand bank account, then obtain an Inland Revenue Department (IRD) number. Download the *IRD number application - non-resident/offshore individual IR742* form from the Inland Revenue Department website (www.ird.govt.nz). IRD numbers normally take eight to 10 working days to be issued.

Transport

GETTING THERE & AWAY

Christchurch Airport is the primary international gateway to the South Island, servicing flights from Australia, Singapore, Fiji and China (Guangzhou). Queenstown Airport is becoming increasingly popular as Australian and Chinese carriers clamour to bring visitors directly into the South Island's premier resort town. The only other airport servicing international arrivals is Dunedin, with three weekly flights to and from Brisbane.

Christchurch is also the South Island's biggest domestic air travel hub, particularly for Air New Zealand flights connecting with Blenheim, Nelson, Hokitika, Queenstown, Timaru, Dunedin and Invercargill. A host of smaller regional airlines reach smaller destinations such as Westport and Stewart Island, with Sounds Air a standout performer

connecting Wellington with airports around the top of the South. Jetstar services Christchurch, Dunedin, Queenstown and Nelson.

Crossing Cook Strait between the North and South Islands is possible with Bluebridge and Interislander ferry services, both offering several sailings daily in each direction. The ferries carry cars and campervans, although it is generally cheaper to pick up a new hire vehicle on each island.

Entering the Country

Disembarkation in New Zealand is generally a straightforward affair, with only the usual customs declarations and luggage-carousel scramble to endure. Under the Orwellian title of 'Advance Passenger Screening', documents that used to be checked after you touched down in NZ (passport, visa

etc) are now checked before you board your flight – make sure all your documentation is in order so that your check-in is stress-free.

Passport

There are no restrictions when it comes to foreign citizens entering NZ. If you have a current passport and visa (or don't require one), you should be fine.

Air

New Zealand's abundance of year-round activities means that airports here are busy most of the time: if you want to fly at a particularly popular time of year (eg over the Christmas period), book well in advance.

The high season for flights into NZ is during summer (December to February), with slightly less of a premium on fares over the shoulder months (October/November and March/April). The low season generally tallies with

---

CLIMATE CHANGE & TRAVEL

Every form of transport that relies on carbon-based fuel generates CO_2, the main cause of human-induced climate change. Modern travel is dependent on aeroplanes, which might use less fuel per kilometre per person than most cars but travel much greater distances. The altitude at which aircraft emit gases (including CO_2) and particles also contributes to their climate change impact. Many websites offer 'carbon calculators' that allow people to estimate the carbon emissions generated by their journey and, for those who wish to do so, to offset the impact of the greenhouse gases emitted with contributions to portfolios of climate-friendly initiatives throughout the world. Lonely Planet offsets the carbon footprint of all staff and author travel.

the winter months (June to August), though this is still a busy time for airlines ferrying ski bunnies and powder hounds.

Airports & Airlines

While **Auckland Airport** (AKL; ☑09-275 0789; www.aucklandairport.co.nz; Ray Emery Dr, Mangere) is the main international gateway to NZ, the South Island has direct international services to the following airports:

Christchurch Airport (CHC; ☑03-358 5029; www.christchurchairport.co.nz; 30 Durey Rd)

Dunedin Airport (DUD;☑03-486 2879; www.dnairport.co.nz; 25 Miller Rd, Momona; ☎)

Queenstown Airport (ZQN; Map p201;☑03-450 9031; www.queenstownairport.co.nz; Sir Henry Wrigley Dr, Frankton)
New Zealand's international carrier is **Air New Zealand** (☑0800 737 000; www.airnewzealand.co.nz). Air New Zealand, **Jetstar** (☑0800 800 995; www.jetstar. com) and **Virgin Australia** (☑0800 670 000; www.virgin-australia.com) fly into all three airports, while Qantas flies into only Christchurch and Queenstown. Christchurch also welcomes year-round flights on Cathay Pacific, China Southern Airlines, Emirates, Fiji Airways and Singapore Airlines.

Sea

Ferry Regular ferry services between Wellington and Picton link the North and South Islands.

Cruise Ship If you're travelling from Australia and content with a slow pace, try P&O (www.pocruises.com.au) and Princess (www.princess.com) for cruises to New Zealand.

Cargo Ship If you don't need luxury, a berth on a cargo ship or freighter to/from New Zealand is a quirky way to go. Freighter Expeditions (www.freighterexpeditions.com.au) offers cruises to New Zealand from Singapore

(49 days return) and Antwerp in Belgium (32 days one way).

Yacht It is possible (though by no means straightforward) to make your way between NZ, Australia and the Pacific islands by crewing on a yacht. Try asking around at harbours, marinas, and yacht and sailing clubs. March and April are the best months to look for boats heading to Australia. From Fiji, October to November is a peak departure season to beat the cyclones that soon follow in that neck of the woods.

GETTING AROUND

Air

Those who have limited time to get between NZ's attractions can make the most of a widespread (and very reliable and safe) network of intra- and inter-island flights.

Domestic Airlines

The country's major domestic carrier, Air New Zealand, has an aerial network covering most of the country, often operating under the Air New Zealand Link moniker on less popular routes. Australia-based Jetstar also flies between main urban areas. Between them, these two airlines carry the vast majority of domestic passengers in NZ. Beyond this, several small-scale regional operators provide essential transport services to outlying islands and smaller centres. There are also plenty of scenic- and charter-flight operators around NZ, not listed here. Operators include the following:

Air New Zealand (☑0800 737 000; www.airnewzealand.co.nz) Offers flights between 20-plus domestic destinations, plus myriad overseas hubs.

Air2there.com (☑0800 777 000; www.air2there.com) Flies between Nelson and Blenheim.

Golden Bay Air (☑0800 588 885; www.goldenbayair.co.nz) Flies regularly to Takaka in Golden Bay from Nelson. Also connects to Karamea for Heaphy Track trampers.

Jetstar (☑0800 800 995; www.jetstar.com) Joins the dots between key centres: Christchurch, Dunedin, Queenstown and Nelson.

Soundsair (☑0800 505 005; www.soundsair.co.nz) Flies from Blenheim to Christchurch and Kaikoura.

Stewart Island Flights (☑03-218 9129; www.stewartislandflights.co.nz) Flies between Invercargill and Stewart Island three times daily.

Air Passes

Available exclusively to travellers from the USA or Canada who have bought an Air New Zealand fare to NZ from the USA, Canada, Australia or the Pacific Islands, Air New Zealand offers the good-value New Zealand Explorer Pass (www.airnewzealand.com/explorer-pass). The pass lets you fly between up to 37 destinations in New Zealand, Australia and the South Pacific islands (including Norfolk Island, Tonga, New Caledonia, Samoa, Vanuatu, Tahiti, Fiji, Niue and the Cook Islands). Fares are broken down into four discounted, distance-based zones: zone one flights start at US$99 (eg Auckland to Wellington); zone two from US$129 (eg Auckland to Queenstown); zone three from US$214 (eg Wellington to Sydney); and zone four from US$295 (eg Tahiti to Auckland). You can buy the pass before you travel, or after you arrive in NZ.

Bicycle

Touring cyclists proliferate in NZ, particularly over summer. The country is clean, green and relatively uncrowded, and has lots of cheap accommodation (including camping) and abundant freshwater. The roads are generally in good nick, and the climate is usually not too hot or cold. Road traffic is the biggest danger: trucks overtaking too close to cyclists are a particular threat. Bikes and cycling gear are readily available to hire or buy in the main centres, and bicycle-repair shops are common.

By law all cyclists must wear an approved safety helmet (or risk a fine); it's also vital to have good reflective safety clothing. Cyclists who use public transport will find that major bus lines and trains only take bicycles on a 'space available' basis (in cities, usually outside rush hour) and may charge up to $10. Some of the smaller shuttle bus companies, on the other hand, make sure they have storage space for bikes, which they carry for a surcharge.

If importing your own bike or transporting it by plane within NZ, check with the relevant airline for costs and the degree of dismantling and packing required.

See www.nzta.govt.nz/walking-cycling-and-public-transport for more bike safety and legal tips, and the New Zealand Cycle Trail (Nga Haerenga) (p47) – a network of 22 'Great Rides' across NZ.

Hire

Rates offered by most outfits for hiring road or mountain bikes are usually around $20 per hour to $60 per day. Longer-term hire may be available by negotiation. You can often hire bikes from your accommodation (hostels, holiday parks etc), or hire more reputable machines from bike shops in the larger towns.

Buying a Bike

Bicycles can be readily bought in NZ's larger cities, but prices for newer models are high. For a decent hybrid bike or rigid mountain bike you'll pay anywhere from $800 to $1800, though you can get a cheap one for around $500 (but you still then need to buy panniers, helmet, lock etc, and the cost quickly climbs). Other options include the post-Christmas sales and midyear stocktakes, when newish cycles can be heavily discounted.

Boat

NZ may be an island nation but there's virtually no long-distance water transport around the country. Obvious exceptions include the passenger ferry that negotiates Foveaux Strait between Bluff and the town of Oban on Stewart Island.

If you're cashed-up, consider the cruise liners that chug around the NZ coastline as part of broader South Pacific itineraries: P&O Cruises (www.pocruises.com.au) is a major player.

Bus

Bus travel in NZ is easygoing and well organised, with services transporting you to the far reaches of both islands (including the start/end of various walking tracks)...but it can be expensive, tedious and time-consuming.

New Zealand's main bus company is **InterCity** (www.intercity.co.nz), which can drive you to just about anywhere on the North and South Islands. **Naked Bus** (☑09-979 1616; https://nakedbus.com) has similar routes and remains the main competition. Both bus lines offer fares as low as $1(!). InterCity also has a South Island sightseeing arm called **Newmans Coach Lines** (www.newmanscoach.co.nz), travelling between Queenstown, Christchurch and the West Coast glaciers.

Privately run shuttle buses can transport travellers to some trailheads or collect them from the end point of a tramp; advance booking essential.

Seat Classes & Smoking

There are no allocated economy or luxury classes on NZ buses (very democratic), and smoking on the bus is a definite no-no.

Reservations

Over summer (December to February), school holidays and public holidays, book well in advance on popular routes (a week or two ahead if possible). At other times, a day or two ahead is usually fine. The best prices are generally available online, booked a few weeks in advance.

Bus Passes

If you're covering a lot of ground, both InterCity and Naked Bus offer bus passes (respectively, priced by hours and number of trips). This can be cheaper than paying as you go, but do the maths before buying and note that you'll be locked into using one network. Passes are usually valid for 12 months.

On fares other than bus passes, InterCity offers a discount of around 10% for YHA, ISIC, HI, Nomads, BBH or VIP backpacker card holders. Senior discounts only apply for NZ citizens.

Flexipass A hop-on/hop-off InterCity pass, allowing travel to pretty much anywhere in NZ, in any direction, including the Interislander ferry across Cook Strait. The pass is purchased in blocks of travel time: minimum 15 hours ($125), maximum 60 hours ($459). The average cost of each block becomes cheaper the more hours you buy. You can top up the pass if you need more time.

Aotearoa Explorer, Tiki Tour & Island Loop Hop-on/hop-off, fixed-itinerary nationwide passes offered by InterCity. These passes link up tourist hotspots and cost $775 to $1140. Passes with a narrower scope (eg West Coast or Southern Alps) are also offered. See www.intercity.co.nz/bus-pass/travelpass for details.

Naked Passport (www.naked passport.com) A Naked Bus pass that allows you to buy trips in blocks of five, which you can add to any time, and book each trip as needed. Five/15/20 trips cost $159/269/439.

Shuttle Buses

As well as InterCity and Naked Bus, regional shuttle buses fill in the gaps between the smaller towns. Operators include the following (see www.tourism.not.nz/transport/bus-and-coach-services for a complete list), offering regular scheduled services and/or bus tours and charters:

Abel Tasman Travel (www.abeltasmantravel.co.nz) Traverses the roads between Nelson, Motueka, Golden Bay and Abel Tasman National Park.

Atomic Shuttles (www.atomic travel.co.nz) Has services throughout the South Island, including to Christchurch, Dunedin, Invercargill, Picton, Nelson, Greymouth, Hokitika, Queenstown and Wanaka.

Catch-a-Bus South (www.catchabussouth.co.nz) Invercargill and Bluff to Dunedin and Queenstown.

Cook Connection (www.cookconnect.co.nz) Triangulates between Mt Cook, Twizel and Lake Tekapo.

East West Coaches (www.eastwestcoaches.co.nz) Offers a service between Christchurch and Westport via Lewis Pass.

Hanmer Connection (www.hanmerconnection.co.nz) Daily services between Hanmer Springs and Christchurch.

Tracknet (www.tracknet.net) Summer track transport (Milford,

Hollyford, Routeburn, Kepler) with Queenstown, Te Anau and Invercargill connections.

Trek Express (www.trekexpress.co.nz) Shuttle services to all tramping tracks in the top half of the South Island (eg Heaphy, Abel Tasman, Old Ghost Road).

West Coast Shuttle (www.westcoastshuttle.co.nz) Daily bus from Greymouth to Christchurch and back.

Bus Tours

Clock up some kilometres with like-minded fellow travellers. The following operators run fixed-itinerary bus tours, nationwide or on the North or South Islands. Accommodation, meals and hop-on/hop-off flexibility are often included. Styles vary from activity-focused itineraries through to hangover-mandatory backpacker buses.

Adventure Tours New Zealand (www.adventuretours.com.au/new-zealand) Four 11- to 22-day NZ tours of North or South Island, or both.

Bottom Bus (www.travel headfirst.com/local-legends/bottom-bus) South Island nother region tours ex Dunedin, Invercargill and Queenstown.

Flying Kiwi (www.flyingkiwi.com) Good-fun, activity-based trips around NZ with camping and cabin accommodation from a few days to a few weeks.

Haka Tours (www.hakatours.com) Three- to 24-day tours with adventure, snow or mountain-biking themes.

Kirra Tours (www.kirratours.co.nz) Upmarket coach tours (graded 'Classic' or 'Platinum' by price) from an operator with 50 years in the business.

Kiwi Experience (www.kiwi experience.com) A major hop-on/hop-off player with eco-friendly credentials. Myriad tours cover the length and breadth of NZ.

Stray Travel (www.straytravel.com) A wide range of flexible hop-on/hop-off passes and tours.

Car & Motorcycle

The best way to explore NZ in depth is to have your own wheels. It's easy to hire cars and campervans, though it's worth noting that fuel costs can be eye-watering. Alternatively, if you're in NZ for a few months, you might consider buying your own vehicle.

Automobile Association

New Zealand's **Automobile Association** (AA; ☎0800 500 444; www.aa.co.nz/travel) provides emergency breakdown services, distance calculators and accommodation guides (from holiday parks to motels and B&Bs).

Members of overseas automobile associations should bring their membership cards – many of these bodies have reciprocal agreements with the AA.

Driving Licences

International visitors to NZ can use their home-country driving licence – if your licence isn't in English, it's a good idea to carry a certified translation with you. Alternatively, use an International Driving Permit (IDP), which will usually be issued on the spot (valid for 12 months) by your home country's automobile association.

Fuel

Fuel (petrol, aka gasoline) is available from service stations across NZ: unless you're cruising around in something from the 1970s, you'll be filling up with 'unleaded', or LPG (gas). LPG is not always stocked by rural suppliers; if you're on gas, it's safer to have dual-fuel capability. Aside from remote locations like Milford Sound and Mt Cook, petrol prices don't vary much from place to place: per-litre costs at the time of research were hovering above $2.

Hire

CAMPERVAN

Check your rear-view mirror on any far-flung NZ road and you'll probably see a shiny white campervan (aka mobile home, motor home, RV), packed with liberated travellers, mountain bikes and portable barbecues, cruising along behind you.

Most towns of any size have a campground or holiday park with powered sites (where you can plug your vehicle in) for around $35 per night. There are also 250-plus vehicle-accessible Department of Conservation (DOC; www.doc.govt.nz) campsites around NZ, priced at up to $21 per adult. Weekly campsite passes for hired campervans slice up to 50% off the price of stays in DOC campgrounds; check the website for info.

You can hire campervans from dozens of companies. Prices vary with season, vehicle size and length of hire, and it pays to book months in advance.

A small van for two people typically has a minikitchen and foldout dining table, the latter transforming into a double bed when dinner is done and dusted. Larger, 'superior' two-berth vans include shower and toilet. Four- to six-berth campervans are the size of trucks (and similarly sluggish) and, besides the extra space, usually contain a toilet and shower.

Over summer, rates offered by the main firms for two-/four-/six-berth vans booked three months in advance start at around $120/150/230 per day (though they rise much higher, depending on model) for hire for two weeks or more. Rates drop to $60/75/100 per day during winter.

Major operators include the following:

Apollo (☑0800 113 131, 09-889 2976; www.apollocamper.co.nz)

Britz (☑09-255 3910, 0800 081 032; www.britz.co.nz) Also does 'Britz Bikes' (add a mountain or city bike from $12 per day).

Maui (☑09-255 3910, 0800 688 558; www.maui-rentals.com)

Wilderness Motorhomes (☑09-282 3606; www.wilderness.co.nz)

INTERNATIONAL HIRE COMPANIES

The big multinational companies have offices in most major cities, towns and airports. Firms sometimes offer one-way hire (eg collect a car in Christchurch, leave it in Queenstown), but there are usually restrictions and fees.

The major companies offer a choice of either unlimited kilometres, or 100km (or so) per day free, plus so many cents per subsequent kilometre. Daily rates in main cities typically start at around $40 per day for a compact, late-model Japanese car, and from $70 for medium-sized cars (including GST, unlimited kilometres and insurance).

Avis (☑0800 655 111, 09-526 2847; www.avis.co.nz)

Budget (☑09-529 7788, 0800 283 438; www.budget.co.nz)

Europcar (☑0800 800 115; www.europcar.co.nz)

Hertz (☑0800 654 321; www.hertz.co.nz)

Thrifty (☑03-359 2721, 0800 737 070; www.thrifty.co.nz)

LOCAL HIRE COMPANIES

Local hire firms proliferate. These are almost always cheaper than the big boys – sometimes half the price – but the cheap rates may come with serious restrictions: vehicles are often older, depots might be further away from airports/city centres, and with less formality sometimes comes a less protective legal structure for renters.

Rentals from local firms start at around $30 or $40 per day for the smallest option. It's cheaper if you hire for a week or more, and there are often low-season and weekend discounts.

Affordable, independent operators with national networks include the following:

a2b Car Rentals (☑0800 545 000, 09-254 4397; www.a2b-car-rental.co.nz)

Ace Rental Cars (☑0800 502 277, 09-303 3112; www.acerentalcars.co.nz)

Apex Rentals (☑03-595 2315, 0800 500 660; www.apexrentals.co.nz)

Ezi Car Rental (☑0800 545 000, 09-254 4397; www.ezicarrental.co.nz)

Go Rentals (☑0800 467 368, 09-974 1598; www.gorentals.co.nz)

Omega Rental Cars (☑09-377 5573, 0800 525 210; www.omegarentalcars.com)

Pegasus Rental Cars (☑0800 803 580; www.rentalcars.co.nz)

Transfercar (☑09-630 7533; www.transfercar.co.nz) Relocation specialists with massive money-saving deals on one-way car hire.

MOTORCYCLE

Born to be wild? NZ has great terrain for motorcycle touring, despite the fickle weather in some regions. Most of the South Island's motorcycle-hire shops are in Christchurch, where you can hire anything from a little 50cc moped (aka nifty-fifty) to a throbbing 750cc touring motorcycle and beyond. Recommended operators (who also run guided tours) offer rates around $100 per day:

New Zealand Motorcycle Rentals & Tours (☑09-486 2472; www.nzbike.com)

Te Waipounamu Motorcycle Tours (☑03-372 3537; www.motorcycle-hire.co.nz)

Insurance

Rather than risk paying out wads of cash if you have an accident, you can take out your own comprehensive insurance policy, or (the usual option) pay an additional fee per day to the hire company to reduce your excess. This brings the amount you must pay in the event of an accident down from around $1500 or $2000 to around $200 or $300. Smaller operators offering cheap rates often have a compulsory insurance excess, taken as a credit-card bond, of around $900.

Many insurance agreements won't cover the cost of damage to glass (including the windscreen) or tyres, and insurance coverage is often invalidated on beaches and certain rough (4WD) unsealed roads – read the fine print.

See www.acc.co.nz for info on NZ's Accident Compensation Corporation insurance scheme (fault-free personal injury insurance).

Purchase

Planning a long trip? Buying a car then selling it at the end of your travels can be one of the cheapest and best ways to see the South Island. Christchurch is the easiest place to buy a car: scour the hostel noticeboards. Turners Auctions (www. turners.co.nz) is NZ's biggest car-auction operator, with 11 locations.

LEGALITIES

Make sure your prospective vehicle has a Warrant of Fitness (WoF) and registration valid for a reasonable period: see the New Zealand Transport Agency website (www. nzta.govt.nz) for details.

Buyers should also take out third-party insurance, covering the cost of repairs to another vehicle in an accident that is your fault: try the **Automobile Association** (AA; ☎0800 500 444; www.aa.co.nz/travel). New Zealand's no-fault Accident Compensation Corporation (www.acc.co.nz) scheme covers personal injury, but make sure you have travel insurance, too.

If you're considering buying a car and want someone to check it out for you, various companies inspect cars for around $150; find them at car auctions, or they will come to you. Try Vehicle Inspection New Zealand (☎09-573 3230, 0800 468 469; www.vinz.co.nz) or the AA.

Before you buy it's wise to confirm ownership of the vehicle, and find out if there's anything dodgy about the car (eg stolen, or outstanding debts). The AA's LemonCheck (☎09-420 3090; www.lemoncheck.co.nz) offers this service.

BUY-BACK DEALS

You can avoid the hassle of buying/selling a vehicle privately by entering into a buy-back arrangement with a dealer. Predictably, dealers often find sneaky ways of knocking down the return-sale price, which may be 50% less than what you paid, so hiring or buying and selling a vehicle yourself (if you have the time) is usually a better bet.

Road Hazards

There's an unusually high percentage of international drivers involved in road accidents in NZ – something like 30% of accidents involve a nonlocal driver. Kiwi traffic is usually pretty light, but it's easy to get stuck behind a slow-moving truck or campervan – pack plenty of patience, and know your road rules before you get behind the wheel. There are also lots of slow wiggly roads, one-way bridges and plenty of gravel roads, all of which require a more cautious driving approach. And watch out for sheep!

To check road conditions, call ☎0800 444 449 or see www.nzta.govt.nz/traffic.

Road Rules

➡ Kiwis drive on the left-hand side of the road; cars are right-hand drive. Give way to the right at intersections.

➡ All vehicle occupants must wear a seatbelt or risk a fine. Small children must be belted into approved safety seats.

➡ Always carry your licence when driving. Drink-driving is a serious offence and remains a significant problem in NZ, despite widespread campaigns and severe penalties. The legal blood-alcohol limit is 0.05% for drivers aged over 20, and 0% (zero) for those under 20.

➡ At single-lane bridges (of which there are a surprisingly large number), a smaller red arrow pointing in your direction of travel means that you give way.

➡ Speed limits on the open road are generally 100km/h; in built-up areas the limit is usually 50km/h. Speed cameras and radars are used extensively.

➡ Be aware that not all rail crossings have barriers or alarms. Approach slowly and look both ways.

➡ Don't pass other cars when the centre line is yellow.

➡ It's illegal to drive while using a mobile phone.

Hitching

Hitchhiking is never entirely safe, and we don't recommend it. Travellers who hitch should understand that they are taking a small but potentially serious risk. That said, it's not unusual to see hitchhikers along NZ country roads.

Alternatively, check hostel noticeboards for ride-share opportunities.

Local Transport

Bus & Tram

NZ's larger cities have extensive bus services but, with a few honourable exceptions, they are mainly daytime, weekday operations; weekend services can be infrequent or nonexistent. Christchurch has city buses and a historic tramway. Don't expect local bus services in more remote areas.

Taxi

The main cities have plenty of taxis and even small towns may have a local service. Taxis are metered, and are generally reliable and trustworthy.

Train

NZ train travel is all about the journey, not about getting anywhere in a hurry.
Great Journeys of New Zealand (☑0800 872 467, 04-495 0775; www.greatjourneysofnz.co.nz) operates two routes in the South Island,

listed below. It's best to reserve online or by phone; reservations can be made directly through Great Journeys of New Zealand (operated by KiwiRail), or at most train stations, travel agents and visitor information centres. Cheaper fares are likely to appear if you book online within NZ. All services are for day travel (no sleeper services).

Coastal Pacific Track damage during the 2016 earthquakes put this scenic Christchurch–Picton route out of action, but when we went to press it was estimated to return in 2018.

TranzAlpine Over the Southern Alps between Christchurch and Greymouth – one of the world's most famous train rides.

Train Passes

A Scenic Journeys Rail Pass allows unlimited travel on all of Great Journeys of New Zealand's rail services, including passage on the Wellington–Picton Interislander ferry. There are two types of pass, both requiring you to book your seats a minimum of 24 hours before you want to travel. Both have discounts for kids.

Fixed Pass Limited-duration fares for one/two/three weeks, costing $629/729/829 per adult.

Freedom Pass Affords you travel on a certain number of days over a 12-month period; a three-/seven-/10-day pass costs $439/969/1299.

Behind the Scenes

SEND US YOUR FEEDBACK

We love to hear from travellers – your comments keep us on our toes and help make our books better. Our well-travelled team reads every word on what you loved or loathed about this book. Although we cannot reply individually to your submissions, we always guarantee that your feedback goes straight to the appropriate authors, in time for the next edition. Each person who sends us information is thanked in the next edition – the most useful submissions are rewarded with a selection of digital PDF chapters.

Visit **lonelyplanet.com/contact** to submit your updates and suggestions or to ask for help. Our award-winning website also features inspirational travel stories, news and discussions.

Note: We may edit, reproduce and incorporate your comments in Lonely Planet products such as guidebooks, websites and digital products, so let us know if you don't want your comments reproduced or your name acknowledged. For a copy of our privacy policy visit lonelyplanet.com/privacy.

OUR READERS

Many thanks to the travellers who used the last edition and wrote to us with helpful hints, useful advice and interesting anecdotes: Ivo Thonon, Jim Corum, Andrew Wintle, Angus Mackay, Prue Biddle.

AUTHOR THANKS

Brett Atkinson

Thanks to all of the i-SITE, DOC and information centre staff who helped on the road, especially Glenn Ormsby and Mariet van Vierzen in Kaikoura. Cheers to the innovative chefs and inspired craft brewers of New Zealand for surprises and sustenance, and to Carol for support on occasional beach, island and city getaways. Thanks to my fellow authors, and my appreciation to Tasmin Waby at Lonely Planet for the opportunity to once again explore my Kiwi backyard.

Andrew Bain

Thanks primarily to Jason and Megan Hopper, who took me to the heights of the mountains and let me take them to the depths of Queenstown's basement bars. Gracias to Robyn Columbus Pester for a host of information, and the myriad business operators who answered my many queries along the journey. To my

greatest gifts – Kiri and Cooper – a big thanks for rolling with it as ever as I wandered in and out of NZ and our other life.

Samantha Forge

Thank you to the many wonderful Kiwis I met throughout the South Island for giving so freely of your time, knowledge and kindness. Thanks to Karyn, my travelling companion in Central Otago, for the cake and companionship. And finally, huge thanks to the other Team NZ authors for their friendship and generosity, and to everyone at LP responsible for piecing this puzzle together, especially the lovely Tasmin Waby.

Anita Isalska

Huge thanks to Tasmin Waby for bringing me aboard Team NZ, and to my fellow writers for being wonderful to work with – especially the above-and-beyond input from Andrew Bain, Brett Atkinson and Peter Dragicevich. Thanks for helpful suggestions from Nathan Watson and the Mountain Safety Council, patient counsel from numerous i-SITEs, blunt input from Tamara Goodwin, and Jane Atkin's great wisdom. Thank you Normal Matt, not for accidental acrobatics in Cardrona but for energetic driving, cruising and pub-hopping in Fiordland.

ACKNOWLEDGMENTS

Climate map data adapted from Peel MC, Finlayson BL & McMahon TA (2007) 'Updated World Map of the Köppen-Geiger Climate Classification', Hydrology and Earth System Sciences, 11, 163344.

Cover photograph: McLean Falls, the Catlins, Tom Mackie/AWL ©

THIS BOOK

This 6th edition of Lonely Planet's *New Zealand's South Island* guidebook was curated by Peter Dragicevich, and researched and written by Brett Atkinson, Andrew Bain, Samantha Forge and Anita Isalska. The previous edition was written by Charles Rawlings-Way, Sarah Bennett, Peter Dragicevich and Lee Slater. This guidebook was produced by the following:

Destination Editor Tasmin Waby

Product Editors Joel Cotterell, Kate Chapman, Tracy Whitmey

Senior Cartographer Diana Von Holdt

Book Designer Michael Weldon

Assisting Editors Michelle Bennett, Janice Bird, Andrea Dobbin, Jennifer Hattam, Victoria Harrison, Jodie Martire, Lou McGregor, Kristin Odijk, Monique Perrin, Simon Williamson

Cover Researcher Naomi Parker

Thanks to Jennifer Carey, Daniel Corbett, Jane Grisman, Liz Heynes, Andi Jones, Anne Mason, Claire Naylor, Karyn Noble, Mazzy Prinsep, Kirsten Rawlings, Jessica Ryan, James Smart, Angela Tinson

Index

Map Pages **000**
Photo Pages **000**

Map Legend

Sights
- Beach
- Bird Sanctuary
- Buddhist
- Castle/Palace
- Christian
- Confucian
- Hindu
- Islamic
- Jain
- Jewish
- Monument
- Museum/Gallery/Historic Building
- Ruin
- Shinto
- Sikh
- Taoist
- Winery/Vineyard
- Zoo/Wildlife Sanctuary
- Other Sight

Activities, Courses & Tours
- Bodysurfing
- Diving
- Canoeing/Kayaking
- Course/Tour
- Sento Hot Baths/Onsen
- Skiing
- Snorkelling
- Surfing
- Swimming/Pool
- Walking
- Windsurfing
- Other Activity

Sleeping
- Sleeping
- Camping
- Hut/Shelter

Eating
- Eating

Drinking & Nightlife
- Drinking & Nightlife
- Cafe

Entertainment
- Entertainment

Shopping
- Shopping

Information
- Bank
- Embassy/Consulate
- Hospital/Medical
- Internet
- Police
- Post Office
- Telephone
- Toilet
- Tourist Information
- Other Information

Geographic
- Beach
- Gate
- Hut/Shelter
- Lighthouse
- Lookout
- Mountain/Volcano
- Oasis
- Park
- Pass
- Picnic Area
- Waterfall

Population
- Capital (National)
- Capital (State/Province)
- City/Large Town
- Town/Village

Transport
- Airport
- Border crossing
- Bus
- Cable car/Funicular
- Cycling
- Ferry
- Metro station
- Monorail
- Parking
- Petrol station
- Subway station
- Taxi
- Train station/Railway
- Tram
- Underground station
- Other Transport

Routes
- Tollway
- Freeway
- Primary
- Secondary
- Tertiary
- Lane
- Unsealed road
- Road under construction
- Plaza/Mall
- Steps
- Tunnel
- Pedestrian overpass
- Walking Tour
- Walking Tour detour
- Path/Walking Trail

Boundaries
- International
- State/Province
- Disputed
- Regional/Suburb
- Marine Park
- Cliff
- Wall

Hydrography
- River, Creek
- Intermittent River
- Canal
- Water
- Dry/Salt/Intermittent Lake
- Reef

Areas
- Airport/Runway
- Beach/Desert
- Cemetery (Christian)
- Cemetery (Other)
- Glacier
- Mudflat
- Park/Forest
- Sight (Building)
- Sportsground
- Swamp/Mangrove

Note: Not all symbols displayed above appear on the maps in this book

Anita Isalska
Fiordland & Southland, West Coast Anita Isalska is a travel journalist, editor and copywriter. After several merry years as a staff writer and editor – a few of them in Lonely Planet's London office – Anita now works freelance between Australia, the UK and any Alpine chalet with good wi-fi. Anita writes about France, Eastern Europe, Southeast Asia and off-beat travel. Read her stuff on www.anitaisalska.com.

OUR STORY

A beat-up old car, a few dollars in the pocket and a sense of adventure. In 1972 that's all Tony and Maureen Wheeler needed for the trip of a lifetime – across Europe and Asia overland to Australia. It took several months, and at the end – broke but inspired – they sat at their kitchen table writing and stapling together their first travel guide, *Across Asia on the Cheap*. Within a week they'd sold 1500 copies. Lonely Planet was born.

Today, Lonely Planet has offices in Franklin, London, Melbourne, Oakland, Beijing and Delhi, with more than 600 staff and writers. We share Tony's belief that 'a great guidebook should do three things: inform, educate and amuse'.

OUR WRITERS

Peter Dragicevich

After a successful career in niche newspaper and magazine publishing, both in his native New Zealand and in Australia, Peter finally gave into Kiwi wanderlust, giving up staff jobs to chase his diverse roots around much of Europe. Over the last decade he's written literally dozens of guidebooks for Lonely Planet on an oddly disparate collection of countries, all of which he's come to love. He once again calls Auckland, New Zealand his home – although his current nomadic existence means he's often elsewhere.

Brett Atkinson

Marlborough & Nelson Brett Atkinson is based in Auckland, New Zealand, but is frequently on the road for Lonely Planet. He's a full-time travel and food writer specialising in adventure travel, unusual destinations, and surprising angles on more well-known destinations. Craft beer and street food are Brett's favourite reasons to explore places, and he is featured regularly on the Lonely Planet website, and in newspapers, magazines and websites across New Zealand and Australia. Since becoming a Lonely Planet author in 2005, Brett has covered areas as diverse as Vietnam, Sri Lanka, the Czech Republic, New Zealand, Morocco, California and the South Pacific.

Andrew Bain

Queenstown & Wanaka Andrew Bain prefers adventure to avarice and can usually be found walking when he should be working. His writing and photography feature in magazines and newspapers around the world, and his writing has won multiple awards, including best adventure story and best Australian story (three times) from the Australian Society of Travel Writers. He was formerly commissioning editor of Lonely Planet's outdoor adventure series of titles, and is the author of *Headwinds*, the story of his 20,000-kilometre cycle journey around Australia, and Lonely Planet's *A Year of Adventures*.

Samantha Forge

Christchurch & Canterbury, Dunedin & Otago Samantha became hooked on travel at the age of 17, when she arrived in London with an overstuffed backpack and a copy of LP's *Europe on a Shoestring*. After a stint in Paris, she moved back to Australia to work as an editor in LP's Melbourne office. Eventually her wanderlust got the better of her, and she now works as a freelance writer and editor. Samantha also wrote the Plan, Understand and Survival Guide chapters.

OVER PAGE MORE WRITERS

Published by Lonely Planet Publications Pty Ltd
ABN 36 005 607 983
6th edition – Sep 2018
ISBN 978 1 78657 082 6
© Lonely Planet 2018   Photographs © as indicated 2018
10 9 8 7 6 5 4 3 2 1
Printed in Singapore